Ernest Hemingway

The American Critical Tradition

M. Thomas Inge
General Editor

Theodore Dreiser: The Critical Reception
Edited by Jack Salzman
Long Island University

Thomas Wolfe: The Critical Reception
Edited by Pascal Reeves
University of Georgia

Ernest Hemingway: The Critical Reception
Edited by Robert O. Stephens
University of North Carolina

William Faulkner: The Critical Reception
Edited by M. Thomas Inge
Virginia Commonwealth University

Ernest Hemingway

The Critical Reception

Edited with an Introduction by

Robert O. Stephens

Burt Franklin & Co., Inc.

TO HEMINGWAY'S REVIEWERS

© 1977 Burt Franklin & Co., Inc.

Library of Congress Cataloging in Publication Data
Main entry under title:
Ernest Hemingway: the critical reception
(The American critical tradition)
Includes index.
1. Hemingway, Ernest, 1899-1961—Criticism and
interpretation—Addresses, essays, lectures.
I. Stephens, Robert O.
PS3515.E37Z5868   813'.5'2   76-48711
ISBN 0-89102-052-7

Acknowledgements and permissions
are listed on pp. xxxvii-xli,
which constitute an extension of the
copyright page for the purposes
of notice.

General Editor's Preface

When we speak of a writer's reputation in critical terms, we should recognize that he actually has two: the response of book reviewers and critics during his own lifetime to each of his works as it was published, and the retrospective evaluation of his achievement by literary historians and academic critics in the decades after his career is concluded. The primary concern of modern scholarship has been the latter, on the assumption that the passage of time is essential before a writer's achievement can be objectively viewed and assessed. The purpose of the volumes in the American Critical Tradition series, however, is to provide overviews of the critical reputations earned by major American authors in their own times. Such overviews are necessary before the full impact of a writer's influence can be properly evaluated and an understanding of how he related to his contemporary cultural milieu achieved.

The few efforts hitherto made in summarizing a writer's contemporary critical standing have usually been based on a reading of sample reviews or vague impressions retained by veterans of the era. Seldom have literary historians gone back to locate and read all or most of the comment elicited by a career in progress. In the present volumes, the editors have sought to unearth every known review of each book in the contemporary newspapers, journals, and periodicals, and to demonstrate the critical response chronologically through reprint, excerpt, or summary. Exhaustive checklists of reviews not included in the text are appended to each chapter, and the editor has provided an introduction summarizing the major trends observable in the criticism. The results not only elucidate the writer's career, but they reveal as well intellectual patterns in book reviewing and the reception of serious writing by the American reading public. Each volume is, therefore, a combined literary chronicle and reference work of a type previously unavailable.

M. Thomas Inge
General Editor

v

Contents

Introduction

While preparing to review Hemingway's *Men Without Women* in 1927, Virginia Woolf reflected sardonically on the role of critics and on the act of criticism, which involve, she said, one of the greatest feats of human credulity: Critics "shut themselves up in a room, dip a pen in the ink and call themselves 'we'" and "the rest of us . . . believe that they are somehow exalted, inspired, infallible." And the reader "begins to suppose that something actually happens to a book when it has been praised or denounced in print."

Woolf was perhaps too modest in her view of the dynamics of criticism. Although she admitted that the critic is likely to "smooth out all traces of that crab-like and crooked path" by which he or she reaches conclusions, she voiced an essential fact about the role of critics, one of crucial importance to those who view the development of a writer's reputation in retrospect. Something does happen to a book when it comes under criticism, for critics in many ways complete the literary process. One can imagine, if not recall, the piles of books and swarms of authors that have failed to attract critical attention—they fall into that limbo of the unrecognized and are mostly unread. They can achieve no place in that body of thought we call literature. For in a roundabout and cumulative way, literature is what critics say is literature.

That fact is amply illustrated in the case of Ernest Hemingway. Without denying the energy and craftsmanship of his extraordinarily original contribution to narrative art in the twentieth century, we must recognize that his reputation was also the product of those who read him and told others about him. That act, multiplied many times, resulted in the cultural phenomenon of Ernest Hemingway—man, legend, and artist. Hemingway insisted that there were no unrecognized great writers—he believed more in the power of genius to claim its audience than in the power of critics to create an audience. Aloof from and suspicious of critical fashions, he thought one of the worst mistakes a writer could make was to heed his critics. His assumption was that criticism was prescriptive and directed to writers rather than to a reading audience.

His critics, nevertheless, went about their business of telling the world that here was a writer. Their task was complicated by a number of considerations, some relating specifically to the case of Ernest Hemingway, some to the more general problems of reporting to a complex audience. Among those complications were Hemingway's fame as a public personality, the development of a cult of Hemingway admirers and even imitators, the circumstances surrounding publication of particular works, the development of disputes over censorship, the question whether he deserved literary awards, rivalries between critics because of literary and political ideologies, and the shifting expectations of a nation moving towards increasing involvement in world affairs. And although reviewers might have attempted to hide "that crab-like and crooked path" by which they arrived at evaluations, the wide ranging critical frameworks within which Hemingway's books were judged, as well as the issues of the reviews themselves, formed a shifting index of critical taste and of the aesthetic and ideological concerns of American reviewers from 1923 to 1972.

Initial critical responses to Hemingway, running from the Paris-Dijon editions of *Three Stories and Ten Poems* (1923) and *in our time* (1924) to *The Sun Also Rises* (1926), focused on his new narrative style. The Paris edition of *in our time* was a cause celebre for those sympathetic to the avant-garde school of writing. "Here ends the inquest into the state of contemporary prose," wrote Ezra Pound, general editor of the series which included *in our time.* Pound called for new standards of evaluation instead of those applied to conventional and domestic publications. Sponsorship of Hemingway by such expatriate demi-gods as Ezra Pound, Gertrude Stein, Ford Madox Ford, and James Joyce helped to identify him as a different kind of young writer. His renunciation of the relatively secure life as a journalist for the *Toronto Star* in favor of the riskier life of a writer of unconventional fiction made him seem all the more deserving of recognition. And Edmund Wilson conferred critical seriousness on Hemingway's first books with notices in the *transatlantic review.*

Reviews of *Three Stories and Ten Poems* and the Paris edition of *in our time* resulted in a successful debut for young Hemingway. There were not many reviews and they uniformly ignored the poems.

Although notices in the *transatlantic review* praised the emotional realism of the stories, they were even more concerned with Hemingway's sparsely suggestive style. Marjorie Ried thought the minute narratives of *in our time* entirely appropriate for telling the essential moments of a story and leaving the rest to the readers' imagination. In a joint review of both books, Edmund Wilson noted the pictorial qualities of the vignettes and thought them comparable to the lithographs of Goya. The other chief issue, as Wilson saw it, was the artistic integrity of the stories and especially the vignettes. The sketches, whether of war, crime, or bullfighting, represented a harrowing record of the modern world's barbarities rendered in a "strikingly original" and newly invented form.

The reception of the New York edition of *In Our Time* (1925) was best expressed by *Time* as it announced, "Here is a writer!" Most reviewers recognized that the sharp, acrid style was the result of long preparation, and they set out to identify the elements that must have figured in the formation of such a style and vision. Schuyler Ashley in the *Kansas City Star* thought Hemingway shared in the discovery of linguistic ore previously mined by Sherwood Anderson and Ring Lardner. *Time* saw a debt owed to Katherine Mansfield's style, rendered in more masculine language. Allen Tate thought Hemingway shared in the tradition of eighteenth-century and earlier writers like Swift, Fielding, Sterne, and even Defoe. Others related the starkness of the stories to the Paris school of machine-age art and thought the pattern of coordinate clauses reflective of mechanical, not organic, art. Like most later attempts to identify influences, however, these attributions were adjectival in effect. They did not so much provide insight into sources as show comparisons by which the new writing could be characterized. The real issue, then, was to define the style: objective, vital, astringent, brittle, concretely visual, austere, filled with hard bits of truth, presentational, personal, nonderivative. In a way, Scott Fitzgerald summed up the effect in "How to Waste Material" (*Bookman*, 63) when he said Hemingway was unliterary. Hemingway realized, said Fitzgerald, that American writing had to outgrow the obsession to cultivate American backgrounds and had to return to style as the key to the modern vision. Reviewers of *In Our Time* thus continued their praise of a new writer with an exciting style and sounded the theme that would dominate the first response to Hemingway: though not always successful, he was full of promise.

The Torrents of Spring, however, published in late spring of 1926, surprised most critics and was a mixed success. After *In Our Time* most reviewers apparently expected something even more austere and naturalistic. Several, of course, knew the literary gossip that the parody of Sherwood Anderson was Hemingway's method of breaking his publishing contract with Boni and Liveright in order to move to Scribner's. Others saw the book as Hemingway's declaration of independence from Anderson's influence as well as from his publisher. In the *New York World* Harry Hansen noted that Hemingway was clearly not guilty of logrolling and that he did not feel indebted to Anderson for his enthusiastic response to *In Our Time.* Several others noted that Anderson's dreamy, groping repetitions in *Dark Laughter* were easy to burlesque and invited parody. While most called *The Torrents of Spring* amusing, a substantial minority thought it tedious or brutal. Reviewers saw it as an interlude, said that parody was not Hemingway's chief gift, and urged him to get on with his true work.

With publication of *The Sun Also Rises* in the fall of 1926, reviewers welcomed Hemingway back to his true style and subject and to the fulfillment of his promise. In a pace-setting review in the *New York Herald Tribune Books,* Conrad Aiken wrote, "It has been apparent for some time now that Mr. Hemingway is a writer of very unusual gifts; it has merely been a question as to what direction he would take." *The Sun Also Rises,* he said, showed Hemingway as the most exciting of contemporary American writers of fiction. *The New York Times Book Review* thought the effect of the novel beyond analysis, that it put more literary English to shame, and that the novel was "unquestionably one of the events of an unusually rich year in literature." Herbert S. Gorman in the *New York World* saw the novel as a great tale of the postwar spiritual decline and as the complete realization of promises made by *In Our Time.* The *Saturday Review of Literature* also saw promises kept and a "Shakespearian absoluteness" in the writing.

As Fitzgerald had anticipated, the expatriate subject of the novel was not acceptable to those reviewers used to thinking of the novel's promise in terms of American materials, despite Hemingway's engaging style. *Time* thought the novel disappointing after the short stories and, while praising the amusing witticisms and subtle psychology of the sexually frustrated, found the soggy cafe life of expatriate Paris "soon tedious." The *Chicago Daily Tribune* found the talk brilliant and funny but too concerned with people and problems of little consequence. Allen Tate in *The Nation* saw that with the expatriate novel Hemingway would be "the big man in American letters" but at the expense of doing violence to the integrity of *In Our Time*. The novel, he said, was not hard-boiled enough and, because of the central dramatic situation, the narrative tended finally to be sentimental. The overall critical verdict, however, was three to one in favor of the novel.

Dialogue and character were the technical issues most frequently commented on in reviews of *The Sun Also Rises*. Most critics found the dialogue technically brilliant, if not always meaningful or wisely used. In his otherwise laudatory review Conrad Aiken noted that the passages of dialogue were often too long and needed slowing down by descriptive passages. The dialogue, he said, gave a feeling of climax too often and thus missed marking the real crescendo of developing action. Burton Rascoe in the *New York Sun*, however, thought the dialogue so natural it hardly seemed written.

The characters also seemed persuasively real. Several reviewers noted that the characters had probably counterparts in persons living in Europe. But most were concerned with the characters whose reality was in art. Lawrence Morris in the *New Republic* noted Hemingway's casual approach to story development—he dropped the characters into any setting and let them live without labeling their motives. Through the dialogue they revealed a stumbling indecision in contrast to their outward directedness and demonstrated the loss of an integrating mythology for their age. Of all the characters, only Brett seemed literary, said Rascoe. She was derived from Michael Arlen's *The Green Hat*. But identifications of Brett with the green hat syndrome were more adjectival than indicative of a model. Only the *Boston Evening Transcript* noted the key part played by Jake's point of view. Unity of vision was achieved through Jake's insight into the messes people made of their lives, said the *Transcript,* and through that vision the characters rose above their individual lives to show themselves indicative of their times. *The Sun Also Rises* thus became a social document but not a thesis novel. Generally, the *Transcript* spoke for most other reviews in calling the novel possibly great and that in distinctive style and insight it went far beyond Sinclair Lewis and Sherwood Anderson.

With publication of *Men Without Women* scarcely a year after *The Sun Also Rises* and only two years after *In Our Time,* reviewers could compare Hemingway's short story technique with that of his novel. Almost immediately a dispute developed among reviewers.

None denied that the stories were technically brilliant, but the issue now was whether the stories tended to contract or expand in meaning. That issue led to the question whether Hemingway's technique limited his range of subjects or whether the subjects themselves constituted a metaphor for expanded meanings. Virginia Woolf, reflecting the views of one group, wrote that Hemingway's stories, compared with those of Maupassant, Merimée, and Chekhov, were incomplete, that the dialogue was uneconomical and established at length what could be said more briefly and pungently in narrative, and as a result the stories were "a little dry and sterile." Percy Hutchinson put the stories in company with those of Kipling, Maupassant, and Conrad and wondered whether Hemingway could win greatness through technique without philosophy. Lee Wilson Dodd applauded the economy of the stories but lamented the lack of reference to larger aspects of human existence found in Gorki, Shakespeare, and Tolstoy. In Hemingway's work he felt as confined as in the cruel little world of Maupassant or the placid, stuffy little world of Jane Austen. In his review, "The Sportsman's Tragedy," however, Edmund Wilson said that Hemingway's drama "usually turns on some principle of courage, honor of pity—in short, of sportsmanship"—which he discovers in his character. Linking Hemingway's work with that of Byron, Shelley, Hardy, Maupassant, Flaubert, Barbusse, and Dos Passos as expressions of outrage against the repressions of their times, Wilson thought Hemingway showed situations with complex moral values and revealed an "image of the common oppression." N. L. Rothman thought Hemingway's stories had neither hope nor suspense but like Shakespeare's presented a pageant of continuous disaster and led to the beauty that comes after resignation to the bitter facts of loss. *Time* noted that seldom had a writer been able to cut so deeply into life with the twenty-six curved tools of the English alphabet. Again, by a ratio of three to one reviewers praised the collection and noted that if it did not reveal new resources it continued and consolidated a remarkable talent.

Even before *A Farewell to Arms* appeared in book form in the fall of 1929, it had become the center of critical dispute. Published in stallments in *Scribner's* during the late spring and summer of that year, the novel had been banned in Boston and copies of the magazine seized by police on grounds that the story included flagrantly immoral episodes and objectionable language. In the November issue of *Bookman*, novelist-critic Robert Herrick seconded the action of the Boston police. In his joint review of the Hemingway novel and Eric Maria Remarque's *All Quiet on the Western Front,* Herrick argued for justifiable censorship to keep "dirt" our of literature and contrasted the American novel unfavorably with the German. He was answered in the February issue of *Bookman* by Henry Seidel Canby and again in the March issue by C. K. Hare in a rebuttal advertisement paid for by Scribner's. The effect was to place *A Farewell to Arms* in the company of, if not on the same level as, Joyce's *Ulysses* in the continuing controversies over a writer's freedom to use language appropriate to the subject and over the problem of linguistic decorum in new writing.

A *Farewell to Arms*, moreover, prompted comparisons with *The Sun Also Rises,* raising the question whether Hemingway, could create something as impressive as the Paris novel and, beyond that, show novelistic brilliance to match his success in the second book of short stories. By better than three to one, reviewers thought he fulfilled expectations. Henry Hazlitt in the *New York Sun* thought *A Farewell to Arms* wider in scope and deeper in feeling than any of Hemingway's previous work. Percy Hutchinson thought that while *The Sun Also Rises* was a more nearly unique work, the war novel was a highly effective example of the new romanticism, with more drama and more sustained movement. Malcolm Cowley called *A Farewell to Arms* Hemingway's first real novel and *The Sun Also Rises* only an extended episode. Others praised the greater sense of design and purpose and, most of all, the believably modern account of love.

Indeed, a secondary issue developed over the question whether the novel was primarily one of love or war. As it turned out, the issue was as much cultural as critical. Both themes were treated iconoclastically, but which had the greater resonance for America at the close of the twenties? Henry Seidel Canby said the novel was an erotic but not decadent story and that it would have been admired by good Victorians for its frankness as well as its style. Clifton Fadiman thought the novel upset all modern dicta on what a novel could do: it told of a convincing love affair, celebrated male friendship, and proved the possibility of true tragedy in contemporary literature. The military descriptions, said Fadiman, were often dull because they were too much like war dispatches, but the lovers' story was told feelingly, without the self-conscious naiveté of Sherwood Anderson. When reviewers cited memorable scenes, however, they turned most often to those of the Caporetto retreat, although several also cited the last scene in the hospital as particularly affecting. Fanny Butcher of the *Chicago Tribune* told how two hard-boiled women readers were reduced to tears by Frederic's goodbye to Catherine. On the other side of the issue, Lewis Galantière thought that Hemingway's treatment of the love affair showed a Redskin fear of displaying emotion, but that the men at the front were truly imagined characters and the war descriptions preeminently successful. In an especially provocative and acerbic review in the *Nashville Tennessean,* Donald Davidson saw the love story as "Perfect Behavior"—a Watsonian nightmare of behaviorism with the lovers acting out their roles while guided by instinct. They had no sense of good, evil, or decorum, he said—just stimulus and response. The novel to Davidson was a fulfillment of Watson's wish for a novel about people who act in a behavioristically sound way.

To the extent that imitation is a form of criticism as well as flattery, *A Farewell to Arms* verified that Hemingway was, in 1929, one of the most influential examples in American letters. The success of *The Sun Also Rises* marked his identification not only with the expatriate school of writers but also with writers developing a new style. By the time of *A Farewell to Arms,* Henry Hazlitt in the *New York Sun* noted that many new novels sought the stature of the established models—of Conrad, Hardy, Hamsun, Proust, and Joyce. The fall of 1929 brought new novels written in the Hemingway style; Hemingway, he concluded, was the greatest single influence on the modern American novel and short story. There was a danger, he said, in the development of a Hemingway cult that thought Hemingway's the only way to write. At the same time, Malcolm Cowley wrote that in five years Hemingway had achieved almost legendary status and was being imitated by older as well as by younger writers. With publication of *Winner Take Nothing* in 1933, Louis Kronenberger noted that Hemingway had gone beyond fashion in his influence and constituted a virtual tradition.

Death in the Afternoon, however, forced reviewers, in the fall of 1932, to think of Hemingway's literary achievement in new contexts. Although most recognized that the book on bullfighting was a predictable extension of the interest so crucially central to *The Sun Also Rises,* they also had to consider Hemingway as a man of letters as well as a writer of fiction. Most critics dutifully noted the treatment of bullfighting as an art form rather than a sport and approved or demurred as their tastes indicated, but their real interest was in the man who chose the subject and in the style he brought to it. Implicitly or explicitly, they believed that the style is the man, and began distinguishing between Hemingway the writer and Hemingway the man. In *The Nation,* Clifton Fadiman made it an official part of the mythology that Hemingway was the new American Byron. Each generation, he said, had its picturesque and dramatic transformations of moral bewilderment into new heroic types and produced its Werthers, Bazarovs, and Dorian Grays to embody responses of suicide, nihilism, or aestheticism. Hemingway would have created a myth even without good writing, said Fadiman, because he personally served as a model of modern, violent romanticism. Hemingway's admirers could empathize with their hero's experiences and responses in their own worship of primary emotions.

The problem of Hemingway as legendary figure thus became a matter of critical concern. Laurence Stallings noted that Hemingway followed his own daimon and wrote a book defying any of the ordinary categories; perhaps it was a sort of anatomy and was in the manner of Thomas Browne, Lawrence Sterne, and Richard Burton. Robert M. Coates noted that the book was finally more about Hemingway than bullfighting. In his otherwise sympathetic review, Seward Collins thought Hemingway had in his apologia for bullfighting gone into a false pose of truculent he-mannishness, and in mid-1933 Max Eastman charged that the supermasculine pose was really one of wearing false hair on the chest. As literary gossip soon had it, that review prompted a shoving match between Eastman and Hemingway when they next met in Maxwell Perkins' office at Scribner's.

The verdict was mixed on the prose style of the book. The digressions between Hemingway and the Old Lady constituted particular points for attacks on Hemingway's language. *Town and Country* charged that obscenities were included for their own sake. *Yale Review* saw the digressions appealing to specialized bawdy tastes, and Laurence Stallings saw them consistent with the savagery of eighteenth-century wit. *Town and Country* too lamented the overlong and complex sentence patterns after the stylized brevity of *A Farewell to Arms,* and R. L. Duffus in the *New York Times Book Review* thought the prose style bogged down in Jamesian syntax. Ben Ray Redman in the *Saturday Review of Literature,* however, thought the book contained nearly perfect prose written with absolute precision. Reviews in general showed that critics did not quite know what to make of the new Hemingway; they viewed *Death in the Afternoon* as an interlude and waited for new work. The overall verdict was evenly split between disapproval and approval on a wait-and-see basis.

After publication of *Winner Take Nothing* in 1933, however, critical approval began to swing away from Hemingway. He was beginning to repeat himself and to show his limits. A majority of the critics by a ratio of three to two, thought his new stories inferior to the work of the twenties but still in the same vein. In the *New Yorker* Clifton Fadiman explained that the good stories of former years, such as "The Killers," made admirers demand even better stories. But the ironic stories of sports and sudden death lacked new insights and smelled of the twenties. "Why not go on to something else?" he suggested.

Green Hills of Africa (1935) dealt decisively with the concerns of the thirties, but it, too, was judged a disappointment as well as an unsuccessful experiment. To the question posed by Hemingway in the foreword whether an account of a month's hunt could compete with a work of the imagination, most critics answered no. Two to one, they rejected the thesis. Although they cited numerous passages—the description of the Gulf Stream as the measuring point for contemporary civilization, the tributes to Tolstoy and the nineteenth-century Russian frontier, the African evenings, the Masai, and the kudu—reviewers for the most part found the subject either dull or irrelevant. With the depression on most readers' minds, Granville Hicks urged Hemingway to look to contemporary American themes. Hemingway, he said, had ignored Melville's dictum that a great book should have a great theme, and in ignoring the bigger game of society for that of kudus, Hemingway had set himself against the judgment of history. Hicks was writing for *New Masses* then. Other reviewers were more concerned with Hemingway's growing feud with critics and rival writers. In *Green Hills of Africa* Hemingway answered Gertrude Stein's attack on his courage and originality, attacked the newly dominant Marxist school of writing, and delivered verdicts on both classic and contemporary writers. John Chamberlain in the *New York Times* lamented that Hemingway seemed as anxious to add the heads of literary and political victims to his trophy collection as he was the heads of game animals. In the *Saturday Review of Literature* Bernard DeVoto said the literary discussions were mostly superficial, and in an otherwise favorable review in the *New York Herald Trib-*

une Carl Van Doren noted that Hemingway's reflections were as boyish as Byron's.

As with *Death in the Afternoon,* the African book presented a puzzle of genre and style. DeVoto thought the big news was Hemingway's entry into a new stylistic period, that the book was an attempt at an anatomy, and that the long sentences and uncertain grammar sounded like a German translation of Hemingway's other style. In the *New Yorker* Clifton Fadiman thought the book in the genre of those written by retired Indian Army colonels and quipped that it showed how one man's dead meat is another man's poison. In the *New Republic* T. S. Mathews charged that Hemingway now thought he could write anything and call it literature. In a more friendly review, Charles Poore in the *New York Times Book Review* hailed Hemingway for developing a new and richer style, one that showed him ready to write a novel of vast and striking scope.

The fact remains, however, that after *A Farewell to Arms* Hemingway was living on credit with most reviewers. Whether he was following the bullfight circuits, hunting kudu in Africa, writing letters to *Esquire,* or getting into the Spanish civil conflict, he was not producing what most critics were willing to recognize as literature. His tough-minded, precise stories of moral malaise in the twenties had prepared spokesmen of national values to expect even more incisive probes into moods underlying the new malaise of the depression. Both *The Sun Also Rises* and *A Farewell to Arms* had settled into the national mind as novels of social import. *Death in the Afternoon* and *Green Hills of Africa* were accepted not as works valuable in themselves but as preparations for the bigger, better novels to come. By the mid-thirties a critical habit was established that was to last to the end of Hemingway's career: there was always the big novel in preparation.

Publication in 1937 of *To Have and Have Not* was important then because it represented Hemingway's return to the novel after eight years and was occasion enough for *Time* to devote a cover story to Hemingway and his new work. Inevitably comparisons were made—in most instances, to the disadvantage of the new work. Most disappointing was the newly emphatic view of man as a violent animal rather than as a person with social and political consciousness. In "Tiger! Tiger!" Bernard DeVoto noted that the highest praise Hemingway could give a man like Harry Morgan was to say that he is like some noble animal; Hemingway's new characters, lacking conscious-ness, became "sacs of basic instinct." Others said the book included pointless brutality and naturalistic rawness for its own sake. It was a thin, screaming book full of puerile slaughter, said Sinclair Lewis in *Newsweek.*

But if violence was not to most critics' taste, they maintained that Hemingway's fictional technique was still effective. Most who praised the technically superior writing, however, reserved that praise for the first two parts. The third, they thought, defective in writing as well as in structure. The two themes of the Haves and Have-Nots never quite came together, said Malcolm Cowley in the *New Republic.* Hemingway's social thought could not keep up with his technical brilliance, said the *New Yorker* and *Yale Review*; his new villains were clay pigeons and caricatures. Richard Gordon in the novel was a John O'Hara character, not one of Hemingway's, said the *Saturday Review of Literature.*

The minority report on *To Have and Have Not* maintained that the violence was integral, that Hemingway had rediscovered his true subject in Key West without another war, that Harry Morgan was Hemingway's most understandable character, and that in his novel Hemingway made the reading public conscious of how the nonliter-ary public thought. To Elliot Paul, whose own anti-Fascist sym-pathies had been recently expressed in *Life and Death of a Spanish Town,* the novel was Hemingway's best in both subject and treat-ment; the Saturday night barroom scene with the Key West veterans was to him on a par with the Cyclops episode in *Ulysses* or the orgy scene in *Studs Lonigan.* To Edward Weeks of *Atlantic Monthly,* Hemingway's scenes of the poor and rich made him a Hogarth of the times.

In retrospect, it seems strange that few early reviewers commented on Harry's conversion in the closing pages of *To Have and Have Not*, to collective action. Harry's violence and the set-piece descriptions of the Key West rich were the chief concerns of most critics. Little connection was made between Hemingway's new involvement with Spanish leftists and his new novel. It would be difficult, said Bernard DeVoto, for Hemingway's new allies of the literary left to accept his "cult of blood consciousness and holy violence." In the *New York Herald Tribune Books* Alfred Kazin, the first and one of the few to note that Harry was unlike previous Hemingway heroes, said that he was a mass-man, and that through his error of excessive self-reliance he learned the folly of isolation. Malcolm Cowley in *New Republic* noted that the change in Harry from tough guy to proletarian hero hinted at the change in Hemingway's social views. In the *Partisan Review* Philip Rahv noted a tendency towards a new social orientation for Hemingway, but thought it was confounded by his old taste for personal violence. Most of those who noted the new direction thought Hemingway had not demonstrated a grasp of the social and political problems implicit in Harry's change, and they viewed *To Have and Have Not* as a satire containing a curious blend of sentimentality and violence.

But the critical notions of the mid-thirties still prevailed. The book was a promise of better things to come—he might yet write a great novel, said Alfred Kazin. *To Have and Have Not* might not be Hemingway's best, said Malcolm Cowley, but it represented a turn in his career rather than a demise. According to Louis Kronenberger, it was clearly a transitional book.

When *The Fifth Column and the First Forty-Nine Stories* appeared in 1938, the principal critical issue was to distinguish between Hemingway's achievements as a playwright and as a short-story teller. In most cases reviewers chose the short stories. No other living author could produce forty-nine stories as good, said Elmer Davis in the *Saturday Review of Literature*. Clifton Fadiman observed that the new collection proved that Hemingway was the best storyteller writing in English. But given the chance to view retrospectively the three collections of short stories along with the four new stories collected for the first time in book form, some critics found the early ones less impressive than they had originally. In the *New York Times Book Review*, Peter Monro Jack complained that he could not tell whether Hemingway meant to express or suppress emotion and that the stories often evoked a beautifully stylized rigor mortis. Malcolm Cowley thought the early stories defined Hemingway's talent and represented a better grasp of reality than the later ones. The former stood up under countless imitations, Cowley noted, and showed Hemingway to be the confirmed prophet of a violent age.

The Fifth Column was a less impressive work that many thought devalued Hemingway's reputation. For some the problem was one of stage craft; for most it was a matter of false identification of the issues. Elmer Davis thought the play read well and should play well, but he was apparently more persuaded by the timeliness of the subject than by the art involved. If it were judged as one of Hemingway's stories, said the *Kansas City Star,* the play was among the least successful. The characters revealed themselves slowly, the dialogue carried too heavy a burden, and the play suggested that all the important action was occurring off-stage. In *New Masses,* however, Edwin Berry Burgum, while conceding faultiness in the stage craft, expressed the view that Philip's development was an index of the experience of expatriate writers who grew beyond bohemianism to discover better values than those of middle-class respectability. In contrast, Lionel Trilling saw the play as a danger signal that Hemingway the man was becoming dominant over Hemingway the artist. Now he was substituting self-consciousness for conscious control, naiveté for innocence, partisanship for disinterestedness, and fumbling communication for expression. Hemingway had become a victim of "liberal-radical highmindedness," Trilling charged, and had lost the idiom of the artist in that of the man. Accusations during the thirties that he lacked concern for social values had pressured Hemingway to vindicate himself by incorporating his partisan sympathies into such ill-conceived works as *To Have and Have Not* and *The Fifth Column.* As with previous works, though, most critics suspended judgment. The stories had been brought to a culmination, but the play was a warm-up for bigger things to come. After all, noted Edmund Wilson, the play had been written in Madrid while shells were still falling on the Hotel Florida.

Reviews of the stage production of *The Fifth Column* in the spring of 1940 were more favorable than were those of the published play. The verdict, however, was not so much a reflection of new insights into the play as it was of changing times. The European war foreseen in the play had become a reality, and the play gained importance as a declaration of principles, said Brooks Atkinson in the *New York Times.* Most critics remembered the difficulties Hemingway had in getting the play produced and noted that in the process Hemingway's story had undergone Hollywood-style tinkering by Benjamin Glazer. The shift in emphasis from the dirty business of war to the dalliance between Philip Rawlings and Dorothy Bridges was chiefly attributed to Glazer, and Hemingway emerged as the emotional realist beside whom Glazer's sentimentality was measured. Most reviewers saw the harsh first act as real Hemingway in setting up the moral complexities of men doing their distasteful work in the name of a good cause. The early second act faltered as the love interest became paramount, and critical opinion divided on whether the play recovered by the end. If it did, it was because of a series of theatrical speeches rather than because the moral complexities had been confronted and developed convincingly. Critical opinion was evenly split on the success of the play, and the chief issue was whether it was a perceptive war statement or an unconvincing wartime love story. In any case, reviewers noted, Hemingway's new career would not be in the theater.

"The Return of Ernest Hemingway" was the title of Edmund Wilson's welcoming review of *For Whom the Bell Tolls* in the fall of 1940, and it was the way most critics characterized the book. The Spanish Civil War novel appeared to be the "big book" most had been waiting for since *To Have and Have Not,* perhaps since *A Farewell to Arms.* One has to read the reviews themselves to get both the sense of relief and the sense of celebration accompanying publication of the novel. J. Donald Adams noted that it erased doubts about Hemingway's achievements since the Key West novel. It redeemed a decade of futility, said John Chamberlain in *New York Herald Tribune Books.* More was expected of Hemingway than of any other writer who saw the Spanish Civil War, said *Newsweek*—his novel was expected to be *the* book on that war, and *For Whom the Bell Tolls* was "undoubtedly that book." So enthusiastic was the critical welcome that the *Saturday Review of Literature* announced it was the only certain nomination among thirty-nine reviewers for the Pulitzer Prize for fiction.

Inevitably the new novel was compared to *A Farewell to Arms,* not only because both provided comparable materials on the two wars bracketing a generation but also because both provided measuring points in an American literary career. The new novel was Hemingway's best since 1929, said Henry Seidel Canby. It was more than an advance on *Farewell,* wrote Clifton Fadiman: it showed growth rare in an American writer. Indeed, most reviewers agreed that it was fulfillment of the long-delayed promise and one of the major American books of the century.

Such an enthusiastic response has to be seen not only in the light of Hemingway's reputation and the critical preoccupation with maturing careers. In a wider sense, Hemingway's case was an index of national psychology after the depression of the thirties. If he could depict strong and resilient men equal to the demands of global war, there was a place for him in the national pantheon, perhaps in the world's.

Hemingway had indeed proved himself and his age, announced

Howard Mumford Jones in the *Saturday Review of Literature*. Gone was the self-consciousness of *Death in the Afternoon*. In its place was the "sorrowful majesty" of a cause that failed but was not finally lost. The novel was permeated with the feeling that inspired the best pages of Hugo, Dickens, Dostoyevski, and Tolstoy. Hemingway's scenes of Spanish life were equated with Tolstoy's depictions of the Napoleonic campaigns in *War and Peace*. Like *David Copperfield* and *Vanity Fair,* the new novel swallowed its hero in a larger action. Although Robert Jordan and Maria might be lost sight of in the action, Pilar emerged as a Falstaffian titaness. Hemingway's new style had more variety than his earlier austere manner and the new dialogue encompassed the richness of Spain and the Spanish character. *For Whom the Bell Tolls* was an occasional novel in the sense that *Vanity Fair* and *Uncle Tom's Cabin* were and, like them, rose above the occasion. It went beyond partisanship to imaginative comprehensiveness and drew on subterranean sources of artistic energy that put Pilar and her companions in Valhalla, in company with Jean Valjean and Abraham Lincoln.

As reviews accumulated it became apparent that there were areas of disagreement, even if the ultimate verdict was better than three to one that the novel was a major success. Although early reviews praised the book for its balanced view of the war and its recognition of barbarities committed by both sides, they noted that the literary left would not like the report of Soviet cynicism in Spain. In early November Alvah Bessie's review in *New Masses* charged that Hemingway had betrayed the Spanish popular cause by characterizing the Soviet role as ambiguous when it was clear and sympathetic. He betrayed further by concentrating on the personal preoccupations of Robert Jordan to the extent that the political implications of the cause were obscured. By December, however, *Commonweal* charged that the novel focused too little on Robert Jordan in its attempt to encompass the wider war and, as a result, Jordan became a puppet who merely spoke Hemingway's undramatized ideas. Similar criticisms were made by Dwight Macdonald and Lionel Trilling in the *Partisan Review* for January 1941. Hemingway had failed to understand—or make Robert Jordan comprehend—the social and political issues involved. The novel was a poetic success, said Trilling, but Jordan's death was melodramatic rather than tragic because Jordan, like Henry James' Christopher Newman, refused to deal with political intrigue and turned instead to the cult of personal experience.

Jordan's death brought no enlightenment because he finally failed to comprehend the complex issues involved in acting within a community of men.

Criticism from the right focused on the sexual mores of the novel. In the *American Mercury* Burton Rascoe charged that the love story depicted nothing more than rutting, written in the manner of pulp magazines. *Catholic World* praised the immediacy of the narration, finding some passages almost too painful to read, but lamented that Hemingway failed to recognize the value of reticence in great literary work. Indeed, a significant issue developed over the question whether the love story was integral or extraneous to the whole action.

Hemingway's broader, more varied style received praise from most reviewers, though several feared that it could easily lapse into episodic looseness. In employing this new style Hemingway had shed his former artificialities and now presented nothing obtrusive, said J. Donald Adams in the *New York Times Book Review*. *Newsweek* noted that Hemingway's new style built up suspense over 400 pages, developed character, analyzed emotions, and presented an ending that was "almost a physical experience." The heavily detailed though simple style, noted *The Nation*, enabled Hemingway to build up the world of the partisans so that the reader could know intimately both major and minor characters. Edmund Wilson observed, however, that the new copiousness allowed slackness and lacked the tension of his earlier work. Mark Schorer thought the new style more flexible but less brilliant than the earlier manner. It was, however, a style integral to the subject and a major development in modern narrative art. Hemingway's new art, said Wilson, was reassuring evidence of the soundness of our intellectual life at a time of national stress.

That Hemingway had indeed made his return into the national consciousness was verified by a *Saturday Review of Literature* poll of critics in 1944. It showed that Hemingway was clearly the outstanding American novelist of the last twenty years and that *A Farewell to Arms* and *For Whom the Bell Tolls* were among the five most memorable novels produced during that period. They kept company with *Arrowsmith,* the *U.S.A.* trilogy, and *The Grapes of Wrath.* Yet literary prizes as marks of official critical recognition did not come readily, even with the success of *For Whom the Bell Tolls.* Clifton Fadiman had gone on record, in 1929, in favor of *A Farewell to Arms* receiving the Pulitzer Prize, but it had gone instead to Oliver La-Farge's *Laughing Boy.* When *For Whom the Bell Tolls* was nominated for the prize in 1941, objections by the Pulitzer committee's Dr. Nicholas Murray Butler blocked the award and, finally, no prize was given for fiction that year. In November 1941, however, Hemingway received a gold medal from the Limited Editions Club for having written, within the previous three years, the book most likely to become a classic.

During the forties Hemingway's reputation rested largely on *For Whom the Bell Tolls.* Appearing at the opening of the European war and yet telling of the prologue in Spain, the novel endured during the war years as a model for war narratives and a paradigm of war experience. It had a double existence in that it was about both the present conflict and the prototypal war experience. As the war widened and Bataan, Stalingrad, and El Alamein became part of the nation's memory, Hemingway's war in Spain seemed both legendary and prophetic.

His reputation as the consummate writer on war was fundamental to his publishing *Men at War* in 1942. The book contained not only passages from *A Farewell to Arms* and *For Whom the Bell Tolls* as recognized war classics but also his introduction dealing with the rites of war and the validity of literature as part of the experience of war. Most reviewers noted his authority on the subject and thought his views profound, if not always orthodox. But the book did little to advance Hemingway's standing. Most critics regarded it as a time-server while Hemingway, like most Americans, was busy seeing the war through its course. A few critics, like Howard Mumford Jones, suspected that Hemingway was entering another decade of self-indulgence and of emphasizing the man over the artist.

The Viking Portable Hemingway, published in 1944, helped keep Hemingway's reputation current while he produced nothing but a few war reports for *Collier's.* Reviewers were uniformly favorable towards the collection, but more because of Malcolm Cowley's introduction than Hemingway's new work. The book was important, as Granville Hicks and Max Lerner indicated, because Cowley established a new view of Hemingway as a nocturnal symbolist and ritualist in the tradition of Hawthorne and Melville, rather than as a literary naturalist. The new interpretation became important in the postwar years as criticism based on archetypes became dominant; and despite the failure of *Across the River and into the Trees* in 1950, the new approach helped keep Hemingway under consideration by the Nobel Prize committee.

The view since 1950 has been that *Across the River and into the Trees* was a critical disaster for Hemingway. Critics of *The Old Man and the Sea* and later books typically praised these works as recoveries from a major collapse, and it is irrefutable that the contemporaneous critical verdict was slightly better than three to two against the postwar novel. But to understand the critical reception of the work in 1950, one must realize that Hemingway was being judged against his own record, that the book appeared after a decade of suspended critical opinion while reviewers awaited the rumored major work in progress, that critics yearned for a literary renaissance following the Second World War to match the one following the First, and that the burden was on Hemingway, as on other surviving members of his literary generation, to verify his claim to greatness. In addition, many more academic journals had begun reviewing current literature, and their taste for an intellectualized and complex vision of the artist's role helped turn the verdict against Hemingway, although critical response among popular reviewers was about evenly split. At the same time, several novelists of Hemingway's generation entered the dispute in his defense, as if they were somehow defending their own achievements. John O'Hara in the *New York Times Book Review,* Elliot Paul in the *Providence Sunday Journal,* Evelyn Waugh in *Commonweal,* and William Faulkner in a letter to the editors of *Time* all spoke in favor of the new novel or the author.

As the novel was evaluated a number of critical issues developed. Probably the crucial one for Hemingway's reputation was whether he had made a "return" comparable to that of 1940. Most reviewers announced themselves disappointed that *Across the River and into the Trees* was not the big novel of the war, although several, like Charles Poore of the *New York Times,* announced their satisfaction upon reading the real thing after a decade of "road-company Hemingway." Repeating the patterns of the thirties, several reviewers again tempered their disappointment with continued insistence that the novel was a purge of the Hemingway psyche in order to make way for better things. Behind their suspended judgment was, of course, the old theory of the mid-career decline of American writers. A secondary issue involved Hemingway's personal circumstances while writing the novel. Most critics began their reviews by noting that Hemingway had feared death or blindness after a hunting accident in Italy. Their question then was whether *Across the River and into the Trees* was indeed the "big book" or a hastily prepared last testament; or perhaps it was a last fling. Also, did Hemingway identify too closely with his hero Richard Cantwell, did he achieve sufficient aesthetic distance to see his hero objectively, and, consequently, were Cantwell's views to be taken as Hemingway's or as a satiric comment on American postwar obsessions? Several reviewers took pains to show that the questions had been clouded by Lillian Ross's profile in the *New Yorker* shortly before publication of the novel, and they urged that the novel be read for itself, not in light of what reviewers knew of Hemingway the man.

Regardless of whether Cantwell was a successfully realized character, he was to most critics the spokesman for the Hemingway code, and concern for ideology became a widely disputed issue. In effect, the issue concerned the validity of the cult of experience as the representative viewpoint of the American novel, and Hemingway's Cantwell was again caught in the crossfire. Typical views of Cantwell-Hemingway's thought held that it was a mixture of True Romance, Superman, and the Last Frontier, that it showed Cantwell as an aristocratic Rotarian, a defunct Philistine, and a brutal sentimentalist, and that the ideology demonstrated the dead end of the tough school of fiction. J. Donald Adams lamented the implication that manliness was equated with killing one's man. The other side of the dispute was that Cantwell's cynicism was more appropriate to the day's need than was Robert Jordan's idealism and that, paradoxically, Cantwell was the repository of decent feeling and residual chivalry in the midst of a Machiavellian cold war. But as the verdicts on various issues gathered cumulative force, the overall decision was that *Across the River and into the Trees* was not the book readers expected from Hemingway after a decade's waiting. Although a number again suspended judgment, more reviewers were ready to say that Hemingway was finished.

The purgation theory seemed to have been rejustified in 1952 when *The Old Man and the Sea* signaled Hemingway's recovery as both a popular and a critical success. The unusual circumstances of publication in a single issue of *Life* magazine did much to emphasize the recovery, but that it was a recovery that produced almost classic poise and control was even more impressive. A number of critics recognized that the coup of publishing the novel in a single issue of a mass circulation magazine constituted a new development in the making of a writer's reputation. Here was a complete, new, and probably major work to which a vast reading public had immediate access. Part of the critic's work had been undercut: it was not necessary to introduce the book to the public; it was already in the readers' hands. If readers looked at critical evaluations of the novel subsequently, they did so to compare their responses to those of the critics. They had received the work almost at the same time as the critics, and a week before publication in book form. The *Christian Science Monitor* saw not only the calculated risk in jeopardizing sales of the book but also the problem of many uninitiated readers' responses to an essentially tragic experience. Would they see it as defeat or triumph? W. M. Frohock in the *Southwest Review* thought that the millions who read the novel in the barberships of America alongside the *Police Gazette* would put down the story "with a feeling of pride in belonging to the same race as the old Cuban." In any case, the manner of publication was clearly a mark of Hemingway's reputation. *Publishers Weekly* noted that magazine publication of the novel gave fiction-reading "a badly-needed short-in-the-arm," but noted, too, that only the exceptional book could be handled in such a way.

Praise for the novel was overwhelming; and the book seemed even more remarkable in contrast with *Across the River and into the Trees.* Indeed, the dominant note of the reviews was that Hemingway had confounded his critics and set aside the law of collapse; in many reviewers' eyes he had produced his best work. So much emphasis was placed on Hemingway's recovery that the novel itself received remarkably little close analysis. The few analytical commentaries centered on Santiago's heroic attributes, on Hemingway's technical purity of style, on the religious ideology of Santiago's quest, and on the book's place in the tradition of sea novels.

Carlos Baker in the *Saturday Review* presented the most positive view of Santiago's heroism. He thought that Santiago should be admitted to the gallery of permanent heroes, along with Melville's Ahab, Whitman's Columbus, and Sandburg's Lincoln. Other critics, though laudatory, were also more cautious. If several thought the old fisherman too representative to be a fully realized character, others thought his lack of specific individuality was essential to the classic appeal of the story. Still others thought his talking to the great marlin was more sentimental than profound. But William Faulkner, reviewing the novel in *Shenandoah,* praised it as Hemingway's best because it discovered God as the Creator and was written out of knowledge of and pity for all creatures caught in the web of necessity and love.

Appraisals of the prose style emphasized the simultaneous austerity and freshness of the language as well as its almost total consonance with the form of the work. Whether the story was a novel, an extended short story, or an expanded anecdote, most agreed that Hemingway had accepted the limits of his form and accommodated his style to its demands. Similarly, most reviewers recognized that the story was haunted with meanings, even though R. W. B. Lewis doubted it could bear heavy critical examination. It was read variously as a Christian tragedy of Everyman, a mystical experience, a never depressing but classically tragic struggle of man against fate, an extension of the American struggle with the frontier, a fable, a parable of the artist struggling with his craft, and, by extension, an allegory of the artist in conflict with his sharkish critics. Still other reviewers insisted that the novel was best read on its own spare terms and that critics should resist the temptation to read it as a parable.

Santiago's concern with the possible evil of his undertaking, as well as the oceanic setting of his struggle, prompted a significant number of reviewers to compare the novel to the more complex *Moby-Dick* and other classics of sea fiction. Anticipating the comparison, however, Malcolm Cowley emphasized the differences in genres and moods of the two works and contrasted the soaring romantic rhetoric of one with the classic restraint of the other. Mark Schorer thought that Santiago's story evoked a Conradian victory in destruction. Other reviewers placed the novel within the framework of American literature of the hunt and compared it not only to *Moby-Dick* but also to works by Jack London and Walter Van Tilberg Clark, to "The Bear" by Faulkner, and, within an older American tradition, to Thomas Bangs Thorpe's "The Big Bear of Arkansas."

A year after *The Old Man and the Sea* was published, Webster Schott of the *Kansas City Star* expressed satisfaction that the book had brought Hemingway a Pulitzer Prize after twenty-eight years, but like others he was still intrigued by rumors of the big book Hemingway was supposed to have written or be writing. The sea novel was presumed to be a part of the larger work, and Schott thought that if the other parts equaled the sea novel, few could argue against Hemingway's having permanent possession of the title of champion novelist.

But for the remaining eight years of his life, there was little indication that Hemingway was involved in a major work. Two minor pieces in the 1957 centennial anniversary issue of the *Atlantic Monthly* reminded readers that Hemingway had published his first American magazine story in that journal thirty years before, and three installments of "The Dangerous Summer" in *Life* in 1960 prompted critical doubts that he could match his performance in *Death in the Afternoon.* Even that mixed achievement of 1932 appeared legendary beside the later inactivity. Then in July, 1961, came Hemingway's suicide and the world's tributes, many of which were written as if the artist had been dead for years. Readers were reminded that he was said to have left a full vault of manuscripts that were awaiting the fullness of time for publication, but hopes for the big novel were dim.

With publication of *A Moveable Feast* in the spring of 1964, a new dimension entered into critical evaluations. Posthumous works had to be appraised as artifacts rather than as contemporary works; and along with the question whether his place in national and world literature was well served by such publication was the further issue whether the new publication revealed a Hemingway different from the grizzled patriarch of letters known to critics during the preceding decade or more. For the most part, *A Moveable Feast* was a happy surprise. It contradicted the rule that literary remains are disappointing, said the *National Review* and *America*; it showed, said *Newsweek,* that fears of inferior work being published posthumously were unjustified; and the *New York Times* observed that it was greater pleasure to read Hemingway than to cope with the folklorists of his mythology.

Aside from the question of posthumous publication, the principal issue concerned the genre of the new book. Although a number of reviewers accepted the book as a memoir, even more took Hemingway's cautionary preface seriously and thought it best read as fiction, probably as a loosely arranged novel on the order of *Winseburg, Ohio.*

Because of Hemingway's disparaging portraits of his rivals in Paris during the twenties, a number of reviewers doubted that the book should have been published at all. Alan Pryce-Jones thought Hemingway had defied Gertrude Stein's advice and had written an *inaccrochable* work. Others reasoned that the book should not be taken as literary history but as one man's view, biased by competitive instincts, of the petty jealousies at work in the expatriate colony. But most of all it was the poignancy of the memoir or idyl that impressed critics. Regardless of whether it was fair, the statement came from Hemingway's youthful experience but with an old man's sadness, and, as Philip Young observed, it was not a remembering but a re-experiencing. The testament, made poignant by Hemingway's death, said *Time,* sometimes read like his obituary.

In 1967 when William White brought together seventy-seven of Hemingway's previously published journalistic pieces in *By-Line: Ernest Hemingway,* critics recognized immediately that the work constituted a further mining of the vault. To the recurring question whether the pieces should have been republished, knowing Hemingway's 1930 injunction that they be ignored in the estimate of his reputation, most critics agreed that the collection reminded readers of an important part of Hemingway's career. They were first-rate, said Granville Hicks, and according to the *National Observer,* they contradicted the maxim that journalism was the ruin of an artist. The *Christian Science Monitor,* however, thought the book's publication an unfortunate event at a time when Hemingway's reputation was already suffering a decline. To others the book was a telling index to Hemingway's achievement over forty years. It showed, said *Time,* his rise, peaking out, and decline, though some, like *Newsweek,* thought it showed his struggle to develop a unique style usable in his fiction.

The most significant question regarding the relationship of the journalism to Hemingway's reputation, however, was whether the book was more useful to the general reader or to Hemingway cultists. For the general reader, said Granville Hicks and others, the book provided a sense of gusto in living, a mint-fresh response to experience, and a fund of anecdotes on important people of the century. As with *A Moveable Feast,* these critics found Hemingway's joy in absorbing events, people, and places one of his most admirable contributions to the lives of his readers. Aside from the question whether the journalistic pieces enhanced their appreciation of his fiction, the cultists were concerned with what new light the pieces might throw on the sources of his fiction and on the connections between personal experience and imaginative creation. The typical comment was that the journalism would provide a scholarly hunting ground for generations of monograph writers.

When *Islands in the Stream* appeared in the fall of 1970, everyone recognized it as the remains of the big novel rumored to exist since the late forties. Part of it had presumably been published as *The Old Man and the Sea.* The chief question haunting reviewers was whether Hemingway had withheld publication because he believed it good enough to stand as his insurance policy, both literarily and financially, or because he knew it was not on a par with his chief work. Most reviewers thought the latter explanation correct; they found the work disappointing, and the consequent issue again became the wisdom of posthumous publication. Most argued that it was after all only a draft, not a completed novel. The *New York Times* thought it had the smell of exploitation, *Time* thought it "stunningly bad" and said that Hemingway would have cut it by a third, and the *New Leader* thought it a monstrous lapse of judgment by his widow. More indulgent reviewers thought it impressive and haunting but not a masterpiece. Malcolm Cowley, however, called it Hemingway's best work, and in a late review, obviously written with the knowledge that the book was taking a beating, Edmund Wilson said the novel would become more impressive than most critics presently thought.

Sensing that the novel might well provide the last occasion for review of Hemingway's legendary style, critics were as easy on the technique as they were severe on the content of the work. Most noted and applauded the painterly prose but, like *Commonweal,* thought that style was the only thing happening in the novel. Hemingway used style in an attempt to induce meaning, said *Harper's,* and, said *Commentary,* he evoked a dreamlike quality for events otherwise disconnected and emotions otherwise suspended. More positively, the *Virginia Quarterly Review* thought his narrative skills were shown in "staggering splendor." But the verdict in general was that the long-awaited big novel in Hemingway's later career was a disappointment.

After the failure of the posthumously published novel as an art form, reviewers were apparently disposed to think more nostalgically of Hemingway's achievement in the short story form. When, in the spring of 1972, Philip Young collected the Nick Adams stories from *In Our Time, Men Without Women,* and *Winner Take Nothing,* arranged them in the chronological order of Nick's development, and added eight previously unpublished stories or sketches about Nick Adams, reviewers gave the book their heavily qualified approval. The eight new pieces added nothing to an appreciation of Hemingway as a short story writer, most indicated, but the stories and their arrangement provided additional insights into one of his most cryptically elusive characters. They verified Hemingway's early decisions to cut out the material here published. What the new pieces told explicitly of Nick could already be inferred from the previously published stories, said *Time*. Almost all reviewers thought the new stories were second-drawer Hemingway, additions to but not rivals of those previously known.

Viewing together the early as well as the later Nick Adams stories, several critics called for a more definitive introduction than that provided by Philip Young. Bibliographer-critic Matthew Bruccoli in the *Chicago Daily News* called for a detailed introduction that pointed out autobiographical parallels, and for data on when the stories were written and published. The *Washington Post* thought the introduction ought to point out the joys in Hemingway's Michigan experience that were echoed in the stories but missing from his biography. Young had indeed written such an introduction but had been overruled in placing it in the collection; it appeared with some revisions later in the year in *Novel* (Fall 1972). In the *Atlantic Monthly*, however, William Abrahams thought a more compelling book would be the "Complete Stories of Ernest Hemingway," thoroughly edited and arranged in order of composition with the stories Hemingway had chosen not to publish relegated to an appendix. Appropriately enough, with the publication of the last of the material in the vault, fifty years debate on the literary achievements of a key American writer ended on a bibliographical and retrospective note. Following generations would have to make their estimates on a career that was now well complete.

Hemingway's critical reception during the middle half of the century provides more than a profile of a writer's career. It serves also as an index of critical preoccupations through which reviewers could announce that certain works were valid contributions to the imaginative life of the world. In effect, the response to Hemingway became part of America's and the world's response to a half century of violence and anxiety.

That Hemingway was a writer so central to people's image of their time makes their recognition of him all the more impressive. Whether critics dealt with the problem of a writer's early success and long decline as symptomatic of our intellectual health or with the problem of new freedom in literary forms and language, they were judging this writer by what they understood to be the generally accepted criteria of their day. In addition, they had to come to terms with the role of literature in response to an imperfectly understood *Zeitgeist* as well as to more specific crises of depression and war.

That some commentators were more influential than others in the development and application of the criteria has to be recognized if we are to arrive at a judicious view of Hemingway's critical fortunes. Hemingway's reception would undoubtedly have been less favorable without the early acclaim of Edmund Wilson. He was among those who understood the significance of the symbolist movement when others were still under sway of the naturalistic and genteel traditions. Similarly, Malcolm Cowley's re-interpretation of Hemingway in the forties did much to direct criticism away from him as a naturalist at the dead end of a tradition and toward a new view of the novelist as a practitioner of an older and more fruitful tradition of art as ritual. Lionel Trilling's insights into the dangers of art serving sociology came at a time that not only corrected the artist's performance but his reviewers' expectations as well. For in spite of Hemingway's feud with critics and his claims to be unaffected by their admonitions, his writing, however indirectly, seems to reflect their influence. Not the least consideration, also, is the recognition of Hemingway's influence on his fellow writers, whether as a model for the "tough guy" school or as a rallying point for such peers as Faulkner, Dos Passos, O'Hara, and Elliot Paul. To them he was something of a test case, and what happened to him happened to the practice of fiction in America.

Robert O. Stephens
Greensboro, North Carolina
July 1976

Acknowledgements

For such a project as this I am fundamentally indebted to Audre Hanneman for her *Ernest Hemingway: A Comprehensive Bibliography* (Princeton University Press, 1967, 1975). Although I have gone beyond Hanneman both for reviews published since her bibliography and for some earlier ones not listed therein, I acknowledged, with gratitude, her groundwork. Of considerable use for the chapter on *Islands in the Stream* was William R. Anderson, Jr.'s "*Islands in the Stream*: The Intial Reception" in *The Fitzgerald/Hemingway Annual, 1971* (Washington, D.C.: NCR Microcard Editions, 1971). I am grateful to Charles Scribner's Sons for the use of materials drawn from their review files. For its critical point of view and its uses in many ways as a model Roger Asselineau's *The Literary Reputation of Hemingway in Europe* (New York University Press, 1965) deserves acknowledgment.

While it is almost axiomatic that no listing of newspaper reviews can be totally exhaustive, I have attempted to obtain a fair sampling of reviews from newspapers across the country. It was important to note the responses of reviewers removed from the major publishing centers in order to note such discrepancies as may exist between reviews written for general readers of the heartlands and those written for a metropolitan audience. I wish to acknowledge the help of the following libraries and persons in identifying, obtaining, and copying reviews: The Public Library of Nashville and Davidson County and Jeanette McQuitty, Anthony P. Cavender, and James M. Smith; Henry O. Vaag, Literature and History Department, Denver Public Library; Emmie Hayes, Adult Services, Miami Public Library; Marjorie Kinney, Missouri Valley Room, Kansas City Public Library; Michael J. Moffitt, Literature Department, Seattle Public Library; John Mullane, History and Literature Department, The Public Library of Cincinnati and Hamilton County; Irene K. Cronin, Reference Department, Springfield (Massachusetts) City Library; Cleveland Public Library; General Library, *Chicago Tribune;* Mildred Giusti, Providence Public Library; New York Public Library; University of Minnesota Library; Dartmouth University Library; University of Cincinnati Library; University of Pennsylvania Library; Louis Round Wilson Library, University of North Carolina at Chapel Hill; William R. Perkins Library, Duke University; Wesleyan University Library; University of Kentucky Library; University of Wyoming Library; New York State Library; Brown University Library; St. Louis University Library; University of Illinois, Urbana, Library; D. H. Hill Library, North Carolina State University; and especially the Walter Clinton Jackson Library, University of North Carolina at Greensboro. I also gratefully acknowledge the Research Council, University of North Carolina at Greensboro, for providing me with grants, which I used for obtaining materials and for typing the manuscript.

Reviews cited in this study fall into three categories: those reprinted wholly or in part, those summarized, and those listed at the end of each chapter under "Checklist of Additional Reviews." The "Checklist" includes summaries that do not add substantially to the critical evaluation of Hemingway's books, parody reviews more remarkable for their own wit than for reflection on the books in question, and occasional appreciative articles that are not primarily reviews but do contain evaluative comments. Certain reviews presented special difficulties which prevented inclusion. Those summarized would have been reprinted except for the inordinate costs or other technical or legal difficulties posed by controllers of copyrights. In summarizing reviews I have tried to be faithful to the ideas of the reviewers and where possible to the tone of the reviews. In selecting the ones that were reprinted wholly or in part, I have been fairly flexible in defining the limits of the study. Included are a few reviews by British writers published in American journals and some by American writers from British journals. To avoid undue repetition I have deleted plot summaries from many reviews, except where plot summary serves as the vehicle for evaluative comment; such deletions are marked by asterisks and ellipses. Silent corrections have been made in deletion of publishing information (except where it was an integral part of the text), in deletion of sectional headings in newspaper reviews, in correcting obvious typographical errors, and in regularizing punctuation.

Acknowledgment is made to the following newspapers, journals and individuals for permission to reprint reviews: John W. Aldridge, "Hemingway Between Triumph and Disaster," by permission of the author. Reviews from *Best Sellers* by permission of the journal. Alvah Bessie, review of *For Whom the Bell Tolls*, by permission of the author. Henry Seidel Canby, "A Report on *The Old Man and the Sea*," and review of *For Whom the Bell Tolls*; Clifton Fadiman, "Ernest Hemingway," by permission of the Book-of-the-Month Club. Margaret Manning, "Nick Adams—A Reminder," courtesy of the *Boston Globe*. David Madden, "Some Early Hemingway," reprinted by permission of *The Boston Herald Traveller*. Phoebe-Lou Adams, review of *The Nick Adams Stories*, by permission of *The Boston Review of the Arts*. Edwin Berry Burgum, "Hemingway's Development," by permission of the author. Matthew J. Bruccoli, "Return of Nick Adams," by permission of the author. G. E. Murray, "Papa's Tales of Nick Adams," by permission of the *Chicago Sun-Times*. Fanny Butcher, "Short Stories Still Live as Works of Art," "The Old Black Magic That Is Hemingway's," "Here Is Genius, Critic Declares of Hemingway"; Walter Havighurst, review of *By-Line: Ernest Hemingway*, "Hemingway at Sunrise"; "Hemingway Seems Out of Focus in 'The Sun Also Rises,'" reprinted courtesy of the *Chicago Tribune*. Reviews by Melvin Maddocks, Theodore Kalem, Roderick Nordell and Olive Dean Hormel © 1964, 1967, 1950, 1970, 1952 The Christian Science Publishing Society, and reprinted by permission of *The Christian Science Monitor*. Reprinted by permission of the *Cincinnati Enquirer*: reviews of *The Torrents of Spring* and *The Sun Also Rises*; R.A., review of *Death in the Afternoon*; J.R., review of *Winner Take Nothing*; Isabel Ackerman, review of *Green Hills of Africa*; R.M.D., review of *To Have and Have Not*; John O. Chappell, Jr., review of *For Whom the Bell Tolls*; Frederick Yeiser, reviews of *Across the River and into the Trees* and *The Old Man and the Sea*. Stephen Donadio, "Hemingway," reprinted from *Commentary*, by permission; copyright © 1970 by the American Jewish Committee and permission of the author. Philip Rahv, reviews of *Across the River and into the Trees* and *The Old Man and the Sea*, reprinted from *Commentary*, by permission; copyright © 1950, © 1952 by the American Jewish Committee and permission of the author. Robert Emmett Long, review of *Islands in the Stream*, reprinted by permission of Commonweal Publishing Co., Inc. Malcolm Cowley, "Hemingway in Madrid," copyright 1938 by Editorial Publications, Inc.; renewal copyright 1966 by Malcolm Cowley, reprinted by permission of the author. John Dos Passos, review of *A Farewell to Arms*, copyright by H. Marston Smith and Elizabeth H. Dos Passos, co-executors of the estate of John Dos Passos, by permission. H. L. Mencken, "Fiction by Adept Hands" and "The Spanish Idea of a Good Time," by permission of LaVonne D. Furr. Reprinted by permission of Fadiman Associates, Ltd: Clifton Fadiman, "Ernest Hemingway Crosses the Bridge," "News from the Hemingway Front," "A Letter to Mr. Hemingway," "Hemingway," and "Busy Week." F. Scott Fitzgerald, "How to Waste Material: A Note on My Generation," by permission of Frances Fitzgerald Smith. Otis Ferguson, "And There Were Giants on the Earth," reprinted from *The Film Criticism of Otis Ferguson*, edited by

THREE STORIES

Up in Michigan

Out of Season

My Old Man

& TEN POEMS

Mitraigliatrice

Oklahoma

Oily Weather

Roosevelt

Captives

Champs d'Honneur

Riparto d'Assalto

Montparnasse

Along With Youth

Chapter Heading

ERNEST HEMINGWAY

Three Stories and Ten Poems *and* in our time

"K. J."
Transatlantic Review, 1
(April 1924),
246.

Mr. Ernest Hemingway's *Three Stories* shows a sensitive feeling for the emotional possibilities of a situation. His method is realistic, but unlike most of his school he has not killed his work on the shallow hardness of photography. *Out of Season* relies for its effect on the power of suggestion and in spite of its surface crudities is one of the best bits of suggestive writing I have seen.

Marjorie Reid.
Transatlantic Review, 1
(April 1924),
247-48.

"Here ends the inquest into the state of contemporary English prose, as edited by Ezra Pound and printed at The Three Mountains Press." This brief comment is affixed to the sixth and last volume in a series of six select-ed by the editor as most indicative of the present trend in English literary expression. In eighteen chapters the longest of which measures scarcely two pages Mr. Hemingway gives pictures of life in the army, in Italy, in the bull rings of Spain, in the gardens of the King of Greece. He projects the moments when life is condensed and clean-cut and significant, presenting them in minute narratives that eliminate every useless word. Each tale is much longer than the measure of its lines. . . .

Edmund Wilson.
"Mr. Hemingway's
Dry-Points."
Dial, 77
(October 1924),
340-41.

Mr. Hemingway's poems are not particularly important, but his prose is of the first distinction. He must be counted as the only American writer but one—Mr. Sherwood Anderson—who has felt the genius of Gertrude Stein's Three Lives and has been evidently influenced by it. Indeed, Miss Stein, Mr. Anderson, and Mr. Hemingway may now be said to form a school by themselves. The characteristic of this school is a naïveté of language often passing into the colloquialism of the character dealt with which serves actually to convey profound emotions and complex states of mind. It is a distinctively American development in prose —as opposed to more or less successful American achievements in the traditional style of English prose—which has artistically justified itself at its best as a limpid shaft into deep waters.

Not, however, that Mr. Hemingway is imitative. On the contrary, he is rather strikingly original, and in the dry compressed little vignettes of In Our Time has almost invented a form of his own.

* * *

Mr. Hemingway is remarkably successful in suggesting moral values by a series of simple statements of this sort. His more important book is called In Our Time, [sic] and below its cool objective manner really constitutes a harrowing record of barbarities: you have not only political executions, but criminal hangings, bullfights, assassinations by the police, and all the cruelties and enormities of the war. Mr. Hemingway is wholly unperturbed as he tells about these things: he is not a propagandist even for humanity. His bull-fight sketches have the dry sharpness and elegance of the bull-fight lithographs of Goya. And, like Goya, he is concerned first of all with making a fine picture. He is showing you what life is, too proud an artist to simplify.

And I am inclined to think that his little book has more artistic dignity than any other that has been written by an American about the period of the war.

Not perhaps the most vivid book, but the soundest. Mr. Hemingway, who can make you feel the poignancy of the Italian soldier deciding in his death agony that he will "make a separate peace," has no anti-militaristic *parti pris* which will lead him to suppress from his record the exhilaration of the men who had "jammed an absolutely perfect barricade across the bridge" and who were "frightfully put out when we heard the flank had gone, and we had to fall back." It is only in the paleness, the thinness of some of his effects that Mr. Hemingway sometimes fails. I am thinking especially of the story called Up in Michigan, which should have been a masterpiece, but has the curious defect of dealing with rude and primitive people yet leaving them shadowy.

In Our Time has a pretty and very amusing cover designed from scrambled newspaper clippings. The only objection I have to its appearance is that the titles are throughout printed without capitals—thus: "in our time by ernest hemingway—paris." This device, which used to be rather effective when the modernists first used to use it to call attention to the fact that they had something new to offer, has now grown common and a bore. The American advertisers have taken it over as one of their stock tricks. And it is so unsightly in itself that it is rather a pity to see it become—as in the case of Mr. Hemingway's book and Mr. Hueffer's "transatlantic review"—a sort of badge of everything that is freshest and most interesting in modern writing.

Kansas City Star, December 20, 1924, p. 6.

Several years ago Ernest Hemingway was a reporter on The Star. Now, in Paris, as correspondent of the Toronto Star, he is recognized, not simply as a journalist, but as one of the most promising young writers in the English language. When Ford Madox Ford, the distinguished novelist and poet, went to America for a visit, he selected Hemingway as the ablest available man to edit the Transatlantic Review during his absence. In view of Ford's rank as an author and editor and of the position of the Transatlantic as one of the principal literary publications of Europe, the recognition amounts to a great deal.

One does not need to take the word of others, however, for Hemingway's ability. Although his published work, outside of newspaper articles, is slight in quantity, it has the quality that is associated with distinguished talent, if not absolute genius.

A little, unpretentious appearing book, with the simple descriptive title, "Three Stories and Ten Poems," written in English, but published in Paris, contains some of the best writing that I have seen from the pen of contemporary American authors. I say this primarily of the stories. In the poems

one feels some of the excellent quality that appears in the prose, but somehow the verse more or less obscures it. The stories, simple, direct, revealing, one of them set in the middle West, the other two in Europe, are the real stuff.

In them are vividness and the firm sure texture of reality. These, however are not uncommon in the work of a great many good writers. What Mr. Hemingway has added is a certain superior objectivity. He has taken told of the best quality that modern journalism has, and he has carried it forward to a new point. Journalistic objectivity is content with the sense impressions of things, excluding both the opinions of the writer and the emotions of the actors except so far as the latter may be inferred from action.

Exclusion of opinion is all to the good. In many cases, however, the emotions of the actors are needed to make a story complete or significant. The "yellow" newspaper recognizes this and pays a reporter to fake a portrayal of the emotions of a man before execution, for example—a portrayal which the murderer is persuaded to sign as his own. The result is always transparent bunk, for the reason that it requires something approaching genius to present the actors' emotions accurately and keep the author and his opinions and emotions out. It is this that Hemingway achieves. It puts into his work a fine, unsentimental understanding.

Add to this achievement Hemingway's real power in description, in picking out the essentials of an object or a person or an action in much the

same way that contemporary painters
are endeavoring to do; add also the
spare inevitableness of his characters,
and you have fiction which arouses the
definitely esthetic emotions as much
as does good music or good painting.
We are prone to talk about "literature
and art," as if literature were not one
of the arts. When literature gets good
enough, however, any reader sees it as
art. And Mr. Hemingway's work is
good enough.

Checklist of
Additional Reviews

Burton Rascoe. "A Bookman's Day
    Book." *New York Herald Tribune*,
    June 15, 1924, Book Section, p. 20.

Notes

in our time

by

ernest hemingway

A GIRL IN CHICAGO: Tell us about
the French women, Hank.   What are
they like?
  BILL SMITH: How old are the French
women, Hank?

paris:

printed at the **three mountains press** *and for sale*
at shakespeare & company, *in the rue de l'odéon;*
london: william jackson, *took's court, cursitor street, chancery lane.*

1924

In Our Time

Herschel Brickell.
"Tales Galore by Writers
From Lands Far
and Near."
*New York Evening Post
Literary Review,*
October 17, 1925,
p. 3.

Mr. Hemingway's book carries on its dust-covers the enthusiastic recommendations of nearly everybody except Mayor Hylan. That's funnier, perhaps, than fair. For the men who praise "In Our Time" know good work when they see it. Sherwood Anderson is there leading the chorus, and Mr. Hemingway's work is most like his. It is an attempt to get at minds and souls and what goes on within.

Of "stories" in the commonly accepted sense of the word there are few; the best of the lot a beautifully executed tale of the racetracks which Mr. Anderson himself could not have bettered. Most of the others are psychological episodes, incidents, sketches . . . call them what you will. They are soundly and movingly done; Mr. Hemingway uses the vernacular with skill. In the curious brief pieces scattered through his pages he does remarkable things with a mere handful of words.

"Preludes to a Mood."
*New York Times Book
Review,*
October 18, 1925,
p. 8.

Ernest Hemingway has a lean, pleasing, tough resilience. His language is fibrous and athletic, colloquial and fresh, hard and clean; his very prose seems to have an organic being of its own. Every syllable counts toward a stimulating, entrancing experience of magic. He looks out upon the world without prejudice or preconception and records with precision and economy, and an almost terrifying immediacy, exactly what he sees. His short stories, sketches, anecdotes and epigrams are triumphs of sheer objectivity.

The items which make up the collection of "In Our Time" are not so much short stories, in the accepted meaning, as preludes to a mood, composed with accurate and acute finesse to converge in the mind of the reader. Mr. Hemingway is oblique, inferential, suggestive rather than overt, explicit, explanatory. His people and events emerge with miraculous suddenness

and inevitability out of a timeless paradise of their own, to intimate their
own especial and intrinsic incongrui-
ties and ironies and pathos out of an
illimitable fabric of comedies and tragedies.

Mr. Hemingway packs a whole character into a phrase, an entire situation
into a sentence or two. He makes each
word count three or four ways. The
covers of his book should strain and
bulge with the healthful ferment that
is between them. Here is an authentic
energy and propulsive force which is
contained in an almost primitive isolation of images as if the language itself
were being made over in its early directness of metaphor. Each story, indeed, is a sort of expanded metaphor,
conveying a far larger implication than
its literal significations.

The first five stories are linked upon the personality of one Nick. In the
seventy pages or so, Nick, his father a
doctor, and his hypochondriacal Christian Science wife, his uncle, his friend,
his first love affair, his fishing expeditions and his casual adventures serve to
give a unique and unmistakable portrait of a growing boy in a Michigan
backwoods settlement. The first story
might almost be a stripped, matter-of-
fact account of a delicate, tricky surgical operation told with the scientific
finality and reticence of a medical report. Mr. Hemingway does not worry
at the young boy's symptoms, his "reactions" to this terrifying introduction to the mysteries of birth and
death; he states: "Nick did not watch.
His curiosity had been gone for a
long time."

Mr. Hemingway can make the reader see a trout lying on the pebbles of a
clear, swift, cold stream. He can show
you the four-cornered mouth of a
grasshopper and the sudden, disconcerting spurt of "tobacco juice" over
the restraining fingers. He can call up a
whole bullfight, indeed an entire civilization, in a curt epigram. He can present the life and the preoccupations
about a race course—the horses, the
jockeys, the touts, the bettors.

Mr. Hemingway's most noteworthy
gift, however, is for a delightful economy of dialogue. In "The Three-Day
Blow," two boys sit over a wood fire
and talk; the shanty, the gale outside,
their convictions and habitual modes
of being are fully revealed in irrevelant
aimless snatches of conversation. It
seems to be overheard, it is so compel-
lingly actual, yet it gives evidence of
Mr. Hemingway's severely schooled se-
lectiveness. It is merely one afternoon
when these two decided to get drunk,
nothing more, yet it is a friendship of
months and years, dense with common
experiences and impressions. Their
weighing of the relative values of baseball teams, of Hugh Walpole and G. K.
Chesterton, of their respective fathers,
and their philosophizings on life in
general are priceless yet poignant with
a hint of that fleeting, ephemeral quality, youth.

Paul Rosenfeld.
"Tough Earth."
New Republic, 45 (November 25, 1925), 22-23.

Hemingway's short stories belong with cubist painting, Le Sacre du Printemps, and other recent work bringing a feeling of positive forces through primitive modern idiom. The use of the direct, crude, rudimentary forms of the simple and primitive classes and their situations, of the stuffs, textures and rhythms of the mechanical and industrial worlds, has enabled this new American story teller, as it enabled the group to which he comes a fresh recruit, to achieve peculiarly sharp, decided, grimly affirmative expressions; and with these acute depictions and half-impersonal beats to satisfy a spirit running through the age. Hemingway's spoken prose is characteristically iron with a lyricism, aliveness and energy tremendously held in check. With the trip-hammer thud of Le Sacre his rhythms go. Emphatic, short, declarative sentences follow staunchly one upon the other, never precipitously or congestedly or mechanically, and never relenting. The stubby verbal forms are speeded in instances up to the brute, rapid, joyous jab of blunt period upon period. Hemingway's vocabulary is largely monosyllabic, and mechanical and concrete. Mixed with the common words, raw and pithy terms picked from the vernaculars of boys, jockeys, hunters, policemen, soliders,

and obscurely related to primitive impulse and primitive sex, further increase the rigidity of effect. There is something of Sherwood Anderson, of his fine bare effects and values coined from simplest words, in Hemingway's clear medium. There is Gertrude Stein equally obvious: her massive volumes, slow power, steady reiterations, and her intuition of the life of headless bodies. The American literary generations are learning to build upon each other. This newcomer's prose departs from the kindred literary mediums as a youngling from forebears. Wanting some of the warmth of Anderson and some of the pathos of Gertrude Stein, Hemingway's style none the less in its very experimental stage shows the outline of a new, tough, severe and satisfying beauty related equally to the world of machinery and the austerity of the red man.

It comes on the general errand of the group, the realization of a picture of the elements of life caught in barest, intensest opposition. . . . The sheer unfeeling barbarity of life, and the elementary humor and tenderness lying close upon it, is a favorite theme. The amazing single pages previously assembled in a booklet by the Three Mountains Press in Paris, sandwiched between the longer stories in the Liveright volume and connecting these with the doings of an epoch, bring dangerously close in instantaneous pictures of the War, of the bull-ring and the police-world, the excitement of combat, the cold ferocity of the mob, the insensibility of soldiering, the relief of nerves in alcoholic stupor, the naked, the mean, the comic brute in the human frame. Against these principles, set invariably in crude, simple, passionate opposition, the author plays the more constructive elements. . . .

There is little analysis in this narrative art. We are given chiefly, at times with marvelous freshness and crispness, what the eye sees and the ear hears. The conflicting principles are boldly established without psychologizings. Yet Hemingway's acceptance of the aesthetic responsibility of getting his material into action in instances remains near gesturing. His units are not brought into actual opposition in all his pieces. Or, formally introduced, they remain at inadequate degrees of tension, while a youthfully insolent sense of the stereotype in life blinds the author. Soldier's Home is one of Hemingway's forms half left in the limbo of the stencil. The happy relief to this and other incompleted pieces is furnished by stories like Cat in the Rain, Indian Camp, and My Old Man. In these, plastic elements accurately felt are opposed point against point, and a whole brought into view. It is a whole this newcomer has to show. It is one from which the many beauties of his book are fetched. He shares his epoch's feeling of a harsh impersonal force in the universe, permanent, not to be changed, taking both destruction and construction up into itself and set in motion by their dialectic. With the blood and pain, he makes us know the toughness of the earth, able to meet desire, nourish life, and waken in man the power to meet the brutalities of existence. This bald feeling is the condition of an adjustment to life begun in men before the War, but demanded even more intensely of them by its ghastlier train, and natural at all times to the products of primitive America. Through it men are reconciled to perpetual struggle, and while holding themselves tight work in relation to something in the universe. This adjustment is not the sole possible one. It is not necessarily the one of next year or of the year to follow, for any. But it had and still has its reality; and the rhythms, and tempi which communicate it share in its permanence.

Schuyler Ashley. *Kansas City Star,* December 12, 1925, p. 6.

This curious and interesting collection of stories and sketches is distinguished by a discriminating use of modern idiom and argot. The short sentences bite like acid; the infrequent expletives snarl and rumble like loaded trucks under a viaduct.

There are many adjectives which come easily to mind in an attempt to characterize the writing of Ernest Hemingway. Objective is one of them; his stories are almost too artfully disanchored from his own emotions. Vital and astringent they are to a surpassing degree. His phrases are brittle, with mordant edges, and he has the inestimable gift of concrete visualization. In lean, spare sentences he always makes you see the thing he writes about. But what comes nearest to catching his peculiar quality is the everyday vernacular term "hardboiled." This fellow is indubitably a hard-boiled writer. He has a great feeling for the nonchalant, bleak-faced relish for life enjoyed by truck drivers and city detectives. He knows Negroes, prize fighters, ex-marines and lonely men who go fishing. He gets at the very essence of young, fairly tough boys, and he writes with gusto of horse racing and bull fighting.

With Sherwood Anderson and Ring Lardner this author shares a secret. They have discovered a rich vein of linguistic ore that lies just below the surface of every trafficway and freight dock, and they are all realizing on the lode. They seek to let the old, worn, literary metaphors retire to amply earned repose, since from the lips of every irascible towboat captain or badly frightened dockhand they hear vivid, startling figures drawn from the complex mechanical civilization of today.

Of course, "In Our Time" is admittedly a slight and fragmentary enterprise. It is, however, a promise, almost an assurance, of richer and more important things to come. A pianist who supples his fingers before essaying a Brahms sonata, a pitcher warming up craftily in the bullpen, or a fighter shadow-boxing under the arc lights before going to work in a cold ring; these are figures applicable to Ernest Hemingway in "In Our Time." By this collection he has established himself as a colorful and competent performer; when he tackles a real subject he should bring all the stands up cheering. More power to him!

Ernest Walsh. "Mr. Hemingway's Prose." *This Quarter*, 1 (Winter 1925-26), 319-21.

The first impression one gets on reading a story by Hemingway is that this writer has been getting ready inside himself and outside himself for a long time before he began to write for the good job of writing. [sic] I mean getting ready unconsciously. It has been a growing process as natural as a plant getting ready to bloom so that one knows that spring or no spring a blooming is going to come off.

I don't mean ripened because Hemingway has always been ripe. He began life a ripe force. He is no accident of the weather. His stories are too deeply rooted in hard soil to have come out with the first breeze out of the land of promise. His is an intended blooming and what we miss in the praises of Sherwood Anderson, Ford Madox Ford, Gilbert Seldes, Edward J. O'Brien, Waldo Frank, Donald Ogden Stewart and John Dos Passos is a recognition of Hemingway's first distinction among the artists of this period and what sets him apart from most living writers, namely: His clarity of heart. We have vigorous writing in others, and vigorous intellect and vigorous heart and vigor of many other kinds but these are after all words and phrases used to sell books. I'm talking about something a human being made out of his life and which takes its aristocracy from the creator's clarity of heart. . . .

Everyone talks about the beauty of Hemingway's prose. It is a dirty low-down critic's trick to speak of a man's heart as *prose*. It is time it was written that *beautiful prose* as written by Ernest Hemingway is not an accomplishment like playing the piano and which anyone can acquire by sufficient practice and moral application and the possession of a piano. The genius of Hemingway's writing lies somewhere around his getting ready to write since some time back. The rest happened. Hemingway managed to get born in America and born with more sensitiveness than most young men born in America. And then he used that sensitiveness to face life rather than to avoid it. Hemingway is perhaps one of the first young writers in this period to realize the importance of being a young man today. With heart he has gone like a man through his dreams before awakening and a Spartan mind and will has renounced with every footstep until we have an uncanny mixture of boy-fresh perception joined to the personality of an artist whose understanding and sympathy for youth is older and wider while keeping within the circle of youth itself. Hemingway is too much of an artist ever to patronize youth and in this he shows that youth understands itself better than age does itself.

There are lines in Hemingway's stories *that come at one reading them as if they had grown in the reader's heart* out of an old memory or an old wish to remember. It doesn't matter that Hemingway's characters all talk alike regardless of age or race or sex and that in each case the language is Hemingway's language. I say it doesn't matter because this is surmounted by an important contribution to the letters of this day. *Hemingway's characters don't all think alike.* But they all think and think as they ought to think. Thinking characters is a new thing in letters. . . .

You can read Hemingway from beginning to end without the dictionary. Hemingway's vocabulary is mean and bare as a poor monastery and out of this he makes patterns of monastic austerity and richness. His stories are a triumph over material. He has accepted his world. He is the most indigenous of our writers and the least detached, the only young man writing who holds opinions and for that I could pray in a barber shop.

A Hemingway story is told from the inside of the characters not from without. There is not that annoying space between author and characters. One doesn't feel one is reading a book while the author looks over one's shoulder and breathes heavily into one's ear. One is alone with a story by Hemingway. One confesses a pleasure in reading him with more privacy afforded than the confessional box affords. There is no one about but the reader and the words on the printed page. Hemingway is the shyest and proudest and sweetest-smelling storyteller of my reading. His method of simplicity in word and sentence structure is the first thing to catch the critic's eye but other writers have been simple without getting his tone and strength. It is obvious that the use of words with few syllables gives a concentrated effect but Hemingway's strength is not merely in having made use of this truth for that would be just a trick of style. It is the piling up of word for word in the right order to give a homely word more than its meaning, it is the use of *speech* as distinguished from *language* that puts Hemingway among the first men writing today. He can make the slang word "*swell*" purchase more meaning in the mind of his reader than one would think possible without tiring the word. He is no dilettante in slang. He is no snobbish didapper seeking prey in shallow water. Hemingway selected his audience. His rewards will be rich. But thank God he will never be satisfied. He is of the elect. He belongs. It will take time to wear him out. And before that he will be dead.

Springfield Republican, January 3, 1926, p. 7A.

Ernest Hemingway in "In Our Time" has looked on life with keen and clear eyes, and shows ability to set "hard bits" of it forth with meaning. These "hard bits" are not strong in the "story" element, nor warmly touched with emotional color. Mr. Hemingway has, however, plenty of time before him for development. The stories of this collection are realism unmitigated, mostly concerning conventionally unpleasant subjects with the scenes of many laid in Indian camps. One such vividly pictures a skillful physician performing a Caesarian operation on an Indian young woman. with a jack knife as a surgical instrument. Interesting material is these stories but the treatment might be improved.

"Writer." *Time,* 7 (January 18, 1926), 38.

"Here is a writer. . . ." Hemingway is a new American writer who "instinctively differentiates between the hawk of living and the handsaw of existing." He has lived in unusual places and done unusual things. He knows the feel of trout-fishing in Michigan, about Yankee jockeys on European racetracks, about squaws bearing children in abandoned logging camps, about bulls and bullfighters tearing one another, about skiing in the Tyrol, about how it feels to shoot Germans in a garden at Mons, about bumming on Canadian trains, and how it is "to be in love, just at first and then really." You cannot say how he knows such things. He writes directly, without explaining himself, without introspection. His stories are more like facets of color and touch than complete narratives, reminiscent of Katherine Mansfield's but more brutally masculine and natural. "Make no mistake, Ernest Hemingway is somebody; a new, honest, un–'literary' transcriber of life–a writer." (Summary)

Allen Tate.
"Good Prose."
The Nation, 122
(February 10, 1926),
160-62.

Since the last years of the eighteenth century, when the writing, publication, and critical reception of books became a process in which these phases of literature were in fixed relations, only those writers most defiant of notice or most isolated by circumstances from competition in society have written as whole men. Few have been indifferent to the rewards speedily due a "performance" for which the stage has been stiffly set at some loss to the fulness of spirit which is a privilege of detachment and leisure. If style, phrase by phrase even, is not thus corrupted—some, like Cabell and Hergesheimer, do not utterly escape this most insidious reach of the infection—then it is the design, the structure, that suffers; the novel must be done up with a mechanically episodic neatness, externally and too obviously a good job. For the audience has been increasingly the puppet of critical advertisement; writers grow wary of the advertising agent, anxious of success. Swift, Fielding, Sterne, the author of "Moll Flanders" and "Captain Singleton," all popular in their time, were not moved, in their essays into pure letters, toward an extraneous satisfaction—one may say, toward a repudiation of spiritual autonomy for the public advantage of familiar properties.

Mr. Hemingway and Mr. Dos Passos are writers of unusual integrity in this respect, though what they share is not a quality of style or method but simply a seriousness, a care for good prose in itself, that would exclude them from the inquiry of Mr. Stuart Sherman who discovers "significant novelists."

* * *

Ernest Hemingway has developed his chief distinction in prose through a careful rejection of "ideas"; he does not conceive his subject matter; he presents it. You will not be able to separate, in his facile accumulation of *petites sensations,* the observer from the observation, the reporter from the item reported; he never comments in excess of the immediate value of the object as a thing seen, of the event as a focus of observed motions. If he lacks the concept of character, he has an infallible deftness at projecting personality by isolating into typical significance some trivial accident of conduct. He lacks the ostentation of a writer inadequately equipped yet ambitious with a "theory of reality." Most typical of Mr. Hemingway's precise economical method is the story Big Two-Hearted River, where the time is one evening to the next afternoon and the single character a trout fisherman who makes his camp-fire, sleeps all night, gets up and catches a few trout, then starts home; that is all. But the passionate accuracy of particular observation, the intense monosyllabic diction, the fidelity to the internal demands of the subject—these qualities fuse in the most completely realized naturalistic fiction of the age. . . .

Louis Kronenberger. "A New Novelist." *Saturday Review of Literature*, 2 (February 13, 1926), 555.

Ernest Hemingway's first book of short stories comes fortified with the praise of men like Sherwood Anderson, Ford Madox Ford, Waldo Frank, and John Dos Passos. The praise of such men fosters deduction. It indicates that Mr. Hemingway must have merit; it implies that his work is experimental, original, modernistic; it may even suggest that his work stems in part from the modes set by their own creation. All these deductions are to some extent true, but only the first is important. There are obvious traces of Sherwood Anderson in Mr. Hemingway and there are subtler traces of Gertrude Stein. His work is experimental and very modern. But much more significantly, it has sound merit of a personal, non-derivative nature; it shows no important affinity with any other writer, and it represents the achievement of unique personal experience.

I think it should be emphasized that Mr. Hemingway's stories are as much an achievement as they are an experiment. Already he has succeeded in making some of them finished products, whose form is consonant with their substance and whose value is not an implication for the future but a realization in the present. It is true that he has no power of emotion or deep quality of cerebration, but the way he has observed people and things, speech, surroundings, atmosphere, the spirit of our times, constitutes sufficient accomplishment for the moment. When translated into words, this power of observation is doubly effective: it is precise and direct, it is also suggestive and illuminating. Almost wholly through his sense of observation, he gets life into these pages: life at any moment, life at a vivid moment, life at a high and crucial moment. At his best, getting it there for a moment's duration, he somehow sends it running backward and forward, so that whatever must be understood is comprehensible by a discerning reader.

For the rest, his stories are experiments demanding further discipline and art. Between each two he interposes a paragraph of bare incident which further suggests the spirit of our time. Unfortunately some of the stories themselves, in their form and meaning, are like these paragraphs. They imply significance but they do not attain it; their lacunae are greater than their substance. They are not without life, but they lack meaning and intensity. Mr. Hemingway is in some respects an "intellectual" writer—in his culture, his humor, his implicit sophistication, his objectivity; but his work itself is finest when it portrays life, conversation, action. He is a synthetic observer, not an analyst.

Robert Wolf.
"In Our Time."
New York Herald Tribune Books, 2
February 14, 1926,
p. 3.

Ernest Hemingway is something new under the sun in American letters—he is the first representative of that post-war group that calls itself—not alone by accident of common residence—the Paris school.

* * *

Of them all, Hemingway is the most lyrical and the most highly finished artist. He shows the influence of Gertrude Stein very strongly, that of Joyce almost not at all; he is also very strongly under the influence of Sherwood Anderson. But through and around and under this he has produced in his own right some of the most sensitive and subtle short stories that have come from any young American.

Apart from individual variations, the style of all the members of this group has something in common—it is monotonous; it is built after the pattern of a machine rather than, let us say, a tree; it is based on co-ordinate rather than subordinate clauses, with corresponding simplicity of punctuation. As a result it has certain striking advantages in reflecting our modern, stereotyped machine civilization, advantages which once apprehended are hard to forego. It also has certain disadvantages. It is dull. Joyce, from the interest of his subject matter and his sheer exuberance and virtuosity rarely has dull moments, but the same cannot be said for the young Joycians and Steinians. Somehow or other this entire young post-armistice generation seems to be suffering from low blood pressure. I think it is not entirely a criticism of the public that they, who took "Winesburg, Ohio," to their bosom have allowed "In Our Time" to fall flat.

But having said this one must hasten to do justice to Hemingway's conspicuous merit. If he has not the crude vitality, the vigorous journalism perhaps, of the earlier Anderson, he is a much more deft and finished artist. He has a quiet irony that is entirely beyond Anderson—his effects throughout are achieved with entire lack of ostentation. I know of no more clever drunk scene anywhere than the one in which Nick and Bill gradually raise their voices, becoming more and more punctilious and elaborate as the whisky in the bottle disappears. "Mr. and Mrs. Elliot," perhaps the most individual achievement in the collection, has already given rise to a whole school of contemporary narrative of its own. "Out of Season," perhaps the most telling, is the ultimate definition of a futile day—the absence of its lead sinker is more cosmologically depressing than whole quartos of philosophical despair. And finally, I know of no American writer with a more startling ear for colloquial conversation, or a more poetic sensitiveness to woods and hills.

"In Our Time" has perhaps not enough energy to be a great book, but

Ernest Hemingway has promise of genius.

F. Scott Fitzgerald. "How To Waste Material, A Note on My Generation." *Bookman*, 63 (May 1926), 262-65.

Ever since Irving's preoccupation with the necessity for an American background, for some square miles of cleared territory on which colorful variants might presently arise, the question of material has hampered the American writer. For one Dreiser who made a single minded and irreproachable choice there have been a dozen like Henry James who have stupid-got with worry over the matter, and yet another dozen who, blinded by the fading tail of Walt Whitman's comet, have botched their books by the insincere compulsion to write "significantly" about America.

Insincere because it is not a compulsion found in themselves—it is "literary" in the most belittling sense. During the past seven years we have had at least half a dozen treatments of the American farmer, ranging from New England to Nebraska; at least a dozen canny books about youth, some of them with surveys of the American universities for background; more than a dozen novels reflecting various aspects of New York, Chicago, Washington, Detroit, Indianapolis, Wilmington,

and Richmond; innumerable novels dealing with American politics, business, society, science, racial problems, art, literature, and moving pictures, and with Americans abroad at peace or in war; finally several novels of change and growth, tracing the swift decades for their own sweet lavender or protesting vaguely and ineffectually against the industrialization of our beautiful old American life. We have had an Arnold Bennett for every five towns—surely by this time the foundations have been laid! Are we competent only to toil forever upon a never completed first floor whose specifications change from year to year?

In any case we are running through our material like spendthrifts—just as we have done before. . . .

Now the business is over. "Wolf" has been cried too often. The public, weary of being fooled, has gone back to its Englishmen, its memoirs and its prophets. Some of the late brilliant boys are on lecture tours (a circular informs me that most of them are to speak upon "the literary revolution"!), some are writing pot boilers, a few have definitely abandoned the literary life—they were never sufficiently aware that material, however closely observed, is as elusive as the moment in which it has its existence unless it is purified by an incorruptible style and by the catharsis of a passionate emotion.

* * *

"In Our Time" consists of fourteen stories, short and long, with fifteen vivid miniatures interpolated between them. When I try to think of any contemporary American short stories as good as "Big Two-Hearted River," the last one in the book, only Gertrude Stein's "Melanctha," Anderson's "The Egg," and Lardner's "Golden Honeymoon" come to mind. It is the account of a boy on a fishing trip—he hikes, pitches his tent, cooks dinner, sleeps, and next morning casts for trout. Nothing more—but I read it with the most breathless unwilling interest I have experienced since Conrad first bent my reluctant eyes upon the sea.

The hero, Nick, runs through nearly all the stories, until the book takes on almost an autobiographical tint—in fact "My Old Man," one of the two in which this element seems entirely absent, is the least successful of all. Some of the stories show influences but they are invariably absorbed and transmuted, while in "My Old Man" there is an echo of Anderson's way of thinking in those sentimental "horse stories," which inaugurated his respectability and also his decline four years ago.

But with "The Doctor and the Doctor's Wife," "The End of Something," "The Three Day Blow," "Mr. and Mrs. Elliot," and "Soldier's Home" you are immediately aware of something temperamentally new. In the first of these a man is backed down by a half breed Indian after committing himself to a fight. The quality of humiliation in the story is so intense that it immediately calls up every such incident in the reader's past. Without the aid of a comment or a pointing finger one knows exactly the sharp emotion of young Nick who watches the scene.

The next two stories describe an experience at the last edge of adolescence. You are constantly aware of the continual snapping of ties that is going on around Nick. In the half stewed, immature conversation before the fire you watch the awakening of that vast unrest that descends upon the emotional type at about eighteen. Again there is not a single recourse to exposition. As in "Big Two-Hearted River," a picture—sharp, nostalgic, tense—develops before your eyes. When the picture is complete a light seems to snap out, the story is over. There is no tail, no sudden change of pace at the end to throw into relief what has gone before.

Nick leaves home penniless; you have a glimpse of him lying wounded in the street of a battered Italian town, and later of a love affair with a nurse on a hospital roof in Milan. Then in one of the best of the stories he is home again. The last glimpse of him is when his mother asks him, with all the bitter world in his heart, to kneel down beside her in the dining room in Puritan prayer.

Anyone who first looks through the short interpolated sketches will hardly fail to read the stories themselves. "The Garden at Mons" and "The Barricade" are profound essays upon the English officer, written on a postage stamp. "The King of Greece's Tea Party," "The Shooting of the Cabinet Ministers," and "The Cigarstore Robbery" particularly fascinated me, as they did when Edmund Wilson first showed them to me in an earlier pamphlet, over two years ago.

Disregard the rather ill considered blurbs upon the cover. It is sufficient that here is no raw food served up by the railroad restaurants of California and Wisconsin. In the best of these dishes there is not a bit to spare. And many of us who have grown weary of admonitions to "watch this man or that" have felt a sort of renewal of excitement at these stories wherein Ernest Hemingway turns a corner into the street.

Ben Ray Redman. "Old Wine in New Bottles." *New York Herald Tribune Books, 7* November 16, 1930, p. 22.

Readers who made their first acquaintance with Ernest Hemingway in the pages of "The Sun Also Rises," and who passed through a profound emotional experience in the romance and tragedy of "A Farewell to Arms," may now possess themselves of the tales and sketches which, the better part of a decade ago, convinced perspicacious readers of certain "little" magazines that a young American writer of great power and untainted originality had come out of Oak Park, Illinois, and arrived in Montparnasse by way of the Italian front and other intermediate points of interest. For, let it be gladly recorded, Hemingway's fortunate publishers have deemed it fit and proper to bring forth a new edition of IN OUR TIME.

Checklist of Additional Reviews

Donald Davidson. "Firing Line." *Nashville Tennessean,* October 18, 1925, p. 7.
"Contrasting Methods." *Saturday Review of Literature,* 7 (January 24, 1931), 548.

The
Torrents of Spring

A Romantic Novel in Honor of the
Passing of a Great Race

BY

ERNEST HEMINGWAY

AUTHOR OF "IN OUR TIME"

And perhaps there is one reason why a comic
writer should of all others be the least excused
for deviating from nature, since it may not be
always so easy for a serious poet to meet with
the great and the admirable; but life everywhere furnishes an accurate observer with the
ridiculous.
                                HENRY FIELDING.

NEW YORK
CHARLES SCRIBNER'S SONS
1926

The Torrents of Spring

Harry Hansen.
"An American Parody."
New York World,
May 30, 1926,
p. 4M.

This seems to be the open season for authors. First comes Llewelyn Powys, Englishman, and in a brilliant travel record, "The Verdict of Bridlegoose," brings down a whole flock of New York celebrities. Next at the bench, with a steady eye on half a dozen targets, comes Ernest Hemingway, the most promising American author in Paris. Hemingway gained critical praise a year ago when he published "In Our Time," a series of short stories, based for the most part on pathological variations in human beings, told with much economy of language. Hemingway has now elaborated on his own idea of authors and their methods in "The Torrents of Spring," which he also calls a "romantic novel in honor of the passing of a great race." The book is, for the most part, a parody of Sherwood Anderson's style and subject matter; to some extent also of that of D. H. Lawrence. It is published not by Mr. Liveright, who issued Hemingway's first book and also publishes Sherwood Anderson, but by Mr. Scribner. Ergo, Mr. Scribner is able to announce that he will publish Hemingway's first novel in the fall.

Something seems to remind me that when Hemingway published "In Our Time" it was Sherwood Anderson who turned handsprings and welcomed this newcomer to the ranks of America's great men. Anderson trumpeted loudly, and now Hemingway pays him back by making him the principal butt of his parody. We may say, therefore, that Hemingway does not approve of logrolling. At least he is not going to "lay off" Anderson merely because the latter was a hospitable host. He evidently regards Anderson as long-winded and boring, and something of his attitude can be gathered from the frequent quotations from Fielding sprinkled through the pages of the new book. . . .

* * *

Hemingway had in Sherwood Anderson a remarkable subject. Taken superficially, Anderson would be easy to parody. He is always repeating himself, both in his words and in his attitudes. He shows no change, no many-sidedness. He is always the dreamy, searching groper, watching the commonplace facts of life with a sort of boyish amazement on his face. His prose is slow and simple. His stories haunt the reader, as they haunt him. He professes over and over again a love for words, without being able to use them as the dictionary indicates. But he also gives you the impression that he sees a bit beyond this external covering which buries men. He tries to dig down underneath the veneer of conventions. He goes about it slowly. His thoughts mature as slowly on paper as they mature slowly in the mind of the average plodding man.

So when Hemingway starts his story in a pump factory in Michigan and has Yogi Johnson talking to Scripps O'Neil about the weather—Scripps, who has two wives and a daughter he calls Lousy because her name is Lucy—you begin to get a glimmering of what is meant by superficial parody. Short sentences. Repetitious thoughts. . . .

* * *

A few other mannerisms. It is patent that D. H. Lawrence is in the mind of the author when he pictures Scripps marrying the waitress. "He felt vaguely uneasy. Something was stirring within him." Notes by the author to the reader recounting his adventures with literary fellows in Paris: John Dos Passos and F. Scott Fitzgerald. Comment on "The Making and Marring of Americans," perhaps a take-off on Lawrence's studies in American classical literature. I say perhaps. I don't know for sure. Hemingway has caught, I think, a glint of Anderson's professional naivete. Beyond that, however, parody is a gift of the gods. Few are blessed with it. It missed Hemingway. He is better as a writer of short stories.

W. Y.
New York Evening Post Literary Review,
June 12, 1926,
p. 9.

Ernest Hemingway, whom Ford Madox Ford found to be the most significant young American writer in Paris, calls his burlesque "a romantic novel in honor of the passing of a great race." And he writes more especially in the "manner" of Sherwood Anderson, following the moods and incidents of "Dark Laughter."

For the most part, the little book is great fun. Mr. Hemingway has left his special field of more or less grim truth telling to play in genial humor his master's game. And he has caught Mr. Anderson's characteristics much more convincingly and amusingly than any other parodist of him.

* * *

There is a variety of diverting allusion to contemporary figures in letters: an ingratiating informality now and again when the author discusses any number of things, all by the way, with the reader; and Mr. Hemingway permits himself to become as grave as he is like to be in one section devoted to the war.

Delicious fun for the reader of Sherwood Anderson and one of the best recent books we have found for reading aloud (always provided those present know Mr. Anderson's work).

"Mr. Hemingway Writes Some High-Spirited Nonsense."
New York Times Book Review,
June 13, 1926,
p. 8.

* * *

The delightful entertainment of "The Torrents of Spring," if not precisely what might have been expected of the author of "In Our Time," is full-blooded comedy, with a sting of satire at the expense of certain literary affectations. The object of Mr. Hemingway's gravely absurd travesty is somewhat on the side of the advanced intellectual position. The subtle incongruity which he establishes in the character of Scripps and Scripps' banal introspections is almost too keenly edged. It is, therefore, a somewhat specialized satire. It is almost in the nature of a literary vaudeville, which will appeal mainly to Mr. Hemingway's fellow-craftsmen. He is not parodying merely a manner but a philosophy and an attitude, a fundamental approach, as well. That calls for a degree of initiation and sophistication in his reader that may not always be available.

"The Torrents of Spring" reveals Mr. Hemingway's gift for highspirited nonsense. Whatever its effect on literary foibles, it contributes to that thoughtful gayety which true wit should inspire. While he ridicules certain extravagances by pushing them to the logical conclusion, Mr. Hemingway obviously entertains a robust respect for the object of his allusive gibes. In the last analysis, the book sets out to amuse. This it does.

"Laughing at Authors."
Cincinnati Enquirer,
June 19, 1926,
p. 8.

* * *

This is hardly the sort of thing one would expect to come from the author of "In Our Time." But the book bears Mr. Hemingway's name and must be his. But is it? One wonders. After all, does it really matter?

The trend of thought illustrated in the foregoing paragraph indicates the style of Mr. Hemingway's sprightly burlesque on the affected methods of certain popular authors of the day.

* * *

... The caption of the first chapter, "Red and Black Laughter," is more than a hint as to what writer Mr. Hemingway is burlesquing. The remainder of the story of Scripps O'Neil and Yogi Johnson, who worked in the pump factory, is of the same cloth. The tale of Scripps' love affairs with first one waitress—whom he marries because she reads the Mercury and the Dial—and then with the other, of Brown's Beanery, "Best By Test," is entertaining and made amusing and provocative by edged humor.

W.E.H.
Boston Evening Transcript,
July 3, 1926, Part 6, p. 2.

* * *

This seems to be the age of satire, and it is indeed considered a highly creditable thing for one man to mimic another's personality. The mere attainment of such a task is considered to be a workmanlike job worthy of accomplishment. And to back it up with erudite evidence of the worthiness one only needs to quote Henry Fielding on the title page. . . .

* * *

This reviewer holds no brief for Mr. Anderson: he considers him tedious and dull in his bad moments. But none the less, the man who has by sheer force and determination of will made himself a writer, and the leader of what Mr. Hemingway jocularly calls the "Chicago School," has never for a single line committed himself to "affectation"; his misfortune is that now at the middle period of his days he still casts wild, searching glances at life with the incoherent and mystified eyes of a schoolboy. But respect him at least for his honesty and humility. He is sincere.

Mr. Hemingway, who dedicates himself to the two Menckens, H. L. and S. Stanwood, discloses his purpose in his chapter headings, the most obvious of which seems to be entitled, "Red and Black Laughter," And to give him also his bit of credit, he has written faithfully in the vernacular of Sherwood Anderson. "The School," despite the prefatory words upon the jacket cover, does not interest him so much as does the frowning blackhaired leader. Anderson is a far easier task than Michael Arlen, or any of the others who have founded "schools" and basic patents, at which less able possessors of a long quill pen may thumb their noses, and thumbing call it art. Yet Mr. Hemingway would probably have fared as well with these others. There is little doubt that in his way he finds ready and favorable accomplishment. Indeed no other compliment need be turned his way than to remark that even to the dyed-in-the-wool Anderson enthusiast some of the phrases have the simplicity and ring of the original; not only that, they possess the same wondering, dazed interrogation with only the slightest of satirical barbs interjected.

* * *

Mr. Hemingway, and those who have in several attempts burlesqued "The Green Hat," do not really write to make their subject more understandable; their puspose is humor, good substantial, almost slap-stick fun that will seem because it deals with literary subjects to be so much, much nearer high comedy than it really is.

The only excuse for the rather rough treatment of sensitive if unfortunate writers of the Sherwood Anderson type is to be found in a philosophy of American laughter. If we are progressing beyond the crude, impersonal buffoonery of slap-stick, if this tearing of notable authors into hilarious shreds means that we as a race are approaching the more personal sense of humor, the laughter that can see something more than an old scarecrow, living but unable to arouse human emotions and sympathies in us, and set up merely to be torn down for our amusement, then this satire may mean something. Otherwise it is merely a more brutal form of play than slap-stick or bull fighting, and equally devoid of meaning, since the crowd has not the brains to originate such humors for itself.

* * *

Margery Latimer. "A Burlesque of Sherwood Anderson." *New York Herald Tribune Books*, 2 (July 18, 1926), 16.

* * *

It is hard to read "Dark Laughter" now and keep a straight face, although some claim to have been amused long before Mr. Hemingway's burlesque. . . .

Mr. Anderson's naive heroes and his women who rushed naked into fields of corn demanded the most serious consideration and grave discussion.

"The Torrents of Spring" gives just the right degree of self-consciousness and humor to the reader of Anderson and its superficial way seems to mark the passing of the naive realists. The book is more a burlesque of Mr. Anderson's psychology, his naivete and illusory, down-to-the-bone realism, than of his style. Beneath his own sharp style Mr. Hemingway satirizes the ideas of D. H. Lawrence, Joyce, Anderson and others of the "great race."

* * *

The shell of the book is the obvious and amusing burlesque of the mannerisms, the affectations and the form of Mr. Anderson's novels.

* * *

Perhaps Mr. Hemingway's name, which one hears everywhere now, is more familiar than his prose, which is narrow, robust and excellent in its limited area. He is hard and objective, where Mr. Anderson is vast and oftentimes ridiculously subjective. His writing is neat, controlled and without the abundant naivete of "Dark Laughter." But his robust rites in honor of Mr. Anderson are, in places, as tedious as that writer himself.

Allen Tate. "The Spirituality of Roughnecks." *The Nation*, 123 (July 28, 1926), 89-90.

Ernest Hemingway says he wrote this novel in ten days, and there is no reason for believing that Mr. Hemingway, besides being the best contemporary writer of eighteenth-century prose, is also a liar. The novel is short. But it would have done him or anybody else much credit had its author labored with its perfect style (perfect within honorable limitations) for ten months. "The Torrents of Spring" differs in important features from Mr. Hemingway's first American volume, published last autumn; its differences from "In Our Time" spring from a basically different intention. "In Our Time" is naturalistic fiction done for purely creative ends. "The Torrents of Spring" grew out of a motive a little this side of that; its motive is satire and, if one may produce an undemonstrable but wholly convincing bit of internal evidence, its object is Sherwood Anderson's "Dark Laughter."

"Pamela" is still worth reading; "Joseph Andrews" is better worth reading. "Dark Laughter" is a good novel, but, like "Pamela," it contains emotion in excess of the facts, and "The Torrents of Spring" is better worth reading. Lacking, as Fielding did in "Joseph Andrews," a motive originally creative, Mr. Hemingway has nevertheless written a novel which is on its own account, irrespective of momentary aim, a small masterpiece of American fiction.

Mr. Hemingway's consistently limited performance is not generally due to missed intention. He knows what he wishes to do; he usually does it. His intention is fundamentally opposed to any other naturalism of the age. He gets his effects not by complete documentation but by the avoidance of explanatory statement; he keeps his ex-

plicit knowledge of the characters exactly equal to the reader's knowledge. Neither do the characters ever rationalize or generalize their successive predicaments. His naturalism is modified naturalism, and its principles have become more and more unfamiliar since the influence of Zola caught up with the more difficult method of "Bouvard et Pecuchet" and obscured it; while Zola has actually instructed the American novel since Frank Norris, Flaubert has been simply admired. Mr. Hemingway, apparently careless about the choice of material, exercises the greatest zeal in isolating its significant aspects; his selective naturalism achieves its effects through indirect irony, the irony of suppressed comment. Few of his characters are fools; all of them are Bouvards and Pecuchets in that their conduct is so arranged as to rouse the reader's sense of value to the appropriate judgment of it, while they are themselves immersed in a "pure present" and lack the power of generalizing it at all. "In Our Time" proved Hemingway to be a master of this irony. It is an irony pre-eminently fitted for sustained satire of the sort conspicuous in Defoe and Swift, and Hemingway's success with it in "The Torrents of Spring" is a triumph, but not a surprise.

The material of the story is slight and insignificant in outline; a summary would be impertinent here. But Scripps O'Neil, Mrs. Scripps, Yogi Johnson, the big Indian and the little Indian, "Brown's Beanery the Best by Test," the drinking club of the educated Indians whence Yogi hears the "dark Negro laughter" of the ebony bartender after he is kicked out for being not an Indian but a Swede— these characters and places focus the best genial satire of the "spirituality" of roughnecks, the most deftly tempered ribaldry, and the most economically realized humor of disproportion that this reviewer has read in American prose.

humor, however admirable much of this author's writing may seem. Hemingway, as he gropes to "find himself," is simply getting Anderson "out of his system," and has taken this means of doing so. Anderson's status among modern writers being assured, the younger writer's half-hour of humor can hardly be said to work to his injury.

"The New Books." *Saturday Review of Literature,* 3 (July 31, 1926), 12.

Mr. Hemingway is one of the younger writers whose future may be interesting. In his book of short stories, "In Our Time," he presented some fiction of more than average merit, though the influence of Sherwood Anderson was discernible. "The Torrents of Spring," inasmuch as it burlesques the Andersonian manner, may be taken as a sign that Hemingway is freeing himself of an influence of which he is obviously conscious. The book is slight but amusing in spots. One of the spots is the account of Yogi Johnson in the Indian Club. A *jeu d'esprit*, that is all.

The more serious-minded may feel that one who so evidently chose Anderson as his master in earlier work repays his tutelage but ill by finally poking fun at the deficiencies of the method. But the complimentary character of parody must also be considered. And a true admirer of Anderson's best work must also be aware of tendencies that cannot but stir one's

"An Anderson Parody." *Springfield Republican,* (August 29, 1926), p. 7F.

Those who have read Sherwood Anderson's "Dark Laughter" will enjoy "The Torrents of Spring" by Ernest Hemingway. . . .

Scripps O'Neil is the most amusing character in a book whose purpose is solely to amuse. The style parodies that affected by Anderson. The inane repetition of words and phrases, the superficial psychology and the inadequate descriptive passages are well brought out, and the affectations are followed to their inevitable nonsensical conclusion.

* * *

"The Torrents of Spring" is an elaborate and clever parody, well worth reading by any person who has or needs enlightenment as to the essentials of literary style.

Lawrence S. Morris. "Frolicking on Olympus." *New Republic,* 48 (September 15, 1926), 101.

Last year Mr. Hemingway published his first book, In Our Time. It was a volume of episodes and brief stories, and to this reviewer the most exciting event, in the way of words on paper, which happened during the year. It did not need the blurbs of the half-dozen distinguished writers, led by Mr. Anderson, which covered its jacket, to give it a send-off. (Those blurbs are referred to gaily in the course of The Torrents of Spring.) The book was Hemingway's apprenticeship. In certain of the stories he was leaning heavily on the gruesome, like many writers, to convince us of the sternness of reality; in others he was compressing into a few pages of swift flexible dialogue the essence of the relation between two characters. In all of them he was busy molding a fresh, living first-hand prose of his own. He preferred simple concrete words. He preferred words which had been reborn in him through the experience of living. And so when he put them on paper, they lived there. Although the debt was definitely Hemingway's, he owed an immense obligation in all of this to Sherwood Anderson, whom he parodies hilariously in The Torrents of Spring. Anderson's gently clumsy fingers had been turning over words for a decade with the patience of love, picking off their tinsel

and letting them live their own ways. Hemingway, with less tenderness, but a more incisive intellect, profited by those years of emotional sincerity. Words began to grow at his touch, words that were clean, simple, lithe. The solemn announcement of The Little Review that he is to be "the big man in American letters" may not be far from the truth. We shall see whether his understanding of life keeps pace with his devilish capacity to express it.

In the meantime he has decided that it is time to laugh a little. He knows what he owes to Sherwood Anderson—he has a swift mind—and he knows what heavy things have been said about his future. So he has written a parody of Dark Laughter, with side-swipes at Gertrude Stein, which is also a parody of himself. Psychologically, it is clearly a declaration of independence. He is throwing off the tutorship of Anderson and announcing his literary freedom.

* * *

In writing the Torrents of Spring he has weaned himself. That he had to do it so vigorously is the finest tribute Sherwood Anderson has received yet. That he chose to do it wittily is our good luck.

The Outlook, 144 (September 15, 1926), 91.

This amusing skit presupposes an intimate knowledge of the work of Sherwood Anderson, Lothrop Stoddard, and the American literary colony in Paris. Probably there is also much guile in the dedication to "H. L. Mencken and S. Stanwood Mencken [sic] in admiration," although if any satire is intended in the reference to the president of the National Security League it is not increased by misspelling his name. Primarily Mr. Hemingway is a youthful if irreverent disciple of Sherwood Anderson. Yogi Johnson, with his inchoate yearnings and his bride from the beanery, is like the hero of "Many Marriages" seen through a glass, spoofingly, and the book thus has the approved *al fresco* conclusion which marks the true Anderson hero's emancipation from clothes and other man-made conventions. The publishers have given the book a dress fit for a masterpiece. If the book proves to be the "Don Quixote" of the Chicago School it will be labor well spent on their part.

Checklist of Additional Reviews

"Disrespectful." *Time,* 7 (June 28, 1926), 31.

Richard S. West, Jr. "Generous Laughs." *Nashville Tennessean,* July 25, 1926, magazine section, p. 6.

New Yorker, 2 (July 31, 1926), 50.

Thomas L. Masson, "We Are Bigger, But Are We Funnier?" *Literary Digest International Book Review,* 4 (October 1926), 667.

Town & Country, 87 (February 15, 1932), 21.

THE SUN ALSO RISES

By
ERNEST HEMINGWAY
Author of "The Torrents of Spring," "In Our Time"

NEW YORK
CHARLES SCRIBNER'S SONS
1926

The Sun Also Rises

"Study in Futility."
Cincinnati Enquirer,
October 30, 1926,
p. 5.

Here is a book which, like its characters, begins nowhere and ends in nothing. That is the secret of its incisiveness. It is raw satire, sometimes almost horrible in its depiction of futility. The characters are a group of English and American young people who frequent the Paris quarter. They have been too strongly dosed with the more unpleasant kinds of reality; they retain no illusions and no reticencies. All they have is a sort of blaring frankness of word and act and an intense weariness of life.

One hates to suspect this gifted satirist (see "The Torrents of Spring") of analogy, and one may be wrong; but Jake, the hero—hero!—of the story, has been so wounded in the war that he is impotent. He is in love with Brett, a titled English girl, and the only personable woman in the group, and she with him. Perforce their love is platonic; moreover, it is that rather mild and rather impersonal affection that comes to jaded people. Brett frankly needs and searches for sensation. Cheated of being mistress to Jake, she becomes mistress in turn to a surly Jewish writer, a drunken English-man and a Spanish bullfighter. She might, she confesses, have loved the last.

Most of the author's narrative is employed in ushering his characters in and out of cafes and in recording the number, nature and effect of their drinks. A good part of the remainder is required to recount the drunken protestations of Mike about Brett's various lovers.

"The Sun Also Rises" is a most unpleasant book; it is a fine commentary on Mr. Hemingway's ability that he has been able to make it as interesting as it is. His descriptions of the Pamplona fiesta and the bull fights are especially effective.

"Marital Tragedy."
New York Times Book Review,
October 31, 1926,
p. 27.

Ernest Hemingway's first novel, "The Sun Also Rises," treats of certain of those younger Americans concerning whom Gertrude Stein has remarked: "You are all a lost generation." This is the novel for which a keen appetite was stimulated by Mr. Hemingway's exciting volume of short stories, "In Our Time." The clear objectivity and the sustained intensity of the stories, and their concentration upon action in the present moment, seemed to point to a failure to project a novel in terms of the same method, yet a resort to any other method would have let down the reader's expectations. It is a relief to find that "The Sun Also Rises" maintains the same heightened, intimate intangibility as the shorter narratives and does it in the same kind of weighted, quickening prose.

Mr. Hemingway has chosen a segment of life which might easily have become "a spectacle of unexplained horrors," and disciplined it to a design which gives full value to its Dionysian, all but uncapturable, elements. On the face of it, he has simply gathered, almost at random, a group of American and British expatriates from Paris, conducted them on a fishing expedition, and exhibited them against the background of a wild Spanish fiesta and bull-fight. The characters are concisely indicated. Much of their inherent natures are left to be betrayed by their own speech, by their apparently aimless conversation among themselves. Mr. Hemingway writes a most admirable dialogue. It has the terse vigor of Ring Lardner at his best. It suggests the double meanings of Ford Madox Ford's records of talk. Mr. Hemingway makes his characters say one thing, convey still another, and when a whole passage of talk has been given, the reader finds himself the richer by a totally unexpected mood, a mood often enough of outrageous familiarity with obscure heartbreaks.

* * *

No amount of analysis can convey the quality of "The Sun Also Rises." It is a truly gripping story, told in a lean, hard, athletic narrative prose that puts more literary English to shame. Mr. Hemingway knows how not only to make words be specific but how to arrange a collection of words, which shall betray a great deal more than is to be found in the individual parts. It is magnificent writing, filled with that organic action which gives a compelling picture of character. This novel is unquestionably one of the events of an unusually rich year in literature.

Conrad Aiken. "Expatriates." *New York Herald Tribune Books,* October 31, 1926, pp. VII-4.

It is rumored, with what accuracy I do not know, that Mr. Hemingway has at one time and another fought bulls in Spain as a mode of making a livelihood. Whether or not that is true, he writes of bull-fighting with extraordinary insight; he is clearly an expert. He is also, as clearly, *aficionado*—which is the Spanish term for a "fan." *Aficionado* however, is a profounder word than fan, and suggests emotional intensities, and religious zeals, not to mention psychotic fixations, which the baseball enthusiast does not dream of. If one likes bull-fighting, it has much the effect on one that half a course of psycho-analysis might have. One is thrilled and horrified; but one is also fascinated, and one cannot have enough. Perhaps the bull-fight only operates in this way on one who is too timid to descend into the ring himself —in which case one must absolve Mr. Hemingway from the charge of psychosis. Nevertheless, it is an interesting fact that his best short story, thus far, is a bull-fight story, "The Undefeated," which in tragic intensity and spareness of outline challenges comparison with the very finest of contemporary short stories. And it is further interesting that in his new novel, "The Sun Also Rises," the narrative works up to, and in a sense is built around, a bull-fight. Moreover, the story takes on, at this point, a force and tension which is nowhere else quite so striking.

This is not to suggest, however, that Mr. Hemingway's novel is lacking in these qualities, or that without the magnetism which the bull-fight exerts upon him he would be helpless. It has been apparent for some time that Mr. Hemingway is a writer of very unusual gifts; it has been merely a question as to what direction he would take. In "The Sun Also Rises" he takes a decided step forward and makes it possible for me to say of him, with entire conviction, that he is in many respects the most exciting of contemporary American writers of fiction. To say that his literary debts are obvious is not to mitigate this assertion in the slightest. He has learned something from Mr. Anderson, and something, perhaps, from Mr. Fitzgerald's "Great Gatsby"; he may even have extracted a grain or two of ore from Miss Gertrude Stein—

which is in itself no inconsiderable feat.

But in the accomplished fact his work is not in the least like the work of any of these writers. If one thing is striking about it, furthermore, it is its extraordinary individuality of style. His publishers say of him, with a discernment unusual in publishers, that he has contrived, in his novel, to present his people and his actions not as perceptible through a literary medium but as if immediate, and that is true. If once or twice in his story he slips into something of Mr. Anderson's cumbersome and roundabout explanatory method, with its "what I mean to say" and its "the thing is this," these echoes are few and unimportant. His own method lies at the other extreme. He simply states; he even, as a general rule, can be said to understate. It almost appears that he goes out of his way, now and then, to avoid the descriptive or the expansive methods— one has the feeling that he is a little afraid of being caught with any sort of purple on his palette, whether it be of rhetoric or of poetry. The action, he seems to say, must speak wholly for itself.

This results, as might be expected, in a quite extraordinary effect of honesty and reality. The half dozen characters, all of whom belong to the curious and sad little world of disillusionment and aimless expatriates who make what home they can in the cafes of Paris, are seen perfectly and unsentimentally by Mr. Hemingway and are put before us with a maximum of economy. In the case of the hero, through whose mind we meet the event, and again in the cases of Brett, the heroine, and Robert Cohn, the sub-hero, Mr. Hemingway accomplishes more than this—he achieves an understanding and revelation of character which approaches the profound. When one reflects on the unattractiveness, not to say the sordidness, of the scene, and the (on the whole) gracelessness of the people, one is all the more astonished at the fact that Mr. Hemingway should have made them so moving. These folk exist, that is all; and if their story is sordid, it is also, by virtue of the author's dignity and detachment in the telling, intensely tragic.

If one feature of "The Sun Also Rises" demands separate discussion, it is Mr. Hemingway's use of dialogue. The dialogue is brilliant. If there is better dialogue being written today I do not know where to find it. More than any other talk I can call to mind, it is alive with the rhythms and idioms, the pauses and suspensions and innuendoes and shorthands, of living speech. It is in the dialogue, almost entirely, that Mr. Hemingway tells his story and makes the people live and act. This is the dramatist's gift, and it reminds one of those novels of Henry James which were first projected as plays and then written, with something like an excess of talk, as fiction. Will Mr. Hemingway try his hand at a play? He clearly has the ability to make· his story move, and move with intensity, through this medium. It is possible that he overuses this ability. One occasionally longs for a slowing down and expansion of the medium, a pause for more leisurely luxuriation in the instant, such as Mr. Hemingway

only vouchsafes us in the fishing episode and in the account of the *fiesta* and the bull-fight. James himself, despite his sins in this regard, somewhere remarked that dialogue, the most trenchant of the novelist's weapons, should be used as sparely as possible, to be kept in reserve, its force and edge unimpaired, for those scenes in which the action took a definite and decisive turn; it is above all in dialogue that climax should flower. In a sense, therefore, Mr. Hemingway gives us the feeling of finality and climax a little too often and thus deprives himself and his reader of that long curve of crescendo without which a novel lacks final perfection of form. His spareness and economy, his objective detachment, would be only the more effective for an occasional offset, and his canvas greatly richer.

"Sad Young Men." *Time*, 8 (November 1, 1926), 48.

After Hemingway's biting short stories of *In Our Time,* many people expected a big novel from the burly young writer. He had a calm, terse, accurate way of saying things about what he had experienced as a doctor's son in North Michigan and as one of the self-possessed young wanderers in Europe. His stories showed a celebration of present joys and a determination not to be dismayed by the facts.

But now his interests appear to have grown soggy from too much sitting in cafes in the Latin quarter of Paris. In this first novel, marked by only a few affectations, he depicts "the semi-humorous love tragedy of an insatiable English war widow and an unmanned U.S. soldier." He takes his title from Ecclesiastes, his motto about a lost generation from Gertrude Stein, and his widow from Michael Arlen's *The Green Hat*. The story is told by Jake the unmanned, who during the widow's flings with a Princeton Jew and a Spanish bullfighter, remains patient, generous, and of course very sad.

The accounts of cosmopolitan castaways in their bars and bedrooms in France and at the bullrings in Spain are accurate and lack a certain expectable triteness. Even the ironies are amusing for a while. The expatriates' emotions are sketched with restraint and subtlety; the book may even be a masterpiece of sex-frustration psychology. But finally the reader is inclined to echo Jake's characteristic remark: "Oh, what the Hell! " (Summary)

Burton Rascoe. "Diversity in the Younger Set." *New York Sun*, November 6, 1929, p. 10.

... When you take him sentence by sentence Broomfield is often a careless, flat and sloppy writer. Ernest Hemingway is not. Every sentence that he writes is fresh and alive. There is no one writing whose prose has more of the force and vibrancy of good, direct, natural, colloquial speech. His dialogue is so natural that it hardly seems as if it is written at all—one hears it.

* * *

... This Brett is the only "literary" character in the book. The rest are real. She has really stepped into "The Sun Also Rises" out of "The Green Hat," where she played the role of Iris Marsh. In "The Sun Also Rises" her grand and noble gesture is to renounce her love for a young bull fighter, because she thinks she will ruin his career if she does not leave him. Some Americans familiar around the Dome and Rotondo [sic] in Paris appear in the novel in the thinnest of disguises, and remarkably true to character.

K.J.W. *Boston Evening Transcript*, November 6, 1926, Part 6, p. 2.

The keynote of "The Sun Also Rises" is struck in the impotence of the hero. More in this perhaps, than in Gertrude Stein's oracular dictum, quoted on the flyleaf: "You are a lost generation": more even than in the selection from Ecclesiastes, from which the book takes its title. In the whole novel, there is no single character who is sure of himself or his purpose; all of them are impotent in one way or another, or at best, ineffectual and unable to find adjustment.

* * *

The tale is told, strangely enough, in the first person, but moves with such casual precision, somewhat in the manner of "South Wind," round the teller, that it is not realized until taking thought of the matter, with what mastery Mr. Hemingway has used his rather bare, journalistic style. In this is the sole justification for such a style; but the use of a style is its justification. All immediate irritation at the staccato sentences is smoothed away with the discovery of this fact.

Speaking of the author's style, a mention of his acute sense of the passage of time is not out of place. He has made of it so intimate a part of the unfolding of the story that one wonders if the novel could ever have a-chieved such power without it. He has realized the factor that distinguished the novel from other literary forms. Events in a novel should not take place within a set period, as in the drama, but more with the swift passage of hours and minutes. To have realized this is no small achievement on Mr. Hemingway's part.

* * *

... Each situation springs naturally and spontaneously from the nature of the characters and the change in place and time. The relationships merge and shift with an inconstancy that is inborne in the people, themselves, and emphasized by the change in setting.

New characters enter the story in the manner of strangers coming into a group. They bear with the group while it travels about, introduce new and perplexing problems into the already complicated situations, and depart their own way.... All of this is done with such ease that Mr. Hemingway appears to have hit upon a new method of novel writing. "Critical realism" might serve as a name for such a method.

It is this that gives to the loose structure a unity of a sort. The method permits events to pile up on one another and provides for the lapses and practical cessation of action, in certain portions of the story. It increases the feeling that the action is continuous from minute to minute, with no break; the seemingly irrelevant details that are constantly given serve in a like manner. Only once does it fail, and then, in the description of the mental processes of Belmonte the bullfighter, it is so definitely in bad taste that it jars on the reader.

The essential unity of the tale depends on Jake and his method of relating it. But there is a more subtle cohesion; all of the characters are conditioned by one single limitation, they are ineffective. They make nasty messes of one another's lives and are doomed to live in the mess. Jake knows more definitely than any of the others what is ailing him and his brothers-in-misery. He is sure of what he wants, he is aware, at least sub-consciously, of the solution of his problems and Brett's. Primarily because his is a physical lack. The others are not troubled with physical ills; but they are in a sorry way spiritually. Jake can with effort bring himself to a certain stoical attitude that ameliorates his own perplexities, the resigned attitude of the peace-making steer. The others blindly grope, and succeed only in goring each other, as well as the good-intentioned steer. But without Jake the story could never have been told: the bulls would have torn each other to shreds.

It would be extremely unfortunate if too much attention were given to the bloody details, and the excellent and joyous humor of the book were neglected. The scene between Cohn—nor is this his only miserable moment in the story—and his mistress, Frances, gives more, in a few paragraphs, of the spirit of the shrew and the henpecked husband than all the comic-strips that have appeared since the invention of the printing press. Yet this is only one of many gorgeous moments, which might easily have been created by Donald Ogden Stewart, with no loss to that gentleman's fame.

. . . The author has found apparently in such a group a representation of the world that cuts across his own angle of vision. He has lifted them out of the muck and mire in which they wallow with such desperate gusto, into the pages of his narrative, some of the mud and slime still clinging to their heels and clothing. To their woeful situation he has managed to impart a poignant and aching beauty. The love affair between Brett and Jake has a sordid and futile loveliness, unlike that in any recent novel unless it be the love affair of Leora and Arrowsmith in Sinclair Lewis's novel.

Indeed one is inclined to the view that these are not a lost generation, Miss Stein to the contrary. As spiritual bankrupts they are not so segregated, after all; they are very closely related to the so-called "iron grip" generation now holding forth. Almost any country's condition can be deduced from the vices and virtues of the expatriates. In them the native attributes are in excess, merely because they live outside the fatherland they represent. Our sun also rises with theirs and goes down and hastes to the place where he arose, even as their sun. Considered in this light, the novel might be called—heaven forbid—a "social document."

For this very reason, only scant mention has been made of the matter, lest possible readers be scared away by the "thesis." Let it be said even now, that there is no such danger to be run, in reading "The Sun Also Rises." Instead Mr. Hemingway has wrought a beautiful and searching novel. If this review has erred on the side of too great praise, it is only because the book has called it forth.

To designate a first novel as great may be unwise; it may be overstatement. But when a book appears so distinctive in treatment that it reminds one only occasionally of the school of Sherwood Anderson with which the author is supposed to have affiliations, and so unique that it recalls, and that by contrast rather than similarity, one other novel, namely Gerhardt's "Futility," such a novel deserves at least a great deal of admiration and loud shouts of encouragement for the author to continue. Certainly no one can deny this to Mr. Hemingway or his novel.

Herbert S. Gorman. "Hemingway Keeps His Promise." *The New York World,* November 14, 1926, p. 10M.

The sense of cool repression that permeated Ernest Hemingway's book of short stories, "In Our Time," is again the most dominant aspect of his first novel, "The Sun Also Rises." Here, at last, is a writer who can assume (or, at least, appear to assume) an entirely impartial attitude toward his characters, drawing them with a surprising clarity through which no shadow of the author falls. Not once does the author intervene, either by implied moral or innuendo, between the reader and the group of slightly fantastic and deplorably febrile personages who act out the plotless incidents of "The Sun Also Rises." Neither is there any fine writing as such, any escape to the pleasurable subterfuges of overlarded description or mental analyses. The sentences are cold and direct. They are always statements.

The characters themselves are evolved from their conversations mainly, and it is a tribute to the uncanny skill of Hemingway to note that these people live with an almost painful reality. For those who know the stamping ground of the American expatriates in Paris—that district clustered about the corner where the Boulevard Raspail crosses the Boulevard Montparnasse —it will become speedily patent that

practically all of these characters are directly based on actual people. This may add in some measure to the reality of the book but not enough so to take from Hemingway the credit of having created a group of vividly-conceived people existing in a somewhat febrile atmosphere.

* * *

... "The Sun Also Rises" is, therefore, the tale of a great spiritual debacle, of a generation that has lost its guiding purpose and has been driven by time, fate or nerves (whatever one desires to call it) into the feverish atmosphere of strained passions. Behind the clarified paragraphs of the novel looms the pathetic figure of a great failure. There is hardly a character in the book that is not thwarted. Yet, in spite of this, a cold twilight of beauty informs the action.

... The book rises to its most colorful and dramatic aspects in the account of the bull-fights and fiesta at Pamplona, a portion that is heightened by some of the finest and most restrained writing that this generation has produced, and there the reader has borne in upon him that these people have no more chance against fate than have the bulls against the banderillos of the fighters.

Hemingway has been wise enough to adorn his novel with no moral either stated or implied. But it is there nevertheless, a natural outgrowth of the action, and the reader may take it or leave it. With this novel Hemingway solidly places himself in the first rank of that younger group from whom we may expect so much, a group that has turned its back on pretty writing as such and turned its mind upon the phenomena of post-war life.

"Hemingway Seems Out of Focus in the 'Sun Also Rises.' " *Chicago Daily Tribune,* November 27, 1926, p. 13.

* * *

... "The Sun Also Rises" is the kind of book that makes this reviewer at least almost plain angry, not for the obvious reason that it is about utterly degraded people, but for the reason that it shows an immense skill, a very honest and unimpassioned conviction about how writing should be done, a remarkably restrained style, and is done in an amusing and clever modern technique, a sketching in with conversation and few modelings of description and none of rumination.

* * *

Why then be angry at it? Because the theme itself is so gestury. Just as it was a perfectly fair criticism to say that "Main Street" was a picture out of proportion to gain an end so it is also fair to say that "The Sun Also Rises" is entirely out of focus. The difference between them is that although "Main Street" did gain an end of parts, "The Sun Also Rises" leaves you feeling that an artist has just done something to be smart.

The heroine of "The Sun Also Rises" is another lady of "The Green Hat," except that she is a little more outspoken and a little heavier drinker. All of the characters in "The Sun Also Rises" are prize old soaks, and it is for the drunken conversation that a great many of the passionate admirers will tout the book.

It is funny, you have to admit that. One of the times that the vine does the talking is a dissertation on the modern writer and it is keen and witty. But most of the time the picture is so trivial. It isn't that you mind its being drunken or of a sort of hyper-civilized crudity, but you do mind horribly having a man who has obviously the talent that Ernest Hemingway has doing just that sort of thing.

Except for the fiesta, which is vivid and gross and impressive and worth doing, the book is concerned with such utter trivialities that your sensitiveness objects violently to it. The wasting of a genuine gift on something that is exactly what you would expect a mediocre young man from Oak Park, Ill., and not one with real talent, to write about Paris is what makes you unhappy. Every young man from every Oak Park in the United States probably sets just such an angle on the group of rotters that are to be found in any city any place, and he always writes about them. But rarely with such results. Ernest Hemingway can be a distinguished writer if he wishes to be. He is even in this book, but it is a distinction hidden under a bushel of sensationalism and triviality.

"Seeking Sensations." *Springfield Republican*, November 28, 1926, p. 7F.

"The Sun Also Rises" pictures the life of a group of English and American expatriates in Paris. In choosing a title from the passage in Ecclesiasticus [sic] beginning "Vanity of vanities, saith the preacher," Ernest Hemingway sounds a keynote of disillusionment which echoes throughout the book. His characters belong to that generation (ever dear to the realist) whose ideals were smashed by the war. We find them in the cafes of the Quarter and follow them to Pamplona, where they seek fresh sensations at the bull fights. By his direct and objective accounts of their days, the author tries to give an impression of sickening futility. He succeeds almost too well; after a few chapters, one wearies of the absence of plot or character development.

Mr. Hemingway has a vigorous objective style, as well as humor and accuracy of observation. These qualities, combined with the material of "The Sun Also Rises," might have produced a rather brilliant short sketch; but in a novel, absence of structure becomes a fault, and extreme moral sordidness at such length defeats artistic purpose.

Schuyler Ashley. *Kansas City Star*, December 4, 1929, p. 8.

Ernest Hemingway seems here to have borrowed the Green Hat of Michael Arlen, knocked it out of shape, kicked it across the room once or twice, and then gone off to a bull fight wearing its remains pulled pugnaciously down over one eye. Personally, I prefer Green Hats worn that way; rowdiness is more palatable when it does not simultaneously affect romanticism and sentimentality. Thus described, "The Sun Also Rises" may appear a lesser novel than it really is. Mr. Hemingway, who once served an apprenticeship to letters on The Kansas City Star, writes with a swinging, effortless precision that puts him in the very first flight of American stylists. There is almost no lost motion in his sentences; his phrases carry to their mark with a very flat trajectory.

* * *

To anyone who has watched in out-of-the way parts of the world the backwash of the (first World) war generation living leisurely, reckless lives, there is more truth in Mr. Hemingway's novel than a casual reader might be ready to admit. Ever since 1918 the continent has been home for a good many young Americans who certainly do not take their Europe a la Henry James. Gertrude Stein told Ernest Hemingway once, "You are all a lost generation," and the remark seems to have impressed him unduly. The gentle tug of the ordinary tides of life, business, marriage, getting-on-in-the-world, have set most of the stranded ships afloat again. Jake Barnes' generation is not "lost," though it has suffered heavy casualties. And, as the book demonstrates quite effectively, they are not all dead yet.

* * *

There is an ample dose of rather bleak *joi de vivre* in this book. At will Ernest Hemingway can re-create the good flavor of days in the open air; he knows intimately the smell of early morning at San Sebastian, or the sensation of emptiness and wind that night brings into the mountain villages of the Basque country. He savors the taste and feel and smell of living with a sort of hard-boiled gusto. One must not, he seems to believe, qualify or analyze things good in themselves, like brook trout, *hors d'oeuvres,* cold spring water, coffee and buttered toast, or hard liquor.

Particularly liquor. The amount of beer, wine and brandy consumed in "The Sun Also Rises" runs, I should say, to a higher average per page and per character than in any other fiction since Rabelais. And the conversation! Hemingway reveals what amounts to a special talent for drunken conversation, the logical illogicality of the inebriate, the earnest, disconnected stories that reveal so much of the drinker's own inner personality. Yet this subtle talent runs away with him at times. His dialogue sounds drunken almost always, even at moments when by my careful and envious arithmetic,

his characters have surely not had time to get tanked up yet.

Cleveland B. Chase. "Out of Little, Much." *Saturday Review of Literature,* 3 (December 11, 1926), 420-21.

The sense of unbounded vigor and enthusiasm coolly repressed and controlled that characterized Ernest Hemingway's book of short stories, "In Our Time," is also the most striking feature of this notable first novel. Written in terse, precise, and aggressively fresh prose, and containing some of the finest dialogue yet written in this country, the story achieves a vividness and a sustained tension that make it unquestionably one of the events of a year rich in interesting books.

Nothing, the adjective is used advisedly, that Hemingway describes has ever been more convincingly described. It probably never will be; for while he writes with spareness and economy, his gift for seizing upon the essential qualities of whatever occupies his attention leaves the reader with nothing to learn. There is a truly Shakespearian absoluteness about his writing. But the things he writes about—bull fights, Spanish fiestas, shallow philanderings, and the petty subtleties of café disputes and *amours*—seem scarcely worthy of the care, of the artistic integrity which he devotes to them.

It would have been difficult for Mr.

Hemingway to have chosen a more dreary or aimless setting for a novel. Having picked, apparently at random, a handful of those disillusioned and degenerating expatriates who make their headquarters in the cafés along the Boulevard Montparnasse, in Paris, he sends them on a fishing expedition to the Pyrenees which ends up in a week of riotous drunkenness at a fiesta and bull fight in Pamplona. He describes these people with photographic exactness. Anyone who is acquainted with the habitués of the cafés of the Boulevard Montparnasse will recognize most of the characters at once. Not one of them, I think, is the product of the author's imagination. Even the fishing trip about which the story centers is an actual event that took place, if my memory is not at fault, in the spring of 1924.

If the characters are intrinsically uninteresting, it is the greater tribute to the power of the author's style that the story never loses an almost painful tension. It is a supreme triumph of style over matter, and if the reader be tempted to question whether the triumph is real, let him turn to almost any one of Mr. Hemingway's passages of dialogue.

* * *

Mr. Hemingway's most pronounced gift as writer is the ability to seize upon the precise details in any setting or situation that lend it meaning and individuality. In consequence, he has developed a crisp, terse, staccato style which consists largely in setting down innumerable details, which are left to be fused and blended in the reader's mind.

* * *

... By the very profuseness and precision of his details he achieves an eventual economy that is astounding. There is a cumulative richness in his staccato statements of fact. He says one thing, implies another, while the whole atmosphere of a passage implies infinitely more than is to be found in its individual parts. We find ourselves in the presence of unsuspected subtleties of mood and of emotion which are arrived at not through the medium of an author's hyperbolic and roundabout statement of them, but because their essential qualities are actually present upon the printed page. It is an interesting fact that neither in his short stories nor in this novel does Hemingway make use of a single simile. To him things are not "like" other things. He does not write about them until he has been able to grasp their essential qualities.

Allen Tate. "Hard-Boiled." *The Nation*, 123 (December 15, 1926), 642-44.

The present novel by the author of "In Our Time" supports the recent prophecy that he will be the "big man in American letters." At the time the prophecy was delivered it was meaningless because it was equivocal. Many

of the possible interpretations now being eliminated, we fear it has turned
out to mean something which we shall
all regret. Mr. Hemingway has written
a book that will be talked about,
praised, perhaps imitated; it has already been received in something of
that cautiously critical spirit which the
followers of Henry James so notoriously maintain toward the master. Mr.
Hemingway has produced a successful
novel, but not without returning some
violence upon the integrity achieved in
his first book. He decided for reasons
of his own to write a popular novel, or
he wrote the only novel which he
could write.

To choose the latter conjecture is
to clear his intentions, obviously at the
cost of impugning his art. One infers
moreover that although sentimentality
appears explicitly for the first time in
his prose, it must have always been
there. Its history can be constructed.
The method used in "In Our Time"
was *pointilliste,* and the sentimentality
was submerged. With great skill he re-
versed the usual and most general formula of prose fiction: instead of selecting the details of physical background and of human behavior for the
intensification of a dramatic situation,
he employed the minimum of drama
for the greatest possible intensification
of the observed object. The reference
of emphasis for the observed object
was therefore not the action; rather,
the reference of the action was the
object, and the action could be impure
or incomplete without risk of detec-
tion. It could be mixed and incoherent; it could be brought in when it was
advantageous to observation, or left
out. The exception, important as such,
in Mr. Hemingway's work is the story
of Mr. and Mrs. Elliott. Here the definite dramatic conflict inherent in a
sexual relation emerged as fantasy, and
significantly; presumably he could not
handle it otherwise without giving
himself away.

In "The Sun Also Rises," a full-
length novel, Mr. Hemingway could
not escape such leading situations, and
he had besides to approach them with
a kind of seriousness. He fails. It is not
that Mr. Hemingway is, in the term
which he uses in the contempt for the
big word, hard-boiled; it is that he is
not hard-boiled enough, in the artistic
sense. No one can dispute with a writer the significance he derives from his
subject-matter; one can only point out
that the significance is mixed or incomplete. Brett is a nymphomaniac;
Robert Cohn, a most offensive cad;
both are puppets. For the emphasis is
false; Hemingway doesn't fill out his
characters and let them stand for
themselves; he isolates one or two
chief traits which reduce them to caricature. His perception of the physical
object is direct and accurate; his vision
of character, singularly oblique. And
he actually betrays the interior machinery of his hard-boiled attitude: "It
is awfully easy to be hard-boiled about
everything in the daytime, but at night
it is another thing," says Jake, the
sexually impotent, musing on the futile accessibility of Brett. The history
of his sentimentality is thus complete.

There are certain devices exploited
in the book which do not improve it;

they extend its appeal. Robert Cohn is not only a bounder, he is a Jewish bounder. The other bounders, like Mike, Mr. Hemingway for some reason spares. He also spares Brett—another device—for while her pleasant folly need not be flogged, it equally need not be condoned; she becomes the attractive wayward lady of Sir Arthur Pinero and Michael Arlen. Petronius's Circe, the archetype of all the Bretts, was neither appealing nor deformed.

Mr. Hemingway has for some time been in the habit of throwing pebbles at the great—which recalls Mr. Pope's couplet about his contemporary Mr. Dennis. The habit was formed in "The Torrents of Spring," where it was a-musing. It is disconcerting in the present novel; it strains the context; and one suspects that Mr. Hemingway protests too much. The point he seems to be making is that he is morally superior, for instance, to Mr. Mencken, but it is not yet clear just why.

Lawrence S. Morris. "Warfare in Man and Among Men." *New Republic*, 49 (December 22, 1926), 142-43.

To anyone with an eye on what was coming, Ernest Hemingway's short stories in the volume, In Our Time, were the most stirring pages of imaginative prose by an American which appeared last year. This man was molding an idiom of his own to express his own way of feeling and seeing. Now comes his first novel, The Sun Also Rises, and it is clear that the shorter tales were merely a preparation. No one need be afraid any more that Hemingway's power is going to be limited to episodes. He has shown that he can not only state a theme, but develop it.

His approach to his job is so direct that it appears casual. Any café or hotel room will do him for a setting. He drops his characters in and lets them live. He does not explain them, as a less complete artist would. He does not label their motives with generalizations of love, hate, ambition. He watches their behavior. Seen from without, his people act in hard, direct ways; from within it is plain there is no direction whatever. They are stumbling through life like a man lost in a forest: attracted to this side by what appears to be a clearing, repelled when the clearing is found to be a marsh.

The essential characteristic of our time is that it is a period without a generalization. Without a mythology, if you prefer: we have inherited a hundred mythologies, and our minds flutter among them, finding satisfaction in none. The distress we are all acutely aware of comes from our failure to realize this fact emotionally. Intellectually we have cut down the frameworks into which our predecessors fitted experience. But we have received new information too fast to digest it. We have not yet reached the full realization that these familiar frameworks are gone from our minds; in practice we cling to their shadows and are hurt when they fail to support us. Until we are emotionally convinced that the old values are gone, we shall not begin to lay down our own generalizations. We have reached the stage—familiar in the history of cultures—where we must pass through Ecclesiastes before writing our Revelations. All contemporary art that is vital, that has its roots in our immediate problem, must seem destructive. It is concerned in realizing this desperate purposelessness by objectifying it.

The Sun Also Rises is one stride toward that objectification. The clear boundaries which were formerly assumed to define motives are gone. Very well: Hemingway will not try to make use of them, and will admit in his vocabulary only words which he himself has found solid. By this courageous self-denial—the mark of every genuine originality—he has achieved a style as close to his thought as the bone of which the skeleton is made is close to the skeleton; and firm with the firmness of packed sand and running water. The effect of this accuracy is a great gain in intensity. Between the lines of the hard-boiled narrative quivers an awareness of the unworded, half-grasped incomprehensibles of life.

* * *

Although Hemingway is objectifying the bewildered anguish of an aimless generation, he does not moon about it. His mind is masculine and imaginative. He loves all the hard, stinging experiences of the senses, he loves skill, he can laugh. He knows the intonations and obliquenesses of human speech. No other American, writing today, can match his dialogue for its apparent naturalness, its intimacy and its concealed power of revealing emotions. Ring Lardner's in comparison sounds framed and self-conscious. For something against which to measure the use of overtones in Hemingway's talk one must go to Joyce's account of a Christmas dinner in the Portrait of the Artist or—allowing for the greater intellectual scope and intensity of Joyce's mind—to the quarrel between Leopold Bloom and the Citizen in Ulysses.

Dial, 82 (January 1927), 73.

If to report correctly and endlessly the vapid talk and indolent thinking of Montparnasse café idlers is to write a novel, Mr. Hemingway has written a novel. His characters are as shallow as the saucers in which they stack their daily emotions, and instead of interpreting his material—or even challenging it—he has been content merely to make a carbon copy of a not particularly significant surface of life in Paris. "Mike was a bad drunk. Brett was a good drunk. Bill was a good drunk. Cohn was never drunk." "I knew I was quite drunk." "It's funny what a wonderful gentility you get in the bar of a big hotel." There are acres of this, until the novel—aside from a few sprints of humour and now and then a "spill" of incident—begins to assume the rhythm, the monotony, and the absence of colour which one associates with a six-day bicycle race.

Bruce Barton.
Atlantic Monthly, 139
(April 1927),
12, 14.

For readers bored by current fiction about other people's love affairs and characters less exciting than the real figures of business life, there is good news. "A writer named Hemingway has arisen" and he writes "as if he never read anybody's writing, as if he had fashioned the art of writing himself."

Reviewers have given the impression that Hemingway is one of those writers who delight in chalking smutty words on the back fence of literature. But his new book shows Hemingway exciting beyond such dullness, and his reviewers owe him an apology.

Although the people of his new book have no morals, drink too much, are blown about by their passions, have no religion and no ideals, they are alive, truly real and alive, with courage and honesty.

Hemingway's is the freshest voice since that of Frank Norris and possibly Lardner and Lewis. He doesn't describe. He lets the people enter, talk, travel, and the reader goes with them. They go to watch bull-fighting in Spain. For several nights they hardly sleep, they drink and dance all night and stay tense at the bullfights in the day. Such doings may be reprehensible, but they are so real that you feel as tired as the people do when it's over.

Hemingway may some day write a book about more respectable people, if he escapes going around with other writers, speaking at women's clubs, or getting a good opinion of himself. He may some day discover that respectable people can be interesting, have adventures, and be fun. But he will need to take care of himself. "The world has plenty of almost everything—doctors, lawyers, bankers, merchants. But what a shortage of comedians! And of men who can tell a story that is even half as interesting as a day at the office or a game of golf." (Summary)

Virginia Woolf.
"An Essay in Criticism."
New York Herald Tribune
Books, 4
October 9, 1927,
pp. 1, 8.

... Of Mr. Hemingway, we know that he is an American living in France, an "advanced" writer, we suspect, connected with what is called a movement, though which of the many we own that we do not know. ... But nothing new is revealed about any of the characters in "The Sun Also Rises." They come before us shaped, proportioned, weighted, exactly as the characters of Maupassant are shaped and proportioned. They are seen from the old angle; the old reticences, the old relations between author and character are observed.

* * *

At any rate, Mr. Hemingway is not modern in the sense given; and it would appear from his first novel that this rumor of modernity must have sprung from his treatment of it rather than from any fundamental novelty in his conception of the art of fiction. It is a bare, abrupt, outspoken book. Life as people live it in Paris in 1927 or even in 1928 is described as we of this age do describe life (it is here that we steal a march upon the Victorians), openly, frankly, without prudery, but also without surprise. The immoralities and moralities of Paris are described as we are apt to hear them spoken of in private life. Such candor is modern and it is admirable. Then, for qualities grow together in art as in life, we find attached to this admirable frankness an equal bareness of style. Nobody speaks for more than a line or two. Half a line is mostly sufficient. If a hill or a town is described (and there is always some reason for its description) there it is, exactly and literally built up of little facts, literal enough, but chosen, as the final sharpness of the outline proves, with utmost care. . . . Each word pulls its weight in the sentence. And the prevailing atmosphere is fine and sharp, like that of winter days when the boughs are bare against the sky. . . . Mr. Hemingway's writing, one might paraphrase, gives us now and then a real emotion, because he keeps absolute purity of line in his movements, and lets the horns (which are truth, fact, reality) pass him close each time. But there is something faked, too, which turns bad and gives an unpleasant feeling—that also we must face in course of time.

* * *

Recalling "The Sun Also Rises,"

certain scenes rise in memory: the bullfight, the character of the Englishman, Harris; here a little landscape which seems to grow behind the people naturally; here a long, lean phrase which goes curling around a situation like the lash of a whip. Now and again this phrase evokes a character brilliantly, more often a scene. Of character, there is little that remains firmly and solidly elucidated. Something indeed seems wrong with the people. If we place them (the comparison is bad) against Tchekhov's people, they are flat as cardboard. If we place them (the comparison is better) against Maupassant's people, they are crude as a photograph. If we place them (the comparison may be illegitimate) against real people, the people we liken them to are of an unreal type. They are people one may have seen showing off at some cafe; talking a rapid high-pitched slang, because slang is speech of the herd, seemingly much at their ease, and yet if we look at them a little from the shadow not at their ease at all, and, indeed, terribly afraid of being themselves, or they would say things simply in their natural voices. So it would seem that the thing that is faked is character; Mr. Hemingway leans against the flanks of that particular bull after the horns have passed.

* * *

André Maurois.
"Ernest Hemingway."
This Quarter, 2
(Oct.-Dec., 1929),
212-15.
Transl. Florence Llona.

When I visited Princeton University two years ago, the faculty were discussing a novel which had just been published by—Ernest Hemingway. I wanted to know what it was called. *"The Sun Also Rises."*—"Is it good?"—"It's very hard, cynical, and extraordinarily true to life. I don't know whether you would care for it." I bought it. It was very good indeed.

Not on account of the plot, which was practically non-existent. . . . But any plot will do when a novelist knows how to create live human beings and Hemingway's characters are alive. They do not talk about their souls, they do not unravel their feelings. No, they merely order drinks and dinners, swear, have a good time, and yet you know them as well as you do Odette Swann, or Charlus, or Legrandin. . . . This young American's technique seemed both perfect and mysterious.

I read his two volumes of short stories next. *In Our Time* and *Men Without Women*. *In Our Time* was oddly constructed. The briefest of italicized sketches, more like blunt, cruel epigrams, alternated with stories as long as tales by Maupassant. Unity is achieved by the sameness of the feeling which runs through these tableaux and which is that life is hard. . . .

* * *

Where did he learn to write? What has he read? What does he admire? We do not know. If names were indispensable to give an idea of his style, I should mention Kipling and Mérimée, but the resemblances are slight and the dissimilarities profound. His impassible narration recalls Mérimée, but Mérimée was a man of the drawing-room and library. Even if he rather fancied the rougher aspects of life, he gazed at them from the outside and held aloof. His smugglers are artists and philosophers. Hemingway's jockeys and boxers are jockeys and boxers, as they should be. While he appreciates the poetic value of sports, they appeal to him above all scientifically. His vocabulary is always accurate, riveted and solid like a specialist's. He has Kipling's art of suggesting passions and feelings without calling them by name, with less moral grandeur perhaps than Kipling because until now the scope of his subject matter has been less ample, but in Hemingway's stories there is an almost physical strength that does not exist in Kipling's, and a still sheerer starkness. A story by Hemingway is stripped to the bone. The facts are nearly always intimated by means of dialogue, without any commentaries. His descriptions are condensed into the least possible volume. Whenever he can, Hemingway lets the mere name of a place suggest the setting . . . Boulevard Raspail . . . Hotel Crillon . . . [ellipses Maurois's]. If this means that he is a realist, he is certainly very different from the 1880 school of French realists. His philosophy too is long a way from theirs. His picture of life is less pessimistic than theirs although just as somber. The "miseries" common to us all pervade his work, but he supplies that powerful antidote, humour. The final impression is one of vigour and courage.

* * *

Anderson, who is so familiar with the plains and forest of the Middle West, knows that Hemingway's plains and forests are real. We Frenchmen feel that his Paris is real. There is no faulty drawing to destroy the illusion. He writes of nothing that he does not know.

The virtue of his construction is its simplicity. His dialogue is remarkable, although in *The Sun Also Rises,* somewhat monotonous, unavoidably however, since the vocabulary of the characters is a meagre one. His style is made up of clean-cut, metallic elements. One is reminded of modern buildings—steel beams and cement. He achieves distinction through a horror of distinction. There are no Corinthian capitals nor processions of stereotyped naked women on Hemingway's facades. . . .

Carlos Baker.
"When the Warriors Sleep."
Saturday Review, 36
(July 4, 1953),
13.

Last October 2 "The Sun Also Rises" was twenty-six years old, almost precisely the age of Hemingway when he wrote this memorable first novel. For many older readers this dramatization of the predicament of a small group of Jazz Age D.P.'s in Paris and Pamplona is still the favorite Hemingway novel. New acquaintances who pick it up in bookstores, college classrooms, or public libraries are still likely to find it as fresh, as enthralling, and most of all as undated as it was when it rolled off the Scribner presses in 1926. The news about "The Sun Also Rises" is that it is still new.

* * *

The critical question (in both senses of the word) is why "The Sun Also Rises" has lasted, and by what hidden art and artifice its survival is more or less permanently guaranteed. Four parts of an answer can be readily given. First its language, having been pruned of the temporary, the faddist. and the adventitious, is still in daily use among us. Age cannot wither the possible variations of which this clean, clear denotative diction is capable. Second is the devotion to fact, that debt—as Conrad's wisest preface observed—which the writer always owes to the physical universe. Third, and a corollary of the second, is the skill in the evocation and manipulation of emotional atmospheres. Such a skill is possible only to one for whom the moral and esthetic apprehensions of human situations—their truth and falsehood, their beauty and their ugliness—has the immediate force of a blow to the midriff, or to the quiet leap and stir of the pleasurably astonished heart. Fourth is the symbolic landscape which in company with the diction, the recorded fact, and the deeply implied emotion, sustains and strengthens "The Sun Also Rises" from underneath, like the foundation of a public monument.

* * *

... The real reason for the undiminished light and heat with which Hemingway's "Sun" keeps on shining a quarter-century after its first rising is the unforced and seemingly careless mastery with which its young author faced up to and overcame a problem in practical esthetics.

The basic strategy is a counterpoint between two sets of emotional atmospheres. In the first part of the novel something vexed and potentially vicious (the neurotic triangle formed by Cohn, Campbell, and Lady Brett) is played off against something healthily and naturally masculine (the upland sport of the fishing trip to Burguete). Later, in the lowland around Pamplona, the counterpoint shifts to the comparative study of Cohn and Romero: the former's sentimental fawning egotism shows all the manly self-reliance and natural bravery of the bullfighter. At Pamplona also occurs the pagan-Christian counterpoint, with Jake's unobtrusive piety arrayed against Brett's Circean witch-hood, a brilliant dramatization of the fact that the fiesta of San Fermin combines Christian ceremonial with pagan celebration. Beneath all these oppositions runs Hemingway's moral geography: his consciousness of the permanence of nature as over against the evanescence of the generations of man, his stoic sense of the vanity of the vain, his stoic admiration for the endurance of what is durable.

"The Sun Also Rises" is not a perfect novel. A reader who follows through the sequence of "A Farewell to Arms" and "For Whom the Bell Tolls" should become aware of the increasing subtlety and assurance with which Hemingway employs his language and his facts (the connotative use of facts replaces their denotative use to a much greater degree). Readers may likewise note the livelier dexterity with which he plays off his emotional atmospheres against one another, and the deeper imaginative interpenetration of the author's moral and esthetic sensibilities. Still, "The Sun" is a very good novel indeed; one may confidently predict that it will easily outlast another twenty-six years. Anyone who is curious about its ability to survive beyond 1978 might try writing an open letter to his grandson.

Checklist of Additional Reviews

Henry S. Canby. "Notes of a Rapid Reader." *Saturday Review of Literature,* 3 (December 18, 1926), 445.

Emmanuel Eisenberg. "The Importance of Being Ernest: Irresponsibly Inscribed After a Perusal of *The Sun Also Rises." New York World,* May 9, 1927, p. 13.

Notes

MEN
WITHOUT WOMEN

By
ERNEST·HEMINGWAY

NEW YORK
CHARLES SCRIBNER'S SONS
1928

Men Without Women

Virginia Woolf.
"An Essay in Criticism."
New York Herald Tribune Books, 4
October 9, 1927,
pp. 1, 8.

... "Men Without Women" consists of short stories in the French rather than in the Russian manner. The great French masters, Mérimée and Maupassant, made their stories as self-sufficient and compact as possible. There is never a thread left hanging; indeed so contracted are they, that when the last sentence of the last page flares up, as it so often does, we see by its light the whole circumference and significance of the story revealed. The Tchekov method is, of course, the very opposite of this. Everything is cloudy and vague, loosely trailing rather than tightly furled. The stories move slowly out of sight like clouds in the summer air, leaving a wake of meaning in our minds which gradually fades away. Of the two methods, who shall say which is the better? At any rate, Mr. Hemingway, enlisting under the French masters, carries out their teaching up to a point with considerable success.

There are in "Men Without Women" many stories which, if life were longer, one would wish to read again. Most of them indeed are so competent, so efficient, and so bare of superfluity that one wonders why they do not make a deeper dent in the mind than they do.

* * *

... all of these are good trenchant stories, quick, terse and strong. If one had not summoned the ghosts of Tchekov, Mérimée and Maupassant, no doubt one would be enthusiastic. As it is, one looks about for something, fails to find something, and so is brought again to the old familiar business of ringing impressions on the counter, and asking what is wrong?

For some reason the book of short stories does not seem to us to go as deep or to promise as much as the novel. Perhaps it is the excessive use of dialogue, for Mr. Hemingway's use of it is surely excessive. A writer will always be chary of dialogue because dialogue puts the most violent pressure on the reader's attention. He has to hear, to see, to supply the right tone, and to fill in the background from what the characters say without any help from the author. Therefore, when fictitious people are allowed to speak it must be because they have something so important to say that it stimulates the reader to do rather more than his share of the work of creation. But, although Mr. Hemingway keeps us under the fire of dialogue constantly, his people, half the time, are only saying what the author could say much more economically for them. At last we are inclined to cry out with the little girl in "Hills Like White Elephants" "Would you please please please please please please stop talking?"

And probably it is this superfluity of dialogue which leads to that other fault which is always lying in wait for the writer of short stories; the lack of proportion. A paragraph in excess will make these little craft lopsided and will bring about that blurred effect which when one is out for clarity and point so baffles the reader. And both these faults, the tendency to flood the page with unnecessary dialogue and the lack of sharp, unmistakable points by which we can take hold of the story, come from the more fundamental fact that, though Mr. Hemingway is brilliantly and enormously skillful, he lets his dexterity, like the bullfighter's cloak, get between him and the fact. For in truth story writing has much in common with bullfighting. One may twist one's self like a corkscrew and go through every sort of contortion so that the public thinks one is running every risk and displaying superb gallantry. But the true writer stands close up to the bull and lets the horns—call them life, truth, reality, whatever you like,—pass him close each time.

Mr. Hemingway, then, is courageous; he is candid; he is highly skilled; he plants words precisely where he wishes; he has moments of bare and nervous beauty; he is modern in manner but not in vision; he is self-consciously virile; his talent has contracted rather than expanded; compared with his novel his stories are a little dry and sterile. . . .

"Men Without Women." *Time,* 10 (October 14, 1927), 38.

The stories in *Men Without Women* have the same qualities that made critics a year ago realize at least one American writer living in Paris can do more than sit in cafes. *The Sun Also Rises* had rock-hard sentences as polished as stones smoothed by wind and rain. With a sharp determined rhythm, the story of sad young men in Paris posed no literary gesticulations, wasted no energy, moved without flourishes.

In *Men Without Women* the stories again have their own tempo, unmarred by conceits and artifices. They are "as clear and crisp and perfectly shaped as icicles, as sharp as splinters of glass. It is impossible to read them without realizing that seldom if ever before has a writer been able to cut so deeply into life with the 26 curved tools of the English alphabet." (Summary)

Percy Hutchinson.
"Mr. Hemingway Shows Himself a Master Craftsman in the Short Story."
New York Herald Tribune Books, 4
October 16, 1927,
pp. 9, 27.

Like Lord Byron, who awoke to find himself famous, Ernest Hemingway, after the publication of "The Sun Also Rises," walked out of the door to find his name shouted on every hand. Seldom has a book received such instantaneous recognition or been greeted with greater enthusiasm. This amazing narrative of American and English after-the-war strays, running up and down France and Spain in wistful wildness, with its mixture of precocity and weariness, its mingling of tears and smiles, with its spiritual pathos and its human comedy, struck a new note in American letters and struck it surely. The laughter of fools, we have been reminded, is as the crackling of thorns under a pot. The laughter of Mr. Hemingway's piquant and entrancing novel may be that of folly; if so, these strays of his were terribly wise in their unwisdom; and never was folly uttered more cracklingly.

Ernest Hemingway since the appearance of "The Sun Also Rises" has not been idle. Lynx-eyed readers of the magazines have detected short stories with his name attached and have eagerly pounced on them. Seven of these stories, and six not hitherto published, are now collected under the title, "Men Without Women"; and the book, although not entirely devoid of female characters, for the most part lives up to its title. If one misses from the pages that little wanton, Lady Brett, so irritatingly childlike in her faith, so engagingly reprehensible in her morals, Hemingway has introduced enough of novelty almost to make up. Moreover, he shows himself master in a new manner in the short-story form. His method is not that of Kipling, of Maupassant, of Conrad. His style is his own. And even if its originalities fail to stand the test of time, they are, for the moment at least, secure.

* * *

What is the secret? What is Hemingway's uniqueness that rivets the attention of the reader and commands his acquiescence? To say that it is his realism is not sufficient. Others have been realists before Hemingway. To come on this arresting thing one must define further; for, although to speak of Hemingway's realism is roughly sufficient, the author of "The Sun Also Rises" and "Men Without Women" has so refined general practices that it is in the realistic hint rather than the realistic statement that his power lies. Hemingway's is the art of the reporter carried to the highest degree. Ernest Hemingway is the supreme reporter. His facts may be from experience, and they may be compounded solely of imagination; but he so presents them that they stand out with all the clearness and sharpness (and also the coldness) of pinnacles of ice in clear, frosty air.

* * *

Yet there is more to "Men Without Women" than reporting; more than colloquial speech in staccato, with ever-gathering power. No reporter, not even a supreme reporter, can live by words alone. He must have something to report worthy of his skill. For the man actually in newspaper work the substance is furnished him out of the swiftly played drama of surrounding lives, he finds it in the entanglements of men and women, their passions, their fears, their hopes. These vary in importance, but they are the daily happenings, hence have their own varying news values. For the writer of fiction, who must search experience or call on imagination, what he is to pass on as facts likewise must not fail of importance. And here Hemingway is not wanting. Hurried on by the swift, sharp reportorial writing though he is, the reader is never left unaware of an ever-increasing tension that underlies the words, of a gathering force propelling him to a climax, the exact nature of which is undiscernible.

* * *

His originality, his vitality, his fidelity, his dramatic sense, are forces that combine to indicate for the author of "The Sun Also Rises" and "Men Without Women" a career of remarkable brilliancy. On the other hand, Hemingway is without a philosophy of life; his fidelity is all to surface aspects. Whether he can win through with his present equipment alone is a question for the future. Kipling got through without a philosophy; but he had a creed, the creed of imperialism. Perhaps Hemingway will be as fortunate.

Joseph Wood Krutch. "The End of Art." *The Nation*, 125 (November 16, 1927), 548.

From Oscar Wilde to Aldous Huxley the favorite characters of our cleverest writers have been tired of everything except talk. Commonly represented as too lazy to work, too cynical to feel, and too disillusioned to believe, they have nevertheless never relaxed in their efforts to express themselves. Never weary of describing their weariness and never too bored to be voluble, they have polished their epigrams with a serious assiduity which seemed to belie the expressed conviction that nothing is worth the effort.

In many respects Mr. Ernest Hemingway is the heir of these gaudier sophisticates. He has received much of his education around the cafe table and, apparently, consorted much with the members of a generation which takes a certain pride in proclaiming itself lost. But either he has found them less verbally brilliant than they have commonly been represented or he has himself lost the last of their enthusiasms, the enthusiasm for things neatly said. Sometimes his characters are the illiterate heroes of the prize-fight or the bull-ring, and sometimes they are the bankrupt intellectuals who wander disconsolately from bar to bar in the forlorn hope that a drink will be more refreshing somewhere else, but the two classes have this in common: they are all but inarticulate. The one has never learned to express itself, the other has grown tired of choosing words, and so both talk the lazy, monotonous, undifferentiated idiom which is the common denominator of the relaxed intellectual and the rough neck. Spiritually the distinguishing mark of Mr. Hemingway's work is a weariness too great to be aware of anything except sensations; technically it is an amazing power to make the apparently aimless and incompetent talk of his characters eloquent, to make them say what they seem too inarticulate or too lazy to define with words.

* * *

Here, if you like, is art upon its last legs. For all his scrupulous detachment and his care never to say one word in his own person, Mr. Hemingway tells us both by his choice of subject and by the method which he employs that life is an affair of mean tragedies, and he tells us it as plainly as if he were devoting a treatise to the exposition of his ideas. In his hands the subject matter of literature becomes sordid little catastrophes in the lives of very vulgar people and its language the most undistinguished which can possibly be made by the most skilful [sic] manipulation to convey a meaning. And yet he possesses a virtuosity not short of amazing; once begun, none of his stories will allow themselves to be laid down unfinished. Mr. Hemingway's range may be narrow and his art "un-

important" but within the limits of what he undertakes in the present volume he is a master. These stories are painfully good. No one, whatever his artistic creed may be, can escape their fascination during the moments it takes to read them; and no one can deny their brilliance.

Dorothy Parker. "A Book of Great Short Stories." *New Yorker*, 3 (October 29, 1927), 92-94.

Ernest Hemingway wrote a novel called "The Sun Also Rises." Promptly upon its publication, Ernest Hemingway was discovered....

* * *

A year or so before "The Sun Also Rises," he had published "In Our Time," a collection of short pieces. The book caused about as much stir in literary circles as an incompleted dogfight on upper Riverside Drive. True, there were a few that went about quick and stirred with admiration for this clean, exciting prose, but most of the reviewers dismissed the volume with a tolerant smile and the word "stark." It was Mr. Mencken who slapped it down with "sketches in the bold, bad manner of the Café du Dome," and the smaller boys, in their manner, took similar pokes at it. Well, you see, Ernest Hemingway was a young American living on the left bank of the Seine in Paris, France; he had been seen at the Dome and the Rotonde and the Select and the Closerie des Lilas. He knew Pound, Joyce and Gertrude Stein. There is something a little—well, a little *you*-know—in all of those things. You wouldn't catch Bruce Barton or Mary Roberts Rinehart doing them. No, sir.

And besides, "In Our Time" was a book of short stories. That's no way to start off. People don't like that; they feel cheated.

* * *

Literature, it appears, is here measured by a yard-stick. As soon as "The Sun Also Rises" came out, Ernest Hemingway was the white-haired boy. He was praised, adored, analyzed, best-sold, argued about, and banned in Boston; all the trimmings were accorded him. People got into feuds about whether or not his story was worth the telling. . . . They affirmed, and passionately, that the dissolute expatriates in this novel of "a lost generation" were not worth bothering about; and then they devoted most of their time to discussing them. There was a time, and it went on for weeks, when you could go nowhere without hearing of "The Sun Also Rises." Some thought it without excuse; and some, they of the cool, tall foreheads, called it the greatest American novel, tossing "Huckleberry Finn" and "The Scarlet Letter" lightly out the window. They hated it or they revered it.

* * *

Now "The Sun Also Rises" was as "starkly" written as Mr. Hemingway's

short stories; it dealt with subjects as "unpleasant." Why it should have been taken to the slightly damp bosom of the public while the (as it seems to me) superb "In Our Time" should have been disregarded will always be a puzzle to me. . . . Mr. Hemingway's style, this prose stripped to its firm young bones, is far more effective, far more moving, in the short story than in the novel. He is, to me, the greatest living writer of short stories; he is, also to me, not the greatest living novelist.

After all the high screaming about "The Sun Also Rises," I feared for Mr. Hemingway's next book. You know how it is—as soon as they all start acclaiming a writer, that writer is just about to slip downward. The littler critics circle like literary buzzards above only the sick lions.

So it is a warm gratification to find the new Hemingway book, "Men Without Women," a truly magnificent work. It is composed of thirteen short stories, most of which have been published before. They are sad and terrible stories; the author's enormous appetite for life seems to have been somehow appeased. You find here little of that peaceful ecstasy that marked the camping trip in "The Sun Also Rises" and the lone fisherman's days in "Big Two-Hearted River," in "In Our Time." The stories include "The Killers," which seems to me one of the four great American short stories. . . . The book also includes "Fifty Grand," "In Another Country," and the delicate and tragic "Hills Like White Elephants." I do not know where a greater collection of stories can be found. Ford Madox Ford has said of this author, "Hemingway writes like an angel." I take issue.... Hemingway writes like a human being. I think it is impossible for him to write of any event at which he has not been present; his is, then, a reportorial talent, just as Sinclair Lewis's is. But, or so I think, Lewis remains a reporter and Hemingway stands a genius because Hemingway has an unerring sense of selection. He discards details with a magnificent lavishness; he keeps his words to their short path. His is, as any reader knows, a dangerous influence. The simple thing he does looks so easy to do. But look at the boys who try to do it.

Lee Wilson Dodd.
"Simple Annals of the Callous."
Saturday Review of Literature, 4 (November 19, 1927), 322-23.

---

* * *

The job Mr. Hemingway sets himself is to make a literal report of such aspects of life as happen to have engaged his attention. He writes of what he has seen, heard, touched, tasted, smelled—provided, always, that it has spontaneously caught his interest. He desires to make a direct transcript of facts from his varying environments, to put down on paper a series of artistically accurate statements—statements, that is to say, fitting his immediate impressions and perceptions as

glove fits hand. There are to be no wrinkles and no decorations; the perfect fit is the goal. As for the selection of facts to be transcribed, he leaves that, without further care, to whatever it is that holds him together as an individual, a simple separate person. He did not make himself nor the world as it impinges upon him; but, because he is himself, certain aspects of the impinging world strongly fix his attention and he is strongly moved to reproduce them in prose. To reproduce such things with a spare, hard, undeviating precision is the entire scope and meaning of his art: and in this restricted endeavor he is triumphant. For what they may or may not be intellectually, esthetically, or morally worth, he makes his facts ours.

* * *

To the present critic, then, who is amazed by and genuinely admires the lean virtuosity of Mr. Hemingway, the second most astonishing thing about him is the narrowness of his selective range. His interest in the so variously impinging Universe is a peculiarly restricted interest. It permits him to observe with due attention only certain sorts of people, themselves with oddly limited minds, interests, and patterns of behavior. The people he observes with fascinated fixation and then makes live before us are real, but they are all very much alike: bullfighters, bruisers, touts, gunmen, professional soldiers, prostitutes, hard drinkers, dope fiends.

* * *

I can easily conceive of a great writer choosing to write the short and simple annals of the hard-boiled; what I can not conceive is his doing so virtually without reference to other possible aspects of human existence. For a Maxim Gorki, as I read him, the lower depths are not wholly disconnected from black, bottomless gulfs even more profoundly terrible, nor have they lost all contact with the loftiest, remotest pinnacles of aspiration. And it makes a difference—. In the callous little world of Mr. Hemingway I feel cribbed, cabined, confined; I lack air— just as I do in the cruel little world of Guy de Maupassant—just as I do, though not so desperately, so gaspingly, in the placid stuffy little world of Jane Austen. But there is room to breathe in Shakespeare, in Tolstoy. And—yes—it makes all the difference.

"Mr. Hemingway's Short Stories of Life in the Raw." *Springfield Republican*, November 20, 1927, p. 7F.

The 14 short stories that comprise Ernest Hemingway's latest book entitled "Men Without Women" give us different but always vibrant snapshots of life. Deceit, sordidness, cunning, pathos, are bared to the reader through staccato dialogs and a few crisp paragraphs of explanation. By simplicity of treatment, the author throws these episodes into sharp relief. Situations are suggested, not explained.

* * *

Every page manages to picture the reality of life. As to the emotional or artistic value of the pictures, readers' opinions will, perhaps, differ.

Edmund Wilson. "The Sportsman's Tragedy." *New Republic*, 53 (December 14, 1927), 102-03.

The reputation of Ernest Hemingway has, in a very short time, reached such proportions that it has already become fashionable to disparage him. Yet it seems to me that he has received in America very little intelligent criticism. I find Lee Wilson Dodd, for example, in the Saturday Review of Literature, with his usual gentle trepidation in the presence of contemporary life, deciding with a sigh of relief that, after all, Ernest Hemingway (a young man who has published only three books) is not Shakespeare or Tolstoy; and describing Hemingway's subjects as follows: "The people he observes with fascinated fixation and then makes live before us are ... all very much alike: bull-fighters, bruisers, touts, gunmen, professional soldiers, prostitutes, hard drinkers, dope fiends. . . . For what they may or may not be intellectually, esthetically or morally worth, he makes his facts ours." In the Nation, Joseph Wood Krutch, whose review is more sympathetic than Mr. Dodd's, describes Hemingway as follows: "Spiritually the distinguishing mark of Mr. Hemingway's work is a weariness too great to be aware of anything but sensations. . . . Mr. Hemingway tells us, both by his choice of subject and by the method which he employs, that life is an affair of mean tragedies. . . . In his hands the subject matter of literature becomes sordid little catastrophes in the lives of very vulgar people." I do not know whether these reviewers of "Men without Women" have never read Hemingway's other two books, or whether they have simply forgotten them. Do the stories in "In Our Time" and in "The Sun Also Rises" actually answer to these descriptions? Does "Men Without Women" answer to them? The hero of "In Our Time," who appears in one or two stories in the new volume, and the hero of "The Sun Also Rises," are both highly civilized persons of rather complex temperament and extreme sensibility. In what way can they be said to be "very vulgar people"? And can the adventures of even the old bull-fighter in "The Undefeated" be called a "sordid little catastrophe"?

* * *

It would appear, then, that Hemingway's world was not quite so devoid of interest as it has been represented by Mr. Krutch and Mr. Dodd. Even when he deals with rudimentary types—as he by no means always does—his drama usually turns on some principle of courage, of honor, of pity—in short, of sportsmanship in its largest human sense—which he discovers in them. I do not say that the world which Hemingway depicts is not a bad world; it is

a bad world and a world where much is suffered. Hemingway's feelings about this world, his criticism of what goes on in it, are, for all his misleadingly simple and matter-of-fact style, rather subtle and complex; but he has, it seems to me, made it sufficiently plain what sort of emotions and ideas he intends to communicate. His first book was called "In Our Time," and it was made up of a series of brief and brutal sketches of barbarous happenings mostly connected with the War, alternated with a series of short stories about a sensitive and healthy boy in the American northwest. We were, I take it, to contrast these two series. When Hemingway gave them this title, he meant to tell us that life was barbarous, even in our civilized age; and that the man who sees the cabinet ministers shot and who finds himself potting at the Germans from the "perfectly priceless barricade" has had to come a long way from the boy who, with the fresh senses of youth, so much enjoyed the three days' fishing trip at Big Two-Hearted River. Yet has he really come so far? Is not the very principle of life essentially ruthless and cruel? What is the difference between the gusto of the soldier all on edge to hunt his fellow humans and the gusto of the young fisherman hooking grasshoppers to catch trout? Hemingway is primarily preoccupied with these problems of suffering and cruelty.

* * *

Hemingway's attitude, however, toward the cruelties and treacheries he describes is quite different from anything else which one remembers in a similar connection. He has nothing of the generous indignation of the romantics: he does not, like Byron, bid the stones of the prisoner's cell "appeal from tyranny to God"; nor, like Shelley, bid the winds to "wail for the world's wrong." Nor has he even that grim and repressed, but still generous, still passionate feeling which we find in the pessimist-realists—in Hardy's "Tess," in Maupassant's "Boule de Suif," even in those infrequent scenes of Flaubert where we are made to boil at the spectacle of an old farm servant or of a young silk-weaver's daughter at the mercy of the bourgeoisie. In his treatment of the War, for example, Hemingway is as far as possible from Barbusse or from John Dos Passos. His point of view, his state of mind, is a curious one, and one typical of the time—he seems so broken in to the agonies of humanity, and, though even against his will, so impassively resigned to them, that his only protest is, as it were, the grin and the oath of the sportsman who loses the game. Furthermore, we are not always quite sure on which side Hemingway is betting. We are sometimes afflicted by the suspicion that what we are witnessing is a set-up, with the manager backing the barbarian. Yet, to speak of Hemingway in these terms is really to misrepresent him. He is not a moralist staging a melodrama, but an artist presenting a situation of which the moral values are complex. Hemingway thoroughly enjoys bull-fighting, as he enjoys skiing, racing and prize-fights; and he is unremittingly conscious of the fact that, from the point of view of life as a sport, all that seems to him most painful is somehow closely bound up with what seems to him most enjoyable. The peculiar conflicts of feeling which arise in a temperament of this kind are the subject of his fiction. His most remarkable effects, effects unlike anything else one remembers, are those, as in the fishing trip in "The Sun Also Rises," where we are made to feel, behind the appetite for the physical world, the falsity or the tragedy of a moral situation. The inescapable consciousness of this discord does not arouse Hemingway to passionate violence; but it poisons him and makes him sick, and thus invests with a singular sinister quality—a quality perhaps new in fiction—the sunlight and the green summer landscapes of "The Sun Also Rises." Thus, if Hemingway is oppressive, as Mr. Dodd complains, it is because he himself is oppressed. And we may find in him—in the clairvoyant's crystal of that incomparable art—an image of the common oppression.

K. S.
Boston Evening Transcript, January 7, 1928, Book Section, p. 4.

The art of Mr. Hemmingway [sic] is exposition in the nude. He never writes an unnecessary word. Everything to which he devotes his attention evolves clean and virile, without any drapery. There is nothing about his prose or his subject matter that is effeminate. It is masculine nudity of the starkest sort. Take for example "The

Killers," one of the fourteen short stories in this collection. It is a beautifully executed picture in which the aforementioned qualities of Mr. Hemmingway's art are most apparent. It is a cruel story, but it is told in such a compact way that it is art.

* * *

Mr. Hemmingway has evolved a new form, noticeable a little too much in "Today Is Friday" and "A Canary for One", and he will have his followers. He is the newest thing after Joyce. He is modern art. "The Sun Also Rises" placed Mr. Hemmingway firmly, and now you will find him and his followers everywhere. "Men Without Women" is proof of his "arrival."

* * *

At any rate "Men Without Women" is good reading and when you lay Hemmingway's latest book down, you know he is serious. How it will all turn out one cannot say. But there will, for a long time anyway, be only one Hemmingway. For he has found the secret of how to be modern and coherent, how to be a reporter and an artist all at once. He sees life as something mean and crude, but it is real life nevertheless. And because of this his work is art, not artifice, sincerity, not affectation.

N. L. Rothman. "Hemingway Whistles in the Dark." *Dial*, 84 (April 1928), 336-38.

Unless I am very much mistaken, there is a good deal in the writing of Ernest Hemingway that is being overlooked, in the general commotion over his splendid technique. It seems to be the same penalty that men pay for writing in some startling, new fashion. The brilliance of the originality of expression so dazzles the eyes of the beholders that they see nothing of the source of the brilliance; they forget that the source of light is most often heat. One might easily suggest that this is at the bottom of most literary *débâcles*, for the audience for literary novelties is notoriously fickle, and rushes from author to author with the alacrity of the proverbial bee. Who lives by his style must perish by another's.

* * *

The reviews of Hemingway's work have been profuse and enthusiastic. There are multitudinous references to his "hard, athletic style," his "clean, masculine prose," his modern economy of detail, his classic detachment from his characters. This compendium of tribute to Hemingway's instincts for form and fine writing leaves, it seems to me, much more to be said.

* * *

We must realize, first, that there is no hope and no suspense in any of Hemingway's work. No suspense! cry modern readers, in dismay. May I remind them that there is precedent for such lack? They will search the tragedies of Shakespeare in vain, for a vestige of what we call suspense, in the sense of dubious outcome. There is never any doubt about the inexorable fate that looms large long before the last act. We know, almost at once, that there is no hope for Romeo and Juliet, no hope for Hamlet, none for Cordelia, none for Brutus. We are spectators at a pageant of continuous disaster, where no chance can vary the logical doom of men and women who fail to blend with the world. Once we have become reconciled to this awful certainty, the rest is beauty and calm—the beauty of souls that are unique and therefore especially alive—the calm of bravery approaching the precipice.

I find this in Hemingway, singing out under the constant beat of conversation and reiteration, the constant escape from solitude and soliloquy, for solitude could only be bitter, and soliloquy only an admission of defeat, some modern version of "to be or not to be." There must be no squealing, no quitting. Men must play at being undefeated. Consider Hemingway's short story of that title, The Undefeated, one of his finest. The bull-fighter knows he cannot vanquish this last bull, nor escape the horns. His *picadero* knows it. The crowd, above, knows it, and heaps the imprecations of the galleries upon him. Somehow, too, the bull has come to know it, and seems to await his victory with a grim

ferocity. His energies slipping from him, Garcia holds his ground, snarls back at the crowd, and awaits the charge with sword pointed.

In another story, The Killers, a man, lying upon a bed, has news brought him of the arrival of two gunmen, hired assassins, who are out to kill him. He does not rise, there is no flight, no attempt at self-preservation. There is almost dignity in his quiescence as he stares dully at the ceiling, waiting. These men, the bull-fighter and the hunted man, are lost, and in their refusal to cry out they rise to a few extraordinary moments of significant living. This, I think, is high tragedy, and high art.

* * *

Enough has been said about Hemingway's objectiveness to necessitate no further discussion of it here. If it is true that the spirit of a book is the writer, then Hemingway is partially revealed as one who whistles in a void of frustration. Nowhere does he come to the aid of his inarticulate characters, inarticulate in the sense that every word they utter is subsidiary rubble on the sides of a volcano. His is the reticence of Jake, who says, "I felt pretty rotten," when he was actually frantic.

In the last analysis, perhaps, this is as close as we can get to the actual Hemingway. That life is very much of a mess; that nothing can be done about it; that we had best not talk about how badly things are really going; that the only escape is in triviality that will consume time, laughing or drinking, prize-fights or bull-fights—these we may glean as probably tenets of his stoicism. He refuses to sympathize with his characters, and strips his stories of non-essential detail. I venture to say that he could write a great tragedy. He remains, I think, our outstanding realist.

H. L. Mencken. (Combined review of *Men Without Women* and Thornton Wilder's *The Bridge of San Luis Rey*.) *The American Mercury*, 14 (May 1928), 127.

Mr. Hemingway and Mr. Wilder, huge successes of late, have received much uncritical homage, but they both may be too wise to let it fool them. They have won attention by technical virtuosity, but if they are to make good their high promise, they must know it will take hard and fundamental thinking. To date, despite bravura passages, they are still uncertain in their grasp of character. Although their work charms, it leaves no deep impression and often seems fragmentary. While we wait for years to bring them maturity, though, we can be sincerely thankful for such good things as Mr. Hemingway's "The Killers" and "Fifty Grand" and Mr. Wilder's "The Marquesa de Montemayor" and "Uncle Pio." If they are not masterpieces, they are the stuff that masterpieces are made from. (Summary)

M. R. Rosene. "The Five Best American Books Published Since 1900." *Writer*, 46 (October 1934), 370-71.

To Hemingway, that Byron in bullfighter's pants so idolized by the campus intelligentsia, I award first prize in the contemporary short story. To particularize, I believe that "The Undefeated" is the best American short story since Crane's "Open Boat." Several of the other stories in this collection approach it in calibre, and they, along with the best work in "Winner Take Nothing" and "In Our Time" make up an aggregate of achievement considerably beyond the powers of any other American now writing.

Hemingway is austere where Anderson is sloppy. He has performed technical tricks of amazing brilliance. He sees clearly, deeply, and steadily. He has nothing in common with those writers, now so lamentably numerous, who should be driving a truck instead of a typewriter. Hemingway is genuine.

Checklist of
Additional Reviews

J. M. March. *New York Evening Post,*
    October 27, 1927, p. 13.

Curtis Williams. "Some Recent
    Books." *Town & Country,* 82 (De-
    cember 15, 1927), 59.

North American Review, 224 (Decem-
    ber 1927), front section.

Booklist, 24 (January 1928), 163.

Notes

A FAREWELL TO ARMS

By
ERNEST HEMINGWAY

NEW YORK
CHARLES SCRIBNER'S SONS
1929

A Farewell to Arms

Henry Hazlitt.
"Take Hemingway."
New York Sun,
September 28, 1929,
p. 38.

The books that tumble endlessly over the reviewer's desk have paper jackets and the jackets have blurbs and the blurbs have surprising comparisons. Novels of the sea are like Conrad and novels of the soil like Hardy and Hamsun and stream-of-consciousness novels are like Proust and Joyce and other novels are like Dostoievsky. But in the last few months, it seems, most of the novels have been like Hemingway. Hardboiled novels, monosyllabic novels, novels without commas, novels about morons, are like Hemingway.

The jacket blurbs are symptomatic. The names that they choose for comparisons, the writers that they profess to think their own writer is like, are the writers whose prestige is now highest, the writers who are fashionable. Hemingway is fashionable. Indeed, he is the idol of the young generation of American writers. There is a Hemingway school, with a constantly increasing membership, Morley Callaghan, Josephine Herbst, John Riordan, Viña Delmar, are in the school or on the fringes of the school. In the year of our Lord 1929 Ernest Hemingway is the greatest single influence on the American novel and short story. We have named some of his offspring, direct and collateral; Sherwood Anderson and Ring Lardner are his uncles. And here is a new novel by the young master himself.

* * *

Many things in the novel are magnificently done. The account of the retreat, which never goes beyond Henry's personal experience, is unforgettable. So, for that matter, are the personal episodes, such as the night rowing on the lake, the death of Catherine. The scenes are vividly realized, and the passage of time is conveyed with uncanny skill. There is a somewhat wider range to the characters than in Hemingway's preceding book. The priest at the officers' mess is not what we have come to think of as a Hemingway figure; the girl, Catherine, has a fine courage and a touch of nobility. And throughout the book, under the iron, cynical surface, under the inspiring portraits of Rinaldi and the Italian soldiers, there is a deep vein of tenderness and pity. In depth, in range, in drama, "A Farewell to Arms" is the finest thing Hemingway has yet done.

The dialogue is what we have come

to expect. It is brilliantly authentic; one listens to it rather than reads it. There is no more convincing dialogue being written anywhere. And the army talk makes that in "What Price Glory?" seem almost tame.

With so much that is admirable it may seem ungrateful to speak of Hemingway's limitations, or of the limitations of his style and method. But it is perhaps necessary to do this because of the author's current authority and influence. There is at present not only a Hemingway school but a Hemingway cult. This cult not only believes that the Hemingway is a good way to write, which is true enough; it imagines it is the way to write, and it looks upon more traditional methods with something like contempt. Here, say the members of the new cult, is the dialogue of our time, the prose of our day. Here is something honest, fresh and thoroughly American. Here at last is something indigenous and independent; one could not possibly, for example, imagine an Englishman writing it.

The argument is plausible and not without force. But we soon begin to perceive that many of Hemingway's virtues are bought at a rather high cost. It is not merely his dialogue that is simple and bare, but his writing in between. It is Hemingway's aim, apparently, not to put down any word or even use any sentence structure that would not be used in the common talk of our own day. With this idea and aim he has often achieved great economy and vigor; he has swept out all sorts of incumbering connectives and musty and shopworn phrases, and much of

the writing that results deserves the adjectives so often applied to it—hard, clean, athletic. But in "Farewell to Arms" he has often carried this simplicity to a point where it becomes palpably artificial, with the result that the prose falls off from the level achieved in "The Sun Also Rises.". . . It is a type of writing so "simple" and above all so monotonous that it actually becomes dull. Just as book type when increased beyond a certain size becomes for an adult not easier but harder to read, so descriptions may become less vivid when carried beyond a certain point of naïveté. In reading these separate drops of assertion, unpunctuated, linked by "ands," one feels like a thirsty man compelled to drink a high ball with a teaspoon.

The truth is, I suspect, that Hemingway feels most at home in writing dialogue and that he writes static description half-heartedly and from a sense of duty. Indeed, one wonders constantly, in reading his novels and short stories, why he has never tried his hand at playwriting. For his method is essentially that of the playwright; it is purely behavioristic, sees merely the thing before it, deals with surface and externals, is objective, almost never introspective. Hemingway may possibly have a deficient sense of stage technic, but until he writes a play I for one shall continue to regret that a first rate talent is being lost to American theater, so desperately in need of first rate talents.

Yet even Hemingway's dialogue, brilliant as it is, has important limitations. It is not sharply enough individualized. You could switch many of the remarks from mouth to mouth without having them sound incongruous. The talk is, further, extremely narrow in range; and one may think of this either as cause or result of the narrow range of the characters. Soldiers, bullfighters, bruisers, peasants, gangmen—all these Hemingway puts down superbly, at least from the outside. Hemingway people are for the most part above the level of morons, but their two main interests in life are alcohol and adultery; the whole world of business, public affairs, art, science, literature might almost cease to exist for all the attention they give to it. They are never complicated people, either emotionally or intellectually, for if they were the casual, hard-boiled Hemingway manner would be incapable of dealing with them. Imagine what would happen if a character out of Henry James or Proust were to stray by accident into a Hemingway novel! He would either be treated as a pretender and a fool or left almost completely unrealized.

Such criticism, it may be objected, is not fair. Every writer has the defects of his qualities. It is silly to complain that apples do not grow on grape vines. If Hemingway would feel embarrassed to find a Henry James character walking into his novels how would Henry James have been able to cope with the situation if a Hemingway character had wandered into one of his?

The objection is valid enough so far as it goes. But my criticism is directed not so much against Hemingway as against the Hemingway cult. His offhand manner and mordant humor are admirably adapted to portraying the commonplace and simple; they fall before a character in any way profound or complex. They create an atmosphere in which nuances, shades and subleties cannot exist. As more young writers follow this manner American novels may gain in vigor and life. But if the manner ever becomes the dominating one (as it seems in danger of becoming), it must end by producing a literature monotonous in theme and tone, lopsided and impoverished.

Fanny Butcher. "Here is Genius, Critic Declares of Hemingway." *Chicago Daily Tribune,* September 28, 1929, p. 11.

Technically and stylistically the most interesting novel of the year is a judgment which any keenly critical reader would pass on "A Farewell to Arms." Anyone who thus has watched American writing cannot but find in it a blossoming of a most unusual genius of our day.

Ernest Hemingway has developed— and most especially in "A Farewell to Arms"—a technique which is purely subjective, and a style which is articulate entirely in its bones and not at all in its flesh. There is no flesh whatever to his writing, no solidness, no roundness, no color, no flow of muscle under the skin. There is nothing but uncompromising bone. He sees his writing as an artist sees a human being, a bone structure upon which is superimposed the flesh which the rest of mankind sees.

* * *

Years ago—I don't remember just how many—a woman by the name of Gertrude Stein wrote a book called "Three Lives." It was three short stories done in a technique entirely different from anything else that had been done before in America. It was absolutely subjective. It was written coldly, but it was comprehensible to the average reader. . . .

She was one of the first to champion the modern movement in art. She worked to do in words what the modernists were doing in line and color. I speak thus of Gertrude Stein because Ernest Hemingway is the direct blossoming of Gertrude Stein's art. Whether he consciously was influenced by her no one of course can say. But he does in "A Farewell to Arms," what Gertrude Stein did in "Three Lives," except that he does it in a longer, more complicated medium and with more power.

There are whole pages in this new book which might have been written by Gertrude Stein herself, except that, even in their most tortuous intricacies, the reader is perfectly clear about what Mr. Hemingway is saying and why he is saying it in exactly that way.

That his coldly unsentimental technique and his style are emotionally effective as well as interesting is evidenced by the effect that the ending had upon two women of my acquaintance. . . Both of them, after reading an absolutely brutal, cold blooded narrative, written in a manner which only the word vulgar describes when used in its original Latin meaning, when they came to the last page were seized with absolutely uncontrollable sobs.

Percy Hutchinson. "Love and War in the Pages of Mr. Hemingway." *New York Times Book Review,* September 29, 1929, p. 5.

As in "The Sun Also Rises," Ernest Hemingway lays the scene of his new novel in Europe. But, unlike the earlier novel, he is not concerned with the aftermath of war, but with certain years and phases of the war itself. Consequently, "A Farewell to Arms," if it is to be given classification, belongs to the rapidly crowding shelf of war novels. Later literary historians will doubtless concern themselves with these novels as a group phenomenon. They will dissect the several specimens, and point out differences and similarities. It is too early for this, and even if it could be of interest, it lies beyond the scope of contemporary review. Suffice it to say, however, that Mr. Hemingway has concerned himself with a phase of the war not yet much used, the collapse of the Italian front in 1917, and that, in consequence, so far as his novel is to be regarded solely as a war book, it has the freshness of depiction in a new field.

Dramatic as are the pages dealing

with the Caporetto débâcle, the war, however, is but a background for the real story, and this in spite of the fact that this story is itself an outgrowth of the war. The love of Lieutenant Henry for the nurse Catherine Barkley, a love so great that Henry eventually deserts, as he puts it, "declares a separate peace," could only have come in the war and out of the war. The story of this attachment is poetic, idyllic, tragic.

* * *

There is in "Farewell to Arms" no change from the narrative method of "The Sun Also Rises" and "Men Without Women." Ernest Hemingway did not invent the method, which is chiefly to be characterized by the staccato nature of sentences (an effort at reproducing universal conversational habit), and its rigid exclusion of all but the most necessary description. Yet if Hemingway was not the inventor of the method, tentative gropings toward such a manner having been made by many of his immediate predecessors, the author of "A Farewell to Arms" has, in his several books, made it so strikingly his own that it may bear his name, and is likely to henceforward. The method has its advantages, and also its disadvantages.

The chief result is a sort of enamel lustre imparted to the story as a whole, not precisely an iridescence, but a white light, rather, that pales and flashes, but never warms. And because it never warms, or never seems to warm, the really human in Hemingway (and there is a great deal in Hemingway that is human) fails of its due. It

is not impossible that Ernest Hemingway has developed his style to the extreme to which he carries it because in it he finds a sort of protective covering for a nature more sensitive than he would have one know. . . . But the Hemingway manner is arresting purely as craftsmanship. And if its extreme naturalism borders dangerously on unnaturalism, for the reason that the effect of the printed pages must be, perforce, different from the effect of speech, then it behooves other craftsmen to find the proper modification. Yet it expresses the spirit of the moment admirably. In fact, seldom has a literary style so precisely jumped with the time.

The Caporetto retreat, which forms the background for an entire portion of the book, and furnishes the action, is a masterly piece of descriptive narration. Not static description (which Hemingway abhors), and not merely action, but a subtle weaving of description and narration, this has all the movement of the retreat, its confusion, its horrors, and also makes the reader see the retreat. . . .

* * *

There will be debate as to whether "A Farewell to Arms" is a finer piece of work than "The Sun Also Rises." And there will be cogent arguments advanced on either side. On the surface, the newer story is more effective than the earlier novel. There is more drama, the movement is more nearly continuous and better sustained. And the story of the love between the English nurse and the American ambulance officer, as hapless as that of Romeo and Juliet, is a high achievement in what might be termed the new romanticism. And yet for the present reviewer "The Sun Also Rises" touches a note which Hemingway caught once, and in the very nature of the thing, cannot touch again. In the attachment of Lady Brett for her physically incapacitated lover there is a profound and genuine affection which has something of inspiration. And the pathos of Lady Brett, that she can maintain this only by derelictions, evidences psychology so subtle that it has hitherto evaded the literary worker, and been not always discernible to the scientifically schooled. Others could have done the Caporetto retreat, though perhaps not so dramatically; and others would have imagined the lyric love of "A Farewell to Arms," although perhaps not carrying it through so poetically. "The Sun Also Rises," as it seems to this writer, at least, is more nearly unique as a document and as a novel. Yet he would not wish to lose, therefore, "The Farewell to Arms." [sic] It is a moving and beautiful book.

Malcolm Cowley.
"Not Yet Demobilized."
New York Herald Tribune Books, 6
October 6, 1929,
pp. 1, 6.

Ernest Hemingway during the last five years has won an extraordinary place in American letters. He·has thousands of adherents among the readers of his own age; there are younger writers of talent who accept his leadership; he is imitated by writers much older than himself—a rare phenomenon—and one finds traces of his influence almost everywhere. His name is generally mentioned with the respect that one accords to a legendary figure. From critics he has received a quite special treatment—many of them have praised him equally for his own qualities and for others he never possessed, and a few did not wait for his second novel before comparing him with James Joyce, with Smollett and Defoe, almost with Homer.

Doubtless some of the reasons for this sudden fame are extra-literary: it may partly be attributed to his living away from New York and its literary jealousies, to his ability to surround himself with a legend, to the pride which has kept him from commercializing his work, and also in some degree to his use of rather sensational material; but nevertheless one is forced to conclude that the principal explanation lies in his having expressed, better than any other writer, the limited viewpoint of his contemporaries, of the generation which was formed by the war and which is still incompletely demobilized.

* * *

Most of the characters in Hemingway's stories belong to this category of the undemobilized. Their standards are the very simple standards of men at war. The virtues they admire are generosity, courage, a certain resignation and also the ability to hold one's liquor. The vices they ridicule are vices only to men who have been soldiers: I mean thrift, caution and sobriety. Their simple enjoyments are food, drink, love and perhaps fishing; their tragedies are love, parting, death; and they discuss these topics with the frankness of the barracks—beneath which is not too carefully hidden a martial sentimentality.

To describe these characters, Hemingway has adopted a simple and very appropriate method: we might agree on calling it subtractive. From the novel as conceived by older writers, he has subtracted the embellishments; he has subtracted all the descriptions, the meditations, the statements of theory and he has reserved only the characters and their behavior—their acts, their sensual perceptions, their words. The last he sets down almost stenographically. As for the acts and perceptions, he relates them in very great detail, almost redundantly, in brief sentences that preserve, in spite of certain mannerisms, the locutions, the rhythms and the loose syntax of common A-merican speech. The general effect is one of deliberate unsophistication.

This method, which he developed in his first four books, has been somewhat modified in his new novel. The style has changed first of all: the rhythm is more definite, the sentences are often longer, and the paragraphs are more carefully constructed. In treatment Hemingway has departed to a certain extent from his former strict behaviorism: he has added landscapes and interior monologues to his range of effects, and he has even begun to discuss ideas. In mood he reveals a new

tenderness, and it is interesting to observe that the present volume is his first love story, properly speaking. It is also his first long story about the war, his first novel in the strict sense—"The Sun Also Rises" was an extended episode—and undoubtedly the most important book he has written.

* * *

... The description of the Italian retreat, with its sleeplessness, its hunger, its growing disorganization, its lines of tired men marching in the rain, is perhaps the finest single passage that Hemingway has written. It calls to mind a great description by another writer: I mean Stendhal's account of the retreat from Waterloo. The two are by no means equal, but it is enough that they can be mentioned in the same breath.

* * *

One cannot help thinking that "A Farewell to Arms" is a symbolic title: that it is Hemingway's farewell to a period, an attitude, and perhaps to a method also.... [Cowley's ellipses] As the process of demobilization draws slowly to its end the simple standards of wartime are being forgotten. Pity, love, adventurousness, anger, the emotions on which his earlier books were based, almost to the entire exclusion of ideas, are less violently stimulated in a world at peace. The emotions as a whole are more colored by thought; perhaps they are weaker and certainly they are becoming more complicated. They seem to demand expression in a subtler and richer prose. The present novel shows a change in this direction, and perhaps the change may extend still farther—who knows! Perhaps even Hemingway may decide in the end that being deliberately unsophisticated is not the height of sophistication.

T. S. Matthews. "Nothing Ever Happens to the Brave." *New Republic*, 60 (October 9, 1929), 208-10.

The writings of Ernest Hemingway have very quickly put him in a prominent place among American writers, and his numerous admirers have looked forward with impatience and great expectations to his second novel. They should not be disappointed: "A Farewell to Arms" is worthy of their hopes and of its author's promise.

The book is cast in the form which Hemingway has apparently delimited for himself in the novel—a diary form. It is written in the first person, in that bare and unliterary style (unliterary except for echoes of Sherwood Anderson and Gertrude Stein), in that tone which suggests a roughly educated but sensitive poet who is prouder of his muscles than of his vocabulary, which we are now accustomed to associate with Hemingway's name. The conversation of the characters is as distinctly Hemingway conversation as the conversation in one of Shaw's plays is Shavian. But there are some marked differences between "A Farewell to

Arms" and Hemingway's previous work.

For one thing, the design is more apparent, the material more solidly arranged. Perhaps the strongest criticism that could be levelled against "The Sun Also Rises" was that its action was concerned with flotsam in the eddy of a backwater. It was apparently possible for some readers to appreciate the masculinity of Hemingway's "anti-literary" style, to admit the authenticity of his character, and still to say, "What of it?" This criticism I do not consider valid—there has always been, it seems to me, in the implications of Hemingway's prose, and in his characters themselves, a kind of symbolic content that gives the least of his stories a wider range than it seems to cover—but such a criticism was certainly possible. It is not, however, a criticism that can possibly be directed against "A Farewell to Arms." Fishing, drinking, and watching bullfights might be considered too superficial to be the stuff of tragedy, but love and death are not parochial themes.

* * *

Hemingway has been generally regarded as one of the most representative spokesmen of a lost generation—a generation remarkable chiefly for its cynicism, its godlessness, and its complete lack of faith. He can still, I think, be regarded as a representative spokesman, but the strictures generally implied against his generation will soon, perhaps, have to be modified or further refined. As far as Hemingway himself is concerned, it can certainly no longer be said that his characters do not embody a very definite faith.

... The note of hopelessness that dominated the whole of "The Sun Also Rises" is not absent in "A Farewell to Arms," nor is it weaker, but it has been subtly modified, so that it is not the note of hopelessness we hear so much as the undertone of courage. Hemingway is now definitely on the side of the angels, fallen angels though they are. The principal instrument of this change is Catherine. Brett, the heroine of "The Sun Also Rises," was really in a constant fever of despair; the selfless faith which Catherine gives her lover may seem to come from a knowledge very like despair, but it is not a fever. ...

* * *

Hemingway is not a realist. The billboards of the world, even as he writes about them, fade into something else in place of the world to which we are accustomed, we see a land and a people of strong outlines, of conventionalized shadow; the people speak in a clipped and tacit language as stylized as their appearance. But Hemingway's report of reality is quite as valid as a realist's. The description of the War, in the first part of "A Farewell to Arms," is perhaps as good a description of war just behind the front as has been written; and a fresh report from a point of view as original as Hemingway's is an addition to experience. But this book is not essentially a war-story: it is a love-story. If love-stories mean nothing to you, gentle or hard-boiled reader, this is not your book.

The transition, indeed, from the comparative realism of the war scenes to the ideal reality of the idyll is not as effective as it might be. The meeting of the lovers after Henry's desertion from the army, and their escape into Switzerland, have not that ring of authenticity about them which from Hemingway we demand. We are accustomed to his apparent irrelevancies, which he knows how to use with such a strong and ironic effect, but the scene, for instance, between the lovers and Ferguson in the hotel at Stresa seems altogether too irrelevant, and has no ironic or dramatic value, but is merely an unwanted complication of the story. From this point until the time when lovers are safely established in Switzerland, we feel a kind of uncertainty about everything that happens; we cannot quite believe in it. Why is it, then, that when our belief is reawakened, it grows with every page, until once more we are convinced, and passionately convinced, that we are hearing the truth?

I think it is because Hemingway, like every writer who has discovered in himself the secret of literature, has now invented the kind of ideal against which no man's heart is proof. In the conclusion of "A Farewell to Arms," he has transferred his action to a stage very far from realism, and to a plane which may be criticized as the dramatics of a sentimental dream. And it is a dream. Catherine Barkley is one of the impossibly beautiful characters of modern tragedy—the Tesses, the Alyoshas, the Myshkins—who could never have existed, who could not live even in our minds if it were not for our hearts. In that sentimentalism, that intimation of impossible immortality, poets and those who hear them are alike guilty.

Hemingway himself is doubtless a very different sort of man from the people pictured in his books: he may well have very different ideas about the real nature of life; but as long as books remain a communication between us, we must take them as we understand them and feel them to be. "Nothing ever happens to the brave." It is an ambiguous statement of belief, and its implications are sufficiently sinister, but its meaning is as clear and as simple as the faith it voices. It is a man's faith; and men have lived and died by much worse.

Agnes W. Smith.
"Mr. Hemingway Does It Again."
New Yorker, 5
(October 12, 1929),
120.

"A Farewell to Arms" is to this reviewer Hemingway's greatest work. That rarest of all literary achievements, it is a glowing modern love story, a story of emotion that is so true it is like an intense personal experience. Unlike other modern novelists who can bring themselves to write of love only with cynicism or awkwardness, Hemingway writes with a poetic modern idiom that only a reading of the dialogue in the final tragic episode can convey. In its eloquent simplicity it makes other dialogue seem smirking and stilted.

Besides love, Mr. Hemingway's story is a brutal war. The affair between Lieutenant Henry, an ambulance driver, and the English nurse Catherine Barkley begins as casually as the war on the Italian front. Indeed, the war and the romantic interlude at first have a half-comic air of opéra-bouffe. But as the war grows intense and grim, the love affair becomes equally as desperate and finally as tragic. The early scenes of war life in the barracks and hospitals are gay, pungent, and witty, though they also carry an undertone of bewilderment. But when the agreeable war breaks open with the German attack at Caporetto, Mr. Hemingway really shows he can do great writing. This dramatic and terrible moment is experienced with such clarity that the printed page rivals the moving pictures in vividness. Then we know how well Hemingway has brought new life and new meanings to words that had begun to fade and grow stale. (Summary)

Henry Seidel Canby.
"Story of the Brave."
Saturday Review of Literature, 6
(October 12, 1929),
231-32.

When Mr. Hemingway dawned upon his native land with "The Sun Also Rises" he was received with mingled praise and doubt. His skill as a storyteller was evident, his dialogue was superb, he had that gift of creating a vivid reality which makes any suit trumps for a novelist, but his subject matter troubled the serious minded. So much art seemed wasted upon the lovable but futile revellers who ran from cocktail to cocktail up and down France, self-tortured, but flippant, as unmoral as monkeys yet pathetically appealing for sympathy in their mental woes (which were usually aggravated by a headache).

Since then we have had many short stories and this full-length novel, and now his scope and purpose become clearer....

* * *

... You cannot take too seriously a novel of such vivid reality as "Farewell to Arms," nor an observer and auditor of such uncanny powers. Hundreds of writers have told the story ... [Canby's ellipses] weariness of routine ... a casual love affair ... an obsession with loving ... the subtle change from mistress to wife (Henry never actually marries Catherine, but that is irrelevant) ... tragedy impending upon too much happiness ... the poignant end. But it is not the plot that counts, it is the circumstance and the complete realization of the characters. In this book you get your own times in typical essence to wonder about and interpret.

Yet I do not believe that Hemingway's strength lies in character creation. His Catherine and his Henry have nothing strange or novel in their personalities. Catherine is a fine girl who needs a lover. Henry is an individualist who acts by instinct rationalized not by principle, and makes his friends love him. Hemingway's art is to make

such not unfamiliar characters articulate when he finds them. His minor people, like the pagan and affectionate Rinaldi, or old Count Greffi, playing billiards and discoursing wisdom at 94, are more original than his protagonists. It isn't *what* they are, it is *how* they are that seems important, and of course that is a true principle in art. . . .

Hemingway works almost entirely through a simple record of incident and dialogue which he stretches to include meditation in the rhythm of thought. It is a fine art. He plays upon a principle which Robert Frost stated years ago, that every speaker has his own style and rhythm, unmistakable as his finger prints, and adds a discovery in which Gertrude Stein (who carries it into absurdity) helps him, that the recurrent rhythms of thought carry word repetition with them, so that both dialogue and meditation can be charged with so much personality that further description is unnecessary.

* * *

. . . Hemingway is after voice rhythms and voice contrasts. It is the way these people talk not what they say that lifts the scene into reality.

I see that he is being criticized for writing in English that teachers of writing would despair of because of its devastations of grammar and syntax. If the teachers despair, they are ignorant. Few experimenters are always successful, and when he does go really wrong, which is seldom, it is because in the attempt to make his English more expressive he overstrains an instrument which, at its best, is crude.

* * *

... Hemingway knows what he is about. Let his imitators beware lest they copy him, twisting syntax, not as he does to fit necessity, but out of bravado and freakishness. English is a great language, which makes rules for text-books, and its genius is to become more expressive not more correct.

... It is not all style. There is a focussing of incident in the retreat from Caporetto, in the escape by night of the two on Lake Maggiore, and in the superb scene of childbirth that belongs to the great art of storytelling in general and would be admirable even if written in the straightforward method of the "Arabian Nights." But the vividness is from style.

"Farewell to Arms" is an erotic story, shocking to the cold, disturbing to the conventional who do not like to see mere impersonal amorousness lifted into a deep, fierce love, involving the best in both man and woman, without changing its dependence upon the senses, nor trafficking with social responsibility. It deals with life where the blood is running and the spirit active—that is enough for me. As for Hemingway's frankness of language, to object to it would be priggish. There is no decadence here, no overemphasis on the sexual as a philosophy. Rather, this book belongs with those studies of conjugal love which just now are interesting the French. If you set out to write of the love life of a man and his wife when that love life is central in their experience, why that love life is what you write about and frankness belongs to the theme.

A good Victorian, I think, would have admired the frankness of this book, and also its style, but might have felt it to be narrow to the point of triviality in its concentration. Our most skilful writers today are more interested in vivid snap shots than in cosmologies. They prefer carved peach stones to panoramas. I prefer either myself to the dull tales of "cases" so much admired a few years ago, in which fiction began to look like sociology. Hemingway does lack scope. He is attracted by the vivid, and doesn't care what is vivid so that he gets it right. It's a better way to begin than the opposite method of biographing the universe as one sees it and calling that a novel. Nevertheless, his eroticism will deserve a less specific name when he has learned how to do it (I think he has learned) and begins to use it as a factor in synthesis. Not that "Farewell to Arms" is a "youthful," an "experimental" novel. It is absolutely done; and, even cosmically speaking, the flow of great social resolutions down and away from battle in the Alps to disillusion in the plains until all that is left of emotion is canalized into the purely personal business of love—that is a big enough theme for any novel. It is only that his stories seem to lack experience beyond the baffled, the desperate, the indifferent, the defiant so far. Which means, I suppose, that he is wise not to have written in that penetrative way of his about what has not yet engaged the imagination of his generation. In fiction, he is worthy to be their leader.

"Man, Woman, War."
Time, 14
(October 14, 1929),
80.

Ernest Hemingway's new novel of love and war on the Italian front keeps a sustained, inexorable movement whether chronicling the chaotic sweep of armies or the tenderly quiescent affair of a U.S. ambulance officer and an English nurse. A story preoccupied with flesh, blood, and nerves rather than with intellectual fancy work, it fulfills the promises Hemingway's admirers have been making for him. Though his consciously bold, often mannered style may annoy, there is no denying its pulsing innuendo.

The novel's depiction of war is on a par with its best predecessors. But it is Hemingway's rendering of modern love that gives the story its greatest significance. Resisting the tendency in literature to malign love as a romantic distortion or a carnal appetite, author Hemingway shows it as an honest blend of desire, serenity, and wordless sympathy. His lovers stand together in a world that is shattering and dissolving and convey their feelings in a casual joke, a gesture in the night, even in trite endearments that take on poignancy for all their triteness. Most poignant of all is the hero's perhaps unethical desertion from the battle line to take the woman he has gotten with child in a rowboat across Lake Maggiore to neutral Switzerland. In their escape, their stay in the Alps in hillside lodgings, and in the hospital at Lausanne where they look at each other in torment as Catherine lies dying in childbirth, they become in a vast landscape small images of the pity, beauty, and doom of mankind. (Summary)

Walter R. Brooks.
"Behind the Blurbs."
Outlook and Independent, 153
(October 16, 1929),
270.

* * *

We have just finished Ernest Hemingway's *Farewell to Arms*. "We may be wrong, but we think it's wonderful." It concerns the love of an American lieutenant and an English nurse, set, on the Italian front, against the background of war. It has as you read it that quality of warmth, of actuality, of closeness that only your own personal experiences have for you. It was so real to us that we felt, as we do ordinarily in our own life, that it must go, that nothing very dramatic or tragic was going to happen—could happen. And that disappointed us a little, because after all we were reading a novel. Then when catastrophes come, they have the same quality of awfulness that they do have in your own experience. This book enriches you.

A. C.
"Echoes from the Great War in Ernest Hemingway's Novel."
Boston Transcript, October 19, 1929, Book Section, p. 2.

* * *

The popularity of Ernest Hemingway has been greatly aided by the younger readers of America. Older people, brought up in days when writers often did not say what they meant, or at least heavily clothed their meanings in veiled metaphors and indirect hints, are shocked by modern harshness of dialogue, and discrepancy of style. Whether a writer should transcend in his dialogue the conventions of the contemporary drawing-room, is apparently a live topic of conversation at present. Certainly a writer should be able to present nearly any idea he wishes, as long as, in some vague manner, it fits in with his general scheme. Today, however, with inferior minds attempting to comprehend certain rather superior books, words are counted more heavily than ideas.

At this juncture, it might be well to say, that it is hard to believe that many intelligent and liberal-minded readers of any age can be very much in sympathy with Mr. Hemingway's use of hard words. It is not that such usage would tend to corrupt the youth, for practically every boy of twelve knows all of them, but it is rather that such usage lowers the tone of literature in general. The best writing is not necessarily the most realistic; indeed, in order to be a really fine work, a book should have some little idealism to it.

... Another American writer, a better one, who is nevertheless somewhat in the same boat as Mr. Hemingway, and embarked on the same uncharted seas, is Sherwood Anderson.

* * *

Although both these writers have doubtless thrown off the cloak of European influence which has so strongly dominated our literature in the past, in many ways, they have not developed a style of their own of much portent. Today, and since the war, it is true that America has become increasingly conscious of the vast reservoir of energy that is hers. There is the exultation of youth in the air; we are innovating with a youth's abandon. We are having new everything, even new writers. Ernest Hemingway is one of these, and in the writings there is a certain undeniable force. Yet one feels that he is wasting talent, that because of his assiduousness in realistic detail, he fails to reach higher, and therefore that his works do not matter much. Far too often does he punch out faithful photographs of mediocre people.

To say that "A Farewell to Arms" is a good book is not praising Mr. Hemingway. Aside from certain annoyances that are difficult to overlook, it is an excellent novel of the war, with perhaps too little motivation for its tragic conclusion. . . .

Clifton P. Fadiman.
"A Fine American Novel."
The Nation, 129
(October 30, 1929),
497-98.

Recently there have been laid down a number of dicta anent what the modern novel may not do if it is to remain a modern novel. One of them is to the effect that a representation of a simple love affair is impossible in our day. Another tells us that it is difficult, if not impossible, to reproduce the emotion of male friendship or love, as the present shift in sex conventions tends to surround the theme with an ambiguous atmosphere. A third dictum concerns itself with the impossibility of true tragedy in contemporary literature. A fourth, not so much a stated law as a pervasive feeling, would insist on the irrelevance to our time of the "non-intellectual" or "primitive" novel. Now, none of these generalizations is silly; there is a great deal of truth in all of them. It just happens that Mr. Hemingway, quite unconsciously, has produced a book which upsets all of them at once and so makes them seem more foolish than they really are. Worse still, his book is not merely a good book but a remarkably beautiful book; and it is not merely modern, but the very apotheosis of a kind of modernism. Mr. Hemingway is simply one of those inconvenient novelists who won't take the trouble to learn the rules of the game. It is all very embarrassing.

Take the business of love, for example. Neither Catherine nor Henry in "A Farewell to Arms" is a very complicated person. They are pretty intelligent about themselves but they are not over self-conscious. There are few kinks in their natures. I don't suppose they could produce one mental perversion between them. They fall in love in a simple, healthy manner, make love passionately and movingly; and when Catherine dies the reader is quite well aware that he has passed through a major tragic experience. Their story seems too simple to be "modern"; yet it is as contemporary as you wish. It seems too simple to be interesting; yet it is gripping, almost heartbreaking. I don't think any complex explanations are in order. I offer the familiar one that Hemingway, almost alone among his generation, feels his material very deeply and that he never overworks that material. Understatement is not so much a method with him as an instinctive habit of mind. (It is more or less an accident that it also happens to harmonize with the contemporary anti-romantic tendency.) Consequently we believe in his love story.

Similarly with the second motif of the book: the emotion of male affection, exemplified in the relationship between Henry and Rinaldi. This is the most perilous theme of all. With some of us a fake Freudism has inclined our minds to the cynical. Others, simpler temperaments, inevitably think of comradeship in oozily sentimental terms, the Kipling strong-men-and-brothers-all business. Hemingway seems unaware of either attitude. Perhaps that unawareness partially explains his success. At any rate, without in any way straining our credulity he makes us feel that this very sense of comradeship—nordically reticent in Henry's case, blasphemously, ironically effusive in Rinaldi's—was one of the few things that mitigated the horror and stupidity of the war.

I have rarely read a more "non-intellectual" book than "A Farewell to Arms." This non-intellectuality is not connected with Hemingway's much-discussed objectivity. It is implicit in his temperament. He is that marvelous combination—a highly intelligent naïf. I do not mean that he writes without thought, for as a matter of obvious fact he is one of the best craftsmen alive. But he feels his story entirely in emotional and narrative terms. He is almost directly opposed in temper, for example, to Sherwood Anderson, who would like to give the effect of naivete but can't because he is always thinking about his own simplicity. "A Farewell to Arms" revolves about two strong, simple feelings: love for a beautiful and noble woman, affection for one's comrades. When it is not concerned with these two feelings it is simple exciting narrative—the retreat from Caporetto, the nocturnal escape to Switzerland. The whole book exists on a plane of strong feeling or of thrilling human adventure. It is impossible to feel superior to Hemingway's primitiveness, his insensibility to "ideas," because he strikes no attitude. A large part of the novel deals with simple things—eating cheese, drinking wine, sleeping with women. But he does not try to make you feel that these activities are "elemental" or overly significant. They are just integral parts of a personality which is strong and whole. Therein lies their effect on us. It is impossible to be patronizing about Henry's, or Hemingway's, complete contemporaneity, his mental divorcement from the past, the antique, the classical, the gentlemanly, cultured tradition. "The frescoes were not bad," remarks the hero at one point. "Any frescoes were good when they started to peel and flake off." This is not merely humorous, it is the reflection of a mind reacting freshly, freely, with an irony that is modern, yet simple and unaffected.

"A Farewell to Arms" is not perfect by any means, nor, to me at least, interesting all the way through. I find the military descriptions dull, and for a paradoxical reason. Hemingway's crisp, curt, casual style, so admirably suited to the rest of his narrative, fails in the military portions because of these very qualities. It is too much like a regulation dispatch. Military reports have always been written in a sort of vulgar Hemingwayese; therefore they give no sense of novelty or surprise. But a detail like this does not matter much; the core of "A Farewell to Arms" remains untouched. It is certainly Hemingway's best book to date. There seems no reason why it should not secure the Pulitzer Prize for, despite the Italian setting, it is as American as Times Square. It is a real occasion for patriotic rejoicing.

Mary Ross.
"A Group of New Novels."
Atlantic Monthly, 144
(November 1929),
20.

In *A Farewell to Arms* Ernest Hemingway has drawn an idyll in the midst of war. In light of his earlier work, an idyll is one of the last things one could have expected him to draw. This story of the Italian front has the same strange power of his earlier books to evoke overtones through laconic dialogue. Beyond this technical mastery, Hemingway shows in his account of the affair between Lieutenant Henry and the Scotch nurse Catherine Barkley a wider and deeper reach of emotion than he has ever dared before. One suspects that this novel has been crystallizing in his mind a long time and extends well beyond the smoky clatter of Montparnasse cafés. It glimpses the gold in the war experience and tells how it was lost.

A Farewell to Arms is probably one of the few books that will be valued by both the younger generation of readers and the broadminded among the elders. (Summary)

Bernard DeVoto.
"A Farewell to Arms."
Bookwise, 1
(November 1929),
5-9.

By declaration on the title-page, "The Sun Also Rises" presented a lost generation. "A Farewell to Arms" is a consideration of the causes of that loss. It is, in other words, a novel of the World War. It is not, however, an attempt at explanation. Explanations are no part of Mr. Hemingway's intent. He will describe merely, rigorously holding himself to the limits of one man's experience and the angle of view possible to one man's eyes. If this be true enough and if it be made real enough, there may perhaps be implications. But the author will not be responsible for them, remembering the relation of one man to infinity. Here is how the war happened to a man and what it did to him. It is one experience in the years of chaos and unreason, a chart of the path forced on one atom. It cannot deal with judgments; an atom has no relationship, finally, to the orbit of a sun. A meaningless, disruptive force careened through the world, destroying much, eternally changing much else. To deal with the force entire or with an aggregate of the lives it touched is impossible. Judgments or any kind of generalizations are charlatanry, falsehood, or ignorance. Here is a man in war: make of him what you may.

* * *

. . . Comparison with "The Sun Also Rises" is inevitable. The new book has what its predecessor lacked, passion. It has, too, a kind of sublimity. The clipped sentences, the almost completely maintained objective of style, are here employed on material of greater importance and to a finer end. In the study of a lost generation, the mechanism of wreckage has proved considerably more fruitful than its result. "A Farewell to Arms" has an intensity of conviction that increases cumulatively. The crescendo from the beginning of the retreat to Catherine's death is an almost intolerable suspense, completely imagined and completely communicated. So far as the concept of doom is possible to this—lost—generation, it is here achieved. The last hundred pages go far beyond anything else of Mr. Hemingway's and far deeper into the mysterious loam of existence.

The content of this book, as of his others, may be described as the contemporary introversion of heartbreak—the hard-surfaced sentimentality, that completely epitomizes one phase of the modern mind. In "A Farewell to Arms" Mr. Hemingway for the first time justifies his despair and gives it a dignity of a tragic emotion.

Robert Herrick. "What is Dirt?" *The Bookman*, 70 (November 1929), 258-62.

The censor, whatever he may think of himself, is always a ridiculous figure to the impartial observer. Latterly the censoring spirit has been especially active around Boston, that ancient home of witch-hangers, offering comic relief to the gods. That a community which could perpetrate the Sacco-Vanzetti outrage on justice should try to suppress *Candide* and *Strange Interlude* is but another instance of the marvellous perversion of our mentality when it becomes tangled in the thickets of public morality. A civilization which laps up jazz, even in Boston, and indulges in the semi-nudities of the bathing beach, ought not to be squeamish over a few printed words, no matter how "suggestive" they may be.

What is sexual evil? What "contaminates" the adolescent or even the mature mind? Our generation is still at sea on these points and the efforts of the censor do not make for light. Indeed proscription often advertises and enhances the attraction of a suppressed article. If the authorities really desire to protect the morals and the taste of the public, they go about it in a foolish manner. Frank commercial pornography such as was practised openly in Italy *ante* Mussolini may have less effect on the morals of the race than wiretapping, third degree methods, and universal graft. Unfortunately to the censor there is only one form of evil, sexual license, and only one morality, his own. Therefore open-minded persons like myself who may not care for eroticism in literature are suspicious of every exercise of literary censorship, as likely to be another case of the mote and the beam.

All the same there are instances where the censor's ban seems less grotesque than others, where even the most liberal-minded observer might accept—for his own reasons, never for the censor's!—the hasty suppression of some expressions of the phallic cult, *e.g.,* the above-mentioned pornographic pictures still vended in Europe. The coarse, mechanical representation of what should be a beautiful, a significant, at least an intense, human action is deplorable from any point of view. . . .

* * *

The principle that should govern exclusions, if it is worth while to make any, is, however, simple enough: that is the principle that must govern the creative artist who has a larger ambition than to become a successful pornographist or sensation-monger. Ardent naturalists or realists or expressionists (whatever from generation to generation they prefer to call themselves) seem to forget the elementary truth that while all human activities may have eternal significance and therefore an art value, few actually do bear the sacred mark. It is the fundamental duty of the creator to endow the activities he chooses to present with such an enduring quality. If he fails, as he often does, he should not fall back childishly on the plea, "But it's so in life, it's true." Everything conceivable is so somewhere in life, but what of it? Unless an action or a word reveals something, means something, why burden our distracted attentions with it? Because a man often vomits after over-drinking of what human importance is it—except to the man himself and those who have to care for the swine?

Lately there has been presented in two contemporary novels a fine instance of the elementary thesis I am setting forth: both are war stories, both by young men; one is German, the other American. The American tale is set forth (perhaps symbolically) from the point of view of an ambulance driver—the amateur; the European story, from that of the common soldier, the professional. Boston, with its beautiful lack of discrimination, has condemned them both; that is, the censor forbade the circulation of the magazine containing *A Farewell to Arms,* and the Boston publisher of the American edition of *All Quiet on the Western Front* prudently deleted certain passages and expressions from the English translation which he knew would not pass the Watch and Ward Society. Although the two stories present similar material, although both deal "nakedly" with certain common physiological functions, one, I maintain, is literature and the other it would not be too strong to call mere garbage.

. . . The scene over the sanitary buckets [in *All Quiet on the Western Front*] tells me far more of war than all the vivid pictures of mangled flesh.

The American novel has no passage exactly paralleling the above although it is never chary of odorous references to similar facts. But what Mr. Hemingway does not hesitate to present is vomiting due to drunkenness, which is not peculiar to soldiers nor significant of their terrible ordeal. Granted that the thing is true and common enough, it has no value in the picture: it is just unpleasant garbage.

The other deleted passage of *All Quiet on the Western Front* has a close parallel in *A Farewell to Arms.* The Boston publisher was probably well-advised in not trying to get away with this scene, although any community with a keener sense of humor might well forgive its frankness for its robust amusement. It is a case of a soldier confined to the convalescent ward of a hospital who is visited (for the first time in two years) by his wife with the child born since her husband's last leave. Since everything must be shared in common, the little group of soldiers in that hospital ward know of this event and know what it means to their comrade not to be able to enjoy this brief visit in privacy. They arrange that the forced conditions shall interfere as little as possible with the privacy of the two and with the perfectly natural desires of the reunited couple to enjoy their (legal) relationship. The situation as rendered by Remarque is a delightful mingling of comadraderie and broad humor, without a single vulgar or "suggestive" word. Solely for the fun of it the incident would be worth while, but it contributes richly to the whole picture of what war does to the human being, which the novelist is painting. Also the goodness and good sense of the ordinary man, his homely sound humanity and honest morality, are all finely revealed.

* * *

The parallel passage to which I have alluded in *A Farewell to Arms* is an ordinary boudoir scene, the boudoir being the private ward of an Italian military hospital where the hero is to be operated on for a presumably serious wound. The heroine is an English nurse whom the ambulance driver has flirted with casually at the front.

* * *

This, I maintain, is merely another lustful indulgence, like so many that occur between men and women and have since the beginning of time and will persist to its end. It has no significance, no more than what goes on in a brothel, hardly more than the copulations of animals. There are fewer *gros mots,* perhaps, used by the American writer than by the German, more sentimental wash, but the implications of the situation—and of the following passages in the hospital and at a Milan hotel—are plain enough even for the dull-witted Victorian to grasp: the whole episode smells of the boudoir. Remarque's treatment of the theme is literature, whereas the American's "beautiful love" is mere dirt, if anything. . . . [Herrick's ellipses]

I must confess that I did not stay with the story beyond the Milan episodes and so am not qualified to say whether such a love "conceived in the muck of war" finally evolved into something which I should call beauty. I had had enough of what Mr. Wister quite properly calls "garbage," in which Mr. Hemingway so often wraps his pearls. I gather from a review of the book that the hero finally deserted from his post of ambulance driver for the sake of his "great love," and I am wondering if that action—to quote once more from the publishers' puff— "elucidates the driving purpose of Hemingway's work"?

It is in substance a quite simple matter, this distinction between what is dirt and what isn't in regard to the sexual relation, so obvious one might think as not to require repetition, except for the fact, which every teacher knows, that it is the simplest truth that most needs iteration. All human activities are the rightful property of the creative artist, from the lowest to the highest, on condition that he can endow them with some significance, a meaning—I do not say with beauty. The sun and the rain beat upon the earth, men and women are born to die, love and hate, hunger and lust: there is nothing either new or important in all that. It remains for the imagination to take these commonplaces of sensation and make out of them something, if not beautiful, at least arresting—something of a larger import than the facts themselves. Mr. Hemingway's young man and woman are but another couple on the loose in Europe during the War—there were so many of them! Erich Remarque's soldiers on their sanitary buckets or stealing food or in the convalescent ward of the hospital befriending a comrade, are pitiful and tragic figures of the greatest signifi-

cance to people of this generation. From them even the dullest—even American amateurs—may learn what war really is, what hateful things it does to human souls as well as to their bodies, what an infinite coil of evil the patrioteers unloose in this world. And, incidentally, how pathetically right and lovable the basic instincts of human beings are even in the depths of slime and muck. . . . [Herrick's ellipses]

The censor, by intimidating the prudent publishers of the American edition of *All Quiet on the Western Front* into deleting certain passages and glossing certain coarse terms in others, has done a great harm. Americans more than Europeans need to have their consciousness of the realities of war pricked, and should have received this important story unblemished by prudery, in its full import, literally rendered out of the German. Whereas, to my way of thinking, no great loss to anybody would result if *A Farewell to Arms* had been suppressed.

* * *

Burton Rascoe. "The Fall Books—Read and Talked About." *Arts & Decoration*, 32 (November 1929), 124.

"A Farewell to Arms" by Ernest Hemingway is a distinguished work of fiction by a writer who is to be counted among the best we have. The story is that of the love affair of an American serving in the ambulance corps of the Italian army with an English nurse, and is told with Mr. Hemingway's customary disregard for the pruderies of English fiction and with his firm resolution to make his fiction true to life as he knows and has observed it. When the story first began to appear serially in a magazine it was accorded the distinction of being banned in Boston. It has other merits besides this, however. The story of the Italian retreat is superbly done. The three Italians, who are the Three Musketeers to the hero's D'Artagnan are delightfully drawn and I felt the death of them (shot down, ironically, in the retreat by an Italian) as a personal loss. Indeed, I was a little aghast at the abrupt manner in which Mr. Hemingway dismissed this chap's death from his mind and the minds of his other characters. I know that soldiering is one thing and sentiment is another and that in war a death here and there is a very minor matter but Mr. Hemingway had made this young Italian our friend.

Mary Ross.
Survey, 63
(November 1, 1929),
166.

Ernest Hemingway's Farewell to Arms, more of a romantic idyll than a "war book," is the story of an American ambulance driver on the Italian front and his love affair with a Scotch Nurse. It is as laconic as Hemingway's earlier stories were superficially "hard-boiled," but below this protective shell of nonchalance runs a force of emo-

tion stronger and more direct than this author has hitherto allowed himself. The Victorians would have done it very differently; but to me there is real and moving tragedy in that last chapter—the stillborn child and the death of Catherine in a Swiss hospital,—and the concluding paragraph when Lieutenant Henry finally puts the nurses out of the room: "But after I got them out and shut the door and turned off the light it wasn't any good. It was like saying good-bye to a statue. After a while I went out and left the hospital and walked back to the hotel in the rain."

William Curtis.
"Some Recent Books."
Town & Country, 84
(November 1, 1929),
86, 146.

Mr. Hemingway will go down in the history of English literature as the gentleman who has adroitly transmuted the technique of James Joyce to the tempo of the American general reader. There is the difference between the work of Mr. Joyce and the work of Mr. Hemingway that there is between pure and applied science. Mr. Joyce is the professor in his laboratory, dealing with abstract principles, concerned only with his thesis. Mr. Joyce set out to prove that the separate units which are housed in the English dictionary could be reassembled in a way which bade defiance to every rule of assemblage which has been tediously elaborated since the days of Chaucer. With true professional zeal he set out to create a monument, and he certainly succeeded. "Ulysses" either shocks or bores in about equal proportions, but it is colossal. Mr. Hemingway is a salesman—manufacturing for the market. I am not in the confidence of Mr. Hemingway—who is?—and he might most indignantly deny the statement I am about to make. I give it as my considered opinion, however, that had not that colossal experiment, "Ulysses," been created, the style and manner of Mr. Hemingway's "A Farewell to Arms" would not have been. And in Mr. Hemingway's book, style is everything.

* * *

... The first and the most obvious thing about Mr. Hemingway's writing is its calculated crudity in matters both of grammar and of rhetoric. He deals with the English language almost like one consciously using bad table manners....

... Personally, I don't think I like the type of writing. It is like the modern decorative formula, too barren and too brutal. All very well when used really to express strong emotion, but tending to become just one great big bore when used in too long stretches of straight narrative. One has a feeling that Mr. Hemingway spends a great deal of trouble and an almost infinite amount of time over his sentences and their structure to be very sure that their simplicity is of the utmost, their brutality the most thoroughgoing.

... Probably the answer is that if you like Hemingway you claim too much for him and his style. I doubt whether there is a better passage in the English language to describe the sensations of a rather dumb man when he realizes that the mother of his child is probably about to die. And yet that one manner is not really applicable to all the situations in life. It is the manner of revolt. It is the manner of those uncomfortable years in every big anti-aristocratic revolution, the French of the Eighteenth, the Russian of the Twentieth Century, when it is considered dangerous to be too polite or too clean.

... I may of course, be wrong, but again I would like to say that I have a strong suspicion that Mr. Hemingway works very hard to keep up his sans-culottes manner of writing.... The Hemingway dialogue is hailed by its supporters as the supreme triumph of naturalness. It is, for the type of mind which has never progressed verbally more than half-way through preparatory school....

I perhaps, as much as any other man, have done my frothing at the mouth about Mr. Hemingway. I still think his short story, "The Killers," is one of the most perfect pieces of work in the language. For a short story. I begin to wonder, however, whether his technique has yet gotten beyond the point where it is more than the vehicle for a short story. "A Farewell to Arms" seems to me an interesting experiment, a very interesting experiment, out of which may in time come something very definitely worth while. Don't let anything that has been said discourage you from reading it. Its publication is a very definite milestone in the progress of English writing. Mr.

Hemingway will undoubtedly occupy considerable space in any future development of the progress of style in American letters. "A Farewell to Arms" is one of those things you simply have to read, because everybody else will be reading it. But, as you read, remember that even Mr. Hemingway is not yet God . . . infallible.

Donald Davidson. "Perfect Behavior." *Nashville Tennessean,* November 3, 1929, Magazine Section, p. 7.

Ernest Hemingway's novel, "A Farewell to Arms," is like a direct and most remarkable answer to the recent wish of Dr. Watson, prophet of behaviorism, that somebody would write a novel containing people who act in a lifelike and scientific manner. That is exactly what Mr. Hemingway does, with such astonishing verity as to overwhelm, befuddle and profoundly impress all readers. Mr. Hemingway here is playing scientist, and he is watching people behave. It is a mistake to suppose that the people behave morally or immorally, becomingly or unbecomingly. That is not the point at all: they merely behave. There is no good, no ill, no pretty, no ugly—only behavior. Behaviorism argues that there is a stimulus and response—nothing else; and Mr. Hemingway's books contain (ostensibly, but not quite) nothing else. The novel is a bold and exceptionally brilliant attempt to apply scientific method to art, and I devoutly hope that all the scientists will read it and admire it immensely.

This comment on a book that is apparently taking the public by storm requires further demonstration, which I shall attempt to give.

Look first at the people of the book, who happen to be people, not cockroaches or mice, acting and reacting in war-time Italy rather than in a laboratory. But they are only people, not highly differentiated individuals. That is to say they are, in a manner of speaking, laboratory specimens. In the interest of the scientific "experiment" or observation, they must be as normal and average as possible, and so they are. It is regrettable, perhaps, that they are nice healthy creatures, not without animal charm (even if without souls), but we must presume that their occasional sufferings are in the interest of some scientific investigation which will eventually declare the "whole truth" about something, possibly war and love.

Thus we have first a Male with no characteristics other than might be noted in a description like this: Henry, Frederick [sic]; American, commissioned in Italian ambulance corps; speaks Italian (with accent); reactions, normally human. And then of course a Female: Barclay, Katherine [sic]; nurse; English; normally attractive and equipped with normally feminine reactions. The subordinate characters, too, are just as colorless: Rinaldi, Italian officer, inclined to be amorous; a priest, unnamed; other officers, soldiers, police, nurses, surgeons, bawdy-house keepers and inmates, restaurant keepers, Swiss officials, family folk. All of these people—notice—talk alike and all do nothing but behave, offering given responses to given stimuli.

Then we must have a situation. It is simply this. Put the Male and Female under the disorderly and rather uninviting conditions of war, including battle, wounds, hospitalization, return to the front, retreat, and bring the Male and Female into propinquity now and then. . . .

* * *

The application of the scientific method may be further demonstrated by a scrutiny of other features of the novel. A scientific report of events requires that there be no comment, no intrusion of private sentiments, no depreciation or apology. The "bare facts" must be given—or tabulated.

Therefore style (as style is generally known) is wiped out, or is reduced to its lowest, most natural, terms. It will take the form of simple, unelaborated predications, not unlike the sentences in a First Reader. For instance: The dog is black. The sky is blue. Katherine is pretty. I did not love Katherine. I drank the wine and it did not make me feel good. She was unconscious all the time and it did not take her very long to die.

And that, as I see it, is the gist of Mr. Hemingway's hypothetical case, which by the unthinking may be called an indictment of war or of civilization or an apology for free love or what you will. But its method does not justify any of these interpretations, however intently they may exist.

What of it then? On the surface it is assuredly a most remarkable performance. To those who take pleasure in contemplating a world of mechanisms doing nothing but acting to act, it must be a nearly perfect book. Let us leave them with their admirations, which are no doubt justifiable under the circumstances.

But what of those who, without knowing exactly why, have an uneasy sense of dissatisfaction with Mr. Hemingway's book and ask for something more than a remarkably natural series of conversations, day-dreams, and incidents? Mr. Hemingway's book will have plenty of defenders to fly up and condemn those who are dissatisfied. I want to supply a little ammunition to the dissatisfied, out of pure sympathy for the under-dog, if for no other reason.

First of all, don't complain about vulgarity or obscenity. There you lose the battle. For to a scientist, nothing is vulgar or obscene any more than it is genteel or pretty. And Mr. Hemingway apparently is trying to be a good scientist.

Attack him instead at the point where a fundamental contradiction exists. Can there be such a thing as a scientific work of art?

The nature of the contradiction can be immediately seen. Mr. Hemingway could treat human affairs scientifically only in a scientific medium. That is, he would have to invent equations, symbols, vocabularies, hypotheses, laws, as scientists are in the habit of doing. By so doing he would achieve all the "reality" that science is capable of achieving—which might be of practical use, but could not be vended as a novel, even by so respectable a house as Charles Scribner's Sons.

Obviously Mr. Hemingway did not, could not, go to such a logical limit. He was forced to compromise by using the vocabulary and the forms of art. The minute he made the compromise, he failed fundamentally and outrageously.

His novel is a splendid imitation, but only an imitation, of science. It is a hybrid beast, ill-begotten and sterile. It is a stunt, a tour-de-force, and no matter how blindingly brilliant, no matter how subtle in artifice, it is in effect a complete deception—possibly a self-deception—and can exist only as a kind of marvellous monstrosity.

Note that he falls short even of science. Committed to the form of the novel, he must be selective where science is inclusive. He cannot destroy his own personality and bias, for from his book we get the distinct impression that he wishes us to believe war is unheroic, life is all too frequently a dirty trick, and love may be a very deadly joke on the woman. Even in his effort to get away from style he creates a new style that is in effect a reaction against all decorative or imaginative prose.

"A Farewell to Arms," which is apparently intended to give us a perfect example of pure behavior, turns out after all to be only the behavior of Mr. Hemingway, stupendously over-reaching himself in the effort to combine the role of artist and scientist and producing something exactly as marvelous and as convincing as a tragic sculpture done in butter.

"Poignant Love Story Told by Ernest Hemingway." *Springfield Republican,* November 10, 1929, p. 4E.

In "A Farewell to Arms" Ernest Hemingway has written, despite hard surface realism and an objective and direct manner, a beautiful and moving love story. It is by no means primarily a war novel; it is first of all a narrative which depicts the romance between an American serving in the Italian army and a young Englishwoman with a British hospital unit also serving on the Italian front during the World War. There is war in this novel, an awful drama depicted naturally and vividly, but the war is not the first thing in the mind of Tenente Henry and that is why the conflict is not the dominating motif of the book. The sudden attachment to Catherine Barkley and his later love for her are the things which mean the most to the novelist.

In "A Farewell To Arms," Mr. Hemingway continues to employ the style which has characterized his previous work and he uses it to good effect. It is neither mannered nor obvious. Hemingway relates essentially what his characters say and do. Apparently he writes with the assumption that these words and actions reflect the thoughts of the characters so that it is not necessary neither from an artistic nor a practical point of view to delve into their minds and attempt to reveal what is hidden there. He assumes no doubt that if readers desire they can go behind the words and actions for an explanation as must be done in actual life. The characters in the drama of this existence reveal themselves by their speech and their acts.

By this method Mr. Hemingway achieves a realism which is convincing. And there is no sacrifice of what is considered essential in a novel; his work is unlike that of Proust or Joyce, in which originality is achieved at the cost of certain qualities inherent in the novel form. Mr. Hemingway encompasses his narrative within normal physical limits. His presentation grips the interest, and holds it. Play of emotions and descriptions of scenes are alike made vivid. Yet it is difficult to fit this novel into any definite category. Virtually the only thing American about the work is the author's nationality. The setting and the atmosphere are European, and the thought is individualistic, as is the style. It is the kind of a work which will perhaps inspire young writers to imitation, with unfortunate results.

During publication of the story as a serial, the ban of censorship was imposed upon a number of instalments. This was done, no doubt, because of a certain frankness of expression to be found in the novel. In considering the work as a whole, however, those phrases which aroused the censor evade the memory, and what lingers is that scene of the Caporetto retreat shown with camera-like faithfulness or that idyll in Switzerland, a romantic tragedy poignant and deeply affecting, which brings the reader to the end feeling that "A Farewell to Arms" cannot be only a story.

John Dos Passos. "Books." *New Masses*, 5 (December 1, 1929), 16.

Hemingway's *A Farewell to Arms* is the best written book that has seen the light in America for many a long day. By well-written I don't mean the tasty college composition course sort of thing that our critics seem to consider good writing. I mean writing that is terse and economical, in which each sentence and each phrase bears its maximum load of meaning, sense impressions, emotion. The book is a first-rate piece of craftsmanship by a man who knows his job. It gives you the sort of pleasure line by line that you get from handling a piece of well finished carpenter's work. Read the first chapter, the talk at the officers' mess in Goritzia, the scene in the dressing-station when the narrator is wounded, the paragraph describing the ride to Milan in the hospital train, the talk with the British major about how everybody's cooked in the war, the whole description of the disaster of Caporetto to the end of the chapter where the battlepolice are shooting the officers as they cross the bridge, the caesarian operation in which the girl dies. The stuff will match up as narrative prose with anything that's been written since there was any English language.

It's a darn good document too. It describes with reserve and exactness the complex of events back of the Italian front in the winter of 1916 and the summer and fall of 1917 when people had more or less settled down to the thought of war as the natural form of human existence when every individual in the armies was struggling for survival with bitter hopelessness. In the absolute degradation of the average soldier's life in the Italian army there were two hopes, that the revolution would end the war or that Meester Weelson would end the war on the terms of the Seventeen Points. In Italy the revolution lost its nerve at the moment of its victory and Meester Weelson's points paved the way for D'Annunzio's bloody farce at Fiume and the tyranny of Mussolini and the banks. If a man wanted to learn the history of that period in that sector of the European War I don't know where he'd find a better account than in the first half of *A Farewell to Arms.*

* * *

It's not surprising that *A Farewell to Arms,* that accidentally combines the selling points of having a lovestory and being about the war, should be going like hotcakes. It would be difficult to dope out just why there should be such a tremendous vogue for books about the war just now. Maybe it's that the boys and girls who were too young to know anything about the last war are just reaching a bookbuying age. Maybe it's the result of the intense military propaganda going on in schools and colleges. Anyhow if they read things like *A Farewell to Arms*

and *All Quiet on the Western Front,* they are certainly getting the dope straight and it's hard to see how the militarist could profit much. Certainly a writer can't help but feel good about the success of such an honest and competent piece of work as *A Farewell to Arms.*

After all craftsmanship is a damn fine thing, one of the few human functions a man can unstintedly admire. The drift of the Fordized world seems all against it. Rationalization and subdivision of labor in industry tend more and more to wipe it out. It's getting to be almost unthinkable that you should take pleasure in your work, that a man should enjoy doing a piece of work for the sake of doing it as well as he damn well can. What we still have is the mechanic's or motorman's pleasure in a smoothrunning machine. As the operator gets more mechanized even that disappears; what you get is a division of life into drudgery and leisure instead of into work and play. As industrial society evolves and the workers get control of the machines a new type of craftsmanship may work out. For the present you only get opportunity for craftsmanship, which ought to be the privilege of any workman, in novelwriting and the painting of easelpictures and in a few of the machinebuilding trades that are hangovers from the period of individual manufacture that is just closing. Most of the attempts to salvage craftsmanship in industry have been faddy movements like East Aurora and Morris furniture and have come to nothing. *A Farewell to Arms* is no worse a novel because it was written with a typewriter. But it's a magnificent novel because the writer felt every minute the satisfaction of working ably with his material and his tools and continually pushing the work to the limit of effort

Ben Ray Redman. "Spokesman for a Generation." *Spur,* 44 (December 1, 1929), 77, 186.

* * *

...Many foolish things were said about "The Sun Also Rises," and many readers belonging to a generation still younger than Hemingway's mistakenly embraced it as a bible of disillusion and futility.

But now that "A Farewell to Arms" has appeared, there can be no mistake; there can be no further doubt as to what kind of an author Ernest Hemingway is, as to what he has to say. This representative of a supposedly disillusioned and cynical generation is really a determined and convincing romanticist; a vital romanticist, for his romance is made from the stuff of life rather than from the gossamer of dreams. In telling the story of *Lieutenant Henry* and *Catherine Barclay* [sic], he has written a love idyll that is charged with sentiment, beauty and tragedy. He has said, as unequivocally as any author ever has, that to live is a good thing, that to love is a good thing, and that whatever price we may have to pay for these things is not too

high. To use a now hackneyed term, "A Farewell to Arms" is a yea-saying book; it is affirmation, not negation. It is even probable that its sentiment may some day be set down as sentimentality. Every generation is sentimental, but it insists upon being sentimental in its own way, in accordance with its own scheme of values, at the same time branding the sentimentality of its forebears as tosh. In twenty years Ernest Hemingway's romanticism may be temporarily out of fashion, but it is the kind of romanticism that can never be long unfashionable.

Meantime, whatever the varying verdicts of posterity (there can never be a final verdict), the author of "A Farewell to Arms" speaks for a generation; and he is a spokesman of great gifts.

H. L. Mencken. "Fiction by Adept Hands." *The American Mercury,* 19 (January 1930), 127.

Mr. Hemingway's "Farewell to Arms" is a study of the disintegration of two youngsters under the impact of war.

* * *

The virtue of the story lies in its brilliant evocation of the horrible squalor and confusion of war—specifically, of war *a la Italienne.* The thing has all the blinding color of a Kiralfy spectacle. And the people who move through it, seen fittingly in the glare,

are often appalling real. But Henry and Catherine, it seems to me, are always a shade less real than the rest. The more they are accounted for, the less accountable they become. In the end they fade into mere wraiths, and in the last scenes they scarcely seem human at all. Mr. Hemingway's dialogue, as always, is fresh and vivid. Otherwise, his tricks begin to wear thin. The mounting incoherence of a drunken scene is effective once, but not three or four times. And there is surely no need to write such vile English as this: "The last mile or two of the new road, where it started to level out, *would be able* to be shelled steadily by the Austrians."

Henry S. Canby. "Chronicle and Comment." *Bookman,* 70 (February 1930), 641-47.

Inflammatory Topics.—Two things, it appears, are not permitted in contemporary literary criticism: to attack Ernest Hemingway or to defend censorship. When Robert Herrick did both in his article, "What is Dirt?" (November *Bookman*), abuse was promptly piled on him and on *The Bookman* by an unprecedented number of correspondents and editorial writers. Some commentators, to be sure, expressed the highest praise and gratitude. But most of the comments were inspired by a mingling of rage as at a crime and horror as at a sacrilege.

Since we favor censorship and think that Hemingway has not had sufficient adverse criticism, Mr. Herrick's article seems to provide a good occasion for some remarks on both subjects. But first we ought to make it clear that we are not in entire agreement with Mr. Herrick, and that on at least two points he seems to us to have been unfair. . . .

* * *

The use of the word *garbage* is one place in which Mr. Herrick was unfair, not only to Hemingway, but to Owen Wister, to whom he ascribed the word. Mr. Wister had indeed applied the word to Hemingway's work but in such a way as to result in a compliment. This is from his comment on *A Farewell to Arms:* "He has got rid of this jolty Western Union ten word sentences which he overdid at times, and also of that monotony which came of dealing too much in human garbage. This book is full of beauty and variety, and nobody in it is garbage."

Mr. Herrick was hardly fair, again, in jumping to conclusions about the book's hero from reading a review, after declining to finish the book himself. The result was that he used the hero's desertion from the Italian army as a criticism of the moral quality of the book's characters, when as a matter of fact the desertion as given is made justifiable or at least defensible.

A number of those who came down on Mr. Herrick blamed him for writing at all about a book he had not read to the end. With this we cannot agree, since he made it perfectly clear just how far he had read and, with the exception of the sentence about the desertion, commented only on the part with which he was familiar. In fact we think credit is due to Mr. Herrick for discerning in the early pages of *A Farewell to Arms* the weakest part, not only of that book, but of all of Hemingway's work. . . .

Here, we submit, Mr. Herrick's judgment is far sounder than that of those who have accepted the central relations of *A Farewell to Arms* as a "beautiful love," and "idyll," and so on. Several critics have pointed out that Frederick [sic] and Catherine are less vivid and real than several minor characters in the book, but they do not seem to have pushed their analysis to the point of realizing what the leading pair actually are in relation to each other: embodiments of passion in an erotic fantasy. The central theme of the book is the story of a Scotch nurse made irresponsible by heartbreak and an American soldier apparently irresponsible by nature going on an irresponsible honeymoon and getting away with it. That is the level at which the story was conceived and written, and that is its appeal: a daydream of extreme erotic indulgence divorced from the other normal human emotions and untouched by the normal difficulties and retributions. . . .

It is true, as will be urged, that the story ends dismally with the death of the girl and her baby, and that the final scene is one of concentrated pathos. But this in no way conflicts with our description of the story as a dehumanized love story. Any other ending, in fact, would have broken the spell of the erotic fantasy and brought the affair into the realm of real life. And that realm is consistently avoided

throughout. The book, that is to say, really has a happy ending. It is a "new kind" of happy ending, and the logical conclusion of the hard-boiled school of writing: the harrowing happy ending. You cry, but if you are in sympathy with the story you sigh with relief.

. . . At the same time it should be promptly added that this aspect of Hemingway's work is but one of several and not the most conspicuous, even though it bulks large in *The Sun Also Rises* and forms the principal thread of the plot in this latest novel. We mention it at this length because it has been largely overlooked and because Hemingway is being praised for his very weaknesses. There is much else in *A Farewell to Arms* that comes from Hemingway the superb writer. The retreat from Caporetto, as everyone has recognized, is a masterly piece of reporting. The encampment scenes and the minor characters are presented with all of Hemingway's amazing observation, his unrivalled brilliance of dialogue, his delightful humor, his endless fecundity of revealing invention, his utterly convincing fidelity in reporting many kinds of activity—all the qualities for which Hemingway has won and deserved enthusiasm as the most striking talent in recent American writing.

* * *

We regret that the impression which must remain from devoting so much space to the two aspects of Hemingway's work which we dislike should be so negative. But as we stated at the beginning, it was our purpose to emphasize the points in which Hemingway has been either mistakenly praised or insufficiently criticized. For the rest, we are glad to concur with almost all of the laudatory comments that have been lavished on his work. While reading most of him this prayer to the muse springs to our lips: "Please let Ernest Hemingway go on writing like this forever." To go on like that would be sufficient, but it is more likely that Hemingway will transcend himself. The very parts of his work that seem to us the most faulty are the result of a fine ambition. If he revealed limitations when he essayed a great love story, the attempt shows that he is not content with the lesser triumphs he could so easily repeat. Even the unfortunate tricks of style come from a serious, studious grappling with his art that is far superior to that of most writers today. Hemingway's career has only begun, and begun so strikingly that almost anything may be expected.

M. K. Hare.
"Is it Dirt or Is it Art?"
Bookman, 71
(March 1930),
xiv-xv.

In the November number of *The Bookman* there appeared an article by Robert Herrick which Mr. M. K. Hare, of Tryon, N.C., among others, considered so unfair to Ernest Hemingway and "A Farewell to Arms" that he wrote an unsolicited reply. Mr. Hare's remarks were so reasonable that it was suggested to *The Bookman* that they be printed as the other side of a question which Mr. Herrick, by his own

admission, had judged after reading less than half of the book concerned. Although the editors of *The Bookman* would not publish Mr. Hare's reply they have graciously allowed the presentation of it in the advertising columns as follows:

It seems strange to me that one who terms himself an "open-minded person," as does Mr. Robert Herrick in his categorical condemnation of "A Farewell to Arms," has not kept his mind open long enough to read to the end of the book he subsequently casts into the garbage tin. Bearing it thither, one feels sure, with a pair of stout Victorian tongs, while the other hand protects his offended nasal organ with a pocket handkerchief. The strange part of this is that the perfume with which his handkerchief is rendered more palatable to his somewhat delicate nose is distilled from the undeleted edition of "All Quiet on the Western Front."

* * *

Mr. Herrick rather harps on this alcoholic oversubscription. His objection to it seems to be partly that it is a civilian as well as a military affliction. As a matter of fact, every case of drunkenness in Mr. Hemingway's book might, if one was so minded, be traced directly to war reaction; *le cafard*, an effort to break the tension of waiting or what have you. In the case to which Mr. Herrick refers, the man who got drunk and was ill as a result of it had been seriously wounded, had undergone several agonizing surgical explorations of his wound, had been slated for a major operation. . . .

* * *

Mr. Hemingway in no way dwells upon any particular experience arising out of war. His story tells simply how deeply an "amateur" at the game can become involved in it, and at the same time he recounts, to my mind with amazing sincerity, human actions and their reactions during a period of the most intensely unnatural physical and spiritual disorder.

Had Mr. Herrick finished the book he would have found something more significant to quote from it regarding the sexual relationship (illegal) of Catherine and Henry.

* * *

As Mr. Herrick did not complete the book there is no use expressing an almost personal indignation of his misrepresentation of the manner of Mr. Hemingway's young man's "desertion" of his ambulance. (He left it, by the way, hopelessly bogged in a mudhole during the Italian retreat along the Piave and subsequently, to avoid being shot by the Italian sentries as a German spy, he swam a river and by devious routes arrived in Switzerland, where he was interned on purpose.)

As anti-war propaganda I give the "All Quiet" a very good mark. But I cannot refrain from repeating a concise if somewhat caustic criticism of it and one which bears directly on the question of what is art and what is "dirt."

"After all," said one who had been there, "the war was not fought entirely in the latrines."

Mr. Herrick would have us believe that Mr. Hemingway presents a picture of war being fought almost entirely in beds, and on the wrong side of the sheet too. But, if this matter of sexual relations is no longer to be treated as a guilty secret and is to be allowed to appear in proportionate importance to the rest of the commonplaces of human experience, it seems to me that Mr. Hemingway has presented it in the least affected and one of the most affecting pictures of what man and woman can mean to one another. Possibly this book may not be art, but need it be called "dirt"?

Lewis Galantière.
"The Brushwood Boy at the Front."
The Hound & Horn, 3 (January-March 1930), 259-62.

Hemingway's strongest and most moving writing is still in *Men Without Women*. In those short stories of gunmen, prizefighters, drug addicts, and bullfighters, he was entirely without self-consciousness, unevasively absorbed by the creation of figures in which he found something to admire and much to pity. He projected them confidently out of himself, and these creatures of his imagination stood like models while he drew them firmly, surely, carefully, divining and surprising their most secret changes of countenance and most characteristic movements. The present novel, although in matters relating to "mere" writing and the organization of materials it marks an advance upon the author's earlier work, is fundamentally retrograde: it represents a return to his uneasy concern with himself. . . .

Every fictional composition is of course a compound of experience. But the motive of experience and the motive of art are not the same: we endure experience for ourselves, whereas we re-create it for others, for an imagined and ideally comprehending reader. An experience, and the emotion which accompanies it, are unimportant except to him who is experiencing, for the reason that they are not being shared; and to be made art, there must be injected into the experience a different, indeed a superior sort of emotion, the emotion of the artist over and above that of the protagonist. It is the artist's emotion (not the protagonist's) that we are able to share, and it is likely that the measure of sincerity and seriousness in art, may very well be merely the depth and the genuineness of the artist's emotion. In certain episodes of *A Farewell to Arms* the impression is irresistible that the measure of sincerity and seriousness in art may very well be merely the depth and the genuineness of the artist's emotion. In certain episodes of *A Farewell to Arms* the impression is irresistible that the author has endeavoured not to reveal or traduce emotions he has experienced, while yet retaining the episodic *cadre* of experience, and in so doing he has been forced to substitute sensation for emotion. In a superficial formula, instead of detaching Frederic and Catherine from himself—the artist's creative gesture—he has detached himself from them, in the gesture of

the observer. Born of a desire to evade the autobiographical, there was in him a curious *will to not-create.* The contrary will produced *Men Without Women;* it gave us all the figures save that of Jake Barnes in *The Sun Also Rises;* the will manifest in *A Farewell to Arms* is one which Hemingway cannot be urged too strongly to defeat.

If we examine this will in the light of the data afforded by *A Farewell to Arms* we find at bottom, I believe, a phenomenon which is at once an ideal and a fear: the ideal is that of our boyhood friend the Redskin; the fear is the fear of displaying emotion. We have had the ideal before, in, for example, novels of the Wild West (I doubt that Homer's heroes refrained from crying out when they were in pain); but I do not know an age before our own in which it could be understood that such an ideal might be accompanied by such a fear. In Hemingway's novel, the Brave is not afraid of war, and the Squaw does not flinch at the thought of birth pangs. The story of their young love in the spring of the year is swiftly told, for most of us reminiscentially stirring, and for the young a simulacrum of Tristan and Iseut. Frederic is a somewhat morose young man, and Catherine is a rather desperately happy young woman. He, the male, is served and adored and complacently spreads his peacock tail before her who serves and adores. Beyond this there is no discernible difference between them: they are wraiths, *deux formes qui ont tout à l'heure passé.* Our knowledge of them is limited to their sensations. There is no need that we be shown conflict *between* them (though one has the impression that a woman would find it hard to live nine or ten months with the Frederic of this novel and not have been pretty well tortured by him); but of conflict *within* them, of their personality, their common humanity, we know nothing. Even in what is presented as their bravery they are the same person, avid of sensation, submissive to the flesh and the world (which is war), grimly gay in their unprotesting acceptance of circumstance, seeking and finding a haven in bed, with a bottle of *fine* or Chianti to stand guard over their exaltation. This return to the primitive, accomplished by Hemingway as skilfully and naturally as Voltaire transported Candide about an impossible world, has as movement, as episode, the merit which Barrès used to call credibility, but the protagonists remain insignificant, a pair of silhouettes. Now and then their dialogue possesses a warm charm, is swept by an all too brief wind of sympathetically heedless youth—and charm and breeze vanish before the reader is able to fix these people in his imagination and love them as young lovers should be loved.

The war story, which fills nearly two-thirds of the book, is by far very much more successful. Only one engagement is described, for Frederic was an ambulance officer, not an infantryman, and his experience of war was had just behind the lines. Yet that too was war, and the sound and smell of it in the streets in which this American volunteer and his men were billeted, over the hills and on the highways that led to the line of battle, are ad-

mirably rendered. Fine as they are, and of thrilling actuality as is the magnificent account of the retreat of the Italian horde from Caporetto, one retains a stronger sense of the characters who people the scene than of the war itself. It is these secondary characters of the novel who are the most vivid. The author knew about Catherine only that she was inexplicably in love with Frederic; she was Frederic's creature, not his, and what Frederic knew about her nobody will ever know. But the men at the front are Hemingway's creatures: he imagined them, knew them, gave them personality and life. It is not simply that Rinaldi is intended to be liked, the priest to be stupid and yet too helpless to draw one's rudeness, Passini and Manera to be socialists, Aymo and Piani and Bondello [sic] to be sterling comrades-in-arms. The intention in these and other minor figures is fulfilled; they are what they are purported to be; and moreover it is only when they are on the scene that the novel is lifted above the level of selective autobiography, that Hemingway's creative gift expands and enjoys free play, that his profound feeling for men of simple desires and his sardonic and occasionally subtle humour emerge, and that his work is of a quality commensurate with the unreserved enthusiasm of which he is for the time being the object.

As for the writing, it seems to me the best Hemingway has done. The book is welded together with great care and scrupulous attention to detail. There are surprises in the novel, but only because we do not read attentively enough: the tone of each situation is sounded in advance; the colour of each character is indicated somewhere before he moves completely into view. In the descriptive passages, Hemingway shows for the first time that he can write by ear as well as by eye, so to say. Even the haphazard punctuation is not an obstacle to enjoyment of the fluidity and the rhythmical beauty of many of his periods. He has remembered, besides, all the lessons of his arduous, self-taught apprenticeship. Echoes are here of those steely paragraphs which comprized the first Paris publication of *In Our Time,* and of much that he has learned since. Now and then there is a line of gibberish, of unfortunate Joyce or bad Stein; his eye for objects and excessive concern with detail lead him into dull cataloguing; his meticulousness about *should* and *would* (which does not prevent his using *whom* in the nominative) lures him into affectation; he sprays the words "nice" and "fine" and "lovely" a bit too monotonously through his pages.

There are two Hemingways: the positive, creative talent skilfully at work in a being who sees and understands the anguish and bravery of men struggling with forces whose purpose they cannot divine; and the negative, fearful writer with the psychological impediments of a child afraid of the dark and conjuring it away with a whistle as hopeless as it is off key. From the first of these we may look for work of great merit.

Checklist of Additional Reviews

Jo Pattangall. *Portland Evening News,* October 15, 1929, p. 10.

Cleveland Open Shelf. November 1929, p. 143.

Edward Hope. *New York Herald Tribune,* December 22, 1929, p. 14.

Booklist, 26 (December 1929), 119.

Louis Henry Cohn. "In Spite of Robert Herrick." *Bibliography of the Works of Ernest Hemingway.* New York: Random House, 1931.

Notes

DEATH IN THE AFTERNOON

By

Ernest Hemingway

CHARLES SCRIBNER'S SONS

NEW YORK · LONDON

1932

Death in the Afternoon

Laurence Stallings.
"Dissertation on Pride."
New York Sun
September 23, 1932,
p. 34.

Ernest Hemingway's new book is a basic treatise on the art of the bullfighter, but it is also a superbly colored and capricious essay on human pride. It has grand flashes of ribaldry and wit, with brutal humors and frank compassions, and is shot through with a ruthless profundity. He calls his book "Death in the Afternoon." The pageantries of the arena—that tragedy in three acts of the bull's trial, sentencing and execution, all composed in the caparison of the theater—these are the materials out of which Mr. Hemingway will construct a pattern of life and death. Skill and bravery, bravado and lust, sinister cruelty and cowardice—and, above all, dangers gratuitously invoked by the master—these are the threads of his fabric. The bullring at Madrid holds for him the mysteries of Eleusis.

We are accustomed to economy of phrase and gesture when reading Mr. Hemingway and have not had such as this book from him before. This will naturally discomfit many who have Hemingway properly placed in their own categories. Certain books, notably ones in which authors are constrained to follow their daimon, are definitely without calculation. Such books inevitably get themselves written when the writer follows where his daimon bids him go. A man may, on his own urging, adorn a book with sententious thoughts on urn burial, and still another tramp his way to Mecca and write topping prose of the last syllable of detail he observed. They remain forever out of literary categories and become, according to the depth of originality in the writer, a work unto themselves. Their influence is not to be calculated. So it is with "Death in the Afternoon." It is one of the great vagaries and we have not had another such in a long time.

The Hemingway of his five books of fiction can be glimpsed from time to time in the moiling heat and pageantry of "Death in the Afternoon." This book is by a man who says that "the essence of the greatest emotional appeal of bullfighting is the feeling of immortality that the bull fighter feels in the middle of a great faena and gives to the spectators. . ." It is its purpose to impart to the reader this feeling, to elucidate the arts and graces with which a great faena is culminated, to honor or condemn the natural carriage of man and beast in that culmination.

As Mr. Hemingway is in dead seriousness, completely absorbed and saturated in his solutions, the reader when at
last he puts down the book still has
the dusty many-colored shouting in his
ears.

With a great sense of timing, Mr.
Hemingway breaks this passionate intent of his book with spots of ribald
dialogue, quotable animadversions a-
gainst literary humanists, and such
like. Yet, even in these jibes, he is
gathering force, using them as antipho-
nal catcalls to serve his purposes.
These jibes would have been perfectly
welcome to the bloods of the eighteenth century, who knew Geneva as a
place where Voltaire jested at the conference of professors. They will go a-
gainst the ingrained stolidity of modern readers.

* * *

All his book, whether concerned with
the delicate nuances, the plastic grace,
the sculptural line of the great matadors such as Belmonte and the younger Gaona, or whether taut with the
wish-images of the bull himself, is concerned with the Pagan virtues rather
than the Christian moralities. It has
been long since such a note has been
heard in an essay on life and death.
The author says that, after the war
when he was trying to learn the secret
of writing honestly, the "only place
where you could see life and death, i.e.
violent death, now that the wars were
over, was in the bull ring. . . ."

The moralists, who had driven such
as Hemingway into the temporary profession of administering violent death,
will now castigate him for seeking out

the riddle of it rather than dropping
the question until next we have the
Stars and Stripes decked over pulpits
and are bidden to assume for national-
istic shibboleths once again a pride we
do not have and to suspend our other
qualities to enjoy the moment of killing. There is no such casuistry of murder in "Death in the Afternoon." Essentially it is as simple as are the qualities it states to be the true simplicity
of the killer's pride in a great fight. As
if to show the contrasts, Mr. Hemingway puts into the midst of his book
several war incidents which, though
they sound natural enough to one who
has been in a collecting station after an
attack, come as the most harrowing
episodes in his book; and this though
the book is devoted to violent death,
and is profusely illustrated with photographs of both men, horses and bulls
at the moment the spirit leaves. . . .
[Stallings' ellipses] As an aside, I
should like to hear Dr. Henry van
Dyke of Princeton on Hemingway's
new book. Dr. van Dyke was by all
odds the most bloodthirsty talking
man I heard in the war.

* * *

The book is given a glossary and
many remarkable illustrations to incul-
cate in the reader a sense of the spirit
of a bullfight as an emotional spectacle
which, for all its transient tragedy, pre-
serves within it all the elements of
great art.

It is filled with description of men
and animals, has a running, critical
commentary of the passing generation
of matadors, illustrates with startling
photographs the many nimble sculp-

tures of man and beast in combat and varies in its style of writing to suit its many changes of pace. At times it becomes a guide book to Spain and at others a paean to its passing glories. Above all it contains strength and gusto and honesty. It will not be liked by sciolasts [sic] and pansies, for some of its jests are too deeply barbed to be merciful to the thin hides of the fashionably perverted.

"Death in the Afternoon" is, I must add, quite a testimonial to many manly arts. It will be chopped to pieces in many a literary dissecting before the winter is over. God bless old Dr. Hemingstein!

Ben Ray Redman. "Blood and Sand, and Art." *Saturday Review of Literature*, 9 (September 24, 1932), 121.

This book will meet with three kinds of reviewers, those who dislike bullfighting, those who like it, and those who know nothing about it; and the reviews will be consequently conditioned. To expose the conditioning factors of the present review, let me say at the outset that I like bullfighting to the point of loving it when it is good, and that I know a little about it.

* * *

[Hemingway] has written a book in which technical explanations burn with emotion because of the passion that is mated with the science. And I, having read this book with close attention and continuous excitement, must testify that of the little I now know about bullfighting ten per cent is due to personal experience, and ninety per cent to "Death in the Afternoon," which has clarified the significance of that experience, and transformed into scientific and esthetic certainties many intuitions.

So I take it that, in one case at least, this book has precisely performed half of its intended function: to explain to the person who has seen bullfighting, without really knowing much about it, just what it is that he has seen. The other half, of course, is to prepare those who have never seen a bullfight for their first encounter with the art. This half is the more difficult. . . .

* * *

But, difficult or not, Hemingway has done his best to write a book that will prove at least intelligible to the reader who has not seen a bullfight, that will prepare him for the spectacle and properly orientate his thinking; a book that will truly serve as an emotional and technical introduction to its subject. And he has so written it that, if it is intelligible before, it is nothing less than a revelation afterward. He has written of the art in all its aspects, from every point of view; historical, critical, emotional, and esthetic. He has revealed its glory and its baseness; he has pointed to the heights which the art can reach, and uncovered the depths to which, because it is a commercial art, it descends. . . . And these things he does in a book written entirely to his own liking (he is permitted to say things that no English or American publisher has let an author say before), stuffed with savage wit and enlivened by amusing digressions, and couched in a prose that must be called perfect because it states with absolute precision what it is meant to state, explains what it is meant to explain beyond possibility of misunderstanding, and communicates to the reader the emotion with which it is so heavily charged.

* * *

Indeed, looking back, I see that I have barely hinted at the fun which "Death in the Afternoon" affords. It was probably a mistake. But the fun is incidental to the serious work of a serious literary artist; it is the comic relief to a genuine work of artistic criticism; the froth on the surface of a book that will confirm many readers in their belief that Ernest Hemingway, in the handling of words as an interpretation of life, is not a brilliant and ephemeral novillero, but a matador possessed of solid and even classic virtues.

Herschel Brickell. "What Bullfighting Means to the Spaniards." *New York Herald Tribune Books,* 9 September 25, 1932, pp. 3, 12.

Upward of ten years ago Ernest Hemingway, then an apprentice writer, decided to go to Spain because he felt that the violent death that is the essential feature of bullfighting might help him to understand certain things about the nature of reality. He wanted, he says, to know exactly how he felt about something; not how he wished to feel or how he was expected to feel, and having achieved this honesty of emotion to learn to convey it to his readers.

* * *

He has done an extraordinary job in assembling his material; his book is crammed with information, and explains completely and entertainingly the whole technique of modern tauromachy, omitting no detail, and going from the ABC's of the matter to the most subtle nuances of the matador's art.

"Death in the Afternoon" tells where the fighting bulls, a special breed, of course, are raised and how trained. It is packed with brilliantly done sketches of the bullfighters themselves, portraits of startling liveliness and vitality. It takes the reader through the day of a bullfight from the early morning visit of inspection to the killing of the last bull and afterward; it tells just when and where bullfights are held and what are the best seats to buy. It explains the difference between the classical and tragic style of Ronda and the romantic style of Sevilla, sets forth the contributions of Juan Belmonte and Joselito, greatest of the moderns, to the history of the ring, and shows that great artist, El Gallo, elder brother of Joselito, at the height of his perfection, and also diving over the barrier headfirst in a panic. It ranges far and wide in this peculiar world, and the text, taken together with the stunning photographs bearing Mr. Hemingway's highly original captions, is a manual of bullfighting that leaves nothing to be desired.

This thorough, careful work cannot be lightly passed over. There is no other book in English that can even be compared with it, and few enough in Spanish—none of exactly this nature. Mr. Hemingway does not stop with bullfighting as a public spectacle that occupies the minds of hundreds of thousands of people through several months every year, and is not content with bringing the sun-drenched arena into his pages with almost incredible reality. He takes us behind the scenes also, into cafés with the bullfighters, into their private lives, their diseases, their comedies and their tragedies; their cool courage and their vanity and cowardice. He draws the sharpest of contrasts between the matador in the ring, silken-clad, dominant, the idol of the crowds, and the same matador an unshaven wreck in a hospital, knowing that even if he recovers he may never again have the nerve to fight with pride and honor.

* * *

If "Death in the Afternoon" were no more than a book on bullfighting it would be excellent reading, full of the vigor and forthrightness of the author's personality, his humor, his strong opinions—and language—and his great skill in conveying his undiluted emotions to his readers. But a whole book on bullfighting, be it ever so remarkable, may be somewhat doubtful of a popular appeal, so Mr. Hemingway has cleverly given his readers a great deal more. He has given them the suggestion of a book about Spain and the Spaniards, which, if written, would have been the best thing of its kind by a contemporary American, since Mr. Hemingway knows the country and its people as do few others.

* * *

There may be a doubt in the minds of some prospective readers about their interest in a book on bullfighting, but if they allow this feeling to cause them to miss "Death in the Afternoon" they will be the losers; it is a book teeming with life, vigorous, powerful, moving and consistently entertaining. In short it is the essence of Hemingway.

R.L. Duffus.
"Hemingway Now Writes of Bull-fighting As An Art."
New York Times Book Review,
September 25, 1932, pp. 5, 17.

The emergence of Mr. Hemingway as an authority on bullfighting should not be a surprise to any one who has read the passages in "The Sun Also Rises" which touch upon that peculiarly Latin sport.... One would say that Mr. Hemingway knows bull-fighting at least as well as the specialized sports writer in our own country knows baseball, football, racing or fighting. He knows it so well that on occasion only the introduction of an extremely singular old lady as the author's interlocutor, a few digressions on death, modern literature and sex life, joined with Mr. Hemingway's extremely masculine style of writing, save the reader from drowning in a flood of technicalities.

It may be asked why Mr. Hemingway should infer in American readers a sufficiently passionate interest in bull-fighting to induce them to buy and read a book of 517 pages on the subject. But this would be to put the cart before the horse—or letting the bull wave a red cloth at the matador instead of vice versa. Bull-fighting, one infers, became a hobby with Mr. Hemingway because of the light it throws on Spain, on human nature and on life and death.

But bull-fighting, though as Mr. Hemingway says, "a decadent art in every way," is an art; indeed, "if it were permanent it could be one of the major arts." It does not seem absurd to Mr. Hemingway to compare it with sculpture and painting, or to set Joselito and Belmonte side by side with Velasquez and Goya, Cervantes and Lope de Vega, Shakespeare and Marlowe. Even such refined elements as the line of the matador's body at the critical instant or the "composition" of bull and man enter into the intelligent "aficionado's" enjoyment. Bull-fighting is thus presented as an art heightened by the presence of death and, if the spectator can project himself into the matador's place, in the terror of death. For even the best matadors have their moments of fear—even their days and seasons of fear.

* * *

It may be said flatly that the famous Hemingway style is neither so clear nor so forceful in most passages of "Death in the Afternoon" as it is in his novels and short stories. In this book Mr. Hemingway is guilty of the grievous sin of writing sentences which have to be read two or three times before the meaning is clear. He enters, indeed, into a stylistic phase which corresponds, for his method, to the later stages of Henry James. The fact that a sentence is usually good Anglo-Saxon, with anything but a shrinking from calling a spade a spade, does not make it a clear sentence if one cannot easily distinguish the subordinate verbs from the principal one. And when Mr. Hemingway throws into one chapter, in a kind of reminiscent emotional jag, all the things about Spain and bygone youth that he could not get into the rest of the book, the reader feels like a chameleon on a patchwork quilt. This is not art in the sense in which the final pages of "A Farewell to Arms" were art—it is fireworks.

* * *

The book will certainly find its place on the shelves of Hemingway addicts. One's guess is that it will be less successful than the novels in making new Hemingway addicts. Action and conversation, as the author himself suggests, are his best weapons. To the degree that he dilutes them with philosophy and exposition he weakens himself.

"Olé! Olé!"
Time, 20
(September 26, 1932),
47.

Ernest Hemingway is that rare phenomenon, a popular author who is equally praised by the critics. Exponent of hard-boiled irony, darling of the sophisticates who pride themselves on being tough-minded, he gained Hollywood huzzas and highbrow applause for his last novel, *A Farewell to Arms.* But his latest book may not claim so wide an audience, may even alienate some of his new following. An authentic Hemingway showpiece, though, *Death in the Afternoon* will tell you all you want to know about bullfighting. After reading this compendious guide to *tauromaquia* you may be no *aficionado* (fan), but you will be aware that Spain's national sport is something more than an unexplained spectacle of horrors.

Author Hemingway accounts for his conversion from the usual Anglo-Saxon prejudice on tormenting animals to his current view: by observing the simplest things—and violent death is one of the most fundamental—he was learning to begin all over again how to write. Beyond that, he learned bullfighting is not so much sport as tragedy. And beyond that, bullfighting is an art in which the artist's brilliance is measured by his risk of death.

A leading light of American letters, Hemingway has exerted an influence far out of proportion to his published work. He is among the best-known of the expatriates, an enthusiastic sportsman, an aggressively "unliterary" writer, and at 34 he has become an American legend. (Summary)

Seward Collins.
"Bull-fights and Politics."
Bookman, 75
(October 1932),
622-24.

There will be many readers and reviewers to say, truly enough, that in DEATH IN THE AFTERNOON Hemingway has written the best book on bull-fighting; but few, I fear, to say that he has written the best book on the best of all sports and spectacles.

There is a curious distortion of values in most of the non-Spanish world which insists that bull-fighting is cruel, barbaric, and degrading, whereas prize-fighting and football are noble and manly arts. It should be obvious that a sport which calls upon an almost incredible combination of rare and admirable qualities, for use against an animal, not against one's fellow men, is on a far higher human plane than sports which utilize much more ordinary qualities to injure and incapacitate other men. In this latter respect, of course, prize-fighting is far worse than football, but college football is seldom free from deliberate attempts to hurt players of the other team, particularly the stars. When this element is not present, football can well be considered one of the best of sports; but by whatever tests can reasonably be applied, it seems to me, bull-fighting will be found to excel almost immeasurably.

* * *

But this is not the place to sing the praises of bull-fighting. Nor does anyone now need to: Hemingway has done it superbly in *Death in the Afternoon*. I merely wanted to take the opportunity to pay tribute to Hemingway's subject as well as to his masterly treatment of a most complicated and subtle form of spectacle. I know comparatively little of the finer points of bull-fighting, but I am sure than even those much better versed will have a great wealth of details illuminated for them by the book. Hemingway has gone past the spectator's viewpoint and made his way to the viewpoint of the torero himself—a feat which surely cannot be achieved by a non-Spaniard more than once in a generation, and which has never before been coupled, in English at least, with such skill in writing.

Hemingway is somewhat on the defensive, as any Anglo-Saxon must be, about the charge of cruelty to animals, especially to the horses. But it seems to me he delivers an effective onslaught on the "animal-arians," as he calls them. I have never seen sense in the view that there is something inhuman in giving a fighting animal a short, almost painless fight, which in the end he happens to lose, and in giving a few decrepit nags half a minute of pain which would surely be exceeded by only a few weeks of the rough treatment they would need in order to be made to earn their oats—few horses die in pasture!—but that there is something noble in setting two abnormally powerful men to pounding each other to pulp. But such is the prevailing attitude, and I fear that even Hemingway's book will do little to change it. It can, however, give pleasure to a large number who appreciate good writing and a wealth of good anecdotes; meanwhile giving secret delight to the small company of trans-Pyreneean *aficionados*.

The very factor which gives the chief excellence to *Death in the Afternoon*, Hemingway's acquisition of the bull-fighter's viewpoint, may perhaps also account for what seems to me the main omission of the book: namely, insufficient emphasis on what I can only call the histrionic aspect of the sport. He uses often such words as "emotion," "grace," "style," "elegance" in describing good work, but with these words he is only barely touching one of the most conspicuous of the many ways in which bull-fighting is unique among sports: the extremely close relation between the performers and the spectators. . . .

* * *

Death in the Afternoon does not carry Hemingway beyond his earlier books as an artist, but that is hardly to be expected of an interlude of reporting and miscellaneous comment in a career chiefly devoted to fiction. But if he nowhere excels himself, there is plenty of writing as fine as he has ever done. I think particularly of the marvelously well sustained pages devoted to a tenderly ironic survey of bull-fighting through the last hundred and fifty years, showing that always the Golden Age is said to have ended with so-and-so, that always the bulls of nowadays are much smaller and younger than those of yore, that always we are in a decadent era, and, finally, that always it is only the death of a great fighter that makes the critics realize that he, too, was of the great line, that he, too, created a Golden Age, whereas now we are entering a period of decadence, of smaller and younger bulls, and so on and so on. . . .

Perhaps readers should be warned that *Death in the Afternoon* is far better than the earlier pages would suggest: self-consciousness at his rather exotic theme seems to have numbed the author into his besetting sin of Gertrude Steinese, jumbled sentence-

structure and punctuation, and phoney philosophizing. These diminish as the book progresses. But other blemishes are strewn along the way, notably a constant sentimentalizing of death, as in the book's title (perhaps a non-combatant reviewer should point out that sentimentalizing was not the only attitude toward death good soldiers brought out of the war, even though it is literarily the modish one); and a constant adolescent coarseness. The extreme coarseness of language is indeed an amazing sidelight on publishing conditions today, that a popular author should be able to insist on such disregard of the proprieties usually associated with the general distribution of books though the trade. But more serious is this evidence that Hemingway is still far from outgrowing his truculent he-manishness and attaining anything like the maturity, depth, and breadth suited to his great natural gifts.

* * *

Robert M. Coates. "Bullfighters." *New Yorker,* 8 (October 1, 1932), 61-63.

Ernest Hemingway's long-expected new book, "Death in the Afternoon," is likely to be greeted with enthusiasm by only two kinds of readers: those who long to know the more technical details of bullfighting as a specialized sport, and those with an insatiable interest in Hemingway the writer, the man, and his point of view.

Few of us can claim membership in the first group. For all the exhaustive information about bullfighting, from the breeding ranches to the moment when the dead bull is dragged from the ring, most will find that a little of such goes a long way. Even so skilled a describer of death in the bull ring as Mr. Hemingway makes you realize that it's a thousand times better to see a bullfight than be told about it. Indeed, the illustrations near the end of the book—and there must be almost a hundred—tell far more about what actually happens in a bullfight than does the text.

For those more interested in the man than the bull, Mr. Hemingway's book should be enlightening in its revelation of his rather special point of view. For he reflects what he thinks you think about his writing. Since he believes you think he writes good dialogue, he creates an Old Lady interlocutor who gives him occasion to say some harsh words on readers, other writers, and the world in general. So he tosses rather sharp conversational barbs at William Faulkner, T. S. Eliot, Aldous Huxley, and among others Jean Cocteau. Although such passages mostly have a ring of petulance, there are others, when he talks of his own writing, which are appealing in their candor. Then we are aware of the great labors that go into his search for the particularizing and essential detail.

Such revelations remind us again that Mr. Hemingway is one of our major modern romantics. In spite of the austere mood and imagery of his prose, he is no classicist. Rather we see in "Death in the Afternoon" the culmination of his romantic view that rebellion against the idea of death gives zest and meaning to life. Except for the unfortunate "Torrents of Spring," all his previous six books have dealt with death or the threat of it. Now death seems to take on the nearness of a personal antagonist. And because death is such an affront, his laconic, flatly accented statements make us feel in a newly intense way the bitterness, pity, and injustice of such pain.

With its morbidity and its bitterness toward readers and critics, "Death in the Afternoon" is in many ways an almost suicidal work for a popular author like Hemingway. He is likely to come in for hard words from even his most recent admirers. But popularity aside, he has done some of his best writing since "In Our Time."

(Summary)

R.A.
"Hemingway on Bullfights."
Cincinnati Enquirer,
October 1, 1932,
p. 6.

Until Hemingway, in "The Sun Also Rises," explained what it was to be an aficionado, the fashionable attitude for Americans and other outlanders in Spain was to attend bullfights in the spirit of slummers in thrills, and anyone who did not walk out after the first killing—there are customarily six deaths to an afternoon—was considered not quite a gentleman. But in the last two or three years the Anglo-Saxon tourist, according to Hemingway, has become open-minded on the question, at least to the point of not condemning others for seeing in bullfights what they cannot see.

Hemingway's own interest in bullfighting developed, he says, from his concern as a writer with the describing of death, which he had observed under the emotional stress of war, but of which no actual models could be assured to him in peace-time. But having followed the bullfights now for a dozen years (300 afternoons; 1500 deaths), his point of view has become that of a connoisseur, enthusiastic only over unusual displays of skill, combined with bravery.

* * *

Until one has seen several fights with ugly bulls and second-rate or slacking matadors one is unlikely to experience the thrill of a good fight, Hemingway says. But not all the fans are intelligent, any more than at football games or ballet performances.

What, after the trout-fishing, was a sober interlude in "The Sun Also Rises" is the main theme of this 500-page treatise, which has 64 full-page photographs, 85 pages of glossary, and appendices recording reactions of various non-Spaniards to their fights, discussing Sidney Franklin, the American matador, and listing the chief annual bullfight meetings for the Spanish world. Hemingway goes into all phases of bullfighting, in and out of the ring, from the breeding of bulls to the ad-

vantages and etiquette of each possible seat location, the sea food and wines in the restaurants and the personalities and prospects of the leading matadors. Bullfighting, he shows, has changed in the last few decades as much as football. Its progress or decadence has been toward sculpturesque cape work at the expense of clean sword work, he believes.

Lest too much technical analysis pall on the reader, and lest the subject seem a cruel or unworthy one, Hemingway sprinkles his chapters with flippancies, sarcasms and naughty-schoolboy "wows" with regard to mystical lovers of the epic (like Waldo Frank), the horrors of death in war, the libido of El Greco (Hemingway preferring Goya) and other more or less serious asides regarding literature, philosophy, romantic love and life in general.

"Whole Technic of Bullfighting." *Springfield Republican,* October 9, 1932, p. 7E.

* * *

From being interested in bullfights as an aid to his literary style to being interested in bullfights per se was only a step. It is evident to the reader that Mr. Hemingway is fully entitled to be called an aficionado, or lover of the bullfight. In his book he describes the growth of his interest in the sport, if it may be so called, and goes into the whole subject exhaustively—the various stages of the fight; the matadors, famous and infamous ones, their origins, skill and appearance, even their relaxations; the bulls, where bred, how selected and shipped; the bull ring itself, with all the color and dust and movement that is typical of Spain. After he has done this, he appends a good-sized glossary of terms, a table of dates and places where bullfights are held during the season in Spain, and a case-history-like presentation of the reactions of various persons he has taken to the spectacles, and over 60 illustrations including matadors dead and in hospital, and a bibliography and an estimate of Sidney Franklin, the whole running to over 500 pages. Yet, he writes, in conclusion: "No. It is not enough of a book, but still there was a few things to be said." And so reveals himself as a humorist, though an unconscious one, no doubt.

While it is to be doubted that the average reader will share Mr. Hemingway's absorption in bullfighting, whether seeing or reading about it, it must be admitted that in presenting it in print the author has done a complete job and at any rate has made known that there is much more to it than is commonly supposed. There is a technic to govern every step of the fight, and by his adherence to these conventions the matador's performance is judged.

* * *

Unless one is interested in bullfights or in Spain, their natural home, "Death in the Afternoon" is likely to seem excessive in length and in detail. It is suitably illustrated.

Curtis Patterson. "The Ancients Are the Ancients—." *Town & Country*, 87 (October 15, 1932), 50.

Ernest Hemingway's latest book is "Death in the Afternoon." It is a tripartite work: bull-fighting in Spain, plus semi-autobiographical details of the author, plus smut. The smut is lugged in by the ears, is unnecessary, is not amusing. The semi-autobiographical details make me faintly sick at my stomach. The explanation of, guide book to, apology for bull-fighting is absorbingly interesting.

* * *

One mistake modernism makes, in my mind, is over-fondness for the obscene. Natural enough. The same thing has happened in painting. Cabanel used to be fond of prettiness for prettiness' sake. True. But is not Modigliani fond of ugliness for ugliness' sake? And is one impulse any better than, any different from, the other? The sooner modernism gets over the attitude of mind of the very small boy who scrawls forbidden words upon a backyard fence the better, the more hopeful, for modernism. A second objection I have to "Death in the Afternoon" is more technical. Mr. Hemingway at one time was a master of the short sentence. His short story, "The Killers," is, in my opinion, the best of its kind ever written in English. But in this, his latest, he has abandoned the short, loose sentence for an overlong, highly involved, extremely intricate periodic sentence that is supremely unsuccessful. One wanders about (or one does if one has only my intelligence) in a maze of words trying anxiously to fit noun to verb and find out what it is all about. Not always, but too occasionally to be amusing. After all, one does not look for a picture puzzle when one is reading either for pleasure or profit.

Granville Hicks. "Bulls and Bottles." *The Nation*, 135 (November 9, 1932), 461.

Though no one can doubt the genuineness of Hemingway's interest in bullfighting, "Death in the Afternoon" seems to have been written with one eye on the proverbial wolf. It may be just as well; a book that tried to maintain the level of "The Undefeated" or of the bullfight descriptions in "The Sun Also Rises" would undoubtedly become painful and might become ridiculous. Certainly the uninitiated reader can learn all that he is likely to need or want to know about bulls, fights, and fighters, and he has some fine photographs, an elegant binding, and a certain amount of humor thrown in.

If anyone else had written the book, there would be little more to say; but because Hemingway ranks so high among contemporary novelists,

and because more people will read the book because they are interested in Hemingway than will read it because they are interested in bullfighting, one is justified in going on to talk about the author. Fortunately the author, fully aware of the interest in his personality, has made a vigorous effort to put as much of himself as possible into his book. As a rule these intimate revelations are placed, for the convenience of the author, who obviously prefers to do a craftsman-like job, as well as for the convenience of the reader, at the end of each chapter. At first they take the form of dialogues between the author and an old lady, dialogues that suggest both Frank Harris and A. A. Milne at their most objectionable. Later on—but none too soon, as Mr. Hemingway candidly observes—the old lady disappears, and the author speaks directly to his readers.

We have, then, a series of observations on life and letters that provide glimpses of the mind of Ernest Hemingway; and there are, of course, other less premeditated revelations. The net impression is not unlike that received from the novels and stories. There is, it is true, a suggestion, especially in his comments on his critics, that Hemingway is less sure of himself than might have been supposed. But in general the book confirms previous judgments. It is surely not surprising to learn that he went to his first bullfight because he "was trying to learn to write, commencing with the simplest things, and one of the simplest things of all and the most fundamental is violent death." It is not surprising to find him speaking of "mountain skiing, sexual

intercourse, wing shooting, or any other thing which it is impossible to make
come true on paper, or at least impossible to attempt to make more than
one version of at a time on paper, it
being always an individual experience." It is not surprising to read: "If
two people love each other there can
be no happy end to it"; or to come
across a brutal and quite irrelevant description of the horrors of death in
war time. All these things fit the picture.

There is considerable humor in the
book, but Hemingway always speaks
respectfully of bullfighting and of
writing. In his peroration, which is
largely concerned with the latter activity, he says: "Let those who want to
save the world, if you can, get to see it
clear and whole. Then any part you
make will represent the whole if it's
made truly." This is obviously sound,
and it would be hard to find any novelist who, as novelist, would disagree
with it. The only questions it raises are
concerned with Hemingway's own efforts to see the world clear and as a
whole. Is his literary process one of
selection—a selection based on and dictated by a knowledge of the whole? Or
is it a process of isolation—a deliberate
setting apart of those segments of human experience he understands and
likes to write about? It would take a
good deal of space to answer these
questions, and a good many references
to the stories and novels to support
one's answers. But there is a kind of
answer suggested in a passage in this
book: "After one comes, through contact with its administrators, no longer
to cherish greatly the law as a remedy

in abuses, then the bottle becomes a
sovereign means of direct action. If
you cannot throw it, at least you can
always drink from it." If, in other
words, you are troubled by the world,
resort to personal violence; and if personal violence proves, as it usually
does, to be dangerous, ineffective, and
undignified, console yourself with
drink—or skiing, or sexual intercourse,
or watching bullfights. Now though
this is certainly a poor way to save the
world, it no doubt is a fine way to
"get to see it clear and whole." Yah, as
Mr. Hemingway would say, like hell it
is!

Malcolm Cowley. "A Farewell to Spain." *New Republic*, 73 (November 30, 1932), 76-77.

Just why did Ernest Hemingway write
a book on bull-fighting? It is, make no
mistake, a good book on bull-fighting,
full of technical writing as accurate as
anything printed in Spanish newspapers like El Sol or A. B. C. and general
information presented more vividly
and completely than ever before in
Spanish or English. Hemingway writes
for those who have seen their first
bull-fight, or shortly intend to see it,
or are wondering whether to do so if
they ever visit Spain. He tells them
what, where, when, how—the seats to
buy, the buses or trains to take, the
things to watch for and which of them
to applaud, which to salute with a vol-

ley of oranges, empty bottles and dead fish. He tells how the bulls are bred and tested, how the matadors are trained, glorified and, in the end, killed off like bulls. He illustrates the text with dozens of good photographs. In appendices, he gives further information, the dates of the principal *corridas* in Spain, Mexico and Peru, the reactions of typical Anglo-Saxons and the achievements of Sidney Franklin, the one American matador. Everything is there, even a store of pathetic or hilarious stories to read during dull moments of the fight, if there be any. In a word, he has written a Baedeker of bulls, an admirable volume, but———

Being a good artist, he does a good job, never faking, skimping or pretending. He often talks about himself, but meanwhile keeps his eye on the thing outside, the object to be portrayed; by force of prolonged attention, he makes the object larger than life, fills it with all his knowledge and feeling, with himself. His book about bullfighting thus becomes something more, a book about sport in general and, since this particular sport is really an art, a book about artistic appreciation and literary criticism, yes, and the art of living, of drinking, of dying, of loving the Spanish land. But all this being said———

Like every good artist, Hemingway employs a double process of selection and diversification, of contraction and expansion. He says: "Let those who want to save the world if you can get to see it clear and as a whole." Writing in Anglo-Saxon words of one syllable he is sometimes more difficult than Whitehead or Paul Valéry, but what he

means in this case is made clear enough by the addition of two more monosyllables and a comma. Let those who want to do so save the world, if *you* can get to see it clear and as a whole. Then, he continues, "any part you make will represent the whole if it's made truly." This book, being truly made, represents in its own fashion the whole of life. But all this being said, one must add that the whole it represents is discolored and distorted by the point of view; that the book is full of self-conscious cruelty, bravado, pity and, especially when dying horses are concerned, a sort of uneasiness that ends by communicating itself to the reader. "Death in the Afternoon" is a less important book than "A Farewell to Arms"; its style is often labored and sometimes flowery (and isn't rendered any less so by Hemingway's apologies for fine writing; apologies never help); its best descriptions of bull-fights are less moving than the briefer description in "The Sun Also Rises."

* * *

There are contradictions between Hemingway's ideas and the ideas suggested to readers by his narrative. To give an obvious example, "Death in the Afternoon" is not at all an unmoral book, nor does it treat bull-fighting as an unmoral subject. If Hemingway praises the performance of a great matador, almost all his adjectives are rich in moral connotations: they are words like true, emotional, not tricked, pure, brave, honest, noble, candid, honorable, sincere. Other matadors are not merely inartistic: they are low, false, vulgar, cowardly; they are even "cynical."

A second contradiction is more important. "All art," he says, "is only done by the individual. The individual is all you ever have." But almost from beginning to end, "Death in the Afternoon" is a refutation of this idea. It is true that the art of the matador, the great individual, provides the "moment of truth" which is the climax of a good bull-fight, but Hemingway makes it clear that the matador's performance would be impossible without the collaboration of nameless people, dozens of them, hundreds, thousands, in circles gradually widening till they include almost a whole nation and a culture extending for centuries into the past. The matador, to begin with, must depend on the work of his own team, his *cuadrilla,* which is charged with the function of conducting the bull through the first two stages of the fight, of regulating his speed and carriage, of preparing him for the "moment of truth" when the sword goes in between the shoulder blades and bull and matador are for the moment one. But the bull, too, must play his part; he must be a brave, "candid" bull of a type that can be raised only by breeders of knowledge and integrity, encouraged by audiences which howl at the sight of inferior animals. The audience, moreover, must appreciate the finer points of the art, must know when to throw small dead animals of all sorts, including fish: it must hold a certain attitude toward bravery and death; it must, in short, be the sort of audience that exists only in Castille, Navarre, Andalusia and perhaps in

Mexico City. The government, finally, must grant at the very least an intelligent toleration if the art of bull-fighting is to survive. The government might easily abolish it, not by jailing the matadors, but simply by seizing the ranches where bulls are raised and sending the animals to the slaughterhouse. As for the bull-fighters themselves they grow up unencouraged, "having a natural talent as acrobats or jockeys or even writers have, and none of them are irreplaceable. . ." And so the author has described a complete circle. He began by saying that the individual, in art, is all you ever have; he ends by deciding that the individual, even the greatest matador, is replaceable and nonessential.

Hemingway is a master at not drawing implications. In this respect as in others, it is interesting to compare "Death in the Afternoon" with "Les Bestiaires," a novel about bull-fighting written by a Frenchman of the same age. Henry de Montherlant sees implications everywhere. The modern *corrida de toros* implies the ancient sacrifice of a white bull to Mithra, which in turn leads him to consider the beauties of ritual, the mysteries of sacrifice, the glories of tradition, Royalism, Catholicism, patriotic ecstasy, till shortly the bulls, the author and his readers together are lost in a haze of emotion. Montherlant is inferior to Hemingway in hardness, honesty, freshness, keen perception, and yet in a sense I think he is justified. Bull-fighting really does imply a certain attitude toward life, a willingness to accept things as they are, bad as they are, and to recompense oneself by regarding them as a picturesque tragedy. Bull-fighting does, I think, imply an aristocracy, an established Church, a proletariat resigned to suffering pain in return for the privilege of seeing pain inflicted on others, and a rabble of gladiators, bootlickers and whores; but I am just as glad that Hemingway does not consciously draw these implications.

* * *

In a sense, every book he has written has been an elegy. He has given us his farewell to Michigan, to Montparnasse, his "Farewell to Arms"; his new book is a sort of elegy to Spain and vanished youth and the brave days of Belmonte and Maera. Hemingway's talent is great enough to justify us in making demands on it. Will he ever give us, I wonder, his farewell to farewells?

H.L. Mencken. "The Spanish Idea of a Good Time." *The American Mercury*, 27 (December 1932), 506-07.

Mr. Hemingway has been before the public for ten years and in that time he has published seven books. He has been praised very lavishly, but has somehow failed to make his way into the first rank of living American authors. Nevertheless, he has made some progress in that direction, and his last novel, "A Farewell to Arms," was unquestionably his best. In the present

book, which is not fiction but fact, his characteristic merits and defects are clearly revealed. It is, on the one hand, an extraordinarily fine piece of expository writing, but on the other hand it often descends to a gross and irritating cheapness. So long as the author confines himself to his proper business, which is that of describing the art and science of bullfighting, he is unfailingly clear, colorful and interesting. Unfortunately, he apparently finds it hard to so confine himself. Only too often he turns aside from his theme to prove fatuously that he is a naughty fellow, and when he does so he almost invariably falls into banality and worse. The reader he seems to keep in his mind's eye is a sort of common denominator of all the Ladies' Aid Societies of his native Oak Park, Ill. The way to shock this innocent grandam, obviously, is to have at her with the ancient four-letter words. Mr. Hemingway does so with moral industry; he even drags her into the story as a character, to gloat over her horror. But she is quite as much an intruder in that story as King George V would be, or Dr. Irving Babbit, or the Holy Ghost, and the four-letter words are as idiotically incongruous as so many boosters' slogans or college yells.

Mr. Hemingway's main purpose in "Death in the Afternoon" is to describe bullfighting as he has observed it in Spain. He admits frankly that he enjoys it, and he conveys a good deal of that enjoyment to the reader. The sport is brutal, but there is no evidence that it is any more brutal than football.

* * *

No better treatise on the sport has ever been written in English, and there is not much probability that better ones are to be had in Spanish. The narrative is full of the vividness of something really seen, felt, experienced. It is done simply, in English that is often bald and graceless, but it is done nevertheless with great skill. Take out the interludes behind the barn, for the pained astonishment of the Oak Park *Damenverein,* and it would be a really first-rate book. Even with the interludes it is well worth reading. Not many current books unearth so much unfamiliar stuff, or present it so effectively. I emerge cherishing a hope that bullfighting will be introduced at Harvard and Yale, or, if not at Harvard and Yale, then at least in the Lynching Belt of the South, where it would offer stiff and perhaps ruinous competition to the frying of poor blackamoors.

* * *

A four-page note on Sidney Franklin, the Brooklyn matador, completes the book. Señor Franklin first came to fame in Mexico, but of late he has been enjoying great success in Spain. Mr. Hemingway says that "he kills easily and well. He does not give the importance to killing that it merits, since it is easy for him and because he ignores the danger." But ignoring it has not enabled him to avoid it, for he has been gored twice, once very badly. Mr. Hemingway describes his principal wounds in plain English. They will give the Oak Park W.C.T.U. another conniption fit. The Hemingway boy is really a case.

Clifton Fadiman. "Ernest Hemingway An American Byron." *The Nation,* 136 (January 18, 1933), 63-64.

There is always a lost generation; and there is always a book in which it perennially finds itself. One finds itself in "The Sorrows of Werther," another in "Fathers and Sons," still another in "Marius the Epicurean" and "The Picture of Dorian Gray." These books, by a technique of enlargement, clarify the dissatisfaction of a generation that falls in love with the sensation of believing itself lost. They are popular far beyond their deserts because they make lostness picturesque, beautiful, or dramatic. It is better to die like Werther than to live like a Geheimrat. Lostness is promoted from mere bewilderment to the plane of a program. A transformation formula, applied to disintegrating moral values, yields philosophies of suicide, nihilism, or aestheticism.

Ignoring for the moment his purely literary qualities, I would suggest that Ernest Hemingway and his heroes stand in somewhat the same relation to our time as Dorian Gray and the young Goethe and Des Esseintes and particularly, as we shall note, Lord Byron did to theirs. It seems clear that the brilliance of his writing accounts only in part for Hemingway's success. Had he written half as well, but in the same manner and about the same subjects, his dominance would have been as notable. The fact is that he has triumphed more as hero than as artist. Hemingway is a man born in his due time, embodying to perfection the mute longings and confused ideals of a large segment of his own and the succeeding generation. He is the unhappy warrior that many men would like to be. About him has sprung up a real contemporary hero-myth. Do we not see young men adopting the Hemingway attitude as others do the Noel Coward attitude, or as a certain type of young woman, in a desperate effort to prevent herself from becoming a young lady, does the Dorothy Parker attitude?

Why is Hemingway news? Though he heartily despises newspaper publicity (being, indeed, the very Greta Garbo of novelists), his name is more often and more heatedly mentioned in literary circles than that of any other contemporary American writer. It is because he apparently creates a new tradition for those who have rejected all the old ones. He provides a modern and more violent romanticism to replace the sickly and worn-out romanticism of the nineteenth century. He takes a spiritual malaise and translates it into something vivid, vital, even splendid, giving to bitterness an exuberance that joy itself cannot match.

The generation for which Hemingway so ably speaks has been often described. No one has characterized it with greater shrewdness or warmer sympathy than Malcolm Cowley. To his analysis little can be added, except perhaps in one respect. The generation that lost itself in the Argonne or a-

mong the hassocks of Gertrude Stein's drawing-room was not the only one. A part, very probably the major part, of the succeeding generation is equally lost today, in the crisis. Hemingway's present readers, I would hazard a guess, are largely under thirty. Though to this group the war can mean little more than something in a book, they feel as vitally maimed as the hero of "The Sun Also Rises." They are the defeated and the betrayed, so disillusioned as to have no desire to attack their betrayers. They are too deeply wounded for the easy salve of sophistication. The values with which they have been inoculated they discover to be false. The culture which they have been instructed to flaunt as the badge of their superiority proves hollow. Since most of the grand words have collapsed, they throw them all overboard. They become rebels who smile at reform and offer a bitter shrug to revolution.

Where are these young people to place the animal faith deeply grounded beneath all their tragic rejections? In historical crises, when the flesh of the dominant system has withered away and laid bare the bones of chaos, the superior individual either makes common cause with his fellows in some attempt at a finer order or, as in the novels of Hemingway, retreats upon his instincts. He abandons, as Hemingway puts it, all efforts "to save the world." He cultivates to the point of fetishism those primal emotions which cannot betray him, as his hands and feet cannot betray him. Among these emotions may well be the fear of death and the delight in it, the stoic joy of battle and the pleasurable acceptance of the flesh and the muscles. In the last analysis he worships his reflexes, tending to exalt any activity which the act of introspection cannot corrode. He reverts, however subtly, to the primitive and even the brutal, because on these levels he finds no echo of the culture which has cheated him. He attempts to cling to the hands of the clock, to become a non-political animal, an individualist contemning all creeds, individualism included.

Having forsworn both his national and his class roots, he is at home in all countries. He puts his faith in simple things rather than in complicated words and shakes off all phrases that smack of the metaphysical or the moral. He seeks the companionship and tries to share the experiences of booze-fighters, killers, athletes, and sportsmen, men who lead careers of physical sensation, superficially insulated from the main current of the life of their time. He may even cultivate a special interest in the reactions of animals, creatures unspoiled by the general infection of the world. Above all, he looks for a hero, one who does all this with efficiency and elegance, one who presents a convincing rationale of his behavior and transmutes it into the contemporary eternity of art.

Hemingway is the hero thrown up by the American ferment, as, in a different way and on a profounder level, D. H. Lawrence was thrown up by the industrial ferment of England. Hemingway is the modern primitive, who makes as fresh a start with the emotions as his forefathers did with the soil. He is the frontiersman of the loins, heart, and biceps, the stoic Red Indian minus traditions, scornful of the past, bare of sentimentality, catching the muscular life in a plain and muscular prose. He is the hero who distrusts heroism; he is the prophet of those who are without faith.

If we compare Hemingway with a great poet who died a little over a century ago, we get an interesting insight into the manner in which similar epochs evoke similar dominating personalities. In the imagination of young Europeans, Byron occupied a place startlingly analogous to Hemingway's position today. To call the author of "Death in the Afternoon" the American Byron is a bold gesture for anyone who bears respectfully in mind Mr. Hemingway's ceremonial *espada,* not to speak of that matricidal rifle which must have dowered so many ducks with the gift of death. However, let us chance it, at the same time making clear that the comparison is merely between the impacts the two personalities have made upon their times. I am in no way suggesting that there is any analogy between the works the two writers have produced.

Both Byron and Hemingway awake to find themselves famous at twenty-five. Both cut themselves off at an early age from their native lands. Byron adopts Greece and Italy; Hemingway celebrates Spain. In Greece Byron finds the fatal theater in which to stage his worship of liberty. In Spain Hemingway discovers the shrine for his cult of violence. Both are attracted by the glory of military life, and meet with disillusion. Both are highly prepossessing examples of maleness and both exploit an athleticism which wins for them—as much to Byron's satisfaction as to Hemingway's disgust—a matinee-idol popularity among literary young ladies. Both are attracted to wild and romantic places—Byron to the Swiss mountains and the Greek coast, Hemingway to Montana and the Ozarks.

But these Plutarchian parallels are irrelevant beside the profounder similarity which history itself points out for us. Byron is a product of the post-Napoleonic period. His defiant romanticism focuses the turmoil, the disillusion, and the bitterness which flooded Europe after her first great imperialist civil war. Hemingway is no less clearly a product of the second breakdown, and the hard, tense quality of his romanticism marks the difference in spiritual tone between 1825 and 1925. But the two are distinctly post-war men, typical of a period of violently shifting values. Driven by the surrounding chaos in upon their own sensations, they inevitably charge their work with this very chaos from which they seek to escape. Byron, writhing under the spell of the Judeo-Christian myth, prefers to think himself "damned," whereas the Manfred pose is impossible to the more sophisticated Hemingway. But at the heart of both lies a tragic sense of defeat, vitalized by a burning rebellion.

This rebellion they express in an open defiance of conventional morality—Byron with the grandiose gesture of the aristocrat, Hemingway with the casualness of the hard-boiled reporter. In controversy both employ a brilliantly acidulous style, and each, using the language of his day, goes as far as postal regulations will permit. They bear the hallmark of many outstanding modern romantics—a fascinated concern with the more outré aspects of sex. Byron's florid incest-obsession, though partly rooted in his biography, is as much a reflection of current literary fashion as Hemingway's bitter-comic preoccupation with homosexuality, nymphomania, and impotence. Both laugh off their lostness with a certain wild *morbidezza.* Byron drinks from skulls. Hemingway enjoys a nice cold riot in bloody hospital scenes and Peninsular testicle feasts.

The ethical ideals of the two, apparently dissimilar, are actually very much alike, not only in their picturesqueness but in their internal contradictions. Byron is torn between a very real love for the grand words of his epoch—liberty, freedom, the chainless mind—and Don Juan's aristocratic cynicism which negates them all. In Hemingway a not dissimilar opposition exists. In "A Farewell to Arms" he writes: "Abstract words such as glory, honor, courage, or hallow were obscene beside the concrete names of villages, the numbers of roads, the names of rivers, the numbers of regiments, and the dates." One can see part of his nature—the hard-boiled half—spurning the grand words which have turned out to be deceivers, while another part—the *panache* half—seeks desperately for a new set of phrases, finding them perhaps in the Spanish *pundonor,* in the super-romantic accent he gives to the death-concept, and in the very vocabulary of disillusion itself. Cynicism and mysticism frequently combine in personalities we think of as "modern."

In the value hierarchy of Hemingway and Byron passion, action, and violence reign supreme. Both exalt sport, though with Byron this is owing partly to his clubfoot and partly to his Tory, country-gentleman tradition. Neither has much capacity for logical reflection, and Goethe's oft-quoted remark about Byron's thinking powers may be applied with some justice to Hemingway. This lack of interest in rational analysis, however, is responsible for a great deal of the drive, energy, and emotional power in the work of the two writers. Both admire the noble, the chivalric individual. ("Nothing ever happens to the brave.") This admiration is founded on the notion of the superior virtues of a trained caste —the samurai feeling. Byron finds this ideal in his cloudy Oriental princes, Hemingway in his matadors. There is a very real cousinship between Manolo, the undefeated bullfighter, and Byron's corsairs and giaours. Worship of a highly specialized, arrogant caste is natural to the man of strong and positive emotion who, whether an early nineteenth-century English lord or a twentieth-century Middle Westerner, can find nothing to admire in the banality of bourgeois culture.

Elsewhere I hope to devote some pages to a discussion of Hemingway's books proper, and to indicate why, as a purely literary figure, he must be considered one of the most distinguished living American writers. This brief note has tried simply to bring out that side of him which we might describe as his social function, his significance as a model of behavior. Like Byron, he expresses the aspirations of that portion of his generation which genuinely feels itself lost and is eager to admire a way of life which combines lostness with courage and color. Both Byron and Hemingway have an unforced faculty for creating an aura of violence, waywardness, and independence which dazzles the imagination of those among their readers who suffer, in Charles Du Bos's admirable phrase, from "the need of fatality." This need of fatality—the courting of violence, darkness, and even death—is a kind of splendid, often very beautiful, disease of the imagination noticeable during periods of social decay. It is frequently the most powerful writers of an epoch—Robinson Jeffers is an example—who are afflicted with it; and among them must surely be named Ernest Hemingway.

R. Selden Rose. "Bullfighting in Spain." *Yale Review,* 22 (Winter 1933), 390-92.

---

* * *

Mr. Hemingway was an enthusiast in the days of "The Sun Also Rises"; now he is an authority who writes to tell honestly what he finds true about bullfighting. His book is a defense only in so far as it is the truth. He is obviously eager for us to share his enthusiasm (a good many of us do), but he is enough of a Spaniard to try at least to assume an attitude of "you can take it or leave it, we like it," and to put on paper just what he has seen and felt. He gives you the light, color, movement, and emotion of the spectacle, the grace and beauty of the technique of the actors. . . .

"Death in the Afternoon" presents all the facts worth knowing about the bull ring since 1700, the blood lines of the various strains of bulls, smart, stupid, cowardly, and brave, the education of the bull-fighter from cradle to infirmary (where most of them end), true and false technique. He analyzes the great evolution of accepted styles. . . .

But there is a great deal more to the book than bullfighting. There is the Old Lady who liked to see the bulls hit the horses because it seemed "so kind of homey." Conversations with her furnish plenty of robust irony and robust humor, some of it far too robust for the book and better suited to the Café Fornos and the inexpensive seats on the sunny side of the bull ring. The Old Lady should have made her exit before the story of the young man who hennaed his hair.

Mr. Hemingway loves Spain, especially Castile. . . . He has thought hard about Spain, and he knows a great deal of how Spaniards feel, not only about bullfighting, but about living and dying as well. We thank him for the savage paragraphs about writers who can't see for themselves and can't write, but "who are in touch with the plunging, immobile all and put to paper the wonderful stuff which God sends them about Spain" and then call the book "Virgin Spain"—a tough old virgin. Mr. Hemingway's prose is what he thinks

prose ought to be: architecture, not interior decorating.

Thomas Beer. "Death at 5:45 P.M." *The American Spectator*, 1 (February 1933), 1, 4.

"Reprint" of letter from reader Robert Orth, written from Tours: "I like it when Hemingway solemnly states that baroque is dead, and then writes a baroque song and dance about art in 'Death in the Afternoon,' and makes five howlers in two pages. Well, he killed one admirer at quarter of six on Monday."

* * *

You enjoyed yourself at the *corrida* with Mr. Hemingway?

The Old Lady: Yes indeed! A bullfight is such an amusing parody of society triumphing over the individual that I was much entertained, and Mr. Hemingway's monologues on syphilis and the like filled up the intervals soothingly. Let us now discuss Mr. Hemingway's digression on art in his extraordinary book. . . . Mr. Hemingway tells the cockeyed world on page 203 that only El Greco, of the three great Spanish painters, believed in Christ. In the case of Goya he demonstrates this non-belief by pointing out that Goya's Christ crucified is a dud. This does not seem to prove anything more than that Goya was not interested in the subject. There is feeling in Goya's painting of Christ betrayed by

Judas, and his picture of Christ praying in the Garden of Olives is a—a moment of truth. Goya certainly cared for the beaten man on his knees in the night, and painted him with compassion. F. J. Sanchez Cantón, who is not a fool, has poked some questions at the legend of Goya's agnosticism and suggests that he said his prayer to the Virgin after finishing the most hopeless of the "Disasters of War." Irreligion in Spain is a complicated topic. . . . Having said what is a little dubious, Mr. Hemingway goes on to say what is absurd. He asserts that Saint Sebastian is *universally* represented in art as queer—androgynous, a female structure. The standard Sebastian of early Christian art is the seventh century figure in San Pietro in Vincoli, at Rome, a plain, bearded man, fully clad, and without an arrow to his name. He was that way into the thirteenth century. Then they began to plug in arrows, to strip him, to emaciate him, and sometimes, to give him a female head. His grand lizzification occurred in Italy, of course. But if Mr. Hemingway ever studies art, he'll be surprised by the number of male Sebastians. . . . Mr. Hemingway presently says that Goya "did not believe in costume." Tosh! To see a quantity of Goya's paintings, as we did at the memorial show in Madrid, in '28, is to be irritated by his insistence on costume. He had a peasant's interest in finery. He broke off a business letter in 1810 to brag of painting a lady in a "most precious mantilla" and there it is, on Isobel Cobos de Orcel, and a swell time Goya had with it! He can do tricks with cloth; he uses rags and sheets and strings for emphasis. He binds the sentimental substructure of the "Madhouse" by that ribbon slung around the naked waist of the lunatic and indicates angry pride in the "Disparate Furioso," by the set of a shirt. . . . Goya is a layer cake—the bully *aficionado,* the arrogant country boy who has made good, the opportunist preacher on war, after the event, the masterly designer, the cheap rural moralist scolding old hags for rouge and diamonds, the great journalist of painting, the dyspeptic snob and the enthusiast for fluffy white pups, children's lace collars, Asensi's dressing gown, and the Marquis of Saint Adrian's pants. Stick around with the hard guy from Fuentetodos for ten years and you begin to wonder what he believed in at all.—If you have anything to say, say it!

Madam, you have left me speechless.

Max Eastman. "Bull in the Afternoon." *New Republic,* 75 (June 7, 1933), 94-97.

Despite gorgeous pages of gigantic humor and bold straight talk of what things are real and what are not, Ernest Hemingway's book about bullfights is also filled with juvenile romantic sentimentalizing over a rather lamentable practice of the culture of Spain. Taking the facts that a powerful but stupid animal is tormented and then killed by agile and theatrical monkeys, he tells us that the act is not only artistic but tragic.

But a bullfight is not art. It is not a representation; it is real life—men tormenting and killing a bull, a bull being tormented and killed. Because it is not a representation, the bullfight fails to merit that exemption of art from the rules of decent conduct which make civilization possible. Even less is it "tragedy." To drag in notions of honor and glory and of sustaining elevated emotions to what is essentially a mean, shocking way of killing a noble and powerful animal, and to take them seriously, is sophomoric at best; worse, it becomes romantic nonsense and self-deception. It is the opposite of tragedy; it is killing made meaner, death more ignoble, bloodshed more shocking than it needs to be.

Ernest Hemingway says he went to Spain to study bullfights because Spaniards have a special feeling about giving death and seeing death given and because, now that the wars are over, he wanted to study the simplicity of violent death to learn how to write. He did not understand that the Spanish feeling towards death is a culturally induced callousness of the imagination, one we expect an American poet to see beyond and to see more sensitively than the Spaniards do. And to say that he went to Spain to study the simplicity of violence is only admitting, however unconsciously, that he went there to see not death but killing. It does not take much psychoanalysis to see that in his talk of learning to ignore the shock of pain in bull, horse or man in order to see the larger pattern of preparation for death Hem-

ingway is really confessing his indifference to "the feeling of life and death" and his preoccupation with the art of killing.

Why then does our ferocious realist wrap himself in clouds of juvenile romanticism when he sees and writes of bullfights? The fact is Hemingway lacks the serene confidence that he is a full-sized man. For obscure reasons he feels a continual sense of obligation to show evidence of red-blooded masculinity. More than the swing of his big shoulders or the clothes he puts on, the emotions he permits to rise to the surface of his prose have formed a literary style of wearing false hair on the chest. So Hemingway permits himself to become romantic about bullfights and blind to what they "actually are" because he is enraptured with courageous killing. More than the courage of toreros, his courage is in confessing that he loves killing because killing makes him feel triumphant over death.

Hemingway is of course right in seeing that much of our race takes pleasure, at least in imagination, from killing. The Old Testament is full of reminders that our ancestors could exclude whole groups from tribal sympathy and take delight in slaughtering them. The current popularity of murder stories and of Hemingway's own violent books is more evidence that this thirst is virtually universal. But we also have the record of civilization to show that the tendency of civilized men is to suppress, to sublimate in representative art, even to breed out this taste for violence.

We have recently seen a generation

of young men forced through the insensate butchery of the World War. After a period of numb silence some of these stricken poets have risen to confess their devastation by the discipline of wholesale killing. Their confession is the true aftermath in poetry of the Great War, not the trivialities of the Cult of Unintelligibility or the cheap moral decorum of the genteel or the gin-soaked cries of the new Bohemians or the poetry of new scientific hopes in Russia. They have given us the true poetry of civilized men's unendurable horror at barbaric slaughter.

Hemingway was one of the most sensitive of those poets, passionately intolerant of priggery and unintelligibility. Somewhere in the middle of this book hints begin to accumulate that he is still one of those sensitive young men shocked by the horror of that ordeal. But he seems not to have recognized that himself yet, and we can only hope he grows in self-knowledge to reach his true height. In the meantime his response is not what one would have expected. After he was thrown into the slaughter pit and told to be courageous about killing, he didn't come out weeping and jittering. He came out roaring for blood, shouting the joy of killing, and most pathetic, talking about killing as a protest against death. (Summary)

Checklist of Additional Reviews

F. S. A. "Bullfighting." *Boston Evening Transcript,* November 30, 1932, p. IV-3.

Booklist, 29 (December 1932), 107.

Corey Ford. "And So They Lived Happily Ever After. Part IV: In the Manner of *Death in the Afternoon, Death Without Women, Death in Esquire.* Mr. Ernest Hemingway." *Scribner's Magazine,* 101 (May 1937), 31.

Notes

Winner Take Nothing

By

ERNEST HEMINGWAY

"Unlike all other forms of lutte or
combat the conditions are that the
winner shall take nothing; neither
his ease, nor his pleasure, nor any
notions of glory; nor, if he win far
enough, shall there be any reward
within himself."

CHARLES SCRIBNER'S SONS
NEW YORK   :   :   :   LONDON
1933

Winner Take Nothing

Fanny Butcher.
"Short Stories Still Live as Works of Art."
Chicago Daily Tribune, October 28, 1933, p. 16.

Ernest Hemingway made his reputation with short stories. His final critical history will include them as surely as it includes his novels. And some of the stories in this volume will bedeck that critical brilliance.

By this time the Hemingway method is no enigma to any one. Those who admire his work (and there is no question of its first rateness by critics) admire it for its superb starkness. He can say more in fewer words than practically any other American writer. He never describes what goes on in the minds of his characters, and only in the least adorned manner what happens to them. Even the background he treats in the same way as he treats plot and psychology . . . [Butcher's ellipses] he implies rather than details. And yet, so perfect is that implication that the reader sees the scene, feels the action, and "suffers with" the character to a degree that becomes deep e-motion.

Hemingway has been called a man's writer. Unquestionably there is nothing "feminine" about his work, and it has a virility about it which most modern writing lacks, but it is no more destined for men alone than life or birth or death are wholly male experiences.

Usually he writes about male affairs . . . the war is often in his work . . . but emotionally, if not actually, war is woman's work as well as man's. "A Natural History of the Dead," one of the scenes reprinted from "Death in the Afternoon," is life burned to the quick . . . men's life . . . but those pages tear at a woman's heart as cruelly as ever they would at a man's.

There is one story, the last of the "Homage to Switzerland" trilogy, about a Swiss professor member of the National Geographic Society which shows Ernest Hemingway a humorist of the first water.

Clifton Fadiman.
"A Letter to Mr. Hemingway."
New Yorker, 9 (October 28, 1933), 74-75.

Dear Mr. Hemingway:

I have this week enjoyed the great

pleasure of reading your latest collection of stories, "Winner Take Nothing." Nobody needs to tell you that they are good stories. Unless you started to imitate your imitators, I don't suppose you could write a bad one. It is true that the volume as a whole (more later) seems to me less satisfactory than "Men Without Women." It is true also that not one of the stories approaches "The Killers." Still, even Maupassant wrote only one "Boule de Suif," they tell me.

The stories are so good, however, that the testier among your admirers may well inquire why they are not better. The way we figure is that while honesty and skill may get an ordinary writer by, they are not enough for us in Ernest Hemingway.

* * *

Here's the point: It seemed to many of us that "A Farewell to Arms" marked a triumphant advance over "The Sun Also Rises." After your second novel, we began to place heavy bets on you for the great American Literary Sweepstakes. For me, certainly, "The Sun Also Rises" was the finest novel of the year. Somebody, nevertheless, is still holding my bet. It didn't seem to me that the odds were tilted one way or the other by "Death in the Afternoon," which was perhaps something you simply had to get out of your system.

Well, here are these short stories, as honest and as uncompromising as anything you've done. But that's not enough. Somehow, they are unsatisfactory. They contain strong echoes of earlier work. They mark time, whereas

"A Farewell to Arms" was a magnificent leap forward.

* * *

I can't believe that in "Winner Take Nothing" you are giving your talents a fair show. Nobody ever doubted your ability to provide us with a novel shudder. Why bother to redemonstrate it? A man who could write the billiard-room scene in "A Farewell to Arms" has too much on the ball to worry excessively about third-position exercises in the macabre ("A Natural History of the Dead"), no matter how perfectly done they are.

Then there is this business of dating. It seems a shame that eyes as wide-open and penetrating as yours should continue to fix themselves on things which smell of the early 1920's. Frigidly objective studies of Lesbians and sentimental whores, coldly shocking tales of self-mutilation and sacrilege—aren't they beginning to get just a little high in flavor?

Your irony, too, is something that you appear to have developed to its full possibilities. You can pass beyond it. Your brilliant trick of incongruous juxtaposition—placing two apparently unrelated aspects of life side by side so that each will unobtrusively bring out the horror of the other—it's a good device, beloved of young writers, but it should be only a vestibule leading to a deeper and more inclusive kind of irony. It is true enough that the face of life is grotesque, but surely you are fit for something more than merely showing us its grotesquerie. As a matter of fact, the trouble is that you yourself have educated us so complely in your own peculiar irony that now we almost know it by heart and continued demonstrations of it move us only as brilliant bravura performances. I think that's why stories like "Homage to Switzerland" and "The Mother of a Queen" and "One Reader Writes" leave us, or me at any rate, a bit cold.

So many of the stories, particularly "Fathers and Sons," contain a kind of youthful Red Indian brutality which everyone is happy to admit only you can make interesting. But at bottom it doesn't seem to me very different from the atmosphere surrounding college-boy fraternity initiations. Nobody objects to brutality *per se,* but the trouble is its roots lie in our childhood and they say that among the things good artists do is to help us outgrow our childhood. That's why I can't feel that your stories about sport and sudden death lead to anything large or profound. As literary material, you have developed these things to the saturation point. Why not go on with something else?

* * *

Mr. Hemingway, we are still betting on you.

Henry Seidel Canby. "Farewell to the Nineties." *Saturday Review of Literature*, 10 (October 28, 1933), 217.

We have accustomed ourselves to Ernest Hemingway, and therefore it becomes more possible to estimate his values and to place him in the literary show. His staccato style has had the compliment of much imitation. His themes, drawn from the wreckage of war, or from ruthless analysis of youthful memories, or from the upsurge of savagery or brutal egoism in supposedly civilized man, have become as expected and familiar as the Cinderella plot of the conventional short story. Hemingway, like Ring Lardner, like O. Henry, like Kipling, has created his world and his technique of making it articulate. He is no longer one of the youngsters, and we must praise him now, not for his novelties as such, but for their merit as renderings of life, and for the qualities of that life itself.

And what does one find in a collection of short stories such as this new volume? On the plus side, an extraordinary power of observation, worthy of comparison with Kipling's, an observation that knows no inhibitions, but is as limited as was that earlier master's—who could do the sensational, but not nuances and subtleties of a matured culture. An observation, however, that, because it is not inhibited, brings a fresh range of subjects into the light.

* * *

And yet, and yet, the comparison with Kipling persists. Now that the novelty is off these studies of egoism, brutality, cold lust, and pathetic demoralization, it becomes clearer and clearer that we have not changed so much from the nineties as we supposed. Then it was what somewhere East of Suez had to say to smug Victorianism which excited the younger readers. The lid was on in genteel America and England—even Mark Twain had not dared to lift it, but under the old Chinese pagoda at Mandalay the Westerner became primitive man again. . . . And unquestionably Hemingway has come a step further along the road. Kipling could never have handled his cold killers, for the war had not yet drained humanitarianism from the imagination. Kipling was incapable of such unadorned brutality of natural speech between men and women only their vulgar selves with no overtones of human possibilities given to them by the writer.

Yet Kipling, with more humor, was far less sentimental than Hemingway. He never is so sorry for himself as this man who records struggle where the winner gets nothing. His norm is still a hearty, courageous world in which brutality or degeneracy is an aberration, romantic because it releases the inhibited in man, but transitory. And Kipling is the better story teller. When you cannot reread with the old pleasure a story of Kipling's it is because he so gloats upon and over-emphasizes

the sensations. His style is sometimes all exclamation mark. Yet even then the brilliant plot remains. When you are bored by Hemingway, as I frankly am by a half dozen of these new stories, which are repetitive with the slow pound, pound of a hammer upon a single mood, there is nothing to revive you except flashes of excellent observation. The younger man is at his best precisely when (if one insists upon regarding him as a novelist) he is at his worst,—when he takes one episode, one phase of a temperament, one mood, one moment, and eliminating all context, all verbiage, cuts a stencil of it and stamps it on the page with unforgettable incisiveness. I would cite from this volume the narrative of the doctor at the end of the "Natural History of the Dead" who will not let them kill the dying man. I don't believe that Kipling or anyone of his time could have written those few pages. They would not have dared the language, they would not have been able to keep what they believed was the hearty normal world so completely out of their imaginations.

And yet I cannot see much difference in the history of art between the sensationalism of Hemingway, except that the first (like his business contemporaries) had Asia to exploit, and the second, after the breakup of the great war, finds his horrors at home, and makes his romance out of reversions instead of adventures. Neither man is a novelist, both men deal in specialties eminently suitable to the sketch or the short story. Both depend upon overemphasis. Both will suffer heavily from a change in taste, as Kipling has already suffered from the shift in interest away from the romance of imperialism. Kipling, of course, has a far greater endowment as a writer. Yet I do not believe that it is merely the franchise to speak plainly of things not written about in nineteenth century English which has given Hemingway his great success. His dialogue is limited. It is good only for special people—especially for primitive passionates, for wounded sophisticates where the primitive shows through like an exposed bone, for pathetic inarticulates, and for men of abnormal simplicity whose love of wine, of women, or of murder so dominates as to run the whole machine—but for these it is a superb instrument. Whether Kipling's humor and his superb apprehensions of the beauty of heroism, of the fundamental decencies, of patriotism, of love not merely sexual, do not make him the greater man, depends upon whether the brutality in which the world is just now indulging is, in truth, further from the heart of human desire than what other ages have longed for. But the two belong to the same wave of historical culture. Kipling began what Hemingway, perhaps, is ending. The path seems to lead into a swamp.

Horace Gregory. "Ernest Hemingway Has Put On Maturity." *New York Herald Tribune Books,* 10 October 29, 1933, pp. VII-5.

On the title page of Ernest Hemingway's new book there is this quotation: "Unlike all other forms of lutte or combat the conditions are that the winner shall take nothing; neither his ease, nor his pleasure, nor any notions of glory; nor, if he win far enough, shall there be any reward within himself."

Almost at once there is a new conception of Hemingway thrust before us and Man Ray's portrait of the thick jowled young man with the bandaged head recedes into the distance of the 1920's, the short years in Paris after the war. It is time to remind ourselves that all of his novels and short stories, even the extended essay "Death in the Afternoon" have a single protagonist, himself. In this book of fourteen very short narratives, the young man has grown considerably older, has lost something of his boyish, two-fisted, middle-western manner, is revealed for a half hour as the sensitive disciplined, entirely civilized person that he is today.

The quotation above suggests that he has matured, that his sadness, his nostalgia for the past, evident from the very start of his career, is no longer an overflow of adolescent emotion. Here he has gone beyond saying good-bye even to death, which was the obsession of his essay on bull-fighting.

* * *

In dealing with his best work, I take for granted that his prose always reaches certain levels of excellence, that his art has always been deliberate, and at worst, made conscious to his readers by a mannerism that has become, through repetition, one of the curses of the contemporary short story. The hard, bright surface has been made to cover much hollow thinking and sloppy emotion which had its roots in speakeasy defiance and tears produced by overdoses of fusel oil. In "Winner Take Nothing," however, there are two stories that show a sudden expansion of Hemingway's range, yet both are beautifully simplified and pure. These are "Wine of Wyoming" and "The Gambler, the Nun and the Radio."

* * *

The emotional truth of this story ["Wyoming"] has its source in the most universal of human experiences and because Hemingway has stated it in terms that every one can read and understand, I believe this piece to be one of the few instances in contemporary literature where the short story may be regarded as a superlative work of art. Hemingway is no longer content to present a situation and then let it answer for itself—it is his interpretation rising out of his experiences that makes a story. This is also true of the gambler-nun-radio story, for Mr. Frazer, patient in a hospital, is evidently a

large fragment of Hemingway. He hears that religion is the opium of the people. He attempts to think out the problem and after reducing all nouns —and states of being to opium-taking —concludes that one must make some kind of moral choice: if religion, education, wealth, ignorance, ambition, sex, and bread are forms of opium, then there must be some scale of values present—for him it is knowledge and the understanding of the people whom he tries to know.

In this book Ernest Hemingway has again assumed leadership for a generation that is facing the difficult problems of approaching middle age. If some members of that generation intend to buy but one book this year, let them select "Winner Take Nothing" for they have every reason to be proud of their distinguished spokesman.

"Hemingway's First Book of Fiction in Four Years." *Kansas City Star,* November 4, 1933.

* * *

Mr. Hemingway's first volume of fiction in four years shows him still pretty intimately concerned with the subjects of liquor, blood and sex. Admirers of the raw stuff of the world will find this their book and Kansas City readers in that category will find special interest in a tale of self-mutilation at General hospital under the title of "God Rest You Merry, Gentlemen." [sic]

Mr. Hemingway's staccato prose is

so easy to read, his dialogue style is so effective, that he probably doesn't feel it necessary to bother much about plot and form. Most readers are led to think that such sharply etched strokes must mean something even when they don't. Some of these stories go no further than a scene or two of hard, brilliantly projected human pathology, depending upon irony for whatever significance they may have.

At the same time Hemingway fans will tell you there are some of his finest stories in this collection, particularly "Wine of Wyoming" and "The Gambler, the Nun and the Radio."

J.R.
"Hemingway's Gamy Dishes."
Cincinnati Enquirer,
November 4, 1933,
p. 7.

It would be both unfair and untrue to say that that [Winner Take Nothing] is just what the reader takes from the latest volume of short stories by the famous author of "A Farewell to Arms" and "Men Without Women" (not to mention his serious laudation of the Spanish bull-fighter, "Death in the Afternoon"). There is always something honest, skillfull and undoubtedly sincere in anything written by Mr. Hemingway, enough to make one willingly overlook his crimes against the grammatical code and his independent disregard of the accepted rules of punctuation. These become

matters of no importance in comparison with his insight into human nature and his bold development of human character.

But it must be admitted that "Winner Take Nothing" marks no advance in the author's established art. There is irony a-plenty, hard realism in abundance, and, at times, pleasing imaginative touches. But there is nothing at all equal to the billiard-room scene in "A Farewell to Arms," or "The Killers," which still remains his masterpiece in the short-story line. Perhaps it is too much to expect improvement on, or even parity with, those exceptionally brilliant works of art.

There are 14 tales in the present volume, including a reprint of "A Natural History of the Dead," an excerpt from the rather technical work on the beauties and glories of the lives of matadors, picadors and the horse-contractors of the plazas de toros. Nine of the stories are here published for the first time.

There is action in all of them and in some of them an expression of human sympathy, as in "Wine of Wyoming," in which the sweet and generous natures of Madame Fontan and her husband, home-brewers and illicit wine makers, are contrasted with the rudeness and vulgarity of their American customers, who pour moonshine into their beer in order to get drunk as quickly as possible.

Hemingway is a realist and his tales are invariably true to life, both in plot and character. But he is a bawdy realist, delighting in the exhibition of mental and moral crookedness and extravagance. And one need not be a purist or a prude to experience a weary feeling of nausea over some of the scenes which he evokes and especially over the constant repetition of profane and obscene phrases, which were undoubtedly uttered exactly as related but might better have been permitted to escape the permanence of the written word.

In several of the stories there is a mild tapering off at the conclusion. In other words the characters, boldly and expertly drawn, fail to furnish the final thrill which the reader has a right to expect in this form of literary work.

There is plenty of meat in "Winner Take Nothing," but much of it has reached a somewhat advanced stage of mortification. It is food for strong stomachs only.

Louis Kronenberger. "Hemingway's New Stories." *New York Times Book Review,* November 5, 1933, p. 6.

Hemingway has had so many imitators and his manner has become so familiar in other men's writing that until we get back to his own work we half forget what Hemingway himself is like. He has created a fashion, almost a tradition, but it by no means completely expresses the man; in one respect, indeed, it misrepresents him. What he has bequeathed to others is a highly impersonal, hard-boiled, callous reporting of speech and behavior, and they have tightened the belt a notch and robbed life of the humanity behind it, action of the subtle intuitions behind it and speech of the emotional chaos behind its shortcomings as a mere form of expression. Hemingway's followers have tried to make morons and killers and bullies of a whole generation because they could not use his technique without using the materials it best seemed to fit. Without Hemingway there could hardly have been, for example, a gangster literature as we know it, or so much melodrama disguised as realism or sentimentality disguised as bravado.

But Hemingway's followers learned no lesson from him: they merely took their cue, which is an entirely different matter. And the dead-level impersonality they evolved misrepresents Hemingway in at least one respect. Hemingway has tremendous personality. It is not the usual kind of personality in literature, not D. H. Lawrence's or Chekhov's, or Max Beerbohm's: it isn't magnetic or inflammatory or pervasive or repellent; indeed, it is a personality in retreat, almost in hiding; an implied personality just as Hemingway's sense of values is an implied sense of values. For though he writes with his ear cocked and his eye cooly leveled, he writes with himself tautly withheld, which is not the same as keeping himself in the background. He has superb drive but no gusto, fine perceptions but little sense of identification. One feels that he learns about people by listening to them, not by talking to them. In the end he probably learns more that way, but he remains in some subtle sense a stranger among his characters.

* * *

What, both in his life and his writing, has his highly masculine and often brutal world given to him so that he need not enlarge upon it; and what has it replaced? It has given him the physical sensations of direct action, rude contact, swift pace. It has given him something to be downright and, if necessary, harsh about without exposing himself as inhumane; it has given him somebody else's code to interpret so that he need not formulate (which is a much harder job) a code of his own; it has given him, perhaps, the right to despise. It has replaced a world filled with much more dubiety and anguish, a world whose restraints are more painful than Mr. Hemingway's total holding back, a world whose sentimentality is all loose ends and not a dammed up spate. Mr. Hemingway's nostalgia, it strikes one sometimes, is for that world; the nostalgia of that world itself is something beyond—or behind—it.

In this new book of stories we get close to that world on a few occasions, however casual or gruff or gingerly the approach.

* * *

Yet can any writer go on and on writing about the same things when they are merely things he has observed, overheard, impaled with his intelligence? A subjective writer can tell the same story his whole life long because it means everything to him; a Proust or a Jane Austen can go on

endlessly observing because he observes his own heritage or her own great dream; but the world Hemingway has made so familiar to us is neither heritage nor dream to him; he is simply its consummate reporter. The reporting in almost all these stories is superlative; the dialogue is admirable, the rapidly sketched-in picture is vivid, whole; the way of life is caught and conveyed without a hitch. It is not that the more typical of these tales represent mere virtuosity—they represent something more: it is not that the life they portray isn't worth exploring. But Hemingway has explored it beyond its worth. One does not cavil on moral grounds; one does not cavil on esthetic grounds; one does not cavil on human grounds. It is no doubt on philosophical grounds that one does object—because of the ultimate wastefulness of showing us things without infusing them into a more spacious canvas, without providing them with transcending values. As Hemingway presents his hard, stupid, aimless, greedy people they imply little more than the truth that they exist. Hemingway's world has been compared to many others, but not to one with which it has everything and yet nothing, in common: Villon's. The bitter, melancholy, profoundly compassionate flame that has kept Villon's world alive for 500 years, that has given it permanent meaning, is what Hemingway needs a little of. One reads a story like the first and finest in the present book, a story called "After the Storm," and one deeply regrets that in the main such incomparable equipment as Hemingway's goes off so many times with a proud and clean report—and hits nothing.

"Stiff Upper Lip."
Time, 22
(November 6, 1933),
59-60.

Ernest Hemingway has three different audiences. Professional critics see him as a professional Hard Guy but have begun to suspect he has an inner core of adolescent sentimentalism. His disciples call him one of the legendary giants of literature and see him moving from success to success. Plain readers find his stories sometimes breath-taking in their power to fix on crucial life situations. All three kinds of readers will find something to meet their expectations in his latest collection of short stories, "Winner Take Nothing."

By now a Hemingway story can hardly be mistaken for anything else. His language, apparently "unliterary," is in reality a carefully artificial literary dialect. His subjects are as characteristic as his style and illustrate his recurring theme of the sportsman enduring with stiff upper lip the perils of an unsportingly tight predicament. His creed is stated more explicitly than elsewhere before in the motto on the title page: "Unlike all other forms of lutte or combat the conditions are that the winner shall take nothing; neither his ease, nor his pleasure, nor any notions of glory; nor if he win far enough, shall there be any reward within himself."

As his subjects are so grim, it was predictable that only four of these fourteen stories were previously published in magazines. For sinister atmospheres Hemingway has never been better than in "After the Storm," an eerie story of a Florida beachcomber's discovery of a submerged wreck of a liner. (Summary)

T.S. Matthews.
"Fiction by Young and Old."
New Republic, 77
(November 15, 1933),
24-25.

Why was the arrival of Hemingway such an exciting event for readers of his lost generation? Now that he and they have grown a little older it is easier to see why. Hemingway's generation was very sorry for itself. (In its own language, it had a right to be.) The adolescent outlook on the world is apt to be bitter, and that generation's world was a *reductio ad absurdum*, a pointless joke. Grown-ups too have been adolescents once, and although they cannot altogether remember what it was like, they can be reminded into sympathy—though of course they take a superior attitude if they can. Hemingway made that superior attitude rather difficult for them; he expressed his generation's bitter adolescence in a way that even grownups had to take seriously. But what we are now beginning to see is that it was, after all, an expression of adolescence. We see it more clearly because Hemingway continues to express it.

The War is over, the hospitals are filled with other wrecks, the graveyards with even newer dead. But Hemingway, like a football player who after graduation continues to see life in terms of off-tackle plays, hitting the line and going down under a punt, still writes in terms of an experience which, to its survivors at least, cannot be considered final. His values are still the oversimplified, bachelor values of wartime. Not everything he writes is about the War, but for readers of other generations than Hemingway's the present collection might well have taken the title of one of its stories: "A Way You'll Never Be." To give his peacetime stories as strong a flavor as war rations, Hemingway has had to go nearly as far afield as Faulkner. Some of his current subjects (Lesbianism, insomnia, castration, syphilis) are the kind of abnormalities that fascinate adolescence but really have very little to do with the price of our daily bread.

And what about Hemingway's people? They are impressive simply because he never looks at them directly. If it were not for this oblique gaze, which invests them with a sinister importance, they would often seem pretty ordinary. As they are shown to us, however, they act and talk with the conscious irony of superior people moving irresistibly through swarms of shadowy inferiors. To what gallery are they playing? And where have we seen their like before? Sensitive adolescents whose feelings have been hurt take refuge and revenge in rughless imaginary adventures, often fatal to themselves

but always obscurely heroic. The winner may take nothing (in fact, he may glory in it), but he is still the winner. Hemingway has put that adolescent into American literature.

This may sound like an attack on Hemingway, and it is. I think he is one of the few exciting writers we have, and that consequently we ought to see, if we can, what all the excitement is about. And I think that what it is about is adolescence. I have purposely not echoed any of the obvious congratulations nor mentioned any of the remaining facts: such as that "After the Storm" is an almost magical story, of the kind that will haunt a reader for years; nor that all "Penrod" enthusiasts should be made to read "A Day's Wait."

William Troy. "Mr. Hemingway's Opium." *The Nation,* 137 (November 15, 1933), 570.

It is among Mr. Hemingway's admirers that the suspicion is being most strongly created that the champion is losing, if he has not already lost, his hold. In the current *Contempo,* for example, Henry Hart administers a sharp castigation to those ungrateful people who were the first to applaud him when he was in his prime. Briefly stated, Mr. Hart's thesis is that the generation into whose veins Hemingway poured such a badly needed flow of rich red blood should be the last to revile him now that his task is done. Despite his eloquent recapitulation of the champion's past glories, however, Mr. Hart only succeeds in delivering what is really a politely modulated funeral oration. Similarly, in a review of the newest Hemingway volume, Horace Gregory lauds the author of "In Our Time" and "The Sun Also Rises" for his services to his generation, of which he is still represented as the principal spokesman, without anywhere making clear whether those services ever did, or do now, include an intellectually satisfactory statement of its position. The reason in both cases for this manifest attempt to let the champion down as easily as possible is not very hard to discover. Whatever have been Hemingway's limitations of mind and sensibility, he has stood out for his generation in America as preeminently the type of pure artist, concentrated on experience and on its disciplined expression in literature. His very limitations have seemed at times to be his greatest virtues. At any rate they have saved him from saga-making, from vatic exuberances, and from the mechanical illustration of politico-economic ideologies. To turn against this writer, therefore, seems almost tantamount to turning against art itself or against the artist's role in culture or society. It is to take sides with the Philistines—by whatever name they may now call themselves.

Now some such reservations must be understood when one reports that Mr. Hemingway's latest collection of stories includes what is actually the poorest and least interesting writing he

has ever placed on public view. One cannot but regret, for instance, that a specimen like One Reader Writes should ever have been exposed to that view. As for most of the stories in the volume, their dulness may be traced either to a lack of growth or to growth along what is for Hemingway a new and unfortunate direction. There is, first of all, a recurrence of all the old nostalgias—the nostalgia for Europe (Wine of Wyoming), for the church (The Gambler, the Nun, and the Radio), for adolescence (Fathers and Sons), and for death (A Clean, Well-Lighted Place). There is also the monotonous repetition of the subjects attached to these themes—eating and drinking, travel, sport, coition.

* * *

The new direction mentioned is an increasing fondness for subjects and characters which are usually distinguished by the label "special." Ignoring the preoccupation with death, which in the reprinted Natural History of the Dead almost amounts to an enthusiastic *delectatio morbosa,* there are enough other indications that Hemingway is in danger of becoming as *fin de siècle* as his contemporary, William Faulkner.

* * *

The Gambler story is from every point of view the most successful in the book: Sister Cecilia and the Mexican Cayetano are both admirably realized characterizations, the narrative is dense, and there is one remarkable passage of serious reflection. Examining the statement that religion is the opium of the people, the convalescent Mr. Frazer decides that economics, patriotism, sexual intercourse, the radio, gambling, and ambition, each in its way, are also opiums of the people. The real, the actual opium of the people, he concludes, is bread.

* * *

Fiction is an opium as long as it contents itself with playing over the surface of things. Action, too, is an opium if it is thought of simply as a catharsis and not as an expression. Unless Mr. Hemingway realizes within the next few years that fiction based on action as catharsis is becoming less and less potent as an opium, he will not be able to hold the championship much longer.

"Hemingway's Tales." *Springfield Republican,* November 26, 1933, p. 7E.

Ernest Hemingway's "Winner Take Nothing" is a compilation of work which he has already published together with nine new short stories. The author asked especially to have included "A Natural History of the Dead" because it first appeared in a book— nonfiction that sold for a much higher price than a book of fiction. That story harks back particularly to his "A Farewell to Arms" and is realism to the point of being grewsome.

Doubtless Hemingway would scorn the comparison, but again and again in these short stories one is reminded of O. Henry. There is the same ability seemingly to take one incident and build an imaginative story around it.

* * *

As a whole, the stories, or sketches, are in Hemingway's best vein.

Checklist of Additional Reviews

John Erskine, *Brooklyn Daily Eagle,* November 5, 1933, p. 7.

Burton Rascoe, *Esquire,* 1 (January 1934), 86.

GREEN HILLS
OF AFRICA

By

ERNEST HEMINGWAY

Decorations by EDWARD SHENTON

CHARLES SCRIBNER'S SONS, NEW YORK

CHARLES SCRIBNER'S SONS, LTD., LONDON

1935

Green Hills of Africa

John Chamberlain.
"Books of the Times."
New York Times,
October 25, 1935,
p. 19.

Ernest Hemingway went to Africa to shoot the bounding kudu and the ungainly rhinoceros and to reply to his critics. The result is "Green Hills of Africa."

Truly, Mr. Hemingway is the strangest literary controversialist on record. When Jules Romains, for example, wishes to answer those who have damned his latest novel or his style or his point of view, he writes a pamphlet. The method is too effete for Mr. Hemingway, who cannot engage in dialectics without first sailing for Cape Town or chartering a fishing smack or hiring a guide to the caribou country....

...Mr. Hemingway's "Green Hills of Africa" is pretty evenly divided between big game lore and salon controversy. His hunting companions are thirsty for two things: animals and lectures on the literary art....

...Sometimes dispensing with grammar, Mr. Hemingway decimates the fauna of Kenya, Taganyika, Northern Rhodesia and the Belgian Congo along with Emerson, Hawthorne, Whittier and Thoreau. The carnage is frightful. "Ping," goes the bullet from Mr. Hemingway's rifle and another black-maned lion bites the dust. "Zingo," goes an epigram from Mr. Hemingway's mouth and the reputation of Thomas Wolfe curls up and dies.

As for the Hemingway taxidermy, it is ambidextrous. With one hand he tears out the entrails of a gazelle and strips the skin clean; with the other he rips the hide from Malcolm Cowley or Waldo Frank.

It is the most literary hunting trip on record. A lecture agency could make a fortune out of the words which Hemingway addressed to the empty veldt. And the slaughter is not limited to animals and literary men....

After reading "Green Hills of Africa" one would like to have a look at Mr. Hemingway's museum. One wonders how the mounted carcase of Franklin D. Roosevelt looks in the company of the mounted head of a kudu. Does the bull sable make as resplendent a specimen as the stuffed skin of the lady author who stole the Hemingway method of writing short stories? And the Hemingway zoo ought to be amusing. Hemingway doesn't tell what animals he brought back alive from Africa. But the only literary specimens that he captures on

the hoof are John Dos Passos and Tolstoy and Joyce, whom he refuses to
kill. Possibly he believes in observing
the game laws.

"Green Hills of Africa" is not one
of the major Hemingway works. Mr.
Hemingway has so simplified his method that all his characters talk the lingo
perfected in "The Sun Also Rises,"
whether these characters are British,
Austrian, Arabian, Ethiopian or Kiku-
yu. Pop, a professional guide who has
been hunting ever since Theodore
Roosevelt listened to Selous's first
whopper, converses like a Chicago gun-
man. Karl, who risked all for the kudu,
if not the kudos, babbles with the accent of Hemingway's Wyoming shep-
herds. Even M'Cola, the gunbearer,
Droopy, the native guide, and Kamau,
the driver, echo the Left Bank of Paris.
But at length a great light dawns. Can
it be that Hemingway has been writing
pidgin English from the start?

There are some memorable passages
in "Green Hills of Africa." For example, the one in which Hemingway
draws the analogy between the Gulf
Stream and the stream of human history. Or the passages about Tolstoy and
the Russian countryside. Or the section on the skies of Spain, Italy and
Northern Michigan. And doubtless the
description of the African terrain is
accurate. But I, for one, grow very
weary of monosyllables about stalking
the kudu. Hemingway has no natural
love for the animal pageant; he is only
interesting [sic] in killing cleanly. He
is not a W. H. Hudson or a Henry
Williamson or a Brooks Atkinson; he is
simply a bullfight *aficionado* looking
for variations on death in the afternoon.

And this cult of blind action, this
glorification of the dangerous life of
hunting and fishing, is keeping Hemingway from deserving people, from
writing about the life of his times. His
animus against "New York literary
men" is part of a general animus a-
gainst ideas. He is fretful when his
contemporaries get interested in the
underlying aspects, the fundamental
meaning, of the human comedy—or
tragedy. His book is all attitude, all
Byronic posturing.

. . . Not that one objects to Mr.
Hemingway's diversions. . . . But to offer "Green Hills of Africa" as a profound philosophical experience is
something else again. It is simply an
overextended book about hunting,
with a few incidental felicities and a
number of literary wisecracks thrown
in.

"Africa: Book Hemingway Wrote So He Could Rejoin the Lions."
Newsweek, 6 (October 26, 1935), 39-40.

When Hemingway returned from Africa in 1934 he said he wanted to write
a novel and earn enough money to go
back to Africa to "learn more about
the lions." Taking time out from fishing for tuna and marlin, while living at
Key West, he wrote "Green Hills of
Africa." It should enable America's
leading literary sportsman soon to re-
join the lions.

There are few surprises for Hemingway's readers in this record of a month's hunt in East Africa. His great technical skill makes "Green Hills of Africa" better than the usual big game hunting records. Not many such accounts can equal Hemingway's evocation of African scenery or convey so well what he calls the "feel" of the land. Enthusiasts of hunting will relish his descriptions of rhino, sable and kudu flashing across the terrain.

But even his admirers must feel uneasy at his sophomoric preoccupations with liquor, profanity and violent death. Others will be more pleased with his self-revealing statement of his artistic goal: to write prose that goes beyond poetry to find "a fourth and fifth dimension." (Summary)

E.M.
"Hemingway Goes Farther Astray in the 'Green Hills of Africa.' "
Kansas City Star,
October 26, 1935.

---

* * *

In "Green Hills of Africa," Hemingway has little of interest to say.

Hemingway intended to write "an absolutely true book to see whether the shape of a country and the pattern of a month's action could, if truly presented, compete with a work of the imagination." Never once does he deviate from his intention but he succeeds only in scoring on the side of the imaginative writer.

The conclusion one reaches is that "absolutely true" writing is not his forte or he is only fooling. His attempt to give the reader the actual picture and not confuse him with literary flourishes produces extensive evidence that it is only the imaginative writer who can present the reader a true picture.

* * *

In occasional interludes, Hemingway expresses his views on literary work and people, and is interesting in such moments. The only great American book, he writes, is "Huckleberry Finn" and it is too long. But "Huckleberry Finn," Hemingway might be reminded, was a true picture in which the author lustily exercised his imagination.

So let Hemingway take his pleasures in the kill and curse his guides and his gun to himself and return to that field in which he won his following. . . .

Bernard DeVoto.
"Hemingway in the Valley."
Saturday Review of Literature, 12
(October 26, 1935),
5.

"The writer has attempted to write an absolutely true book to see whether the shape of a country and the pattern of a month's action can, if truly presented, compete with a work of the imagination." So Mr. Hemingway describes his intention, in a preface that is shorter than the average sentence that follows it. . . .

... "Green Hills of Africa" cannot compete with his works of the imagination. It is not exactly a poor book, but it is certainly far from a good one. The trouble is that it has few fine and no extraordinary passages, and long parts of it are dull. And being bored by Ernest Hemingway is a new experience for readers and reviewers alike. The queer thing is that this novelty springs from the same intense literary self-consciousness that has been a large part of the effectiveness of his books up to now. He kills this one by being too assiduously an experimental artist in prose, out to register sensation and find the right words for the countryside and activity and emotion, and, by way of the bush and the campfires and the rhinoceros dung, carry his prose to the "fourth and fifth dimension that can be gotten." He has reverted to his café-table-talk days, he is being arty, and Africa isn't a good place for it.

Only about forty percent of the book is devoted to the shape of the country and the pattern of action. That part isn't too good. He is magnificent when he is rendering the emotions of the hunt and the kill, but those passages are less frequent than long, confusing, over-written descriptions, and these are lush and very tiresome. Besides, there are a lot of tricks and some cheating. Mr. Hemingway plunges into the rhetoric he has monotonously denounced, and he overlays a good many bits of plain brush-work with very eloquent and highly literary researches into past time.

The rest of it runs about twenty percent literary discussion, twenty percent exhibitionism, and twenty per-cent straight fiction technique gratefully brought into this unimaginative effort. The literary discussion, though it contains some precious plums, is mostly bad; the exhibitionism is unfailingly good. Mr. Hemingway is not qualified for analytical thought. His flat judgments and especially his papal rules and by-laws are superficial when they aren't plain cockeyed. He has written about writing, probably, more than any other writer of his time: he is much better at writing and we should all be richer if he would stick to it. But he is a first-rate humorist, and the clowning is excellent. When he gives us Hemingway in the sulks, Hemingway with the braggies, Hemingway amused or angered by the gun-bearers, Hemingway getting tight, Hemingway at the latrine, Hemingway being hard-boiled, or brutal, or swaggering, or ruthless, Hemingway kidding someone or getting sore at someone—the book comes to life. It comes to life, in fact, whenever he forgets about the shape of the country and the pattern of action, and brings some people on the stage.

Working with real people, Pop, P.O.M., Karl, the casuals, he is quite as effective a novelist as he is with imaginary ones. He imparts the same life to the natives, some of whom do not even speak. Droopy, Garrick, and The Wanderobo are splendid creations; one sees and feels them, accepts them, experiences them. They live. And that is creation of a high order, a *tour de force* all the more remarkable since it is done without the dialogue that is Mr. Hemingway's most formidable weapon. When he is being a novelist, he achieves his purpose. His book has the life and validity he tells us he set out to give it; he gets the experience itself into prose. It successfully competes with the imagination—because it uses the tools and technique of an imaginative artist.

The big news for literature, however, is that, stylistically, there is a new period of Hemingway. He seems to be fighting a one-man revolution to carry prose back to "The Anatomy of Melancholy" or beyond. There have been omens of it before now, of course, and Mr. Hemingway, in his café-table days, pondered Gertrude Stein to his own gain. The repetitious Stein of "Tender Buttons" doesn't show up here, but the Stein who is out to get four or five dimensions into prose is pretty obvious. But he also appears to have been reading a prose translation of "The Odyssey" too closely, and something that sounds like a German translation of Hemingway. With the result that whereas the typical Hemingway sentence used to run three to a line it now runs three to a page. And whereas he used to simplify vocabulary in order to be wholly clear, he now simplifies grammar till the result looks like a marriage between an e. e. cummings simultaneity and one of those ground-mists of Sherwood Anderson's that Mr. Hemingway was burlesquing ten years ago.

* * *

An unimportant book. A pretty small book for a big man to write. One hopes that this is just a valley and that something the size of "Death in the Afternoon" is on the other side.

Charles G. Poore. "Ernest Hemingway's Story of His African Safari." *New York Times Book Review,* October 27, 1935, pp. 3, 27.

As the Belmonte of his own hunting cuadrilla Ernest Hemingway has produced a fine book on death in the African afternoon. Incidentally, it is the best-written story of big-game hunting anywhere I have read. And more than that. It's a book about people in unacknowledged conflict and about the pleasures of drinking and war and peace and writing. Particularly writing; pages and pages on the literary life. So even if you do not approve very strongly of men who go out and blast innocent rhinos into kingdom come you can still enjoy "Green Hills of Africa" for many other things.

* * *

Hemingway's early manner of writing has passed pretty thoroughly into a large body of American prose. It has done great good there, keeping down the phony simile, the woolly clause. Who has not read ringing denunciations of him written in a style their writers did not have before they read "The Sun Also Rises"? But it did not have enough range. So now he has left the old four-word sentence each word containing four letters to others. Some of his sentences in "Green Hills of Africa" would make Henry James take a breath....

* * *

... In "Green Hills of Africa" his writing is better than ever, fuller, richer, deeper and only looking for something that can use its full power. There should soon be rousing calls demanding that he go to work on a novel of vast and striking scope instead of wasting time calling shots on the kudu. There's a lot in that. He should. ...

... The honesty he uses in tracing the exact way he feels toward Karl, the "lucky hunter"—jealous, admiring, angry, very friendly, according to the fortunes in their hunting rivalry—is the most skillful writing in the book. Karl plays Joselito to his Belmonte. That tension, and the dialogues, and the characters, black, white or brown, and the descriptions of country help to make the book compete successfully with many novels. But there's not tension, development, conflict enough to make it compete successfully with the best novels. No one would say it was as good as "A Farewell to Arms." And, as a matter of fact, there's no good reason for setting up any such standards of comparison. It's the best trophy any writer has brought out of the big game country in many years.

Carl Van Doren. "Ernest Hemingway, Singing in Africa." *New York Herald Tribune Books*, 12 October 27, 1935, p. 3.

* * *

... He has attempted "to write an absolutely true book to see whether the shape of a country and the pattern of a month's action can, if truly presented, compete with a work of the imagination."

Of course they can and his book does. If he had called it a novel it would have made little difference. Most of his readers will read it as if it were. They will not know how truthful he is about the African landscape or about the habits of the men and animals that live there. They will not know whether the persons of the story are actual or invented, what they do and say and appear to feel and think. The story is built like a novel, goes back like one after beginning in the middle and then moves forward to a calculated climax of romantic ecstasy and ironic disappointment. The persons talk like characters in a novel; that is, a Hemingway novel. All it lacks is lovers, and Mr. Hemingway in his Foreword says that "any one not finding sufficient love interest is at liberty, while reading it, to insert whatever love interest he or she may have at the time."

What makes "Green Hills of Africa"

history or autobiography, not fiction, is that Mr. Hemingway is in his own person the hero. The minor figures, his wife, the other hunters, and the various natives, are characterized and differentiated with lively skill. The country through which he hunts not only looks real, but sounds, feels, smells, and tastes real. He has used all his senses in perceiving it and he communicates it to all the senses of his readers. But it frankly exists as it existed for him. He is the center of the action, the sensorium on which the action is recorded. His book about Africa is a book about Ernest Hemingway in Africa.

* * *

"Green Hills" makes it plain once more that Mr. Hemingway is not tough and strong, as in the legend about him. The strongest kind of man, like Pop in the story, would not have such ups and downs of spirit as Mr. Hemingway's. The next strongest kind would not be so conscious of them, if he had them, as to be able to turn them to literary use. Mr. Hemingway belongs to a third class of strong men. Or rather, he is what is better for him to be, a very sensitive man, subtle and articulate beneath his swaggering surfaces. He is an artist who likes best to deal with the deeds of strong men, because they stir him and fit his talents.

When he reflects or argues he is often as boyish as Byron, and he is often tiresome when he goes in for talking and writing tough. He is mature only as an artist, expounding his own art and exhibiting it in prose that sings like poetry without ever ceasing to be prose, easy, intricate, and magical.

Edward Weeks.
Atlantic Monthly, 156
(November 1935),
30, 32.

Green Hills of Africa tells of Hemingway's recent trip to East Africa, where he led the vigorous life in the best manner of T. Roosevelt. Although I am not hunter and have a city man's aversion for bloodletting and safari camps, I found the book absorbing. Besides its candor and its skillful writing, it tells better than anything before Hemingway's beliefs as a writer.

Like most readers, I will never track kudu, check the windage to make my shot, or know the elation of killing well. But that I participated in the experience with Hemingway is a tribute to his narrative skill. It is engrossing without the least distracting pomposity. The dialogue is so real yet so unexpected that it reveals the tensed minds of the hunters. Hemingway's "landscape painting" blends sensuous and intellectual details into a perfectly focused picture for the mind. His descriptions of the African evening, the Masai tribesmen, the final approach to the kudu, and the Gulf Stream are among the best he has ever written. Because Hemingway's own personality so dominates the book, the portraits of the other white hunters come off less well than do those of the Africans, especially M'Cola and Garrick, his gun bearers.

Some readers will be put off by the rough talk of the hunters, but that's how men talk whether they hunt, fish, or play golf. Others may be distracted by the awkward transition between the first two chapters. But the good parts dominate the book, and the best is Hemingway's underlying credo. Here is a frank self-revelation by a powerful and sensitive writer. (Summary)

Clifton Fadiman.
"Busy Week."
New Yorker, 11
(November 2, 1935),
80-81.

I realize that Mr. Hemingway cannot write books just for me. So all I can say is that if you like talk about the killing of large, heavy animals whose meat you do not need and which bleed excitingly after you have pumped shells into them, "Green Hills of Africa" is your book. It is not mine. I'll wait patiently and quite happily for the next Hemingway. Not all of this book, by the way, is about Mr. Hemingway's happy days among antelopes, rhinoceroses, and reedbuck. There are a few amusing conversations, very truculent, in which Mr. Hemingway carries on his feud with the reviewers and insists on his right—I have never heard any one deny it—to lead his own life in his own way. There's some talk, very well done too, about war and revolution, which Mr. Hemingway apparently thinks of as spectacles designed entirely to deepen the experience of

writers. And there is a constant use of the word "bloody," giving an interesting cockney tinge to his style. But "Green Hills of Africa" is mainly a successful demonstration of the author's hunting prowess. My narrow mind puts it down as a well-written tale of the sort ferocious, retired Indian Army colonels generally write before they die. There's no reason why Mr. Hemingway shouldn't do this sort of thing as often as he wishes. He likes the idea of killing animals; others don't. What is one man's dead meat is another man's poison, and let's stop arguing.

"Hunter's Credo."
Time, 26
(November 4, 1935),
81.

In the eleven years since *In Our Time* Hemingway has published two novels, a parody on Sherwood Anderson, a book on bullfighting in Spain, and two other volumes of short stories. Although in these books he showed his distaste for literary pretentions and his admiration for courageous endurance in times of peril, he never got around to saying what system of belief, if any, guided his writing. *Green Hills of Africa* contains at least part of his credo. Consequently, it shows a new stage in his development and sheds more light on his personality than anything he has previously published.

Ostensibly the account of a hunting trip for big game in East Africa, the book provides sharp description of encounters with buffalo, kudu, rhino, and lions and with the African mind seen at work in the native guides and in Masai herdsmen. And not least are the evocations of the sunlit and wild African terrain. But even better are Hemingway's comments on politics, revolution, literature, and man's fate.

Hemingway sets for himself the test to write "an absolutely true book" to see if it can compete with a work of the imagination. Whether in comparison with most contemporary "works of the imagination" or even with his own, Hemingway's book is a successful experiment. The rapid narration, the personal conflicts between the hunters and within each huntsman, the sweeping but detailed landscapes, and Hemingway's own total absorption in the hunt give it not only the organization of a good novel but also the vivid immediacy of an intense experience.

Running through this realistic treatment of the emotions and actions of the hunt is Hemingway's statement of convictions. Often expressed in a half-defiant way, they suggest he is really defending his views against some unseen critic. He defends his life away from the center of literary and political wars by asserting that life is to be savored, not worried about. Nevertheless he does worry about the bitterness and jealousy of literary life, the tendency of good American writers to be destroyed by the conditions of authorship in the U. S., and especially about the way a new generation of writers has to live and work in groups rather than nurture their talents in courageous isolation.

The dominant mood running through these discussions is the fear that modern civilization has become too complex and too chaotic to be controlled or even understood. The reformers only show their immaturity, their failure to realize the complexities. For Hemingway the solution is to know as much and to be as sensitive as possible to the tremors of the world but to keep one's distance by responding to a new and fresh environment—now it's East Africa. And then one finds his satisfaction in making his own work as near perfect as he can. Unfortunately, he does not say for what end one must work. (Summary)

Isabel Ackerman. "Hemingway on the Hunt." *Cincinnati Enquirer,* November 9, 1935, p. 5.

Granted that "Green Hills of Africa" is prime entertainment, but that's not all. It's not only a word-cinema of the "countries" Hemingway hunted, landscapes with fauna and figures, native and foreign (the latter being Hemingway and party), a cinema with asides in sound Hemingway would make out to be casual.

Here we have Ernest Hemingway, the sportsman, stalking big game in African hills, chalking up two lions, a buffalo, a rhino, and two kudu, and enjoying life. His happy hunting is to convince us that here is no sick modern (no more, "The Sun Also Rises"), but a healthy confident primitive. He passes the famine exodus on the road; he sees the locusts overhead, but Ernest's joust with Karl, his friend and fellow-hunter, goes on with all the chivalric importance of being earnest. Around the campfire with whisky and soda comes conversation, another European throw-back; then nature's nobleman talks of writers, of revolutions, and the good life. Hemingway sees the last this way: "Let the others come to America, who did not know that they had come too late. Our people had seen it at its best. . . . A continent ages quickly when we come. . . . Now I would go some where else. . . . I knew a good country when I saw one. . . . Sure, you couldn't make a living" in Africa, but he's always found it easy to make money. So we have one solution of the world crisis: A new pioneer, the squire of Africa, hunting, fishing, exporting literary manufactures and importing beer.

Hemingway's experience in the World War he values highly for its literary stimulus. "Those writers who had not seen it were always very jealous, and tried to make it seem unimportant or abnormal, or a disease as a subject, while really it was just something quite irreplaceable that they had missed." In any case he seems to have been left with a masochistic fascination for shambles. "Death in the Afternoon," the bull-fighting rhapsody, is followed by "Green Hills of Africa," in which he writes of nothing with more zest than hyenas ludicrous in dying.

The hunter's wife is with him, playing such a role as the wife's in Dashiell Hammett's "The Thin Man."

Behind the reporting of adventure, and star reporting it is, too, behind the Hemingway dialogue sometimes degenerating into gags and patter reminiscent of Hollywood breeziness, is a man trying to answer for himself.

Granville Hicks. "Small Game Hunting." *New Masses*, 17 (November 19, 1935), 23.

It ought to be said that I approached *Green Hills of Africa* with a sincere desire to find something to praise in it. Hemingway's piece in *The New Masses, Who Murdered the Vets?*, put me in a frame of mind to forgive everything, even *Death in the Afternoon.* I have always admired most of *The Sun Also Rises,* some of *A Farewell to Arms* and several of the short stories. I have always felt that Hemingway was by all odds the clearest and strongest non-revolutionary writer of his generation. The passion of *Who Murdered the Vets?* not only strengthened my conviction; it made me want to emphasize the good things that can be said about Hemingway, not the bad. This was not because I had any notion that Hemingway would become a revolutionary novelist if *The New Masses* patted him on the back; it was because *Who Murdered the Vets?* had a quality that has been disastrously absent from his previous work. A reviewer has a right to interpret an author's work in terms of his direction. *Who Murdered the Vets?*

suggested that Hemingway was going somewhere, and I hoped to find further evidence in *Green Hills of Africa.*

This autobiographical preface is advisable, for what I have to say about *Green Hills of Africa* is that it is the dullest book I have read since *Anthony Adverse.* There are perhaps ten pages that are interesting, and of these I shall speak later on. The rest of the book is just plain dull. Hunting is probably exciting to do; it is not exciting to read about. . . .

After a good deal of thinking about why the book is dull, the only reason I can see is its subject-matter. On pages 148-150, Hemingway has a very long sentence—which proves that he does not have to write short ones, and that, I suspect, is what it is intended to prove. The sentence begins by talking about the feeling that comes "when you write well and truly of something and know impersonally you have written in that way and those who are paid to read it and report on it do not like the subject so they say it is all a fake, yet you know its value absolutely." Now I do not like the subject of *Green Hills of Africa,* but it would never occur to me to say that it is in any respect a fake. It is a perfectly honest book, and that is why I think it is dull, because the subject is dull. Another clause in the same sentence concerns the feeling that comes "when you do something which people do not consider a serious occupation and yet you know, truly, that it is as important and has always been as important as all the things that are in fashion." This applies, I suppose, to either bull-fighting or hunting, and the only possible comment is that though they may be important to Hemingway, they aren't to most people. The proof is in the response to *Death in the Afternoon* and *Green Hills of Africa.* Since they are, it seems to me, as good books as are likely to be written on bull-fighting and hunting, the trouble must be with the subject.

A certain amount of nonsense is written about the subject-matter of literature. No critic in his right mind will try to prescribe an author's subjects; the author has to start with what he feels and knows. But that is not equivalent to saying that one subject is as good as another. "To write a great novel," Herman Melville said, "you must have a great theme." The whole history of literature proves that he was right. When an author, starting out to write on some trivial theme, has produced a great book, it is because the trivial theme hitched on to a great one. (You might have a great novel about people who were hunting, but it wouldn't be about hunting.) A great theme concerns the issues of life and death as they present themselves in the age in which the author lives.

It comes down to an argument over values, in which Mr. Hemingway's judgment is set against the judgment of history. The ten interesting pages in the book are all given over to discussion of the nature of literature and the function of the author. It is a subject on which Mr. Hemingway feels deeply, and when he feels deeply he writes well. But he is always on the defensive, just as he was in the literary conversations in *Death in the Afternoon.* He is very bitter about the critics and very bold in asserting his independence of them, so bitter and so bold that one detects signs of a bad conscience. No one will deny that sports are pleasant and even important but to be wholly wrapped up in them is not a sign of intellectual maturity. And the truth is, as he constantly reveals, that Hemingway is not wholly wrapped up in them. He has ideas about war, revolution, religion, art and other adult interests, ideas that the readers of *The New Masses* wouldn't always like, but ideas. And still he goes on writing about bulls and kudus.

Would Hemingway write better books if he wrote on different themes? *Who Murdered the Vets?* suggests that he would, for in that piece all his talents were suddenly lifted onto a higher level. That is why a great theme is important: it calls out so much more of what is in an author. I should like to have Hemingway write a novel about a strike, to use an obvious example, not because a strike is the only thing worth writing about, but because it would do something to Hemingway. If he would just let himself look squarely at the contemporary American scene, he would be bound to grow. I am not talking about his becoming a Communist, though that would be good for the revolutionary movement and better for him. I am merely suggesting that his concern with the margins of life is a dangerous business. In six years Hemingway has not produced a book even remotely worthy of his talents. He knows that the time is short and that it is difficult in this age and country for a writer to survive. There is bigger game in the world than kudus, and he had better start going after it now if he ever wants to get it.

T. S. Matthews.
"A Hemingway You'll Never Be."
New Republic, 85 (November 27, 1935), 79-80.

It used to be pretty exciting, sitting down to read a new book by Hemingway, but now it's damn near alarming. I can remember the time when he was just a big brother, and we thought his strong-arm stunts were swell, especially as they upset our elders considerably. We thought it was great stuff to have a he-man writer on our side for a change. And it wasn't just that he turned the tables on the grown-ups (they're always pushovers sooner or later), but the way he thumbed his nose at his highbrow playmates—the boys that led the class in composition—and made them like it.

Of course he had it all over us little post-war boys, but we knew that and we didn't really mind it. We hadn't had his advantages and there was no use kidding ourselves. We hadn't been to war and we hadn't learned how to write by cabling newspaper dispatches and picking the kernels of sense out of Gertrude Stein's earnest chaff—how to put irony in your sentences and pity in your paragraphs. We knew there was only one Hemingway and it was a good way to be and it was a way we'd never be. O.K., that was all right with us, mister. And what's the trouble now?

Well, the trouble seems to be that he's gone on a month's shooting trip in Africa and then written a book about it. And why not? No reason, no reason at all; only the things he says in the book would have gone just as well (better) in a letter to some pal. He thinks he can write a piece about anything and get away with it. He probably can, too. But it isn't the hot stuff he says he knows it is. It's no news to us "critics"—that's a violent word, boy, a violent word—that we're the lice on literature; but it's news when a writer announces that nobody can share his feelings but it's literature to announce the fact.

And speaking of literature, which Hemingway seems to be getting fond of doing—he can't keep it up much longer, this front of being the square-shouldered outdoor guy who just puts down what he sees. Sees? That fellow knows how to read, just like T. S. Eliot, and don't let him fool you. He has somebody in his book say, "It was wonderful when we heard him bellow. It's such a sad sound. It's like hearing a horn in the woods." Hell, I know that line myself. ("Dieu, que le son de cor est triste au fond des bois."). . . .

You might think I didn't like the book. Well, in a way I didn't; it kind of griped me. I kept wishing he'd quit telling us what a hot shot he is and do a little real shooting—at something more alive than fellow pot-hunters or kudu-snatchers. That fellow can write when he really tries. There are spots of first-rate reporting in "Green Hills of Africa." In fact, the book is lousy with

them—if you see what I mean.

Checklist of Additional Reviews

Sinclair Lewis. "Rambling Thoughts on Literature as a Business." *Yale Literary Magazine,* 101 (February 1936), 43-47.

THE
SPANISH EARTH

≫

ERNEST HEMINGWAY

≪

With an introduction by Jasper Wood

Illustrations by Frederick K. Russell

THE J. B. SAVAGE COMPANY
CLEVELAND · 1938

The Spanish Earth

John T. McManus.
" 'The Spanish Earth,' at
the 55th St. Playhouse,
is a Plea for Democracy."
New York Times,
August 21, 1937,
p. 7.

... By comparison with the picture's commentary, written and presented by Ernest Hemingway, the camera would seem to be mightier than the pen. Hemingway's narrative is, of course, superb. It is terse, powerful, and at times informative; but it is vengeful, bitter and unreasoning. In its contemplative way, the film argues its point much more effectively. Its technique is that of the film document, but Hemingway's narrative makes it a definitely propagandist effort.

"The New Pictures."
Time, 30
(August 23, 1937),
48-49.

When writers Archibald MacLeish, John Dos Passos and Ernest Hemingway decided last winter to aid the Spanish Republic by producing a film showing the Leftist point of view they were confronted by a lack of source materials in the U.S. To obtain the dramatic and pictorial footage they needed they organized Contemporary Historians, Inc., sent their own team to Spain. There writer Hemingway, Dutch director Joris Ivens and cameraman John Ferno spent several months filming sequences in Madrid, at the village of Fuenteduena 60 kilometers from Madrid and at various fronts. The film they made is being released in Manhattan this week. Previewers judged it well worth waiting for.

The Spanish Earth tells the story of the Spanish Revolution in terms of people rather than action. The human face becomes the key register of meanings for the events now shaking Spain. The succession of faces—of speakers at meetings, workers in the villages, old women refugees from Madrid, men going into battle, faces full of grief and determination—all become a veritable portfolio of portraits of the human soul in the presence of disaster and distress. Unposed and unacted, the scenes were recorded by nand-held camera close to the action of attacks on a bridge, the city under bombardment and always back to the village to show the quiet, steady work of people continuing their lives while the war goes on about them. Accompanying the pictorial image is author Hemingway's unforgettably eloquent narration. Altogether it is a record of high achievement for the cause of Spanish democracy. (Summary)

Otis Ferguson.
"And There Were Giants on the Earth!"
New Republic, 92 (September 1, 1937), 103.

Top place in importance for the week goes to the set of pictures Joris Ivens brought back from the Madrid area and has finally got edited, scored for music and ready to go. His camera was in the fields, the rocking streets of the city, behind redoubts and with the tanks, sometimes in the advancing front line. He got as much of it as he could under such difficulties, sizing up not only perspective, sufficiency of lighting, the best points of shelter and focus, sizing up as well how each thing would fit with his idea. Then he took what he had and worked his idea through it.

* * *

Much of the carrying power in understatement should be credited to Ernest Hemingway's commentary. His voice doesn't come over too well, and what with his suggestion of some overrehearsed WNEW announcer in an embarrassment it isn't vintage Hemingway; but with his knowledge and quiet statement of the odds against survival, that feeling for the people of Spain which comes from his heart, the combination of experience and intuition directing your attention quietly to the mortal truth you might well have missed in the frame, there could hardly be a better choice.

* * *

It isn't so much in the outward drama of the attack, the rattling trucks and tanks, breastworks and machine-gun placements and range-finders. These things are here but subordinated to a purpose, which is recorded in this camera simply because it is there in Ivens' and Hemingway's people—the serene grim cast of feature or carriage of the body, the fine figure of a man who comes up to address his brigade or parliamentary body. Men for the most part whose clouds of doubt and petty worry have burned off before a confident power imposing its symmetry from within. Relaxed, haggard or plain dirty, one after another is seen on the screen going through his heavy job as though in very token of the fact that a million or ten thousand or even fifty such cannot be wrong. There is no need for vilification and babble of glory here; showing the Spanish land and the people related to it, the film does not have to raise its voice to be undeniable, its report a plain testimonial to the way men can be lifted clear beyond themselves by the conception of and full response to the epic demand of their time.

Notes

TO HAVE
AND
HAVE NOT

ERNEST
HEMINGWAY

NEW YORK

CHARLES SCRIBNER'S SONS

1937

To Have and Have Not

Fanny Butcher.
"Horror Packed Into New Novel by Hemingway."
Chicago Daily Tribune,
October 16, 1937,
p. 17.

Starting and ending, Ernest Hemingway's first long novel since "A Farewell to Arms" is revolutionary Cuban politics—incidental only, however, to the life story of Harry Morgan, Key West fisherman.

The book opens with one of the most vivid descriptions of a street riot that has been put on paper. It progresses through uncompromisingly realistic descriptions of human baseness, cupidity, and brutal insensibility such as literature seldom has known. It is a profoundly shocking book because Mr. Hemingway is the artist that he is. A lesser writer would have given the impression of sticking in his thumb and pulling out one plum of brutality after another and whacking himself on the back and saying, "What a great horror guy am I." Mr. Hemingway says tacitly, "Of such is the earth" (if not heaven), and it is shocking in a terrible way to be convinced, as he does convince the reader, that it is true.

"To Have and Have Not" is a loosely articulated novel. It is like a series of bomblike episodes, told sometimes by the hero, sometimes by others, each one leaving havoc in the reader's mind.

"Two Kinds of Life."
Saturday Review of Literature, 16
(October 16, 1937),
6-7.

* * *

The story of Harry is so fast and exciting that you read it without caring, at the time, whether it's just a glorified pulp or whether it really says something. What it gives you is Harry's character, inside out, and always in Harry's own words. Harry's speech, and that of the Negro and the rummy who ship with him, cannot be improved upon for vigorous, natural American. It is the talk as much as the action that carries you along, if not breathless, certainly well stimulated.

But Harry is a very simple character. There is not much about him, or about the three short stories in which he figures—and which do not quite add up to a novel—to stick with you. There is an excellent two-page scene between

Harry and his wife, written in human terms, which illuminates the subhumanity of many other scenes. But on the whole I remember less about "To Have and Have Not" after weeks than about "A Farewell to Arms" after eight years or "The Sun Also Rises" after eleven. The idea of the book seems to be that you either live dangerously or you walk around dead. This idea doesn't have to be phony, as it was in "The Green Hat," for instance, and it isn't phony in Hemingway; but it is less than profound and short of impressive. In the third volume of "Men of Good Will," "The Proud and the Meek," Jules Romains explored the same dichotomy of haves and have-nots, with incomparably more subtlety, and with immeasurably superior results, both intellectually and artistically.

Hemingway has such vituperative contempt for people who do not live dangerously that he presents all of them—the "haves"—in caricature. These rich people are not without actual counterparts among the lunatic fringe of economic royalty, but as object lessons in Hemingway's book they are tiresome, because they are all alike.... The scenes in "To Have and Have Not" which do not involve Harry Morgan seem like interruptions, as if they didn't belong in the book at all. One such episode, concerning a third-rate but wealthy writer on the skids, is not so much bad Hemingway as bad John O'Hara. Hemingway's implicit, but belligerent, intolerance of complex personalities has come nearer and nearer the surface in his last three books, but he seems to have abandoned the

450-word sentence; so whatever it may not be, "To Have and Have Not" is good reading.

Bernard DeVoto. "Tiger, Tiger!" *Saturday Review of Literature,* 16 (October 16, 1937), 8.

So far none of Ernest Hemingway's characters has had any more consciousness than a jaguar. They are physiological systems organized around abdomens, suprarenal glands, and genitals. They are sacs of basic instinct. Their cerebrums have highly developed motor areas but are elsewhere atrophied or vestigial. Their speech is rudimentary, they have no capacity for analytical or reflective thought, they have no beliefs, no moral concepts, no ideas. Living on an instinctual level, they have no complexities of personality, emotion, or experience.

Working exclusively with such people, Mr. Hemingway has created the most memorable prize-fighters, bullfighters, literary hangers-on, fishermen, duck-shooters, and thugs that American literature has ever seen. With Frederic Henry, a man without consciousness caught up in a catastrophic mob-panic, and Catherine Barkley, a woman who lives in completely unconscious obedience to instinct, he has composed a novel that will last as long as any in its generation. No one else writing in America today can give a scene the reality that Mr. Hemingway gives it, or can equal his dialogue, which reaches the reader as living speech.

* * *

But if his characters are incapable of ideas, Mr. Hemingway is not. Their mindlessness is itself the assertion of an idea. It is one of Mr. Hemingway's root ideas and has come to dominate his work. Every so often it should be taken out and scrutinized.

Since the thinking of the Hemingway characters has been confined to a form of omphalic irritation, they have not usually had any social awareness. The social significance of "To Have and Have Not" is also negligible. The dice which Mr. Hemingway is rolling are so openly and flagrantly loaded that he cannot mean us to think of his sterile millionaires and his gonadotropic "conchs" in economic terms. The social assertions and findings are so naive, fragmentary, and casual that they cannot be offered as criticism of the established order: beside them, the simplest of the Blue-jeans-and-solidarity Cinderella stories that *The New Masses* was praising three or four years ago would seem profound. . . .

* * *

One wonders if refusal to pity himself is enough to make Harry Morgan so admirable as Mr. Hemingway considers him. He breaks faith with and murders the Chinaman who employs him; after rum-running and miscellaneous violence, he becomes an accessory to bank robbery and more murder; and

he finishes up with a quadruple murder. But floods of adrenalin are always surging into his blood stream, and when he is wounded, both his central and his sympathetic nervous systems are polarized in support of his will to live. Mr. Hemingway is in the position of saying that nothing else matters.

* * *

We have reached the end of a path that Mr. Hemingway has been traveling for a long time. The highest praise he can give a man is to say that he is like an animal.

* * *

What gave the death of the bull its tragic beauty was the fact that it perished at the moment of total aggressiveness, charging at its mortal enemy with all the physiology of its animal nature concentrated in the instinctive, self-justifying act of destruction. And now, compared with the human world which gives the sterile dominion over the potent, how beautiful is the long curve of the shark diving for gouts of blood.

Every man to his preference. Mr. Hemingway is certainly entitled to fall in love with sharks if he wants to, and our literature is the richer for his admiration. There has been, of course, much anthropophobia in modern literature. If the admirers of D. H. Lawrence, for instance, have not consciously loved alligators, they are at least accustomed to praise the faculties of alligators that may be discerned in man. But it is hard to see just how man himself may profitably employ the idea and just what reference either the alligator or the bull has to the problems man is working with in the modern world. And it will be interesting to see how the literary left, which temporarily regards Mr. Hemingway as an ally, will adapt his conclusions when adopting them. The cult of blood-consciousness and holy violence, as well as the clean beauty of the shark, has so far been the property of their political opponents.

It would be even more interesting to find out what Mr. Hemingway thinks of Mr. Robinson Jeffers. Utilizing the diseased secretion of thought to the utmost, Mr. Jeffers has also reached the conclusion that the animals are superior to man, but he finds the waving grasses still more admirable. Unpitying alligator or undeluded chlorophyll—which shall we prefer, which shall be the measure of things?

W. M. R.
"Hemingway's Strong Man in Defeat."
Kansas City Star,
October 16, 1937.

Ernest Hemingway's recent activities in Spain in connection with the civil war have been followed with particular interest because of the considerable part the World war played in his development as a novelist and because of a growing suspicion that another war was needed to arouse him once more to the production of memorable prose. "To Have and Have Not" appears now, however, with conclusive evidence that

Hemingway was not merely a war novelist and that he had made his own recovery before Generalissimo Franco started his Fascist attack on the Iberian peninsula.

But the reviewers who deplored Hemingway's earlier preoccupation with bull-fighting and his pursuit of the elusive African bull kudu were not altogether wrong. Although the novelist did not require another suicide by civilization as a stimulant, apparently he had to come upon a real struggle in the contemporary world in combat and make the experience equally impressive to his readers.

Hemingway found such a conflict in the Florida coast region where he lives. He has recounted it in the life of one man, Harry Morgan, a native of Key West.

* * *

The adventure ends in one of the most violent scenes ever described by Hemingway. It is superbly done. The novelist's terse style is used to its best effect. His sense of contrast is sure, his eye for significant and arresting details almost flawless, his ear acutely sensitive to the tone and idiom appropriate to the action, thought and feeling of his characters.

In this direct manner, Hemingway presents a modern version of the old tragedy of the man who contends alone against the hard conditions of his time. . . .

* * *

Harry Morgan is Hemingway's strong, passionate, ruthless, self-contained and lonely individual in work clothes. He also is the novelist's most clearly defined character, a credible embodiment of the pronounced masculine qualities that Hemingway always has emphasized. Harry therefore is interesting not only as an original character but as one with whom the novelist reveals an attitude that is fully realized.

The masculine standard by which Hemingway measures humanity is observable throughout the novel. Marie, Harry Morgan's wife, is a big, vigorous, capable woman, worthy of a lusty man like Harry. The love of Harry and Marie is a physically splendid affair. In two brief chapters in which Marie figures importantly, the physical attachment between a man and a woman and the grief of a woman whose man has died attain remarkably eloquent expression in the common language of husband and wife. . . .

* * *

The lyrical paganism of Harry and Marie is related to deep feeling, and emotionalism that also manifests itself in compassion, in tenderness even, in generous measure.

* * *

The dramatic and poignant struggle is convincingly sustained so long as Hemingway writes of Harry, Marie and their associates. The effect largely is lost when the author breaks the thread of the narrative to drag in the story of Richard Gordon, the novelist, and skip around the harbor for brief glimpses of yacht owners and their guests. In employing this awkward device, he not only deprives his novel of unity and consistency, but fails to relate Harry Morgan to this other environment, or to develop adequately that environment.

Hemingway succeeds with Morgan and his kind because he describes them faithfully in their own terms. He mostly fails in his excursion among the better dressed individuals roundabout because he selects them as types rather than characters, confines his exploration too largely to the libido, and exposes his poor victims with a savagery that will help only his reputation as a "hard-boiled" writer.

Clifton Fadiman. "Hemingway." *New Yorker,* 13 (October 16, 1937), 76, 77.

Mr. Hemingway's new novel, "To Have and Have not," is his first since "A Farewell to Arms," which appeared eight years ago. . . . Taken by and large, this is Mr. Hemingway's most violent book, and some smarty who should know better will doubtless rebaptize it "A Hello to Arms."

* * *

Solidly portrayed, worthy of admiration, Morgan is a remarkable character, and his defeat and death, even if they are a trifle along Victor McLaglen lines, pluck at the heart. To his creator he seems an important symbol; to others he may seem only a fine piece of characterization. I string along with the others, and that is one reason that, for me, this new book cannot rank with "A Farewell to Arms" and "The Sun Also Rises."

The fact is that the opposition between the lusty, integrated, animal Harry Morgan and the soft world against which he is posed—a world of deadbeat sportsmen, dried-out millionaires, degenerate Hollywood mistresses, neurotic novelists (how Mr. Hemingway hates novelists!), and wealthy parlor pinks—is not a crucial opposition, but only a partial one. Harry Morgan is an outlaw; so are the millionaires and the rich sportsmen that Mr. Hemingway now almost Jacobinically hates. But the millionaires got into the right racket, Harry into the wrong one. That's all. Under slightly more favorable circumstances—say, a Fascist *Putsch*—Harry might have risen to power. He's simply had the bad luck to play the individualist's game badly, whereas the others, despised by him and Mr. Hemingway, have played it more luckily, or at a fortunate season. Thus the contrast implied in the title is not one between the leisured and the submerged but merely between two kinds of men: those with *cojones,* those without.

The book is further weakened by the excess, as it seems to me, of melodrama and by the friability of its masonry. Three episodes in the life of Harry Morgan make up the story. They are tied together only by the fact that they are dominated by a single character. One suspects that they were chosen in part for their melodramatic appeal, and because they give Mr. Hemingway a chance to demonstrate

once more that no one now writing English can equal him in the tense narration of scenes of violence.

One further comment and I am through carping. Mr. Hemingway is wasting his time getting furious with literary fake Bolsheviks, filleted writers, and flabby Harvard aesthetes. They are clay pigeons, not worthy either of his art of his ire. It's all been done before. . . .

I don't think the book as a whole will stand up with his best work. Still, in addition to the character of Harry Morgan himself, there are some extraordinary things in it. Technically it is a joy: as finished, as controlled in its prose as anything Mr. Hemingway has done. . . . He has the true bazaar tale-teller's touch. You are drawn at once into the charmed circle of narrative.

* * *

Suppose we have been waiting eight years for a Hemingway novel. There's no rush. We're all his friends, quite willing to wait several more if necessary. There's something transitional, tentative about this book, not technically, but intellectually. It seems interlude work, half-confident, caught confused and blinking-eyed between two worlds.

R. M. D.
"Tough 'Have-Not.'"
Cincinnati Enquirer,
October 16, 1937,
p. 7.

Harry Morgan, with whose life this novel is entirely concerned, is perhaps the most completely real masculine character Ernest Hemingway has created.

Morgan is a native of Key West, Florida—that paradise of the "haves" and purgatory of the "have nots." He owns a fast motor boat in which he takes out fishing parties and runs rum, guns, and sometimes human contraband. His life is a lonely struggle to keep himself, his wife, and his daughters away from the edge of the "have not" category.

His friends see him as a man of no pity, least of all for himself. All his life he has played a lone hand in a hard world, and it is only in the climax of the novel, as moving a scene as Mr. Hemingway has ever written, that he realizes the failure of his philosophy.

The reader sees him in the round— through his own words and thoughts, through the eyes of Albert, the friend Harry Morgan unwittingly sends to his death, through his adoring but baffled wife, and through the series of dramatic incidents that make up the book.

As a contrast to Morgan and his "conch" associates, Mr. Hemingway portrays the wealthy wasters, literary weaklings, oversexed women, and languid men who, with their palatial yachts, make up the "haves." Their lives and that of Harry Morgan, although on different levels, frequently touch, and when they do the contact is electrical in effect.

J. Donald Adams.
"Ernest Hemingway's First Novel in Eight Years."
New York Times Book Review,
October 17, 1937,
p. 2.

"To Have and Have Not" is Mr. Hemingway's first novel since "A Farewell to Arms" eight years ago. He has in the meantime published a book of short stories, a book on bullfighting in Spain and a book on big game hunting in Africa. While he has demonstrated a normally productive career so far, he has not, unfortunately, grown in stature as he has in reputation.

Paradoxical as the case is, Mr. Hemingway has moved steadily toward mastery of his technique without showing evidence of corresponding mental growth. He has shown that technique is not enough to make a great writer; even his highly-praised technical achievements have not always been the perfect instrument for what he needed to say. But more important, he has given no evidence of increasing his power to illuminate experience. The result is that his new novel is an essentially empty book.

For some years Mr. Hemingway has been a leading figure in American literature and has influenced men a little younger than himself so that they pay him the tribute of imitation. He has unquestionably a commanding talent, and what he does with it is always of interest.

But his story of Harry Morgan fails to gain our sympathy, despite repeated invitations to the reader to agree with the novelist that society is to blame for Harry's outlawry and death. All Harry asked of a job was whether it would pay and whether he could get away with it. He felt no obligation to society, society owed him nothing, and in the end, he got what he gave. As there is no ground for compassion, there is likewise no ground for tragedy.

Mr. Hemingway's thinking about the idle rich is similarly adolescent. For all their being hand-picked specimens, the yachtsmen and other parasites are simply the selfish rich who have existed in every age. They do not prove anything about the evils of economic royalism.

One wishes that such a narrative talent as Mr. Hemingway's could have found a better use. Such economy of phrase and driving action deserve a better narrative conception. Finally, though, the famous Hemingway dialogue reveals itself as essentially sterile. Like the thought, the dialogue is a purely mechanical formula, false to life, and all the characters seem to talk alike.

"To Have and Have Not" is clearly below the standard of "A Farewell to Arms." Despite its strength as action narrative, it has nothing comparable to the Caporetto retreat or the final hospital scene of the earlier novel. Mr.

Hemingway's reputation would have been stronger if it had never been published. (Summary)

Alfred Kazin. "Hemingway's First Book on His Own People." *New York Herald Tribune Books,* 14 October 17, 1937, p. 3.

In the eight years since the publication of "A Farewell to Arms," the Hemingway legend has lost its luster with the gradual recession of a world that nourished that legend with emulation and empty flattery. He has written books, but they have been elaborate and sometimes threadbare excuse for one solid book; and as the years have gone by, we have grown accustomed to him standing like Tarzan against a backdrop labeled Nature, while little men with nothing of his stabbing talent and pride of craftsmanship have done the work. One wondered if the end of 12, Rue de Fleurus, Gertrude Stein like some immense priestess of nonsense expounding her text in nonsense syllables, dear Ezra Pound and all the rest, was not his end, too. Had the lost generation gone down with a whimper? Would it never go beyond the pat theatrics of saying America, farewell?

The answer—troubled, sketchy, feverishly brilliant and flat by turns, and only a little heartening—is "To Have and Have Not." It happens to be the first full-length book Hemingway has ever written about his own country and his own people; and that explains a good deal. In the earlier books America was the last frontier of his Michigan boyhood, a mountainous jumble of forest against which we saw him as the inquisitive but tight-lipped youth, the doctor's son, violently athletic, hard, curt, and already a little sad. And then America went out of the picture altogether, and there was the dry crackle of the boozed cosmopolitans eating their hearts out in unison, with a shift of scene to Malaga or Paris or the African jungle, with the famous style getting more mechanical book by book, the sentences more involved, the head-shaking over a circumscribed eternity more obvious.

It is significant that the America of "To Have and Have Not" is Key West. For like the Paris of 1925, Key West is at once an outpost of a culture and its symbol. It is a home for disabled and unemployed veterans, a night resort for writers who talk great books, a harbor for the sleek yachts of the newer millionaires. Being a tip of the continent, it is an open door to Cuba, a window on the Gulf Stream, the Florida of the boom all over again, albeit a little tarnished; and a bit of Latin America. It is by Key West that Hemingway went home, and it is Key West, apparently, that remains America in cross-section to him: the noisy, shabby, deeply moving rancor and tumult of all those human wrecks, the fishermen and the Cuban revolutionaries, the veterans and the alcoholics, the gilt-edged snobs and the hungry natives, the great white stretch of beach promising everything and leading nowhere.

For this is a Hemingway who can get angry and snarl with his heart open. It means a novel thrown together with a fury that leaps from one page to another, a succession of styles instead of a chopped, frozen manner; it means that as he wrote the book he was forced to see his way through in terms of his own position, so that chapters are broken nervously, speeches are begun but never finished, characters enter from all sides and at all times. . . .

The hero of the book is not, like most of Hemingway's heroes, an elaborately selfconscious man against society; he is rather a mass-man, a man like any other, whose life has a beginning, a middle, and a significant end. Harry Morgan's vice is his excessive self-reliance, the pride in his own tough loneliness; but he differs from Jake and Frederick as much as he differs from those sullen, tight-lipped men of action who play the role of natural man, the present version of the romantic savage, in Hemingway's works. Harry is unique because he is capable of struggle and casual about annihilation; and through his effort, though it consists largely of hard-fisted industry, chances taken at night, terrible suffering, he learns the folly of isolation.

* * *

A new Hemingway? Not altogether. There are pages and pages in which the old icy brilliance comes through, with the slippery rhythm, the virtual assonance, the artful grace of phrases fused with such laborious cleverness that the click-clack of the beat is like a hiss. But where before there was one style for one chill elegy on the war and wasted youth, here there are many new twists and turns, even an unusual clumsiness, for this is a Hemingway who is rather less sure of himself than usual, but a good deal more intense. That clumsiness makes uncomfortable reading; it contributes to the impression one gets as a whole that the book is hardly up to snuff; but it tells us that here, in a country notorious for its one-book geniuses and despite an interminably autobiographical generation, is a genuine artist who has worked his way out of a cult of tiresome defeatism; and who may, on this path, yet write a book worthy of him. There's just a chance that Ernest Hemingway is a promising young novelist.

"Hemingway's Tale: 'To Have and Have Not' Raw and Unreal." *Springfield Republican,* October 17, 1937, p. 7E.

Ernest Hemingway's new work, "To Have and Have Not" shows a disappointing lack of development and reveals the weakness of his method. His aim is to picture phases of life that have new intensity, either through being primitively rough or sophisticatedly degenerate. . . .

The beginning is all incident, expressed in conversation, and lacking in background—even in sufficient clarity as to the characters. Toward the end, when he devotes a few pages to degenerate scions of wealth and education, he supplies thumbnail biographical sketches. The incidents lack essential drama, and the author falls back upon profane and bawdy talk, which exists for no recognizable purpose of delineation.

In Mr. Hemingway's treatment excess of naturalism creates an impression of unreality, and the rawness exists for its own sake. In short, there is a labored sophistication both in the direct action and the psychological analysis. It is true that equally raffish persons, both uncivilized and over-civilized, (even a professor of economics), may be found in real life, and that Mr. Hemingway has probably known individuals approximating to these types. But this impression is derived by inference, not by contemplation of the scenes described.

The characters in Norman Douglas's "South Wind" or Aldous Huxley's "Those Barren Leaves," are equally disgusting, but when the reader has finished with those books he believes in the characters and the environment. Instead of portraying offensive persons significantly, Mr. Hemingway too often falls back upon a literal report of offensiveness, and even then employs language that seems artificial rather than inevitable.

"All Stories End . . ."
Time, 30
(October 18, 1937),
79-85.

In the eyes of the genteel literary world Ernest Hemingway is due for his comeuppance. Master of one of the most vigorous prose styles of the century, he has used his literary powers to decimate the comfortable assumptions of the polite practicioners of literature. His critics have called him a bullying bravo and claimed that his attacks on what was already a declining tradition were not such remarkable feats after all. Gaining his first fame as spokesman for the "lost generation," he has aged with his contemporaries and begun to seem dated as the brave world of the twenties has receded. Some have even called him another aged-out but garrulous veteran whose great day is no longer of interest to a younger generation.

Among more serious observers of American letters, though, the question of Hemingway's literary fame still remains unanswered. Assuming an author's limitation to his chosen subject and his decline once that subject has been exhausted, they continued to see him as spokesman for the violence and disillusionment of the postwar generation. But that vein of literary ore was exhausted, they said, and therefore Hemingway too was played out. Where could he go from there?

What the observers overlooked, however, was that Hemingway is emphatically not the run-of-the-critics

writer and not necessarily subject to such rules. Missed also were the clues in *Green Hills of Africa* and *Death in the Afternoon* that Hemingway himself was aware of the traps for the fashionable writer and was busy working his way past them. In the bullfighting book he was announcing an almost Elizabethan view that all stories end in death and that death becomes one's other self in the midst of life.

In his newest novel, *To Have and Have Not*, published last week by Scribner's, death is both the background knowledge and the present action. For the easily shocked, it is worth noting there are at least twelve killings, all carried out in the goriest manner, not to mention direct presentation of all the better known four-letter words and scenes of copulation and masturbation vividly suggested. But readers will also find a more serious Hemingway emerging in the novel after the maturing period of the last year.

Most of the book is given over to recounting the saga of surly, rough-talking, brutal Harry Morgan, sometime charterboatman to big game fishermen, smuggler of Chinese coolies, rumrunner, and ferryman to Cuban insurgents. The end of Morgan's career of double-dealing and carnage, however, is his recognition that playing the game alone is playing against unbeatable odds. Besides the episodic chronicle Hemingway affords snapshot views of other forms of life along the waterfronts at Key West: war veterans from the work camps brawling their Saturday nights away in the saloons, artists' colony writers, rich yachtsmen and the local "conchs," as the Key West natives call themselves. Too much written from the "slice-of-life" point of view, often intrusive in the rushing failure of Harry Morgan's struggle, they are less convincing than Hemingway's Morgan, who is the author's most thoroughly consistent and deeply understandable character so far. (Summary)

Sinclair Lewis. "Glorious Dirt." *Newsweek,* 10 (October 18, 1937), 34.

America has a new philosophy, recently announced by President Roosevelt in his Cleveland speech of Oct. 5 and by Ernest Hemingway in his new novel, "To Have and Have Not," published by Scribner's Oct. 15. Philosopher Roosevelt told us that excellently educated men and women have the least worthwhile opinions with respect to national problems. Philosopher Hemingway in his alleged novel of tough sailors and tougher beachcombers on the Florida Keys demonstrates that all excellently educated men and women are cowardly and boring degenerates, but that such unlettered rumrunners as Harry Morgan are wise and good and attractive. It seems that they gain virtue not merely because they smuggle rum but because they find no place for a decent man in industrial America.

With such spiritual guidelines we have now only to eliminate Groton, Harvard and all reading—including Mr. Hemingway's books—to produce a nation of noble and blissful people.

Mr. Hemingway is so concerned with demonstrating this new nobility that he fills his book with manly killings, so many and so sadistically done that the saloon floors and boat decks are awash with blood. After three or four such inspirational killings, accompanied by the four-letter words which in Sauk Center 45 years ago we thought to be brave and original, it all gets pretty dull. And that is the eventual criticism of this "novel," which is not even a novel but a thinly connected group of tales. It is not only dull, it is annoying.

This thin, screaming little book of 75,000 words is Mr. Hemingway's first novel since the rich and exhilarating "Farewell to Arms" of eight years ago. A logical continuation of the puerile slaughter with which Mr. Hemingway filled his hunting chronicle "The Green Hills of Africa," it begins to show a senile weariness in the man who could have been the greatest novelist in America. Perhaps he still can be, if he will stop trying to save Spain and start saving Ernest Hemingway. (Summary)

Malcolm Cowley. "Hemingway: Work in Progress." *New Republic*, 92 (October 20, 1937), 305-06.

* * *

During the last ten years Hemingway has been imitated more widely than any other American or British writer, even T. S. Eliot. You find his influence everywhere from the pulp-paper true-detective-story weeklies to the very little magazines making no compromise with the public taste. You find it in newspapers and movies, in English highbrow novels and even in this weekly journal of opinion. Partly it has been a bad influence. It has made people copy the hard-boiled manner of "The Killers" and "Fifty Grand"—this latter being the cheapest story that Hemingway ever signed. It has encouraged them to boast in print of their love affairs and drinking bouts—though God knows they needed little encouragement. Worst of all, it has caused many young writers to take over Hemingway's vocabulary and his manner of seeing the world—thereby making it impossible for them to be as honest as Hemingway. But in general I think that his influence has been excellent. It has freed many writers—not only novelists but poets and essayists and simple reporters—from a burden of erudition and affectation that they thought was part of the writer's equipment. It has encouraged them to write as simply as possible about the things they really feel, instead of the things they think that other people think they ought to feel. Critics in particular owe a debt to Hemingway; and many of them, including myself, have been slow to acknowledge it. So let me put the record straight. I don't think that he is as great as Tolstoy or Thomas Mann, but I do think that he is perhaps as good as Mark Twain, and that is saying a great deal. In our own generation, he is the best we have.

His new novel I found easy to read, impossible to lay down before it was finished, and very hard to review. It contains some of the best writing he has ever done. There are scenes that are superb technical achievements and other scenes that carry him into new registers of emotion. As a whole it lacks unity and sureness of effect.

Part of its weakness is a simple matter of plot structure, a department in which Hemingway was never strong. The book falls apart at the beginning and the end. It begins with two long stories about Harry Morgan—both of them, I think, were first published in The Cosmopolitan—and it ends with a fine soliloquy by Harry Morgan's widow. In the intervening pages, Hemingway deals with his principal theme, which is really two themes in counterpoint—on the one side, the life of the Have-Nots, that is, the Key West fisherman and relief workers who surround Harry Morgan; on the other side, the life of the Haves, that is, the wealthy yachtsmen and the drunken writers who winter in the Key West bars. These two themes never quite come together.

But a more serious weakness lies in the characters themselves, or rather in the author's attitude toward his characters. Some of them—the writers for example—are the same sort of people, leading the same sort of lives, as he described in "The Sun Also Rises." In those days Hemingway was unhappy about the lives they were leading, yet he approached the people with real sympathy, going to great pains, for example, to explain to himself why Robert Cohn was really a villain in spite of all his admirable qualities. But this time Hemingway really hates the people; he pictures them not as human beings but as the mere embodiments of lust or folly, as wolves or goats or monkeys disguised with little mustaches and portable typewriters.... But since Hemingway is a writer himself, this aversion is also a self-aversion, and prophesies a change in his own career —not from literature to fishing, for example, but rather from one kind of writing to another kind. And that change, that transition, is already foreshadowed in his characters. Among the very few that he portrays sympathetically are two Catholics and a Communist war veteran. Harry Morgan himself begins as a tough guy capable of killing people in cold blood, either to get money or to save his hide; but he dies as a sort of proletarian hero.

* * *

As a whole, "To Have and Have Not" is the weakest of Hemingway's books—except perhaps "Green Hills of Africa"—but it is by no means the least promising. For some years now the literary hyenas have been saying that Hemingway was done for, but their noses have betrayed them into finding the scent of decay where none existed. From the evidence of this book, I should say that he was just beginning a new career.

Louis Kronenberger.
" 'When He Thinks—.' "
The Nation, 145 (October 23, 1937), 439-40.

Hemingway's new novel—his first since "A Farewell to Arms"—will strike many people as confused and some people as transitional. For despite a living hero and a handful of superb scenes, it is a book with neither poise nor integration, and with shocking lapses from professional skill. It splits up in the middle, not simply as a narrative, but also as a conception for a narrative: Hemingway, having told the story of a man, suddenly reinterprets it, and finds it necessary to contrast his hero with other men. Having shown us a lone wolf beaten down by the forces of a protected society, he goes on to picture a whole gallery of creatures drawn from that society.

Structurally all this is awkward and incompetent. It is like writing a letter and then adding to it an appalling number of postscripts. But the structural defect proceeds out of something more serious—out of an intellectual naïveté which goes so far as to imagine that an explicit contrast between Harry Morgan and society is required. Actually the relationship has been obvious, not only in all the incidents of the story, but also in the very theme. It was implicit so soon as Hemingway ever conceived of Harry Morgan as an incorrigible individualist. Harry Morgan is doomed by the nature of his own conflicts and experiences; is doomed as his type has been doomed since it first arose in fiction; is doomed as the heroes of Balzac and Stendhal, or Dreiser and Conrad, were doomed. To drive the point home, Harry Morgan and society have only to interact, indeed they must interact; whereas Hemingway has thought to solve the problem by presenting them separately. But an even greater blunder on Hemingway's part was to suppose that he was presenting a true contrast. In reality Harry Morgan and the kind of society pitted against him were not divided in aim; they were merely unequal in strength.

Between the lines, however, one can read an *intention* on Hemingway's part which appeared to make the second half of the book a valid contrast with the first half. For by the time he had created Harry Morgan he had changed his conception of Harry Morgan's place in the scheme of things: the lone wolf had turned into the poor slob, the rebel had turned into the victim. The victim, to be sure, was there from the beginning; but not for Hemingway. Hemingway began by exalting Harry Morgan as the good type of hard guy—the fellow who pitied no one, least of all himself; the husband whose wife adored him extravagantly for his guts and his *cojones*; the fighter who knew how to take it on the chin. Then slowly the buccaneer began to

dwindle, and someone who was a social problem, who had a social significance, began to take his place. And as Harry Morgan, the man born to stand alone, was about to go down to defeat, he came to realize that in this world the victims of society cannot stand alone.

This shift in values, coming as it does well after the book is under way, results in artistic ambiguity and confusion. But offstage we have advanced from the Hemingway who went to Spain to watch the bullfighters to the Hemingway who went to Spain to join the Loyalists. Death in the Afternoon has taken on a sterner meaning, and in that sense "To Have and Have Not" would seem to mark a transition to the kind of book that Hemingway will write in the future. In that sense it was no bad thing to convert a successful novelette about Harry Morgan into an unsuccessful novel about Harry Morgan and society. But I must go on to say at once that I still find more of the old than of the new Hemingway in this book, and that in many respects he has still to come to grips with important social and ethical problems. The old love of violence—or is it no more than an unconscious exertion toward violence?—is as marked here as ever; the interest in sport is still too ritualistic; the harping on masculinity and potency is still a proof of either not enough perspective or not enough self-confidence; the hysterical exultation of a woman in her potent male is still a form of sentimentality.

Meanwhile, with Hemingway taking on new and more significant interests, one is left wondering how well he will be able to cope with them. He is a very talented writer, but it remains to be proved how intelligent a one. When Clifton Fadiman some years ago drew the parallel between Hemingway and Byron, I am sure that he extended it to include Goethe's celebrated remark about Byron: "When he thinks, he is a child." Nothing could be more inept here, more lacking in true insight, than Hemingway's brand of satire against literary loafers and the complacent rich. It is not only crude and slapdash, misunderstanding its own ends, but some of it is hardly professional. When one encounters such a remark as "A man tapped for Bones is seldom tapped for bed," one is back on the Yale campus hearing one undergraduate wisecrack with another. Similarly, once action in the story is over, and reaction sets in—as with Harry's wife after he is dead—the sentimental note is sounded no more convincingly than the satiric was. Hemingway is writing, not as the woman felt, but as he would like her to feel. For he does not understand the woman.

These may seem like artistic rather than intellectual matters, but their failure as art is based on a defect of intelligence. And upon Hemingway's intellectual growth, it seems to me, his social and ethical growth—and hence his place as a really serious novelist—must hinge. As a writer he can portray scenes with what is little less than genius. As a thinking being he has still a very great deal to learn. His intentions in the matter are fairly clear. His qualifications are more in doubt. His temperament, I think, is in most doubt of all.

Edward B. Schriftgiesser. "The Struggle Between the Have and Have Nots." *Boston Evening Transcript*, October 30, 1937, Part 4, p. 2.

Violence is no new thing in Ernest Hemingway's stories, but anger is. The spectacle of this chronicler of murder and sudden death losing his Olympian indifference over the eternal struggle between the Have and the Have-nots, is a little startling; and adds an unexpected point of interest to his first full-length novel in the eight years since "A Farewell to Arms."

* * *

There is nothing artificial, nothing false, in the violence of Hemingway's tale, any more than the melodrama of Macbeth is false. For the people with whom he deals, whether he is writing of Spanish bullfighters or American soldiers or the conchs of Key West, are elemental beings, possessed of a primitive vitality that inevitably generates drama when they come in conflict with the forces of life and fate. The ancients knew that great tragedy called for protagonists of greater stature than common men and women; they elevated their actors on buskins or made their characters kings and queens. The modern way, not essentially different, is to choose men mentally or biologically equipped with sovereign vigor. Heroes have never lived in subtle worlds; the classic tragedies are not subtle; and those who decry the clamor and naked crying aloud in Hemingway's novels overlook the fact that he is writing of a world where lines are still drawn sharply and without shading.

Hemingway's great gift to contemporary literature, whatever else he may have contributed, has been to drill into the consciousness of the reading public some realization of the way the great non-literary majority think and talk and feel. His work in battering down the taboo against the language they use daily—in this book he apparently has reached the ultimate freedom—is a secondary contribution; the realism of his scenes has been matched by other writers, but he alone is able to light what is happening inside the bodies and souls of such men of action as have survived into this devitalized time. And it is the men of action, Hemingway implies, who alone matter, even when their actions serve only to trap them more inescapably in a tragic doom.

* * *

Edward Weeks.
Atlantic Monthly, 160
(November 1937),
front section.

In the eight years since *A Farewell to Arms* the world has changed from a time when a novelist could live his own life, preoccupied with his own view of art and unconcerned about the surge of events, to the vastly different climate of the artist today. During that period Ernest Hemingway has seen the Spain he loved vanish in a civil war, ignored the world while he hunted big game in Africa, and then watched from his vantage point in Key West while the American depression widened the gap between the "haves" and the "have nots." Now the inequalities in the community have entered Hemingway's artistic consciousness even while he retains his old love for blood-quick action, his terse dialogue, and his preoccupation with death. So much is evident in his new novel *To Have and Have Not*.

Action, characterization, and satire dominate the novel. Action is Hemingway's forte. He does it better than any other living American writer. The shooting of Pancho and the boys, the struggle with the blue marlin, the smuggling of the Chinese, the confrontation with the bank robbers are all swift-moving and wholly absorbing episodes. Characterization comes through clearly whether in the dialogue of the rummies, the Vets, Harry and Marie, or in the introspective flashes of Hemingway trying to think through the feelings of his people. In social satire his sketches of oversexed women and literary flabbies are exercises in cool contempt. But in these sketches the contrast between the rich and the "have nots" is often too theatrical and too obvious to be wholly convincing.

If one asks whether the pitiless killing of Mr. Sing, the excruciating pain of Harry Morgan's last moments, the denunciation by Richard Gordon's wife, or the bed talk of Harry and Marie is defensible, the answer is that we have our humiliations at home in South Chicago and Harlan County. We need not turn to the bombings in Spain or China to discover this is not a pretty world. Hemingway mirrors its brutality in prose as Hogarth did with his brush. (Summary)

Elliot Paul.
"Hemingway and the Critics."
Saturday Review of Literature, 17 (November 6, 1937), 3-4.

When a book by Ernest Hemingway is published it should be received gladly. He is a talented artist, one of the best we have. Nothing he has written has been without interest. Some readers like one short story better than another. Personally I prefer "Hills Like White Elephants." And of the novels I think the new one "To Have and Have Not" is by far the best—style, subject matter, dialogue, and all. That is not the point. What I mean to say is that he is entitled to respectful consideration. Instead, a considerable portion of the reviewers become surly, flippant, in some cases insulting. . . .

* * *

Of course, the public pays no attention to these distinguished professionals but buys the book merrily, enjoys it, and understands it. Nevertheless, the manifestation of bad taste and unfairness meted out to Hemingway by those who are paid to keep the public informed is disgusting. No other American writer would be subjected to such an impertinent barrage, no matter what he published. The same men who carp about the degree of greatness of a sincere and sensitive writer whose talents are no longer in question, each week are extraordinarily gentle with the most abject tripe. No one is deceived.

* * *

"To Have and Have Not" must mean a great deal to Hemingway. I cannot go along with those who believe that he hates most of his characters. Quite to the contrary. He is almost dangerously fond of them. There is not a writer in America who treats his people with such extraordinary, almost feminine, delicacy or who is capable of so many shades of meaning, in the lines and between them.

Harry Morgan, the hero of "To Have and Have Not," has the qualities which characterized the builders of this nation in happier days. He is strong and courageous, ambitious and proud. Men respect and fear him. He lets nothing stand in his way. He would not harm a fly unless it seemed imperative to do so. To his wife he is loyal and affectionate, and she loves him and follows him unquestioningly. Other women are frightened and attracted by his force and virility. He is poor but resourceful and instead of choosing a moderate and conservative path (such as running a filling station) he wants to take greater risks for greater gain.

* * *

tion moves by itself, without comment or interpretation on the author's part. While he works easily and effectively with this technique, Mr. Hemingway has all the old-time romantic zest for reckless daring, robust passion, and the desperate loyalty of the outlawed Robin Hoods. For the more languorous interludes in which the spoiled wasters appear, he has no special knack—John O'Hara does them better. But no one now writing sets up so well the scenes of violence that give body to the book, from the first shooting in Havana to the final horror. If *To Have and Have Not* is intended to stand or fall by anything more than the substance of these successive scenes, I do not think it stands. The cases are too hand-picked to convince the professional social worker or the plain citizen seeking to clarify his thinking on fundamental social problems and to work with them towards their reduction.

"Hamer Fights Hemingway Ban."
Publishers Weekly, 133 (May 14, 1938), 1935.

Fighting the attempt of Detroit authorities to ban the bookshop sale and library circulation of Ernest Hemingway's most recent novel, "To Have and Have Not," Alvin C. Hamer of Hamer's Book Service has secured a show cause order against Wayne County Prosecutor Duncan C. McCrea and the Police Department. The order, issued by Judge Robert B. Toms, presiding judge of the Wayne County Circuit Court, directs McCrea and the police to appear May 14th to show why they should not be enjoined from attempting to suppress the book.

The legal battle is the result of a decision by the prosecutor that "To Have and Have Not" is obscene literature, a decision based on complaints by the Detroit Council of Catholic Organizations. . . .

The County Prosecutor said that he would seek the assistance of church organizations in defending his case, while Mr. Hamer announced that he had invited such celebrities as Alexander Woollcott, Carl Sandburg, Sinclair Lewis, Dorothy Thompson, Theodore Roosevelt, Jr., Rose Wilder Lane and Bennett Cerf to testify at the injunction hearing.

Prosecutor McCrea has also called upon the Detroit Library Commission to take the book off the circulating shelves. The Commission, according to the Detroit *News*, agreed to keep the book from the curious or casual reader, but announced that it would preserve it among examples of works by "writers of some standing."

* * *

"Case to Be Tried on Its Merits."
Publishers Weekly, 133 (June 25, 1938), 2434.

Alvin C. Hamer's suit for an injunction to prevent the Prosecutor of Wayne

County, Michigan, from interfering with the sale of Ernest Hemingway's "To Have and Have Not," will come to trial shortly. On June 18th Judge James E. Chenot of the Wayne County Circuit Court declined the Detroit bookseller's plea for a temporary injunction but agreed that the question whether the book violates the State obscenity statute may now be tried on its merits. The Prosecutor had argued that the Circuit Court had no jurisdiction in the case at all, but the court denied this contention and accepted jurisdiction. Recently Mr. Hamer broadened the basis of his appeal by contending that the Prosecutor was not elected or appointed to act as a censor and therefore had no right to issue a censorship order.

* * *

Checklist of Additional Reviews

Van Wyck Brooks, Archibald Mac-Leish, and Thornton Wilder. Letter to the Editor on Detroit's ban of the novel. *Nation,* 147 (July 23, 1938), 96.

Hershel Brickell. "Mr. Brickell Replies." *Saturday Review of Literature,* 17 (November 20, 1937), 9.

Earle Birney. "The Importance of Being Ernest Hemingway." *Canadian Forum,* 17 (December 1937), 322-23.

"Faces of the Month." *Fortune,* 16 (December 1937), 224.

Notes

THE FIFTH COLUMN

AND THE FIRST
FORTY-NINE
STORIES

By

ERNEST

HEMINGWAY

NEW YORK

CHARLES SCRIBNER'S SONS

1938

The Fifth Column
and the
First Forty-Nine Stories

W. M. R.
"Hemingway War Play
with Short Stories."
Kansas City Star,
October 15, 1938.

Ernest Hemingway has had poor luck getting his first play produced. "One producer died after he had signed a contract to put it on and had gone to California to cast it. Another producer signed another contract and had trouble raising money."

Uncertain himself as to the merit of the play, Hemingway explains it was written under the difficult conditions of war, during the time when the Spanish hotel in which he was living and working was struck by more than thirty high explosive shells. . . .

Judged from its effect in print, the play was not helped by the shells.

* * *

The psychological conflict frequently is allowed to dominate the play. The unseen enemy is forgotten while Philip, the American, tries to decide between his love for the beautiful Dorothy and devotion to the cause he has espoused. The situations are not designed to consistently express the atmosphere of war and maintain suspense. The characters are a bit slow in revealing themselves. The dialogue is brisk but too heavy a burden is placed on it, the talk failing to convey a sound impression of important action occurring offstage that is related to the play.

Perhaps a good director and competent actors will give an entirely different effect to "The Fifth Column," imparting the impact demanded of wartime drama. In the reading it is no more than one of Hemingway's less successful stories. It is worth reading, however, as is almost everything the former Kansas Citian has written.

All the short stories that Hemingway has produced are included in this volume. There are stories in the collection that fall below the standard of first-rate fiction, but it would be hard to pick three that should never have been published. Most of them bear the mark of high talent and some of them —notably, "The Short Happy Life of Francis Macomber," "Big Two-Heart-

ed River," "The Killers," "The Undefeated" and "The Snows of Kilimanjaro"—are the work of genius.

Elmer Davis.
"He Has Ground a New Edge."
Saturday Review of Literature, 18 (October 15, 1938), 6.

The news is that Hemingway is back
again, and you can write off "To Have
and Have Not" along with "The Prodigal Parents," "A Double-Barreled Detective Story," and other errors by
men with a high fielding average. "The
Fifth Column" is a play which was not
produced because the first man who
was going to produce it died and the
next couldn't raise the money. (Let us
hope the jinx wore out before it
reached Mr. Maxwell Perkins at Scribner's.) But Hemingway had it published because he thought it might
read well, and he is right. Also, his
preface would serve as a pretty good
review, except that he only says "if it
is good." Well, it is good; no need to
worry about that.

* * *

Enough about the plot; the plot is
that these people are all alive—Philip
and Dorothy, and Antonio the hard-
boiled Colonel in command of counter-espionage, and Max the German
revolutionary whose face had been
spoiled by the Nazis. Max and Antonio
didn't like people who weakened; but
Max at least could understand it.
These people (except Dorothy) are all
doing something; whether you agree
with what they are doing a hundred
per cent, or only fifty-one per cent, or
no per cent, they are worth reading
about. So far as a layman can see, the
story ought to play well too.

Just for good measure are included
Hemingway's forty-nine published
short stories. There is not much to say
about them, except that nobody else
now living could show forty-nine stories that good. Hemingway says that
while he was writing the play, more
than thirty high-explosive shells hit the
Hotel Florida, and that if the play is
good, perhaps those shells helped write
it. Maybe and maybe not; of his last
four stories two were written in Africa
where things were peaceful, two in
Spain; the two from Spain are only
so-so, the two from Africa, "The Short
Happy Life of Francis Macomber" and
"The Snows of Kilimanjaro"—are right
up among the best. Every middle-aged
author has played with the idea of the
man who dies before he got around to
doing the things he always meant to
do, but I cannot recall anybody else
who has done it so well as it is done in
"The Snows of Kilimanjaro."

* * *

Alfred Kazin.
"What Spain Has Made of Ernest Hemingway."
New York Herald Tribune Books, 14 October 16, 1938, p. 5.

"The Fifth Column" is hardly a great play; it is an interesting Hemingway period piece—I almost said Hemingway short story, so nimbly do his stage people talk the clipped Hemingway speech—for it tells us more about him that it does about Spain. The heroism and the hunger of Spain flow a little into it, and a little of the treachery and the slow panic of Realpolitik; but above and against the spectacle of martyrdom there is the old Hemingway hero, witty and sick, and the old Hemingway heroine, with her heart behind a Maginot line, though this girl comes from Vassar, and Vassar ought to be mad at Mr. Hemingway for keeps. . . .

* * *

When some years ago Clifton Fadiman so shrewdly noted Hemingway's resemblance to Byron, he could not have known that our Byron would find his own Greek war of independence, and that, as for his handsome prototype, war would mean the adventures of the eternally disillusioned among dead masterpieces. They sing "Bandera Rossa" downstairs in the Hotel Florida, and Philip says: "The best people I ever knew died for that song." But he's not one of the best

people; he may die with the mantle of a new world before his eyes, but sullenly, it's the thing to do, drinking's no longer any fun. He's Mr. Hemingway's Philip, sick in peace and sick in war, sick in the hearts of too many country-women. It's a good war, yes, but war is what the Hemingway soul has moved through for fourteen years, the war against sobriety and against twentieth-century fate, the long, embattled journey by which Hemingway has gone around the world to find a little heroism in Madrid.

What it comes to is that this play—witty, noisy, full of crackle and home-driven insight—fails to master, because Hemingway has not yet mastered, that contemporary drama of which the Spanish war is but the most violent episode. . . .

* * *

When will Hemingway in his vigorous, hopeful middle age reach up to the times that have in all their complexity made him the writer he is, given him his stage, displayed his forte, distinguished him from the others?

So much and so little for "The Fifth Column." With it are all of Hemingway's short stories of which the first four—"The Short Happy Life of Louis [sic] Macomber," "The Capital of the World," "The Snows of Kilimanjaro," and "Old Man at the Bridge" (dated Barcelona, 1938)—are new, and of which at least a half-dozen, as no one needs to be told, are simply terrific. They're printing Hemingway short stories in schoolbooks these days, and their author, it seems, is a little embarrassed. Ah, for the days when even the Treaty of Versailles was young!

"Dramatist of Violence." *Time*, 32 (October 17, 1938), 75.

In some Hemingway tales, particularly "The Killers" and "Fifty Grand," the dialogue carries the narrative so strongly that the stories read like plays. Characters reveal their tormented inner lives in pungent, unexpected lines that break through ordinary talk. So much does dialogue carry the burden of the story that many readers have speculated how Hemingway would do as a dramatist. They can now get a good idea in his newly published play of the Spanish Civil War, *The Fifth Column*.

On almost any stage several scenes would rank as spine-tingling melodrama. New to Hemingway's writing is the nightmarish aura of confusion in which events take place. Unfortunately, though, the pace falters just as it gets well underway. Hemingway's temptress Dorothy Bridges is such a dunce that only an extraordinarily beautiful actress could make her hold on Philip Rawlings seem plausible. Philip's overlong explanations on why he works with the Loyalists, too, make one suspect their clarity even in his own mind. Further dissipating the effect: too many big scenes—like the execution of a captured Nazi—take place off-stage.

If the play is disappointing, the stories make the book one of the best literary bargains of the year. The 49 tales, which include several newly published ones as well as those from Hemingway's three previous collections, add up to a large volume of superb prose. "The Short Happy Life of Francis Macomber" is the best of the new stories; it epitomizes Hemingway's basic creed as well as anything he has done. Beside such brief but polished pieces, combining as they do both physical action and psychological subtlety, *The Fifth Column* appears ragged and confused. Which makes readers of the play hope Hemingway will keep his drama within the confines of stories and novels. (Summary)

Clifton Fadiman. *New Yorker*, 16 (October 22, 1938), 82-83.

News from the Ernest Hemingway Front: All the published short stories, together with four that have never appeared in book form, are now available in one volume. There's Mr. Hemingway's play, too, "The Fifth Column," about espionage and counter-espionage in contemporary Madrid. Two weeks' work on this play ought to turn it into a producible affair, but even as it stands it makes exciting reading. Some scenes will make you gasp and a few, I regret to say, may make you snicker.

Among the four new stories is "The Snows of Kilimanjaro," as good as anything Hemingway has done, and two brilliant little sketches that come out of his Madrid experiences. I don't see how you can go through this book (it's called "The Fifth Column and the First Forty-Nine Stories") without being convinced that Hemingway is the best short-story writer now using English.

Peter Monro Jack. "Hemingway's Plays and Stories." *New York Times Book Review*, October 23, 1938, p. 4.

In his new book Ernest Hemingway reprints the collected stories from *In Our Time, Men Without Women,* and *Winner Take Nothing* and, in addition, four new stories and his three-act play about the war in Spain. Unable yet to get the play produced, Mr. Hemingway has included it as a story, and it reads well. The play appears as the first story, but the real first story, "Up in Michigan," was written in Paris in 1921. It reveals the strong influence of Gertrude Stein: repetitive patterns and whole paragraphs with the rhythms of *Three Lives* (1909) provide clues to the origin of such narrative style. The last story is as recent as April of this year. Cabled from Barcelona, the story of an old refugee who worries more about his animals left behind than about his own luck shows that Mr. Hemingway's chief recent development is in being able to cable his stories.

From 1921 to 1938 Mr. Hemingway has told the same story—of pity, pride and loneliness, all conveyed in terse reportage of the cruel facts. Always professional, they seem letter-perfect in their exactness. His gallery of killers, gangsters, soldiers, bullfighters and big-game hunters shows a monotony of range throughout the book, a monotony of feeling which the surgically exact prose accentuates rather than conceals.

Whatever emotion charges the stories, it is carefully muted. Whether Mr. Hemingway means to suppress or express emotion, however, is not always clear. Sometimes the perfect style seems to prevent an effect that a lesser writer could achieve by less remarkable technique. But where emotion is expressed by indirection, it is all the stronger for Mr. Hemingway's high degree of control.

As for the play, the author is right. It reads like a collection of his stories. Some scenes come off very well. At least two characters reveal dialect and manners that should make for some amusing moments on stage. And the dialogue, like that in his stories, has a casual but perfect understatement about it. But because it begins and ends casually, neither with a bang nor a whimper, it is doubtful the story dialogue will be his gift to the stage. In addition, Mr. Hemingway's sense of characters shows itself to be surprisingly derivative. His hero Philip Rawlings is imagined in movie terms—a cross between Ronald Coleman and Raymond Massey. His lady correspondent is from Vassar and from any one of a number of Mr. Hemingway's other stories by way of Noel Coward. In the big scene—the capture of the German officer and the Spanish politician who have been directing the bombardment of the city—Hemingway drops his magazine story and gets to the real business of the play. If this scene is successful, it can rescue the rest of the play, for on it depends all the meaning of the otherwise indulgent scenes of loving, quarreling and conniving.

For the moment, the play is more easily imagined as another story than as drama to be performed. The people of the play are the emotional successors to all the Parisian drifters, the Italian soldiers, the big-game hunters, the Spanish bullfighters—all now brought to Madrid for their latest confrontation with the world. Essentially unchanged by the war, they bring their style with them and the short stories show them as they have always been— caught in a kind of beautifully stylized rigor mortis. (Summary)

"The Fifth Column and the First Forty-Nine Stories."
Nashville Tennessean, October 23, 1938, p. 6.

Ernest Hemingway has taken time from his martial activities in Spain to write a play called "The Fifth Column." His output has slowed down a little of late, and apparently the play was not enough for a book.

So all his short stories have been assembled, four new ones have been added.

About the stories little need be said, for those who like Hemingway know all about them in advance. It's an advantage to have them all under the same roof, as it were, and the new ones are fairly typical of their creator, and that's about that.

The play is a different story. In the first place it is about Loyalist activities in Spain, and therefore controversial. Hemingway's sympathies are so generally known, and his prejudices as well, that they too may be skipped. The question is whether or not the play is a good play. It probably is, although it may not be as effective on the stage as in print.

Its grave defect is that it is political, and is not removed even a little from reality. Therefore those who read it will at once identify themselves with the side they admire and Hemingway's effort will be distorted at the outset. He is too discerning a writer not to know this, so the inference must be that "The Fifth Column" is intended as propaganda, and the verdict must be that it is as effective as propaganda plays ever are.

* * *

Malcolm Cowley. "Hemingway in Madrid." *New Republic,* 96 (November 2, 1938), 367-68.

---

* * *

I should judge that "The Fifth Column" would need a little playdoctoring before production. There is too much commotion offstage, there are scenes that wouldn't be effective for lack of the proper timing, and no great skill is shown in the playwright's business of getting people in and out of doors. But the play reads like one of Hemingway's short stories, which is to say that it reads very well. The plot jumps ahead, the dialogue is sometimes tough, sometimes outrageously funny, and the minor characters are real creations—especially Max, the secret agent with a very tender heart and a face horribly deformed by torture.

The hero, Philip Rawlings, is the latest in a long line of Hemingway heroes, all of them brutal and reckless by day but wistful as little boys when alone at night with the women they love.

* * *

The trouble is that although long-legged, bright-haired Dorothy is a symbol of the hero's nostalgia, and might be a symbol of ours if we saw her in the flesh, she is nothing of the sort when we read "The Fifth Column." She is presented there as a chattering, superficial fool, a perfect specimen of the Junior Leaguer pitching woo on the fringes of the radical movement, with the result that she keeps the play from being a tragedy or even a valid conflict between love and duty. If Philip hadn't left her for the Spanish people, he might have traded her for a flask of Chanel No. 5 and still have had the best of the bargain.

* * *

During the seventeen years of his literary career, Hemingway's short stories have changed very little. He has broadened the range of his technical effects, and his geographical background, and to some extent his human sympathies. The new stories are not published like a few of the earlier ones, in the effort to be lurid or shocking. Yet those first stories defined his talent as a writer, and some of them I still prefer to his more recent work. When he wrote them he seemed to be closer to his material and more directly moved by it. Has he ever shown more compassion than in "The Battler" and "Indian Camp" and "My Old Man," all included in his first volume?

Reading the stories over again, you are impressed by how well they stand up in the face of a thousand products advertised to be just as good. You are also impressed by the number of them that deal with lust or violent death. In the first story—taking the order in which they are printed, not the order of writing—a rich woman shoots her husband in the back of the head with a hunting rifle. In the second, a Spanish boy plays at bull-fighting and is killed by an accidental thrust from a butcher knife. In the third, a writer dies of gangrene after reliving his violent past. In the fourth, an old man waits for death in the midst of a general retreat. Some of the others deal with suicide, abortion, self-mutilation, wartime insanity, lesbianism, death on the racetrack, death in the bull ring; one story is called "A Natural History of the Dead." People used to say that this choice of subjects was due to some unhealthy quirk, but I think there is another explanation. Every great writer—as Robert Cantwell said in his fine essay on Henry James—is a prophet in spite of himself. He tries to express the underlying spirit of his age, and that spirit will sometime be carried into action. Hemingway's violence seemed excessive during the relatively quiet decade that followed the War. But now, after the fighting in Spain and China and the great surrender at Munich, it seems a simple and accurate description of the world in which we live.

R. W. N.
"Hemingway Writer of Short Stories."
Springfield Republican,
November 6, 1938,
p. 7E.

The name Ernest Hemingway has come to have wide publicity value. Whether his work has merits of the lasting kind remains to be seen. That is true of the work of any currently prominent writer. The assertion that "today Hemingway is recognized as the greatest contemporary practitioner of the short-story writer's art" is criticism of the blurb type. It may be true, but the critical discernment of those who think they recognize in him "the greatest practitioner" has yet to undergo the test of time.

To some observers it seems more probable that he owes his contemporary prominence in the field of short fiction writing to qualities that may not ultimately be found to foot up into permanent preeminence: brevity, variety (plus novelty to the reader) of subject-matter; wide range of personal experience; an excellent memory coupled with ability to draw quickly upon his "morgue" of filed impressions; the manner often of the ready reporter or the easy and spontaneous raconteur.

The entire body to date of Mr. Hemingway's published short fiction-esque work is now obtainable in a single volume, together with, for good measure, four such pieces not previously published and an unproduced play. The volume is "The Fifth Column and the First Forty-nine Stories." Enjoyment of the play ("The Fifth Column") may depend to a certain extent upon the reader's experience in following dramatic continuities in printed form, but there is little doubt that he will read the 49 "stories" with enjoyment. Indeed, the play is probably much easier to follow in print than it would be to produce.

The chief difficulty in reading it lies in the fact that a somewhat complicated stage-set must be kept in mind and that the numerous and sometimes rather long stage-directions require close attention to understand what would be instantly apparent in the physically staged and acted piece. The "fifth column" is the name given by the Spanish loyalists to the enemies working within the loyalist lines.

Contrary to the opinion sometimes expressed, Mr. Hemingway is not a distinguished stylist. He writes, as already said, in the manner of the ready reporter or the ready raconteur (not infrequently, indeed, he is a raconteur). His diction has the merit of uncomplicated directness, but it is not always free of incorrectness or careless or obscure constructions—a remark that sometimes applies also to the construction of longer passages, compelling one to return and reread to clarify or readjust his understanding.

One of the pleasingly noticeable things in Hemingway is his ability to handle commonplace, trivial, and fragmentary material so that it carries point and discloses its significance. His superiority over many of the writers who affect this genre is obvious, and accounts in a very considerable degree for his hold upon readers. Yet even brevities and fragmentary lengths that convey meaning lack substantiality— what Aristotle quaintly characterized as "magnitude"—and do not build up cumulations of effect that grow into impressive substance. The glance, however keen and discerning, is not the equivalent of a sustained look.

Edwin Berry Burgum. "Hemingway's Development." *New Masses*, 29 (November 22, 1938), 21-23.

The preface which Ernest Hemingway has written for his play about the war in Madrid *(The Fifth Column and the First Forty-nine Stories)* is one of the important literary documents of our time. It is not simply the apology that

an honest craftsman might write for a play he has not succeeded in getting produced. The preface is a statement about the broader matter of his intentions and attitudes, such as could only come from an author without a trace of meretricious purpose.

* * *

Whatever may have been true of the past, Hemingway's recognition is now serious that art must have its roots in social events. He renounces the easy success of reduplicating past molds in favor of loyalty to the changing shape of things. When a writer who has been sensitive to style and technique of expression chooses the risk of esthetic failure because he will not allow himself to degenerate into the insignificant and the outmoded, his action becomes an important sign of the times. But it is especially significant for those who have aligned themselves with the left. They have been warned often enough by the high priests of Culture of the dangers that lurk in the doctrinaire, and now an American writer who is certainly as good as we possess tells his fellow writers it is a danger they must run. In the language of politics, they must "take sides against fascism."

About his own play, Hemingway, I think has been too modest. The success of his turn to the dramatic form in *The Fifth Column* may have been embarrassed by lack of familiarity with practical stagecraft. We may leave this judgment to the event. But it is otherwise with his turn to an anti-fascist theme, for the play makes good reading. . . .

If *The Fifth Column* were only another story of violence and intrigue in time of war, it would be of little moment. But its sensational events are the mechanism through which a typical Hemingway character gets a grip on himself. Externally Philip resembles the familiar type, Middle class, wearing his education lightly, and unaccustomed to treating money with veneration, he has lived from one love affair into another, never expecting more than sensuality and never satisfied when he got it. . . . But now his disgust has for the first time found its reason, and he contrasts the grace and luxury of the proposed debauch with the struggle that thousands of men and women around them are making to safeguard such elemental needs as life and food and freedom. Philip turns away in preference to an illiterate Spanish courtesan in whose love he recognizes the broader element of a common interest in the fight for the survival of Spanish democracy.

The success of such a story obviously does not lie in the nature of a theme which might easily have been treated with banality or sentiment. Philip's seriousness of purpose grows with his participation in the hunt for spies. It is not the result of any reading of treatises or long theoretical discussions. It is the gradual, quite unintellectual response to his admiration for Spanish friends. . . .

* * *

The whole of Hemingway's development from the beginning of his career as a writer is implicit in the character of Philip Rawlings. The collection of his short stories appended to the play graphs a course the direction of which the play can now be said to have defined. Their arrangement from stories of Nick's boyhood in the Midwest to his mature experience in European or American cities suggests the interpretation. Hemingway has always been absorbed by certain elementary concerns of men. Influenced by the revolt against intellectualism and respectability led by Dreiser and Anderson, but for him principally by the early work of Gertrude Stein, he has cherished beyond all else the cultivation of the body. The quality he has consistently admired in men has been physical competence. Indifferent to class lines, he has ignored the ideals that Americans have associated with them: success in business, public esteem, the austerity of the puritan, the effeminacy of the dilettante. . . .

Hemingway wrote of this world so freshly and frankly as to take his audience unawares. He made them like the direct experience of his stories by furnishing them no excuse for the *arrière pensée* of the moralist. He profited, it is true, from the more tolerant attitude that prevailed in literary circles as a result of the propaganda in the works of Mencken, Dreiser, and Anderson. But he never stimulated criticism, as some of his predecessors had done, by justifying his interpretation. He kept himself out of sight as carefully as Flaubert, never indulging in a phrase of open comment, so that the flavor of irony or disillusionment or whatever it might be, seemed to reside in the very juxtaposition of events. . . .

* * *

But for those who were watching for social connotations in Hemingway's development, disquieting symptoms had appeared. The constant question in our minds, I remember, was whether Hemingway was going esthetic, was going to follow to its end the road that Gertrude Stein had shown him. His style had been without parallel in American writing for flawless achievement in what he sought. It isolated as only fine prose can do the sentence intonation, the slangy penetrating metaphor, which prove how superficial are the differences in linguistic pattern between the American of the middle class and the proletariat.

But now that all this sensitiveness was turned, however beautifully, into lamentation that bullfighting was becoming a lost art, that economic insecurity and the demands of the poor were responsible for the decay of another old Spanish custom, it seemed to adumbrate the cultural orientation of fascism, which is obtuse to the cruelty and vulgarity of the present because it lives in dreams of feudal perfection. Knowing also as we did that the ethos of the gangster about whom Hemingway had written was only that of the fascist vigilante not yet systematized, we hesitated about his direction.

We had forgotten, as events showed, that Hemingway had always lacked the principal ingredient of fascist culture. This is, I take it, to see persons not of one's class from the outside, to fail to penetrate into understanding of the complexity of their psychology and the real nature of their aims. It should not be ignored that there is a kind of fascist interest in the proletariat.... But, though Hemingway's characters have often been callous in this fashion, he has never been similarly callous in his relation to them. Indeed, quite the contrary; if he has continually shocked the respectable reader, it has been precisely by the authenticity of his disclosure of other *mores* than their own. He has not sentimentalized the worker or the sportsman. He has put himself on their level and made them articulate. Nor has he ignored what is often the reckless generosity of their characters.

In fact, he has come more and more to recognize that the underprivileged have a resiliency of resistance to degenerating pressures that is lacking in the coddled rich, though the resistance, as in *To Have and Have Not,* may in the particular case be partial and end in failure. Hemingway's irony, indeed, proceeds from his recognition that the real kindliness and generosity in human relationships is less likely to be found in the reputable classes; just as his cynicism was in large measure a consequence of his absorption in the *mores* of the dominant class and those it had corrupted. But at bottom he had always taken for granted the democratic tradition of freedom and equality. Life in Europe after the war had this salutary effect upon many of our expatriate writers. Bohemianism in these individuals promoted the rediscovery of neglected human values. The sentimental ideal of equality and fraternity, detached from its mooring in middle-class respectability, became for them a real conviction. Though confused enough at first, this reaction to accepted values became more significant as the accepted values continued to degenerate. After Prohibition, in "Wine of Wyoming," Hemingway feels more at home with the family of poor French farmers in Wyoming who hospitably offer him their friendship and wine they are periodically arrested for making, than he does with the dominant class. The Spanish war immensely expanded these displacements of class feeling, completed the shift from Bohemianism to democracy, and clarified the enigma that the sophisticated and esoteric artist sometimes has the strongest appreciation of the virtues of the common man. It was so with Elliot Paul, and it has been so with Hemingway. And this collection of his short stories is the record of the road that Hemingway has traveled through the confusions of modern life to a clearer insight into the relation between democracy and art.

Edmund Wilson. "Hemingway and the Wars." *The Nation,* 147 (December 10, 1938), 628, 630.

Little did the critics of Hemingway know what they had in store for them when they were urging him a few years ago to interest himself in the large forces of society. Mr. Hemingway had a period of scathing indignation, during which he defied the "world-savers" in the interests of his art and hobbies, and gibed fiercely at the insincerities of phony radicals; then he became aroused by the struggle of the Loyalists in Spain, the Stalinists took him in tow, and the first results are before us.

The earliest signs of Hemingway's new social consciousness had shown themselves in his book before this, "To Have and Have Not," in which he added nothing to the effect of several short stories by attempting to solder them together as a long story. . . . The literary fellow-travelers wrote as if "To Have and Have Not" were the most creditable thing Hemingway had written, though from the literary point of view it was certainly by far the worst book he had written.

"The Fifth Column," a play, is almost as bad. It opens very amusingly and rather dramatically, and it is good reading for the way the characters talk. But one can't see that it does very much either for Hemingway or for the revolution. The hero, though of Anglo-American origins, is a member of the Communist secret police, engaged in catching Fascist spies in Spain. . . .

This heroic Anglo-American secret police agent is the same old Hemingway protagonist of "The Sun Also Rises" and "A Farewell to Arms," though now rather more besotted and maudlin; but we never doubt that he will do his duty. Indeed, the more besotted and maudlin this familiar old character gets, the more completely he behaves like the hero of a book of adventure for boys. It does not make things any better for Hemingway to tell us in his preface that during the time when he was writing this play the hotel in which he himself was living was struck by "more than thirty high-explosive shells." In fact, it makes it worse.

The recent political activity of Hemingway has thus unquestionably its unfortunate aspect in that the spy hunt of the Loyalists in Spain has given him a pretext for turning loose without check in his writing the impulse to contemplate cruelty which has always played such a large part in his work. This impulse has been balanced in the past by the complementary impulse to show suffering; and he has made himself the master of a peculiar moral malaise, the source of much of the beauty of his stories, which derives from his identifying himself at once with the injurer and the injured. But here he is simply free to let the sadistic impulse have its way. . . .

Now the bad news is told. Let us get on to the good. This book contains four new short stories which are among the best that Hemingway has written. The Short Happy Life of Francis Macomber seems to me to be one of his masterpieces. A story of big-game hunters in Africa, it is as good as "Green Hills of Africa" was bad. The difference between Hemingway's work when he is writing, on the one hand, objectively and when he is writing, on the other hand, directly about himself with a consciousness of what his public expects of him or about some character with whom it is easy for him to identify this public personality, is one of the odd phenomena of literature. The Short Happy Life of Francis Macomber deals with a theme that was implicit in "Green Hills of Africa," but it disengages and fully develops his theme.

So the story, in three pages, of the war in Spain—which might have been written about any war—is as telling as "The Fifth Column" is silly. Hemingway's hand is as firm, his taste as sure, in his handling of this little anecdote, where he is concentrating artistically on something outside him, as they are inept in his dispatches from Spain, now collected and published in England in the series of left monographs called "Fact," where he is always diverting attention to his own narrow escapes from danger (though these, too, contain a couple of excellent anecdotes). So the story called The Capital of the World, another of Hemingway's very best, projects and judges in a poetic symbol those very adolescent obsessions which tend to spoil his other work. A young boy who has come up from the country and waits on table in a pension in Madrid gets accidentally stabbed with a meat knife while playing at bull-fighting with the dishwasher. This is the anecdote, but Hemingway has built in behind it all the life of the pension and the city: the priesthood, the working-class movement, the grown-up bull-fighters who have broken down or missed out. . . .

The fourth story, The Snows of Kilimanjaro, another tragedy of African hunting, has some elements of the trashy moral attitudes which did such damage in "The Fifth Column" and "To Have and Have Not." Here the central male, formerly a seriously intentioned writer, has allowed himself to marry a rich woman and now is dying in futility in Africa. He goes back poignantly to his early days in

Paris, when he was happy, earnest, and poor, and he blames bitterly the rich bitch who has debased him. Yet this story, too, is one of the good ones. This new group of stories in general has more body than the last batch published in book form. There is a wonderful piece of writing at the end of The Snows of Kilimanjaro, in which the reader is made gradually to realize that what seems to be an escape by plane with the sick man looking down on Africa is only the dream of a dying man.

When Loyalist Madrid is as far behind Hemingway as his former adventures in Africa, he will no doubt get something out of them as much better than the melodrama of "The Fifth Column" as The Life of Francis Macomber is than "Green Hills of Africa." And in the meantime this omnibus volume, which contains all of Hemingway's short stories, represents one of the most considerable achievements of the American writing of our time, and ought, as they say, to be in every home.

Lionel Trilling. "Hemingway and His Critics." *Partisan Review*, 6 (Winter 1939), 52-60.

Between *The Fifth Column,* the play which makes the occasion for this large volume, and *The First Forty-Nine Stories,* which make its bulk and

its virtue, there is a difference of essence. For the play is the work of Hemingway the "man" and the stories are by Hemingway the "artist." This is a distinction which seldom enough means anything in criticism, but now and then an author gives us, as Hemingway gives us, writing of two such different kinds that there is a certain amount of validity and at any rate a convenience in making it. Once made, the distinction can better be elaborated than defined or defended. Hemingway the "artist" is conscious, Hemingway the "man" is self-conscious; the "artist" has a kind of innocence, the "man" a kind of naivety; the "artist" is disinterested, the "man" has a dull personal axe to grind; the "artist" has a perfect medium and tells the truth even if it be only *his* truth, but the "man" fumbles at communication and falsifies. As Edmund Wilson said in his "Letter to the Russians about Hemingway," which is the best estimate of our author that I know, "... something frightful seems to happen to Hemingway as soon as he begins to write in the first person. In his fiction, the conflicting elements of his personality, the emotional situations which obsess him, are externalized and objectified; and the result is an art which is severe, intense and deeply serious. But as soon as he talks in his own person, he seems to lose all his capacity for self-criticism and is likely to become fatuous or maudlin."

Mr. Wilson had in mind such specifically autobiographical and polemical works as *Green Hills of Africa* (and obviously he was not referring to the technical use of the first person in fictional narrative) but since the writing of the "Letter" in 1935, we may observe of Hemingway that the "man" has encroached upon the "artist" in his fiction. In *To Have and Have Not* and now in *The Fifth Column* the "first person" dominates and is the source of the failure of both works.

Of course it might be perfectly just to set down these failures simply to a lapse of Hemingway's talent. But there is, I think, something else to be said. For as one compares the high virtues of Hemingway's stories with the weakness of his latest novel and his first play, although one is perfectly aware of all that must be charged against the author himself, what forces itself into consideration is the cultural atmosphere which has helped to bring about the recent falling off. Insofar as we can ever blame a critical tradition for a writer's failures, we must, I believe, blame American criticism for the illegitimate emergence of Hemingway the "man" and the resultant inferiority of his two recent major works.

It is certainly true that criticism of one kind or another has played an unusually important part in Hemingway's career. Perhaps no American talent has so publicly developed as Hemingway's: more than any writer of our time he has been under glass, watched, checked up on, predicted, suspected, warned. One part of his audience took from him new styles of writing, of love-making, of very being; this was the simpler part, but its infatuate imitation was of course a kind of criticism. But another section of his audience responded negatively, pointing out that the texture of Hemingway's

work was made up of cruelty, religion, anti-intellectualism, even of basic fascism, and looked upon him as the active proponent of evil. Neither part of such an audience could fail to make its impression upon a writer. The knowledge that he had set a fashion and become a legend may have been gratifying but surely also burdensome and depressing, and it must have offered no small temptation. Yet perhaps more difficult for Hemingway to support with equanimity, and, from our point of view, much more important, was the constant accusation that he had attacked good human values. For upon Hemingway were turned all the fine social feelings of the now passing decade, all the noble sentiments, all the desperate optimism, all the extreme rationalism, all the contempt of irony and indirection—all the attitudes which, in the full tide of the liberal-radical movement, became dominant in our thought about literature. There was demanded of him earnestness and pity, social consciousness, as it was called, something "positive" and "constructive" and literal. For is not life a simple thing and is not the writer a villain or a counterrevolutionary who does not see it so?

As if under the pressure of this critical tradition, which persisted in mistaking the "artist" for the "man," Hemingway seems to have undertaken to vindicate the "man" by showing that he, too, could muster the required "social" feelings in the required social way. At any rate, he now brought the "man" with all his contradictions and conflicts into his fiction. But "his ideas about life,"—I quote Edmund

Wilson again— "or rather his sense of what happens and the way it happens is in his stories sunk deep below the surface and is not conveyed by argument or preaching but by directly transmitted emotion: it is turned into something as hard as crystal and as disturbing as a great lyric. When he expounds this sense of life, however, in his own character of Ernest Hemingway, the Old Master of Key West, he has a way of sounding silly." If, however, the failures of Hemingway "in his own character" were apparent to the practitioners of his critical tradition, they did not want Hemingway's virtues—the something "hard" and "disturbing." Indeed, they were in a critical tradition that did not want artists at all; it wanted "men," recruits, and its apologists were delighted to enlist Hemingway in his own character, with all his confusions and naivety, simply because Hemingway had not declared himself on the right side.

And so when *To Have And Have Not* appeared, one critic of the Left, grappling with the patent fact that the "artist" had failed, yet determined to defend the "man" who was his new ally, had no recourse save to explain that in this case failure was triumph because artistic fumbling was the mark of Hemingway's attempt to come to grips with the problems of modern life which were as yet too great for his art to encompass. Similarly, another critic of the Left, faced with the aesthetic inferiority of Hemingway's first play, takes refuge in praising the personal vindication which the "man" has made by "taking sides against fascism." In other words, the "man" has been a sad

case and long in need of regeneration; the looseness of thought and emotion, the easy and uninteresting idealism of the social feelings to which Hemingway now gives such sudden and literal expression are seen as the grateful signs of a personal reformation.

But the disinterested reader does not have to look very deep to see that Hemingway's social feelings, whatever they may yet become, are now the occasion for indulgence in the "man." His two recent failures are failures not only in form but in feeling; one looks at *To Have and Have Not* and *The Fifth Column,* one looks at their brag, and their disconcerting forcing of the emotions, at their downright priggishness, and then one looks at the criticism which, as I conceive it, made these failures possible by demanding them and which now accepts them so gladly, and one is tempted to reverse the whole liberal-radical assumption about literature. One almost wishes to say to an author like Hemingway, "You have no duty, no responsibility. Literature, in a political sense, is not in the least important. Wherever the sword is drawn it is mightier than the pen. Whatever you can do as a man, you can win no wars as an artist."

Very obviously this would not be the whole truth, yet saying it might counteract the crude and literal theory of art to which, in varying measure, we have all been training ourselves for a decade. We have conceived the artist to be a man perpetually on the spot, who must always report to us his precise moral and political latitude and longitude. Not that for a moment we would consider shaping our own political ideas by his; but we who of course turn for political guidance to newspapers, theorists, or historians, create the fiction that thousands—not, to be sure, ourselves—are waiting on the influence of the creative artist, and we stand by to see if he is leading us as he properly should. We consider then that we have exalted the importance of art, and perhaps we have. But in doing so we have quite forgotten how complex and subtle art is and, if it is to be "used," how very difficult it is to use it.

One feels that Hemingway would never have thrown himself into his new and inferior work if the necessity had not been put upon him to justify himself before this magisterial conception of literature. Devoted to literalness, the critical tradition of the Left took Hemingway's symbols for his intention, saw in his stories only cruelty or violence or a calculated indifference, and turned upon him a barrage of high-mindedness—that liberal-radical highmindedness that is increasingly taking the place of thought among the "progressive professional and middle class forces" and that now, under the name of "good will" shuts out half the world. Had it seen what was actually in Hemingway's work, it would not have forced him out of his idiom of the artist and into the idiom of the man which he speaks with difficulty and without truth.

For what should have been always obvious is that Hemingway is a writer who, when he writes as an "artist," is passionately and aggressively concerned with truth and even with social truth. And with this in mind, one might begin the consideration of his

virtues with a glance at Woodrow Wilson. Hemingway has said that all genuine American writing comes from the prose of Huckleberry Finn's voyage down the Mississippi and certainly his own starts there. But Huck's prose is a sort of moral symbol. It is the antithesis to the Widow Douglas—to the pious, the respectable, the morally plausible. It is the prose of the free man seeing the world as it really is. And Woodrow Wilson was, we might say, Hemingway's Widow Douglas. To the sensitive men who went to war it was not, perhaps, death and destruction that made the disorganizing shock. It was perhaps rather that death and destruction went on at the instance and to the accompaniment of the fine grave words, of which Woodrow Wilson's speeches were the finest and gravest. Here was the issue of liberal theory; here in the bloated or piecemeal corpse was the outcome of the words of humanitarianism and ideals; this was the work of presumably careful men of good will, learned men, polite men. The world was a newspaper world, a state-paper world, a memorial speech world. Words were trundled smoothly o'er the tongue—Coleridge had said it long ago—

> *Like mere abstractions, empty sounds to which*
> *We join no feeling and attach no form*
> *As if the soldier died without a wound . . .*
> *Passed off to Heaven, translated and not killed.*

Everyone in that time had feelings, as they called them; just as everyone has "feelings" now. And it seems to me that what Hemingway wanted first to do was to get rid of the "feelings," the comfortable liberal humanitarian feelings: and to replace them with the truth.

Not cynicism, I think, not despair, as so often is said, but this admirable desire shaped his famous style and his notorious set of admirations and contempts. The trick of understatement or tangential statement sprang from this desire. Men had made so many utterances in such fine language that it had become time to shut up. Hemingway's people, as everyone knows, are afraid of words and ashamed of them and the line from his stories which has become famous is the one that begins "Won't you please," goes on through its innumerable "pleases" and ends, "stop talking." Not only slain men but slain words made up the mortality of the war.

Another manifestation of the same desire in Hemingway was his devotion to the ideal of technique as an end in itself. A great deal can go down in the tumble but one of the things that stands best is a cleanly done job. As John Peale Bishop says in his admirable essay on Hemingway (which yet, I feel, contributes to the general misapprehension by asserting the evanescence of Hemingway's "compassion"), professional pride is one of the last things to go. Hemingway became a devotee of his own skill and he exploited the ideal of skill in his characters. His admired men always do a good job; and the proper handling of a rod, a gun, an espada or a pen is a thing, so Hemingway seems always to

be saying, which can be understood when speech cannot.

This does not mean that Hemingway attacks mind itself, a charge which has often been brought against him. It is perhaps safe to say that whenever he seems to be making such an attack, it is not so much *reason* as it is *rationalization* that he resists; "mind" appears simply as the complex of false feelings. And against "mind" in this sense he sets up what he believes to be the primal emotions, among others pain and death, met not with the mind but with techniques and courage. "Mind" he sees as a kind of castrating knife, cutting off people's courage and proper self-love, making them "reasonable," which is to say dull and false. There is no need to point out how erroneous his view would have been were it really mind that was in question, but in the long romantic tradition of the attitude it never really *is* mind that is in question but rather a dull overlay of mechanical negative proper feeling, or a falseness of feeling which people believe to be reasonableness and reasonable virtue. And when we think how quickly "mind" capitulates in a crisis, how quickly, for example, it accommodated itself to the war and served it and glorified it, revulsion from it and a turning to the life of action—reduced, to be sure, to athleticism: but skilful physical effort is perhaps something intellectuals too quickly dismiss as a form of activity—can be the better understood. We can understand too the insistence on courage, even on courage deliberately observed in its purity: that is, when it is at the service of the most sordid desires, as in "Fifty Grand."

This, then, was Hemingway's vision of the world. Was it a complete vision? Of course it was not. Was it a useful vision? That depended. If it was true, it was useful—if we knew how to use it. But the use of literature is not easy. In our hearts most of us are Platonists in the matter of art and we feel that we become directly infected by what we read; or at any rate we want to be Platonists, and we carry on a certain conviction from our Tom Swift days that literature provides chiefly a means of identification and emulation. The Platonist view is not wholly to be dismissed; we *do* in a degree become directly infected by art; but the position is too simple. And we are further Platonistic in our feeling that literature must be religious: we want our attitudes formulated by the tribal bard. This, of course, gives to literature a very important function. But it forgets that literature has never "solved," though it may perhaps provide part of the data for eventual solutions.

With this attitude we asked, Can Hemingway's people speak only with difficulty? and we answered, Then it surely means that he thinks people should not speak. Does he find in courage the first of virtues? Then it surely means that we should be nothing but courageous. Is he concerned with the ideas of death and of violence? Then it must mean that to him these are good things.

In short, we looked for an emotional leader. We did not conceive Hemingway to be saying, Come, let us look at the world together. We supposed him

to be saying, Come, it is your moral duty to be as my characters are. We took the easiest and simplest way of using the artist and decided that he was not the "man" for us. That he was a man and a Prophet we were certain; and equally certain that he was not the "man" we would want to be or the Prophet who could lead us. That, as artist, he was not concerned with being a "man" did not occur to us. We had, in other words, quite overlooked the whole process of art, overlooked style and tone, symbol and implication, overlooked the obliqueness and complication with which the artist may criticize life, and assumed that what Hemingway saw or what he put into his stories he wanted to have exist in the actual world.

In short, the criticism of Hemingway came down to a kind of moral-political lecture, based on the assumption that art is—or should be—the exact equivalent of life. The writer would have to be strong indeed who could remain unmoved by the moral pressure that was exerted upon Hemingway. He put away the significant reticences of the artist, opened his heart like "a man," and the flat literalness, the fine, fruity social idealism of the latest novel and the play are the result.

The Fifth Column is difficult to speak of. Summary is always likely to be a critical treachery, but after consulting the summaries of those who admire the work and regard it as a notable event, it seems fair to say that it is the story of a tender-tough American hero with the horrors, who does counter-espionage in Madrid, though everybody thinks he is just a playboy, who fears that he will no longer do his work well if he continues his liaison with an American girl chiefly remarkable for her legs and her obtuseness; and so sacrifices love and bourgeois pleasure for the sake of duty. Hemingway as a playwright gives up his tools of suggestion and tone and tells a literal story—an adventure story of the Spanish war, at best the story of the regeneration of an American Pimpernel of not very good intelligence.

It is this work which has been received with the greatest satisfaction by a large and important cultural group as the fulfilment and vindication of Hemingway's career, as a fine document of the Spanish struggle, and as a political event of significance, "a sign of the times," as one reviewer called it. To me it seems none of these things. It does not vindicate Hemingway's career because that career in its essential parts needs no vindication; and it does not fulfill Hemingway's career because that career has been in the service of fine feelings. Nor can I believe that the Spanish war is represented in any good sense by a play whose symbols are so sentimentally personal* and whose dra-

matic tension is so weak; and it seems to me that there is something even vulgar in making Spain serve as a kind of mental hospital for disorganized foreigners who, out of a kind of self-contempt, turn to the "ideal of the Spanish people." Nor, finally, can I think that Hemingway's statement of an anti-fascist position is of great political importance or of more than neutral virtue. It is hard to believe that the declaration of anti-facsism is nowadays any more a mark of sufficient grace in a writer than a declaration against disease would be in a physician or a declaration against accidents would be in a locomotive engineer. The admirable intention in itself is not enough and criticism begins and does not end when the intention is declared.

But I believe that judgments so simple as these will be accepted with more and more difficulty. The "progressive professional and middle class forces" are framing a new culture, based on the old liberal-radical culture but designed now to hide the new anomaly by which they live their intellectual and emotional lives. For they must believe, it seems, that imperialist arms advance proletarian revolution, that oppression by the right people brings liberty. Like Hemingway's latest hero, they show one front to the world and another to themselves, know that within they are true proletarian men while they wrap themselves in Early American togas; they are enthralled by their own good will; they are people of fine feelings and they dare not think lest the therapeutic charm vanish. This is not a political essay and I am not here concerned with the political con-

---

*In fairness to Hemingway the disclaimer of an important intention which he makes in his Preface should be cited. Some people, he says, have objected that his play does not present "the nobility and dignity of the cause of the Spanish people. It does not attempt to. It will take many plays and novels to do that, and the best ones will be written after the war is over." And he goes on: "This is only a play about counter espionage in Madrid. It has the defects of having been written in war time, and if it has a moral it is that people who work for certain organizations have very little time for home life." I do not think that this exempts the play from severe judgment by those who dislike it, just as I think that those who admire it have a right to see in it as they do, a "sign of the times."

sequences of these things, bad though they be and worse though they will be, but only with the cultural consequences. For to prevent the anomaly from appearing in its genuine difficulty, e-motion—of a very limited kind—has been apotheosized and thought has been made almost a kind of treachery; the reviewer of *The Fifth Column* to whom I have already referred cites as a virtue Hemingway's "unintellectual" partisanship of the Spanish cause. The piety of "good will" has become e-nough and Fascism is conceived not as a force which complicates the world but as a force which simplifies the world—and so it does for any number of people of good will (of a good will not to be doubted, I should say) for whom the existence of an absolute theological evil makes non-existent any other evil.

It is this group that has made Hemingway its cultural hero and for reasons that need not be canvassed very far. Now that Hemingway has become what this group would call "affirmative" he has become insufficient; but insufficiency is the very thing this group desires. When Hemingway was in "negation" his themes of courage, loyalty, tenderness and silence, tangentially used, suggested much; but now that they are used literally and directly they say far less than the situation demands. His stories showed a great effort of comprehension and they demand a considerable effort from their readers, that effort in which lies whatever teaching power there is in art; but now he is not making an effort to understand but to accept, which may indeed be the effort of the honest po-

litical man but not of the honest artist.

An attempt has been made to settle the problem of the artist's relation to politics by loudly making the requirement that he give up his base individuality and rescue humanity and his own soul by becoming the mouthpiece of a party, a movement or a philosophy. That requirement has demonstrably failed as a solution of the problem; the problem, however, still remains. It may be, of course, that politics itself will settle the problem for us; it may be that in our tragic time art worthy the name cannot be produced and that we must live with the banalities of *The Fifth Column* or even with less. However, if the problem will be allowed to exist at all, it will not be solved in theory and on paper but in practice. And we have, after all, the practice of the past to guide us at least with a few tentative notions. We can learn to stop pressing the writer with the demand for contemporaneity when we remember the simple fact that writers have always written directly to and about the troubles of their own time and for and about their contemporaries, some in ways to us more obvious than others but all responding inevitably to what was happening around them. We can learn too that the relation of an artist to his culture, whether that culture be national or the culture of a relatively small recusant group, is a complex and even a contradictory relation: the artist must accept his culture and be accepted by it, but also—so it seems—he must be its critic, correcting and even rejecting it according to his personal insight; his strength seems to come from the tension of this ambiva-

lent situation and we must learn to
welcome the ambivalence. Finally, and
simplest of all, we learn not to expect
a political, certainly not an immediately political, effect from a work of art;
and in removing from art a burden of
messianic responsibility which it never
has discharged and cannot discharge
we may leave it free to do whatever it
actually can do.

Checklist of
Additional Reviews

Richard Croom Beatty. *Nashville Ban-
    ner,* November 2, 1938, p. 4-X.
Booklist, 35 (November 15, 1938), 98.
Russell Maloney. "A Footnote to a
    Footnote." *New Yorker,* 15 (July
    15, 1939), 26.

Notes

THE FIFTH COLUMN

A PLAY IN THREE ACTS

By

ERNEST

HEMINGWAY

NEW YORK
CHARLES SCRIBNER'S SONS
1940

The Fifth Column

John Mason Brown.
" 'Fifth Column' Opens
with Ulric and Tone."
New York Post,
March 7, 1940,
p. 10.

It is a pity Cupid has to pull so long and fabulous a bow in the war in Spain as Benjamin Glazer makes him do in his freely rewritten version of Ernest Hemingway's published drama, "The Fifth Column." Because Cupid does not take his place in the ranks . . . [sic] even behind local footlights . . . as a reliable combatant against General Franco and the forces of Fascism. His darts and his "darlings," his love potions and his boudoir crises, appear somehow irredeemably irrelevant, as trivial at the Alvin, at least from this safe distance, as they now seem very much beside the point compared to what was at stake in Spain.

If Cupid's promotion to the status of commandant in Mr. Glazer's adaptation of Mr. Hemingway's play is doubly regrettable it is because "The Fifth Column" (as written, rewritten, and produced) has its undeniable virtues. It may lack to an incredible extent the magical touches of Mr. Hemingway's authorship. It may dawdle for scene after scene over a love story which is at best unconvincing. Its form may be far from perfect.

But obviously it has something to say. And no less plainly, in spite of its ineptitudes, it does possess its unmistakable authenticity whenever it deals brutally with the brutalities of modern war. Furthermore, it proves far more interesting, even in its in-and-out manner, than the printed script would have led one to expect. . . .

* * *

As it reached the stage last night it is a many-scened dramatization of those very principles of idealistic devotion which Maxwell Anderson stated in his much better and more passionately written prologue to "Key Largo." In this case Mr. Tone plays an American journalist in Spain turned second rate cop, as he puts it, who finally decides to abandon marrying the American girl with whom he has fallen in love (after raping her in this version) to sacrifice himself in the fight against Fascism. Just why he could not have married the girl and stayed in Madrid, even to die, is something Mr. Glazer and Mr. Hemingway never quite get around to making clear. But their presidential point is that the frontiers of democracy begin wherever liberty is threatened. And this they manage to get stated far more effectively than they do to dramatize their long-winded and extraneous romance.

* * *

But the sorry truth is that, though the script is excellently acted in most cases and holds the attention fairly well, its virtues are mainly deceptive because of the lack of distinction and genuine relevance in its writing. Somehow at the end of an evening which is only pretty good, you feel as if a very skillful magician had been trying to make you believe that 1 and 1 makes 5, and as if at moments you had been fooled into believing that they did.

Richard Watts, Jr. "The Theatres." *New York Herald Tribune,* March 7, 1940, p. 16.

Mr. Hemingway's play has had many adventures of one sort or another since he wrote it in the shell-wracked Hotel Florida in besieged Madrid back in the grim and terrible days of the Fascist war in Spain. Now, after a long and troubled sojourn in Philadelphia, Boston and Baltimore, it reaches town in an adaptation by Benjamin Glazer as a Theater Guild production, and it can be said that the result is surprisingly impressive. Something of Hemingway has gone out of it and something of Hollywood has gone in as a natural result of the author's willingness to leave his script unprotected in the hands of others and "The Fifth Column" shows resulting signs of discomfort in its determination to tell a sort of love story. In fact, whenever it goes into its romance, the play has an unhappy way of standing still. Yet happily a great deal of the spirit and heroism and horror of valiant wartime Madrid clings to the drama and, splendidly played by an excellent cast, it emerged in its Theater Guild manifestation as a striking and powerful, if not always satisfying, work.

Unquestionably "The Fifth Column" is at its best in its earlier sections, although it pulls itself together in time for a proper ending. . . .

So much war and international chicanery and shifting of allegiance have taken place since the days of the assault on Republican Spain that "The Fifth Column" might seem in danger of appearing outmoded to current audiences. Perhaps, too, as a guest of the hospitable Hotel Florida during the siege of Madrid, I found an additional personal interest in the new play. It seems to me, however, that not only has something of a heroic atmosphere been captured by the drama, but that something of the importance of a struggle, which, had it turned out differently, might conceivably have kept the present war from Europe's doors has been suggested. In at least one character too—that of the stalwart German anti-Fascist, who has been tortured by the Nazis—a quality of true valor and gallantry of spirit has been set down. Most of the minor characters are vividly drawn, also, although the role of the central figure has been less clearly presented than it should have been and the part of the heroine seems completely vapid.

* * *

"The Fifth Column" has its share of defects but it is an interesting play for all that.

Brooks Atkinson. "Ernest Hemingway's 'The Fifth Column' Put on by Theatre Guild–Drama of Spanish Civil War." *New York Times,* March 7, 1940, p. 18.

After passing through so many hands that many of us despaired ever seeing it produced, Ernest Hemingway's "The Fifth Column" opened at the Alvin Theatre last evening. Adapted by Benjamin Glazer and produced by the Theatre Guild with an excellent cast, it was well worth the wait. Most of it is a strikingly convincing drama of the deadly night and day struggle of Madrid under siege, and it rings with a metallic resonance of Hemingway writing on a contemporary subject.

In this tense story of love and war Hemingway's hero Philip Rawlings is engaged in the business of tracking down fascist agents inside the besieged city. In his more desperate moments of tormented conscience Rawlings turns to a politically indifferent American girl and is briefly tempted to desert the cause and leave with her to a neutral country. The love affair,

though it has a certain genuineness about it, seems commonplace beside the intensely harrowing struggle of Rawlings and his fellow counter-espionage agents to do their dirty but necessary work. When Hemingway tells how they bring themselves to do their sickening business against all their natural instincts and sympathies, his story blazes with sincerity. In contrast with these scenes the second act of love quarrels and debates on doing one's duty seems less dramatic and relies too much on stump speech rhetoric.

The play never fully recovers the grim candor of the beginning after the early second act. In spite of its unevenness, though, Mr. Hemingway's play has gotten under the skin of a vital subject and he has turned his emotionally raw theme into a courageous statement of principle. (Summary)

Joseph Wood Krutch. "The Fifth Column." *The Nation,* 150 (March 16, 1940), 371-72.

"The Fifth Column" was written and published in play form by Ernest Hemingway. It was "adapted" by Benjamin Glazer and has now been performed by the Guild at the Alvin Theater. If a consensus of reviewers' opinions is sufficient evidence, it is a fine play and ought to be a great success. In my judgment, however, it is not quite the first nor very likely to become quite the second.

Mr. Hemingway's report on the war

in Spain begins well. In fact, the first of the two acts is, in its entirety, tense and absorbing. But the expectations created by that first act are never fulfilled, and despite sincere, perhaps even brilliant acting and staging the very subject matter itself seems to elude the authors, and what had begun as a complex picture of life in a war-torn city ends stagily as the love story of a hard-boiled hero whose grandiose gestures may be authentic but are too familiar and expected to carry very deep conviction. The fault does not seem to lie where one would have been most inclined to expect a fault, for the writing in the first act at least is not only vivid and terse but little marred by the tendency toward exhibitionism which is its author's besetting sin. He does not wear his lack of heart on his sleeve; he is not, to revive the familiar taunt, too overwhelmingly aware of the hair on his chest. But he does abandon a complex and difficult subject for one that is relatively easy and already stereotyped, with the result that the spectator finds his interest declining step by step after the midpoint of the play has been reached and as the themes which had been brilliantly suggested in the first half of the piece recede farther and farther into the background.

These themes are all concerned in one way or another with the difficulty of reconciling the aims of a holy war with the methods which it must inevitably use, and with the contrast inevitably apparent between the cause for which one is fighting and the individuals in whose name the cause is fought for. It is not merely that the hero, a young American correspondent who has been drawn by his sympathy for the Loyalist government into the dangerous business of counter-espionage, cannot fail to realize that the drunken electrician of the hotel in which he lives is no very inspiring specimen of that proletariat for which he is endangering his life; it is also that his superior, the officer in charge of espionage, has been completely dehumanized by the process of fighting for humanity, and that the ruthlessness which he himself believes to be necessary remains nevertheless debasing when it is translated into a concrete instance—when, for instance, he has to bully a frightened boy wrongly suspected of treachery or shoot a fat German general in the back when the latter, a captive, will not walk fast enough. But these themes, brilliantly suggested, are never fully treated, and they are, I think, left undeveloped, not because they are not what the author is really interested in, but because it is plainly so much easier to develop instead the easily managed story of the hero's love affair with an American girl and his final decision not to follow her out of Spain to safety. Probably both original author and adapter are familiar with the fact that puzzled critics of the drama often fall back upon the statement that a play under discussion "doesn't come to a focus." The trouble with "The Fifth Column" is that it does—at the wrong place. In the opening scenes several themes are in solution, and it is the least interesting of all that crystallizes.

In the past, when Mr. Hemingway has been beset with doubts he has sometimes seemed to imply that the sensible thing for any modern man faced with a difficult problem to do is just to forget all about it and go out and kill somone, or failing that, some animal—even if it is only a lion in Africa or a skilfully tortured bull in an arena. In the present instance there is little suggestion of that attitude, and he ends instead with a careful debate in which the girl who argues that Americans should leave dying Europe to wallow in its own blood is answered by a German refugee who explains that fascism cannot be fought with any chance of success except upon its own frontier. But the difficulty with this last conclusion is simply that by the time one has got around to it in the last few minutes of the performance the whole play has become so artificial that the argument has ceased to seem very real and has become merely the inevitable end of a play.

* * *

Wolcott Gibbs. "Saint Dorothy." *New Yorker,* 16 (March 16, 1940), 44.

In his published version of "The Fifth Column" Mr. Hemingway presented his heroine Dorothy Bridges as a beautiful and expensive embodiment of nostalgia, a half-contemptuous, half-rueful symbol of what men give up to spend their lives working for a cause. A figure out of Anita Loos and *Vogue* and *Harper's Bazaar,* she wants to take her man away to some glittering place where they can enjoy skiing and champagne cocktails and associate with other people in nice clothes.

In Benjamin Glazer's adaptation of the play there is not much left of the original Dorothy but her political vagueness. In his new version of Dorothy the final impression is that she would rather take Philip Rawlings home to Scarsdale and have him join the Chamber of Commerce. In the big renunciation scene she talks like a female Sidney Carton, except that instead of wanting to exchange duty for pure love she wants an exchange of duty for old pleasures. That is something of the subtle shift of values that takes place in this Broadway version of Hemingway's war play of Madrid under siege.

Mr. Glazer also seems to have forgotten the words of another and earlier Hemingway hero. In "A Farewell to Arms" the author's half-articulate narrator tells how he is always embarrassed by such words as "sacred," "glorious," "sacrifice," and "in vain." In this adaptation too many expressions like these seem to have crept into the script. Some of the speeches sound much nobler than they did when Hemingway wrote the originals as shells slammed into the Hotel Florida.

Despite these exchanges of values, the play is astonishingly good. The quality of Hemingway's dialogue is still present even if it has been slicked up for Broadway. Even more important it retains the sense of sickness and disgust of Philip Rawlings as he does what has to be done. It is emphatically worth seeing. (Summary)

George Jean Nathan. "Oscar Bait." *Newsweek,* 15 (March 18, 1940), 52.

The new production of *The Fifth Column* at the Alvin reveals some strange literary-dramatic associations. Movie scenarist Benjamin Glazer's adaptation of Hemingway's published play results in a Hollywood-style prettying up of the novelist's austere drama of anti-Francoism. On the whole the enterprise lacks such inner organization and clear directness that it could profit from the model of even a William Saroyan production.

As anyone knows who read it, the Hemingway play was far from being dramatically satisfactory. In the Glazer amendment it is even further from being critically satisfactory. Glazer's attempt to develop the stage action around the boy-meets-girl element puts him in even more difficulty than Lawrence Stallings found himself some years ago with his dramatization of *A Farewell to Arms.* When he lets Hemingway have his own say, the play takes on an urgent sincerity, but when he perches Charlie McCarthy-like on Hemingway's lap and speaks for him, the sincerity takes on a strained, mechanical quality. As a playwright Hemingway may throw away his dramatic opportunities in his urgency to make his point. As his adapter, Glazer is too concerned with keeping the dramatic niceties to keep the issues alive. Of the two, I prefer the Hemingway approach, whatever it may cost him theatrically. (Summary)

"Revamp Till Ready." *Time,* 35 (March 18, 1940), 65-67.

When Ernest Hemingway finished *The Fifth Column* in November 1937, the Spanish war was big news and Hemingway was there in Madrid covering it. The provocative question was who would be the lucky producer to do the play.

Since then the news has changed and so have the fortunes of the play. When it was published in the fall of 1938, *The Fifth Column* won critical acclaim and producers were dickering for it. It looked as if Producer Jed Harris had won, but Hemingway and Harris couldn't agree on revisions. Harris bowed out. Austin Parker died a few days after taking an option on the play. After more revisions and refusals Hemingway agreed to let Hollywood writer Benjamin Glazer rewrite it. In December the Theatre Guild announced forthcoming production.

When it opened last week *The Fifth Column* sounded more like a too-familiar gramaphone record of the Spanish war story than a news broadcast from Madrid. Neither did it sound much like Hemingway's play. In Glazer's adaptation it was more a general tale of war than a personal memoir. It included melodrama as well as drama, romantic love in place of sexual passion, moral crises instead of psychological conflict.

The play that Hemingway wrote was a more somber picture of Madrid at war. In stage terms it was less dramatic but more real, it lacked "big scenes" but showed Death in the Afternoon with a new and casually horrifying meaning. The acting version achieves exciting theater in the first half as it explores Hemingway hero Philip Rawlings' struggle between the idealism that made him take on a sickening job and the nausea induced by the job itself. The second half develops the worn-out conflict of love versus duty and its romantic twaddle nearly sinks the play. The love affair is flimsy and unreal and not all Glazer's theatrical expertise can bring it to life. After that only eloquent rhetoric holds the play together and nothing is less like Ernest Hemingway than eloquent rhetoric. (Summary)

Stark Young. "Mr. Tone and Mr. Hemingway." *New Republic*, 102 (March 25, 1940), 408.

* * *

Nearly everyone at times reading some book of Mr. Hemingway's must have noted its dramatic quality and felt that it would make good theatre. There is not space to go into the discussion, but only to note that a thing's being highly dramatic does not necessarily mean that it is to that degree theatric. It may in fact be dramatic without being even possible for the stage at all. As for the Hemingway writing, I have of course read many pages where the stage possibilities seemed immense. At the same time, however, it was plain what a rare method would be needed to create the stage elements that must be added, and especially to do the necessary projection. In such a style of writing the matter of projection is a special problem, quite beyond the method and concentration of most of our directors and players.

The play tells the story of a newspaperman who has gone to Spain to join the fight against fascism. He serves as a sort of "second-hand cop," has a Spanish prostitute on the side, finds an American girl in the same hotel with him, rapes her—he is drunk at the moment—and falls in love with her. She too finally confesses her love for him; the war ends with fascism victorious under Franco; the two lovers plan to marry, they are to meet in France; she learns that the brother she came to find is dead; her lover arranges her departure. The German fighter, with the scarred face, has a final say about devoting his life all through the cause of liberty, and the American decides not to join the girl as promised.

Such a dénouement gets nowhere. The character may behave as he likes, but the author is expected to see and judge his matter in scale as it were, and with reference to some point of view. And with all this coming overseas to Spain to die for liberty, for its sake giving up marriage, etc., etc., we should get some further definition of what this liberty is. Otherwise what remains has a very good chance of being largely gush, or cant, or impotent thinking, or some rehash of adolescent idealism and pubic vitality.

At its best this writing has at times the sense of some thrilling combination in reactions: at times it achieves a blaze of single motif, a complete isolation, that is unforgettable; and sometimes a handling of life, blood, sex, raw force that at its fullest pitch achieves a certain orgastic clarity that is superb. At its less good, or its worst, this writing can give the sense of mere canceling and tricky simplification; at times it gives a far too tricky impression of the glamor of the libido. The appeal then is obviously that of a certain effeminate virility.

As compared with the published text, Mr. Glazer has re-written the play with more space given to the love story, and has added rape. These love scenes often lack the character and excitement and so on of Mr. Hemingway's style; but the point of view, or attitude toward love between men and women, the approach to the subject, seem to me quite in accord with that found in the novels.

Many of the play's admirable qualities are so closely bound up with the directing and acting that it is practically impossible to distinguish which is which and where the credit most lies. Certainly this is the case with Mr. Tone, who achieves the finest effects of tenderness—sudden insight into the quick heart, and conveys to us perfectly that sort of lyrical shock method that the writing employs, and that nos-talgia for life—sweet wings that pass, that pass away.

And yet on the whole this play, whatever its limitations, is about something; about something even if now and again it is too much about something that is left out. Sometimes the writing itself is magical and thrilling, the interspaces of its mood filled with a breathless miracle....

* * *

It is interesting to consider what effect might have derived for Mr. Tone's role if the heroine had been left as she is in the original. There she is the predatory young woman journalist, looking for her own where she may find it—in this case near the battle lines in tortured Spain. She is, after a fashion, then, another horror; and the sex motive would thus have become an added complication harrowing the situation for him. His resolving not to join her in France would then be quite another thing. The dénouement would make for much better sense and unity of tone. At the same time the leading male role would become to a greater extent the central interest in the play, the medium through which war's character is portrayed; and for the actor playing it the source of greater singleness and concentration. The Glazer version, however, provides another sort of variety....

Rosamond Gilder. "War, Sacred and Profane." *Theatre Arts*, 24 (May 1940), 310-14.

Quite suddenly, at the wrong end of a sagging season, *The Fifth Column* crashed into town and the theatre woke up. Ernest Hemingway's play has been on the verge of production ever since it was written under shell fire in Madrid in 1937. Published in 1938, it now emerges, in Benjamin Glazer's adaptation, as the Theatre Guild's third offering of the season and one of the few plays of the year that demand serious consideration. Superbly acted, sensitively directed and effectively staged, *The Fifth Column* brings the breath of things lived into the close atmosphere of Broadway's show shop.

It is far from being a perfect play, but it is a good play, if a good play is one that rivets the attention of the listener, enlists his sympathy and drawn him into participation in the spiritual combat which takes place on the stage. The nature of that combat is clearly defined in Ernest Hemingway's text and further clarified—if somewhat sentimentalized—in Mr. Galzer's adaptation. It lies in the struggle in Philip Rawlings' mind between his normal desire for a decent, peaceful, kindly way of life, and the brutal necessities of action in a war-ridden world. . . .

Much of the effectiveness of the play lies in the forthright, pungent impact of Hemingway's dialogue. He can use the ordinary language of ordinary people, with its limited vocabulary, its worn formulas, its repetitious phrases and catchwords, with cumulative effect. His is not the organ note of an Odets, the *Kindersymphonie*—from pipes to double bass—of a Saroyan. He plays a single percussion instrument, but he plays it with remarkable variety—harsh, poignant, violent, tender, comic,—but always with a stroke that tells. Structurally Mr. Glazer's play is far more theatre-worthy than Mr. Hemingway's original version. In it scenes have been transposed; the character of Dorothy changed from that of a rather silly, selfish fool to a 'noble' if colorless creature, thereby creating a sharper contrast between Philip's actual life and the nostalgia for the wholesome and the good which she represents; the part of Max has been enlarged and the bases of his arguments broadened. But most of Hemingway's dialogue has been preserved, the chief character is his, as is the picture of war and its effect on those who wage it. Above all, the passion and horror of Hemingway's writing, the sense of desperate men engaged in desperate and perilous undertakings, the disgust with war, are preserved.

* * *

Checklist of Additional Reviews

Life, 8 (March 25, 1940), 100-01.

FOR WHOM
THE BELL TOLLS

By

ERNEST
HEMINGWAY

NEW YORK
CHARLES SCRIBNER'S SONS
1940

For Whom the Bell Tolls

Henry Seidel Canby.
"For Whom the Bell Tolls."
Book-of-the-Month Club News,
October, 1940,
pp. 2-3.

This is Hemingway's best book since *Farewell to Arms.* As that famous novel, now regarded as an American masterpiece, has been inaccurately described as a story of the Italian defeat at Caporetto in the last war, so *For Whom the Bell Tolls* will be, with equal inaccuracy, spoken of as a story of the Spanish Civil War. . . .

Like *Farewell to Arms,* this is actually the narrative of the reactions of a young man to danger, and a conflict of ideas and tense emotion. As in *Farewell to Arms,* a love story enters, quite accidentally, and becomes a vital part of the narrative. And let me say that Hemingway who has been celebrated for his toughness and brutality, has written in the sudden love story of Robert Jordan and his "rabbit" one of the most touching and perfect love stories in modern literature—a love story with a tragic ending which lifts rather than depresses the imagination.

The proper background for understanding a description of this fine romance is the famous series of drawings by the great Spanish artist, Goya, of a century ago, illustrating the horrors and realities of guerrilla warfare. In those celebrated prints one sees the strange Spanish peasant; cruel, yet capable of infinite loyalty; brave, because expecting suffering; ignorant of and indifferent to culture as we know it; but with an immense zest for living and an unexampled homely wisdom. These pictures show them with their fierce native emotions aroused by forces from the world outside, torturing and fighting and rescuing each other.

* * *

It is exceedingly difficult to make the prospective reader of this book feel the interest and tensity of these few days, because so much that happens results from the remarkable characters with whom Jordan finds himself associated, and from his own precarious position, an outsider in almost hourly danger of death or betrayal. At the end of it all, he says that the life of this band has become his life; among these peasants are his closest friends and most dangerous enemies. Both past and future seem shadowy in comparison with this life in hiding on the mountain. And that is the way the reader feels. These striking personalities, disengaged from the Spanish type by Hemingway's unequalled power of dramatization in dialogue, become so intimate and so self-expressive under the pressure of the events, that you have lived, felt, and thought with them—a triumph for a novelist. I do not know how true they are to a Spanish type; perhaps Hemingway does not. I do know that here is a group of fully realized human beings, real beyond question, even though the story in which they are involved is a psychological romance.

* * *

War is the scene of this novel, as of pretty much everything else nowadays; but it is a magnificent romance of human nature quite apart from and above its environment of civil war.

John Chamberlain. "Hemingway Tells How Men Meet Death." *New York Herald Tribune Books*, 17 (October 20, 1940), 1, 2.

In one sense Ernest Hemingway's long-awaited novel of the Spanish civil war is a simple reworking of the basic theme of "A Farewell to Arms": boy meets girl amid the detritus of war, boy and girl manage to live an idyll for a brief, surcharged moment, and so on, with appropriate Hemingway philosophizing about guts. . . . In "A Farewell to Arms" it was the ability of two waifs to snatch a moment of love amid a senseless carnage that was important. In "For Whom the Bell Tolls" the idyll remains the same, but the warfare is

no longer an idiot's delight, it has become meaningful and important—and love must always be secondary to honor. Hemingway may once have blushed for the world's hypocrisy when he heard the words "heroism" and "patriotism"; as intellectual coinage he rated them as clamshells or wampum. Now, however, he seems certain they are the real valuta. . . .

The new "return to arms" is a story that has something for everybody. On one level it is a thriller which yields nothing to Malraux's "Man's Fate"—or, for that matter, to Nick Carter or "The Perils of Pauline." It moves along from high spot to high spot with tumultuous abandon, the style purged of all the early Hemingway preoccupation with finicky Steinesque internal rhyme schemes. The "lean, hard, athletic" prose is less a matter of biceps now, and more a matter of nervous drive. On another level "For Whom the Bell Tolls" is a political novel: Hemingway believes that the battle for Spain was the first battle in the war that is now raging in the eastern Mediterranean and over the English Channel. (The title is a cryptic reminder from John Donne that a human loss anywhere hurts the human race everywhere.) And on still another level the novel is a paean to the landscape and spirit of Spain, a country which Hemingway knows far more intimately than he does his own. The Spanish character, with its urge to the auto da fé and its delight in blasphemy, fascinates him; he likes people who think the imminent prospect of death is the only thing that can add a real fillip to life. Finally, the novel has a faint touch of a very terrible satire: Hemingway seems to be hinting that all noble causes must end in the triumph of the bureaucrat, the routineer and the heresy-hunter. Nevertheless, men must fight for what they believe: that is the glory and the tragedy of man and the material for great art. Ahab may never triumph over the whale, yet the chase must go on.

* * *

It has taken Hemingway a long time to reach the point of writing this superb series of annotations on how a great variety of men go to meet their Maker. In his stories of the First World War death is something to be avoided and forgotten; one must not be yellow, of course, but bravery was a personal matter and had nothing to do with the needs of society. . . .

The new Hemingway, however, redeems a decade of futility. With the writing of "For Whom the Bell Tolls" it becomes apparent that Hemingway is not made for a peace-time world; he is born to be the chronicler of warring man, and he must have a war in which he can believe to lend dignity to an art that degenerates the minute it is touched with skepticism. Fortunately for both Hemingway and his reader, the Spanish loyalists fought a worthy war. And because the end in view justifies the deaths of Anselmo and Fernando and Robert Jordan and El Sordo, the deaf guerrilla, Hemingway can follow these fated and noble human beings through their last moments with a passionate regard that enables him to plumb the depths and scale the heights of human existence on a lim-

ited planet under an ultimately pitiless sky. Robert Jordan and Maria living in a suburban town in America would never make sense, but Robert Jordan and Maria as a pair whose lives are dedicated to the Spanish Republican cause even more than they are dedicated to each other makes for some tense, beautiful and infinitely tender writing.

* * *

J. Donald Adams. "The New Novel by Hemingway." *New York Times Book Review,* October 20, 1940, p. 1.

This is the best book Ernest Hemingway has written, the fullest, the deepest, the truest. It will, I think, be one of the major novels in American literature.

There were those of us who felt, when "To Have and Have Not" was published, that Hemingway was through as a creative writer. That is always a dangerous assumption to make regarding any writer of much innate ability, but it did seem that Hemingway was blocked off from further development. We were badly mistaken. Technical skill he had long ago acquired; the doubt lay in where and how he could apply it, and that doubt he has now sweepingly erased. The skill is even further sharpened than it was, but with it has come an inner growth, a deeper and surer feeling for life, than he has previously displayed. Whatever brought about this growth— whether his experience of the Spanish war, out of which this novel was made, or something else, it is plainly to be seen in this book, from beginning to end. There are no traces of adolescence in the Hemingway of "For Whom the Bell Tolls." This is the work of a mature artist of a mature mind.

* * *

The title derives from John Donne....

It is a fine title, and an apt one, for this is a book filled with the imminence of death, and the manner of man's meeting it. That is as it should be; this is a story of the Spanish war. But in it Hemingway has struck universal chords, and he has struck them vibrantly. Perhaps it conveys something of the measure of "For Whom the Bell Tolls" to say that with that theme, it is not a depressing but an uplifting book. It has the purging quality that lies in the presenting of tragic but profound truth. Hemingway has freed himself from the negation that held him in his other novels....

...And as "For Whom the Bell Tolls" is a better story of action than "A Farewell to Arms" so too is this a finer love story than that of Lieutenant Henry and Catherine Barkley. That is saying a good deal, but it is true. I know of no love scenes in American fiction and few in any other to compare with those of "For Whom the Bell Tolls" in depth and sincerity of feeling. They are unerringly right, and as much beyond those of "A Farewell to Arms" as the latter were beyond

the casual couplings of "The Sun Also Rises."

The book holds, I think, the best character drawing that Hemingway has done. Robert Jordan is a fine portrait of a fighting idealist and the Spanish figures are superbly done, in particular the woman Pilar, who should take her place among the memorable women of fiction—earthy and strong, tender, hard, wise, a woman who, as she said of herself, would have been a good man and yet was a woman made for men. The brutal, unstable Pablo, in whom strength and evil were combined, the good and brave old man Anselmo—these and others are warmly living in this heroic story.

I wrote once that Ernest Hemingway can see and describe with a precision and a vividness unmatched since Kipling first displayed his great visual gift. There are scenes in this book finer than any he has done. The telling of how the Civil Guard was shot in Pablo's town and how the fascists were beaten to death between rows of men armed with flails and hurled over a cliff into the river 300 feet below, how the fascists walked out one by one from their prayers in the City Hall and severally met their deaths, has the thrust and power of one of the more terrible of Goya's pictures.

In all that goes to make a good novel "For Whom the Bell Tolls" is an advance beyond Hemingway's previous work. It is much more full-bodied in its drawing of character, visually more brilliant, and incomparably richer in content. Hemingway's style, too, has changed for the better. It was extraordinarily effective at times before, but it is shed now of the artificialities that clung to it. There is nothing obtrusive about the manner in which this book is written; the style is a part of the whole, there is no artifice to halt the eye. It has simplicity and power, delicacy and strength.

This is Hemingway's longest novel, and it could be, I think, as most books can, a little shorter, and with benefit. It seems to me that some of the long passages in which Robert Jordan's mind turns back to his days in Madrid retard the narrative unnecessarily and could well have been omitted. If there are other flaws in this fine performance, I have not yet found them. A very good novel it unquestionably is, and I am not at all sure that it may not prove to be a great one. That is not something to determine on a first reading. But this much more is certain: that Hemingway is now a writer of real stature, not merely a writer of abundant talents whose work does not measure up to his equipment. "For Whom the Bell Tolls" is the book of a man who knows what life is about, and who can convey his knowledge. Hemingway has found bigger game than the kudu and the lion. The hunter is home from the hill.

Dorothy Parker.
"Mr. Hemingway's Finest Story Yet."
PM,
October 20, 1940,
p. 42.

* * *

This is a book, not of three days, but of all time. This is a book of all of us alive, of you and me and ours and those we hate. That is told by its title, taken from one of John Donne's sermons. . . .

This is a book about love and courage and innocence and strength and decency and glory. It is about stubbornness and stupidity and selfishness and treachery and death. It is a book about all those things that go on in the world night and day and always; those things that are only heightened and deepened by war. It is written with justice that is blood brother to brutality. It is written with a wisdom that washes the mind and cools it. It is written with an understanding that rips the heart with compassion for those who live, who do the best they can, just so that they may go on living.

It is a great thing to see a fine writer grow finer before your eyes. *For Whom the Bell Tolls* is, and beyond all comparison, Ernest Hemingway's finest book. It is not necessary politely to introduce that statement by the words "I think." It is so, and that is all there is to it. It is not written in his staccato manner. The pack of little Hemingways who ran along after his old style cannot hope to copy the swell and flow of his new one. I cannot imagine what will become of those of them who are too old for the draft.

There are many authors who have written about love, all along the gamut from embarrassment to enchantment —there are many who have written about sex and have got rich and fat and pale at the job. But nobody can write as Ernest Hemingway can of a man and a woman together, their completion and their fulfillment. And nobody can make melodrama as Ernest Hemingway can, nobody else can get such excitement upon a printed page. I do not feel that the creation of excitement is a minor achievement.

For Whom the Bell Tolls is nothing to warrant a display of adjectives. Adjectives are dug from soil too long worked, and they make sickly praise and stumbling reading. I think that what you do about this book of Ernest Hemingway's is point to it and say, "Here is a book." As you would stand below Everest and say, "Here is a mountain."

Ralph Thompson. "Books of the Times." *New York Times*, October 21, 1940, p. 15.

"For Whom the Bell Tolls" is our finest major novel of the Second World War and the most impressive work to date on the Spanish Civil War. A tremendous piece of work, it tells a su-perb story filled with the matter of picaresque romance: adventure, blood, lust, vulgarity, comedy and tragedy. For the young American Robert Jordan the lust and adventure are soon submerged in blood. As in other Hemingway fiction, the comedy comes out of the vulgarity, this time from a rich and indigenous peasant tradition. The tragedy is that which began in Madrid four years ago and is now felt everywhere.

Although Mr. Hemingway has always been a serious writer he has never seemed more a master than he is in "For Whom the Bell Tolls." His dialogue is incomparable in its echo of the Spanish idiom, his characters are modeled in high relief, his scenes are beautifully varied in intensity, ranging from the almost pastoral (though occasionally a bit too sweet) to the alarm of awakening to the sound of a strange horse thumping through the snow and into camp and on to the high tension of the last battle scene.

Mr. Hemingway has taken his theme from John Donne of three hundred years ago: that no man is an island and when the bell tolls it tolls for all. Out of this text and his own experience, belief, and great talent he has made his finest novel. (Summary)

"Hemingway's Spanish War."
Newsweek, 16 (October 21, 1940), 50.

More was expected of Ernest Hemingway than of any other writer who saw the Spanish war. He knew and loved Spain and the Spanish people long before the coming of the war. He believed in the Spanish Republic and thought it worth fighting for. And because they knew him as one of the great writers of our time most people thought the book he must inevitably write about it would be *the* book on the Spanish Civil War. *For Whom the Bell Tolls* is undoubtedly that book.

For more than 400 pages Hemingway accumulates suspense, develops his people, dissects their fears and courage like some spiritual anatomist, and brings the reader with the little band of guerrillas to the final action of the bridge. The last few pages are so intense that the end is almost a personal experience. And that is great writing. (Summary)

"Death in Spain."
Time, 36 (October 21, 1940), 94-95.

After Ernest Hemingway began expounding the mystique of big game hunting in *Green Hills of Africa* many of his admirers feared he carried his legendary virility to the point of developing a new Byronism. He seemed to be too obsessed with killing for the sake of killing, with boxing, riding, hunting, fishing while his depression-conscious critics called for greater social involvement. The feeling was abroad that if he did not soon find another experience big enough to make him write another *A Farewell to Arms*, he would continue his falling off past the point of recovery. Both his critics and admirers failed to recognize that his apparent obsession with killing was keyed to the dominant experience of this age—violent death.

In 1936 the Spanish Civil War became that great experience for Hemingway and out of it he published this week his great novel *For Whom the Bell Tolls*. Taking his title and theme from Elizabethan preacher John Donne's meditation that no man is an island, that the bell of death tolls for all mankind, he made his novel a great love story, a story of tense adventure in war, a sombre tragedy of Spanish peasants caught in the war, and most of all, a meditation on death.

The greatness of the story lies in the lovers' and peasants' triumph over their knowledge of coming death if they blow up the bridge. Robert Jordan carries out his assignment because he is convinced that doing so will help defeat the fascists. Pilar proceeds despite all omens of disaster because she believes in the revolution. Pablo, despite his strong instinct to live and his desertion with the detonator, realizes he is too lonely away from mankind's struggle and returns to help destroy the bridge. Unlike other novels of the Spanish war, *For Whom the Bell Tolls* avoids the dubious heroics and equally dubious politics of the International Brigades to focus on the simple human struggle of the Spanish people.

Though leftists may claim the novel, they will not relish the portraits of cynical Soviet agents or the realistic descriptions of Spanish peasants liquidating their local bourgeoisie. Whatever he may think of himself as a leftist sympathizer, Hemingway has emerged as a great and sensitive artist well over his Red rash. His bell tolls for all mankind. (Summary)

W. A. M.
"Hemingway's Searching Human Document."
Nashville Tennessean, October 25, 1940, p. 8-B.

With an objectivity all the more remarkable because he hardly could have been classed as an impartial observer while the war in Spain was being fought, Ernest Hemingway has written a searching human document dealing with that struggle.

There is a frankness often brutal but sometimes beautiful in this story of four days in the life of an American volunteer working for the Republican cause behind the Fascist lines. The raw emotions brought into play by any war but accentuated by such a conflict as this between two elements within the same nation are mercilessly bared.

The characters are made to live and to die before the reader's eyes so realistically as to give point to the quotation from John Donne to which the book owes its title: "Never send to know for whom the bell tolls; it tolls for thee."

The net result is a book which compares most favorably with "A Farewell to Arms," even though memory may have accented the virtues and obscured the faults of that earlier Hemingway work.

* * *

Hemingway too makes the reader see the actions of the bloodthirsty mob into which a cowardly leader turns the normally kindly Republican peasants. It is not a pretty picture, certainly not the kind that would be painted of his own side by a true partisan.

About as close as the author comes to propaganda is in a passage where Jordan describes the American economic system to one of the Spaniards and is queried about possible reactions to the income and inheritance taxes.

* * *

It is not necessary, however, for a reader to consider the political and social implications of the book at all.

There is a story sufficiently interesting to stand on its own merits. It moves on inexorably to an end that seems as appropriate as it is inevitable. There is an intimate study of the diverse little group of central characters and occasional glimpses of the pre-war Spanish life of fiestas and bull fights about which Hemingway has written so effectively in the past.

And set against the stark and bloody background of war is a little idyl of passionate love, drawn with a delicacy which avoids offense and yet lacks none of the frankness of the other threads of the story.

Margaret Marshall. "Notes by the Way." *The Nation,* 151 (October 26, 1940), 395-96.

If you remember Ernest Hemingway's last novel, "To Have and Have Not"—it was not very memorable—you will recall that in midcourse the first exponent of the hard-boiled school of fiction, later an *aficionado* of bullfighting, "got religion" and forced his hero, arbitrarily and quite unconvincingly, to die a proletarian. Meanwhile Hemingway had gone to Spain, where the first act of Europe's civil war was being played out. The first yield of his experience there as interested observer was a group of excellent short stories and a brief play, "The Fifth Column," which was not only a bad play but flaunted, in its handling of human character and values, the sentimental-brutal immaturity of the enthusiastic amateur of war and revolution.

His present book, "For Whom the Bell Tolls," also has for its background the Spanish civil war. It is a long book; it has obviously been written with care and love; it is in a straight line from "A Farewell to Arms" and superior to it; and happily it not only removes the bad taste left in the mouth by "The Fifth Column" but sets a new standard for Hemingway in characterization, dialogue, suspense, and compassion for the human being faced with death—and with the necessity for imposing death on other human beings. . . .

Within the frame of tension set up by this relatively simple plot, Hemingway has projected in great detail the world of the *partizans;* we enter it with Robert Jordan, whose compulsion to gain their confidence and command their help in carrying out his assignment generates part of the action and suspense. We come to know intimately the characters and lives of Pilar and her husband, Pablo, and see the conflict between them played out; there are less detailed but vivid portraits of half a dozen minor characters; the landscape is made palpable—Hemingway communicates not only the physical but the emotional impact of a spring snowstorm in the mountains. Yet through 471 pages one seldom feels that the primary plot is being held in abeyance. The exposition is accomplished almost entirely by means of dialogue and action. The suspense is continuously heightened, and the impact of the final action at the bridge is of course greatly intensified by our involvement in the human beings who take part in it.

The most striking as well as the most interesting character in the book is the woman Pilar; one of the finest single passages is her account of the terrible events which occurred in her native village when the civil war began. This account, in the Hemingway economy, also helps to characterize Pablo. Robert Jordan is adequate but he does not touch the imagination as Pilar does, even though, or perhaps because, he is presented more subjectively. The only unreal character for me, is Maria. The romantic great-love-at-first-sight between Jordan and the girl whom the *partizans* have rescued from her fascist captors is not convincing, never seems integral. If it was intended to have the quality and force of fantasy—which seems possible—the intention has failed.

The book's title is taken from John Donne: ". . . any man's death diminishes me, because I am involved in mankind; and therefore never send to know for whom the bell tolls; it tolls for thee." It indicates the spirit which informs the book, but Hemingway cannot compete with Donne, and the reader will not find any fresh or overpowering expression of this theme. Nor will he find a "revolutionary" novel as the term applies, for instance, to Franz Hoellering's "The Defenders." The understanding of social forces which underlies Hoellering's story of Vienna in 1934 remains only a vague perception in Hemingway's story of Spain in 1937—unprojected save in the personal and far from profound musings of Robert Jordan. . . .

* * *

The novel which embodies the deeper social meanings of the Spanish war has yet to be written, and I doubt that Hemingway will write it, but he has given us as moving and vivid a story of a group of human beings involved in that war as we are likely to have.

Clifton Fadiman. "Hemingway Crosses the Bridge." *New Yorker,* 16 (October 26, 1940), 66-68.

It's not inaccurate to say that Hemingway's "For Whom the Bell Tolls" is "A Farewell to Arms" with the background, instead, the Spanish Civil War. The hero, Robert Jordan, a young American loyalist sympathizer, recalls to mind Frederic Henry. Like Henry, he is anti-heroically heroic, anti-romantically romantic, very male, passionate, an artist of action, Mercutio modernized. Though the heroine, Maria, reminds one rather less of Catherine Barkley, the two women have much in common. Also, in both books the mounting interplay of death and sex is a major theme, the body's intense aliveness as it senses its own destruction.

But there, I think, the resemblance ends. For this book is not merely an advance on "A Farewell to Arms." It touches a deeper level than any sounded in the author's other books. It expresses and releases the adult Hemingway, whose voice was first heard in the groping "To Have and Have Not." It is by a better man, a man in whom works the principle of growth, so rare among American writers.

* * *

Hemingway is no fool. He portrays many of the Loyalists as cowards, brutes, and politicians—as they undoubtedly were. He portrays some of the Fascists as men of twisted nobility —as they undoubtedly were. But he knows that the war, at its deepest level (the first battle of the war now on your front pages) is a war between those who doubt life and those who affirm it. And if it is not yet such a war, it must become so, or it will, no matter who wins, have been fought in vain. I take that to be the central feeling of "For Whom the Bell Tolls," and that is why the book is more than a thrilling novel about love and death and battle and a finer work than "A Farewell to Arms."

It is interesting to watch in this new book a certain process of etherealization. Just as the Wagnerian death fascination of "Death in the Afternoon" changes here into something purer, so the smallboy Spartanism and the parade of masculinity which weakened the earlier books are transformed into something less gross, something—Hemingway would despise the world—spiritual. And yet this is by far the most sensual of all his books, the most truly passionate. . . .

Dignity also is what each of the characters possesses, from Fernando, who wears it like another skin, down to Augustín, whose every third word is an obscenity. Each has his own dignity, which means worth, and that dignity is gradually lifted to the surface by the harsh touch of death, as the grain of a fine wood reveals itself with polishing . . . —each of these (all of them flawed, some of them brutal, one of them treacherous) has a value, a personal weight that Hemingway makes

us feel almost tangibly, so that their lives and deaths are not incidents in a story but matters of moment to us who are "involved in Mankinde."

"For Whom the Bell Tolls" rises above "A Farewell to Arms" in still another way. The love story in "A Farewell to Arms" *is* the book. Chapters like that describing the retreat from Caporetto or that beautiful scene of the conversation with the old man at the billiard table are mere set pieces and might conceivably have been used in some other book. But the love of Robert and Maria is a structural part of "For Whom the Bell Tolls." It is not "love interest," nor is it the whole story, either; it is an integral portion of three days and three nights of life lived by two young people facing death. Furthermore, though this love does not rise above passion, it endows passion with an end and a meaning. . . .

Fine as the Italians were in "A Farewell to Arms," these Spaniards are finer. . . . They are in some ways like Russians, the pre-Soviet Russians, very philosophic and confessional and poetical. But they are not soft; indeed, the Spanish fury to kill, to kill as a pure act of faith, is one of the dominating emotions of the book. And their language is superb, translated literally out of its elegant and formal original, a trick which sounds as if it might be atrocious and turns out one hundred per cent effective. As a matter of fact, I would imagine "For Whom the Bell Tolls" to be as excellent a Spanish novel as it is an American one.

I have no idea whether this is a "great" book, for I have read it only once, and too quickly. But I know there are great things in it and that the man who wrote it is a bigger man than he was five years ago. There are some technical flaws. For example, I think the chapters describing the disorganization and political chicanery of the Loyalist command impede the story. But the faults are far outweighed by a dozen episodes that invade the memory and settle there: El Sordo's last fight on the hilltop; any of the love scenes; the struggle at the bridge; Pilar's dreadful story of Pablo's killing of the Fascists; Maria's recital of the noble death of her mother and father; Pilar's memories of her life among the bull-fighters; the astounding conversation—this is a set piece, but it's forgivable—about "the smell of death;" and the final scene, in which Robert, his left leg smashed, alone and on the threshold of delirium, trains his machine gun on the advancing Fascists and prepares himself, knowing at last why he is doing so, to die.

So I do not much care whether or not this is a "great" book. I feel that it is what Hemingway wanted it to be: a true book. It is written with only one prejudice—a prejudice in favor of the common human being. But that is a prejudice not easy to arrive at and which only major writers can movingly express.

* * *

Howard Mumford Jones. "The Soul of Spain." *Saturday Review of Literature*, 23 (October 26, 1940), 5, 19.

I think "For Whom the Bell Tolls" is as great an advance over "A Farewell to Arms" as "A Farewell to Arms" was better than "The Sun Also Rises." "The Sun Also Rises" was a striking book, but it was also something of a stunt. "A Farewell to Arms" was a moving book, but it was also sentimental. "For Whom the Bell Tolls" is not a stunt and is not merely sentimental. It is on the contrary, the finest and richest novel which Mr. Hemingway has written, it is one of the finest and richest novels of the year, and it is probably one of the finest and richest novels of the last decade. Gone now are the brittle surface, the clever concision of the early books. Gone is the self-conscious "little Hemingway" of "Death in the Afternoon." Gone is the Hemingway manner. Manner has been replaced by style, and the mere author has died out in the artist. Hemingway disappears, and in his place is the sorrowful majesty of a cause in which he believed and which did not triumph, at least superficially. But it is only superficially that this lost cause is to be identified with the Spanish Republic. More deeply, the cause is *not* lost, because (and I am not trying to be magniloquent), it is the cause of Humanity itself—that vague and splendid cause in which the nineteenth century liberal believed with a faith that we have almost lost, and which inspired some of the best pages of Victor Hugo and Charles Dickens and Dostoievski and Tolstoy. . . .

* * *

The whole book is bounded in the little lapse of time between Roberto's arrival and his death three or four days later. He has been in Madrid, and in his reminiscences we learn something about municipal life in Spain. Hemingway occasionally interpolates the story of somebody else on the Republican side—usually I wish he wouldn't. But in general it is the lives and experiences of this small group of guerilla fighters, men and women, caught in these few days between the upper and the nether millstones, which serve as the vehicle for his imaginative triumph. Through them I think Hemingway has done for the Spanish Civil War the sort of thing that Tolstoy did for the Napoleonic campaigns in "War and Peace." At the end of "For Whom the Bell Tolls," the reader has not lived in Spain, he has lived Spain.

It is sometimes the mark of an imaginative and moving novel that the hero should vanish into the book. David Copperfield, for example, to all intents and purposes thus disappears. In "Vanity Fair" the death of that half-hero, George Sedley, is merely trivial and incidental, though he dies at Waterloo; and yet "Vanity Fair" is *par excellence* the English novel of Waterloo. In such cases the book is so vital it swallows up the character. Something of that sort happens in "For Whom

the Bell Tolls." Roberto Jordan is neither a David Copperfield nor a George Sedley, but he is in the main merely another Hemingway young man. Though we follow his adventures and the play of his mind with interest, though it is a matter of breathless consequence that he shall destroy his bridge, he is mainly the vehicle which calls into being the life of Spain.

The heroine just escapes being merely another Hemingway heroine. She is named Maria. Dreadful things have happened to her, and they are movingly told; she is tenderly presented—a new Haidee for a relatively chaste and very republican Don Juan; and the love-making is beautiful and frank. But even Maria is little more than pathetic. Perhaps if she were not the technical heroine, she would escape into a fuller life. For, just as Amelia is dwarfed by Becky Sharp, so Maria is dwarfed by another woman. In the rich and Falstaffian figure of La Pilar, wife of Pablo, disillusioned chieftain of the guerillas, Hemingway has created a character like a mountain. Whether Pilar is cooking, studying human nature, instructing Maria in the facts of life, cursing with the fulness of a Shakespearian shrew, inspiriting her husband, aiding Roberto, or philosophizing, she moves like a Titaness. Grouped around her, the other members of the gang are presented with a minute and sympathetic fidelity, a simplicity and sympathy, an intuitive insight into the mental processes of "uncultivated" people that make them almost incredibly vivid. They dwarf the titular leads. The death of the old man at the bridge is, for example, much more pathetic than the love tale.

I have spoken of the style. In the descriptive and narrative portions Hemingway achieves a wider variety of effects than, I think, in any other story. But it is particularly in dialogue that the novel scores. The conversation is carried over almost literally from the Spanish, and it would appear that colloquial Spanish permits a combination of dignity, rhetorical precision, and wild poetry unattainable in a Germanic tongue. It is also rich in curses. Hemingway has solved the important problem of rendering the profanity and obscenity of the common people by using a device so simple and yet effective that I must leave it for the reader to discover. An immense part of the vitality of "For Whom the Bell Tolls" lies in the imaginative force of its dialogue.

Everybody knows what an occasional poem is, and everybody knows that very few occasional poems survive the event which called them into being. I wish we had in criticism the phrase, "occasional novel." I refer to those books which, produced by such an event as the Spanish Civil War, are impassioned and journalistic, and no more. Like occasional poetry, occasional fiction may often be impassioned, but the passion is not often shaped into enduring bronze. But somehow, sometime, somebody comes along and lifts the occasional novel out of contentiousness into the world of Humanity. Such a book is "Uncle Tom's Cabin." There is a small library of fiction on Negro slavery—who reads it today? But who doesn't know the story of Little Eva and Uncle Tom?

There were a hundred novels about Waterloo—and only "Vanity Fair" remains. Who doesn't know about Becky Sharp? I think it at least possible that "For Whom the Bell Tolls" may be the "Vanity Fair," the "Uncle Tom's Cabin" of the Spanish War. If the guess should prove accurate, the book will last, in my judgment, because it rises out of partisanship into imaginative comprehensiveness.

For, although Hemingway like Roberto is enlisted on the side of the Republic, neither he nor his hero blinks the truth that a good deal of the material on that side is pretty sorry stuff. He has not omitted the drunkenness, the disorder, the cruelty, the selfishness, the confusion. The hero dies because of stupidity and treachery on his own side. Interpolated into the main action, there is a long and dreadful narrative about the murder by Pablo and others of twenty fascists in a Spanish village which is among the scenes of fiction I would rather forget. And yet, at the end, Pilar and her companions join the immortals. Their ride up the mountain is like riding into Valhalla—a Valhalla inhabited by Jean Valjean and Uncle Tom and the hero of "Redemption" and the legend that is Abraham Lincoln. Mere reporting, mere realism, mere enlistment on the right side—we have had dozens of books that could show these excellences only. "For Whom the Bell Tolls" seems to me at least to spring from this great subterranean source of artistic energy.

"Hemingway's Power in Finer Revelation." *Springfield Republican,* October 27, 1940, p. 7E.

Ernest Hemingway always has been more interested in people under extraordinary stress than those who are leading lives disciplined only by normal events. His most famous book is a story of lives twisted by the World war. "For Whom the Bell Tolls" is the story of lives twisted by another war, the one in Spain, and in many respects it is superior to "A Farewell to Arms." Although less compact, with 471 pages, it approaches the classical dramatic tradition by compressing all its action into less than 96 hours, and for all its focus on the familiar pattern of a man and woman in love in war time goes beyond these two in an effort to picture all humanity in the grip of evil.

Mr. Hemingway has here produced a work of shining literary merit, a novel of beauty and unrelenting tension, and to a degree unusual for him, has divorced his characters from himself and wedded them to humanity as the rest of us understand humanity. His people are no less filled with grimness and vitality than they ever were, but they are less harsh and easier to understand. Somewhere in the transition from the battlefields of France to those of Spain, Mr. Hemingway's jagged, cynical edges have been dulled, and the result is fortunate.

* * *

The two main themes, the importance of the individuals to each other and the importance of the bridge to humanity as a whole as a blow against fascism, then race together to an inevitable collision with the mounting suspense that only a master novelist can design.

This tension, which continually heightens from the first chapter, is slowed little, if at all, by frequent cutbacks to previous experiences of several of the characters—digressions which Mr. Hemingway has introduced to complete his picture of the Spanish war. Although there is no question as to where the author's sympathies lie, this is not a propaganda novel, and neither is it a war correspondent's account of what one man saw. Although fascism receives no laurels whatsoever, the account of the elimination of rightists from a village at the start of the war was certainly not included with a calculation to make friends for either side.

* * *

This is an unusually inspiring novel of Mr. Hemingway's. There is hardly a serious novelist nowadays who defends war, but there are very few who can derive from it and pass on to others a great tenderness for humanity rather than a passion for one nation or one flag. Mr. Hemingway has magnificently brought to us his understanding of what John Donne said, in the 17th century: "No man is an Island. . . ."

Edmund Wilson. "Return of Ernest Hemingway." *New Republic*, 103 (October 28, 1940), 591-92.

This new novel of Hemingway will come as a relief to those who didn't like "Green Hills of Africa," "To Have and Have Not," and "The Fifth Column." The big game hunter, the waterside superman, the Hotel Florida Stalinist, with their constrained and fevered attitudes, have evaporated like the fantasies of alcohol. Hemingway the artist is with us again; and it is like having an old friend back.

This book is also a new departure. It is Hemingway's first attempt to compose a full-length novel, with real characters, and a built-up story. On the eve of a Loyalist attack in the Spanish civil war, a young American who has enlisted on the Loyalist side goes out into country held by the Fascists, under orders to blow up a bridge. He directs with considerable difficulty a band of peasant guerillas, spends three nights in a cave in their company, blows up the bridge on schedule, and is finally shot by the Fascists. The method is the reverse of the ordinary method in novels of contemporary history, Franz Hoellering's or André Malraux's which undertake a general survey of a revolutionary crisis, shuttling back and forth among various groups of characters. There is a little of this shuttling in "For Whom the Bell Tolls," but it is all directly related to the main action: the blowing-up of the bridge. Through this episode the writer has aimed to reflect the whole course of the Spanish War, to show the tangle of elements that were engaged in it, and to exhibit the events in a larger perspective than that of the emergency of the moment.

In this he has been successful to a degree which will be surprising even to those who have believed in him most. There is in "For Whom the Bell Tolls" an imagination for social and political phenomena such as he has hardly given evidence of before. The vision of this kind of insight is not so highly developed as it is with a writer like Malraux, but it is here combined with other things that these political novels often lack. What Hemingway presents us with in this study of the Spanish war is not so much a social analysis as a criticism of moral qualities. The *kind* of people people are rather than their social-economic relations is what Hemingway is particularly aware of.

Thus there is here a conception of the Spanish character, very firm and based on close observation, underlying the various social types; and in approaching the role of the Communists in Spain, Hemingway's judgments are not made to fit into the categories of a political line—since he has dropped off the Stalinist melodrama of the days of 1937, a way of thinking certainly alien to his artistic nature—but seem to represent definite personal impressions. The whole picture of the Russians and their followers in Spain—which will put The New Masses to the trouble of immediately denouncing a former favorite at a time when they are already working overtime with so many other denunciations on their hands—looks absolutely authentic. You have the contrast between the exaltation of the converts and recruits of the headquarters of the International Brigade, and the luxury, the insolence and the cynicism of the headquarters of the emissaries of the Kremlin. You have the revolutionary stuffed shirt, André Marty, hero of the 1918 mutiny of the French fleet in the Black Sea, who has been magnified and corrupted in Moscow till he is no longer anything but a mischievous bureaucrat, obsessed with the idea of shooting heretics; and you have the Moscow insider Karkov, cold of head and serious of purpose while he repeats for the sake of conformity the venomous gibberings of Pravda.

You have in the center of the stage the sincere fellow traveler from the States, teacher of Spanish in a Western college; and you have, traced with realism and delicacy, the whole chronicle of his reactions to the Communists, of his relations with the Spaniards he has to work with, and of the operation upon him in Spain of the American influences he brings with him. In the end, realizing fully the military futility of his mission and balked in his effort to save the situation, by the confusion of forces at cross-purposes that are throttling the Loyalist campaign, he is to stick by his gun sustained by nothing but the memory of his grandfather's record as a soldier in the American Civil War. In view of the dramatic declamations on the note of "Look here, upon this picure, and on this!" that the Stalinists were making a year

or two ago over the contrast between Dos Passos' attitude and Hemingway's in connection with the Spanish war, it is striking that the hero of "For Whom the Bell Tolls" should end up by cutting a figure not fundamentally so very much different from that of the hero of "The Adventures of a Young Man."

Thus we get down out of the empyrean of Marxist political analysis, where the leaders are pulling the strings for the masses, and see the ordinary people as they come. And we see the actual layout—mile by mile and hill by hill—of the country in which they have to struggle. One of the most highly developed of Hemingway's senses is his geographical and strategical vision—what may be called his sense of terrain. It is no doubt from the Western frontier that he has inherited his vivid perception of every tree, every bush, every path, every contour and every stream that go to make up the lay of the land. He derives and he can communicate an excitement from the mere exploration and mastery of country that goes back to Fenimore Cooper and he has succeeded in getting it into this new novel as he got it into his early stories. We are shown the Spanish conflict in its essential and primitive aspect of groups of imperfectly equipped and more or less groping human beings maneuvering over the surface of the earth.

The novel has certain weaknesses. A master of the concentrated short story, Hemingway is less sure of his grasp of the form of the elaborated novel. The shape of "For Whom the Bell Tolls" is sometimes slack and sometimes bulging. It is certainly quite a little too long. You need space to make an epic of three days; but the story seems to slow up toward the end where the reader feels it ought to move faster; and the author has not found out how to mold or to cut the interior soliloquies of his hero. Nor are the excursions outside the consciousness of the hero, whose point of view comprehends most of the book, conducted with consistent attention to the symmetry and point of the whole.

There is, furthermore, in "For Whom the Bell Tolls" something missing that we still look for in Hemingway. Where the semi-religious exaltation of communism has failed a writer who had once gained from it a new impetus, a vacuum is created which was not there before and which for the moment has to be filled. In Hemingway's case, there has poured in a certain amount of conventional romance. There is in "For Whom the Bell Tolls" a love story that is headed straight for Hollywood. The hero falls in with an appealing little girl who has been captured and raped by the Fascists, who has never loved before and who wants him to teach her love. She adores him, lives only to serve him, longs for nothing but to learn his desires so that she can do for him what he wants, talks of her identity as completely merged in his. She is as docile as the Indian wives in the early stories of Kipling; and since the dialogue of the characters speaking Spanish is rendered literally with its *thees* and *thous* and all the formalities of a Latin language, the scenes between Robert and Maria have a strange atmosphere of literary medievalism reminiscent of the era of Maurice Hewlett. Robert keeps insisting to himself on his good fortune and on the unusualness of his experience in acquiring a girl like Maria; and, for all the reviewer knows, there may be a few such cases in Spain. But the whole thing has the too-perfect felicity of a youthful erotic dream. It lacks the true desperate emotion of the love affairs in some of Hemingway's other stories. And in general, though the situation is breathless and the suspense kept up all through, the book lacks the tensity, the moral malaise, that made the early work of Hemingway troubling.

But then this early work was, as it were, lyric; and "For Whom the Bell Tolls" is an effort toward something else, which requires a steady hand. The hero of this new novel is no romantic Hemingway cartoon: his attitude toward his duty and the danger it involves are studied with more coolness and sobriety than in the case of perhaps any other of the author's leading juveniles. The young man is a credible young man who is shown in his relation to other people, and these other people are for the most part given credible identities, too. The author has begun to externalize the elements of a complex personality in human figures that have a more complete existence than those of his previous stories.

That he should thus go back to his art, after a period of artistic demoralization, and give it a larger scope, that, in an era of general perplexity and panic, he should dramatize the events of the immediate past in terms, not of partisan journalism, but of the common human instincts that make men both fraternal and combative, is a reassuring evidence of the soundness of our intellectual life.

Robert E. Sherwood. "The Atlantic Bookshelf." *Atlantic Monthly*, 166 (November 1940), front section.

One has to be cautious how he applies the word "artist" to so virile a writer as Ernest Hemingway, but his new novel *For Whom the Bell Tolls* is such a rare and beautiful work that artist is the word for the man who produced it. It includes not only all the "blood and guts" characteristic of earlier Hemingway books but also a high degree of delicacy. Unlike some other works of skilled American writers, the novel shows Hemingway capable of self-criticism and self-development, able to work hard and intelligently to give form and substance to his huge natural talent. In his new novel he has succeeded wonderfully and at precisely the right moment.

For Whom the Bell Tolls includes not only the immediately fresh perceptions for which Hemingway has become known. It provides also a sense of permanence and elevation of spirit. The people of the story are common folk, the people who always fight the wars and are the victims. They are those for whom a lost cause is never really lost nor a sacrifice ever completely futile. Through them the novel justifies its use of John Donne's declaration that the fate of all is clear in the fate of one.

The novel is another story of the Spanish Civil War. Hemingway was active in that prologue to this war and he sensed its meaning in a way too few others felt. But now he writes of that war objectively and disinterestedly and with hardly a trace of rancor. In his union of passion and reason he has created a work of art that goes beyond the precipitating event.

On a relatively small canvas he has painted the story of a minor partisan operation of seventy-two hours, but with his few characters he has been able to tell the story behind the Spanish tragedy and its effects on Europe and the rest of us. In one superb chapter he tells how the Republican movement started in a small town, and in another sequence how the important message is carried through the lines but delivered too late. And he shows how, in a masterful portrait of political commissar Marty, the tragedy is complicated by the man's greater eagerness to detect unreliability among his comrades than to win victory over the Fascists.

Hemingway's hero Robert Jordan superficially resembles other Hemingway heroes in his resistance to illusion, but he is better than they are, more mature, clearer of conscience and capable of a more complete love. The love scenes between Jordan and the girl Maria are among the rare ones in modern literature, where the merely skillful can write knowledgeably about sex but few can write truly and beautifully about love.

Though he writes without rancor Hemingway has written with great sympathy for the victims of Fascism, including the Fascists themselves. In showing, not telling, how Fascism kills man's spirit he has produced his finest work and dispelled our doubts about any limits to his great powers. (Summary)

Edwin Seaver. *Direction*, 3 (November 1940), 18-19.

It is interesting that now, when the double-crossers have been double-crossed, when the betrayers of Spain have turned out to be the betrayers of their own people, when what was foretold has come to pass and London is suffering the same fate as Madrid—it is significant that just now two of the best novels of the season should appear, accusing ghosts, to haunt us with memories of the international crime committed against the Spanish people. That the crime has turned upon the perpetrators and the criminals are now the victims is one of the few things around that help one to believe there may be such a thing as divine justice after all.

In his magnificent preface to Gustav Regler's *The Great Crusade*, Ernest Hemingway refers to the Spanish War "as the greatest holding attack in history." For that holding attack, he says, the Spanish people were killed in vast numbers, starved out, deprived of weapons and betrayed.

But there were victories, and they were not only spiritual. *The Great Cru-sade* deals with a period of the Spanish War when what happened around Madrid stiffened the backbones of millions of people and they knew that this thing called Fascism could be stopped; when the International Brigades wrote a glorious page in a day that was maggoty with corruption.

* * *

It is this that makes both *The Great Crusade* and *For Whom the Bell Tolls* optimistic tragedies. It is this that makes both books monuments that say: Here lie men who died for what they believed in at a time when belief in peace and justice was a crime against society.

* * *

"The greatest novels," writes Hemingway, "are all made up. Everything in them is created by the writer. . . . But there are events which are so great that if a writer has participated in them all his obligation is to try to write them truly rather than assume the presumption of altering them with invention."

For Whom the Bell Tolls lies somewhere between these two types of novels. Hemingway has written truly of real events; he was in Spain and he knew that country and the defenders of the Republic, knew them as a poet knows them, which is what counts. At the same time, his novel is "all made up"; he did not dynamite a bridge at the moment of attack, nor remain alone, with a broken thigh, on the mountain, holding off the enemy single-handed while his comrades escaped. He did all this and more with his imagination, with his imagination rooted in reality, with that peculiar quality of imagination that so heightens reality that we percieve it as we might had we ourselves the good fortune to be so gifted.

I am writing this several weeks in advance of the publication of *For Whom the Bell Tolls*, when it is being said the new novel is Hemingway's best book since *Farewell to Arms*. It is this, but it is so much more. The present novel surpasses the previous one, in the same proportion that Hemingway himself has grown in experience in the interval, which is considerable. Here are no bewildered, snatching a moment of life while the watchdogs of hell are asleep; no defeated, wringing a moment of ecstasy from that defeat.

The protagonists of *For Whom the Bell Tolls* are not bewildered nor are they defeated. They know what they are fighting for and dying for. The hard-boiled pose is no longer necessary; we have gone beyond all that sort of thing, because life itself, the political situation, if you will, is so much more hard-boiled than we can ever pretend to be. And there is a political situation, and this is most important to realize, for no longer is it I against the world, or we two against the world, but the people against their aggressors, the Republic against the Fascists, the cause bigger than myself, bigger even than my feelings for my beloved, the cause that is myself and my beloved, and who kills it kills me.

What a farce to label Ernest Hemingway an "irresponsible"; never has a writer shown a greater sense of responsibility, to his art, to his generation, to his people, to the cause of liberty and justice. This sense of responsibility was always there; but never before, in any of his novels or stories, has Hemingway understood it so clearly, or written so plainly in the shadow of history.

* * *

Ernest Hemingway owes much to the war in Spain; it enormously deepened his experience, widened his horizons. It saved him from "death in the afternoon." Now he has repaid some of that debt and we are all the richer for it.

It seems only fair to mention, in passing, that *For Whom the Bell Tolls* is a Book-of-the-Month Club selection, and that with *Native Son*, a similar such selection, the Club has to its credit two of the really important American novels—and how many are there? —of the current year.

John O. Chappell, Jr. "Adventure, Love, Death." *Cincinnati Enquirer,* November 2, 1940, p. 5.

"For Whom the Bell Tolls" is a novel about the Spanish Civil War and its ingredients are three—adventure, love, death.

Robert Jordan, a young American, has come to Spain to fight against the Fascists. He has been ordered to blow up a bridge over a deep gorge just before a Loyalist offensive begins.

He seeks the aid of a band of guerrillas living in a cave near the bridge. There is Pablo, the piggishly treacherous leader of the band; Pilar, his foul-mouthed, kind-hearted wife who has known little but hardship and poverty; Maria, the beautiful young middle-class girl who has taken refuge with the band after escaping from the Fascists.

The story's action takes place during a three-day lull before the offensive begins. These men and women, peasants, gypsies, and bourgeois, know they face death. Pablo, a cynical changeling, is concerned with saving his skin; other members of the band, unfaltering in the belief that their fight is that of all mankind against oppression, await what the fortunes of war may bring them with almost mystical courage.

Pilar, the "wise woman," smells death-to-come and in a terrible scene describes the odor to Robert, telling him that he has the smell of death-to-come.

Although Pilar has jealously protected Maria from the advances of the guerrillas, she gives her to Robert—because they love each other and their time together will be so brief. Maria has seen her father and mother murdered by the Fascists. To her Robert means the first and only personal happiness she has known. For Robert, Maria represents the love of his lifetime, a love transcending even death. And so it is that Robert and the guerrillas, Pablo, Pilar, and Maria, in three days of life together, taste all human experience as it reaches its highest concentration in war, love, death.

"For Whom the Bell Tolls" is the mature work of an artist at the peak of his powers. I don't think Hemingway will write a better novel. His former brittle, meaningless objectivity has been displaced by a new insight and understanding.

"Hemingway Novel a Smash." *Publishers' Weekly*, 138 (November 2, 1940), 1751-52.

The biggest sales news of the past week is the immediate and nationwide success of Ernest Hemingway's new novel, "For Whom the Bell Tolls." No Scribner book has gotten such a tremendous break within the memory of anyone in the firm. Other people in the trade are saying that the novel has started off faster than any recent book, the immediate response being similar only to that received by "Gone with the Wind," "The Grapes of Wrath" and possibly the early start of "Native Son."

* * *

The first edition of "For Whom the Bell Tolls" numbered 210,000 copies, including those for the Book-of-the-Month Club. . . . The advance distribution of the novel was heavy; and within less than a week after publication it was necessary to order another printing of 50,000 copies, making the total number printed up to October 28th 260,000 copies.

"For Whom the Bell Tolls" started off with no slackness whatever. On the morning of publication, several book-stores reported customers waiting for the doors to open to buy copies. Before the end of the day stores in New York and vicinity were sending messengers for new stock. On the following day telegrams and registered letters were received from more than 70 stores. This number steadily increased until on Monday, October 28th, 128 stores sent in orders, many of them second and third re-orders, each one doubling or tripling the number of copies ordered before.

* * *

"Selling the Hemingway Novel to the Movies." *Publishers' Weekly,* 138 (November 2, 1940), 1752.

Several weeks before the actual date of publication of Hemingway's "For Whom the Bell Tolls" it became pretty evident that the novel would have the big success that the story above indicates it is having. Naturally the movie companies became keenly interested in the film rights. The competition for the book was keen and resulted in its sale to Paramount for what is probably the highest price ever paid by the movies for a book—and the sale was completed only three days after publication. . . .

The deal with Paramount called for the payment of $100,000 plus 10 cents a copy for each of the first 500,000 copies sold, including Book-of-the-Month Club copies. As noted above, the first printing was 210,000 and another printing of 50,000 has been ordered, making 260,000 in print. If all these were sold and no more, the price for the film rights would amount to roughly $125,000.

* * *

Naomi Bender. "Ernest Hemingway Rises." *Miami Herald,* November 3, 1940, p. 4-E.

It gives me great pleasure to see that the critics, who once vied with each other to see how many insults they could heap on author Ernest Hemingway, are now crawling over each other in their haste to acclaim his latest novel.

So venomous were they where Hemingway was concerned that one thought it was Hemingway the man who was under dissection rather than his books. When "To Have and Have Not" was published they pounced upon Hemingway with glee, flourishing this book as proof that he was finished as an author, that his success had gone to his head and ruined his exciting talent. Poor Hemingway, they mourned, shaking their heads with delight. So keen were they to find fault with this author that instead of pointing to the qualities in "To Have and Have Not" which were good and indicative of literary virility far exceeding that of the average writer, they tore it to pieces, refusing to concede it any virtues.

Now they must admit that Hemingway has produced a fine, perhaps even a great, novel. "For Whom the Bell Tolls" is final proof that in Hemingway we have a modern American novelist who exemplifies the best of our literary tradition; in whom there is strength and comprehension and humanity; who can write from the head as well as from the heart, with discipline as well as romantic fire.

* * *

This is a story not only of love, though the relationship between Maria and Jordan is beautiful and tender, it is not a story of war alone, though the descriptions of battles are grimly realistic; it is not even a story of the cruelty of man, his weaknesses and his loss of faith, though there are hideous descriptions of all these things on the Loyalist as well as the Fascist sides. This is a book that dramatically and heartrendingly fulfills the meaning of John Donne's quotation in the frontispiece. . . .

Alvah Bessie.
New Masses, 37
(November 5, 1940),
25-29.

* * *

Many expected that Hemingway's experience in Spain would so inflame his heart and his talents, that his long-announced novel of that war would be both his finest achievement and "the"

novel about Spain. It is not. It is his finest achievement only in the sense that he has now perfected his extraordinary technical facility and touched some moments of action with a fictional suspense that is literally unbearable. But depth of understanding there is none; breadth of conception is heartbreakingly lacking; there is no searching, no probing, no grappling with the truths of human life that is more than superficial. And an astounding thing has happened, that anyone who was even remotely concerned with what happened in Spain will find almost incredible: Hemingway has treated that war (in an essential way) exactly as he treated the first world war in *A Farewell to Arms.* Touched in his own flesh and spirit by the horror of that first great imperialist conflict, struck into a mood of impotent despair by its utter lack of meaning and its destruction of everything all decent human beings value, Hemingway proclaimed the futility of life and love and happiness. . . .

* * *

This is a story of action, and the action is fast and furious, fused with a suspense that is magnificently handled in every incident. But this is also *A Farewell to Arms*, slightly in reverse. For the total implication of the novel is, again, the necessity for virility, the pervasive horror of death, the futility —nay, the impossibility of love. Given only seventy-two hours in which to live, Robert Jordan must live his life within that span. He accepts that fate, but the reader's disappointment in his fate is Hemingway's disappointment with life—for there is no tragedy here, merely pathos. Here, again, are long and fruitless and somewhat meaningless disquistions upon the significance of death and killing (in war, in murder, in the bull-ring, by accident, by design). Here again is the small and personal (and the word *personal* is the key to the dilemma of Ernest Hemingway's persistent lack of growth) frustration of the individual, and here again is the author's almost pathological preoccupation with blood and mutilation and sex and death—they all go together and are part and parcel of his attitude toward life, and they are the *only* facts of life with which he has consistently dealt. I do not mean to imply that these subjects are unworthy or incapable of profound treatment, singly or together; I do mean to insist that in Hemingway's hands they have never achieved the stature of universality, perhaps because Hemingway cannot see them in perspective, cannot see them more than sentimentally.

It must be clearly stated that Hemingway's position in this novel is unequivocally on the side of the Spanish people; there can be no question of his defection from that cause. It is, however, a tragic fact that the cause of Spain does not, in any *essential* way, figure as a motivating power, a driving, emotional, passional force in this story. In the widest sense, that cause is actually *irrelevant* to the narrative. For the author is less concerned with the fate of the Spanish people, whom I am certain he loves, than he is with the fate of his hero and his heroine, who are *himself*. They are Hemingway and Hemingway alone, in their (say rather *his*, for Jordan is the mainspring of the narrative, and the girl Maria is only lightly sketched) morbid concentration upon the meaning of *individual* death, *personal* happiness, *personal* misery, *personal* significance in living and their personal equation is not so deeply felt or understood as to achieve wide significance. For all his groping, the author of the *Bell* has yet to integrate his individual sensitivity to life with the sensitivity of every living human being (read the Spanish people); he has yet to expand his personality as a novelist to embrace the truths of other people, everywhere; he has yet to dive deep into the lives of others, and there to find his own.

This personal constriction has long been evident and has made inevitable other aspects of Hemingway's personality that are, to say the least, reprehensible. I refer to his persistent chauvinism, as referred to the Italian People, and to women; to the irresponsibility he has shown in publishing in Hearst's *Cosmopolitan* such a story as *Below the Ridge*, a story whose implications gave deadly ammunition to the enemy—Hemingway's enemy, the fascist-minded of America; to the irresponsibility he demonstrated in permitting his play, *The Fifth Column*, to be mutilated and distorted out of all semblance of what he originally wanted to say, to the point where it was actually a slander of the Spanish people.

There are many references in the *Bell* to various political aspects of the struggle in Spain. And few of these references do more than *obscure* the nature of that struggle. Robert Jordan, his American anti-fascist fighter, wonders "what the Russian stand is on the whole business." If Jordan, who is pictured as an utterly inflexible anti-fascist, did not understand what the Soviet Union felt about Spain, surely his creator did and does. And just as in his story *Below the Ridge,* Hemingway's sins of omission in the *Bell* allow the untutored reader to believe that the role of the Soviet Union in Spain was sinister and reprehensible. For certainly he must himself know—and it is his obligation to clearly state—that that role was clear and well-defined, and so honest as to command the entire respect and adherence of the Spanish people, who hung banners in their towns which read: *Viva La U.R.S.S.*; *Mejor Amigo del Pueblo Español* (Long Live the Soviet Union, Best Friend of the People of Spain!)

Now this concentration, this constriction of Hemingway's indubitable genius, to the purely personal, has resulted in a book about Spain that is not about Spain at all! It has resulted in the intensification of his idiosyncratic tendencies to the point where he, an inflexible supporter of the loyalists and an avowed admirer of the International Brigades, can conceive and execute as vicious a personal attack upon André Marty, the *organizer* of the International Brigades, as could be and has been delivered upon him by French fascist deputies themselves! . . .

* * *

This is the trap into which the individualism Hemingway's bourgeois critics so admired, has led a man who is still one of our most greatly endowed creative artists. For he has written a novel of Spain without the Spanish people, a *Hamlet* without the Dane. . . .

It seems certain that Hemingway did not intend to write a *Cosmopolitan* love story against a background of the Spanish Civil War; yet this is what he has done. It is certain that he did not intend to slander the Spanish people or the Soviet Union; yet his method of telling the story has resulted in both. With minor exceptions, the Spanish people portrayed here are cruel, vindictive, brutalized, irresponsible. Throughout the long narrative there is evidence of much confusion: Hemingway praises the individual heroism of individual Communists, and impugns and slanders their leadership, their motives, and their attitudes. He admires the Brigades, and assails their leadership (and surely he knows enough about military affairs to realize that no soldier can fight well unless his officer commands his respect).

Already this greatly endowed writer, who on innumerable occasions has placed himself without equivocation on the side of the people against their enemies, has been readmitted by the most reactionary critics to the Valhalla of the Literary Giants. . . .

But this is strange company for a man like Hemingway, a man who transcended the futility created in him by the first world war, was vitalized, as a man and as an artist, by Spain; a man who won the respect and admiration of almost every International Brigade man who met him, and who gave liberally to these men of his own substance. For at the moment he is found in bad company; in the company of his enemies, and the people's enemies who will fawn upon him and use him, his great talents and his passion for the people's cause, to traduce and betray those talents and those people.

Burton Rascoe.
"Wolfe, Farrell and Hemingway."
American Mercury, 51 (December 1940), 493-98.

In his latest novel, *For Whom the Bell Tolls*, Ernest Hemingway demonstrates all over again that he has the least mature mind of any writer of great talent in our day. For a while it seemed that Thomas Wolfe would claim that dubious distinction with James T. Farrell as a close second. But at age thirty-five Wolfe finally outgrew his adolescence; and by the time he had finished the second volume of his Studs Lonigan trilogy, that is at about age thirty, Farrell passed out of his childhood.

That Hemingway still suffers his adolescence can be seen in his masculine fantasy of love. The rutting in this novel can hardly qualify for the terms "romance" or "love." His hero is rather a self-centered nympholept whose idea of love is best seen when he is alone in bed after spending an evening at the movies. The essence of love in *For Whom the Bell Tolls* is not fundamentally different from what one

finds in such pulp magazines as *High Adventure* and *Red Star True Confessions*. Admittedly Hemingway has a greater sense of style, but they are all still "pulp" love stories.

His grasp of politics is no better. Though he describes the brutalizing effects of war on its makers and victims, he deludes himself into believing it does not matter that one gives his faith to a corrupt cause so long as he has faith. The Loyalists did not win Robert Jordan's war. The ideal for which he and all the other foreigners fought was sabotaged by the Moscow communists even while they pretended to believe in it. Even Hemingway knows now that he was wrong when he denounced Dos Passos for exposing the Stalinist "liquidations" of those who put the cause of the Loyalists above that of Stalin.

The pointlessness of the novel becomes clear when we realize that Hemingway began to write it with one set of illusions, then lost them as he wrote. His point of view vanished and he was left with only half realized doubts that it is good to die for what one believes regardless of its validity. (Summary)

John Chamberlain.
"The New Books."
Harper's, 182 (December 1940), front section.

In Ernest Hemingway's *To Have and Have Not* there is a grim episode: Harry Morgan, the hard-bitten rum-runner of the Florida keys, forces a group of helplessly chattering Chinese overboard from his boat after he has promised to smuggle them from Cuba into the United States. In the latest Hemingway novel, *For Whom the Bell Tolls*, there is a curious reworking of this motif. Instead of the bilking of the luckless Chinese a whole group of Spanish Fascists are forced to run a gauntlet between two walls of Republicans armed with flails. At the end of the gauntlet, at the edge of the town plaza, there is a cliff—and death waits below on the bank of a river.

When I read the Chinese episode in *To Have and Have Not*, I felt faintly sick; the whole scene seemed to stamp its creator as one who loved violence and torture for their own sake. . . .

The comparable scene in *For Whom the Bell Tolls*, however, evokes an entirely different kind of response. As horror, it has details that are infinitely more gory and harrowing than anything in *To Have and Have Not*. But the episode is related to human motives that have some connection with honor and ethics, even if, from a cosmic point of view, they seem misguided. Pablo, the Republican guerilla chieftain who orders the death of the Fascists, has Lenin's or Grant's or William Tecumseh Sherman's justification: he is convinced that a good stiff administration of horror in the beginning will, through its deterrent force, save many more lives later on. Harry Morgan's skulduggery is purely selfish and mean, even though he tells himself it is done to turn a penny for the wife and kiddies. But Pablo's butchery is linked up with a noble cause; and if it

is ultimately self-betraying, as I think it is, it at least forces one to meditate upon the tragic destiny of man. The difference in reader response to what is, after all, the same mechanical operation in the two novels is the measure of Hemingway's artistic rehabilitation. After ten years the bright hope of America's post-war literature has come back.

The new novel has been called Hemingway's best. Maybe it is, and maybe it is not; in any event, we will not know until the passions of the present epoch have subsided.

* * *

If it is adventure that you are looking for, it is here. If it is vivid reporting—the best pictorial writing in modern American literature—well, that is here, too. And if you are searching for a book to explain the Spanish temperament, with its tragic acceptance of death as the one thing which, by its imminence, can lend sweetness to life, then you don't have to go beyond *For Whom the Bell Tolls*. But these are more or less incidental virtues. The main idea of the book is to report, in terms of dramatic action, how a variety of men and women face killing and the probability of being killed. Pablo, one gathers, kills from mixed motives: he believes in the Republican cause, yes, but he is also a welterer in blood. Eventually the butchery begins to pall on him; he sees the Fascists becoming stronger by the month, and he meditates on the uselessness of it all.

* * *

When he is writing of death, Hemingway is always convincing. He is convincing, too, in his elaboration of the character of Pilar, the grand, ugly, forceful, and wise old woman who is living with Pablo and noting the progressive steps in his degeneration. And when Hemingway writes of the Stalinist bureaucrats, who pursue policies that can only wreck Republican morale, he is truthful enough to revise his tough-guy judgment of two years ago, when he went about trying to justify the Kremlin's devious ways. In terms of character portrayal this is Hemingway's most solid novel; the minor characters are as real as the major. And in terms of straight thinking, *For Whom the Bell Tolls* is certainly Hemingway's most mature work to date.

The only flaw in the whole beautiful performance is the love story of Robert Jordan and Maria, the girl who has been raped by the Fascists. As Edmund Wilson has said, this has the too perfect felicity of an erotic dream. Hemingway pictures Robert Jordan as indulging in reveries about Jean Harlow and Greta Garbo; and the actual affair between Robert and Maria reads like a projection of these reveries. True, the affair is all very lovely; Hemingway's literal translation of Spanish abounds in "thees" and "thous" and "little rabbits," and if you want an idyl Jordan and Maria provide a perfect one. But the idyl seems trumped up; Maria's character remains shadowy to the last. . . .

* * *

The Jordan-Maria fantasy, however, does not greatly detract from the effect of *For Whom the Bell Tolls*. Once upon a time, just before the American Civil War, Herman Melville wrote novels whose greatness was securely based on acceptance of the tragic sense of life. Now, a hundred years later, Hemingway has made at least a fair stab at competing with Melville. With the world in flames, and the imminence of death a palpable thing with everyone of us, Hemingway has both his subject and his audience. The objective conditions are right for him; and with his powers rescued from the débâcle of *To Have and Have Not* he is probably only on the threshold of a new career.

J. N. Vaughan. *Commonweal*, 33 (December 13, 1940), 210.

As a conservative estimate, one million dollars will be spent by American readers for this book. They will get for their money 34 pages of permanent value. These 34 pages tell of a massacre happening in a little Spanish town in the early days of the Civil War. The killing was done by loyalists, peasants, communists, republicans, anarchists. Those killed were correspondingly rebels, propertied people, fascists, monarchists. The 34 page value however does not depend on the ideological identity of either the killers or the killed. In civil war neither side proves too delicate to be incapable of what is here described. We have fully known this since the days of Thucydides. Hemingway's 34 page narrative is a bill of particulars supplementing the story of Corcyra as told by the great Greek historian. What we never had before Hemingway was a full portrayal of actual massacre being done and suffered by identified people whom we have known. Personal participation in massacre in order to know it "from the inside" is no longer indispensable. You can now get it from pages 96 to 130 of "For Whom the Bell Tolls."

Of the main story little be said. It is infinitely inferior to Hemingway's prior work.... Attention is so often drawn away from Jordan that the reader cannot feel himself comfortably at home in the capital of Hemingway, prepared temporarily to live, eat, act, think and aspire the way the Hemingwegians do these things. So long as one feels alien to the imaginary country of Hemingway, so long must one view Jordan as a kind of visible Charlie McCarthy.

As to the love affair in this novel— phooey!

When I suffer nostalgically for repetition of the things Mr. Hemingway could tell me once upon a time, I shall return to the Story of Nick, to the Story of Francis Macomber, to a "Clean and Well Lighted Place." [sic] Mr. Hemingway: please publish the massacre scene separately, and then forget "For Whom the Bell Tolls"; please leave stories of the Spanish Civil War to Malraux; above all please tell us more stories to show that only the brave enjoy an existence fit to be had. We do not demand of you that you show us the way to peace and order. If we had them, could the land of Hemingway survive? Hemingwegians are

not adapted to a stable, moral, peaceful world.

E. VR. W.
Catholic World, 152 (January 1941), 502-03.

The hallmark of genius of the highest quality is reticence. As an actor can, at times, make a pause mean more than any words, so a poet; but "the rest is silence—" is a line to which Mr. Hemingway has never paid much attention. Although a curious modern attitude confuses frankness with strength, any survey of the classics will prove that the great masters understood both the power and dignity of restraint.... This is the responsibility that an author with Mr. Hemingway's power and social consciousness should face squarely. His influence is great among the motley of his readers and many writers are bound to shape their style upon a man whose pen has such magic of reality and who can sell his book at the highest price ever paid by Hollywood.

* * *

The band of Loyalist peasants and gypsies whom Jordan joins in hiding are drawn with the rounded detail of a Breughel.... Some of the detail is impossible reading nor could the present reviewer finish the agonizing narration of the Loyalist purge of a Nationalist village or Maria's relation of her own tortures by the Phalangists. Mr. Hemingway has made the unspeakable qualities of rough Spanish speech very vivid by interpolating "obscenity" for dashes.

For Whom the Bell Tolls is written out of the heart of a man who has plumbed the depths of human suffering, who has faced disillusion and struggled to be tolerant and compassionate even toward such brutes as Pablo, the bully. The undertones seem to be wrung out of mental weariness and a certain bewilderment. The Communist peasants begin to say their prayers again when death approaches and when Jordan fears he may be driven to suicide by the pain of his crushed leg, he cries out, "Listen, if I do that now, you wouldn't misunderstand, would you? *Who are you talking to? Nobody,*" as he had said to himself before "It's only missing it [religion] that's bad."

Nothing is finer than the theme chosen from John Donne: "No man is an Iland, intire of it selfe; . . . any man's death diminishes me, because I am involved in Mankinde: And therefore never send to know for whom the bell tolls; It tolls for thee." As a story this book offers not pleasure but mounting pain; as literature it lacks the reserve that steadies genius and that lack not only dims its brilliance but makes it dangerous in its influence.

Malcolm Cowley. "Death of a Hero." *New Republic*, 104 (January 20, 1941), 89-90.

In addition to being a fine novel, "For Whom the Bell Tolls" is also an interesting and very complicated political and moral document. More attention should be paid to this side of it, for all the able reviews that the book has already received. The truth is that Hemingway has always been concerned with ideas, even when his critics took it for granted that he was dealing with purely visceral processes; and for many years his work had more effect on the thinking of young Americans than that of any professional philosopher. In his latest book, the ideas are handled more directly. He is trying here not only to write his best novel, but also to state and justify an attitude toward the Spanish revolution, and toward the whole set of beliefs that dominated the 1930's, besides implying an attitude toward what has happened since his story ended. It is an ambitious undertaking, but then Hemingway has written a very long book, and everything is there if you look for it.

* * *

We can take for granted that "For Whom the Bell Tolls" is the sort of "true book" that Robert Jordan would have written if he had survived. And because he belongs to the long

line of Hemingway's semi-autobiographical heroes, we can take for
granted that he is speaking for the
author, who also played his part in the
Spanish war. But this, once again, is
not the whole story. Jordan cannot
speak for him completely, since the
author himself has changed since the
defeat of the cause for which his hero
died. Something of his later philosophy or his changed feeling toward life
has also gone into the book, and that
is what makes it such a complicated
document.

The new attitude is never directly
expressed, but it is implicit in the
choice of characters and events and in
the whole mood of the story. From
the first chapter to the last, one feels a
continual sense of doom, so that reading the book is almost like watching an
express train pounding full speed toward an open drawbridge. The hero
has to die by emotional necessity, because he has become the symbol of a
dying cause. But most clearly of all,
Hemingway's new feeling about the
war is revealed by the double irony of
this death. Robert Jordan pays with
his life for dynamiting a bridge, in
order to assure the success of a Loyalist offensive, although he already
knows that the offensive will be a failure. That is the first irony. But even at
the moment of his death, he wants to
carry on the fight, telling himself that
if he holds the enemy back a little
while or merely shoots the officer,
"that may make all the difference."
Painfully wounded, fighting back the
desire to kill himself and thus avoid
being taken and tortured, he lies there
with his submachine gun pointed at

the road. Now it happens that among
the Rebels mentioned in the book, one
officer has been singled out as a modest, brave, and religious man, exactly
the sort that Jordan admires. And by
the second irony, this is the officer
killed with Jordan's last clip of bullets.

Years ago, in an often quoted passage of "A Farewell to Arms," Hemingway had said that he "was always
embarrassed by the words sacred, glorious and sacrifice, and the expression
in vain." Now apparently he has written a whole book to explain the meaning of the word "sacrifice" and the
phrase "in vain." Yet even that is not
the whole story. For Hemingway also
seems to be saying that human beings
are not in vain; that they are always
worth more than any cause for which
they die. He seems to be saying, less
persuasively, that love is not in vain,
especially when enjoyed in the face of
danger. And finally, by the immense
care with which he has written this
book, certainly the best and richest of
his novels, he seems to be saying that
honesty and careful craftsmanship are
not in vain. These apparently are the
principles to which he clings in the
ruin of our times.

Dwight Macdonald. "Reading from Left to Right." *Partisan Review*, 8 (January-February 1941), 24-28.

Hemingway's publishers advertise his new book as "the novel that has something for everybody." This seems to be an accurate statement. It is the biggest publishing success since *Gone With the Wind*. . . .

In the face of all this enthusiasm, I have to note that my own experience with *For Whom the Bell Tolls* was disappointing. The opening chapters promised a good deal: they were moving, exciting, wonderfully keen in sensory description. They set the stage for major tragedy. But the stage was never really filled, the promise wasn't kept. The longer I read, the more of a letdown I felt, the more I had a sense that the author was floundering around, uncertain of his values and intentions, unable to come up to the pretensions of his theme. One trouble with the book is that it isn't a novel at all but rather a series of short stories, some of them excellent—Pilar's narratives of the killing of the fascists and of her life with the consumptive bullfighter; the description of Gaylords Hotel; Andres' journey through the Loyalist lines; and the final blowing up of the bridge—imbedded in a mixture of sentimental love scenes, too much talk, rambling narrative sequences, and rather dull interior monologues by

Jordan. So, too, with the characters; they are excellent when they are sketched in just enough for the purposes of a short story, as with El Sordo, the dignified Fernando, and the old man Anselmo. But when Hemingway tries to do more, he fails, as with the character of Pilar, which starts off well enough but becomes gaseous when it is expanded.

The worst failure is the central character, Robert Jordan. Like previous Hemingway heroes, Jordan is not an objectively rendered character but simply a mouthpiece for the author. The earlier heroes had at least a certain dramatic consistency, but Jordan is a monster, uniting—or trying to—the nihilism and cynicism of the usual Hemingway hero with a rather simpleminded political idealism—a sort of Hemingwayesque scoutmaster leading his little group of peasants. For the Hemingway who speaks through Jordan is a Hemingway with a hangover, a repentant Hemingway who has been in contact with a revolution and has accepted it enough to be ashamed of his old faith and yet who cannot feel or understand deeply the new values. The result is that Jordan as a character is vague and fuzzy, destroyed by the continual friction of these irreconcilable viewpoints.

Jordan's confusion is shared and not understood by his creator, and this confusion is the root of the failure of the novel. Although Hemingway himself denies it frequently in the course of the book, and although most of the critics take his denial at face value, *For Whom the Bell Tolls* is a political novel, both in that it deals with a great political event, the Spanish civil war, and that its author takes a definite (though largely unconscious) political attitude towards this event. And it is a failure because Hemingway lacks the moral and intellectual equipment to handle such a theme. Instinctively, he tries to cut the subject down to something he can handle by restricting his view of the war to the activities of a small band of peasant guerillas behind Franco's lines (and hence safely insulated from Loyalist politics) and by making his protagonist—in Karkov's words—"a young American of slight political development but . . . a fine partisan record."

But such limitations negate the pretensions of the book. Hemingway's peasants have been so depoliticalized that it seems little more than chance that they are Loyalists rather than Rebels, and so the long novel is reduced to the scale of an adventure story. . . .

I think the novel is a failure for precisely the reason that many critics seem to like it most: because of its rejection of political consciousness. . . .This false antithesis, between politics and 'art,' or even between politics and 'life,' attractive enough always to the empirically-slanted American consciousness, is doubly seductive today when political creeds have been so discredited by the events of recent years. . . .

* * *

It is notable that in his attempts to define to himself why he finds it increasingly harder to believe in the Loyalist cause, Jordan often blames the Spanish national character (which he feels is treacherous, provincial, cruel, etc.) and sometimes even certain disturbing moral characteristics of individual Stalinists. But he never gives a thought to the really disillusioning development: the slow strangling, by the Stalino-bourgeois coalition, of the revolutionary upsurge of the Spanish masses. The most politically revealing thing in the book is Hemingway's vindictive picture of the Anarchists—"the crackpots and romantic revolutionists," "the wild men," or, most often, simply "the crazies." . . .What worries Hemingway about the Anarchists is that they were undisciplined and armed, which is a good short description of the masses in process of making a revolution. . . .

* * *

I find it significant that the Communist Party seems to be undecided as to just what line to take towards *For Whom the Bell Tolls*. While the book has been roundly denounced in classic C.P. style in the *Daily Worker*, it is being sold in the Party bookshops. And Alvah C. Bessie in the *New Masses* writes more in sorrow than in anger, taking the line that Hemingway, while still sincerely enlisted in the fight against "our common enemy" (reaction), has been misled so that "at the moment he is found in bad company." The Party has evidently not given up hope of welcoming back the straying sheep into the fold at some future (and happier) date. I should say this is a shrewd political judgment.

Lionel Trilling.
"An American in Spain."
Partisan Review, 8
(January-February 1941),
63-67.

To anyone who has been at all interested in its author's career—and who
has not?—*For Whom the Bell Tolls* will
first give a literary emotion, for here,
we feel at once, is a restored Hemingway writing to the top of his bent. He
does not, as in the period of *To Have
and Have Not* and *The Fifth Column*,
warp or impede his notable talent with
the belief that art is to be used like the
automatic rifle. He does not substitute
political will for literary insight nor
arrogantly pass off his personal rage as
social responsibility. Not that his present political attitude is coherent or
illuminating; indeed, it is so little of
either that it acts as the anarchic element in a work whose total effect is
less impressive than many of its parts.
Yet at least it is flexible enough, or
ambiguous enough, to allow Hemingway a more varied notion of life than
he has ever before achieved.

With the themes that bring out his
skills most happily Hemingway has
never been so good—no one else can
make so memorable the events of sensory experience, how things look and
move and are related to each other.
From the beginning of the novel to the
end one has the happy sense of the
author's unremitting and successful
poetic effort. So great is this effort,
indeed, that one is inclined to feel that

it is at times even too great, that it
becomes conscious of itself almost to
priggishness and quite to virtuosity. A-
bout some of the very good things—
they are by now famous—one has the
uneasy sense that they are rather too
obviously "performances": I mean
things so admirable as the account of
the massacre of the fascists by the
republicans as well as things so much
less good because so frankly gaudy as
the description of the "smell of
death." The really superlative passages
are more modestly handled and the
episodes of El Sordo on his hill and
Andres making his way through the
republican lines are equal to Tolstoy in
his best battle-manner. But the sense
of the writer doing his duty up to and
beyond the point of supererogation is
forced on us again in the frequent occurrence of that kind of writing of
which Hemingway has always allowed
himself a small and forgivable amount
to deal with emotions which he considers especially difficult, delicate or
noble. Obtrusively "literary" and oddly "feminine," it is usually used for
the emotions of love and it is always in
as false and fancy taste as this:

Now as they lay all that before had
been shielded was unshielded.
Where there had been roughness of
fabric all was smooth with a
smoothness and firm rounded pressing and a long warm coolness, cool
outside and warm within, long and
light and closely holding, closely
held, lonely, hollow-making with
contours, happy-making, young and
loving and now all warmly smooth
with a hollowing, chest-aching,

tight-held loneliness that was such that Robert Jordan felt he could not stand it. . . .

Yet the virtuosity and the lapses of taste are but excesses of an effort which is, as a whole, remarkably successful. And if we cannot help thinking a little wryly about how much tragic defeat, how much limitation of political hope was necessary before Hemingway could be weaned from the novel of arrogant political will, neither can we help being impressed by what he has accomplished in the change.

I speak first and at some length of the style of *For Whom the Bell Tolls* because it seems to me that the power and charm of the book arise almost entirely from the success of the style —from the success of many incidents handled to the full of their possible esthetic interest. The power and charm do not arise from the plan of the book as a whole; when the reading is behind us what we remember is a series of brilliant scenes and a sense of having been almost constantly excited, but we do not remember a general significance. Yet Hemingway, we may be sure, intended that the star-crossed love and heroic death of Robert Jordan should be a real tragedy, a moral and political tragedy which should suggest and embody the tragedy of the Spanish war. In this intention he quite fails; he gives us astonishing melodrama, which is something, but he does not give us tragedy. The clue to the failure is the essential, inner dulness of the hero, which, in historical fact, the events he lives through actual-

ly did have. Because Jordan does not reproduce in himself the moral and political tensions which existed in the historical situation, his story is at best cinematic; and since his story must provide whatever architectonic the novel is to have, the novel itself fails, not absolutely but relatively to its possibility and implied intention.

This failure illustrates as well as anything could the point of Philip Rahv's essay, "The Cult of Experience in American Writing" (*Partisan Review,* November-December 1940). For here again we have the imbalance which Mr. Rahv speaks of as characteristic of the American novel, on the one hand the remarkable perception of sensory and emotional fact, on the other hand an inadequacy of intellectual vitality. Consider as an illuminating detail the relation which Hemingway establishes between Robert Jordan and the leaders he admires, Goltz the general and Karkov the journalist. Both are cynical and exceptionally competent men, wholly capable of understanding all the meanings of the revolutionary scene. But they are Europeans and Robert Jordan is not; like the hero of Henry James's novel, *The American*, he knows that there are machinations going on around him, very wrong but very wonderful, which he will never be able to understand. Nor does he really want to understand as his friends do; he wants, as he says, to keep his mind in suspension until the war is won. He wants only to feel emotions and ideals, or, as a technician and a brave man, to *do* what he is told; the thinking is for others. Yet, like a

Henry James character again, he must penetrate the complex secret; but he has no wish to use it, only to "experience" it, for he likes, as he says, the feeling of being an "insider," which is what one becomes by losing one's American "chastity of mind" telling political lies with the Russians in Gaylord's Hotel.

Hemingway himself, then, is wholly aware of the moral and political tensions which existed in actual fact. Again and again, and always pungently, he brings to our notice the contradictions of a revolutionary civil war—describes the cynicism and intrigue and shabby vice of the Russian politicos, pointedly questions the political virtue of La Pasionaria, paints André Marty, in a brilliant and terrifying scene, as a homicidal psychopath under the protection of the Comintern, speaks out about the sins of Loyalist leaders and has only a small and uncertain inclination to extenuate the special sins of the Communists. Indeed, there is scarcely a charge that anti-Stalinists might have made during the war whose truth Hemingway does not in one way or another avow. Yet by some failure of mind or of seriousness, he cannot permit these political facts to become integral with the book by entering importantly into the mind of the hero. Robert Jordan, to be sure, thinks a good deal about all these things but almost always as if they were not much more than—to use the phrase of another anti-fascist—a matter of taste. He can, in Mr. Rahv's use of the word, "experience" all the badness, but he cannot deal with it, dare not judge it.

In the end it kills him. And Hemingway knows, of course, that it kills him, for it is certainly true that of all the things that prevent Robert Jordan's despatch from arriving in time to halt the ill-fated attack and preserve his own life, it is the atmosphere of Gaylord's Hotel that is ultimately culpable; it is Marty's protected madness that makes it finally impossible to cancel the attack and that seals Jordan's fate. Were this kept in focus we should have had a personal tragedy which would have truly represented the whole tragedy of the Spanish war—the tragedy, that is, which was not merely a defeat by superior force but also a moral and political failure; for tragedy is not a matter of fact, it is a matter of value. To Robert Jordan his own death is bitter enough, but it is only the last incident of his experience; of its inherent tragic meaning, of its significance in relation to its cause, he has no awareness. Nor is his lack of awareness an intentional irony of which the reader is to be conscious; Hemingway lets the significance fade and the event becomes very nearly a matter of accident. It is, I find, rather terrifying to see where writing from naked experience can take an author; Hemingway knows that his hero must die in some moral circumstance and he lamely and belatedly contrives for Robert Jordan a problem of—courage. And so we get what we all like in the movies, a good fighting death, but in the face of all the potential significance of the event it is devastatingly meaningless. Courage, we are told as a last word, is all: and every nerve responds to the farewell, the flying hooves, the pain and the pathos, but we have been shuffled quite away from the tragedy, which is not of fact and the nerves but of judgment and the mind.

What is the major movement of the novel is, then, a failure and a failure the more to be regretted because it has so many of the elements of great success. But there is another movement of the novel which does not fail—I mean all that part which deals with the guerilla bands of the mountains. One has to understand the genre of this to understand its success; one has to see that this part of the story is a social romance. I should like to draw on Mr. Rahv again: he remarks in another of his essays ("Paleface and Redskin," *Kenyon Review*, Summer 1939) that Hemingway may well be understood as a descendant of Natty Bumppo; certainly in each of Hemingway's heroes there is a great deal of the Leatherstocking blood, though "crossed" (as Leatherstocking himself would say) with the gentler, more sensitive blood of Uncas. And as Leatherstocking-Uncas, the perfect scout, Robert Jordan is all decision, action and good perception, far more interesting and attractive than in his character of looker-on at the political feasts of the Russians where he is a kind of Parsifal, the culpable innocent who will not ask the right question. But more than the character of its hero takes its rise from Cooper—more, too, than Hemingway's "sense of terrain" which Edmund Wilson speaks of as being like Cooper's; for when we think of how clear a line there is between Uncas, Chingachgook and Tamenund, the noble Indians, and

El Sordo and Anselmo and the rest of the guerilla band we see how very like Cooper's is Hemingway's romantic sense of social and personal virtues. With Cooper, however, the social idealization is more formal and more frankly "mythical" and perhaps it is Hemingway's greater realism which makes his social romance suspect, if not as fact then as feeling. For in a love affair with a nation, a people or a class, such as between Kipling and the sahibs or— to speak of a minor but socially interesting writer of today—between Angela Thirkell and the English upper middle class, there is pretty sure to appear, sooner or later, a hatred of the outlander. Even when, like Hemingway, the lover is not himself a member of the beloved group, one cannot help sensing the implied rejection of the rest of humanity.

There is something suspect, too, I feel, in the love-story of his novel, which has so stirred and charmed the reviewers. By now the relation between men and women in Hemingway's novels has fixed itself into a rather dull convention in which the men are all dominance and knowledge, the women all essential innocence and responsive passion; these relationships reach their full development almost at the moment of first meeting and are somehow completed as soon as begun. Most significant, one feels of love in the Hemignway novels that it exists at all only because circumstances so surely doom it. We do not have to venture very deep into unexpressed meanings to find a connection between Hemingway's social myth and the pattern of his love-stories; in both there is a desperation which makes a quick grab for simple perfection, a desperation which, at the same time, makes understandable the compulsive turning to courage as the saving and solving virtue. The whole complex of attitudes is, we might guess, a way of responding to the idea of death.

About Hemingway's concern with death I do not find myself in agreement with the many critics who have found it irritating that anyone should deal with death except as a simple physical fact. I am not sure that our liberal, positive, progressive attitudes have taught us to be emotionally more competent before the idea of death, but only more silent; I cannot assume that anyone who breaks our habit of silence is, by that, doing wrong. But in Hemingway's treatment of death there is something indirect and thwarted, as though he cannot entirely break through our cultural reticences to speculate and poetize creatively upon the theme, as could, say, a death-haunted man like John Donne, from whom Hemingway takes the epigraph and title of his novel. For Donne, death is the appalling negation and therefore the teacher of the ego, whereas for Hemingway it is the ego's final expression and the perfect protector of the personality. The great power of mind in Donne saved him from this sentimental error, just as it taught him how little the ego can exist by itself, how "no man is an *Ilande* intire of itselfe." The nature and power of Hemingway's mind are such that he cannot exemplify in art the idea of the community of men, however moving and important it seems to him; he is wholly at the ser-

vice of the cult of experience and the result is a novel which, undertaking to celebrate the community of men, actually glorifies the isolation of the individual ego.

Mark Schorer. "The Background of a Style." *Kenyon Review*, 3 (Winter 1941), 101-105.

What was for long the sign of Ernest Hemingway's work—the curious tension between subject matter and style, between the themes of violence and the perfectly controlled prose—has gone. Hemingway was extraordinary among modern prose writers for exactly this reason, that he pressed his style into the service of his subject matter in a rather special way: the style was the immediate representation of the moral attitude of the author toward his material, it objectified the author's values and thus in itself was comment in writing otherwise unhampered by comment. When, however, the subject matter began to change—from violent experience itself to the expressed evaluation of violence—the manner began to change. The separation seems to take place in the story, "The Snows of Kilimanjara," [sic] but it is in the novel *To Have and Have Not,* that the fumbling transition is clearest. The first third of this book is superb narrative in the old manner; but as Hemingway lets himself into the theme proper thereafter, the book begins to break down, and the end is a debacle, the noisy collapse of a style and technique simply unable to support their matter. Before, the style in itself was moral comment; with a change in moral attitude, that style was necessarily disrupted. In *For Whom the Bell Tolls* we may witness a new style, less brilliant but more flexible, as it integrates itself. That is a very exciting literary spectacle.

* * *

The style which made Hemingway famous—with its ascetic suppression of ornament and figure, its insistence on the objective and the unreflective (for good fighters do not talk), its habit of understatement (or sportsmen boast), the directness and the brevity of its syntactical constructions, its muscularity, the sharpness of its staccato and repetitive effects, "the purity of its line under the maximum of exposure," that is, its continued poise under the weight of event or feeling—this style is an exact transfiguration of Hemingway's moral attitude toward a peculiarly violent and chaotic experience. His style, in effect, is what he had instead of God.

Until God came.

Now that the evidence is in, the position taken by Edmund Wilson some time ago in *The Atlantic Monthly* is indefensible. Mr. Wilson argued that Hemingway's political persuasion was no persuasion at all, but a simple transfer from object to object of the desire to kill: kudu to fascist. No one would seriously contend, I think, that the very motive of *For Whom the Bell Tolls* is not a tremendous sense of man's dignity and worth, an urgent awareness of the necessity of man's freedom, a nearly poetic realization of man's *collective* virtues. Indeed, the individual vanishes in the political whole, but vanishes precisely to defend his dignity, his freedom, his virtue. In spite of the ominous premium which the title seems to place on individuality, the real theme of this book is the relative unimportance of individuality and the superb importance of the political whole. (For fascists are men, too, and even when the bell tolls for them, it tolls for me, I believe; but the fascists in this book have scarcely any meaning as personalities, merely represent The Enemy.) Hemingway's title portends nothing more than that which we have all known: that the doom of Republican Spain was our doom. This novel is no *War and Peace*, no *Dynasts*; it is realistic, political, and deeply partisan. The defects of characterization are the conventional defects of partisan novels, in which personalities always threaten to vanish in abstractions, as, half the time, the woman Pilar becomes a Spanish Gaea, Robert Jordan any vaguely attractive American, and Maria that perfect sexual creature of the private Hemingway mythology. As in so many partisan novels it is the minor characters, who bear no burden but their own, who are excellent: Sordo, the good old man Anselmo, the insane Marty, the politically exhausted Pablo, this last a magnificent portrait, and a dozen more. About their cause, which is his, Hemingway writes with a zealot's passion. And the old mould is as useless to him—as meaningless—as the old insistence on the individual's isolation, on the private pursuit of his pleasures, and on the exercise of his wholly private virtues. If the early books pled for sporting conduct on violent occasions, this book pleads the moral necessity of political violence. A different thing; indeed, a different writer.

Here is none of the grace of *The Sun Also Rises*, none of the precise perfection of stories such as *A Clean, Well-Lighted Place*. This is by no means a perfect technical performance. The severe compression of the old work gives way to nearly complete relaxation. The first effect of this relaxation is evident in the pace of the narrative itself, which is leisurely. The second effect is in the fulness of detail, which Hemingway's sentences can suddenly accommodate. And the third effect is in the sentences themselves, which employ a wide variety of cadences, almost entirely new, and which are short and long, truncated and sinuous, bare or copious as they are needed. To my taste, this syntactical loosening up is almost excessive, for it quickly ramifies in many directions. Understatement is gone and overstatement too often replaces it; we are reminded of Hemingway's own remark that "the dignity of movement of an iceberg is due to only one-eighth of it being above water." The older objectivity of style held the narrative in check in a way that this narrative is not held in check; and to this fact we may attribute many long passages of reflection not particularly well-written and not particularly necessary to the story, long reveries with which the old-

er Hemingway would have had nothing to do. This easy method of exposition is a technical device which the older style made a luxury; here it is everywhere, and largely wasted.

Thus we gain and we lose. Because it is another story, this story could not have been told at all in the older style, and so, in the future, the flexibility of this new style, with its broader subject matter, gives us a bigger writer. How much do we care if, in relaxing, this style also sprawls sometimes, sometimes even snores a little in the sun? It is possible that moral greatness and the best manners are incompatible.

Robert Littell. "Outstanding Novels," *Yale Review*, 30 Winter 1941, vi, viii.

* * *

Here is a book which people are going to be reading a long time from now, so long a time perhaps that the book may eventually be preceded by an introduction, recalling, to a generation that will certainly remember the greater drama, how this hideous Spanish curtain-raiser came about, and who fought in it, and where, and why. It is Mr. Hemingway's best novel, and one of the best novels about that carrion angel, man, which any American has written. . . .

* * *

There are in it many moments of suspense and danger so excruciating that one is torn between a desire to pull the trigger quick before turning the new page and a desire to run away. Literature is full of harrowing and hair-raising pages, but I don't know anyone who so well as Mr. Hemingway forces one to share the intimate, personal, dry-in-the-mouth, pit-of-the-stomach feelings of a character in a very tight corner. That may be because of Mr. Hemingway's peculiarly microscopic truthfulness and his queer lack of detachment; it may also be because he has an uncannily accurate eye and nose for sights and smells, for feelings and parts of the human body which have usually been beneath the notice or beyond the reticence of other writers.

And yet somehow he can make ignoble objects and coarse words sing. For this book is in its total effect a long way from the flat-in-the-mud realism of so many war books. It's also much more than a breathtaking thriller; the excitement in it, no matter how brutal, how physical, how murderous, somehow manages to soar, distilled by agony into something finer than, on the face of it, it is.

* * *

Some of his earlier books had in them a little of the child staring at a pool of blood. But in this book that side of him has grown up; the pool of blood still interests him for itself, but he also cares deeply whose blood it was, and in what cause shed.

Not that the cause of the Spanish Loyalists—though he was on their side —seems to him "the Cause" with a capital C. Far from neutral or *au*

dessus de la mêlée, Mr. Hemingway cares even more for the truth than for his side. And he pulls no punches in telling about the horrible things that were done by the people on his side. For pitiless, unbearable brutality, the description of the beating to death of the fascists as told by that extraordinary character, Pilar, is very hard to match outside of reality.

"The Nation's Book Reviewers Nominate Their Pulitzer Prize Favorites." *Saturday Review of Literature*, 24 (April 26, 1941), 7.

This is the fourth year *The Saturday Review* has asked the book reviewers of the nation's press to state their nominations for the annual Pulitzer Prize awards. In no year has there been such a wide margin of disagreement as in the present poll. Thirty-nine reviewers participate in the selections, but in only one classification—fiction—are they able to muster a bare majority in support of a particular title. In the categories of biography, history, and poetry, the leading titles fall short of anything resembling an overwhelming vote.

The outstanding book on the list, from the standpoint of vote totals, is Ernest Hemingway's "For Whom the Bell Tolls." Kenneth Robert's "Oliver Wiswell" is runner-up, but the voting behind the leader is somewhat scattered. The only other title, in addition to "For Whom the Bell Tolls," to receive a clear margin of preference is Van Wyck Brook's "New England: Indian Summer," in the history category. . . .

"Out of Oak Park by Madrid."
The Monthly Letter of the Limited Editions Club, September, 1941, pp. 1-4.

It was just a year ago. Mr. Sinclair Lewis, Mr. Clifton Fadiman and Mr. Sterling North were stuffing roast-beef hash into themselves, at The Plaza in New York: where the roast-beef hash costs a whole lot more than it costs at any hashjoint to which *you* may be addicted—and tastes a whole lot better. Mr. Lewis was in New York at the time, although he is now in Minnesota contemplating his novel; Mr. Fadiman was in New York, where he usually is; but Mr. Sterling North had come to New York from Chicago, especially in order to eat the roast-beef hash and to serve on a Committee.

It was part of a game, a game which we, the members and the directors of The Limited Editions Club, had dreamed up nearly ten years ago. For it is the function of the members and the directors of The Limited Editions Club to prepare for themselves new and fine editions of the classics of the world's literatures, new and fine editons of books which we all want to

have on our shelves to read and to re-read. In the discharge of that function, we are continually asking ourselves what a classic is and how to recognize it.

* * *

Now the Selecting Committee was met. Mr. Sterling North, the Literary Editor of *The Chicago Daily News,* had come on from Chicago for the meeting. Mr. Fadiman and Mr. Lewis met him at The Plaza. As they stuffed enormous portions of roast-beef hash into themselves, they went over the list of nominations.

For some little time, they discussed Carl Sandburg's four-volume tome, *Abraham Lincoln: The War Years*; and each of the three advanced a reason why this tome should be considered a classic of the future.

But then they got off onto *For Whom the Bell Tolls.* Mr. North said he thought *For Whom the Bell Tolls* a truly great book because it is a great love story. Mr. Fadiman said that, if *A Tale of Two Cities* is a classic, if *Ivanhoe* is a classic, then *For Whom the Bell Tolls* is a classic: because it is a galloping chronicle in that tradition.

These remarks only served to inspire Mr. Lewis. He trumpeted that *For Whom the Bell Tolls* is definitely a masterpiece, definitely a classic; and he set forth his reasons in an oration which enchanted every diner within hearing distance, the head-waiter, the waiters; and would surely have enchanted Ernest Hemingway.

Ernest Hemingway had written *For Whom the Bell Tolls.* He wrote the book in 1940, and it was published toward the end of that year. It was a triumphant success. Chosen for distribution among its members by The Book-of-the-Month Club, it was reviewed for the members by Henry Seidel Canby, who said: "This is a magnificent romance of human nature, a triumph for the novelist. It is Hemingway's best book since *A Farewell to Arms*, that famous novel which is now regarded as an American masterpiece."

When the book was distributed to the reviewers, they jumped upon Dr. Canby's bandwagon. Here, they said, is an American *masterpiece*. The American reading public jumped upon the bandwagon, too, and bought hundreds of thousands of copies of the book. So, when the time came for the announcement of the Pulitzer Prizes, everyone agreed that the Pulitzer Prize, for the best novel published in the year 1940, would go to Ernest Hemingway for writing *For Whom the Bell Tolls*.

Well, the Pulitzer Prize was not given to Mr. Hemingway. It was given to nobody at all. The members of the Pulitzer Prize Committee declared that they thought *For Whom the Bell Tolls* "vulgar, revolting and obscene." A vulgar and revolting story went the rounds, to the effect that the committee wanted to give the award to Mr. Hemingway; that they were prevented from doing so by a denunciation uttered by Dr. Nicholas Murray Butler, who has been since what seems like 1492 the President of Columbia University; and that, in yielding to Dr. Butler's pressure, the committee decided to make the award to nobody at all.

Be that as it may, Mr. Lewis and Mr. Fadiman and Mr. North voted to award The Limited Editions Club's Gold Medal to Ernest Hemingway for writing the book, published in the preceding three years, which they considered most likely to attain the stature of a classic.

* * *

"Hemingway Gets Gold Medal for Book." *New York Times,* November 27, 1941, p. 21.

Author Ernest Hemingway was awarded the Limited Editions Club gold medal yesterday for his last year's novel "For Whom the Bell Tolls." In a meeting at the Waldorf-Astoria attended by 250 leading literary figures the novelist was acclaimed for writing the book published during the previous three years most likely to become a classic.

The Hemingway novel of the Spanish Civil War was selected from a list of nominations by fifty book critics. The board of judges was headed by Sterling North, literary editor of The Chicago Daily News; Clifton Fadiman, literary editor of The New Yorker; and Sinclair Lewis. It was the third gold medal given by the Limited Editions Club. Previous recipients were Donald Cultrose Peattie in 1935 for his "Almanac for Moderns" and Van Wyck Brooks for "The Flowering of New England" in 1938.

Author Sinclair Lewis addressed the group, said he was reluctant to call

Hemingway the greatest living writer but ranked the gold medalist among the half dozen best writers of today. At 42, said Lewis, Hemingway may still have the best part of his career before him. Others ranked with Hemingway by Lewis included Theodore Dreiser, Willa Cather, Somerset Maugham, H. G. Wells and Jules Romains.

Speaker Lewis described Hemingway as a man without academic ties and indifferent to academic acclaim, including honorary degrees. He characterized Hemingway as a major interpreter of the world-wide revolution but not a professional revolutionist. Rather, he said, the novelist showed in "For Whom the Bell Tolls" how men see violence as a key human trait and turn to violence without apology. He said Hemingway wrote about war without coyness or cuteness, without Kipling's celebration of war as a young men's diverson.

Vacationing in Sun Valley, Idaho, Mr. Hemingway sent a telegram saying the award made him "very happy." (Summary)

J. Donald Adams. "Speaking of Books." *New York Times Book Review,* August 1, 1943, p. 2.

Distribution of the movie version of Hemingway's "For Whom the Bell Tolls" sends this reviewer back to the novel to check his earlier impressions. Three years ago I thought the book "the fullest, the deepest, the truest" of all Hemingway's novels. I find little to modify in that judgment. It still seems the least adolescent, the freest of negation of all his fiction. His notable descriptive powers still have their sharpest edge, his characters are fully realized (Robert Jordan perhaps less so than Pilar, Pablo and Anselmo), his style his least obtrusive, his thought at its most mature level. Then as now it left me alive with anticipation of his next work. And that is what its predecessors did not do. (Summary)

"SRL Poll on Novels and Novelists." *Saturday Review of Literature*, 27 (August 5, 1944), 61.

The *Saturday Review* has asked a number of its contributors to nominate the leading American novelist and the leading novel of the last twenty years. Ernest Hemingway wins hands down as the leading novelist, receiving twice as many votes as Willa Cather, the runner-up, with John Dos Passos third on the list. Sinclair Lewis was fourth, Thomas Wolfe fifth, Ellen Glasgow sixth, and Theodore Dreiser seventh. John Steinbeck, Kenneth Roberts, William Faulkner, and Marjorie Rawlings were tied for eight place.

Judging from the balloting, it is apparent that the critics have taken into account the sum total of a writer's work, for the leading novelist and the leading novel do not coincide. Sinclair Lewis's "Arrowsmith" was chosen the outstanding novel, with Hemingway's "A Farewell to Arms" a close second. Dos Passos's "U.S.A." was third; Steinbeck's "The Grapes of Wrath" fourth; "For Whom the Bell Tolls" fifth. "Arrowsmith" picked up a large number of ballots through the "split-ticket" system of voting, while the voters for Mr. Hemingway, for the most part, selected the works of other writers for their choice of best novel.... Mr. Hemingway, apparently, has caused some confusion in the minds of those who thought him the greatest novelist over two decades. Less than half of his followers gave him credit for writing the best novel, and they were divided between "A Farewell to Arms" and "For Whom the Bell Tolls."

The editors of *The Saturday Review* did not contribute to the poll, but in the estimation of at least one of them, the votes for the first four of the outstanding novelists might have read, Ernest Hemingway, Sinclair Lewis, John Steinbeck, and Ellen Glasgow. The novels might have been "Arrowsmith," "For Whom the Bell Tolls," "The Grapes of Wrath," and "Barren Ground."

Checklist of Additional Reviews

Adeline T. Davidson. *Library Journal*, 65 (November 1, 1940), 923.

Booklist, 37 (November 1, 1940), 90.

Bookmark, 2 (January 1941), 12.

Gilbert Highet. "Thou Tellest Me, Comrade." *Nation*, 152 (March 1, 1941), 242.

"Hemingway Novel Wins Critics' Vote." *New York Times*, April 26, 1941, p. 13.

"Eirie Bans Hemingway Book." *New York Times*, June 12, 1941, p. 3.

Otis Ferguson. "Double Talk Tales: For Whom is That Bell For? "*Saturday Review of Literature*, 24 (September 27, 1941), 10.

Notes

MEN AT WAR

*The Best War Stories
of All Time*

EDITED

with an Introduction

BY

ERNEST HEMINGWAY

Based on a plan by William Kozlenko

CROWN PUBLISHERS
NEW YORK

Men at War

Howard Mumford Jones.
"Minority Report on
Hemingway."
*Saturday Review of
Literature*, 25
(September 12, 1942),
11.

I regretfully turn in a minority report.

The Hemingway who wrote greatly in "For Whom the Bell Tolls" writes the preface to this collection with an air of self-righteousness that is most intolerable and not to be borne. The general tone of the wandering introduction is that almost everybody else is wrong about war, and that only now has the Great Interpreter collected the few immortal narratives, real and imaginary, that tell you what war is really like. But as soon as we open to the first page of the introduction and read the sentence: "This book will not tell you how to die," we know that we are back at the old stand, and that what we have is a collection of pieces to satisfy Mr. Hemingway's curious obsession with death.

Having said so much, I cheerfully admit there are some gripping narratives in the book. But I affirm also that the interest of the collection is factitious. . . . No, the anthology is a hodgepodge; and once its immediate appeal has faded, it will be seen to be such. And I think Mr. Hemingway is too important an artist to permit himself to "author" (the book deserves the word) so shapeless a collection.

Vincent McHugh.
"Hemingway on War."
New Yorker, 18
(October 24, 1942).
80-81.

The blurb on this book calls it "the best war stories of all time." Within limits it comes close to deserving the term, given the wide sampling ranging from Joshua's horn assualt on Jericho to Walter B. Clausen's story on Midway, with Stephen Crane, Prescott, Caesar, Hugo, Stendhal and Marbot included. Included also are Hemingway's descriptions of the Caporetto retreat and El Sordo's fight on the hilltop.

Most of editor Hemingway's selections are from the work of professional writers. While this affords interesting and often true-sounding views by authors rising to their opportunities, it leaves a desire for the words of ordinary soldiers recorded in diaries, memoirs, letters and reports: one wishes, for example, a part of Colonel Freemantle's reminiscences of Gettysburg in place of some of Mr. Hemingway's fictional selections.

In the twenty-page introduction Mr. Hemingway says as usual some profound things on war. Some are extraordinary. He suggests that "the only ultimate settlement" for the Nazis is to sterilize them, which he means in the most literal sense. (Summary)

Herbert Gorman.
"How Men Have Fought and Died."
New York Times Book Review,
November 8, 1942, pp. 1, 37.

Hemingway's "Men at War" is a thundering battlewagon of a book, almost 1100 pages long. It is impressive, sometimes frightening and at some points almost unbearably touching. Much may be familiar to more comprehensive readers, but there are still many fine pieces one may have somehow missed. Hardly an aspect of men's bravery, tenacity and endurance under fire is omitted. Some is in fiction, some in straight narrative history, some in memoir form.

In his selections Ernest Hemingway avoids the sentimental, the flag-waving patriotic and the comically shoddy accounts of military action. His writers are those who became possessed by their subject and made it an aching moment in a lasting and convincing form. Not that everything here is a permanent contribution to letters.

Some pieces appear to have stolen in because of a momentary lapse on the compiler's part. But on the whole the book is an impressive monument to men's ability to endure moments of greatest stress.

Mr. Hemingway's twenty-one page introduction is interesting but too discursive and rather badly put together. Besides assuring the reader that no worse things are to be gone through than have been endured before—that only the tools of war are new—he confronts the old question of censorship and public morale in wartime and tries to explain why no really good books on war were written during the last great war. His reports on the present war suggest, however, that we have moved a long way towards frankness since 1914-18. (Summary)

Marshall Bragdon.
"From Jericho to Midway."
Springfield Republican,
December 5, 1942, p. 6.

During a war, during this war, it is easy to lose historical perspective; to feel and to say, "Nothing like this has happened ever before." That may be true as to the technics, ideologies and dimensions of the struggle. Yet the human ingredients change little: the agonies of body and mind, the strengths and weaknesses nakedly tested in conflict.

That is why a recent book is worth

having at hand: "Men at War: The Best War Stories of All Time." Edited with an introduction by Ernest Hemingway, this 1072-page battleship of an anthology contains more than 80 selections. Its array of short stories and excisions from novels, histories and memoirs forms a turbulent processional, revealing the warriors of almost every century at grips with one another in every form of combat.

* * *

The American battle scene is represented by Crane's "Red Badge of Courage" in its entirety, by Edmonds's picture of Oriskany, Lloyd Lewis's descriptions of Shiloh and Atlanta, by several other Civil War episodes, and by a memorable sheaf of World War pieces by Thomason, Stallings, Col. Roosevelt the younger, Fletcher Pratt and Frazier Hunt. And from the last year come three brief but vivid glimpses of Pearl Harbor and certain events in the South Pacific.

These last inclusions bring up Mr. Hemingway's assertion that no good (and true) war book was written between 1914 and 1918. After leafing through that wartime harvest he felt constrained to select only from books that appeared after the armistice.

"The only true writing that came through during the war was in poetry," he says, and explains, "One reason for this is that poets are not arrested as quickly as prose writers would be if they wrote critically, since the latter's meaning, if they are good writers, is too uncomfortably clear."

He suggests that if such a period of censorship and self-censorship comes now in tempting writers to betray their integrity as truth tellers, then it would be best for the strongest and best of them not to publish but to continue writing privately for a better and freer day; if necessary to work at something else for bread and butter.

He is speaking, of course, of "creative" writing. There have been fine war books already but they have been chiefly war correspondents' second thoughts. "They Were Expendable," for instance, is a magificent job of interviewing. "Suez to Singapore" lambasts our Brittanic allies, but no one has attempted a similar broadside against any part of the American effort. In any case, we cannot predict confidently what would happen until the unpalatable, unsparing book has been written about us.

Mary Stahlman Douglas. *Nashville Banner*, December 16, 1942, p. 42.

This volume contains 82 great war stories, from Julius Caesar's account of his invasion of Britain to Blake Clark's story of Pearl Harbor. I like Mr. Hemingway's forthright and rather unorthodox introduction. There were simply some things he had to get off his muchly publicized chest. . . .

* * *

Let no one think this is strictly a man's book. I read from it avidly far, far into several nights. The proof of the excellence of the selections is that each story, however old it may be, reads as though it might have been written today. So whether it is Oman's "Battle of Hastings," or Malory's "Last Battle of King Arthur," or Xenophon's "March to the Sea," or Stendhal's view of Waterloo, or Hemingway's stories of the civil war in Spain, or Frank Richards' description of the Battle of Ypres, or Walter B. Clausen's account of Midway, it will hold you spellbound and it will leave you very, very humble in the sight and sound of so much that has proved men now and again very like the gods.

Walter Millis. "The Red Face of War, From Goliath to Hitler." *New York Herald Tribune Book Review,* October 25, 1942, p. 3.

This remarkable anthology presents in one volume the red face of war as it has been recorded upon the imaginations of men—of those who have seen it and of those who have not, of ancient men and modern, of fighters and artists and historians. . . .

In many of these narratives one sees war in the large, as the bloody, grandiose, almost impersonal catastrophe; in many others one sees it in the small, narrowed to the ancient and mysterious problem, of its impact upon the individual. . . .

* * *

About the impression as a whole many things might be said. Hemingway himself says in his introduction: "This book will not tell you how to die. This book will tell you, though, how all men from earliest times have fought and died." It will almost, but perhaps not quite. There is the old difficulty that fighting men are not, as a rule, writers, and writers for the most part are not fighting men; and while this book collects the work of the most notable exceptions, even their picture, if not imaginary, is still imaginative. The soldier artist is not writing of battle, but of his memory of battle, heightened, intensified, given a shape and form which may go beyond the actuality. This is war as seen by the unusually sensitive, observant and creative mind, which may be rather different from war as seen by the great mass of any army. It is suggestive that the authors who were primarily soldiers are rather consistently less agonized, more matter of fact, more zestful, than the soldiers who were primarily authors. It is interesting to compare Marbot with Hemingway. It would have been interesting had the book included material, like the superb "Fighting at Jutland" or like many battle reports, from men with no pretense to being writers or artists at all who were simply telling what happened to them in the first moments after the happening. Many of these are very great stories, and true to another side of war.

* * *

It seemed to me, like so many other attempts to deal with war as a whole, angry, chaotic, rambling and pointless. It falls back on the cliches about the stupid politicans who produce these disorders and the stupid generals who augment them—justified cliches, no doubt, but of little use in understanding either why wars come, how they can best be waged or how they are to be prevented. Through his shrewd and sound remarks on war literature and war writers, he scatters at random his resentments against the whole business of war and his convictions as to the necessity of fighting this one. He seriously wants to sterilize all Nazis, but explains that advocacy of this idea will only increase German resistance. He gets mixed up in his facts about the Battle of Midway. I suspect that he is, like so many others of us, a victim of the violent conflict of the emotions which war engenders and that his anger is as much with himself as with the things he castigates. It is not a helpful mood. But it is a familiar one, and out of it has come a remarkable collection, giving a remarkable panorama of man in conflict.

Carlos Baker.
"Anthologies of Mars and Midas."
Sewanee Review, 51 (January-March 1943), 160-63.

* * *

Mr. Hemingway long ago decided that he belonged properly if not continually with Mars, and this anthology of men at war is evidently a compromise between what Mr. Hemingway wanted to include, and what the times made it expedient to exclude; between what Mr. Hemingway thought was sentimental trash, and what his publishers or nameless co-editors were set on putting in. It is a thematic anthology, and its theme is war. Insofar as it is a group effort, it falls short of the hopes of Mr. Hemingway; insofar as it falls short of his hopes, it corroborates his standards, those (I mean) that underlie the best of his own writing.

The latest restatement of these standards is what renders valuable Hemingway's introduction to the anthology. "A writer's job," he says, "is to tell the truth. His standard of fidelity to the truth should be so high that his invention, out of his experience, should produce a truer account than anything factual can be. For facts can be observed badly; but when a good writer is creating something, he has time and scope to make it an absolute truth." Hemingway does not, of course, mean a transcendental absolute. He does mean something like unremitting conformity to the probable actual, that truth which is greater than the sum of its observed parts, the "news that stays news" because it is true both to itself and to its constituents, which feed but do not compel it. . . .

Although relatively few of the selections conform to Hemingway's standards, the surprise is that so many should come so close. Among the two dozen which do conform, I should unhesitatingly include Crane's *Red Badge of Courage* (here given complete),

Hemingway's account of El Sordo's last fight from *For Whom the Bell Tolls*; the extract from *Her Privates We*; the two episodes from Lawrence's *Seven Pillars of Wisdom*; one or two by Colonel Thomason; Stendhal's *Personal View of Waterloo;* Bierce's *Owl Creek Bridge*; Hillary's *Falling Through Space*, and perhaps a dozen others including one by Tolstoy. These twenty-odd are based on fact, accurately observed and recorded with the utmost fidelity, but illumined from within by a quality which goes beyond reporting as a good statue goes beyond stone. They contain the general in the particular; experience is rather a referant than a comptroller. They have in common the factual flavor of eyewitness accounts, but have been matured by the artistic process beyond the level of reporting. They have shaped forms which are recognizable as actuality from rough blocks of carefully ascertained fact. Their matter, to put it one more way, is informed with spirit.

Many, if not most of the remaining stories are history, approaching the others at various levels and to various degrees of nearness, yet always remaining history, tied to particularized fact. The rewards they offer are various: information about the great battles; demonstration of the part played by chance, ignorance, stupidity, or forethought (or these in combination) in the outcome of world-shaking issues. It is odd how flat some of them seem beside the genuine works of art. But the art of writing, like the art of war, has come a long way since David slew Goliath.

Checklist of Additional Reviews

Booklist, 39 (November 15, 1942), 102.

"Ample Anthologies." *Newsweek*, 20 (November 16, 1942), 92.

Cleveland Open Shelf, November 1942, p. 24.

Notes

The Viking Portable Library

HEMINGWAY

◇◇

Edited by Malcolm Cowley

NEW YORK · THE VIKING PRESS
1944

The Viking Portable Hemingway

Max Lerner.
"On Hemingway."
PM,
September 28, 1944,
p. 2.

* * *

I have just finished reading the *Viking Portable Hemingway*, edited by Malcolm Cowley, and I want to cheer for it. In it a great writer and a perceptive critic have combined to produce a delightful anthology. Many Americans know Hemingway only through his bestselling novel, *For Whom the Bell Tolls*, and through the somewhat dubious movie version of it. They would do well to go back to the earliest work—*The Sun Also Rises, A Farewell to Arms*, and the short stories from *In Our Time*.

There have been two strains of Hemingway criticism. One has been to exalt or damn him as a "tough guy," the creator of the hard-boiled realistic school of American fiction, the chronicler of the excesses of life and the poverties of speech of the "lost generation," the explorer of violence and bull-fighting and revolution. Malcolm Cowley's introduction to this volume, the finest piece of critical writing that has been done on Hemingway, breaks away from this strain. Hemingway, says Cowley, must not be taken as "the fruit of a misalliance between Dreiser and Jack London." He is rather in the tradition of Poe and Hawthorne and Melville—one of "the haunted and nocturnal writers, the men who dealt in images that were symbols of an inner world." And he makes out a good case for his view.

Yet after reading this volume I cannot see Hemingway wholly as a Poe or a Hawthorne. Cowley has given us a half-truth, as had the other critics. The Hemingway I have just read is both a tough guy *and* a nocturnal writer. He is the man who celebrates the virile pursuits of men, and at the same time he is haunted by the sense of their inner meaning. In that fusion of the muscular and the symbolic lies his essential and viable quality.

The young people who have talked about Heminway to me have seen him mainly, I think, as a Byronic figure of our own day. He is the man who, in the great words of Justice Holmes, must "share the passion and action of his time at peril of being judged not to have lived."

* * *

281

There are some who put Hemingway into the tradition of the political novel: and there is a sense in which Malraux's *Man's Fate* and Koestler's *Arrival and Departure* and Silone's *Bread and Wine* claim Hemingway's novel of Robert Jordan and the Spanish war in their company. They deal with political ideas, handled by men who have sought to shape history as well as to probe the human mind.

Yet, it is only in his latest phase that Hemingway belongs with these men. It is hard to think of any of them as the writer of the stories of Nick Adams in *In Our Time*.

For all of Hemingway's recent insistence that no man is an island, the lasting impression one gets from him is of a writer intensely absorbed with the individual. Cowley has an interesting suggestion that Hemingway is a "primitive" in the sense that he is obsessed with ritual—the ritual of fishing, of bull-fighting, of death, of love. One can carry the suggestion further. Those who have read the anthropologist Van Gennep, will know that he divides rituals into two groups. One consists of the "rites of passage"—the rituals performed at times of crisis in the individual's life. The other consists of the rituals performed during crises in the life of the group or tribe.

Hemingway is a ritualist in the first sense only. It is because he has a keen eye for the crises of the individual life that one can find in each of his stories the brave show of toughness combined with a scarcely hidden agony.

Dan S. Norton. "Eclectic Hemingway," *New York Times Book Review,* October 8, 1944, p. 3.

In the twenty years he has been writing Ernest Hemingway has given in his novels and short stories the most remarkable account of living in our time provided by any American author. "The Portable Hemingway" edited by Malcolm Cowley purports to sample that account by showing the interrelationships of Hemingway's chief works.

Although it is a fine collection it fails to show the connections claimed for it. Mr. Cowley does very well with the short stories, reprinting all of "In Our Time" and a representative selection of the later stories. He is correct in omitting "Green Hills of Africa" and would have done better to omit the epilogue from "Death in the Afternoon." In both, Hemingway shows that in writing about himself he is too likely to substitute pose for insight. In handling the novels Mr. Cowley succeeds less well. Limited no doubt by space considerations, he has settled for reprinting excerpts from the novels, except for presenting all of "The Sun Also Rises." In doing so, he demonstrates all over again how a novel cannot be represented by an excerpt, no matter how good the excerpt or how helpful the context. A comprehensive anthology of a novelist is an editorial paradox.

Although Mr. Cowley's introduction provides excellent literary comment, it fails to show, as announced, how the novels tell a more or less connected story. The pairings of excerpts result in a meeting of virtual strangers in many cases. What the collection does show is that Heminway is best seen as a latter day romantic. His temperament meets almost any textbook definition of nineteenth century romanticism. Like Byron, he is in revolt against society's artificial rules and makes romantic despair his dominating mood. Like Keats he is half in love with easeful death. Like Wordsworth he sees the simple peasant living closest to truth. Feeling the romantics' desire to escape the present, he turns not to the past but to the primitive. In this he reaffirms the basic romantic belief in emotion and instinct and distrust of the mind.

Despite these objections Mr. Cowley's anthology has value. A rich and generous collection, it recalls many fine moments for those who know Hemingway's work. For those who do not, it provides an interesting and extensive introduction that should send them on to read "A Farewell to Arms" and "For Whom the Bell Tolls." Until they do they cannot measure his achievement or recognize the recent changes in his interpretation of our experience. (Summary)

Marshall Bragdon. "Rereading Hemingway." *Springfield Republican*, October 14, 1944, p. 6.

It is a striking experience at this stage of this war to sample again the work of Ernest Hemingway. The last war made him and marked him; in turn he set down some essences of that war, and even more searingly some of its consequences in human lives. "Farewell to Arms" and "The Sun Also Rises" convey powerfully the immediate and the delayed-action costs of it all.

"The Portable Hemingway," edited by Malcolm Cowley, offers a convenient means of acquaintance or of rereading. . . .Malcolm Cowley's introduction is luminous and searching, and his prefaces to various sections are helpful. Not unexpectedly, the reader will find the novel excerpts least satisfactory. Good novels bleed when cut.

The past work of Hemingway (who has most recently been reporting this war at a reported dollar a word) is significant for his technics, his general attitudes toward life, and most difficult to measure, the change in those attitudes.

His craftsmanship is great, as evidenced by his imitators' obvious failures. By laborious apprenticeship, he strove to describe accurately "the sequence of motion and fact" of a situation; to see things clearly and report them honestly. This was a special kind of realism. Hemingway contrived to select those sharp details of a scene or conflict which produced in a reader the same emotion that he felt as first-hand observer. Such disciplined suggestiveness is a very difficult achievement; lesser writers who reach for it often end by merely aping this author's incidental mannerisms.

* * *

Rejection of society's rules and half-hypocrisies is a central theme of Hemingway. And it has made him a limited but superb observer of the negative aspects of life between 1919 and 1939.

The Spanish war, however, brought a new element to Hemingway's attitude. It was a new thing when Robert Jordan, dying in Spain, felt a "social purpose," an obligation to an alien but beloved people, and even a devotion to an ideal. How much this element will be strengthened in Hemingway's future work remains to be seen. It necessarily depends upon the degree of decency or obscenity (to borrow his famous euphemism) that characterizes our peacemaking, and that marks the next two decades. If renewed despair engulfs us, Hemingway will record it with terrible honesty.

Granville Hicks. "Twenty Years of Hemingway." *New Republic*, 111 (October 23, 1944), 524, 526.

Mr. Cowley's "Portable Hemingway" contains the whole of "The Sun Also Rises," the description of the retreat from Caporetto from "A Farewell to Arms," the account of Harry Morgan's slaughter of the Cubans from "To Have and Have Not" and the story of El Sordo's battle from "For Whom the Bell Tolls." It also contains the whole of "In Our Time," nine other short stories, and a brief passage from "Death in the Afternoon." I do not know for whom such a book is published, and I do not suppose it matters. People buy it and read it, and then perhaps they go and read the novels from which the extracts are taken and the other short stories, and that is all to the good, or else they read only what is in the book, and that is a good deal better than reading nothing. The selection is in some ways a strange one, but presumably it was dictated in part by practical considerations of publishing. The important thing is that there is nothing here that is not worth reading or rereading, and nothing has been omitted that is conspicuously better than what is here.

For people who have been reading Hemingway these twenty years, the book's great value—aside from the pleasant temptation to reread what one has always been promising oneself one would reread—lies in Malcolm Cowley's introduction and notes. The introductory essay, much of which appeared in The New Republic last summer, is the best critical discussion of Hemingway I have read. Curiously and even shockingly, it is one of the first discussions to examine Hemingway on his own grounds.

Hemingway, Cowley maintains, is not a naturalist, as the textbooks have said, but one of "the haunted and nocturnal writers" in the tradition of Poe, Hawthorne and Melville. Like everyone else, I have always known that Hemingway did not describe fishing and skiing, and boxing and bull-fighting, drinking and sexual intercourse for their own sake. I have thought and said that violent physical activity was for Hemingway the only possible escape from a world grown too complicated and difficult and disheartening. This is partly true, but the point Cowley makes is that the acts Hemingway so often describes have for him the quality of rites. Rites are a form of escape, too, I suppose, but when one reaches this level—the level, I mean, on which all primitive and most civilized men have lived—"escape" cannot be used as a term of abuse. Hemingway, that is to say, though he appears to be dealing with the surface behavior of bored and not very representative individuals, is actually touching upon a profound and almost universal phenomenon. Perhaps that is why so many critics have felt in his work power and significance that their analyses did not account for.

Even writing, Cowley suggests, is a

form of incantation or exorcism for Hemingway, and he quotes some of the many passages in which autobiographical characters speak of the cartharsis writing can give .

* * *

In discussing ritual and symbol, Cowley makes an interesting point about the influence of Hemingway's early contacts with Indians. He neglects, however, a greater influence, Hemingway's Catholicism. I do not know whether Hemingway has ever been a "good" Catholic, but surely the fact of his being a "bad" Catholic—like Jake Barnes and Frederic Henry—has to be reckoned with. As the lovely dialogue between Frederic Henry and Count Greffi in "A Farewell to Arms" indicates, his fears and doubts are sharpened by an awareness of a conceivable faith in the order and purpose of the universe. This awareness is always present, but the response to it broadens from the anguish of Frederic Henry, who is *croyant* at night, to the stoical affirmation of Anselmo in "For Whom the Bell Tolls." "Let *them* have God," Anselmo says. "Clearly I miss Him, having been brought up in religion. But now a man is responsible to himself."

Cowley is right in emphasizing the strain of primitivism in Hemingway, but it will not do to make too much of that particular theme. Next in importance to his concern with death, and closely related to it, is his concern with human loneliness. In the early work it is only in a rare kind of sexual relationship and in brief moments of male companionship that a man escapes loneliness, and both experiences are transient. Harry Morgan's discovery in "To Have and Have Not" that a man cannot stand alone is not wholly convincing in terms of the novel, but its meaning for Hemingway became apparent in "For Whom the Bell Tolls." Here for the first time a Hemingway hero has a rich sense of the support that a beloved woman, a group of comrades and a cause can give—in death as well as life.

Now it is this sense of living in the group and surviving in the group that is the primitive sense, whereas the feeling of isolation is sophisticated. Individualism in the philosophical sense is rare in most primitive societies and apparently nonexistent in many. Primitive man confronts all the experiences of life, including death, as part of a group, and his rituals—never private affairs like Hemingway's—grow out of and intensify the feeling of group solidarity. Civilization breaks down the small, integrated groups, and man comes to feel that he is alone. For us, the sense of belonging is something to be achieved, not a heritage, and, as is clear in "For Whom the Bell Tolls," it is always precarious.

It is strange that Hemingway, who has always hated pretentiousness, has found pretentious titles for all of his novels. If the titles are to be accepted at face value, he has written about a generation, about a war, about the struggle between rich and poor and about human solidarity. As a matter of fact, only the fourth of the novels lives up to the wider implications of its name, and even "For Whom the Bell Tolls" is not wholly or with perfect

success what it purports to be. It is perhaps unfortunate that his novels should have seemed to attempt so much. If one admits at the beginning that his men and women are in many respects not widely representative, one is more likely to see them for what they are, and to discover, as Cowley has discovered, that it is not their outward behavior that makes them important but their fears and their adjustments to their fears. If, that is, Jake Barnes is not representative of the postwar generation—and outwardly I don't see how he can be—he may, looked at closely, stand for an even larger segment of humanity.

To call Hemingway a great writer is not, it should be needless to say, to express agreement with all or any of his views. But Cowley has put this as well as it can be put:

By now he has earned the right to be taken for what he is, with his great faults and greater virtues, with his narrowness, his power, his always open eyes, his stubborn, chip-on-the-shoulder honesty, his nightmares, his rituals for escaping them, and his sense of an inner and outer world that for twenty years were moving together toward the same disaster.

In the recent Collier's articles one sees pictures of Hemingway, the bearded, self-confident veteran surrounded by apprehensive kids in uniform, and one can smile, thinking of what he has said about war, thinking about his love of poses; but here, too, his demon is driving him, and some day we may be glad that he has again gone where his demon bade.

Checklist of
Additional Reviews

Kirkus, 12 (August 15, 1944), 347.
Booklist, 41 (October 15, 1944), 60.

ACROSS THE RIVER

AND

INTO THE TREES

BY

ERNEST HEMINGWAY

CHARLES SCRIBNER'S SONS
NEW YORK
1950

Across the River and into the Trees

Lewis Gannett.
"Books and Things."
New York Herald Tribune,
September 7, 1950,
p. 23.

"Across the River and Into the Trees" is a story about a day in the life of a man very like the Ernest Hemingway whom Lillian Ross reported so devastatingly in "The New Yorker" a few weeks ago—a self-conscious tough boy, proud of the soldier's trade—"the oldest and the best, although most people who practice it are unworthy," proud of his drinking, proud of his woman, angrily proud of his "old wild-boar truculence," and a little in love with "sleep's other brother," death.

* * *

There are wonderful flashes of the old Hemingway in the book—the tacit understanding between the colonel and his American driver, for instance. . . . There is the old Hemingway passion for good shooting, and there is the dream-girl who is a dream of all fair women and never more than a dream, like almost all the Hemingway women. Best of all are the passages of deep respect for the honest profession of soldiering, so seldom represented by men in command.

The old "wild boar truculence" is appealing; it has its charm. The truculence is, indeed, the heart of the book. Some of the moonlight romance sounds as if it had been written for "Esquire," and paid for by the line. Some of the book is Hemingway at his worst, and the whole does not add up to Hemingway at his best. You remember, halfway through, that there was always some bad Hemingway mixed up with the best Hemingway, but before you come to the end, you forget. You are too conscious of a tired young-old man, in love with lost youth, and rather moony about it.

Colonel Cantwell knew that a man who, like Ernest Hemingway with the 4th Division, had really known and felt the war, could not write about it . . . .

That is the good Hemingway, saying that the good Hemingway cannot —not yet, at any rate—write the real Hemingway book about the war.

289

Charles Poore.
"Books of the Times."
New York Times,
September 7, 1950,
p. 29.

Ernest Hemingway, who has probably
made a deeper mark on the world's
literature than any other modern A-
merican writer, is publishing a new
novel, "Across the River and into the
Trees," today. It is his first since "For
Whom the Bell Tolls," which appeared
in 1940, and it is his best love story
since "A Farewell to Arms," which
appeared in 1929. A lot of contemporary history—the Age of Hemingway—
is suggested in those dates, those titles,
and the astounding memories they can
stir in all our yesterdays.

I have read "Across the River and
into the Trees" twice now, in Cosmopolitan magazine and in book form,
and I like it very much, though I am
not unaware that it is heavily weighted
with the foolishness of grandeur.

* * *

After a decade of reading road-company Hemingways, it is a great pleasure to be reading Hemingway himself
again. There really is no true substitute
for his novels, no matter how wide the
popular demand. The swarming Hem-
ingwayfarers have never matched his
gift for stinging comedy, his cadences
and his profoundly tragic sense of life.
Though the world at large, which used
to think he was rather too preoccupied
with death, has by now seen how mild-

ly he prophesied the dilemma of war-
haunted humanity.

The wonderful descriptions of
Venice in "Across the River and into
the Trees" may send Hemingway-
pilgrims there as numerously as they
once went to Pamplona and Madrid. A
measure of his stature as a writer is the
fact that he could even write about
Paris as if no one had ever written
about Paris before.

The Spanish influence, though, is
strongest always. In reading the story
of the colonel and Renata you may
occasionally feel that it is a parable of
Goya and the Duchess of Alba. For
Cantwell is really much more an artist
than he is a soldier, and Renata is
more like a Spanish duchess than an
Italian countess. And I suspect, though
I have not counted them, that there
are more Spanish than Italian words in
the text. The whole business about the
mock heroic Ordine Militar, Nobile y
Espirituoso de los Caballeros de Brusa-
delli, to which a very select group of
characters belongs, is done in Spanish,
since "the colonel and the head waiter
both spoke Spanish, and since that is
the best language for founding orders." And the book itself is a memorable series of Caprichos and Dispar-
ates, or like the drawings Goya made
between Madrid and Sanlucar.

Hemingway's capacity for finding
characters who improbably want to be
informed interminably about all sorts
of things within his spokesman's prov-
ince of opinion serves him well here.
(You may remember the Old Lady in
"Death in the Afternoon" or the fellow in the Tyroler hat in "The Green
Hills of Africa," for example.) What

with the head waiter's chiming reminiscences and Renata's singular curiosity about E.T.O. figures and campaigns, the colonel has a loquacious field day.

In the gondola or at the bar of the Gritti Palace, Richard and Renata are lovers in the immemorial Hemingway manner; somewhat more rank-conscious than usual; talking the fabulous dialogue that would not surprise Lady Brett Ashley of "The Sun Also Rises" or Maria of "For Whom the Bell Tolls"; figures in a deceitvely simple and yet amazingly complex commentary on life and love and death and art and war and peace and Venice.

It is a short novel, but if you follow all its forays and judgments and allusions it will last you a long time. The prodigal talent of Hemingway, which has so often given in a paragraph or a line a scene that other writers would laboriously fatten into a chapter, was never more apparent than here. And so are the snap judgments, which, once uttered and committed to type, will always be there to plague him—or, at any rate, be brought up and worried and fretted and refuted by others. For example, I think his remarks on Eisenhower, the man who had the incomparable capacity to command Montgomery, de Gaulle, Bradley and Patton in a victorious quadriga, show a certain lack of imagination. And that is all the more disappointing when you consider that Hemingway can still write our Tolstoyan novel of the war.

Well, after all, we might remember that it is Cantwell, the imaginary character, the valiant, dying colonel, who is speaking, not Hemingway. Just as it is Cantwell, not Hemingway, who

seems to remember a war-correspondent's briefing in Paris in the grim winter of 1944 much more angrily than so many things that must have happened to him between the Piave and Normandy.

Far from incidentally, some of Hemingway's best descriptions of modern war are here . . . . Hemingway knows what he's talking about better than many a novelist-soldier of the chair-borne paragraph troopers who went into the Army with a copy of "A Farewell to Arms" in his musette bag.

Here, then, is Hemingway's new novel, a little less than perfect, but proof positive that he is still the old master. All those who came to praise him after "The Sun Also Rises" and "A Farewell to Arms" and "For Whom the Bell Tolls" will praise him again. All those who came to bury him after "Death in the Afternoon" and "The Green Hills of Africa" and "To Have and Have Not" will come to bury him again. All short-story anthologists will continue to choose between "The Killers" and "The Snows of Kilimanjaro." And, as usual, everybody will want to read Hemingway's new book.

Joseph Henry Jackson. "The New Hemingway." *San Francisco Chronicle*, September 7, 1950, p. 18.

Some months ago, in a flurry of publicity releases, Charles Scribner's Sons, long publishers of Ernest Hemingway's books, announced that there would be a new Hemingway novel, and somewhat sooner than had been expected.

The story was that Hemingway, at work on a full-lenth fiction, had had a sudden illness and that in his awareness that just perhaps he might not pull through it had decided to drop the long novel temporarily and do a shorter one that he had had in his mind for some time. Tied in with this was the announcement that the shorter novel would appear in magazine serial form.

The serialization took place, and this time there was a different kind of flurry—a series of rumors that Mr. Hemingway was "writing extensively" for book publication, and that the book, when it appeared, would be quite a different matter from the serial version.

Not having read the serialization, I am not competent to report on this aspect of it. Having read the book, "Across the River and Into the Trees," I can report that the Scribner hint of some months past—that this one was not "the important book"—is justified. There is no question about the Hemingway touch, so to put it. That is here, though too often it resembles a parody of Hemingway at his best. But the test comes when you finish the book and ask yourself what its author had to say this time. The honest reader, with the best will in the world, will have to answer: "Not much, if anything."

* * *

The publishers suggest that this is a "mood novel," and that's about it, of course. Unfortunately the mood is extremely close—almost uncannily close—to that created by Lillian Ross in her piece on Mr. Hemingway himself in The New Yorker last spring—a piece that kicked up quite a how-de-do in literary circles. No one has the right to say that Colonel Cantwell, in this tale, is the author's own projections of himself, and it would be going too far to say so flatly, anyway. But it is a fact that the rough-talking, shadow-boxing, duck-hunting, retread officer, with his tags and odds and ends of World War I memories, his interest in the techniques of war and his politico-philosophical views, is weirdly like the picture Lillian Ross drew of the Hemingway she talked to. . . .

As for the rest, I would add only that, along with many others who have lived and read through the decades in which Mr. Hemingway has been a unique literary influence, I shall wait for the longer, more important novel on which he is reported to have been engaged for some time. It should provide the clue to whether the old Hemingway is still—as the Colonel might put it—"operating."

Lee Cheney Jessup. "A Sadder and Wiser Hemingway." *Nashville Banner,* September 8, 1950, p. 34.

Ernest Hemingway's first novel in a decade is indeed a literary event anticipated most eagerly by those with the nostalgic longing for another "Farewell to Arms." They have reckoned, however, without consideration for the intervening years, and the fact that "Farewell to Arms" is the product of a young man's enthusiasm and vitality.

The latest of Hemingway's is the product of a sadder and wiser personality. It is difficult to compare it with his previous writings although the situation is the one most often employed by Hemingway—the manifestation of deep and passionate love against a background of sudden death. The shadow of death here is not the violence and uncertainty of war but the dark and inexorable shade of personal infirmities, brought on by war's ravages, and the hero is not young and handsome, but in middle years with a body scarred and marred by the two wars of the past.

* * *

Here it seems that Hemingway becomes autobiographical and though it is the "skin of Esau it is the voice of Jacob," and the illusion of the love scenes dissolves under the vitriolic outbursts of Col. Cantwell's biographer. These indictments may be fair and true but they seem dissonant and awkward, strewn among the mechanism of love-making.

Also, the story carries a heavy burden in the special and obscure figures of speech attributed to the army colonel, and the ambiguity of many of the references in the dialogues which cloud the meaning. But against these trivialities is the mood, flawlessly projected as only Hemingway can do it: vibrant life against death, Venice, the

beautiful surrounded by the remnants of war, the perfection of youth against the handicaps of age, gaiety and laughter shielding heartbreak, and over it all the brooding awareness of the approach of the tragic moment. Whatever the middle may lack, the beginning and the end are unmistakably and satisfyingly Hemingway magic.

* * *

Theodore M. O'Leary. "In Mood of Sadness and Futility." *Kansas City Star,* September 9, 1950

In "Across the River and Into the Trees," his first novel in ten years, Ernest Hemingway has chosen, as he did in his three most famous novels, to write about an American against a European background.

* * *

Colonel Cantwell has had his share of disappointments but the keenest of all is his realization that he has won the complete and unselfish love of this beautiful girl of 19 too late. Both he and Renata know that the colonel will live only a short time longer, that their two days in Venice, will probably be the last they will ever have together. It is this plain fact that casts over "Across the River and Into the Trees" the mood of sadness and futility so characteristic of "The Sun Also Rises" and Hemingway's other novels.

In fact, and not very surprisingly, execpt for evidence of a growing cryptic quality in his work, "Across the River and Into the Trees" displays almost the same faults and virtues as Hemingway's other novels, if we exclude his generally unsuccessful "To Have and Have Not."

The descriptive writing in it is nothing less than wonderful, with its completely simple clarity and its strong appeal to all the senses. A duck blind on a cold morning, a windy night in a gondola on a Venice canal, a road through the Italian countryside, the look of the wind-swept Grand Canal from the open window of a hotel room at sunset—these things and many others Hemingway conveys as well as anybody ever has.

The casual conversations between Colonel Cantwell and boatmen and barmen and waiters are perfect little segments of life, reaffirming the dignity of men regardless of station, and the true meaning of good manners.

On the other hand, the vaunted Hemingway dialogue disappoints in many of the exchanges between the colonel and Renata. Some of their lovers' conversation is downright embarrassing, not because of its intimacy but because of its improbability, even phoniness. At such times Hemingway seems on the verge of writing a parody of Hemingway.

That sadness to which reference has been made sometimes almost descends to pathos, but always at the last dangerous moment Hemingway retrieves the situation, usually by putting a hard and sardonic remark in the colonel's mouth. Hemingway's completely unnecessary and juvenile fondness for the more vulgar 4-letter words is also unhappily evident.

To borrow Hemingway's own device of using sporting terms to deal with nonsporting subjects, it can be said that every time Ernest Hemingway writes a book he climbs into the ring and is in a sense defending his championship against scores of imitators and challengers, who are not necessarily synonymous. In "Across the River and Into the Trees" he has missed a knockout, but he has almost certainly scored a decision. And, excluding maybe a sour round or two, he's given the ringsiders their money's worth while hanging on to his title.

Maxwell Geismar. "Across the River and Into the Trees." *Saturday Review of Literature*, 33 (September 9, 1950), 18, 19.

This is an unfortunate novel and unpleasant to review for anyone who respects Hemingway's talent and achievement. It is not only Hemingway's worst novel; it is a synthesis of everything that is bad in his previous work and it throws a doubtful light on the future.

It is so dreadful, in fact, that it begins to have its own morbid fascination and is almost impossible, as they say, to put down . . . .

The sex is oral and anatomical mainly; the passion, so far as I can see, is purely verbal. There is not one scene of genuine feeling; what is even more curious on the part of the artist who could understand Lady Brett or Catherine Barkley is the heroine's complete lack of sensuousness or feminine perception. She is a fantasy of the completely docile, pliant child bride and is useful in the novel merely as interlocutor for the Colonel's overwhelming narcissism . . . .

* * *

The ideological background of the novel is a mixture of *True Romances,* Superman, and the Last Frontier. And the setting of the novel is a perfect instance of Veblen's conspicuous consumption. The Colonel drinks to Leclerc's death with a magnum of Perrier-Jouet Brut 1942 and knows the feeding habits of lobsters from the Dalmatian coast. His companion, the young countess, speaks casually of her butler and maid while she impulsively slips her lover the family jewels. But the Colonel moves warily from duck shoot to duck shoot and even at his favorite cafe, after the tourists and diplomats have gone, he is alert for plots, intrigues, sudden death, and makes sure he has both his flanks covered.

As is the case of Sinclair Lewis, the late phase of Hemingway's work—this vulgar and snobbish vision of social superiority and luxury—is essentially middle class. And yet what marks this psychological universe is precisely the lack of any sort of middle ground. Just as the Colonel's friends range from waiters to the Italian nobility, but exclude an average citizen, the only alternative to "fun" is desperation. He is himself either barbarous or kind, a good boy or a bad boy; everything is either wonderful or dreadful, and the love affair oscillates between these precarious poles of emotion . . . .

* * *

But all that is left here is the scab and the pus, as it were, of true insights. The suffering and anguish are a mark of superiority, not of human communion; the double identification in Hemingway's best work with both the hunter and the hunted has been resolved into the code of the snob and the killer. This is a cosmos of jerks, this is Winner Take Everything, this is to Have and to Have and to Have. There are still good things in "Across the River and into the Trees," and it is possible that the novel will serve as an emotional release for an intricate and tormented talent, very much as "The Torrents of Spring" did in the earlier phase of Hemingway's career.

But surely this, to use his new lingo, is not the work of the man who was there. Nor did Walt Whitman's original phrase of compassion—"I was the man. I was there"—mean what Hemingway now means.

Morton Dauwen Zabel. "A Good Day for Mr. Tolstoy." *The Nation,* 171 (September 9, 1950), 230.

* * *

This is the novel—Hemingway's fifth in thirty years of writing—we've awaited for ten years, certainly with every hope that it would augur the renewal of a talent that has given us several of the memorable books of the century. Briefly, it doesn't. What might, in say, thirty pages, have been an effective *conte* on the order of "Francis Macomber" or "The Snows of Kilimanjaro," has been stretched, beaten out, and enervated to the length of three hundred. The drama is almost static. The talk, retaining only a few of its old living accents, develops unbelievable prodigies of flatness, mawkishness, repetition, and dead wastes of words. The Colonel, advertised as "perhaps the most complex character that Hemingway has ever presented," proves to be a stereotype of earlier heroes: another existential man at his rope's end, faithful only to the ritual of soldiering and love; and the girl Renata repeats the submissive childlover of "For Whom the Bell Tolls," serving also as counterfoil to another familiar type, the bitch exwife—an ambitious woman journalist in this case—who has sealed Cantwell's scepticism of all but the most rudimentary forms of human or sexual traffic.

The reader inevitably arrives at this book with a complex conditioning. It is, first of all, offered as a by-product of the larger novel Hemingway has been writing since 1940. We remember how the earlier novels and tales stamped the modern imagination with some of its most memorable fables and images. But we are also perforce reminded of how many other assaults the force and stubborn integrity of these have met in the last twenty years—confused performances like "Death in the Afternoon" and "To Have and Have Not"; fiascos of ineptitude like "Green Hills of Africa" and "The Fifth Column"; the muddled power of "For Whom the Bell Tolls"; not to mention the dismal exhibitionism of the *Esquire* articles in the thirties or the self-exploiting public character of the interviews and photographs .... The resentment induced by all this has hardly been improved on hearing Hemingway deliver himself of statements like the following: "I started out very quiet and I beat Mr. Turgenev. Then I trained hard and I beat Mr. de Maupassant. I've fought two draws with Mr. Stendhal .... But nobody's going to get me in any ring with Mr. Tolstoy unless I'm crazy or I keep getting better." The modesty *vis-a-vis* Tolstoy is appreciated, but one wonders if a little less certainty about having worsted the Messrs. Turgenev, Maupassant, and Stendhal might not, to put it mildly, have been tactful, or done Mr. Hemingway a little good. Of course there was also that *New Yorker* profile last spring. With every allowance for calculated malice, one was left wondering what could possibly survive for the serious business of art and writing. The only answer provided by "Across the River" is: very little.

The obvious truth is that this new novel is the poorest thing its author has ever done—poor with a feebleness of invention, a dulness of language, and a self-parodying of style and theme even beyond "The Fifth Column" and "To Have and Have Not." It gives no sign of the latent rigor that has permitted Hemingway, in tales like "The Undefeated," "Old Man at the Bridge," "Macomber," and "Kilimanjaro," to pull himself together after he had given every evidence of having gone to pieces, and to declare his old powers. For a few small favors one must be grateful: this book at least lacks the supremely silly "(obscenity)" device that disfigured the pages of "For Whom the Bell Tolls." What one is left with (the analogy of Kipling once suggested by Edmund Wilson is again pertinent) is the impasse of routine mechanism and contrivance a talent arrives at when an inflexibly formulated conception of experience or humanity is pushed to the limits of its utility, excluding any genuine exploration of human complexity or any but the most brutally patented responses to character and conduct.

We are left to conclude that this talent, while nothing can efface what it acheived in at least two novels and a score of brilliant tales, will be subjected to some severely revised judgments in the coming years, and that when it is measured against some of its closer rivals—Fitzgerald, for instance, or Faulkner—it will meet rougher tests than the unlikely cases of Turgenev and Stendhal provide. "Across the River and into the Trees" (the title badly mars the fine rhythm of Stonewall Jackson's last words) is an occasion for little but exasperated depression. But we are promised another novel soon. We must wait for it. And see.

Frederick Yeiser. *Cincinnati Enquirer,* September 9, 1950, p. 5.

The charitable thing would be to write off Ernest Hemingway's new novel, his first in 10 years or so, as a minor effort and let it go at that. Its chief faults, it seems to me are two: dullness and silly writing—neither of which one expects from such an experienced novelist as Hemingway. So much of the time he lapses into a kind of sports and outdoor writer's jargon. The dialogue (once his strong point), page after page of it here, verges on adult infantilism.

It seems with "Across the River and into the Trees" that Hemingway has attempted to revert to the manner of "The Sun Also Rises" and the spirit of "A Farewell to Arms," but somehow winds up creating a parody of both. He is still fighting the Italian campaign of World War I, this time through the agency of Col. Richard Cantwell, his mouthpiece in the story, who, as a general in the second war, has much to say about that, too. On wild duck shooting, which also comes into this picture, Hemingway is, as always, excellent.

Richard Cantwell, regular Army, reduced to Colonel, stationed in Trieste, takes a short leave to do some shooting north of Venice. In the duck blind, he goes over his past, but in particular the last few days in Venice, where he has had a lovely time with his lady love, Renata, a beautiful young contessa. The chronology is confused. Cant-well, the beat-up soldier with a bad heart, realizes that his number is up, so makes the best of his last fling, as it turns out to be.

The novel derives its title from a statement Stonewall Jackson was said to have made just before his own death: "No, no, let us cross the river and rest under the shade of the trees." There are flashes of the old-time Hem-ingway in writing about Venice. If the rest had been as good as that, he would have had a good book. And I believe most readers may find it diffi-cult to keep from identifying the au-thor with his principal character.

Malcolm Cowley. "Hemingway Portrait of an Old Soldier Preparing to Die." *New York Herald Tribune Book Review*, 27 September 10, 1950, pp. 1, 16.

This is not the big novel for which his public has been waiting and on which Ernest Hemingway has been working at intervals for the last ten years . . . .

An early draft of "Across the Riv-er" was serialized last spring in five issues of the "Cosmopolitan." Since then Hemingway has revised the text and has added new scenes that make it more impressive in its honesty and bit-terness. It is beautifully finished as a piece of writing; in that sense it is what we expect of Hemingway; but it is still below the level of his earlier novels, which we studied so eagerly and from which we learned so much.

* * *

Death—or rather the preparation for a good death—is the subject of the novel . . . .

* * *

The preparation for death has been completed or nearly completed; when he says good by to Renata he is ready for what the day will bring. That is the theme of the novel and the plot, too, in its essential outlines. Hemingway has always had an instinct for rituals and ceremonials and here he has given us, in secular and even shocking terms, a long rite of confession and extreme unction.

Colonel Cantwell is in some ways the most fully realized of Heming-way's heroes. At every moment, in each new situation, he is the old sol-dier who loves the military profession, loves to command, loves fighting for its own sake and even loves his ene-mies, if they are dangerous men like Rommel and Ernst Udet, but who jeal-ously hates the commanding generals on his own side. He doesn't step out of character even when embracing his girl in a gondola; it is as if he was carrying out a military maneuver, landing on a friendly coast but with due attention to secrecy and surprise. When he dines in a restaurant it is always at a table in the far corner, "where the Colonel had both his flanks covered, and he rested solidly against the corner of the room."

His language is that of an old soldier who has had time to read books, look at many pictures and form his own judgments, but prefers to express them in the words of soldiers at the front. . . . In general he uses rougher words than any other character in American fiction, except possibly some of those in "The Naked and the Dead"; but the words seem less objectionable than they might in other situations, because they are part of the Colonel's personality.

* * *

A weakness of the book is the absence of secondary characters. Hemingway is excellent at thumbnail sketches, as always, and one remembers the Colonel's driver, the boatman, the room waiter with a glass eye and other persons who are caught briefly but permanently, as in one of Goya's etchings. At the same time one feels the lack of characters like Rinaldi (in "A Farewell to Arms") and Pilar and Anselmo (in "For Whom the Bell Tolls") who are not merely shown in a glimpse but reveal themselves progressively by the part they play in the action. In the new novel only the Colonel and Renata are essential to the action; the other characters are a sort of background that could be changed without changing the plot.

There is a scene or chapter missing from the novel and even the careless reader will be obscurely worried by its absence. Before he is ready for death Colonel Cantwell has to be purged of his bitterness; and we feel in reading the story that he cannot be completely purged until all the causes of bitterness have been confessed or at least

brought into his conscious memory, so that they can be acknowledged and exorcised. One cause of bitterness is the failure of his marriage and that is briefly but adequately handled. . . .

But a deeper cause of bitterness is that the Colonel, who had always wanted to be a general officer in the Army of the United States, had been a general for only a few months at the front and then had been reduced in rank. Hemingway mentions the fact often, but he never gives us the scene in which—or as a result of which—this general was reclassified. Perhaps he was being punished for one of the three mistakes that he speaks to Renata of having made. "Can you tell me about that and why?" she asks. The Colonel says, "No," flatly—"And that was the end of that," the author adds. He is justified in keeping the information from Renata, but not in keeping it from the reader.

* * *

Until this unwritten scene, or one like it, has been brought into the foreground of his mind—brought there, considered in all its aspects and then dismissed from memory like the unhappy marriage—the Colonel cannot be completely purged of his bitterness and prepared to accept his fate. The result of its absence is that the Colonel's death—for which we have been prepared by the title of the book and by intimations in every chapter—leaves us with less than the liberating sense of tragedy that Hemingway must have wished to achieve.

There are fine things in the book that I haven't mentioned. The first scene, of duck shooting in the Venetian marshes, is one of those sporting prints with a somber undertone that Hemingway has always done better than any other writer. The approach to Venice is marvelous and so are the characters seen briefly in Harry's Bar. There are fine memories of the fighting in both world wars and in fact there is something quotable in every chapter.

What one misses in "Across the River" is the sense of adventure and exploration that marked his earlier novels. Each of them treated a new subject in a new fashion and, except for "To Have and Have Not," each of them marked a real advance, so that "A Farewell to Arms" and "For Whom the Bell Tolls" were both the great novels of their respective decades. For all its skill and honesty, "Across the River and Into the Trees" is a tired book compared with those others. To see what the new Hemingway can do we still have to wait for his big novel.

Elliot Paul.
" 'Thanks to Ernest.' "
Providence Sunday Journal,
September 10, 1950,
p. VI-8.

Hemingway's first great novel was "A Farewell to Arms" in which he told the story, made truly of the fabric of World War I, which later he was to discover in the shameless betrayal of Spanish democracy by fascists and democrats elsewhere, and now he has surpassed in its recurrence in World War II.

* * *

Now comes "Across the River and into the Trees," and the decade of experience Hemingway has gathered into his best telling of the familiar, touching sad story. In former days, for instance, he was rather insistent that he knew nothing of art and implied that those who did had been squandering time. Today he has shed all that and writes of Goya, Greco, Degas and Hieronimus Bosch with understanding. His taste has improved with his imagining.

* * *

Hemingway will, no doubt, get the usual disrespectful reception from the boys of English "A" who have spent their years in New York offices and hate those who have seen or felt other things. Thanks to Ernest and nuts to his disparagers.

Hemingway is widely read and proportionately little understood. That is because his prose, sentence by sentence, is clear and precise, and his grasp of contemporary situations is profound and a decade ahead of his public's. For me the greatest American writers now living and writing are Hemingway, Faulkner, Christina Stead (born Australian but one of us from choice) and Maritta Wolfe. And the poets are E.E. Cummings and, before he went dotty about religion, T. S. Eliot.

Clyde Throckmorton.
"Widely-Heralded
Hemingway Novel
Falls Short of Author's
Major Work."
Nashville Tennessean,
September 10, 1950,
p. 4-E.

It must be observed at the outset that "Across the River and into the Trees" is not a completely successful novel.

Nor is it of the stature of "For Whom the Bell Tolls" or of some of Mr. Hemingway's shorter work, the often reprinted "The Snows of Kilimanjaro," for example, which also deals with approaching death.

The publication (the work has undergone considerable revision since its magazine serialization earlier this year) of Ernest Hemingway's first novel in 10 years has been widely heralded. For those of his admirers who expected a major work, perhaps even a great novel, it will be a disappointment.

There is some distinguished and some beautiful writing in it. The celebrated Hemingway style—which consists of stripping every sentence to its barest essentials, hard, bare, amounting almost to a denial of style—is often very effective in evoking a particular mood or in establishing a scene with a minimum of detail so that the trees do not obscure the forest.

Thus the automobile journey from Trieste to Venice early in the book projects the mood of melancholy and inexorable tragedy that broods over the whole work. Man is helpless against circumstances and nothing awaits but annihilation.

But on the whole Col. Cantwell and his Italian countess never emerge as real people although they are the only people in the book with whom the action is concerned. What they say and do never becomes quite believable. A lot of it is interesting; much of it appears contrived.

* * *

There is a duck shoot which is up to Papa Hemingway's best descriptive writing but the greater part of the novel is about Colonel Cantwell and Renata and their last meeting, because the colonel dies in his car on his way back to Trieste.

* * *

Strangley enough, much of the talk is about war, however unlikely it is that a young girl in love would want to hear so much about military matters. Hemingway, the war correspondent, supplies the speeches for the colonel, and a number of British, American and French generals are pulled down from pedestals in the course of the Colonel's reminiscences.

Mr. Hemingway might conceivably have written a bitter novel based on his war experience or a tender love story. "Across the River and into the Trees" fails to be either.

John O'Hara.
"The Author's Name is Hemingway."
New York Times Book Review,
September 10, 1950, pp. 1, 30.

The most important author living to-day, the outstanding author since the death of Shakespeare, has brought out a new novel. The title of the novel is "Across the River and Into the Trees." The author, of course, is Ernest Hemingway, the most important, the outstanding author out of the millions of writers who have lived since 1616.

* * *

Books do not necessarily represent an author's activity, but the new novel is Hemingway's thirteenth book in what appears to be twenty-seven years of writing and knocking around for a rough average of one book every two years. Hemingway has not been idle, and most of the items in his bibliography come alive by merely calling up their titles.

The reasons that Ernest Hemingway is important are not easy to search for, although they are easy to find. Once you have skipped the remarks of the pedants, the college professors, the literateurs, and of Hemingway himself, and have examined his background and his still immediate history, you can relax down to the fine, simple, inexplicable acceptance of being in the world-presence of a genius. . . .

* * *

The truculent, self-pitying hero of "Across the River and Into the Trees" is a busted one-star general called Col. Richard Cantwell. He seems to have traversed the same territory as the charming Lieutenant Henry of "A Farewell to Arms." It is impossible to believe that the lieutenant and the colonel are the same man, and therefore the autobiographical aspect must be ruled out one time or the other. The present reviewer, whose age is 45, is unwilling to concede that Enrico and Ricardo are the same infant with years piled on. In any event, Colonel Cantwell is in Venice to see his girl, a beautiful and quite incredible countess named Renata. The colonel is full of junk, against the bad heart condition he has, and the story is hardly more than a report of their last love-making, to the accompaniment of a threnody on and by the dying warrior. That great, great man and fine actor, Walter Huston, was in my mind all the time I read this book. Huston, singing "September Song," you know. But Hemingway, the inimitable, has written a 308-page novel out of a "September Song" situation, and not one syllable of what Hemingway has written can or will be missed by any literate person in the world.

* * *

The novel opens with the colonel on his way to his ultimate rendezvous with the countess. . . . She is, on this reviewer's oath, practically all that a middle-aged man with a cardiac condition could ask for. Not yet 19 years old, a countess who need not worry about consequences, Renata (whose name sounds like lasso to me) is so much in love with the colonel that she takes his rudeness and gives him emeralds in return.

It is so easy to kid that aspect of Hemingway's writing and it is so foolish to do so. Go ahead and disbelieve in Catherine Barkley, as I disbelieve now in the Countess Renata, as I did too in Maria, of "For Whom the Bell Tolls." But the Hemingway heroines, as distinguished from the Sinclair Lewis ones, have a way of catching up with you after you have passed them by. You read them; you see them played by Helen Hayes, Elissa Landi, Ingrid Bergman; you put them away. And yet in later years you form your own non-theatrical picture of them out of what you remember of what Hemingway wrote, and what you have seen of living women. . . .

It is not unfair or unjustifiable, this casting of the novel's characters. The novel was written as a serial for Cosmopolitan, whose demands and restrictions are, I should say, almost precisely those of the movies. Now that the novel is available between boards, a great many touches that most likely were in Hemingway's working manuscripts have been restored. They don't add much, they don't take much away. At the same time they do make a difference: they make the bound volume authentically Hemingway, and not Hemingway plus (or maybe minus is the word) the Cosmopolitan editors. And in any case the touches never would appear in the movies. They would not even appear in the most rudimentary "treatment" that might be submitted to the Johnston Office.

* * *

In the new novel, Hemingway, rather regrettably, has done nothing to protect himself against personal attack, or, more accurately, counter-attack. He has named some names, and made easily identifiable some others: Patton, Eisenhower, Montgomery, Ney, Custer, Truman, Dewey, as well as an author or two, a journalist or two, and probably a few non-celebrated individuals who will recognize themselves or think they do.

This does not sound like a *roman à clef*, any more than it is an autobiography (Hemingway is still alive, Dick Cantwell ends the book by dying), and that doesn't matter either way. What matters is that Ernest Hemingway has brought out a new book.

To use his own favorite metaphor, he may not be able to go the full distance, but he can still hurt you. Always dangerous. Always in there with that right cocked.

Real class.

Beatrice Washburn. "Hemingway's Art Collides with Time." *Miami Herald,* September 10, 1950, p. 4-G.

Hemingway is more than a popular modern novelist. He is a Trend, an Influence, an Original.

Thousands of little Hemingways the

country over have copied the master's terse, monosyllabic style, his short sentences, four-letter words, and his trick of depicting character through dialogue. His people do not need to act, though they are exceptionally active.

They fight, drink, shout, kill, die and make love. But what they do best is talk. . . .

This is Hemingway's great gift, one that no one has been able to imitate. He can, by a line of conversation, a turned phrase, a brief description, lift a character off the printed page and make him into a human being.

"Across the River," is not up to the master's best. That is the danger of writing so well that you have to continually top your own standard. But it is intensely readable, if for nothing else, because it probably depicts Hemingway's own point of view at the present time.

* * *

The colonel is no longer young and his romance with the young Italian countess is that of a sick and disillusioned man. The hero's love for Venice seems greater than his love for a beautiful woman and is there any greater proof of age, when we begin to love places better than people?

A wistfulness has crept into Hemingway's famous style, the style that made "Death in the Afternoon" seem like a shout. He is beginning to doubt that blood and battles and violent death are really worth the energy they take. He is even beginning to doubt love and he has at last found, like many a lesser man, that youth and sun and glory, battle and violent death

simmer down in the long run to memory and dreams.

"The New Hemingway." *Newsweek*, 36 (September 11, 1950), 90-95.

Ernest Hemingway's new novel "Across the River and into the Trees" is unusual in contemporary fiction, particularly unusual in writing having to do with the war, and exceptional in the war fiction of the man from Oak Park. A novel of atmospheres, blues and grays and shaded light, quiet talk, a sense of ease, suddenly captured and just as suddenly lost, it celebrates a love of life in poignant images of girls walking with the sea wind blowing their hair, children playing at dusk, ducks flying through the gray dawn— all against the lovely magic of Venice, the ancient city.

Hemingway's early lyricism of morning-fresh sensations is almost totally missing from his story of Colonel Cantwell's last visit to the city of his youth. It would be almost too poignant if it were present in this sombre account. For the drama of this novel depends almost entirely on the interplay between the colonel's memory of his dreamlike youth and his present savoring of the last good sensations with his haunting knowledge of war with its fears, guilts, outrages in the middle distance. His memory of some incident of battle breaks into his quietness like a present reminder of the fighting in Korea.

His Venice is finally dreamlike in its idealization. So is his young mistress, a nineteen year-old Italian countess who gives him her portrait, likewise a dream portrait in its flesh-toned reality and its ethereal beauty. In such scenes it becomes clear that Hemingway's novel has depths beneath its surfaces. Here are mingled America and Europe, a tradition where art is an attribute of life juxtaposed with a society that has no art; a legendary story of youth and age, innocence and experience, love in confrontation with death, the beauty and the beast. Thus, at 52, with thirteen books to his credit, Hemingway has mastered a new subject and a new style.

This new style, however, may not be as effective as his old one has been. Forming some of the most powerful and most sensitive stories in the English language, that older style featured the first-person-singular, tough-guy, hard-boiled technique which produced a revolution in popular American culture. It had its echoes in gangster stories, detective sagas, movie and radio scripts. Compact and restrained, the new style lacks the repetitions and staccato sentences that made the earlier manner so well known.

But in many respects—the new tension that underlies its almost undramatic events, the high degree of concentration—Hemingway's "Across the River and into the Trees" is his best and most carefully thought out book. His subtle characterization of Richard Cantwell may help fill a blank spot in contemporary war fiction. Where other accounts have centered on the plain soldier and treated higher officers sa-

tirically or ironically, Hemingway's colonel tells how it was from another and equally sensitive angle of vision. (Summary)

"On the Ropes."
Time, 56
(September 11, 1950),
110, 113.

When he talked with Lillian Ross for his *New Yorker* portrait some months ago, Ernest Hemingway characterized his forthcoming novel as a defense of his title. He was still champ at 50, said author Hemingway, and ready to take on all challengers. But only the most sentimental referee could call him a winner after reading "Across the River and into the Trees." He hardly wins a round. His fans can only hope that the self-styled champ had an off day.

In this heavily autobiographical story of Colonel Richard Cantwell's last, best weekend in Venice, Hemingway writes a carefully arranged language of tough-guy sentimentality as his hero savors the wine of the country, delivers himself of ill-considered opinions on fellow officers, war book writers, women correspondents, art and hunting. Between harangues he talks tough and tender to his young Italian mistress, who is wise and old in the ways of Venice.

From one of the few great writers of his generation, this novel gives Hemingway admirers little to cheer about. Occasionally, as in the description of the duck shoot, the writing provides flashes of the old superb exactness.

And even the thin story manages to stay in motion and carry a sense of potential explosion, though the explosion never occurs. The poetic blend of tension and despair, once a hallmark of the Hemingway style, here gives way to a virtual parody of itself. The love talk is embarrassingly artificial rather than restrained; the colonel's juvenile arrogance and his truculent toughness make him a bore who soon deserves no sympathy from readers, no matter how loyal his girl.

It will be hard for Hemingway loyalists to believe the champ's claim that this is his best novel. They will hope that in the more ambitious work he is reported to be busy with he will recover his Sunday punch. (Summary)

Harold C. Gardiner. "He-Man Whimpering." *America*, 83 (September 16, 1950), 628, 630.

Ernest Hemingway has been the "great bronze god" of American fiction for many years, but his utterly trivial *Across the River and into the Trees* will surely tarnish the sheen on the idol.

To be sure, Hemingway still retains something of his old touch. He can still convey a sense of human fellowship among men under stress, a sense of the futility of war, an appreciation of the heartbreaking beauty of the natural world. But he looses these traits in an atmosphere of unmanly griping and whining. His colonel is a whipped man

from the outset, and he knows it. So do the readers. One cannot help remembering the defensive claims Hemingway made for the book some months ago in the classic profile in the *New Yorker*. Even then he seemed not at all confident about the book but seemed to be preparing a groundwork of excuses for the failure.

Some reports have it that Hemingway wrote the novel hastily as a possible last book, fearing he would never finish his more ambitious work. If this turns out to be so, he will have ended not with a bang but a whimper. (Summary)

Theodore Kalem. "Hemingway: Victim of an American Fallacy." *Christian Science Monitor*, September 16, 1950, p. 11.

It is the fate of a major writer to be judged by the standard of his best previous work. By that standard Ernest Hemingway's "Across the River and Into the Trees" disappoints. Yet, within the context of the current enfeebled state of American letters, it is a pretty remarkable performance. Barring a miracle, no American novel will top it this year, because no other American can write this well.

To use the terminology Hemingway delights in, he is the winner and still champion. But the opposition is not exactly formidable. The wonder kids from Truman Capote to Frederick

Buechner have flashy techniques but no subject matter. The only serious challenger, the greatly gifted William Faulkner, writes with a lavish carelessness that blunts his best efforts.

Hemingway has always been a perfectionist, and in "Across the River and Into the Trees" only his superb verbal discipline arrests a case of incipient parody. For in his new novel Hemingway is repeating himself, and repetition is a form of parody. The familiar themes are recapitulated—time and love, war and death, virile sports and favorite cities—but in a muted minor way.

In this sad, nostalgic, autumnal book, Hemingway is reciting the names of the things he has loved. Its felt quality derives less from a sense of immediacy than from the poignance of things passing and past. . . .

Because there is nothing essentially new in this novel, it affords an interesting opportunity for differentiating Hemingway's authentic from his ostensible subject matter. His egotistic hedonism, his romantic attitudes, his small-boy-heroics and tough-guy poses have obscured the nucleus of his work. His ability, in T. S. Eliot's words, "to tell the truth about his own feelings at the moment when they exist" has fostered the assumption that he celebrates only the life of the senses. That is not entirely correct, though he has undoubtedly "saturated his books with the memory of physical pleasure, with sunshine and salt water, with food, wine, and making love, and with the remorse which is the shadow of that sun." But the core of Hemingway's work, the hub around which it resolves is the problem of value.

* * *

Unlikely as it may seem to the superficial reader, Hemingway has been posing in fictional terms some of the same questions with which moral philosophy concerns itself. How does one live the good life? How does one face death and disaster? How does one deal honorably with other human beings? In sum, what are the values by which one lives and, if necessary dies?

* * *

"How can one make the best of one's life? " André Malraux asks in one of his novels. "By converting as wide a range of experience as possible into conscious thought." It is here that Hemingway fails, and fails badly. It is not that he has a weak mind. The deep-seated, anti-intellectual tradition in American life and letters has made him coy before ideas. He is a victim of the fallacy that sensation is somehow "realer" than thought. And so he brings to the large, complicated questions which he is sensitive enough to raise, oversimplified instinctual answers which are embarrassingly primitive. One can see in "Across the River and Into the Trees" that the law of diminishing returns has begun to operate against him. Even "his rare mastery of the sensuous element" will not sustain him in further repetitions. Form and style go a long way, but they will not redeem a writer who is on the brink of no longer having anything vital to say.

Fanny Butcher.
"The Old Black Magic That Is Hemingway's."
Chicago Sunday Tribune,
September 17, 1950,
pp. IV-3, 14.

* * *

Ernest Hemingway has that old black magic with words which few writers have ever had, a magic which his imitators have dreamed of but which is truly his alone. He can say more in fewer words than any man writing today. To some readers WHAT he says doesn't matter particularly. The way he says it, the fine, almost mystical overtones of meaning which a sentence of his can convey, are enough to make any book of his an intellectual experience.

Unlike most magicians with words, Ernest Hemingway has no use for "moods" or "atmosphere" or any of the other literary charms with which literary magic is usually wrought. He writes realistically of the most realistic subjects. His books are male, almost aggressively so, and the effects which he creates are the more unexpected. War, war, and war again, a doomed love and death are not subjects which most readers would expect to be irresistible, and they may not be to many readers. But "Across the River and Into the Trees" will hold countless readers in a kind of literary vise by the sheer power of technique.

This is going to be a much discussed book for what it says rather than for the way it says it, for the dying colonel has many bitter things to say about the conduct of the two wars in which he participated. He names names, he makes specific accusations. And, altho it should be no surprise to devotees of Hemingway, the hero's language is sometimes the kind that is usually kept from delicate ears. The author's constant use of "old" in connection with his 50 year old hero will be unconvincing to those readers who feel more vigorous at or past 50 than they ever felt in their lives. But no one, whatever the sins of omission or commission which he or she thinks Ernest Hemingway has indulged in, can deny that "Across the River and Into the Trees" shows its author's sheer magic in the use of words.

Kate Simon.
"Old Age of a Hero."
New Republic, 123
(September 18, 1950),
20-21.

Hemingway's new novel takes both its title and its tone from Stonewall Jackson's dying words: "No, no, let us cross over the river and rest under the shade of the trees." A slight, sad book, it is a muted, brooding twilight story brushed by autumnal mists.

The speaker of Jackson's elegiac words is Colonel Richard Cantwell, a re-embodiment of Hemingway's Jake Barnes-Frederic Henry-Robert Jordan hero. Like his predecessors, he is tough, proud, inwardly sentimental, has a hold on morality that is almost totally esthetic, struggles to keep his integrity in a world of shapeless banalities and brutalities. He is a passionate hidalgo, exquisitely sensitive and gracefully cruel, whose inward gaze is always watchful for flaws in the perfection of his own identity. But unlike Barnes-Henry-Jordan, he has grown older, mellowed, become more gentle. He has consorted too much with death and, still gallant, sees blood and brutality as only the incidental evils of his work as a soldier.

In structure not much more than a long love scene and a farewell, *Across the River and into the Trees* cultivates the ambience of doom as Richard Cantwell and the girl he loves, a nineteen-year-old Italian countess, savor the last warmth of love and dreams together. Talking of love, art, wine, war, and Venice, they live out their last weekend under the shadow of dissolution, for the colonel's imminent death is not only his own but every man's and the decay of his civilization.

Hemingway brings to his writing the same care and discipline Cantwell invests in acting out his life and death. With sure, spare strokes the minor characters come to life and into clear, separate identities. The prose itself borders on poetry in its sentence rhythms, its resonant words and phrases that often quiver with emotion. He makes the one major love scene restrained and delicate even within its erotic feeling. And the farewell is a truly bittersweet experience. Occasionally Hemingway's artistic hold on his story slips and one finds repetitions serving no esthetic purpose, and useless obscenities. Irritating also is the characteristic rejection of thought in favor of sensation and arrogant instinct.

The canvas of Hemingway's story is smaller and grayer than we are used to having from this writer. It is possible readers will still want the bright color and restless excitement of his earlier works. But there is no less art than before. On a minor scale there is still magic in the mixture and the Hemingway spell still works. (Summary)

Alfred Kazin. "The Indignant Flesh." *New Yorker,* 26 (September 19, 1950), 113-18.

Reports are that "Across the River and into the Trees" was written while Hemingway, believing in 1949 that he might die of an eye infection from a hunting accident near Venice, turned away from a more ambitious work to have his say in the little time left. Obviously written under considerable tension, the book has autobiographical overtones. But it must distress those who have admired Hemingway's work for the past quarter century. One feels torn between embarrassment—even pity—that so important a writer can make such a travesty of himself and astonishment that he can celebrate the world's beauty so wonderfully and be so vulgar.

Written as if it were a premature summary of the author's own life and work, the novel includes most of those situations, motifs, dialogue sequences, character types and scenic descriptions familiar to readers of Hemingway. At times he seems to be quoting some of his more famous lines, reliving some of his better known horrors. The gamy prose indulges his compulsion to use dirty words but more with an air of bullying than with his old satiric gaiety.

The Colonel is an amalgam of all Hemingway's prizefighters, soldiers, hunters and drinkers. In some ways the Hemingway hero has never been more distinct than he is in this portrait just before his death. But the man, like the book, seems held together more by blind anger than the lyric emotion that gave Hemingway's earlier books their special poignance. Triggered by outrage at the betrayal by his body and by the memory of some obscure mistake that caused his demotion from brigadier to colonel, his truculence extends to his army chauffeur, to the army top brass, to American women and even to the White House. He likes nothing and nobody but the few of his select circle and the wine and food he associates with his earlier and better days. Listening to him, you realize that he is not finally the embodiment of despair against death and bureaucracy but an oracular and self-important American big shot who has seen all the wars and come to believe that toughness is the same as valor.

The book is the Colonel's and it is not a satiric portrait but an indulgence of petty and irrelevant opinions. It may be the Colonel's last word but it is good to know that Hemingway has recovered and it is not his last book. (Summary)

Serge Hughes. *Commonweal*, 52 (September 22, 1950), 585.

It has been ten years since we had a new Hemingway novel, and it has seemed longer than that. Now in *Across the River and Into the Trees* Hemingway has produced a competent and interesting story that has all the well-known elements of his kind of book—war experiences, violence, sex, nostalgia. There are no unexpected developments, no new twists, but there is a sense of something different too. A kind of indecision has come to the writer who could so deftly impart form to these elements.

In his story of Richard Cantwell's last few hours in Venice, Hemingway sketches a background of gray, poor, sad, tired Venice which mirrors the hero's mood. So too the minor characters, all neatly drawn and well placed, reflect different dimensions of Cantwell's personality. But Hemingway's faltering skill begins to show when he characterizes the heroine, Cantwell's young Italian mistress, she of the long beautiful hair and the tight black sweaters. In her total perfection as beautiful woman and adoring lover she lacks reality. Hemingway's difficulty here is not the same as he has shown in earlier heroines. In Renata he has given her such a heavy symbolic function that she lacks autonomous artistic value.

What her symbolic function is becomes clear as the character of Richard Cantwell emerges. He is a man so completely disillusioned about politics, culture, patriotism, even love, that he can only carry out his assignments and hope to die without pretensions. The girl with all her simplicity, animal integrity, lack of moral complexity and remoteness from corruption becomes less a person than a symbol of beautiful, amoral bliss.

Not that Hemingway has tried to write a novel of ideas with characters as symbols. The girl might be meaningful to Cantwell if he released the poet in himself, but since he is disillusioned about poetry too, he cheats the poet in himself to speak in banalities and wisecracks. And here Hemingway loses control of his character, has him speak a false, hybrid language of bathos and elegy that tells not so much of interior struggle as of author-imposed limitations on his ability to believe and feel. So the hero becomes a false register of moods and values instead of a tormented man.

But all is not waste. The superb war reminiscences show that when Hemingway has hold of his real subject he is peerless. Such writing almost makes ignorable the poses, the phony language, the unworkable symbols. Because Hemingway has blended the sordid and elegiac with a hero whose complexity has extended beyond his grasp, he has made a novel meriting more respect than enthusiasm. (Summary)

J. Donald Adams. "Speaking of Books." *New York Times Book Review,* September 24, 1950, p. 2.

As I remarked last week, the latest version of the Hemingway heroine carries the dream-girl type to an ultimate conclusion. Beside her, even Catherine Barkely and Maria of the cropped head are vibrant with identity. All three are abstractions as compared with the heroine of the first Hemingway novel, Lady Brett Ashley, but she was not of their company; Brett belongs in the other main group of female characters favored by American male novelists, the horde of hussies to which contemporary fiction has given birth. Because they are positive rather than negative personalities, they more readily assume an air of reality than do their pliant and worshipful sisters.

Hemingway abandoned the type in his longer works of fiction, though she continued to make an occasional appearance in the short stories. All the novels since "The Sun Also Rises" have enshrined the dream girl. Her complete insubstantiality in "Across the River and Into the Trees" was pointed out in nearly all the reviews I have read. In what seems to me to be the best of them, Maxwell Geismar's, she is described as "useful in the novel merely as interlocutor for the Colonel's overwhelming narcissism." In that last word you have the key to all the Hemingway novels as well; in this book the narcissism stands fully, and for the reader, painfully revealed.

So far I have read eleven reviews, plus the publisher's quotes from two others I have not seen. Of the eleven, only three were definitely favorable (and two of these had minor reservations). . . .

* * *

These varying reactions seem to me worth noting because of the indubitable fact that Hemingway has, since his first success, exercised more influence on American fiction than any other contemporary novelist. My own feeling about him has always been that he is one of the best descriptive writers in English, surpassed only by Kipling and a very few others; a master in the evocation of mood—most perfectly displayed in some of the short stories, and in certain situations of the novels. He is not, and never has been, a creator of character in the sense that novelists like Balzac and Tolstoy were, and has never come remotely near the understanding of human life and the values of which it is composed that are essential to great fiction.

Those who take this view of Hemingway must hope that his book is an aberration, and not what the reading of it, without regard to the circumstances under which it was written, would seem to indicate: that it is a crystallization of his attitude toward life and his understanding of it. . . .

To me, the terrible thing—and I use that adjective with deliberation—about "Across the River and Into the Trees" is that a writer could hold, at the center of this thinking about life, the belief that unless a man has killed he has not lived. To believe that is to renounce one's human birthright; it is to surrender all hope of ever creating a better world than the one in which we live. For it is nonsense to pretend that this view of life is that of a Hemingway character only; when a writer has identified himself, consciously or unconsciously, with the man or woman about whom he is writing, one does not have to be psychic to be aware of the identification, particularly when the process of arrival at that point of view has had so clearly marked a trail. To me, "Across the River and Into the Trees" is one of the saddest books I have ever read; not because I am moved to compassion by the conjunction of love and death in the Colonel's life, but because a great talent has come, whether for now or forever, to such a dead end.

John K. Hutchens.
"Nobody on the Fence."
New York Herald Tribune Books, 27
September 24, 1950,
p. 3.

All around the country, since September 7, the big literary conversation topic has been the new Hemingway novel, and the first thing you may have noticed is that people like it or don't. No middle ground at all. Now the first critical returns on "Across the River and Into the Trees" are in, and they, too, are sharply divided, with the anti's apparently in a slight majority. A sampling:

The reviewers for this newspaper, Lewis Gannett (daily), Malcolm Cowley (Sunday), were disappointed. The reviewers for "The New York Times," Charles Poore (daily), John O'Hara (Sunday), were enthusiastic. "Time" said, "The famed Hemingway style is hardly more than a parody of itself." "Newsweek" said, "In many respects . . . Hemingway's best and most carefully thought-out book." "Can only distress anyone who admires Hemingway," wrote Alfred Kazin in "The New Yorker," while Maxwell Geismar, in "The Saturday Review of Literature," thought it "an unfortunate novel and unpleasant to review for anyone who respects Hemingway's talent and achievement." "The Providence Sunday Journal" (Elliot Paul): "Thanks to Ernest and nuts to his disparagers." "The San Francisco Chronicle" (Joseph Henry Jackson): "Too often it resembles a parody of Hemingway at his best."

And so it went, while the House of Scribner—with an eye on those sales that such controversy is likely to stimulate—stepped up its printings from 100,000 copies to 125,000. . . .

Richard H. Rovere. "New Books—Hemingway to Howells." *Harper's*, 201 (September 1950), 104-106.

Ernest Hemingway's *Across the River and into the Trees* is a disappointing novel. Though it has moments of strength and beauty, it also has moments of tawdriness. The work of most novelists is not irreparably damaged by an occasional lapse from taste and consistency, but along the hard, clear surface of Hemingway's prose, a junky phrase is a road block. . . . It is an incredibly talky book. It is almost garrulous, a strange thing for a Hemingway novel to be. The reason, I think, is that Hemingway is here using dialogue not as a tool of narrative but simply as a means for the author to unburden himself of opinions. The male talker is Colonel Richard Cantwell, a typical Hemingway hero but closer to the writer in temperament and experience than any he has ever drawn before. Cantwell is just Hemingway's present age, fifty-one. Like Hemingway, he believes that the full impact and meaning of life can be known only through mortal combat and mortal love of woman, both of which he happens to have known abundantly. . . .

* * *

What predestined the novel to failure, I think, is the closeness of Hemingway's identification with his hero. Because Cantwell is Hemingway, he is static, a known and fixed quality throughout the book. He is always credible but seldom interesting, because Hemingway, writing of himself, has nothing to learn of himself in the process of composition. He does not obey Henry James's law of "emergence," which, as Vincent McHugh says in his *Primer of the Novel*, a treatise on fiction that is often very brilliant but sometimes only smart, should be at work in every novel and, more than that, should be "simultaneous with growth—not merely the growth of a character in the reader's mind but his growth in *himself*. Thus the revelation of character is no mere assembly of parts but a stream of becoming, a continous flowering in which the whole plant goes on growing while each sepal opens."

What we know of Cantwell at the end of this book is hardly more than what we knew at the start. This is a particular disappointment in a Hemingway novel, for Hemingway's most conspicuous gift has always been for placing his characters in the stream of becoming. Even in such short works as *The Short Happy Life of Francis Macomber* and *The Snows of Kilimanjaro*, both of which have points in common with *Across the River and into the Trees*, his characters undergo continuous change and growth. Enough friction is generated in the dialogue and confrontations to wear down several finishes and destroy several resistances. There are, certainly, some writers who can deal with themselves as Hemingway can deal with others; there are, indeed, some who can deal with no one but themselves. But Hemingway is not one of them, for although he is as much concerned with the depths of personality as anyone else, he can learn about personality and explain it only in terms of movement and open conflict. He is a superb instrument of observation. But like any other instrument of observation, he can observe anything on the horizon except himself; no matter how much he is pivoted and adjusted, he cannot turn himself inward. . . .

Hemingway, of course, cannot put pen to paper without getting certain interesting results. Though much of the dialogue in this novel is only talk, some of it, particularly when Cantwell is speaking with one of the minor figures, is very fine talk. Some of the narrative and descriptive prose is as good as the best. Two minor figures, a Venetian maître d'hôtel and a young and rather prissy enlisted man, a comic book reader who seems to be Hemingway's judgment on the young Americans he is old enough to be a father to, are worthy additions to the gallery. But a Hemingway novel is not redeemed by its occasional successes. Moreover, this work is shot through with an atrabiliousness of mind that Hemingway has not shown in many years. As Cantwell plays out his almost Socratic role, he unloads a number of opinions on living persons, some named, others not, that are informed by almost everything but charity. In some cases, perhaps, these are merely expressions of the brutality Cantwell sought to shed. "For a while," Hemingway writes, "he was [Dante], and he drew all the circles. They were just as unjust as Dante's, but he drew them." But whatever they express in Cantwell, and whether they are more or less just than Dante's, they are unavoidably Hemingway's and they are, to say the least, unattractive.

Melwyn Breen.
"Afterglow."
Saturday Night, 65 (October 3, 1950), 24.

Most reviewers of the Master's latest have tossed the book into the wastebasket with one hand and seized either a smoldering or a sorrowful pen with the other. The violence of opinion expressed by Hemingway's central figure has prevented objectivity. This has been especially so for those who maintain that an author's character must necessarily reflect his own opinions. Others, less concerned with the political and military knowledgeability of either Hemingway or Colonel Cantwell, are not so sure.

* * *

All of these opinions have been laid by one or another of the critics at the feet of the author himself. One story goes that Hemingway, feeling physically as the Colonel did, abandoned work in progress in order to set his own house in order. The book, therefore, is said to be a thinly disguised catalogue of his final fling at the world's expense. But Hemingway lives to answer for his opinions for what they are

worth. One valid literary problem he does present: is Colonel Cantwell a character who stands on his own feet?

It is certain that he does. It will be easy to forget the self-consciousness of phrases ("Daughter"), the absurdly coy conversations with the portrait of the *inamorata* and even to forget some notably dull passages. But with the book finished and put down the figure of Colonel Cantwell begins slowly to come to life. There is a peculiar distillation arising from the story that has a delayed action. It is in the memory, rather than in the telling, that Cantwell becomes a full-length figure.

As the irritating aspects disappear some of the old image is reformed. What can be seen is Hemingway's unique power of presenting a picture of universal sadness without a coincidental feeling of futility. The Colonel becomes alive through the very pattern and process of his thinking. As with a good friend, the reader finds it easy to forget the annoying and infuriating human being and to be very sad indeed over the life and death of Colonel Cantwell. Here is the sure touch of the literary artist.

"Across the River" is not a great novel in the sense of "A Farewell to Arms." The Colonel's universal sadness is not that of Frederic Henry's. The Colonel was always a professional soldier with thinking never apart from doing. Henry, on the other hand, came into soldiering as a temporary task. His was the sadness of isolation in a world insane. The Colonel never believed at any time that he would be "through with the war."

The Colonel's isolation comes from

his feel of death. For a man of action the threat comes as the act itself; the attempt and not the deed confounds him. In his death is represented his final penetration to the core of life. Whether, for all mankind, that is of the quality of universality, is the problem Hemingway has set. For Cantwell, it sufficed.

R. F. H.
"After 10 years."
Springfield Republican,
October 15, 1950,
p. 19A.

Through continued exposure to the Rover Boys, Terry and the Pirates and Just Plain Bill, the American public has become accustomed to sequels and thus may not take kindly to Ernest Hemingway's first book since "For Whom the Bell Tolls" 10 years ago. The new novel, "Across the River and into the Trees," is not a continuation of the adventures of Robert Jordan, Maria, Pilar or anyone very much like them. And it will not make a good movie.

* * *

It is by no means a thrilling story, nor is it intended to be, but is a searingly effective reconstruction of the mood of hopelessness which seems to be darkening most of the world.

The young countess is one of those supremely beautiful, intelligent, artistic and understanding Hemingway women never met in the bars frequented by this department, but Col. Cantwell

is known to most of us, if not liked or fully understood—a man embittered by human stupidity, including his own, and doomed by life to a final irony worse than any that have gone before. His personality is complicated, too much so for the short acquaintance granted by the novel, but he is very real.

As remarked before, this is not a thrilling story, nor is it, at the moment of reading, as effective as the usual Hemingway novel. It is, however, a fine piece of work, absorbing and provoking of thought, better answering today's cry for understanding than would another crusading "For Whom the Bell Tolls," which after all was a decade ago. We are 10 years and a world war older now, and so is Hemingway.

Norman Cousins.
"Hemingway & Steinbeck."
Saturday Review of
Literature, 33
(October 28, 1950),
26-27.

* * *

Hemingway's book is a bleating boast for the sentimental brute. All the familiar Hemingway ingredients are brought together in a disturbingly autobiographical summation. Hemingway selects for his theme the death of a hero in what appears to be a one-volume distillation of all his ideas. Death is always the biggest act in the Hemingway drama, and he seems to be saying to the reader: "If you want to know how a real man dies, this is the way it is, and I tell you true."

In the few days before he dies Hemingway's real man revisits the scene of his military glory, for reality with Hemingway seldom excludes the soldier's experience. The real man also proves his capacity and proficiency as a male mating machine, for reality with Hemingway most certainly is related to a prodigious conceit over potency, real or feigned. The hero-soldier also gets into a raw fist fight and has the deep male satisfaction of being able to crash his fists into the hard but yielding faces and bodies of two sailors. Here, too, reality with Hemingway is inseparable from empty violence, best expressed in the natural weapons of muscular strength and the straight and true punch. The main witness to all this in the book is a soft and lovely and pliant and supremely fulfilling young girl who is otherwise unrecognizable as a person and who exists solely for the reminiscent intellectual and sensual pleasures of the hero-soldier. Again, Hemingway reality regards the female as a functional repository in which a truly wise and strong man can find long ease for mind and body; but the female herself never lives beyond the purely passive. Any inventory of Hemingway reality is incomplete, however, unless it also includes truly superior knowledge of and access to rare and subtle liquids and foods.

In sum, the Hemingway hero or real man is the spectacle of the ego run riot. It is a diseased and elephantine assertion of self. It is a world trying to drown itself in its hormones, a world in which people exist only in biological pairs—for the benefit of the male. It is a world naked and bereft of any comprehension of the higher reaches of mutuality in love or kinship. It is a world of ponderous bulls preening and parading themselves in the open arena.

* * *

Ben Ray Redman. "The Champ and the Referees." *Saturday Review of Literature*, 33 (October 28, 1950), 15, 16, 38.

All the reviewers of Ernest Hemingway's latest novel are in happy agreement—up to a point. They agree that the book is entitled "Across the River and Into the Trees" and that it is the story of the last two days in the life of an American colonel, aged fifty-one, reduced from the wartime rank of brigadier, who spends these days in Venice, where, with a rapidly failing heart, he keeps himself alive on pills and very dry martinis, makes love to the most beautiful girl in the world—an eighteen-nineteen-year-old Italian countess, named Renata—, talks a great deal, drinks a great deal, goes duck shooting in the Venetian marshes, and dies. But, once this point has been reached and passed, agreement is left behind. . . .

* * *

What does it all add up to? Well, one might shrug cynically and repeat some old sayings: "That's what makes horse racing." "It takes all kinds to make a world." "You get out of a book only what you bring to it." "We all believe what we wish to believe." "What paper do you read?" Indeed, the old sayings are quite serviceable at this point. But I think it is fair—whatever the merits or demerits of "Across the River"—to add that our survey provides a remarkable example of a great many reviewers having failed to keep their eyes on the ball. Too many of these reviews were written with one eye on the book and the other on what the reviewers thought they knew of Hemingway's character, and what they did know of his publicity—*The New Yorker* article very much in particular. Too many reviewers were affected by the information that Hemingway had interrupted the writing of a "bigger" novel to write this comparatively small one. . . . Too many reviewers fixed their gaze not on "Across the River," and its central character, but on an inextricable, twinned, double-exposure image of Cantwell-Hemingway. (Cantwell, by the way, thought of himself as a failure, whereas Hemingway, even now, proably thinks of himself as a success.) Hemingway was damned for Cantwell's puerilities and ideas; Cantwell was damned for Hemingway's ideas and puerilities. In many, if not most, reviews moral judgments took precedence over literary judgments or swept them from the board. . . . In hardly a single case was the book itself viewed in critical isolation; in few cases did it occur to a reviewer that Cantwell's character might be precisely the character that

Hemingway was determined to put into a novel, that it might be a masterpiece of knowledgeable drawing. No critic, apparently, asked himself: "What would I think of this novel if it had been written by a man of whom I know nothing?" But, comes the answer: "The question is silly. We know all about Ernest Hemingway.". . .

Perhaps we really do know too much about Hemingway, or at least his public poses, to judge his work impartially. If this is so, all of us who find ourselves reviewing his books and those of other authors similarly situated, should do our heroic best to thrust aside our knowledge, or half-knowledge. Otherwise we shall never be able to see clearly the book in hand, the book-in-itself.

Mary Sandrock. "New Novels." *Catholic World,* 172 (October 1950), 72-73.

"The boatman lifted the combination shooting stool and shell box out of the boat and handed it to the shooter, who leaned over and placed it in the bottom of the big barrel." That sentence from *Across the River and Into the Trees,* with but one word of more than two syllables, is the quintessence of Hemingway's self-consciously simple style. It has not changed. But Hemingway, who came to the fore two post-war eras ago, has grown old. He had an early infantile fascination for naughty words and the animal workings of the human body, and still thinks that to spray a character with them will make him a "man."

* * *

Grand guy, Cantwell. Hemingway has him freely spitting, relieving himself, barking out four-letter words, appreciating poetry and Venetian architecture. In the last war, Cantwell had briefly risen to Brigadier General; the demotion has made him bitter. His heart is giving out on him. He drinks mightily, shoots duck, copulates with eighteen-year-old Countess Renata who can match him drink for drink, then dies.

Hemingway presents them as accomplished lovers. Just how did they first come together? But, then, there is no reasoning why with Hemingway characters. They are toughly, ludicrously amoral. Uninteresting to read except as a clinical study of the failure of a behind-the-barndoor mentality to cope with maturity.

Philip Rahv. *Commentary*, 10 (October 1950), 400-402.

The first thing to be remarked about *Across the River and into the Trees* is that it is so egregiously bad as to render all comment on it positively embarrasing to anyone who esteems Hemingway as one of the more considerable prose artists of our time and as the author of some of the finest short stories in the language. Hence the dis-

appointment induced by this latest work of his, a work manifestly composed in a state of distemper, if not actual demoralization.

This novel reads like a parody by the author of his own manner—a parody so biting that it virtually destroys the mixed social and literary legend of Hemingway that has now endured for nearly three decades. For it can be said that not since the days of Dickens and later of Mark Twain has the writer of fiction in English succeeded in beguiling and captivating his readers to the extent that Hemingway did; and his success had a quality of ease and naturalness that was essentially exhilarating. In this latest book, however, the legend suffers irremediable damage. Here he really goes too far in the exploitation of it, indulging himself in blatant self-pity and equally blatant conceit, with the result that certain faults of personality, and the moral and intellectual immaturity which he was never able to overcome but which heretofore, in the greater part of his creative work, he managed to sublimate with genuine artistry, now come through as ruling elements, forcing the reader to react to Hemingway the man rather than to Hemingway the artist. And the man in Hemingway—in his literary appearances at any rate—has nearly always struck one as the parasitical double of the artist in him.

* * *

In fact there is hardly any aesthetic distance between the author and Colonel Richard Cantwell, the hero of the novel. They have so much in common, in their private history and war experience no less than in their opinions, tastes, attitudes, and prejudices, that there is no telling them apart. Thus the author intrudes everywhere, violating the most elementary specifications making for verisimilitude in a work of fiction. . . .

The stated themes of love and death are unrealized in this novel. The Colonel dies of heart disease as the action ends, but we are prepared for his death only factually, not imaginatively. It is an occurrence, nothing more, devoid of expressive implications, since the story turns on no significant principle of honor or valor or compassion such as invested some of Hemingway's earlier narratives with value and meaning. This could not but happen once the author became involved with his hero in exactly the wrong way, shifting from the role of creator to that of devotee pure and simple. He is unaware, or only dimly aware, of his hero's vanity and brutality and of the ugly competitiveness exhibited in his relations to other human beings. There can be no evaluation of character or behavior in such a contest, and no intelligible meaning to the action.

It is true, of course, that Hemingway has always been more closely involved with his hero than most novelists. The relation in which he stood to him, however, was not that of literal and helpless identification but that of the ego to the ego-ideal. Seeking to "find himself" in this leading character, he endowed him with all the qualities he considered admirable; and the world into which he turned him loose to do or die, though real enough, was none the less specially selected and ordered so as to provide him with the conditions he needed for self-fulfillment. These were conditions of relative freedom from normal circumstances and routine compulsions, for it is only within the special ambience of combat and virile sports that he performed his part, discovering the fate that awaited him. It seems to me that a good many qualities of Hemingway's prose are accounted for by this disengagement of his hero and his typical situation from the thick coils of environment, from its confusion of objects and facts. It certainly helped Hemingway to form a style of unusual lightness and freshness, but it did not make him a novelist of the first rank.

There is a certain kind of freedom which the greater novelists can neither afford nor care to solicit. Still, the fact that the binding agent of Hemingway's work was the personality of the hero, who alone held sway and in whom all the compositional elements were merged, made for a unity and concreteness of effect matched by very few of his contemporaries. But within this creative process there always lurked the danger of a possible merger between ego and ego-ideal that would disrupt the delicate balance allowing the author to live through his leading character imaginatively while standing apart from him as a man. That this balance has been lost is now evident. Colonel Cantwell is not Hemingway's ego-ideal, like Jake Barnes and Lieutenant Henry: he is the ego-ideal taken as achieved and absorbed into the ego of Hemingway, who is thus turned into his own complete ego-ideal. It is greatly to be hoped that in his future work the man recedes as the artist regains control.

Edward Weeks. "The Busted General." *Atlantic*, 186 (October 1950), 80, 81.

Stonewall Jackson's dying words set the key as well as furnish the title for Hemingway's mordant story of the dying colonel in the new novel, *Across the River and into the Trees*.

The hero Colonel Richard Cantwell, U.S. Army, is a consistent and exciting character despite his bitter and self-disparaging talk that he is a busted general. His brutal and brusque talk even when trying to be fair, his habit of command, his deceptive toughness, his sardonic condemnations of Eisenhower, Montgomery, Patton and Le-Clerc all take shape in the matrix of his confession that he wished to be and was a general officer in the Army of the United States and that he failed. But even with his sense of failure he is still quite a man. He would be so if he could drink only half as much and make love half as well.

The Colonel's portrait, however, has its blank spots, experiences for which Hemingway has not accounted well enough, and all the parts do not blend or fit together at all points. Why was he a lieutenant with the Italian army during the first great war and not with the Americans? What was he doing between the two world wars that

he could have such a close knowledge of the American West, such a quotable grasp of Shakespeare, such a taste in art, all suggestive of a civilian career? Why would such a great lover wait until his forties to marry, even if he is paying alimony to an American war correspondent? Such blanks fail to show the blending of his burly and sensitive sides. And too, his coarse talk and his bravado in counting his number of killed and possibly killed men seem less than true for the really tough soldier he seems to be.

But this is a great love story, not just love for the girl Renata but also for the infantry, for Venice and the Venetians, for the gusty love of food and wine, and that is finally what one remembers most about Hemingway's dying colonel. (Summary)

Evelyn Waugh. "The Case of Mr. Hemingway." *Commonweal*, 53 (November 3, 1950), 97-98. [Previously published in *Tablet*, 196 (September 30, 1950), 290, 292.]

As Ernest Hemingway's long-awaited novel has been published for some weeks now and has been widely reviewed, it is almost impossible to approach the book without feeling prejudice against either the book or its reviewers. For the most part, it seems, critics have indicated disapproval, some with derisive glee and others with a pretense at pity. The reception seems to be the culmination of a long campaign to show that Hemingway is finished.

Having read the reviews before I read the book, I expected the worst and intended to make the best of it. Even if he has written a totally fatuous book, Mr. Hemingway must still be recognized as one of our time's most original and powerful writers. *Across the River and into the Trees* is quite possibly his worst book, but it is better than most of the works now applauded by critics.

Even if Mr. Hemingway's hero is a boor and a bore, arrogant, humorless and self-centered, he is presented in a full, strong portrait. And as the critics have been telling us for some years now, we cannot judge novels by the attractiveness of their heroes. His heroine shows Hemingway's troubador instinct to ennoble his ladies. But in this respect his treatment of Renata is not greatly different from his treatment of Lady Brett Ashley a quarter of a century ago. If we were impressed then, why should we accept the gifts so thanklessly today?

One can of course cite the hordes of imitators between then and now. But the imitators could only copy the technique, not the mood, of Hemingway. He has a melancholy and a sense of doom at odds with the philistine insistence on happy characters. His new novel shows the nemesis of the philistine. His colonel has been through sports and drink and love-

making and professional success and found nothing at the end of it all. Though he thinks himself cultured and sophisticated, he shows the philistine self-delusion in thinking he knows Europe because he knows the barmen, in believing he knows all about the Old Masters and to hell with the art experts.

The faults as well as the merits of this book have been evident in Hemingway from the first. One wonders why critics have decided now to make such a concerted attack. Undoubtedly, the portrait of Hemingway in the *New Yorker* a few months ago by a female reporter did much to show him making a complete and not very lovable ass of himself. Before that he had disappointed all those who expected him to write the Modern War Epic. After he described Socialist atrocities, certified the presence of Russians in Madrid and made comic spectacles of Marty and La Pasionaria, he was on the wrong side of the Socialist barricades. At the same time, his sense of superiority to Americans and American urban commercial developments and his sense of inferiority to Europeans pleased no one. And his interest in the technicalities of every trade but his own, combined with his nausea for the talk of other writers, left him with few friends among his fellow writers.

If we ask why his critics hate him so, I believe we have to see that they have detected in him an unforgivable thing—Decent Feeling. After we look past all the bluster and profanity, we find an elementary sense of chivalry—respect for women, pity for the weak, a love of honor. That is what affronts the fashionable supercilious caddishness of literary types and this is why their complaints are so loud and insistent. (Summary)

William Faulkner.
"Faulkner to Waugh to Hemingway."
Time, 56
(November 13, 1950),
6.

Sir:

Re Waugh on Hemingway [Waugh criticized the critics of Hemingway's new novel, *Across the River and into the Trees*] in *Time,* October 30:

Good for Mr. Waugh. I would like to have said this myself, not the Waugh of course but the equivalent Faulkner. One reason I did not is, the man who wrote some of the pieces of *Men Without Women* and *The Sun Also Rises* and some of the African stuff (and some—most—of all the rest of it too for that matter) does not need defending, because the ones who throw the spitballs didn't write the pieces in *Men Without Women* and *The Sun Also Rises* and the African pieces and the rest of it don't have anything to stand on while they throw the spitballs.

Neither does Mr. Waugh need this from me. But I hope he will accept me on his side.

William Faulkner
Oxford, Miss.

Ellen Violett.
Theatre Arts, 34
(November 1950),
5-7.

* * *

Through the eyes of the hero one sees that war, even justifiable war, brings inevitably in its wake such incredible mismanagement, injustice, and waste as beggars description. Yet one learns from watching him that war is attractive to the hero; to be a good soldier appears to him to be part of man's normal competence; to be a war casualty is a distinguished sort of martyrdom; to die in battle is glorious. This, of course, is an important and real enigma in man. In the face of war it helps if he can work himself up to this pitch. But without this pitch in men there might not be war. In the intervals where there has not been a war on his horizon, Hemingway tests his heroes, if only vicariously, in the bull ring, or, as in "The Short Happy Life of Francis Macomber," in the jungle. The moral problem is man's attitude towards fighting. The causes of war or of bull rings are secondary. "I must fight," the heroes tell themselves, "mustn't I? "

There is no need to condescend or lament because the problem which has badgered Hemingway all these years is a small boy's problem. It exists. It recurs in the most complicated and sophisticated of modern men. It is a man's dilemma and women—great Hemingway readers—never tire of speculating about it. Hemingway has wailed the dilemma in a sort of male siren song: he speaks with the voice of angels. His self doubt is the most natural one in the world and his style is a triumph of naturalness. How else could one say what Hemingway has said over and over again, but childishly, despairingly, with a love of the permanent, physical, apparent world that verges on lyricism.

His latest book, one is led to believe, was written when Hemingway thought he really was going to die. Death was no longer something that might be his lot as a fighting foreign correspondent. It was actual and it came in the form of an illness, now happily arrested. His book concerns a middle-aged general who comes through the war only to be threatened by death through heart failure. The "I must fight" routine is of no service to him. The danger this time lies inside him rather than outside. It cannot be faced down and grappled with. The man, Hemingway's inviolate creature, is threatened. The hero of all those wars and all those women will be no more. It is a thought which stuns. To prove that it is not so, that the man exists, Hemingway through his General must retreat. There is no looking ahead to the proving ground of battle because the battle will be an unequal one in which courage is not enough. He looks back. And the central moral problem becomes "I was a fighter. Wasn't I?"

* * *

If Hemingway had seen his book for what it is the outcome might have been different. But he did not. He wrote it absolutely straight. This the General said, did, drank. The author has no point of view but the General's. When his heroes were young and full of the pitiable poses of youth this lack of viewpoint did them no disservice. But now Hemingway is dealing with a man who has lived his whole life. And still there is the same twenty-two year-old reaction to disaster. The problem is no longer universal. It has become a special, arrested case. And the style that was once the crowning glory suffers accordingly. It is a parody of the old voice of angels. The former naturalness is now grotesquely unnatural. The wine is ordered to keep the General going, not out of a youthful zest for living. One feels he has the conversations with waiters just to keep in practice and shoots ducks only to prove there is death in the old boy yet. All spontaneity is gone.

It is sad to think that a writer, who has, above all, the power to move his reader, should have been allowed by his own artistic conscience, by his advisers or his publishers, to make public a book that is without one line of genuine emotion. Self pity does not qualify and lack of self knowledge is no excuse. The man who has spoken through lovers so wistfully, so arrogantly, and with such romanticism, now appears before the audiences of the world, in the act of throwing his voice rather sloppily into two stuffed dummies, dressed as the bride and groom.

But this mistake is presumably only a break in a longer conversation. Hemingway was at work on another project which he interrupted for "Across the

River and Into the Trees." His most devoted critics will probably await it no less eagerly because of one slip of the golden tongue.

Charles Angoff. "Ernest Hemingway." *American Mercury*, 71 (November 1950), 619-25.

Future literary historians are likely to see Hemingway's *Across the River and into the Trees* as a marker of the end of the "tough" school of fiction in American literature. It is such a caricature of his method and so offensive to literary taste that it will probably end whatever influence the method still has over younger writers.

The literary *mores* of our time have been shaped by Hemingway's style and outlook, however dubious they may have been considered, more than by any other writer. None in the last fifty years has been so much imitated. In spite of their great appeal to the general public, not even Howells, Crane, Norris, Dreiser, Wharton, Cather, Fitzgerald, Lewis or Steinbeck prompted schools of writing as did Hemingway.

Like Tolstoy, Flaubert, Maupassant and Hardy, they believed in character and in probing its roots in environment and heredity. They followed its struggles, triumphs, failures in the mysterious tangle of good and evil, beauty, despair, horror, and ecstasy and assumed that the inner man was the real man; characters' external attributes were significant only insofar as they showed the inner man. These writers thought character was the most important element in life and art. As creative artists they thought it their function to show the variety of character by presenting the differences as clearly, accurately and completely as possible and to show that these differences related, however mysteriously, to something spiritual in man's nature. They thought that physical elements of human experience are more effectively indicated by suggestion than by being made explicit and that they should be kept subordinate to the spiritual ends to which they pointed.

Such concepts of character have been denied in effect by writers of popular fiction. More interested in the external man, in dramatic exploits and in violent passions, they analyze only the physical elements of experience and find murder more real than a broken heart, violent sex more revelatory than a shy kiss. Although Hemingway has never considered himself such a writer, his concentration on the external attributes of men has had much in common with the work of what must be called pulp writers. If his views of the inner man's importance are different, his writings have yet to prove it. His ability to write masterfully of the world of things has produced some ringingly true and exciting fictional dialogue. And in telling the conversation of some of the less complicated types of humanity, he has revealed a deep and genuine love for them, often without the condescension shown by more conscientious writers. But his pulp characters are still largely things in a world of things.

This is perhaps most apparent in his writing about women and about love. He shows no real awareness of interpersonal relationships. His women are only posters, only womanly moods, females with breasts but no hearts, curves but no inner softnesss, cooperative but not comforting in the timeless womanly way. Except for their powers of speech, they have little to distinguish them from females of other animal species.

In *Across the River and into the Trees* Hemingway has made the great error of ignoring the inner man and his limitless, dazzling mystery. In his desire to be "realistic" he has carried his brand of realism to a dead end. His hero is no more than an assemblage of mechanical impulses, his heroine no more real than a talking doll. In doing so he has dramatized his failure to grasp inner reality and has showed the abysmally vulgar depths to which his shabby fictional philosophy can push one. It is hard to believe that a school of fiction based on such a view will survive the disaster of *Across the River and into the Trees.* (Summary)

Philip Young.
Tomorrow, 10 (November 1950), 55-56.

With its title, which is taken from Stonewall Jackson's last words, "Let us cross over the river and rest under the shade of the tress," Hemingway's new novel announces itself as a story about dying. . . .

In many ways, this is the mixture as before. Death is the subject that has long preoccupied Hemingway, as he once admitted: Cantwell muses, "I have lived with it nearly all my life. . . . " Here are the characters as before. The Colonel is that man known to our own time as the "Hemingway hero," now grown into middle age. We once knew him, in his youth, as Lt. Henry, of *A Farewell to Arms*; for it was Frederic Henry, "a lieutenant then, and in a foreign army," who was wounded at the place where Cantwell "builds a monument" to his worst wound, identifying himself with it, in a primitive ritual. And as always the hero is Hemingway himself, the eccentric, war-ravaged, fifty-one-year-old soldier with high blood pressure, who takes his pills with gin. The only big change is that Cantwell is a professional soldier and a very literary one at that. Here too is the heroine as before, the highly idealized girl who so exists for her lover that she nearly ceases to exist as a person. Here in short are all the Hemingway ingredients, and a characteristic compound of love and death that we are coming to know him by.

The situation in the novel ("a girl nineteen years old in love with a man over fifty years old that you knew was going to die") is perilous. But that fact does not fully explain why, using the methods and materials which have been in other Hemingway novels so satisfying, this is a pretty bad book. The failure is the sum of many errors —the outrageous and irrelevant attacks on recognizable living writers for instance; and the wholly embarrassing conversations with Renata's portrait, and—nearly as discomforting—with Renata herself. At times, Hemingway seems under the delusion that he is being interviewed: T/5 Jackson, Renata, and others act as straight men, setting up questions so Cantwell can pontificate; when obliging reporters are not about, Hemingway interviews himself. Thus we get estimates of prominent generals, admirals, presidential candidates, and Red Smith, the sports columnist (the Colonel likes *him*). Also the Russian situation, the Tito situation, and "inside" bits about various battles. None of this is extraordinarily interesting to read: "Nobody would give you a penny for your thoughts, he thought. Not this morning." But the reader is giving three dollars.

Hemingway has quite patently indulged a desire to write out, in novel length, a dream of how he himself would like to die. He envisions an ideal girl who adores him, and ideal meals with perfect wines in an ideal hotel in his favorite city, and—fabulously important to him—"the best run duck shoot I have ever shot at." Then when it is over he gets the signal from his heart, speaks the appropriate last words and dies.

There is no telling what urge prompted Hemingway to make Cantwell a colonel who had once been a general, but perhaps the demotion has its obscure parallels in Hemingway's own literary career: he has frequently been demoted by the critics. We must not forget, however, that right after *The Torrents of Spring* came *The Sun Also Rises;* after *To Have and Have Not, For Whom the Bell Tolls.* This book gives Hemingway's detractors another opportunity to attack him for the "narrowness of his vision," for his "obsession with violence," and the like. Where in him, one can ask once more, do you find a mature, brooding intelligence, a sense of the past, the grown-up relationships of adult people, and all the other qualities we look for in a first-rate novelist? All we get are battles, or their aftermath, and Hemingway still under the spell of his own war chants. This new novel, in addition to all the faults peculiar to itself, brings up stronger than ever the old objections, for although the book —like *The Sun Also Rises*—has to do less with battles than their results, never has Hemingway's stubborn insistence on the essential and profound significance of violence "in our time" been more emphatic.

It is true that in all of his work Hemingway's vision has opened largely on a world of violence and evil. The conditions of his world—its atmosphere of urgency and despair—are such as are imposed by war. Its hero is a soldier, its heroine a girl the soldier usually meets, loves and parts from forever, all in a space of days. They leave no children behind them; they exist in the shadows of death, the essential preoccupation of those at the front. The stuff of their everyday lives are bottles, hotels, munitions, battalions, corpses, broken bones, fractured love affairs. The background is always war; for even when one escapes the world of war one ends up by imitating it—one kills, instead of humans: ducks, fish, kudu, bulls and horses.

We do very well to protest this picture. It does not represent the kind of world we wish to live in; it is not one, ultimately, in which some of us are even very interested. But if we review our time, what facts stand out stronger than the facts of violence, evil, and death,—countless "minor" wars, and two major slaughters, and a third holocaust, beyond which we cannot see at all, approaching? We may argue the utter inadequacy of this world Hemingway has refracted and recreated. But we should be hard pressed to prove that it is not the one we inhabit.

Robert Warshow. "The Dying Gladiator." *Partisan Review*, 17 (November-December 1950), 876-84.

This is the saddest story Hemingway has written, for in it he has abandoned the one supreme virtue that gave his work distinction. That virtue was the clarity and immediacy of his identification of language and vision, the almost absolute congruence of form and content whereby his prose seems to be contained in the language. It is true that this near-perfection is sometimes the product of oversimplification, as can be seen in Hemingway's denial of ideas, but it is an oversimplification resulting from the limitations of personality rather than from language. One feels in general that whatever "realities" are available to the personal vision, they find their inextricable unity in language and perception.

In such constructions of vision Hemingway is closer to Kafka than is any other American writer. Both get their strongest and most characteristic effects by a perverse tone of innocence. Where Kafka can abruptly convince a reader that a man has turned into a monstrous insect, Hemingway can just as persuasively tell of a monstrously factual act of man on man, as in the shooting of six cabinet ministers at half-past six in the morning against the wall of a hospital. But because Hemingway's world is the more accessible of the two, he has been more popular and has served as a dangerous temptation to other writers. Still, both are cult writers in effect and belong to the class of writers who transform the universe by the brilliance of their technique.

For such a writer language is everything. If he for a moment ceases to maintain the illusion that every word is heavily weighted with care and seriousness, if he for a moment lets it be felt that the words are only instruments he manipulates, his "universe" becomes a pose, his structure falls apart. Hemingway's lapses have been frequent. The boring talk of "cojones" and the fastidiousness of wine tasting in *The Sun Also Rises* showed his tendency to let personality intrude between the subject and the language. The cute "obscenities" and false rhetoric of Spanish in *For Whom the Bell Tolls* told that language was a kind of joke, even if on the level of art. In *Across the River and into the Trees* the language is more clearly a joke but more on the level of a Broadway columnist than of art, and it shows the writer indulging his personal obsessions in the most flagrant way yet.

The book is an epitome of Hemingway's favorite themes, opinions and prejudices—of death, war, love, hunting, good food, good wine, the comradeship of those who have been wounded, the corruptness of intellectuals, journalists, and the bourgeoisie, especially the new rich, of snobbery on every subject from wine to military tactics. Its love scenes have the same mawkishness and its "rough" language the same coyness as those of *For Whom the Bell Tolls.* And it is all so vulgarized that one wonders how the author could have let himself slip so far. (Summary)

Isaac Rosenfeld. "A Farewell to Hemingway." *Kenyon Review*, 13 (Winter 1951), 147-55.

It is not enough to say that *Across the River and Into the Trees* is a bad novel, which nearly everyone has said (the fact is, a good deal of it is trash), or to ascribe its failure to Hemingway's playing Hemingway. Such judgments fail to go deep; they make an artificial separation between the man and the artist, and attribute to the former, as though these were superficial mistakes, shortcomings which are the very essence of Hemingway's art. It seems to me that no writer of comparable stat-

ure has ever expressed in his work so false an attitude toward life. Now this is more than a matter of temperament, though the pompous boasting, the sounding off on life, love and literature in baseball, prize-ring and military metaphors (the purpose of which is to demonstrate that Hemingway is so great a literary figure that he is primarily an athlete, a hunter, a soldier, a lover of fine wines and women—anything but a writer; this is what I consider trash) that run all through this book, do help to create the impression that Hemingway has gone on a bender and deserted his art. But these monkey-shines are defenses, and to ignore the serious principle while criticizing Hemingway's legend of himself is to succumb to the strategy: at the expense of the man, to flatter the art.

It is easy to understand how Hemingway took hold of our imagination. The characters he created of the lost generation gave us an image of ourselves which we were glad to accept; it was a true image, and in the long run, ennobling. With considerable courage, he continued the work of realism in judging an old social order whose wars were not of our making, and for the wreck of whose values we were not responsible. Jake and his friends did not run out on life, they were pushed out; the separate peace which Frederic Henry concluded was the only sensible thing to do, and only the reactionary and the philistine would blame him for it. These characters, in their main outlines, were seen as the result of external force; the action of the world on them was recorded in the form of a wound. . . .

It was only natural that a whole generation should seize on the wound in justification of itself. The success myth, as the not yet successful Hemingway had the insight to observe, was overthrown, and nothing besides the wound had offered itself. He had no false comfort to give and he told, as far as it went, the truth. It was not the time to examine this argument closely; to do so would have seemed like compromising with society. It passed unnoticed that Hemingway himself was offering a compromise; not the kind the world desired or which it even recognized. All the same, in the character structure which he gave his heroes—an entity by itself, which we now call "the Hemingway character" —the old values were never seriously questioned, and such clichés as manliness, courage and self-reliance remained unchanged. There is no objection to these values as such; the objection is to the meaning society has given them. Hemingway never examined their social meaning; he merely cut the traditional world of application out from under these values and put something unexpected in its place. He did not tell the lost generation to go out and in the name of these values sell, conquer, succeed, or otherwise overwhelm the world. He did tell it, in so many words, in his books and in the concomitant legend of himself, to attack and refashion itself in character, to be, precisely, self-reliant, courageous and manly—in a word, hard. It is here that he has been a misleading influence on a whole generation of American writers and their audience; and while he is not to be blamed for the army of imitators that has followed him or made (not without his example) an alliance, through the hard-boiled tradition, with bad taste, he is to be judged for what he himself has done. He has created his own subsection of the Myth of the American Male, supporting everything in this myth which is lifeless, vicious and false—the contempt for women and for every tender feeling, as for something effeminate and corrupt, the apotheosis of the purely forceful, tense and thrusting component of maleness as a phallic bludgeon to beat the female principle into submission, the perpetual adolescence of the emotions with its compensatory heroics to cover a fear, and consequent hatred, of sexual love; and this, not as a lapse from his art, but in its best practice.

In Hemingway's work there has always been a great lag between characterization and expression; the lives and characters of his heroes are set down to mean one thing, but they express something entirely different, frequently the opposite. Hemingway's men are hard, they contain their emotions; so runs their title to manliness. They contain their emotions because of a natural dignity and restraint, and this restraint becomes all the more appropriate as the strength of the emotion increases; it is only the trivial feeling that one can afford to let out freely. . . .

* * *

The style covers up this starvation with the honorific leanness. Dividing its skill between the suppression of feeling and the presentation of the clear, clean impression for which Hemingway is famous, it becomes a paraphrase of his philosophy, which considers emotion a disgraceful epiphenomenon, and holds a man to be most human when he is most like wood. This always happens. What was meant to be a full engagement with life, turns out to be a fear of life. All the softer emotions having been eliminated from the character structure of his heroes, the capacity for love and surrender vanish for good, leaving no counterpart in the outer world. Reality is to be read only in terms of violent action, the only kind of which his characters are capable; the world is that which answers to a man's capacity for dealing a blow. The only possible contact in such a world is that of devouring, the only yielding, death. Behaviorism is the only psychology, sickness, the only norm. There is nothing in this scheme to allow for growth, development, education of the feelings, since these do not exit. Hemingway is therefore one of the most static of novelists. His characters either learn nothing or, like Harry Morgan and Robert Jordan with their great discovery that there is some connection between man and man, reach, at the very end, the usual starting-point of the novel. Without this education, which is one of the basic patterns of life, there can be neither a great form nor a great subject in the novel. But in behaviorism there is nothing more to learn; once the reflex is conditioned, it is fixed.

If this were no more than a false philosophy and psychology, it would still be possible for Hemingway's art to succeed, in virtue of its own insight, unacknowledged in the doctrine. But this philosophy—as with all such anti-intellectualisms—is irrefutable. It has no theory, which one can correct by drawing the example from the practice; this is the practice. The philosophy is but another way of expressing the limitation and the falsehood of the art. It is only when Hemingway's style is freed of its defensive obligations that it reaches its best level, as when he writes of landscape and machines; there are no emotions to fend off with the latter, and with the former, the emotions are not suspect, since they have only symbolic reference to the feminine.

* * *

The curious thing about *Across the River* is that while it is his worst novel, in one respect—but only in this respect—it is an improvement over all the earlier works. For once the severed halves of the characterization are joined, and the conscious and unconscious images of the hero closely resemble each other.

Richard Cantwell, Col., Infantry, U.S.A., who has come to Venice for several days to see his mistress and shoot ducks, is a man of fifty with a weak heart. He has the same structure as the earlier characters, with the same ascription of the inner anxiety to external causes, and the same discharge of that anxiety through substitutive behavior. He exists for the most part in conversation. Hemingway's clipped dialogue, which had always served the purpose of direct characterization (and of reflecting the unintentional characterization by keeping affect to a minimum), has now been loosened somewhat; it has a more complicated function—that of reducing the character to an even further simplicity. The gap between consciousness and behavior is now completely closed; at least, there is no language left to express it, as the displacement of tension through physical behavior (in Cantwell's case, battle) has been read back into the character, where it becomes the basic language. . . . But now, though the hero is still meant to exemplify Hemingway's attitude toward life, he is presented as a sick man; he swallows pills all through the action, he must avoid excitement and strain, and he dies of a heart attack. . . . Cantwell has also a touch of the Shriner. He plays a game with the head waiter of his hotel, complete with Secret Order, passwords, etc., and gladly interrupts his conversations with Renata, in which he treats her to encyclopedic pontifications, for a mystical pass or two with the *Gran Maestro.*

This may be a serious disintegration in the conception of character, a boring and pathetic attempt in and out of character to play the great man, but it is not a total loss. For once the hero, a man of the same cut and cloth as all the rest, is identified for what he is. The claims to universality are abandoned: Cantwell is not a figure of the lost generation, he is not the representative of something going on in our time, he is not learning through fatal experience what everyone with natural feeling knows to begin with, that no man is an island. He is a man on his own, lonely, grown old, demoted from

the rank of General to nobody, in love or persuaded he is in love (there can never have been much difference for him) with a girl who may or may not exist (again no difference), prattling of war, of the good life and the true love with an unfeeling, monotonous, heartsick narcissism, not yet having learned what he is doing, having learned nothing from life, nothing beyond the one thing he knows now—that he is about to die. The defenses are down, the myth is overthrown. This is a poor sick bum, giving himself airs; as sick as all his brothers have been, and like them empty, compulsive and deluded, incapable of love. But for once Hemingway knows his man and for once it is possible to believe in his hero for what he is. He has come home, ruined, to something like humanity, the humanity, at least, of self-betrayal. What he acts out and what he expresses in his action, for once, are one.

This is the most touching thing Hemingway has done. For all the trash and foolishness of this book, perhaps even because of it, because he let himself be lulled and dulled by the fable of himself, he gave away some of his usual caution and let a little grief, more than ordinarily and not all of it stuck in the throat, come through his careful style. A little of the real terror of life in himself, with no defenses handy, not even a propitiatory bull to offer in sacrifice, nothing to kill but the hero. And a little real courage, more than it takes to shoot lions in Africa, the courage to confess, even if it be only through self-betrayal, the sickness and fear and sad wreck of life behind the myth. Wish him luck.

Northrop Frye. "Novels on Several Occasions." *The Hudson Review*, 3 (Winter 1951), 611-12.

The theme of *Across the River and Into the Trees* is death in Venice, with Colonel Cantwell, a reduced brigadier and a "beat-up old bastard," as a military counterpart of Mann's beat-up old novelist.... It is a great theme, and in the hands of someone competent to deal with it—say Ernest Hemingway—it might have been a long short story of overwhelming power.

It is pleasant to dwell on the idea and postpone the fact. In the opening scene and in the curt description of the colonel's death, there is something of the old Hemingway grip. In between, however, the story lies around in bits and pieces, with no serious effort to articulate it. The colonel is entitled to rancorous prejudice—the reader doesn't expect him to be a Buddhist sage, and in his political and military reflections one wouldn't mind the clichés of a commonplace grouch if they built up to something bigger, but they don't. We expect to find the love scenes stripped of eloquence, but not to encounter a cloying singsong of "I love you truly" and a repetitiousness that looks like padding. The role of the Contessa is that of a more attractive version of a deferential yesman. The colonel wanders in an empty limbo between a dead and an unborn world, at no point related to other human beings in a way that would give his story any representative importance. As far as anyone can be, he is an island entire of itself.

This last, of course, is part of Hemingway's point. His story is intended to be a study in isolation, of how the standards of a decent soldier are betrayed by modern war. The colonel is not a writer, and the things that are happening to him he assumes to be incommunicable, because he has found them so. And he dominates the book so much that something of his distrust of communication seems to have leaked into the author and paralyzed his will to write. In this kind of story the hero's loneliness must be compensated for by the author's desire to tell the story and, to adopt one of his own cadences, tell it truly. But this involves the total detachment of author from character which comes when sympathy and insight are informed by professional skill. This detachment has not been reached, and the book remains technically on the amateurish level in which the most articulate character sounds like a mouthpiece for the author. Hence all the self-pity and egotism which have been thrown out the door reappear in the windows between the lines. The reader is practically compelled to read the story the wrong way, and the result is a continuous sense of embarassment.

Deb Wylder.
"Ernest Hemingway and
the Rotary Club."
Western Review, 15
(Spring 1951),
237-40.*

* * *

The world, *Cosmopolitan* asserts, has waited ten long years for Hemingway's new novel. "How do you like it now, gentlemen?" Mr. Hemingway constantly asks in a recent article by Lillian Ross in *The New Yorker*. Probably the most frequent answer to this question will be, "We don't." And the tone of the answer will vary with the reader. For a generation that went to war feeling that what Hemingway had said about the first World War and its aftermath was as valid for their own generation as for his, the answer will be in the shocked voice of the betrayed. The voice of the critic and scholar, whom Hemingway has used every opportunity to badger these past few years, will be the voice of one who has long awaited a chance for reprisal. But even this voice may sound a bit startled at the change in Hemingway. For Hemingway has finally joined the "lost generation" that has recently become totally lost.

If the generation of the "twenties" could be classified as "lost," we must at least admit that they were searching. They were searching for an answer to the problems that an earlier generation had, without preparing them, created and thrown in their faces. . . .

With *Across the River and into the Trees,* Ernest Hemingway has concluded his search, but from what Hemingway has found, one might say that he has finally become lost—irrevocably lost—at least in the world of values. He has, in effect, joined the ranks with Sinclair Lewis and John Dos Passos in an acceptance of those same institutionalized values which he had rejected in his youth.

Not that Hemingway accepts the "American way of life" in a blind faith like Dos Passos. Not that Colonel Richard Cantwell, the new Hemingway hero, does not have his personal code which embodies honesty, integrity, and action; for he does. . . . But, underlying all this overt statement of Colonel Cantwell's integrity, we find an acceptance of both the military and aristocratic hierarchies which becomes almost fascistic. True, the Colonel rejects the workings of the military hierarchy because it has become inefficient due to, primarily, its complexity. However, we are even more aware of the Colonel's personal dislike of the higher-ups who have refused to grant him a general's command in the regular army. The reason for this confusion lies, perhaps, in Hemingway's having forgotten some of the lessons taught him by Gertrude Stein. . . . When Hemingway intended to publish his stories with his own meditations as additional material, Gertrude told him, "Hemingway, remarks are not literature." She was right, then; she is still right. Unfortunately, Hemingway seems to have forgotten this advice, for his new novel is filled with his own remarks thrust into the mouth of Colonel Cantwell. For example, Eisenhower is described as "strictly Epworth League" and a good politician. The other war leaders are classed as Rotarians, in general, and now and then Cantwell pauses to make specific charges against them as individuals. Which really, I suppose, doesn't seem such a terrible indictment when we learn a little more about Cantwell; he is not only an aristocratic Rotarian, but a legionnaire as well.

* * *

Ray B. West, Jr. has stated that "ideology is not imposed upon the material, it grows out of it, and any attempt to impose it results in artistic failure." But in *Across the River and into the Trees*, the ideology has not only been forced upon the material, the ideology has been superficially attached to the protagonist. In other words, what is usually called the Hemingway "code" no longer acts as a set of rules to aid the protagonist to live in the world—it has now become an excuse for an embittered old man (excluding his sexual virility and adolescent outlook) to separate himself from the world.

Hemingway has tried, in this novel, to present a more complicated and more subtle development through repetition and concentration on unimportant detail rather than through a corresponding complexity of style. . . . And it is enough to say that the dialogue of *Across the River and Into the Trees* sounds like an imitation of Hemingway's worst imitators. The dialogue, moreover, is often used as a device to allow the unbelievable Colo-

nel Cantwell to make Hemingway-inspired remarks about war and literature. The tone is closer to *Green Hills of Africa* and *Death in the Afternoon* than any of his novels. The result is a failure, for the imposition of such authoritative (and Hemingway *is* authority in this novel) material disrupts the novel form.

Hemingway has recently used every means in his power to strike at the critic. His introduction to Vittorini's *In Sicily* was as much of a personal attack against critics as what it was intended to be—an introduction to a novel. His new novel bears a strong resemblance to this introduction. Forgetting Miss Stein's advice, he has misused the form of the novel as a vehicle for his own remarks.

*Mr. Wylder would like it noted that his position has changed a great deal since this original review was written. See his book *Hemingway's Heroes* (Albuquerque: University of New Mexico Press, 1969).

Joseph Warren Beach. "How Do You Like It Now, Gentlemen?" *Sewanee Review,* 59 (April-June 1951), 311-28.

With his latest novel, Ernest Hemingway has caused a good deal of embarrassment to the many eminent critics and the large body of readers who have whole-heartedly admired him and defended him against all who challenged his perfection as an artist. Indeed, he has rather put his admirers on the spot. He is making it necessary for them to pass his earlier work in review in the light of his latest performance and satisfy themselves whether the faintly disagreeable odor that emanates from *Across the River and Into the Trees* is an evidence of decay already present in the work they have admired so much, or simply an accidental feature of a story turned out in a moment of weakness.

* * *

It has often been noted that the hero of Hemingway's novels is always much the same person—that Jake Barnes and Frederick Henry and Robert Jordan are grown-up versions of the boy Nick Adams of *In Our Time,* who is so obviously a rendering of the boy Ernest Hemingway. Well, Colonel Cantwell is the oldest of all these avatars of Nick Adams; but one is not sure that he is actually the most adult in his attitude toward himself. And the sense of psychological regression here is one thing that makes us hesitate to rate this book among the best of his work.

Apart from incidental talk about fighting and brass hats, the action of the story consists of three things: the love-making of Renata and the Colonel, the duck-hunt on the following day, and the death of the Colonel on his way back to Venice. It is a slight ground of substance for so long a piece. This is not the serious book about the war on which Hemingway has been at work for many years. It is

something thrown off in passing. Hemingway began the present work as a short story. "Then I couldn't stop it," he says. "It went on into a novel." The question is whether he would not have been wiser to stop it. The situation of the man of fifty, with a bad heart, falling in love with a beautiful young girl, and realizing that here, too late, is the true love of which he has always dreamed, is entirely plausible and deeply moving. The question is whether, as it stands, this subject is big enough, strong enough, for the weight he puts upon it.

For one thing, it has proved a considerable strain on his stylistic resources, which have generally been adequate to all his needs. He has seldom allowed himself so many soft, blank-check adjectives for characterizing towns or persons or feelings. The distant view of Venice was "wonderful" and "beautiful" to the Colonel as it was when he was eighteen.

* * *

You may say that the belated discovery of true love is a tragic circumstance, not unknown in human experience, and one that may well draw our tears. Draw our tears, yes. But whether it is correct to use the word tragic in this connection depends on one's conception of tragedy. According to Aristotle tragedy is associated with an important action and one in which the character of the participants is a main determinant in the catastrophe. Hemingway does not succeed in giving this abortive love the sort of importance that Aristotle calls for and Shakespeare exemplifies. And it is not the character

of Renata or the Colonel that pro-
vokes the tragedy here, but the accidental circumstance that they have
met thirty years too late. It is more
exact to say that this story is *pathetic,*
and that the pathos is rather too much
drawn out for the happiest effect.

* * *

In *To Have and Have Not* the pleasures of the marriage bed are a conso-
lation prize for the valiant man who
has lost out in the unfair battle of life.
In *Across the River and Into the Trees*
the belated discovery of love by the
old campaigner proves too thin a subject for a book of three hundred pages
and leaves us with the feeling of having
fallen into sentimental self-indulgence.

* * *

Checklist of
Additional Reviews

Kirkus, 18 (July 15, 1950), 390.

Booklist, 46 (July 15, 1950), 345.

Booklist, 47 (September 1, 1950), 13.

H. W. Hart. *Library Journal,* 75 (September 1, 1950), 1407.

Emmett Dedmon. *Chicago Sun,* September 10, 1950, p. 9.

William J. Parker. *Denver Post,* September 10, 1950, p. 6-E.

"British Call Hemingway Book 'Evil,
Adolescent.' " *Chicago Sunday Tribune,* September 17, 1950, Magazine of Books, p. 14.

Bookmark, 10 (October 1950), 8.

E. B. White. "Across the Street and
into the Grill." *New Yorker,* 26
(October 14, 1950), 28.

THE OLD MAN
AND
THE SEA

ERNEST HEMINGWAY

CHARLES SCRIBNER'S SONS, NEW YORK
1952

The Old Man and the Sea

Henry Seidel Canby.
"An Unforgettable Picture of Man Against the Sea and Man Against Fate."
Book-of-the-Month Club News,
August 1952,
pp. 2-3.

This is one of the best stories that Ernest Hemingway ever wrote. I believe it is the best fishing story in English. If not so short as the story of Jonah and Whale, it is nevertheless not very long; and it is at once both superbly placid and superbly exciting, with something of the irresistible subsurface power that one can always sense beneath the long swells of a calm tropical sea. It has no superiors in the art of writing about the sea in any language I know, unless it is the great conclusion of Melville's *Moby-Dick.*

* * *

Hemingway himself has always been known as a great hunter and a great fisherman. Here again he is a major writer, for no minor writer could so put into words the ancient magic of the sea, or thus take a simple old man like Santiago (though not simple in character, or in understanding) and by him and through him give articulate expression to basic human dreams, hungers and terrors. For it is terror, among other things, that besets the old man before he reaches Cuba again. . . .

Through Hemingway's matchless skill, a fishing story becomes a masterpiece of the sea. Quiet yet passionate, nervously alive yet always superbly controlled, it is an unforgettable picture of man against the sea and man against fate.

Orville Prescott.
"Books of the Times."
New York Times,
August 28, 1952,
p. 21.

Several weeks ago Life magazine sent galley proofs of the new Hemingway novel "The Old Man and the Sea" to several hundred critics and newsmen along with the announcement of publication of the novel in a single issue of Life eleven days before appearance of the novel in book form. Ordinarily book reviewers are little concerned with what magazines publish. But here was a major work by a world-famous author being presented to a mass audience for the price of 20 cents, days before the book could be bought at $3 from the booksellers. What the booksellers who have distributed his books for twenty-six years had to say of Mr. Hemingway is not on record. What Mr. Hemingway has to say is on record in several Life advertisements. He is happier about having a world-wide audience than he would be at having a Nobel Prize.

The new novel shows Hemingway at the top of his form. It is a short work of only 27,000 words, and in it he has accepted the sharp restrictions imposed by the nature of the story. Written with sure skill, it shows the master technician doing superbly what he can do better than anybody else. A much simpler book than "Across the River and into the Trees," it avoids the glamour girls and bullying braggarts, the sentimentality, the outbursts of spite, the false theatricalism of the earlier book in favor of an honest and elemental theme. Here are the excitement and tension of the old man's adventure with the magnificent marlin and the beauty of days and nights alone on the Gulf Stream. Here again Hemingway shows himself unexcelled in descriptions of physical action and its emotional atmosphere. Here too is his celebration of the old man's dogged courage, better even than that of "The Undefeated," which it most resembles.

With all its mastery, the new novel has its limitations. Most markedly, the old fisherman lacks full characterization as an individual. He is presented more as a symbolic attitude toward life than as a man. His thoughts are so poetically rendered as to seem at times artificial. Poetic and beautiful as they are, they seem more Hemingway's than the old man's. (Summary)

Theodore M. O'Leary. "Ernest Hemingway at His Best." *Kansas City Star,* August 30, 1952.

To come quite simply to the point, as Ernest Hemingway himself usually does, Hemingway has written a great book. You can call "The Old Man and the Sea" a long short story or you can call it a short novel, but no matter what you call it, it is one of those perfectly executed pieces of fiction that appear at great intervals and are destined to endure.

* * *

The tragic ending which Hemingway has given the story of the old man and the great marlin is inevitably right. As you read it and consider other possible alternatives, you realize that no other ending would have been possible, that any other conclusion would have robbed the book of its perfection. And the tragedy is softened as the relation of the old man and the boy seems destined to resume its old aspect.

* * *

Most of Ernest Hemingway's great literary assets and none of his liabilities are displayed in "The Old Man and the Sea." His prose is simple and beautiful but much less mannered than that of his last previous book, "Across the River and Into the Trees," in which certain passages seemed almost like parodies of Hemingway by Hemingway. Hemingway is never content until he tells you exactly how something looks, or smells, or feels; yet present behind that exactness are almost limitless intimations and suggestions which set off in every reader's mind his own train of thought.

The dialogue between the old man and the boy is Hemingway's best, which means it is the best written in our time. . . .

Death, usually violent death, has always been a primary interest of Hemingway and that interest is present here. To him the supreme drama of life is concerned with such death, whether it be the death of a man or a woman, or of a fish, a bull, a duck or a lion. But there is no evidence here of his tendency to write of death and violence for their own sake and to present characters who admire and overdramatize their own personal tragedies, an essentially juvenile tendency which has marred some of Hemingway's books.

So the man who has given us some of our greatest modern novels and many of our greatest short stories has now given us a kind of combination of the two, which as much as anything he has ever written should help assure him of his place among the topmost literary figures of our troubled century.

Carlos Baker. "The Marvel Who Must Die." *Saturday Review*, 34 (September 6, 1952), 10-11.

The admirable Santiago, Hemingway's ancient mariner and protagonist of this triumphant short novel, enters the gallery of permanent heroes effortlessly, as if he had belonged there from the beginning.

* * *

Once more, in his lengthening career as one of the few genuine tragic writers of modern times, Hemingway has memorably engaged a theme familiar to tragic literature. Santiago belongs among all those who have the strength and dignity to fight against great odds and to win moral victories, even though the tangible rewards may be lost in the process of the battle. On the heroic level, one thinks of Melville's Ahab, Whitman's Columbus, Sandburg's Lincoln. But the great skill here has been to take a simple fisherman and by setting his struggle against the background of the ancient and unchanging sea, and pitting him against an adversary worthy of his strength, to bring out his native ability and indomitability until, once having known him, we can never afterwards lose sight of him. . . . It approaches, as a tragic pattern, the story of King Lear, whose shark-hearted daughters bled him of his dominions and his hundred

knights, yet left his dignity unimpaired
and his native courage unshaken. . . .

"One cannot hope to explain," says
the publisher's commentary, "why the
reading of this book is so profound an
experience." One can, however, at
least begin to explain the essence of
the experience by making two related
observations about it. The first is that
the story not only shows a natural
tragic pattern (which is no doubt why
Hemingway was drawn to it); it develops also as a kind of natural parable.
Like human life, for which it easily
stands as an extended image, the struggle commences, grows, and subsides
between one sleep and another. The
parable of Santiago Agonistes works
upon our sensibilities like a heroic
metaphor achieved naturally and without manifest heroics. The result, a divi-
dend above and beyond the pleasure
of reading a fine story, is the discovery
of an open-sided trope in which every
man may locate some of the profounder aspects of his own spiritual
biography.

The second point enters the region
of religious experience. The theme of
what is Christlike in every good man
has grown in upon Hemingway since
1940, when the Christian Anselmo, another aged man, was established as the
moral norm in "For Whom the Bell
Tolls." The ancient Santiago, stumbling out of his boat with dried blood
on his face from a partly healed
wound, and with the deep cord-cuts
like stigmata on his hands, carries the
mast over his shoulder up the hill.
Sleeping exhaustedly face down on the
spread newspapers that cover the
springs of his bed, he lies cruciform,

with arms out straight and palms
turned upwards. *In hoc signo vinces.*
He has entered the Masonic order of
Christian heroes. In short, Hemingway
has enhanced the native power of his
tragic parable by engaging, though unobtrusively, the further power of
Christian symbolism. Somewhere between its parabolical and its Christian
meaning lies one important explanation of this book's power to move us.

* * *

Brendan Gill.
"Not to Die."
New Yorker, 28
(September 6, 1952),
104.

Ernest Hemingwy's new novel "The
Old Man and the Sea" is such a short
and simple story and so dominated by
a mood of unexpected tenderness that
one is tempted to read it as a parable.
To do so, however, would diminish
and vulgarize it. Finding parables is
better left to the professors. The wiser
reader must take it on its own spare
terms and let its meanings become as
large and as manifold as he can sense
them.

The old fisherman who has chosen
skill over luck and has won his great
marlin, then lost him to the sharks, is
the embodiment of a whole cluster of
themes announced and returned to by
Hemingway through the whole body
of his work. He has never done so
more gravely and candidly than here.
For what he shows in Santiago, even
more clearly than in Manuel Garcia,

Harry Morgan or Francis Macomber, is that the price of enduring is great and must be paid again and again until finally no one has the means to go on paying it. (Summary)

Harvey Breit.
"Hemingway's 'Old Man.'"
The Nation, 175
(September 6, 1952),
194-95.

In recent years the literary journals have reflected with evident, if uneasy, satisfaction the phenomenon known as the decline of Ernest Hemingway. Behind the critical demolition when it was executed in good faith—and this was not always the case—existed a too easy notion, really an assumption, that Hemingway was immature. And behind this assumption there was another: Kafka was mature. In Kafka the critic saw the arch-contemporary; in Hemingway he saw the obsolescent. . . .

What Hemingway has attempted throughout his mature career is his own synthesis. Sometimes he has brought it off wholly; sometimes he has failed to bring it off except in part. What he has attempted to do—it is a metaphysical rather than an aesthetic aim, because it is related to his fundamental attitude toward all of life—is to fuse under a sustained pressure the opposite elements of experience and vision, of prosaic event and dramatic or poetic insight. Say it how you will, in his continuous, exacting, and independent operations in prose Hemingway

has attempted to annihilate that shadow which, according to T.S. Eliot, falls between the idea and the reality, between the essence and the descent. In his effort to deliver the essence intact, Hemingway has fashioned an instrument of power that goes beyond beautiful writing, beyond the bare, spare, stripped prose, beyond the exact hearing of the quintessential speech. What he has fashioned is a kind of try-works, to borrow a figure from Melville, a vast cook stove that burns away all matter except the essence of the chase, the sperm oil, the dead center.

In his new short novel, "The Old Man and the Sea," Hemingway is working with fluent, controlled, and astonishing power. It ought not to cause surprise; the power was operative even in "Across the River and into the Trees." Only then the cook stove was stoked too high and much that mattered was burned off. The Hemingway shorthand was too intense, too much was suppressed, and therefore it called attention to itself.

Ultimately it is a question of limits. Hemingway's art unfolds peerlessly when he operates within the limits he sets for himself, another way of saying the limits his story sets for him. In "The Old Man and the Sea" Hemingway manipulates his own boundaries and is obedient to them, and the result is a great and "true" novel, touching and terrible, tragic and happy. It is not the most complex or exacting or challenging novel Hemingway has ever written, but it is perhaps the warmest and the most beautiful.

* * *

It is Hemingway's great art that he teaches whatever it is he is concerned with, whether it be shooting game, fighting bulls, planning a military campaign, or plotting a prize fight. It has little to do with pedantry; it has everything to do with reality and concreteness. And more: in all his best work, and it is true of the new novel, these special areas, these particular professions and occupations are transposed inexorably into universal meanings. In "The Old Man" the mystique of fishing, with its limited triumphs and tragedies, is transposed into a universal condition of life, with its success and shame, its morality and pride and potential loss of pride.

On so many counts the book is momentous and heartening. For one thing, the "law" of the collapse of the American artist after his first books is canceled out—if one holds with the law at all. For another, this small book reveals the artist as having gained in stature. Though in his past work Hemingway suggested compassion and humility and love, in "The Old Man" he gives expression to them in a directer and bolder way, without sacrificing the strength and toughness of the earlier work. And for a final thing, it suggests that the big book Hemingway has been working on in the past, and is still working on, may be his greatest.

Malcolm Cowley. "Hemingway's Novel Has the Rich Simplicity of a Classic." *New York Herald Tribune Book Review*, 29 (September 7, 1952), 1, 17.

---

* * *

The publishers called it a classic, even before it was printed in "Life," with a hastiness of epithet that suggests the speed of modern times; in more backward ages it took three or four centuries to make a classic. There is one sense, however, in which the publishers' claim is justified. "The Old Man and the Sea" is classical in spirit if we think of "classical" as a term applied to those works in all fields that accept limitations of space, subject and treatment while trying to achieve faultlessness within the limitations: Greek temples as opposed to Gothic Cathedrals. In its own terms the book is as nearly faultless as any short novel of our times.

Its length of less than thirty thousand words would seem to place it with earlier long stories like "The Undefeated" and "Francis Macomber" and at first glance it seems to be simpler than either of these. It has no complications of plot and it presents only three characters, counting the fish. When read carefully, however, it proves to have a power of suggestion that gives it more weight and scope than any of the early stories. There are single phrases that imply a way of life. *"Qué va,"* says the boy when he is roused and set to work long before dawn. "It is what a man must do." The old man felt that "no man was ever alone on the sea." I remember one sentence among others: "They walked down the road to the old man's shack and all along the road, in the dark, barefoot men were moving, carrying the masts of their boats." In twenty eight words, all of them short, each of them right, it gives a background to the characters by evoking the life of a whole community.

At cocktail parties you already hear the book described as the poor man's "Moby Dick." . . . In the present instance it is justified by a surface resemblance in plot, but by absolutely nothing in the essence of the two books. "Moby Dick" is still our greatest novel and the other is a long story; if they illuminate each other—and they do—it is only by contrast.

Where "The Old Man and the Sea" is classical in spirit, "Moby Dick" is quintessentially romantic; it accepts no limits of any sort. . . . Demon and titan, whale and whalesman, are described in a fashion that strains the resources of the English language, as if the author, like Captain Ahab, were in perpetual pursuit of the never attainable.

Hemingway's hero, instead of being a titan, is an old man reduced to living on food that is begged or stolen for him by a teen-age boy. He is even "too simple to wonder when he had attained humility," but he still takes pride in his skill and resolution as a fisherman. Therefore, when his luck turns bad, he goes farther out into the Gulf Stream than anyone else from his village had dared to go alone. The fish that takes his bait is not a great gliding demon, a natural force personified, but simply the largest and noblest of the marlin. There is no hint in the story of Melville's essentially romantic feeling that God is immanent in man and nature. When the old man prays it is to an orthodox god transcending nature, but he and the fish are both in nature; they are even brothers in nature.

* * *

As simple as the story seems to be, it implies a complicated system of meanings and values. I might mention a few of these, if only to combat the notion that Hemingway writes about nothing but physical sensations. The lonely old man, whose only moral support has been the sense of his calling as a fisherman, broke the rules of his calling by going out too far. That was the sin of presumption or *hubris* for which he was punished by losing the fish. But he had fought and loved and killed the fish as a fisherman should and therefore he wasn't defeated in his ultimate purpose. It hadn't been to sell the fish for money enough to support him through the winter, but rather to win a battle over loneliness by proving his right to human companionship. He wins the battle in his humble fashion. Seeing the huge skeleton, other fishermen respect him once more and the boy defies his family by coming back to the old man's boat.

I couldn't write even a short report

on the book without paying tribute to Hemingway's prose. It is as different from Melville's prose in "Moby Dick" as anything could be and still remain English. There is no attempt in it to express the inexpressible by inventing new words and turns of phrase; instead Hemingway uses the oldest and shortest words, the simplest constructions, but gives them a new value—as if English were a strange language that he had studied or invented for himself and was trying to write in its original purity.

* * *

I remember reading about one of Louis XIV's courtiers, a consummate horseman who believed that his art was best displayed, not in cantering or galloping or jumping, though he excelled in all, but simply by walking his horse across the courtyard at Versailles; it was by so doing that he displayed his ease, his perfect seat, his mastery of the steed. There is something of the same spirit in "The Old Man and the Sea." One could never say that it was Hemingway at a walk, since that would imply that he was relaxed, whereas the story is tense, concentrated and full of excitement; but it is Hemingway displaying his strength and richness in simplicity.

Frederick Yeiser. *Cincinnati Enquirer,* September 7, 1952, p. IV-15.

Every good writer should be permitted a lapse or two. Ernest Hemingway had his with "Across the River and into the Trees," which was below his standard, so much so, in fact, as to cause anything else he should write subsequently to seem to be above it. That may be the case with his new book, "The Old Man and the Sea," which has had a build-up that few others have had, thanks to its appearance in "Life."

Admirable is it is from the standpoint of craftsmanship, it does not strike me in any way superior, except in style, to a half-dozen of his other works of greater or shorter length. I am not certain either that he strikes his richest vein in this story of the battle between an old fisherman and a marlin, or that its theme—the nobility and courage of man in strife—needs further restatement and development. In so far that it does, no one could have done it more resourcefully than Hemingway has. I must say the "The Old Man and the Sea" impresses me less as a story than as a piece of writing. In the second instance it is comforting to know that Hemingway has lost none of his mastery.

Someone—Somerset Maugham, I believe—has called "The Old Man and the Sea" "vintage Hemingway." That does not miss the mark by much.

Emmett Gowen.
"An Epic Struggle of
Man, Fish."
Nashville Tennessean,
September 7, 1952,
p. 23-C.

A Cuban sailor beached by old age and
the blue marlin he catches for the market are the characters in the simplest
work of fiction ever to be put forward
as an achievement by a master of the
art.

The old man fishing boldly in a
skiff far out from land in the Gulf
Stream hooks a great fish and the action begins, this single incident and its
aftermath being presented as a novel,
although ordinarily this one-incident
pattern is a little bare even for a short
story.

The descriptions of the fishing are
perfect and the fascinating forms of
Gulf Stream life, the teeming tropic
ocean, give a setting of beauty to a
struggle between an old man and a
fish. It is a struggle as meaningful, as
full of symbol and allegory in its relative space as Herman Melville's great
"Moby Dick." Indeed, the phrase "a
sort of miniature Moby Dick" is
inevitable and inescapable.

* * *

The struggle with the fish is absolutely
dramatic; both the old man and the
fish are fighting as champions of their
respective species, both fighting for
their lives. The old man plays a championship game, or, rather, plays life
that way.

The tale makes us aware of the in-
souciance and bravery of life. We
know as we read that we, too, are
gallant heroes and that the old man's
indomitable spirit resides in all men, to
emerge in some vital struggle. This
makes the story gratifying indeed to
read: half an hour of relishing true
human pride.

* * *

Hemingway has probably "convinced" as many big fish as any man—
his famous rule is that you must CON-
VINCE the fish. But to hold a reader
on the book, to CONVINCE through a
description of catching is a gallant
feat.

Nevertheless Hemingway has done
this with brevity and amazing simplicity. The old maestro is magnificent in
his venerable days: No venery, no alco-
holism, but the thrilling game of fishing pure and clean, and an epic fish
story.

He has recaptured the old undiluted
Hemingway magic and will recapture a
host of his former readers who knew
all the time he would come back with
a book like this some day.

Robert Gorham Davis. "The Story of a Tragic Fisherman." *New York Times Book Review*, September 7, 1952, pp. 1, 20.

In his tale of the old Cuban fisherman who goes out too far beyond ordinary limits to risk everything for the great catch, Ernest Hemingway emphasizes the skill and craft the old man must show to prove he is still champion. One senses before long that he has another craft in mind as well. When he speaks of the strange powers of the old man and his need to prove himself again and again, Hemingway too is using all his tricks and all his discipline to win the great contest. He has been preparing for it a long time.

Back twenty-five years before, he told in "Big Two-Hearted River" of young Nick Adams who wrestled with his thoughts as he struggled with the fish in that river in Michigan. But then his hero refused to go into the deep water of the swamp to make the ultimate test. In "The Old Man and the Sea," a tale written in his full maturity, Hemingway takes his fisherman into the deep water and into an adventure as close to tragedy as fishing may go. In the novella, as in the earlier story, he knows that art and insight come from a sense of limits, but now his hero exceeds the limits and learns the price that includes more than his own suffering. Now the line of dramat-

ic action curves up and down with a classic purity of design and the result is a suggestion of something new about Hemingway's thought, a definition of attitude never so clearly seen before.

Like earlier Hemingway heroes, Santiago maintains the code of right feeling toward his struggle even while he suffers defeat or death or loss of what he most loves. But earlier heroes like Lieutenant Henry walking home in the rain from the hospital, Robert Jordan dying at the bridge, or Harry Morgan dying with a bullet in his stomach were largely alone in their defeat. And others like Belmonte in "The Sun Also Rises" and Richard Cantwell in "Across the River and into the Trees" have been profoundly bitter in their loss. With Santiago it is all quite different. He has learned humility and knows it is not disgraceful to lose; through humility he has also learned that the worth of what a man must do and suffer depends on his sense of community with other men and with nature. And Santiago, through the formalized idioms of a Romance tongue, has the language to express his feeling of community, as Harry Morgan and Richard Cantwell did not. For Santiago has his town and his fellow fishermen including the boy Manolin and he is their champion too. What he brings back at the end of the story implies a human continuity that far transcends an individual relationship. And what he feels while alone on the sea is a knowledge of kinship with the great marlin and the sea and all the creatures of the deep.

The action of his adventure is wonderfully particularized but Santiago's simplicity and the articulateness of his soliloquies seem more the personified attitude of his creator than the objective personality of a man in his own right. The old man's references to sin, which is almost the only thing he is not willing to think about, inevitably recall that other story by Melville of the man who knew the sea as an object of fear as well as of love.

But such depersonalization is an acceptance of the limits of the story rather than a fault of a short and magnificently told tale. In his eloquent simplicity Santiago, like Nick Adams in "Big Two-Hearted River," goes back to something good and true in himself that has always been there. And in writing the story Hemingway too has gone back to what has always been good and true in himself. He has shown new indications of humility and maturity and a deeper sense of the work of a great writer. After the unfortunate interruption of "Across the River and into the Trees" it promises well for that long and major work which may go far out and far down for the truly big story. (Summary)

Fanny Butcher. "Hemingway at His Incomparable Best; New Novella Ranked with 'Moby Dick.' " *Chicago Sunday Tribune,* September 7, 1952 pp. 3, 11.

Ernest Hemingway, whose pen seemed less mighty than the sword in his last book, "Across the River and Into the Trees," has touched again the eternal source of his incomparable descriptive writing nature, as did the giant Antaeus who, when thrown to the ground, arose with his strength renewed sevenfold by contact with his mother, Earth.

"The Old Man and the Sea" is the record of a life and death struggle between an ancient fisherman of Cuba and a giant marlin. It is an epic which will inevitably be ranked with "Moby Dick" as a great American classic of man's battle with a titan of the sea. It is Hemingway at his incomparable best, with every word as vital to its pattern as each serrated piece is to a jugsaw puzzle, and with the pattern as sure and as full of strength and beauty as a porpoise's path thru the ocean.

* * *

Nowhere in literature will you remember any picture of man's struggle with a fish to compare with this except in the tale of the pursuit and capture of the great white whale in

"Moby Dick." That is why "The Old Man and the Sea" will inevitably be compared to Herman Melville's great classic. It can proudly stand beside Melville's chapters which describe that other epic battle between man and one of the sea's noble creatures.

Joseph Henry Jackson. "Hemingway at His Best in a Story of a Fisherman and His Catch." *San Francisco Chronicle*, September 7, 1952, pp. 20, 22.

The way to approach the new Hemingway, it seems to me, is to consider first its story—the simplest level of the narration and the surface conflict which is what makes it a story. There are other meanings here, of course, which is as Hemingway wants it, and those meanings are clear, direct, vigorous, for Hemingway—after his less successful experiment with "Across the River and Into the Trees"—is back again at the old stand, the Hemingway who produces at the top level his readers have come to expect of him.

* * *

To be sure, you can call this a fishing story if you like. So, in a way, it is. So, if you want to put it that way, "Moby Dick" is a fishing story.

What Hemingway is talking about, however, is what has always been in one way or another his theme when he is at his best. He is talking about courage, but he is also saying something else. What interests him is what is beyond the courage, the necessity in a man to meet the challenge whatever and wherever it is. As he has always said, it is the striving that is important, and though the courage is part of it, what counts is putting up the fight, and going on with the fight with all a man has, and Hemingway means "all." That, and only that, is what counts, whether the fate is a giant marlin or a whale or simply a set of circumstances.

And, Hemingway reminds his reader, it makes no difference at all if the reward is lost, if the implacable evil of the sharks in that sense beat a man out of what he has won. This a man must fight too, and again it makes no difference even if he knows he cannot beat it.

Hemingway does not say this in the way of a man pointing a righteous moral. He simply saw, long ago, that it was the way things are. And here once more, as always in his best writing, he says what he has seen.

As for the telling of the story, Hemingway has never written more clearly, more precisely, with less waste—not that he is very often a man to waste a word. Here, because he knows so well the background against which he stages his miracle-play of Man against Fate, he evokes both struggle and sea with a skill that very few—oh, well, what few, then? no one else writing today—could touch.

Perhaps best of all is the perfect judgment of the man who knows exactly what he is doing; the story is written at its own length, neither cut to a "short story" nor blown up into a "novel." In its way this is as perfect a piece of work as Hemingway has done. And a lot of people, professional readers and those who read simply because they want to, will feel a warm glow of pleasure when they see that Hemingway has lost nothing of the powers that made him the writer he is and have kept him up there where he belongs.

"Clean & Straight."
Time, 60
(September 8, 1952),
114.

Ernest Hemingway says that he wanted for a long time to write *The Old Man and the Sea* but did not think he could. He did write it though and the short, 27,000-word novel may well be, as he thinks it is, the best work he has ever done.

The new work has almost none of the old Hemingway tough sentimentality and truculence that frequently brought twinges of discomfort to even his most enthusiastic admirers. It is a clean, straight story with a strong claim to being called a masterpiece by those who admire craftsmanship. Its meanings will probably be as plentiful as there are cults of readers. But all will find it a poem of action celebrating a brave man, a great fish, the sea and, perhaps, the Creator of such wonders. Not fundamentally different from what Hemingway has done before, it is distinctly better.

For years the U. S. publishing world has buzzed with rumors that Hemingway was at work on a "big" novel that would dwarf all he had done before. Asked last week what part *The Old Man and the Sea* played in that grand scheme, Hemingway replied that he has written and re-written some 200,00 words of a long book about the sea. Divided into four books, the work is still subject to decision whether it is to be published separately, but, said Hemingway, any of the parts could be so published. Beyond that, he prefers not to talk of his writing because it is bad for a writer to talk about what he is doing. (Summary)

Olive Dean Hormel.
Christian Science Monitor,
September 11, 1952,
p. 11.

On the surface, it would be easy to join the chorus of critics and go lyrical about Mr. Hemingway's new novel—thus echoing also the author's own paean; for Mr. Hemingway is quoted as saying: "I have had to read it now over 200 times and every time it does something to me. It's as though I had gotten finally what I had been working for all my life."

A tale so intensely felt and so carefully wrought by a master craftsman is endowed with strange power. One reads and is haunted by the quest for meanings in the stripped simplicity of the telling.

* * *

By the time this review appears, nearly

everyone at all interested will have been able to read "The Old Man and the Sea," since it was published in full in a magazine on September 1st, one week before its release in book form this Monday, September 8th. More than five million magazine subscribers will have been confronted by that artfully premonitory paragraph with which the story opens. How have they responded to the rhythm of Hemingway's portentous prose?

This is an interesting speculation, as the author himself has remarked. Certainly, it represents a unique opportunity for the artist to reach a mass audience with his message—an opportunity which Mr. Hemingway embraced at the risk perhaps of greatly diminishing the sale of his story in book form, even as a dual selection of the Book-of-the-Month Club.

How many of this vast potential readership will follow the old man in his adventure, as he is swept "too far out" by the Gulf Stream through his lone three-day battle with the huge marlin he has hooked—when he has confidence, because he has "learned humility"? And through his long night's sortie with those "moving appetites," the sharks—until the trade winds and the lights of Havana bring him home to harbor at dawn with only the skeleton of his great fish in tow? And will these millions see this as defeat or triumph?

In a work of art of the dimensions the critics now acclaim there could be no uncertainty upon so all-important a point. But even the critics disagree. And there have been few times in history when the artist's affirmation of

man's dominion would have been more salutary.

I believe that Hemingway meant this as a triumph for the old man, and that it marks a definite advance in his philosophy. His god, however, is still only "the principle of good sportsmanship," as Mr. Edmund Wilson once said—and his man just "a guy that can take it," as any Hemingway fan will tell you. His old man of this story has also a craft—learned the hard way. Given courage and craft—and, yes, humility—he comes through with his skin and a certain amount of self-respect.

This is a better report than any of Hemingway's books has yet given. It's by no means the "dead end" that critics sorrowfully termed its predecessor.

Is it the best that the artist can say to the millions today?

Melwyn Breen. "Man, Nature and Nothing." *Saturday Night*, 67 (September 13, 1952), 26.

There is nothing in the new book that was not there before. There is the same pre-occupation with suffering, violence and death; there's the same central figure, the man of complete simplicity, the type that Hemingway admires most; there's the same relation between one man (who in different disguises is always himself) and a menacing alien universe. All the themes—except one—that pervade the earlier books and make them successes or failures according to his shifts of attitude toward them are present in the short space of 30,000 words.

The only difference is the apparent shift away from what has been described as Hemingway's succumbing to his own myth. This does much to eradicate the impression of sophomoric preoccupation with prolonged and unconvincing sexual stamina that characterized the work from "For Whom the Bell Tolls" to "Across the River and Into the Trees."

* * *

In action and narrative it is superb, always controlled by Hemingway's certain authority over the subject matter. In style it is Hemingway at his most stripped, exercising the peculiar discipline he inherited with a difference from Flaubert. . . .

With regard to the book's philosophic overtones—or, in Hemingway's case, "undercurrents" is probably the apter word—they too have always been there. They mar the book's final effect in exactly the way they have done in books of his before this. Once again, it is his complete admiration for "integrity" that is on display; "integrity" being courage, the will to endure through suffering, to get done what must be done regardless of violence and death.

* * *

After the death Hemingway's profound pessimism—and the fundamental weakness of the story—becomes apparent. It is clear that the whole thing was a grim joke; it was all much ado about *nada*. It was actually much worse, for not only is Santiago poorer than before but during the struggle he became identified with the marlin: though he kills to live he must die a little with every killing. For all creatures are one and the antagonistic principle of the universe is a force that works through man *and* Nature, destroying through all of them. In the end no one wins except the sharks (who swallow the chunks in the very act of dying).

The tragedy, according to Hemingway, is that this integrity on the part of both the marlin and Santiago is doomed to be wasted.

* * *

So for Santiago no chance against the sharks because the dice are loaded against him, nothing but his integrity.

In "To Have and Have Not" there was an attempt to crusade, even to present an aspect of class warfare and even a sense that the time might be when the isolation might be overcome. In "For Whom the Bell Tolls" there was the same violent inactivity for a cause that was hopelessly lost. In "Across the River and Into the Trees" there was a kind of posturing, a narcissistic belief in the long-lasting of one's own integrity. In "The Old Man and the Sea," the game, even the game of integrity, isn't worth the candle. It has become the will to live that keeps the dumb ox revolving around the treadmill.

Harold C. Gardiner.
"Pathetic Fallacy."
America, 87
(September 13, 1952),
569.

If the champ has not staged a complete comeback in *The Old Man and the Sea* after losing the heavyweight title in *Across the River and Into the Trees,* he has at least made it back to the light-heavyweight title. Which is to say, he has written one of his better stories, a very simple one as most of his master works are.

No word is wasted in this tense, lean, completely functional narrative. Even the sentence rhythms convey the atmosphere of struggle. Add to that an extraordinary feel for clean sea winds, for the mystery of life beneath the waves and the lonely majesty of sunsets.

Both man and fish in this story are so simple and elemental there is little to choose between them. Each is noble in his way, and they develop in their struggle a similarity tantamount to kinship. But the fact that their nobilities get blurred tells partly why the champ is still in the light-heavyweight division. It is Hemingway who does the blurring. He puts into the mouth of the old fisherman romantic and sentimental language when he talks to the great fish. Some years ago, Ruskin coined the term "pathetic fallacy" to indicate "undue attribution of personality to impersonal objects." When Hemingway does so, he dilutes the

content of a superb form. In this sense he misses true greatness.

Hemingway has here adapted his unique style to a form that is unusual but not, as the publisher's blurb claims, a new form. It is nonsense to say he has "improvised in effect his own new mode" and set a "new pattern for generations of followers." It has been done before in our own time by Steinbeck in *The Pearl* and by Paul Horgan in *The Devil in the Desert.* (Summary)

P. S. J.
" 'The Old Man' and
the Book."
Publishers' Weekly, 162
(September 13, 1952),
1011.

Now that "The Old Man and the Sea" is safely ashore as a book in the bookstores, what does all the excitement add up to?

To begin with, "The Old Man and the Sea" is Hemingway at his masterful best, an opinion we share with the majority of reviewers. *Life* has every reason to be proud of the excellence of its presentation of the novel, achieved with imagination and good taste, and disappointing only to those who predicted that readers would be put off by having to stalk the story along a circuitous paperchase between columns of advertising.

Certainly this advance publication has caused some confusion and not a little grief in the trade. But it is unfair to criticize the publishers, who did not engineer the arrangement, or those reviewers who timed their columns to coincide with *Life's* appearance on the newsstands; and one can hardly blame those booksellers who broke the publication date set for them and put the book on sale when it was news.

What does matter very much is that here we have a book that has been brought dramatically into focus for millions of readers, the mass-market that ordinarily only a segement of the industry taps. . . .

When the final figures are added up, there will, of course, be no way of determining how many more copies of the book would have been sold through bookstores had *Life* not published it first. But we suspect that the Hemingway fans will buy the book anyway and that a good many non-bookbuyers who read the novel in *Life* for 20 cents will even dig down for the $3 the book is worth to preserve for themselves and to share with others, in enduring form, a deeply moving experience.

The net result of this spectacular experiment will be watched closely by the trade; and one thing that booksellers are not likely to forget is that for thirty years they have been helping Hemingway and his books establish the reputation that caused *Life* to publish its first piece of fiction.

One thing is clear: for once, the public has been introduced to a book, rather than a book to the public. Reading and books, particularly fiction, have been given a badly needed shot-in-the-arm; "The Old Man and the Sea's" wide penetration into the public's awareness may well be felt to the trade's advantage for some time to come. Only the exceptional book, however, can be handled in this way and have such an effect, for too much bypassing of the normal methods and channels of publication and distribution will inevitably cause the further weakening of the outlets upon which the success of the majority of books depends.

Seymour Krim. "Ernest Hemingway: Valor and Defeat." *Commonweal*, 56 (September 19, 1952), 584-86.

The beauty and the terror of art are that sooner or later an artist must reveal everything he is and has, including much he would, as a private person, conceal. His limits as well as his strengths show themselves because he draws on his total experience. And there are no rules, no agreed upon lines, to mark off what the literary artist can write about and what he should leave alone.

As a serious and independent artist, Ernest Hemingway must be judged by the highest standards of expectation. As a man he has often made an embarrassing spectacle of himself with his posturings, his mooning over adolescent things, sports writers, movie actors and actresses, his antics at the Stork Club. Judged also by the total demands of art, he has shown himself to be a remarkably limited writer. Within his limitations, however, he has made a conspicuous contribution to American letters, much like that of Turgeniev in Russian literature.

He has written with great love and clarity about men and their relation to the physical environment and has invented a style which could make a reader experience that aspect of life. His writing has been such that one could have the experience only as a result of his art. He gave his readers a fresh and intense sensitivity to certain things which other writers took for granted. And he did so with an art that has been imitated by more American writers than ever followed any of our other artists. When you think about it, that is no small contribution.

But as *The Old Man and the Sea* has shown again, this intense freshness has its limitations and admits Hemingway only a narrow range in which to do his best work. Readers' familiarity with the limits of his range makes his new book seem to be only more of the same. We know our Hemingway too well. We can anticipate much of the new book because he seems to have few mysteries left that we don't already know.

True, the book is moving and written and felt with romantic dignity. It has an earnest personal concern with courage in defeat and has that aura which has made Hemingway a kind of literary knight of the twentieth century. His story is consistent with his themes of the last twenty-five years— of "grace under pressure" raised to nobility, of one of the Undefeated struck down by overwhelming forces but of one retaining the code of virtue which brings honor in defeat.

The trouble is that these themes are no longer as fresh and effective as they once were. To the long-time reader of Hemingway, that is the difficulty. He has not developed as a major artist. He is still fighting the old wars with the same old spears, and to invoke the totality of experience, that is not enough. It is likely that he has already done the significant part of his life's work. If history is any guide, his reputation will probably go into a rapid decline and be revived much later by men not as close to him as we are, men who will see him differently. We have gotten all we can from him now. Even if he writes several more good books, he is unlikely to extend our sensibilities or refresh our vision. One wishes he could be like a few wise athletes who know when to quit, before their reputations become tattered and dull. But chances are he will merely repeat and embellish the best of his earlier work, as he has done in *The Old Man and the Sea*. (Summary)

J. Donald Adams. "Speaking of Books." *New York Times Book Review*, September 21, 1952, p. 2.

Sometimes great works are recognized immediately for what they are; sometimes they have to wait for full recognition. The Gettysburg address is an obvious example of delayed response. Ernest Hemingway's new story probably belongs with those gaining immediate recognition. Like most great writing, it has an impact that is cumulative as well as immediate. Having read "The Old Man and the Sea" three times, I know it has a lasting effect that goes beyond what I might be doing or where I might live at a particular time.

The story shows again what we have always known about tragedy. Greatly presented, tragedy or even persistent frustration is never depressing in effect. Inferior handling of such material may be. But since men have begun to set pen to paper, they have found that such a theme is heightened by an artist through the mastery of his language and the prism of his personality. Tragedy brings us again to an awareness of ancient and ennobling truth.

Hemingway's story is tragic. It elevates, not depresses; it increases, not decreases, one's appetite for life. That is one reason why Hemingway at his best is greater than Faulkner. One of the great qualities of his writing is its pervading aliveness. Each time I read the story I find vitalities missed before. Sometimes they are deceptively small things but they spread into wider circles like those made by a pebble thrown into water.

The story is classic in spirit and design, unsprawling and rigidly confined. The old Greeks would like Hemingway's handling of the action and the central character. The old fisherman lacks individualizing traits, but it is part of the story's strength that he is Everyman. He has been liberated from photographic reality in his delineation. He takes us away from what O'Faolain has called the modern "tangle of sophistication" and back to the roots of literature in epic and folksong.

There is here too another quality largely lost in modern literature and absent even in Hemingway's earlier work. The old man's sense of oneness with nature is like what would have been felt by an American Indian, had his life been lived on the sea. He sees the marlin as a part of nature within himself, feels the need for apology when he kills the fish, feels respect and sympathy for his adversary as they struggle for life on the Gulf Stream.

This is Hemingway's most mature work both in craft and attitude. It will bulk large in his career. (Summary)

Edward Weeks. "Hemingway at His Best." *Atlantic*, 190 (September 1952), 72.

Ernest Hemingway has returned in *The Old Man and the Sea* to the stripped, lean, objective narrative of his best work. The short novel of the old Havana fisherman wastes not a word and suffers not a single intrusion by the author or any personage who might be Hemingway. Rather it is all the old fisherman's story—of his response to the sea, his sureness in piercing its depths with line or sight, his admirable resourcefulness in hanging on to the giant marlin through agonizing days and nights, his rage while defending his prize from the sharks. He has none of the braggart in him that made that other fisherman, Harry Morgan, finally unbelievable. The old man and the boy Manolin are in perfect harmony with Hemingway's bare story: their affection and their language are true to themselves, their attitude at one with the sea. This is a story of clean thrusting power and beauty of description. I have put this book on the top shelf of Hemingway's work and am grateful for it. (Summary)

Mark Schorer. "With Grace Under Pressure." *New Republic*, 127 (October 6, 1952), 19-20.

The only guts that are mentioned in this story are the veritable entrails of fish, but we are nevertheless reminded on every page that Hemingway once defined this favorite word, in its metaphorical use, as "grace under pressure." Grace, in the fullest sense, is the possession of this old man, just as grace was precisely what Colonel Cantwell, in *Across the River and Into the Trees*, was totally without. But here it is, complete and absolute, the very breath of this old man, so thoroughly his in his essence as in his *ambiente*, that it can only be there under pressure as at all other times, and indeed, even under the greatest pressure, he hardly alters. Grace, by which one

means now not the old stiff upper lip (this old man's upper lip is not so very stiff) which came to some of the older heroes a little easily sometimes, a quality more nearly a manner of speaking than of being; not that now, but benignity, nothing less, and beautifully, masterfully presented, so that the satisfaction one has in this creation is plain happiness, and then I suppose, gratitude.

* * *

Everywhere the book is being called a classic. In at least one sense, the word cannot be applied, for here and there, where the writing wavers, its pure lucidity is muddied by all that hulking personality which, at his worst, Hemingway has made all too familiar. I do not have in mind the talk about baseball, which has bothered at least one reviewer. "The baseball" is a near obsession with most Caribbean natives, but we do not have to know this to accept the old man's interest as his own rather than as Hemingway's. (After all, DiMaggio's father *was* a fisherman, as the old man tells us, and the sword of the marlin is "as long as a baseball bat.") But a murky paragraph that has to do with "mysticism about turtles" is a case in point.

* * *

But the Old man seldom lapses into dramatic falseness. In his age, alone at sea, he has taken to speaking aloud, and instead of dialogue between characters by which most fiction moves, this story moves by little dialogues in the old man himself, the exchange of what is spoken and what is not spoken. This is almost a running drama between that which is only possible and that which is real. . . .

The threat of over-generalization is almost always in the spoken words, which, then, are immediately rooted in actuality by the reservations of the unspoken. And of course, Hemingway's incredible gift for writing of the natural life serves the same function. Whether he is describing plankton, jelly fish, the sucking fish that swim in the shadow of the marlin, the gutting of a dolphin that contains two dying fish, or turtles, they are all always there before us, actualities, and the old man is an actuality among them.

The novel is nearly a fable. The best fiction, at its heart, always is, of course, but with his particular diction and syntax, Hemingway's stories approach fable more directly than most, and never so directly as here. It is the quality of his fiction at its very best, the marvelous simplicity of line. (" 'Be calm and strong, old man,' he said.") There has been another strain in his fiction, to be sure—his personal ambition to become a character in a tall tale, folklore as opposed to fable. That is the weaker man pushing aside the great novelist. The strain glimmers once in this story, when we are told of the old man's feat of strength in his youth: "They had gone one day and one night with their elbows on a chalk line on the table and their forearms straight up and their hands gripped tight." Take it away.

The true quality of fable is first of all in the style, in the degree of abstraction, which is not only in some ways Biblical but is always tending toward the proverbial rhythm. ("The setting of the sun is a difficult time for fish.") Next, it is in the simplicity of the narrative, and in the beautiful proportion (about three-fourths to one-fourth) of its rise and fall. Finally, of course, it is in the moral significance of the narrative, this fine story of an ancient who goes too far out, "beyond the boundaries of permitted aspiration," as Conrad put it ("You violated your luck when you went too far outside," the old man things), and encounters his destiny. . . .

In this isolation, he wins a Conradian victory, which means destruction and triumph. We permit his martyrdom because he has earned it. His sigh is "just a noise such as a man might make, involuntarily, feeling the nail go through his hands and into the wood." He stumbles under the weight of his mast when he carries it across his shoulder, up a hill. He sleeps, finally, "with his arms out straight and the palms of his hands up." There is more than this, and for those who, like this reviewer, believe that Hemingway's art, when it is art, is absolutely incomparable, and that he is unquestionably the greatest craftsman in the American novel in this century, something that is perhaps even more interesting. For this appears to be not only a moral fable, but a parable, and all the controlled passion in the story, all the taut excitement in the prose come, I believe, from the parable. It is an old man catching a fish, yes, but it is also a great artist in the act of mastering his subject, and, more than that, of actually writing about that struggle. Nothing is more important than his craft, and it is beloved; but because it must be struggled with and mastered, it is also a foe, enemy to all self-indulgence, to all looseness of feeling, all laxness of style, all soft pomposities.

* * *

Hemingway, who has always known the tricks, is strong enough now to have mastered his greatest subject. "I could not fail myself and die on a fish like this," the old man reflects. They win together, the great character, the big writer.

Philip Rahv.
Commentary, 14 (October 1952), 390-91.

Hemingway's new story happily demonstrates his recovery from the distemper that so plainly marked his last novel, *Across the River and Into the Trees.* In *The Old Man and the Sea* the artist in him appears to have recouped some of his losses, curbing the overassertive ego so easily disposed to fall into a kind of morbid irritability of self-love mixed with self-pity. It is to be hoped that the recovery is more than temporary.

But free as this latest work is of the faults of the preceding one, it is still by no means the masterpiece which the nationwide publicity set off by its publication in *Life* magazine has made it out to be. Publicity is the reward as well as the nemesis of celebrities, but it has nothing in common with judgment. Though the merit of this new

story is incontestable, so are its limitations. I do not believe that it will eventually be placed among Hemingway's major writings.

Moreover, it is in no sense a novel, as the publishers would have us believe. At its core it is actually little more than a fishing anecdote, though one invested with an heroic appeal by the writer's art, which here again confirms its natural affinity with the theme of combat and virile sports. This art is at its best in the supple and exact rendering of the sensory detail called for by its chosen theme; and in telling of the old fisherman's ordeal on the open sea—of his strenuous encounter with a giant marlin, the capture of him after a two-day struggle, and the loss of the carcass to the sharks in the end—Hemingway makes the most of his gifts, turning to good account the values of courage and endurance and discipline in action on which his ethic as an artist depends.

* * *

When all this has been said, however, one is still left with the impression that the creative appeal of this narrative is forceful yet restricted, its quality of emotion genuine but so elemental in its totality as to exact nothing from us beyond instant assent. It exhibits the credentials of the authentic, but in itself it promises very little by way of an advance beyond the positions already won in the earlier phases of Hemingway's career. To be sure, if one is to judge by what some of the reviewers have been saying and by the talk heard among literary people, the meaning of *The Old Man and the Sea* is to be sought in its deep symbolism. It may be that the symbolism is really there, though I for one have been unable to locate it. I suspect that here again the characteristic attempt of the present literary period is being made to overcome the reality of the felt experience of art by converting it to some moral or spiritual platitude. . . . Perhaps this latter-day tendency accounts for the inflationary readings that Hemingway's story has received, readings that typically stress some kind of schematism of spirit at the expense of the action so lucidly represented in its pages. Hemingway's big marlin is no Moby Dick, and his fisherman is not Captain Ahab nor was meant to be. It is enough praise to say that their existence is real, and that their encounter is described in a language at once relaxed and disciplined which is a source of pleasure. . . . And I would suggest to the ingenious interpreters that they look to the denotations of a work of literature before taking off into the empyrean of pure connotation.

Gilbert Highet.
"New Books."
Harper's, 205
(October 1952),
102-104.

Ernest Hemingway's *The Old Man and the Sea* is a good story. It is about courage. It tells of a fisherman who fights old age and the loss of his strength, poverty and the loss of his luck, loneliness and the gigantic sea in which he hunts, almost completely solitary except for the birds, the flying-fish, and the friendly dolphins. It tells how he caught a huge fish: how the fish fought him, pulling him many miles out to sea; how he killed it; how the sharks attacked his magnificent prize before he could get it home; and how bravely and hopelessly he fought them—even the sharks are brave, in their way.

This always was a good story. It was good when Mr. Hemingway first told it, in an essay called "On the Blue Water," on page 184 of *Esquire* for April 1936. It was good when variations of it were told by other American writers. Walter Van Tilburg Clark did it proud in *The Track of the Cat*. Mr. Hemingway's closest predecessor, Jack London, made fun of it in a mammoth-hunt called "A Relic of the Pliocence." There was also a long novel about a sea captain and a whale.

Mr. Hemingway's feelings do not change much, so it is natural that this should be a plot familiar to his readers. It is an epic pattern. A hero undertakes a hard task. He is scarcely equal to it because of ill luck, wounds, treachery, hesitation, or age. With a tremendous effort he succeeds. But in his success he loses the prize itself, or final victory, or his life. Still, his gallantry remains. Mr. Hemingway has used this pattern in "Francis Macomber," *For Whom the Bell Tolls,* and several other tales. What is new here is his thinking about age and about death: not the energetic death of the fighter or hunter, nor the silly chance death of the pedestrian, but the inevitable death of which old age is a degrading part. A number of his early stories had aging athletes in them: "My Old Man," about racing; "The Undefeated," about bullfighting; *To Have and Have Not,* about smuggling. His last book, about the garrulous colonel, approached this problem again, from the point of view of the sufferer, not of the spectator. But the colonel was elderly, boozy, and a bore. The lonely fisherman here is old, ascetic, and noble.

William Faulkner.
Shenandoah, 3 (Autumn 1952), 55.

His best. Time may show it to be the best single piece of any of us, I mean his and my contemporaries. This time, he discovered God, a Creator. Until now, his men and women had made themselves, shaped themselves out of their own clay; their victories and defeats were at the hands of each other, just to prove to themselves or one another how tough they could be. But this time, he wrote about pity: about something somewhere that made them all: the old man who had to catch the fish and then lose it, the fish that had to be caught and then lost, the sharks which had to rob the old man of his fish; made them all and loved them all and pitied them all. It's all right. Praise God that whatever made and loves and pities Hemingway and me kept him from touching it any further.

Paul Pickerel.
"Outstanding Novels."
Yale Review, 42 (Autumn 1952), viii.

Ernest Hemingway should be encouraged to write poor novels because it is such a joy to read those in which he recovers himself and confounds his critics. Like many others who read *Across the River and Into the Trees* two years ago, I thought it a failure, though (happily) limitations of space kept me from taking up the reviewers' popular pastime of lamenting the end of a great career. Now, with *The Old Man and the Sea*, Hemingway demonstrates that the critical keening was premature. . . .

For sheer daring in prose style this book equals anything Hemingway has written. There are passages where the sentences are played out as taut and supple as the action itself. This is the Hemingway who can sweep the slime of words off things and give us—separate, erect, bright in their fresh-created newness—the objects of the physical world and the feelings of men.

Some will think there is a softening of Hemingway's vision in this book. I think it is a deepening. The life of struggle he portrays is terribly hard, but not brutal; it is as much a contest of love as of enmity. That much is not perhaps new. But the old man's remark near the end of the book, "I live in a good town," catches the subdued sense of the world's goodness that suffuses the closing pages of the story and, in retrospect, the whole of it.

Perhaps the story is longer than the material really warrants, and there are traces of that self-pity and sentimentality which are Hemingway's besetting sins. The brief dialogue between the tourists at the end of the book is certainly unfortunate. Yet *The Old Man and the Sea* offers in a high degree the kind of pleasure proper to fiction: an image of life, intense and passionate, its meaning self-contained yet universal.

Delmore Schwartz. *Partisan Review,* 19 (November-December 1952), 702-703.

The ovation greeting Hemingway's new novel has had a note of insistence in its desire to continue admiring a great writer, a note of relief because his previous book was so ominously bad. The insistent praise for *The Old Man and the Sea* is not so much for the work itself as for a virtuoso performance that reminds us of Hemingway at his best. One needs only remember "The Undefeated" or the Caporetto retreat in *A Farewell to Arms* to see how the new novel falls short. It has great vividness in the narrative of physical action, but the old man's emotions are rendered with a margin of self-consciousness and mannered assertion. The old fisherman becomes too generalized; he lacks a personal history. It is as if Hemingway cannot get free of his knowledge that he is a great writer, that he needs to speak to the reader directly.

Taken in the context of the author's work as a whole, the book provides new definition and new clarity. One sees how with Hemingway the beatitude within us is moral stamina, how experience without illusion is unending threat. That new clarity tells us more forcefully than ever how much Hemingway is a purely American writer. His men alone against nature, his soldiers, sportsmen and hunters are essentially pioneers facing the terror and isolation of the forest again. The hunting and fishing which once were necessities have now become games, but they are pursued with energy and passion. Only in sport can his men be truly themselves, pitting isolated will against the whole of experience. When Hemingway tried to go beyond that condition in *For Whom the Bell Tolls,* his power was under control in those parts where the partisan hero was another Daniel Boone. In *Across the River and Into the Trees* his hero lost his role as isolated individual in modern warfare and could assert his will only in hysterical fury. After the bluster and bravado of that book Hemingway has regained his own sensibility and the possibility of a new masterpiece. (Summary)

R. W. B. Lewis.
"Eccentrics' Pilgrimage."
The Hudson Review, 6
(Spring 1953),
146-48.

Hemingway's brief parable of the old fisherman, the giant marlin and the sharks has an authentic beauty, but I doubt if the book can bear the amount of critical weight already piled upon it. . . . The work is not, somehow, altogether and finally *serio* (the Italian word distinguishes, better than its English translation, between the good quality and its corruptions into the stuffy and pretentious); and our assent has to be partially withheld. Yet it has its rare and gentle humanities.

The story (I assume it need not be rehearsed) is an autumnal song celebrating anew and in his old age the staunch, solitary and self-communing figure who has attained to the qualities Hemingway thinks necessary for survival in a wolfish world. In his own right, so to speak, the old man is a moving and even a noble individual; love has gone into him, and goes out of him; he is really, and without insistence, at home with the weather. It is only when his inventor tampers with him, makes him dream of lions on the beach, and the like, that he verges on the antic. His crisis is the classic contest between *virtu* and *fortuna*: between the old man's skill and tenacity ("I know many tricks and have resolution") and the unpredictable swerve of things which Hemingway calls "luck"

("Luck is a thing that comes in many forms and who can recognise her? "). Hemingway has remarked rather often that such is also the crisis of every creative enterprise; and we may be supposed to take the story as an allegory of its own history. If so, however, it is an allegory too banal to warrant much analysis. . . .

Although *The Old Man and the Sea* is not absolutely persuasive, Hemingway regains in it much of the poise so vexatiously missing in the unlucky *Across the River*. The distinction of Hemingway's best work has rested upon the insight by which he managed to avoid the tempting alternative I have mentioned. "Let those who want to save the world," he once wrote, "if you can get to see it clear and as a whole." In *Across the River*, Hemingway seemed intent on the world's salvation, though for what hodge-podge of purposes, one scarcely dares to guess. Now, with this curiously peaceful account of the old man's splendid failure, Hemingway returns to the role of the perceiver; and what he perceives is once again the stimulating and fatal relation between integrity of character and the churning abundance of experience. His style catches this perception with a good deal of its old power: in the relation (mentioned by Harry Levin) between an abundance of nouns, the signs of things in experience, and the simplicity and paucity of adjectives—signs of the ways we clutch at experience, seek to punch it into shape and hang on to it. The old man's old man is realised in prose that honors them both.

John W. Aldridge. "About Ernest Hemingway." *Virginia Quarterly Review*, 29 (Spring 1953), 311-20.

I confess that I am unable to share in the prevailing wild enthusiasm for this new book of Hemingway's, "The Old Man and the Sea." It is of course a remarkable advance over his last novel; and it has a purity of line and a benignity, a downright saintliness, of tone which would seem to indicate not merely that he has sloughed off his former emotional fattiness but that he has expanded and deepened his spiritual perspective in a way that must strike us as extraordinary. But one must take care not to push these generosities too far, if only because they spill over so easily into that excess of blind charity we all tend to feel for Hemingway each time he pulls out of another slump and attains to the heroism of simply writing well once again. It should be possible for us to honor him for his amazing recuperative powers and his new talent for quasi-religious revelation and still be able to see that it is not for either of these qualities that his book must finally be valued, but for the degree of its success in meeting the standards set down by his own best previous achievement as an artist. I have these standards in mind when I say that "The Old Man and the Sea" seems to me a work of distinctly minor Hemingway fiction.

I have come to this conclusion after noticing, first of all, that the style of the book, in spite of its antiseptic clarity and restraint, is oddly colorless and flat, as if there were nothing sufficiently strong within its subject to resist it at any point and provoke it into fully alert dramatic life. In the best of the early Hemingway one always felt that the prose had been forced out under great pressure through a tight screen of opposing psychic tensions; and one read it with the same taut apprehensiveness, the same premonition of hugely impending catastrophe, as that with which it was written—quite as if one were picking one's way with the author through an uncleared minefield of language. But now the prose—to change the figure once again—has a fabricated quality, as if it had been shipped into the book by some manufacturer of standardized Hemingway parts.

It soon becomes clear, however, that this weakness of style is merely a symptom of a far more serious weakness in the thematic possibilities of the material itself. The theme of the strong man struggling to survive amid the hostile pressures of a purely physical world has never been the central theme of Hemingway's greatest fiction; in fact, when one thinks back over his recent novels, one is tempted to conclude that it fails him miserably as a central theme each time he tries to use it in anything more ambitious than a short story. What has always served Hemingway best has been the theme of the shell-shocked, traumatic man struggling to preserve himself not from physical but from psychic destruction. This was the theme of his great early work; and it provided him with a formula for dramatic success on which he has never been able to improve.

* * *

Webster Schott. "In Pulitzer Prize Novel, Hemingway Symbolized Own Battle Against Odds. *Kansas City Star,* May 16, 1953.

A seldom-quoted passage in the author's preface to Ernest Hemingway's "The Fifth Column and the First Forty-Nine Stories" comments:

> In going where you have to go, and in doing what you have to do, and seeing what you have to see, you dull and blunt the instrument you write with. But I would rather have it bent and dulled and know I had to put it on the grindstone again and hammer it into shape and put a whetstone to it, and know that I had something to write about, than to have it bright and shining and nothing to say, or smooth and well-oiled in the closet, but unused.

This was written in 1939, but it more accurately describes Hemingway's position after the publication of "Across the River and Into the Trees" in the fall of 1950. Apparently written under fear of death from a serious eye infection, the novel was almost a caricature of Hemingway's great gifts, of

Hemingway himself, too. In a frenzy to get out what he thought was the last he might say, Hemingway did blunt the instrument he wrote with. It did need serious honing and hammering if Hemingway were to produce novels worthy of comparison to "A Farewell to Arms" and "For Whom the Bell Tolls."

Some critics, almost happily, decided Hemingway was through—getting older, he could only repeat and exaggerate what he had said in his twenties and thirties. Others were cautiously hopeful, while wondering where Hemingway could go from the dead-end street of "Across the River."

Hemingway, of course, turned in a new direction which led to the beautiful short novel "The Old Man and the Sea" (published last September) and the 1952 Pulitzer prize for fiction which he was awarded—the first time in a 28-year career of novel writing—last week.

* * *

Victory is always a matter of morals for Hemingway, and Santiago is perhaps the most victorious man Hemingway has ever given us.

Yet—unlike the great Hemingway heroes of previous novels—Santiago survives.

On the surface, "The Old Man and the Sea" is a simple, terse and forthright story of an ancient mariner who almost achieved what he had strived for all of his life: to catch a truly magnificent fish. Nothing is brought into this parable to alter its course. The biblical-like narrative is probably as technically perfect as Hemingway is ever likely to write. The English of the novel is very close to a literal translation of what it might have been in Spanish, the old man's tongue. Commands, the imperative voice, are delivered in the delicate form of the Romance languages, "Let no one disturb him." Possessives are constructed as prepositional phrases, like "the head of the fish" rather than "the fish's head."

The novel is indeed a "pure" work of fiction, but it is deceptively simple and full of subsurface meanings. They are not, as is frequently the case, meanings inferred by book reviewers and critics with overworked imaginations. Hemingway himself said after the book was published that "It's as though I had gotten finally what I had been working for all my life . . . all the things that are in it do not show, but only are with you after you have read it."

On one level the novel might be the story of Hemingway, the Old Writer, who is trying to create the finest book of his life. All he knows, all that he has ever hoped for is to be in it. Like the old fisherman, his previous achievement is not important. He must prove again that he is No. 1, for his feats are of a time long past, and there are those who doubt his skill. Possibly the sharks who cannibalize the fish are critics at work on the supreme Hemingway novel. Perhaps the novel (the fish) is destroyed by Hemingway's weakness, magnified as he grows older, in making his intention clear.

On another level, "The Old Man and the Sea" might be the whole story of life itself, the eternal competition to survive as man battles nature, himself and his fellow man. Santiago, one

will remember, felt a kinship, even love, for the giant marlin and called the fish "brother." It's almost as if Hemingway were saying there is a fellowship between mankind and all the creatures of the globe. At times the novel seems like a hymn to humanity, contrasting man's endurance with an ambition so tremendous and so nearly attained that he becomes heroic in his failure. The relationship is not as neatly worked out as a credo, but this reverence must also be linked to Hemingway's attachment in the novel to Christian symbolism. . . .

It's almost as if Hemingway had made some sort of spiritual peace with himself in "The Old Man and the Sea." He has not written a book so affirmative in conclusion, so gentle with man, or so simple while so complex. It may not be a great novel, but it has elements of greatness. And if the other three parts of the long 4-part novel about the sea Hemingway is working on are comparable to "The Old Man," Hemingway may be persuaded to forget the "title" he feels he is constantly having to "defend." He might win it permanently.

F. W. Dupee. "Hemingway Revealed." *Kenyon Review*, 15 (Winter 1953), 150-55.

Across the River and Into the Trees was, despite its poor reception, a powerful expression of the Hemingway legend. In the new novel, *The Old Man and the Sea*, Hemingway shows a determination to shake off the legend and a resolve to return to his original capacity as an exacting artist, a visionary of man's relationship to other men, to nature and to human nature within himself. In doing so he is an artist not so much exposed as revealed.

The Old Man and the Sea is one of his best stories and at the same time a first-rate contribution to American literature of the big hunt. Like Melville's *Moby-Dick* or Faulkner's "The Bear," this story affirms through the image of the hunt our frontier values and the natural basis of our life. Certainly Hemingway's story is not the complex performance these older works are, but it is ambitious in its own way. It is a quintessential tragedy, not of an enchanted boy in the forest but of an aging man whose urgent simplicity is like a cry of alarm at night or a command shouted across the water.

The story of Santiago and the giant marlin he follows too far out and loses to the sharks tells, through the mouths of his fellow fishermen, that a man's excellent performance does not compensate his failure to bring back the great catch. But neither does a man's failure compromise his performance. Committed to a careful accounting of the profit and loss in life, Hemingway knows that in general the two entries must occupy to infinity their separate colums in the ledger. But at moments of intense experience they compose a sum, as if magically, as in a dream or in art. In the old man's story, as in many of Hemingway's stories, there are such moments.

Santiago is both a preeminently natural man, entirely human with traits that make him an individual—his brown face splotch, his peculiar idiom, his taste for big-league baseball, his dreams of lions—and, at the same time, a superior man. Like all such heroes, he suffers abysmally but is equal to his suffering because he has freely chosen to endure that suffering for a good cause. Though his story may be the saddest Hemingway has written, it is perhaps the least painful. To the extent that his suffering is commensurate with his circumstances, Santiago's story is also among Hemingway's least theatrical. He agonizes in the name of all superior individuals of his time, as did Hemingway's earlier heroes, and thus keeps to the historical pattern of Hemingway's line of vision. But his loneliness is his own; he requires the companionship and help of others, and in this circumstance is sadness but not theatrical suffering. His portrait emerges perfectly from the minutiae of his conduct in action.

The portrait shows the consciousness of humane naturalism Hemingway shares with Faulkner and other American writers of their generation. The old man's hatred of the sharks echoes Hemingway's hatred of acquisitive and destructive men. Though his feeling for nature receives an unusually ideal expression in the story, his anger is not lessened. Rather that anger has reached a stage of ineffability that finds its expression in a dream like that of the lions on the yellow beach. (Summary)

W. M. Frohock.
"Mr. Hemingway's Truly Tragic Bones."
Southwest Review, 38 (Winter 1953), 74-77.

* * *

If it is true, as Hemingway has always claimed, that a writer writes "truly" only about what he knows well, we have the reason right here why *The Old Man and the Sea* is such superior stuff. The central character is the Old Champ; Santiago is not the man he was when he fought the big Negro in the "hand game" and beat him in a twenty-four-hour match; he has everything he has always had except the strength, which is the one thing whose absence makes the contest with the fish so unequal. Hemingway was studying this type as long ago as "Fifty Grand" and "The Undefeated" and as recently as *Across the River and Into the Trees*. . . . The locale is the Gulf Stream, off Cuba, where Hemingway has fished for everything from mackerel to submarines, and the action is built around a type of game fishing on which Hemingway is more than merely a competent authority. Out of such familiar stuff he has fashioned a piece of writing which is as effective, all in all, as anything he has ever done.

I have had no luck finding a name for this kind of writing. To call the piece a novel is a confusion of terms. It comes closer to being a poem, and because its principal themes are human endurance and the defeat of human endurance, the poem is tragic. It follows the standard outlines of classical tragedy; there is a first struggle that the hero seems to stand a chance of winning (the fight with the marlin); then comes the realization that what seemed to be the whole conflict was only the first round (the fish must be taken back to land) and now that we see what the whole conflict really is, the hero turns out to be up against an invincible opponent; so we watch the rest of the hero's vicissitudes (the sharks) knowing that he must inevitably lose, yet admiring and respecting him in his defeat.

The Old Man is also a tragedy in the sense that what defeats Santiago is his being human. It is human to grow old and not have the strength one once had, and human not to be able to cope with all the forces that nature can muster out of the Gulf Stream. A man can do only so much; after he has done that he must lose, because he is a man and not more than a man. Even though one defeats and kills the great fish, the sharks always come. It would be prudent to concede the struggle, but one gains stature and becomes admirable to the degree that one is not prudent and does not concede, but rather refuses to recognize the limitations of being human. Santiago refuses—and the reader puts down the book with a feeling of pride in belonging to the same race as the old Cuban.

The above facts can be checked with anyone who has had his hair cut since September 1, 1952, on which date *Life* put this tragic poem on the subject of human endurance beside the *Police Gazette* on the reading tables of the barbershops of America.

* * *

That so fine a piece of writing should be made available on such a scale is a good thing. It is good, too, that a writer should be so well paid for good work as, according to the papers, Hemingway was. . . .

Even so, the appearance of *The Old Man and the Sea* is an opportunity for critics to review what they have been saying about the writer who, with Faulkner, stands out as the best we have. One very common critical error, in particular, needs revision. Too many have been saying, for too long, that Hemingway's characters are too simple and elementary to be capable of any but the simplest and most elementary emotions. As if that settled anything! We owe it to ourselves to realize that while the emotions of the characters are frequently elementary, those of the attentive reader are not elementary at all. *The Old Man* offers an excellent illustration of this. In his own eyes, old Santiago is nothing but a tough old man who needs to catch a big fish; for him to perceive himself as any sort of tragic figure would be the sheerest nonsense. But for us not to perceive him as such would be to fail to recognize the extremely complex emotions that build up in us as we read about him. And truly tragic emotion, since it involves our complete awareness of our predicament as human beings and our whole understanding of life, is at the opposite pole from the primitive.

* * *

The real significance of *The Old Man* is that Hemingway had it in him to do the story. It gives clear evidence that he has all his powers. We had been waiting for something of such quality from him since 1940. . . . John O'Hara may have overstated the case when he referred to Hemingway as the finest manipulator of English since Shakespeare, but there is no contesting the fact that when Hemingway is right he is very good indeed. *The Old Man and the Sea* is all we need to prove that he can still be right, extremely right, and perhaps even righter than he has ever been before.

Checklist of Additional Reviews

Paul Sann. *New York Post,* August 31, 1952, p. 12-M.

E. F. Walbridge. *Library Journal,* 77 (September 1, 1952), 1401.

Booklist, 49 (September 1, 1952), 2, 13.

William J. Parker. "The Old Champ Can Still Write." *Denver Post,* September 7, 1952, p. 22.

Jack Kofoed. "Hemingway Proves Again He Is a Strong Man." *Miami Herald,* September 7, 1952, p. 4-F.

"Hemingway's Gimmick," *Newsweek,* 40 (September 8, 1952), 102-103.

Bookmark, 12 (October 1952), 10.

Riley Hughes. *Catholic World,* 176 (November 1952), 151.

M. C. Scoggin. *Horn Book,* 28 (December 1952), 427.

Solomon B. Freehof. *Carnegie Magazine,* 27 (February 1953), 44-48.

Vance Bourjaily. "The Big Come-

back." *New York Times Book Review*, February 28, 1965, pp. 1, 49.
John W. Aldridge. "Two Poor Fish on One Line." *Book Week,* 2 (June 20, 1965), 16, 19.

Ernest Hemingway

THE
HEMINGWAY
READER

SELECTED

with a Foreword and twelve Brief Prefaces

by CHARLES POORE

CHARLES SCRIBNER'S SONS

NEW YORK 1953

The Hemingway Reader

Ben Ray Redman.
"Gallantry in the Face of
Death."
Saturday Review, 36
(June 6, 1953),
18.

Ernest Hemingway has long enjoyed a popular reputation as a tough naturalistic writer, but as far back as 1926, when I first read "The Sun Also Rises," I began to suspect that he was a Romantic. The suspicion was confirmed by "A Farewell to Arms," and was transformed into conviction by the books that followed. Now that I have just read for the third or fifth time "The Sun Also Rises," "A Farewell to Arms," "To Have and Have Not," and "Green Hills of Africa"—in new editions recently published by Scribner's—the romantic character and power of Hemingway's work have again impressed me with all the liveliness of a fresh discovery. Naturalism does not respond to life; it adds nothing, and subtracts only because selection is unavoidable. It reproduces, copies, as best it can. But it does not respond. Hemingway's writing, on the other hand, has from the beginning—from the time of "Three Stories and Ten Poems" (1923)—been an active response, a gallant response. In this gallantry, however disguised, we find the most vital of Hemingway's own vital juices, and the key to all the characters whom he admires. . . . It is inevitable that the moralists should find the Jake Barneses and Brett Ashleys and Harry Morgans of Hemingway's world pitiable at best and loathesome at worst; that critics who live only by the light of a social conscience should find Frederick Henry and Catherine Barkley and the hunters of "Green Hills of Africa" socially irresponsible; that readers who believe that their lives rest securely on supernatural sanctions should sneer at the code which provides Hemingway's best characters with the only meaning that they can discover in existence. But all this has nothing to do with literature or literary criticism. It is the writing that counts, and it is some of the very best of our time. For Ernest Hemingway, at least, the code has worked. And for us, too—for we have the books.

Stanley Edgar Hyman.
"A Hemingway Sampler."
New York Times Book Review,
September 13, 1953,
p. 28.

It was almost inevitable that sooner or later the Viking "Portable Hemingway" would be succeeded by a Scribner compendium of Ernest Hemingway's thirty years publishing with that house. Now Charles Poore has edited a comprehensive selection of Hemingway's work including all of "The Torrents of Spring" and "The Sun Also Rises," well chosen chapters from five other books, and eleven short stories. They have been chosen with intelligence and discrimination and are accompanied by prefaces which are brief and relevant if somewhat too generous in approval.

One can always quibble with the choices and the reasons for their inclusion. One suspects that "The Torrents of Spring," really a crashing bore, was included because it is not otherwise available, and so too for "The Fable of the Good Lion," an awkward piece of whimsey from Holiday. As for the stories, Mr. Poore's taste for narratives of physical action over those of more complicated and elusive rituals seems to predominate.

Such a book raises the larger issue, though, of Hemingway's development over three decades. The compilation is a merciless test of a writer competing against his own best work. Except for

a few pages of puerile private joking and an unsatisfactory ending, "The Sun Also Rises" survives untarnished. So do the parts reprinted from "A Farewell to Arms" and "To Have and Have Not" and a decent proportion of the stories. But the self-indulgence as early as "A Way You'll Never Be" gave omen of the egocentrism of the later war correspondence; the sentimental Hispanophilism of "Death in the Afternoon" was later to mar "For Whom the Bell Tolls"; and the dogmatic opinions of "Green Hills of Africa" were to reappear just as obtrusively in "Across the River and Into the Trees." The tough economy and fresh skill of most early works make the later performances almost painful to read.

One cannot expect a writer always to be at his best, and even at his worst Hemingway is better than most of today's writers. But when his pieces are presented chronologically, they graph a neat parabola of sinking into self-parody. And that makes a gloomy portent for the literary fate of Ernest Hemingway. (Summary)

George F. Whicher.
"An Indivisible Writer."
New York Herald Tribune Book Review, 30
September 27, 1953,
p. 21.

In his Foreword to "The Hemingway Reader" Charles Poore states very cogently the reason why it is next to impossible for any one to make a satisfactory book of excerpts from this author. "No part of Hemingway's work," he says, "is only an island, entire in itself; every part is a piece of a continent, a part of a main, created in a new prose for a new world." This is a highly perceptive remark, albeit somewhat damaging to the book Mr. Poore has compiled. . . . The effect is to emphasize Hemingway's skill as "the finest stylist" among contemporary story tellers, but at the cost of obscuring the pattern, the double response to experience, that runs through all his books and forms the chief significance of his writing. On the one hand, he shows us over and over men of keen sensibilities wounded both physically and psychically by life in our time, and on the other hand, repeated instances of men who have learned to take the worst that life can offer with tight-lipped stoical endurance. Sometimes the two are fused in one person, and then we have Hemingway at the top of his form as in "The Old Man and the Sea."

Theodore M. O'Leary. "Volume of Excellent Hemingway Selections." *Kansas City Star*, February 6, 1954.

The selections from the writings of Ernest Hemingway which the New York literary critic, Charles Poore, has chosen for "The Hemingway Reader" are on the whole of such uniform excellence that the reader, dazzled by their brilliance, is disposed to acqui-esce when Poore asserts in a foreword that Hemingway is "one of the three principal men of letters of our time." The other two named by Poore are Yeats and Joyce.

* * *

The selections which he has put into this book, Poore says in his foreword, "together represent a body of work that has changed the course of storytelling and given new cadences to the language. They are not gathered here, though, to illustrate academic principles or to pepper elegies. They are alive, a part of experience that tells us more vividly than any casual actuality ever can, where men and women have been, and what they have done and left undone in this brightest and bloodiest of centuries."

This foreword and Poore's brief prefaces to each of his selections are informative and intelligent and on the whole more restrained than the writings of some other Hemingway admirers. Only occasionally do you sense that perhaps Poore shares a belief prevalent with some that to acknowledge the presence in the world of other good and scrupulously honest writers is somehow to detract from Hemingway's stature.

Hemingway, himself, has sometimes seemed to impugn the literary honesty of other writers. His own standards of craftsmanship and honesty are certainly of the highest and he always strives with his whole heart and mind to adhere to them. But sometimes he mistakes the intent for the accomplishment. That is seldom the case with anything in "The Hemingway Reader."

This is a real big league, all-star line-up, but there is some good ball played every day of the season in the minor leagues too. And there are other ways to tell a story besides the Hemingway.

Checklist of Additional Reviews

E. F. Walbridge. *Library Journal,* 78 (July 1953), 1231.

Edward Wagenknecht. "A Collection of Hemingway." *Chicago Sunday Tribune,* August 30, 1953, p. 6.

New Yorker, 29 (September 12, 1953), 145.

Booklist, 50 (September 15, 1953), 34.

Wisconsin Library Bulletin, 49 (October 1953), 212.

Christian Century, 70 (October 14, 1953), 1169.

Notes

ERNEST HEMINGWAY

A Moveable Feast

❖

If you are lucky enough to have lived
in Paris as a young man, then wherever you
go for the rest of your life, it stays with
you, for Paris is a moveable feast.

ERNEST HEMINGWAY
to a friend, 1950

CHARLES SCRIBNER'S SONS, *New York*

A Moveable Feast

Clifton Fadiman.
"Ernest Hemingway."
Book-of-the-Month Club News,
May 1964,
pp. 1-5.

* * *

These autobiographical recollections of the Paris of the early '20s seem to be part of a long soliloquy, Hemingway talking to himself, nostalgically evoking the days of his youth, before *The Sun Also Rises* had made him a world figure, before the legend had achieved any clear form. No better summary could be devised than the book's ending: "This is how Paris was in the early days when we were very poor and very happy."

It does not seem possible that Hemingway's Paris (limited to the Left Bank, and indeed to two or three quarters of the Left Bank) can ever be revived. It seems almost as far away as the Paris of François Villon, with which indeed it had much in common. . . .

* * *

Pervading all these reminiscences, whether joyful, vengeful or even funny, is the special Hemingway sadness, the sense that all this was to end, that "nothing was simple." The year during which he was working over the manuscript of *The Sun Also Rises*—while off at a little skiing center in Austria—was also "the year that the rich showed up," the year that was to mark the beginning of the end of his happy first marriage, the year that was to propel him into a world of cheap publicity and genuine fame. He was always to return to his beloved city, but 1925-26 marked "the end of the first part of Paris," and things would never again be quite the same.

How good, however, to have the early days of struggle and poverty and solid, happy married love preserved for us in these frank and moving recollections. Later on he was to write wonderful books, perhaps even one or two great ones, but it was in the early '20s that it was bliss to be alive. It was then that he discovered the heart of his esthetic faith: "All you have to do is write one true sentence"—and follow it with another. . . .

In these simple, flowing pages, written without much thought for the famous Hemingway "effects," is an invaluable portrait of the artist as a young man during that most interesting of all periods—the period when mere living and mere loving and mere writing were enough, and the contagion of the world's slow stain lay, though not far distant, still in the future. No writer could be less akin to Virgil, yet these pictures of the past enclose the Virgilian sense of mortality, the memory of what was and can never be again, when all the world was young and youth seemed to be all the world.

George Plimpton. "When Papa Was Apprenticing." *New York Herald Tribune Book Week,* May 3, 1964, pp. 1, 12-13.

Thinking back on it, there were two subjects Hemingway detested talking about. He felt any discussion of his craft was a waste of time, possibly injurious, and he was particularly sensitive to questions put to him on the subject. . . .

* * *

And similarly, his apprenticeship as a writer, his years in newspaper work, the Paris of the Twenties, his tutelage with Gertrude Stein, his friendships with Ezra Pound, Archibald MacLeish, the literary life there—such questions though not met with as violent a reaction, were answered, if at all, with reluctance. "The literary gossip of 30-odd years ago is disgusting and boring," he said.

His attitude seemed less inflexible after the African plane-crashes. His injuries were serious, and his friends re-marked that their effect seemed to make him turn inward, particularly to the past—never in any maudlin sense, or as a refuge, but that the stories and reminiscences seemed to come more easily from him. The early Paris years had been a very good time for him. Some of the stories were essentially comic, but almost all are extremely personal, and one can see why he would want to harbor them. He finally decided to let them go, to record them—finishing them in Idaho in 1960—and they are now available in *A Moveable Feast.* . . .

* * *

The Paris sketches are absolutely controlled, far enough removed in time so that the scenes and characters are observed in tranquillity, and yet with astonishing immediacy—his remarkable gift—so that many of the sketches have the hard brilliance of his best fiction. Indeed, in a short prefatory note Hemingway says the book may be regarded as fiction—by which he means not that the incidents described are imaginary, but that the techniques utilized are those of the fiction writer. . . . He informs not as a sociologist might look at the period, or a literary historian—which will disappoint those expecting to find portraits-in-depth of Joyce or Stein or the others. He makes no pretense of exploring their complexities. Instead, the portraits, vivid and sharp, are used as a short story writer might use them—as characters in a set piece, so that their names could be substituted without diminishing the value of the whole. It is better, of course, to have them as they are, if only to watch Hemingway settle old scores with his detractors. . . .

But mainly the tone of *A Moveable Feast* is reflective and comfortable as Hemingway returns to one of the basic themes of his early work—the release that comes with the relish of sensation, the gratification of appetite. In many ways, the book is close to the concept of the famous short story, "The Big Two-Hearted River," in which Nick Adams returns in near shock from the wars to find release, perhaps sanity, in the carefully relished sensations of trout fishing in the timber country, a refurbishing through a lucid and aesthetic appreciation of the physical world.

Hemingway's return to Paris in *A Moveable Feast* suggests the same sort of therapeutic visit—his health crippled in the plane-crashes, his consciousness sensing decline, a robust middle age behind him—returning in print to the ties of Paris to touch down at specific landmarks, certain streets, cafes, even remembered bottles of wine and long past meals, as if these physical entities could bring serenity and order. It is a therapeutic measure Hemingway has often put his characters to: one remembers the night walk in *The Sun Also Rises* through a directory of streets, and the fishing near Pamplona. . . .

Boris Pasternak's wife once complained that this aspect of Hemingway—the acute consciousness of sensation—bored her finally, particularly the directories of streets, the endless meals and drinks with little else happening to the heroes. Pasternak disagreed. "The greatness of a writer," he said, "has nothing to do with subject matter itself, only with how much the subject matter touches the author. It is the density of style which counts. Through Hemingway's style you feel matter, iron, wood."

Madame Pasternak would have her troubles with *A Moveable Feast,* aptly named, since literally dozens of meals, with attendant wines, are chronicled with such "density of style" that one's stomach moans. . . .

* * *

But for all the cataloguing of meals, of wines, of Paris streets (over 30 are identified), and even pervading the fine humor of the sketches (both Faulkner in certain sections of *The Reivers* and Hemingway seem to have done their best humorous writing in their last years) there is a note of impending chaos and death. The therapy does not work. Hemingway sees ruin in the faces of his Paris friends—Ernest Walsh, Ford, Pascin, and the smell of it seems to be with many others.

* * *

Walter Havighurst. "Hemingway at Sunrise." *Chicago Tribune Books Today,* May 3, 1964, p. 1.

* * *

Others have written about Paris in the '20s. But Hemingway, the central character in that story, writes it better than anybody. To one who knows the literature of the expatriates, this is a book of familiar places and people seen more clearly, in a truer light, than before. If the subject is new, here is a beguiling chapter of our literature.

An American chapter in Paris. More than any other expatriate account, Hemingway's is American. Here he is writing his Michigan stories, recalling his American boyhood, and shaping an American language for it. At the same time he is seeing Paris with wholly American eyes. At 26 he was both disillusioned and zestful, and Paris gave him nearly everything.

This is not a book about the lost generation, tho it contains wonderfully sharp vignettes of Pound, Eliot, Fitzgerald, and the others. Mostly it is a book about Ernest Hemingway at "the fulltime job of learning to write prose." He would be the last to write a handbook on story writing, yet here it is—the honest, candid, careful account of how one young writer learned to do his work.

* * *

All of Hemingway's books are about himself. This one especially, and its last six pages most of all. "During our last year in the mountains new people came deep into our lives and nothing was ever the same again." It was insidious. "All things truly wicked start from an innocence." Those last pages, the only ones told in the third person, end this bittersweet book on a note of endless regret.

Charles Poore.
"Ernest Hemingway's Memoir of Paris in the Twenties."
New York Times, May 5, 1964, p. 41.

The importance of beating Ernest, someone once said, gave a hopeless target to industrious lit'ry careerists. How cheerfully Hemingway was aware of that—and how early—appears quite clearly in this memoir of what I can only call his brilliantly obscure emergence as a man of letters. Here is Hemingway at his best. No one has ever written about Paris in the nineteen-twenties as well as Hemingway. Thousands, of course, have given their own bright versions of that unaccountably perpetual springtime, but too many lost parts of their own identities in taking on some of Hemingway's. And they could not precisely share his astounding fugue of interests, which wove Tolstoy out of Sylvia Beach's bookshop with days at the great race tracks, skiing expeditions to the Alps and the study of Cezanne, noticing that F. Scott Fitzgerald was wearing a British Guardsman's tie and boxing with Ezra Pound, forays to Pamplona and living above a sawmill at 113 Rue Notre Dame des Champs.

* * *

It would be a shallow mistake to take this book as a return only to the past. "If the reader prefers," Hemingway suggests at the end of a preface dated a year or so before his death in 1961—"this book may be regarded as fiction. But there is always the chance that such a book of fiction may throw some light on what has been written as fact."

There you have it. And the light these pages throw on what has been written by and around and about Hemingway is extraordinarily various. "A Moveable Feast" decidedly would not have the tone of the twenties as he put it to his ear in the nineteen-fifties if Hemingway had not subsequently written the books that led to the Nobel Prize and read the things about himself that sometimes made him wonder whether he was a figment of his critics' odd imaginations.

The Society of Those Who Knew Hemingway When—a motley if there ever was one—is here in silhouette. But there are Goyesque portraits in full color of Pound and Gertrude Stein and Scott and Zelda Fitzgerald and James Joyce. It would be unkind to ask the forever undemobilized pallbearers of Ford Madox Ford to cheer Hemingway's view of Ford-double-Ford. However, several writers who may have fattened their portfolios by remembering that they knew him rather more extensively than he remembered having known them will probably be content to remain incognito at "A Moveable Feast."

Any book by or about Hemingway suddenly becomes the occasion for another full-scale review of his career and I don't think this one is going to prove a conspicuous exception. The St. Vitus dancers among his critics who are maz-ily on record for changing their minds about him are always good for one more swing. But, once again, it is a greater pleasure, for the reader at large, to read Hemingway than to cope with the folklorists of his mythology.

Alan Pryce-Jones. "Hemingway: 'Poor and Very Happy.'" *New York Herald Tribune,* May 5, 1964, p. 23.

Early in Hemingway's acquaintance with Gertrude Stein, she warned him, he tells us, against writing anything that is *inaccrochable,* meaning by that anything that sticks out like a sore thumb and so cannot be used, because all it does is to hurt. "There is no point in it," she said. "It's wrong and it's silly."

In this absorbing book of Paris recollections there is a certain element of the *inaccrochable,* along with much that is bright-colored and occasionally touching. It covers "the early days when we were very poor and very happy," legendary days which have already been copiously recorded by everyone, it sometimes seemed, whoever bought a drink in the Select or Lipp's. But Hemingway's is the book we have been waiting for, and the first question to be asked is: How does he emerge from it?

As a rather anxious college kid; newly married, newly emancipated, deeply introverted in spite of all the boxing and horse-racing and poker-playing; curiously unaware of Paris and the French, except as a succession of visual or gastronomic experiences; desperately keen to keep up with the big boys, yet at the same time, blushing, one judges, if they spoke to him without warning.

A nice kid, on the whole, but with a black streak to him which evidently made it hard for him to give his friendship, except to those whom he could regard as his inferiors. . . .

* * *

All the time he writes a bony, unwasteful prose which is a joy to read. . . .

He is at his best in evocation of being young and in love, writing of wife, child and cat as though from a great distance, yet with a tenderness far more convincing than the nervous masculinity with which he faced the outer world. . . .

These sketches were written between 1957 and 1960, more than thirty years after the events they describe. The Hemingway who wrote them was very different from the young man out of Michigan who was beginning life in that most tricky of periods and places, Paris immediately after the World War. We should not read them for insight into Paris, but for insight into one of the processes, often harsh, sometimes delightfully high-spirited, by which a difficult personality, full of high talent, edges its way into the world.

"When Papa Was Tatie." *Time*, 83 (May 8, 1964), 98, 100.

Instead of the glum reminiscences and tedious memorabilia most men leave to the world, Ernest Hemingway bequeathed an invitation to laughter. In *A Moveable Feast* he takes the reader into the scenes of the author's youth in Paris, where he was happier than he would ever be again. It reads like a last-minute appeal to see him as he was before he was caught in his later legend of "Papa."

A peculiar thing about the book is the way the people seem to talk like Hemingway characters. That effect was perhaps not unintentional. In his introduction he says the book may be read as fiction if the reader likes and "it may throw light on what has been written as fact." Some people and some fictional characters did come to talk that way, but it was later, after the enormous influence of *A Farewell to Arms*. That Hemingway knows what he is doing shows in the fact he does not let better-known figures have a say of their own. Ezra Pound, James Joyce and Wyndham Lewis had a recognizable style and are presented here only by indirection.

The portraits of Gertrude Stein and Scott Fitzgerald are another matter. Besides putting himself on record as having developed conversational rhythms independent of and parallel to Stein's, Hemingway shows her as a monster of obtuse egotism presiding over her salon as over a shrine dedicated to herself. His account of Fitzgerald's troubles with Zelda is irresistibly funny but leaves doubt that the author of *The Great Gatsby* could be so simple or fatuous.

Ostensibly gay and artless, the sketches have a lifetime of craft behind each line and in effect a heartbreaking quality when one remembers that they were fashioned by a man soon to take his own life. In a nature that seemed all gallantry and confidence one searches for the clue. It is there probably in the vast pride that required others to live by Hemingway's own austere and complex code even when they did not know the rules. With a need to win even when others were unaware anything was at stake, Hemingway assumed a mask of gentle or sardonic humor that was the armor of his severe stoicism. He sought the natural grace of the truly simple man but lived by something closer to the contrived spontaneity of the method actor.

When he describes the doomed painter Pascin drinking with two tart-models at the Dôme cafe, Hemingway praises Pascin for laughing while the seeds of his death were in him. One .wonders whether this is a man writing his own obituary. (Summary)

Mary Stahlman Douglas. "Hemingway Recalls Paris in Twenties." *The Nashville Banner*, May 8, 1964, p. 29.

This self-portrait of a writer as a young man in Paris in the early 1920's is as fresh and vibrant and pulsing with life as if written at the time in the friendly cafes where Hemingway actually did much of his writing. As a matter of fact, it was written during the last three years of his life, but his powers of evocation were still strong and his readers will be grateful that he has set down these recollections of his early struggles, his fascination with Paris, his friendships with Gertrude Stein, Sylvia Beach, Ezra Pound, Scott Fitzgerald and many others, and his life with his wife, Hadley and their son, Bumby.

* * *

"A Moveable Feast" is a tender, nostalgic, humorous, sharp and occasionally bitter (when he is scoring writers he did not like) retelling of a young writer's life in Paris in the Twenties "when we were very poor and very happy."

Granville Hicks.
"Oh to Be Poor in Paris."
Saturday Review, 47
(May 9, 1964),
29-30.

According to a note by his widow, Ernest Hemingway began writing *A Moveable Feast* in Cuba in 1957, and finished the revision of the book in Idaho in 1960. It comes out of his last literary phase, and since it concerns his first literary phase, 1921-1926, during which time he wrote *The Sun Also Rises* and some of his best short stories, the early Hemingway and the late are instructively juxtaposed. The comparison is not in favor of the later Hemingway.

The book begins:

> Then there was the bad weather. It would come in one day when the fall was over. We would have to shut the windows in the night against the rain and the cold wind would strip the leaves from the trees in the Place Contrescarpe. The leaves lay sodden in the rain and the wind drove the rain against the big green autobus at the terminal and the Café des Amateurs was crowded and the windows misted over from the heat and the smoke inside.

This is Hemingway, all right, omission of commas and all; but it is Hemingway imitating himself, whereas there was once an inimitable Hemingway. The passage suggests that in this book, as in *The Old Man and the Sea,* the author was relying on technique and sheer will, instead of being able to count on spontaneous imagination.

* * *

As for happiness, one can see that there were many happy times, but this is by no means a happy book. Much of it is made up of Hemingway's distaste for people he met, or his eventual disillusionment with them. . . .

He is peculiarly nasty on the subject of Ford Madox Ford. . . . Although he seems never to have met T. S. Eliot, he makes an unpleasant crack at him, as he has done elsewhere. He tells an unpleasant story about Ernest Walsh, whom he describes as an editor of the *Dial*. (Walsh is not mentioned in William Wasserstrom's *The Time of the Dial*.)

The most disturbing section of the book is that devoted to Scott Fitzgerald. . . .

Although he says more than once how fine everything was in Paris in the early Twenties, the only passage in which one feels real nostalgia, a true passion to recapture the past, has nothing to do with Paris, but is an account of skiing in Austria. . . .

Hemingway's strong concern with sports of many kinds has often been commented on. But what was even stronger was his preoccupation with his job as a writer. Although what he says here about his apprenticeship is not particularly revealing, one does feel his seriousness, his determination, and his ability to discipline himself. Regarded at the beginning of his career as a primitive, a natural, he now seems to have been, above everything else, a sophisticated craftsman.

He remained a craftsman to the end, and there is some first-class Hemingway in the book, but there is little of the evocative power one finds in *The Sun Also Rises. A Moveable Feast* does, however, contribute to our understanding of Hemingway. It suggests that in the early Twenties, when he was shaping himself so rapidly as a writer, he was full of uncertainties. His uneasiness with people persisted, and indeed, became greater and greater as his eminence was more and more widely recognized and as he became more and more self-conscious. If, then, we read between the lines, we can see the development of the talents that were to take him so far, but we also see within him qualities that were to limit his growth. The least one can say of the book is that, in the old phrase, no one who is interested in Hemingway will want to miss it.

Stanley Kaufmann. "Paris and Hemingway in the Spring." *New Republic*, 150 (May 9, 1964), 17-18, 20-21, 23-24.

Camus' observation in his *Notebooks* that one can, without romanticism, feel nostolgia for lost poverty might serve as an epigraph for Hemingway's posthumous memoir. Paris in the twenties was Hemingway's moveable feast and he returned to it in the late fifties to write this affecting and biographically invaluable book. Something of an anomalous performance in literature, it is a reminder of earlier greatness by an author who slipped in critical esteem during the last half of his writing career.

Gertrude Stein and Sherwood Anderson once agreed that the confessions of the real Ernest Hemingway would be quite a different book from those he wrote, but it would have to be for another audience. This book is probably not the one envisioned by Miss Stein and Anderson, but their intuition was sound. It is for a different audience and these twenty sketches give an intimate view of the young writer as he was evolving his famous style. It provides information and insight that he never revealed during his life. One assumes it was to be deliberately posthumous.

Much of the book is up to Hemingway's best. True, there are distractions in the embarrassingly awkward conversations between Hemingway and his wife and in the snobbism of the chivalrically poor looking down at the rich, the cowards, the cheapjacks, but the rest is a small diamond mine of portraits—friends, acquaintances, enemies. Some are almost forgotten figures, remembered only because Hemingway and a few other memoirists knew them. Better known ones like Ford Madox Ford, Wyndham Lewis, Gertrude Stein, Ezra Pound, Scott Fitzgerald are sketched with dazzling malice, unforgiving condenscension, and occasionally, gratitude.

Hemingway unquestionably has a mean streak; he admits to a bad, quick temper at that time. His mockery of Gertrude Stein can at least be understood, possibly justified, after she called him yellow in the *Autobiography of Alice B. Toklas.* But his treatment of Fitzgerald, after the older (three years) and successful author sponsored him to Scribner's, admired him and finally envied his continued success, can only be explained as deeply impelled abscission from those to whom he was indebted.

Above all the engrossing biographical detail, portraiture, anecdotes and even the sad, lovely, moving warmth of the doomed marriage looms Hemingway's account of how he developed the ability to write so affectingly. Besides the sheer happiness which existed in memory if not fact, he felt the rock-deep rightness of his decision to give up newspaper work and settle firmly into his true vocation. In this book one is present at one of the epochal moments in twentieth century literature. Hemingway was forging his prose style. It was the high period of his life, and looking back to the time after thirty-five years he seems to know that he knew then he would never be happier, stronger in his work, more imperial.

Younger readers who came to Hemingway after World War II cannot possibly see him in the same way his own generation saw him: a powerful and incredibly timely writer, almost a savior bringing curt truth to an overformalized and windy society. Those same readers saw him write lesser books as the years went on and saw the artist replaced by Papa, but if he was not a god anymore, he had been

once. Younger readers missed this transition. From the start he was a mixed blessing in their eyes. To them this latest book may be a happy surprise, a clear view back through the forest of his own self-imitation and the imitations of others. It may help them (as Gertrude Stein's other audience?) sense what the earlier generation sensed. Although there may be other posthumous books by Hemingway, it is unlikely they will sound more strikingly this strong note of rejuvenation. (Summary)

Lewis Galantière. "There is Never Any End to Paris." *New York Times Book Review,* May 10, 1964, pp. 1, 26.

The twenty sketches of "A Moveable Feast" give it the appearance of a random compilation, but it is in fact a calculated production based on two premises: one is that it includes cryptic messages with meanings known only to a few readers; the other is that the artist in Hemingway never allowed him to appear in undress.

It is a book which has emotions as its facts, the emotions of love and loathing, sometimes bitterness. Hemingway here tells of his love for Paris as the place for a young writer to find himself, of his young wife, of Ezra Pound, Sylvia Beach, Bill Bird, "Chink" Dorman-Smith, and the poet

Evan Shipman. But the objects of his love were relatively few. Hemingway did not love easily. Beneath his often boisterous gaiety he was wary, secretive. The book is mostly about the choices he made among his people.

Despite his prefatory note that his judgments were made "for reasons sufficient to the writer," Hemingway leaves unexplained and perplexing his reasons for including an obscure painter or an anonymous homosexual in savage pieces that serve no literary purpose. Nor does he tell why he disliked Ford Madox Ford but instead depicts him in a thin and stupid anecdote detailing Ford's habit of telling harmless fables. Reasons for his harsher treatment of Gertrude Stein and Scott Fitzgerald remain similarly unexplained.

But the purport of the book becomes clearer in the lyrical final section called "There is Never Any End to Paris." Flaubert would have cried "Bravo" at the literary architectonics with which Hemingway gives unity to the book, pleads his case with the young wife he left, and pronounces a curse from the grave on the invading rich and their "pilot fish" who corrupted his purity as an artist. Especially this last section becomes a chant of love for his first wife. Because his own two natures struggled in a Faustian agony over his treatment of her, his chant evokes finally not pathos but tragedy. Not at all the fragmentary book it first appears, "A Moveable Feast" should be read as a novel. It belongs among his better works and for the sheer writing is vintage Hemingway. (Summary)

"The Torrents of Spring." *Newsweek*, 63 (May 11, 1964), 102.

After all the conflicting rumors at the time of Hemingway's death that a treasure of manuscripts had been left behind, one certainty is his book of "sketches of the author's life in Paris in the '20s." Yet anyone who cares about books, especially posthumous ones, must have had mixed feelings: fear that Hemingway's gift may have failed him when he needed it most, hope that by some miracle it had returned. Either way, the book must be of intense interest, as Hemingway deals here with the decisive years when he worked out his famous style, perhaps the most influential style in the modern novel.

To those looking for literary gossip the book will be a disappointment; it adds little to the overfamiliar chit chat about the "lost generation." There are harrowing glimpses of Gertrude Stein's personal life and artistic decline; a malicious but funny portrait of Ford Madox Ford; a loathing view of Wyndham Lewis as the "nastiest man" he ever knew. It is not the judgments themselves but their intensity that is so startling. In Hemingway's vivid feelings and their immediacy lies the abiding interest.

To read the book for its vignettes, however, is to miss its real significance. The twenties in Paris were Hemingway's banquet years, and looking back to that time over nearly four decades, he did not so much remember it as re-experience it. Despite passages of leaden dialogue and some unwitting self-parody, he tells it as he felt it then and provides a sense of utter fullness and confidence as he came into possession of all his power as man and writer.

He must have instinctively feared then what in 1960 he knew could not be denied: that the power could not last. So he made his memoir a kind of novel about the end of innocence and the death of spring. The book is pervasively haunted by a sense of irrecoverable loss. Like a chant for the dead, his refrain goes, "It was there . . . it was there." Near the end the power was gone, hope receded, and the years must have seemed unendurable. (Summary)

Stanley Edgar Hyman. "Ernest Hemingway with a Knife." *New Leader*, 47 (May 11, 1964), 8-9.

A Moveable Feast, the first posthumous publication from the fifty pounds of manuscript Ernest Hemingway left, is his most insignificant book. Yet at its best it has the interest of a minor work by a major writer; at its worst it is interesting in the way a bitchy remark is when overheard at a party.

The portraits of Gertrude Stein, Ford Madox Ford, Wyndham Lewis, and F. Scott Fitzgerald are cutting and malicious. But Hemingway's preface poses the possibility that the accounts may be more fiction than fact. If they are fact, he was indiscreet and cruel to write them. If they are invented, he must be judged contemptible for spending his last years attacking former friends no longer able to answer him. One wonders what sort of man was this hear-and-tell or invent-and-tell friend.

The rest of the book proposes to answer the question but finally fails to do so. One gets a better sense of the older Hemingway than of the real Hemingway in his twenties. With a sort of weepy self-idealization he sees himself as a poor but happy young husband, a courageous writer working his solitary way through the jungle of art, a sensitive young athlete admired by the peasants. He seems so concerned with his potency both in the conjugal bed and in his writing that finally one suspects he protests too much.

Hemingway might well have been worried about the writing. It has real marks of impotency. It exaggerates his characteristic mannerisms to the point of self-parody, has a maddening second-person point of view, uses arch and often labored figures of speech, and sometimes is simply inept. The unfortunate title, for example, confuses the term "moveable feast." He makes it mean a portable feast rather than one that does not come on the same day each year. This is not to say the book is completely without good writing. He tells movingly of a sad professional fire-eater he encountered in a café and recreates a wonderfully funny conversation with a young writer whom he tries to convert to literary criticism. But for the most part the book is his worst piece of writing.

A Moveable Feast markedly diminishes Hemingway's reputation. Other books like it will destroy his standing. His widow and her advisers should be advised to temper their publication plans with mercy. (Summary)

Melvin Maddocks. "Hemingway's Paris Legend." *Christian Science Monitor*, May 14, 1964, p. 11.

---

* * *

This slim 211-page volume is . . . by turns an unabashed lyric poem and a swaggering final curtain call for a literary showman still preoccupied at 60 with boasting in sniggering terms about his alcoholic capacity and sexual prowess.

At its best it is also an expert piece of impressionism, recovering not so much the exact look of Paris as the unique way it looked to a hungry young man who feasted on life as if each day were the last meal.

This is a dialogue between a veteran artist and his romantic memories, with Paris deployed like a stage setting. Hemingway had the simple, monstrous egotism of the healthy young writer: the world existed in order that he might write about it. . . .

In these pages Paris serves as an environment publicly supporting the privacies of one man's youth and ambition. Every day seems magically endowed, from the moment in the early morning when the sun dapples the glistening cobblestones and the goatherd proceeds across them, like the introductory figure in a legend, blowing his pipes and milking his black goats for the sleepy customers that materialize, all Paris ultimately leading to its destiny: another page of Hemingway.

The sadness of this memoir—and it is a peculiarly sad book—lies in its failed and soured personal relationships. Hemingway is hugely romantic about his first wife and one or two other people—rather typically, a waiter and a couple of bicycle racers. He is harsh with most people—particularly other writers, particularly other American writers (the securely unpopular Ezra Pound may be the only exception).

Indeed he is as hard on people as he is soft on places.

* * *

For it is the human beings that jarringly break the spell of Hemingway's fairyland Paris: "The only thing that could spoil a day was people. . . . People were always the limiters of happiness." When Paris ceases to be a personal objection [sic] of charmed moods and becomes a place where other, unenchanted people live, it loses its clear value to him. The Hemingway Paris is a fairy castle with no princess to rescue—only a prince watching himself in the great hall's trick mirror.

Or, to accept the Hemingway metaphor, it is like one of those huge, mul-

ticourse meals one sits down to in determined solitude. (There are, in fact,
dozens of meals almost ritualistically
detailed.)

The trouble is, the feasting is being
described with the sharp-palated nostalgia of an old man surviving on milk
and soda crackers.

Here was youth. Here was Paris.
And nothing afterwards was to be half
so good. "A Moveable Feast" has the
querulous, haunting pathos of a boy's
world about to go flat. It is an affecting but despairingly self-willed indulgence in savoriness past.

Charles A. Brady.
America, 110
(May 16, 1964),
680.

A Moveable Feast contradicts the rule
that literary remains are disappointing.
It is far more satisfactory than Hemingway's other two personal records,
Death in the Afternoon and *Green
Hills of Africa.* A memoir of his Arca-
dian years in Paris, the book is a first-
rate autobiographical revelation that
presents its Paris-scapes with the feeling of Utrillo, provides sometimes
startling insights about the author's
contemporaries, and is a poignant personal confession.

Besides the shuddering glimpse he
provides into Gertrude Stein's private
hell, conversations with Ford Madox
Ford on the definition of a gentleman,
and the saintliness of Ezra Pound,
Hemingway celebrates the waiters of
Paris as culture heroes in his affection-

ately nostalgic treatment. Confession-
ally, he acknowledges his betrayal of
his young wife but tells of their real-
life love with all the tenderness of *A
Farewell to Arms.*

Keeping simultaneously the hard,
clear immediacy of his fiction and the
long elegiac view of memory, Hemingway achieves an almost pastoral simplicity in the account of his youth and
the world of his youth. Evoking the
days when he was still "Hem" to his
friends and not yet "Papa" to the
world, he paints an attractively sardonic self-portrait with careful Braque
strokes. It owes much to his masters:
to Stendhal for sensibility, Flaubert
for craftsmanship, and most of all,
James and Conrad for the ability "to
make instead of describe." (Summary)

Richard Ellmann.
"Under the Ritz."
New Statesman, 67
(May 22, 1964),
809-10.

In the last decade of his 61 years Hemingway fell into writing about veterans
who knew the ropes only too well. In
Italy and then in Cuba, the centre of
attention was an unvanquishable old
man, dressed up in martial or littoral
costume, condensing into new saws for
the benefit of some devoted novice
(the younger the better) a lifetime's
know-how. Hemingway was so eager
to depict characters tired, opposed,
yet indomitable, that he seemed to be
displaying his own toughness to the
critics—by this time numerous—who

thought he was no longer out in front. The sense of being himself under test led him to those dreams of senile glory in which decrepit heroes triumphantly outfaced old age and death—harshest critics of all. His books took on the air of ripostes, conceived in defiance, executed in mawkish gestures monosyllabically enforced, that Hemingway as well as his imitators had sterotyped.

The new book comes as a relief because the defensive tactics of the old man are left out, and we are back among the up-and-coming. . . .

* * *

In writing about the early Twenties, Hemingway returned to what reads more like the account of a battle than a feast. The participants, savagely articulate to a man, have nearly all written books about the time and more often than not they converge on Hemingway as a favourite target, partly because he was so much more successful than they. Gertrude Stein, Robert McAlmon, Wyndham Lewis and Harold Loeb (better known as Robert Cohn in *The Sun Also Rises*) struck at Hemingway in turn, and during his lifetime he offered no direct reply. Among these assailants, Gertrude Stein (as Hemingway's brother Leicester confirms) particularly annoyed by depicting him as an ungrateful pupil, a coward, and (to cap it all) a bad boxer. Hemingway saved his retort for more than 25 years, and now offers a counter-image of Gertrude Stein as a woman formidable in talk but lazy and corrupt, piqued at his not remaining subordinate and unknown, quick to instruct (though his style had already

been formed) but suspicious of her pupils after their graduation. . . .

The most amusing part of the book describes Hemingway's meeting with Scott Fitzgerald, especially a drive they took by car from Lyons to Paris. . . .

* * *

From external colouring to inner substance, the two men were opposites. Hemingway's posture was impregnability, while Fitzgerald's was the admission of more weaknesses than he had. He made no scruple about assessing himself as "very second-rate"; he printed stationery identifying himself as "Hack Writer and Plagiarist." He recognised later that his own tendency was toward self-disparagement (he called it "melancholy") as surely as Hemingway's was towards megalomania. Their early association must have been a continual pummelling of Fitzgerald, who would confess changing his stories' endings to suit the market, only to have Hemingway claim total indifference to such considerations. Fitzgerald called himself an "old whore," while Hemingway, on higher and higher wages, still claimed virginity. By Hemingway's standards, Fitzgerald should not have been able to write at all, but he acknowledged with surprise that his friend could sometimes write well.

While Fitzgerald was expending his subject-matter prodigally in his early years, Hemingway was always gathering, absorbing, hoarding, withholding. He prided himself, *The Moveable Feast* [sic] makes clear, on his secrets, such as a method of giving his stories added power by not mentioning a large part of their subject. . . .

For Hemingway writing was a kind of suppression with only partial release, and this book inadvertently reveals many examples of this habit of mind. He would go without food in order to save the money, then indulge later in some gush of expense, and at the same time keep a secret money heap in reserve. This propensity goes beyond good housekeeping. His capacity for retention of his notebooks for so many years, for storing manuscripts in bank vaults for future exploitation, seems connected with this mode of writing and living. Even his method of composing paragraphs in circles around key words suggests a kind of peristaltic movement. Though he wanted to be known as swash-buckling, his strength came from self-containment.

As an ant he could not bear grasshoppers—mistimedly drunk, ungainly, ill-smelling, bad-spelling people. The quality for which he has been so dispraised, by Morley Callaghan and others—his competitiveness and reluctance to recognise value in his rivals' work (a quality he noted in Stein but not in himself)—seems to have been more than anything an attempt to protect his winter stores. . . .

* * *

Evidently good literature can be written by ants and grasshoppers alike. In Hemingway there is more to stir respect, in Fitzgerald more to evoke sympathy. At his best, in the edged dialogues of this book, Hemingway exhibits the intensity Fitzgerald admired

in him. The language, seemingly simple, has poetic undertones, as when he writes of Paris, "in those days, though, the spring always came finally," or describes Fitzgerald in a fancied illness. . . .

Occasionally, it's true, Hemingway lapses into the flaw of his manner, the rather precious winding about with words such as "wonderful" or "true" or "warm." But as a rule the style is eccentric, narrow, powerful, and all his own. Fitzgerald's manner, less concentrated, somewhat diffuse, a little careless, but slipping in and out of distinction, is now attracting the imitators who grew tired of the old battered idol.

Geoffrey Wagner. "Hemingway Playing Hemingway: Victim of a Manner." *Commonweal*, 80 (May 29, 1964), 302-303.

A Moveable Feast makes it appear that the Hemingway estate is prepared to publish some very minor work in the name of the master. For all the good it is likely to do Hemingway's reputation, it would have been better to keep it in the vault. Subtitled "Sketches of the Author's Life in Paris in the Twenties," the book is a group of literary reminiscences of dubious accuracy and even more dubious value.

The memoir has the old hedonist emphasis on the senses—of sight, taste, touch, smell—but uses the senses as a tool of doctrinaire anti-intellectualism. At points the book becomes a virtual anthology of insults to the intellect in the name of the senses. Like Gertrude Stein who, according to Hemingway, never spoke well of any writer not reflecting favorably on her work, he attacks his old critics not with reasoned discourse but with epithets and innuendo. Wyndham Lewis, thus, was the nastiest looking man he had ever seen. Ford Madox Ford smelled appallingly bad.

When Hemingway began writing, American prose cried for the sort of reform he brought it. He revived romanticism by writing romantic tales in the famous flat style. It was almost too easy. He made the manner important and in the end let the manner take over. He could not be blamed because his method was commercialized, but he suffered a failure of self-consciousness in parodying himself in the guise of realism at the close of his career. In his accounts of Paris street life, for example, his realism is only map-reading. The anti-ornamental deadpan narration was a limited style-as-vision technique, and he never realized he lacked a vision to support the style. The result was to exalt his style for its effects rather than for its content. His early work did a great deal but one is not sure just what it was.

Such a style ends up as a fairly virulent form of skepticism, and the anti-intellectualism of this book pays court to it. Hemingway is revealed pushed into a pose buttressed by hedonist rhetoric. It smells of the Rotten-Apple syndrom—all tough on the outside and mushy in the middle. (Summary)

Maxwell Geismar. "When He Was Good." *Cosmopolitan*, 156 (May 1964), 8-9.

This memoir of Hemingway's Paris years deals with those apprentice days when he was writing those first famous short stories, meeting almost daily such figures as Ezra Pound, Gertrude Stein, and Scott Fitzgerald, reading the Russian masters, and coming into possession of his literary powers. His Paris was a cauldron of the arts and of exciting literary movements. To read a good writer on his own life and times is an exciting prospect, and the book starts out with the glow of that time. We are still hungry for Hemingway's great moments of fiction and the light he can shed on himself and his period.

But after the initial glow we become aware of the real tone of the book. In accounts of sexual gossip and sexual scandal about Gertrude Stein, for example, we recognize that beneath the nostalgia is a merciless, satiric, wholly self-centered, and uncompassionate mind at work. Toward those like Sylvia Beach who were not his competitors, Hemingway could be entertainingly accurate. He writes well of the Paris food, the fishermen, the waiters too. But when he writes of old rivalries, he shows a malicious and phony side of his character. The older Hemingway, feeling his own decline, is not so much the man obsessed with death and killing, as the truism has it, but the writer indulging his killer instinct. In his funny but devastating and cruel sketches of Ford Madox Ford and Scott Fitzgerald he produces a strange and finally disappointing book.

This memoir confirms the psychic transformation in Hemingway that has haunted the American literary and critical imagination. In his earlier days Hemingway was a great poet of pagan pleasure and stoic suffering. But later he reverted to a blind and sharkish Darwinian cosmos. He was denied, or he denied, the intellect which might have made up for his failing physical powers. Through his own method and style of fiction he was denied, or he denied, the human concern which might have absorbed his own consuming egotism. Now all one can do is be thankful for what he could do when he was good. (Summary)

Nelson Algren. "Who's Who at the Lost & Found." *The Nation*, 198 (June 1, 1964), 560-61.

The vital difference between this youthful American in love with his wife, his writing, food, wine and racehorses, was that the others had arrived at the Moveable Feast directly from a picnic in Kansas City or St. Paul, but he had come to his place by way of death.

Paris to the Fitzgeralds was only a farther place on a meadow of endless sun. But Hemingway had so narrowly missed having no place at all—"I'd felt my life flutter like a handkerchief in the wind"—that he knew how swiftly all good days are taken away. Hemingway was a young man learning how to sleep again.

But his hold on life having once been loosened, it now became all the more tenacious for that. The tension that began to pervade his writing derived from this tenaciousness, and lent him a perspective larger than that indicated by a phrase like "lost generation." . . .

* * *

Hemingway wasn't lost. He would have been an expatriate even if he had never left Oak Park. His exile, like Villon's, was not from a land, but from the living. His need was not for a country, but for the company of men. Spiritually, therefore, he was closer to Villon than to Scott Fitzgerald. . . .

If we consider that Hemingway, like Villon, was forging a a style not out of literature, but out of his need, we see not only what style is, but what Hemingway was.

The man and the style were one: the style was the instrument by which his need was realized; and the need was for light and simplicity. Thus, in achieving this for himself, he touched multitudes enduring a murky complexity.

* * *

The light he throws here is upon others. It is the harsh light of exposure: he reserves a soft, blurring glow for himself. Reporting a dialogue between two raving dikes, overheard accidentally thirty-five years before, is a bit the book could have done without. He might have let the poor brutes be. But the spotlight is useful when he recalls Fitzgerald's relationship to Zelda, because it reveals the fashion in which Fitzgerald was cut down. It does not have that justification with Gertrude Stein.

* * *

Hemingway was a tolerant opponent and a mean competitor, both. Henry Strater, the artist whose portrait of Hemingway illustrates the back cover of *A Moveable Feast,* and who was close to Hemingway in Paris because he could knock Hemingway down as often as Hemingway could knock him down, remembers that their friendship ended on a fishing trip in a quarrel over a marlin. "I hated his guts for twenty years over that," Strater now recalls their feud, "I never hated any man so much in my life." Then he added: "But of all the friends I've had, now dead, the one I most wish were alive today is Hemingway."

Jeffrey Hart. "Hemingway's Code." *National Review,* 16 (June 2, 1964), 450-52.

In *A Moveable Feast* Hemingway evokes that ideal Paris most of us have, lodged somewhere in our minds, safe from time and peopled with the likes of Joyce, Fitzgerald, Pound, Ford and Hemingway himself. It is the Paris of sipping cognac at the Dôme, walking among the bookstalls by the Seine or meeting at Sylvia Beach's bookshop, the Paris where some of the major poems and books of our age were being written. It was the Paris where Hemingway lived a kind of idyllic literary life of acceptable poverty, even hunger at times, but alive in all his senses, learning from his contemporaries and from the old masters, and realizing the confidence of his growing powers as an artist. Evoked here in one of Hemingway's most moving and beautifully written books, that Paris has all the freshness of a first experience with a fabled time and place.

Further, the memoir contradicts all those theories about the decline of Hemingway's powers. In places devastatingly funny, sometimes affectionate as with Pound or cruel as with Wyndham Lewis, the book rises through malice to insight in the small masterpiece on Scott Fitzgerald, a strange compound of the marvelous and the outrageous which darkens at times with the knowledge of Zelda's insanity. The book has the effect of re-directing us to Hemingway's achievement and seeing again what in the man and the style was most distinctive.

Hemingway once observed that real American writing derived from the earthy, unliterary, circumstantial language spoken by Huck Finn. That language was the antithesis of language spoken by the Widow Douglas and was the moral equivalent of a correction of her pious, respectable, well-intentioned viewpoint that was nevertheless unequal to the facts. After the First

World War, as Lionel Trilling has noted, Hemingway had to do for the rhetoric of Wilsonian idealism what Huck had done for the Widow Douglas. The rhetoric of good intentions had to be corrected through bare, declarative statement emphasizing the importance of fact.

But Hemingway's problem was more complicated than Twain's. The war and his infantryman's knowledge of the terror of facts made the necessity of correction more drastic. Where Twain could pose a deliberately "uneducated" style against the middle-class uplift of the Widow Douglas, Hemingway had to bring to bear not only the importance of fact against Wilsonian uplift but also a sense of fact so painful that presentation was not enough. His knowledge of *nada* haunted the facts. In addition to lower-class vocabulary he had to combine an essentially aristocratic discipline of irony and understatement to deal with emotions of terror and disgust.

He had to adopt an aristocratic code of manners to embody that language. It is significant then that Hemingway appeared those days looking oddly British and, as Ford described him, with an Eton-Oxford air of a young captain from an English midland regiment. Significant also was Hemingway's admiration for Kipling as a literary source. Hemingway brought to American literature a classic Tory strategy which combines upper and lower against middle class, aristocrat and peasant against the social climbing moral idealist.

The sustaining discipline was the key skill, a way of meeting experience through prose. It was always a contingent thing, subject to circumstances, and Hemingway could not always bring it off. He shows in *A Moveable Feast* how he learned it and his death in 1961 shows that he lost it. (Summary)

Gouverneur Paulding. "Postcards From Paris." *Reporter*, 30 (June 4, 1964), 40-43.

These memories of Hemingway's young writing years in the Paris of the 1920's show a wonderful craftsman at his best; they are also cruel, devious, and at the end overwhelmingly sad. For at the end a young man comes forth from the garden of Eden, but not with his Eve; he sees himself naked, and is ashamed.

* * *

From the very beginning of the book, when the Hemingways are working so hard and are so happy, there is the premonition of sadness. Hemingway can divert his thoughts, and ours, by being rude to Ford Madox Ford, or cruel to Miss Stein, or vaguely superior to T. S. Eliot, or loyal to Ezra Pound; he can even put his thoughts altogether aside by writing about horse racing, or bicycle racing, or fishing, or skiing on his vacation trips to Austria; he can find relief by concentrating on his problems as a writer; but in the end he has to face, without dissimulation, honestly, with all candor, what from the beginning he knew he would have to face if he were to write "truly," the final results of those Paris years.

One was a triumph: he had learned to write; he had finished *The Sun Also Rises*. The other he blamed on "the rich" who had broken into his privacy —a "pilot fish" had brought them to draw sustenance from the integrity of his effort—and he also blamed it on his bad luck. But in the end, to his very great credit, he blamed only himself for betraying his wife.

Frank Kermode. "Hemingway's Last Novel." *New York Review of Books*, 2 (June 11, 1964), 4-6.

A Moveable Feast is in some ways Hemingway's best book since the 1920's. It is, in fact, about his apprenticeship in Paris during the twenties, when he was training for his contests with life as well as with Mr. Turgenev and Mr. Stendhal. It tells how he learned to purge his writing in order to make, not describe; to omit, not to invent. It tells also how he learned to purge his acquaintance as well as his prose. But though he tells what he learned about Ford Madox Ford and Wyndham Lewis and Gertrude Stein and Scott Fitzgerald, all told with more than a little malice, it is mostly about his heroic effort in the struggle for style. It is the older Hemingway

writing about his younger self but in the prose of the latter.

The book reveals the coexistence in Hemingway of technical and personal ambitions that at times seemed at odds with each other. The technician struggled to purge his prose of *littérature* in order to represent accurately the structure of experience and the texture of the world. The style became a painful stripping away of any but the declarative. What went in should have the authority of a manual of instruction in some manly technique. But the technique involved the technician, human material emotionally involved in the demands of harsh, difficult skills. Finally the behavior of this human material under stress came to interest him more until the hero and not the skill became the focus. To learn to do a difficult craft was heroic. There is an intelligible relation between the self-denial of the writing and the self-indulgence in being the hero, the big-game man, the *aficionado*, the marksman. The man who makes such technically authoritative prose develops an increasingly simplistic theory of manliness; he is drawn to pay attention to the life of honor, perhaps even of the mystic. The later Hemingway was marred by this disingenuous simplicity, and one sees how it related to his virtues and developed from them.

So this posthumous book is very moving. Written by a man who had over the years disciplined his technique to the point where he could deal with fourth and fifth dimensions, it also recognizes that in the last ten years, except for one crystalline novella, he had written nothing of the arduous prose of the first heroic period. And then he wrote this book about the heroic apprenticeship.

From start to finish this is the work of a great writer. The total authenticity of his remembered or invented life has a structural function in the book. Hemingway suggested it might better be considered a work of fiction, and it ought to be judged with his novels. A deliberate and ingenious way of revisiting the sources of his strength, it displays that strength as very little else of his had done in thirty years. And that makes it altogether exceptional. (Summary)

Benjamin DeMott. "The Need for Watering Places." *Harper's,* 228 (June 1964), 114, 116, 118.

Everything in its place, was the 'twenties' motto: Larks in Life, Agony in Art. And, judging from the record, many writers took the motto perfectly straight. Happy or otherwise on the beaches, slopes, and courts, novelists specialized at their desks in breakdowns and defeats of ambition. Critics harped on pain and "imagination of disaster."

* * *

That the author of *A Moveable Feast*, a memoir of Paris pleasures, made light of this obligation can't, in candor, be argued. Hemingway's novels abound in agony—mean minds, wounds, and worse; and students long ago learned how to read a death wish in practically every good story he told. Still, it is undeniable that Eden does have a place in his work. Time and again, Hemingway set heroes and heroines down in a holiday world of pure simplicity and innocence, and more than once they could be seen actually enjoying themselves.

* * *

The point at stake, which is that few twentieth-century novelists are richer than this one in evocations of states of happiness, can't be zipped neatly into critic-ese about Hemingway and doom and death, or Hemingway and *anomie* and *Angst*. But it has substance nevertheless. There is just a chance, indeed, that when the sinking time arrives for "Papa's" reputation, it will be his wealth in the courage of pleasure that finally keeps him afloat.

Readers with a feeling for Hemingway as a master of revels will find little to surprise them in the work at hand. The book's period is 1921 to 1926, and, for reasons that are convincing even when abstractly stated, its quality is that of an idyl. Young Ernest from Illinois is hopeful, energetic, independent. He is impecunious—but in a good cause, that of Literature. His Muse is consistently generous. And, additional advantages, he has commerce both with traditions of his art and with worthy living practitioners, enjoys an attractive and manageable domestic life, and possesses, besides friends and recreations, an enviable clarity about his own needs and ambitions.

But this *is* an abstract rehearsal of blessings; *A Moveable Feast* demands a different sort of account. For the book is a bill of particulars first of all; the writer is laying down The Facts. He lays down facts about his dwelling place: 74 rue Cardinal Lemonie on the Montagne Ste. Genevieve, six flights up, two rooms, heated by fireplace, no hot water or inside toilet, furnished with mattress and springs, table and chairs, cheerful pictures, wife, infant son, and cat. He lays down facts about food and drink. . . .

* * *

As is evident, *A Moveable Feast* is a sentimental book. The voice that speaks in it, moreover, is the sloppy-avuncular voice which, as early as *A Farewell to Arms*, lent an air of self-parody to Hemingway's work. ("Paris was never to be the same again, although it was always Paris and you changed as it changed" etc.) And the view of experience is practically weightless. (Original sin turns out to be a rich man's disease. Evil is what other people do. And belief in a twentieth-century industrial metropolis as a great happy valley for all is a sign not of nasty obliviousness but of lovable innocence.) Here, as often elsewhere in his writing, the Nobel prize-winner retreats to a time made simple by the loss of details, steps "back out of all this too much for us," and trusts a fantasy to make him whole beyond confusion. And here as elsewhere, the evidence indicates that such retreats are at once less instructive and interesting when puffed out with cotton-candy nostalgia and and tears than

when trimmed in decent irony, after the manner of Robert Frost.

But if the meal in *A Moveable Feast* isn't transportable—is, in truth, rather sticky and stale, an affair of flyblown frosting and melting molded minarets —it is, nevertheless, a monument of a kind: a memorial to Appetite. And such memorials have their uses. They preserve the ideas of simplicity and freshness as well. No doubt the "proper" way to like Hemingway is in a carefully restrained vein, as Henry James liked Matthew Arnold—"with an affection that is proof against anything [the man] may say or do, and proof also against taking him too seriously." But the Eden for which the author of *The Sun Also Rises* boyishly, likably yearned had, in his best glimpses of it, a luring power—the power to coax people out of habitual states of complex non-feeling into the embarrassing simplicity of desire. To forget it altogether would be too much like forgetting youth itself.

Brooks Atkinson. "Critic at Large: Gertrude Stein and Scott Fitzgerald are Defended Against Hemingway's Attacks." *New York Times,* July 7, 1964, p. 32.

Since Gertrude Stein and Scott Fitzgerald are no longer able to defend themselves against Hemingway's defamation of their character in "A Moveable Feast," one has to answer for them, even though Hemingway too is no longer able to answer back. Unfair's unfair.

There is no avoiding it. His posthumous book of reminiscences about Paris in the 1920's is extraordinarily mean; his portraits of Gertrude Stein and Scott Fitzgerald, both of whom extended friendship and hospitality to the young writer, are cruel and humiliating. Such treatment might seem less sanctimonious if Hemingway's self-portrait acknowledged flaws, but he depicts himself as a chivalric figure patiently suffering their imperfections. In one sketch he presents Ford Madox Ford worrying about who was a cad. Ford assured Hemingway that he was not a cad, but this book shows he became one.

Betraying friends was not new for Hemingway. In her book "At the Hemingways," his sister Marcelline Hemingway Sanford tells of her pained surprise at finding two close family friends made characters in "a vulgar, sordid tale," one of the "Three Stories and Ten Poems." It should have been no surprise to Fitzgerald, then, to find himself hurt by the patronizing use of his name in "The Snows of Kilimanjaro," and if he were now alive, to see himself treated poisonously in this memoir.

Hemingway speaks in "A Moveable Feast" about the nobility and difficulty of writing a true sentence, one that eliminates adjectives and makes a blunt statement of fact. The harshness of life and the martyrdom of human beings with limited choices for survival were to be conveyed in the overtones

of such sentences. They needed the background of war to provide the illusion of resignation. When there were no wars, when the subject did not support the style, Hemingway had to look for other subjects of conflict and other victims. He told Gertrude Stein that one had to be prepared to kill a man. In "A Moveable Feast" he does it by poisoning at least two of the dishes. (Summary)

Virginia Quarterly Review, 40 (Summer 1964), cvi-cvii.

The short sketches making up this book of reminiscences of Paris in the twenties where young Americans like Hemingway and his first wife, Hadley, lived, as someone said, like babes in the Bois, were not written until 1957-1960. Yet the reminiscences could be of yesterday, so fresh they are, so precisely remembered. They make a wonderful memorial to a great writer; the writing is Hemingway at his very best as he was in the beginning before the corn came up and without the braggadocio. The reader is given the essence of observation whether of the smell of new bread, the taste of ice-cold beer on an empty stomach, the sound of dry snow underfoot, the speech of the rich, the dialogue of available blondes. The only difference made by the thirty years between the event and the recording is in the candor the author allowed himself about real acquaintances of those days—most of them now dead. . . . Yet what seems most interesting of all about this posthumous volume is the light it throws on Hemingway's mode of writing and the way he went about perfecting his famous style. . . . Hemingway made it clear that he applied his literary judgment, as opposed to his creativity, always to the surface aspects of writing, never to an understanding or assimilation of what he was writing. Of meanings he appears terrified, and he speaks with serious contempt of criticism and critics. His motto might have been, Save the Surface and you Save All. Yet within the area for development he did allow himself, he accomplished a remarkable thing. His style, much imitated in its time, less so at present, surely made a permanent mark on the language. Looked at objectively, the present book of reminiscences reveals that the style Hemingway—who so loved the Latin peoples—created sounds like nothing so much as a translation from a Romance tongue. . . . They may not read like English, those beginnings, but they are almost hypnotically readable. In fact they are irresistible.

Philip Young.
"Touching Down and Out: *A Moveable Feast*." *Kenyon Review*, 26 (Autumn 1964), 697-707.

Most of us can remember without much trouble the discovery Hawthorne imagined having made in the storeroom of "The Custom-House." Among "aged cobwebs," "bundles of official documents," "musty papers" and "similar rubbish" he came upon a "small package . . . done up in . . . ancient yellow parchment" and tied with "faded red tape." The package contained "the record of other doings and sufferings," "the groundwork of a tale" that became, after the author had allowed himself "much license" with the record, *The Scarlet Letter*. (He thought eventually to deposit the package with the Essex Historical Society.)

Now, as related by Mary Hemingway, we have a sort of counterpart to that happy event. This is in the discovery of some notebooks, packed away in two old trunks recovered from the storage basement of the Paris Ritz, where they had rested for some thirty years. The "trunks" were "two small, fabric-covered, rectangular boxes, both opening at the seams," wherein were found, amidst "ancient newspaper cuttings . . . a few cracked and faded books, some musty sweatshirts and withered sandals," several "blue-and-yellow covered penciled notebooks." After Hemingway had transformed them into what he says "may be regarded as fiction," these notebooks became *A Moveable Feast*.

* * *

In life Hemingway maintained where he could a pretty steady vigilance against the slightest injury to his reputation. And though he often let down the bars himself he was quick to take offense at any uninvited invasion of his privacy. Whatever principles lurked in these attitudes seem to have applied only to the living, and to have existed chiefly for the benefit of himself alive. But reputations do not end with the death of writers, as he was ever well aware, and several are going to suffer from the holes fired into them here. So descendants of the dead live on, and a few people at least are going to be hurt. What Fitzgerald confided to Hemingway after lunch at Michaud's, the dialogue with Ford Madox Ford in the Closerie des Lilas, what Hemingway overheard in Miss Stein's apartment one spring morning —these bullets are likely to keep on hitting home as long as the targets are up. In each of these cases Hemingway has already been taken severely to task for telling tales out of school.

All the jokes in *A Moveable Feast* are on other people; Hemingway comes out—steadily, effortlessly— smelling like a *vin rosé*. Underneath his well-known openness and generosity there was a mean, wary streak. He couldn't have been all that good nor they, perhaps, all that vulnerable. It is possible to make exactly the same objection to this book that many people, including Hemingway, made to Lillian Ross's once-notorious profile of him (which, incidentally, some of his chapters rather resemble). This objection would be that the sketches do not give much sense that the writers attacked were, much of the time anyway, serious and hard-working people. If his cruelty is to be excused, and it will be as Miss Ross has been, it will have to be with reference to the fierceness of competitive spirit without

which he, at least, could not have been champion at all or ever, and to the *éclat* with which these people are shot down. This was the fighter he said he was and, considering the infirmities of the late years, this is perhaps his most remarkable comeback, following as it does on the abortive "Dangerous Summer," which he himself did not think well enough of to publish in full. We will eventually forget the belligerence and arrogance, along with a lot of other things, by summoning up the same "strange excuse" with which Auden let off Yeats: "Time . . . Worships language and forgives/Everyone by whom it lives."

Hemingway shared in this devotion, and his success is with language. It is the shock of immediacy, the sense of our own presence on the streets he walks or in the cafés where he writes, talks, or drinks, that makes the book. When he is hungry so are we. And when, for instance, a small check enables him to break the fast at Lipp's, thought then as now to have the best beer in Paris, and he orders a great one, a *distingué*, and *pommes à l'huile* and a large sausage, this reader, who was only reading (it's not all *that* immediate), was driven ravenous. Or take the first little sketch in the book. It is too cold to write in his room so he goes to a café, sees a pretty girl there, works on a story, drinks a *café au lait* and decides to go where there will be snow instead of rain. Nothing has happened, the girl is wholly anonymous, the story is not named. But the scene is etched in the reader as if a diamond had scratched glass.

There are flaws in the diamond.

Some of the dialogue with Hadley is unreal and a little embarrassing; sometimes the borders of sentimentality are skirted if not transgressed. But for the most part the prose glitters, warms, and delights. Hemingway is not remembering but re-experiencing; not describing, making. In several cases the results are comparable to his fiction. So much have things changed that he could have invented names for the characters and called the sketches stories, reversing the process whereby editors once rejected the stories as sketches. Then the book would seem like a book of stories, but a little like a novel, too, as does *Winesburg*, which he once called his first pattern, or *In Our Time*. And the novel would pick up a little more than the unity of place from the sense of irretrievable loss that haunts it—loss of the spirit of youth, innocence and springtime, soon to pass.

* * *

In part the appeal of this little, almost trivial book lies in the fact of Hemingway's active and communicated presence in the great years of Americans in Paris, an ideal expatriation that thousands of literary people, born too late, have dreamed of ever since. There was never for us anything like it; never such a sense that the arts were being born anew, or such exhilaration at having escaped this country. The wine was nearly free, the food was excellent and cheap, it was a good place to work, or not work; a couple could live well in this then-finest of cities on $25.00 a week. Many have tried to re-establish it all in Paris, or

Rome, or elsewhere, but the arts are not being born anew, things have come to cost as much in many places as they do at home, and now we are teaching them how to drink.

But if it were simply a matter of time, place and nostalgia other writers would have been able to turn the trick, which they have notably failed to do. The difference is that this little collection of anecdotes and reminiscences is a minor work of art. The principles and particulars of poverty, the pleasures of food and drink disciplined by the shortage of cash, always how the weather was—these things and others are the texture of the book functioning almost thematically under the word-by-word spell of the style. This gentle effort toward unity is climaxed in the last scene, "There Is Never Any End to Paris," which is set mainly in Austria and has mostly to do with the skiing there: the magician has moved the activity so far to the side that you are not watching what else he is up to, and you do not see how he does it when suddenly there is the book, wrapped up and ending on the same sad loving note with which it began.

Then the tones of malice and superiority ring fainter, and one remembers the terrible need for reassurance that caught Hemingway up during the months of acute depression in his last two years, when he felt that after all he had been knocked out and nothing he had ever written was worth a damn. As George Plimpton guessed in an early review, one function of this book was probably therapeutic. It was as if by "touching down" at these places and times, and even specific bottles and meals, the author could bring back the serentiy and order that were failing him so badly. We know he had done this sort of thing before, as in "Big Two-Hearted River." And now he must touch down once more, with the same fanatical precision. We know, again via Mary Hemingway, how she and her husband walked over and over the routes he walks in this book, partly to check their accuracy. Everything must be absolutely and exactly right. Many months later she got a friend to re-check the itinerary. Finally she herself "flew over and retraced all the steps Ernest wrote he took, first by myself and then with my friend. . . ." It turned out that Hemingway had mis-spelled the names of two streets. Noth-ing else was amiss. But it was a loyal, worthy thing for her to do. She hon-ored the therapy even though the pa-tient was deceased.

Andrew Lytle.
"*A Moveable Feast:*
The Going To and Fro."
Sewanee Review, 73
(Spring, 1965),
339-43.

A great hazard to an artist is his repu-tation. Except to that small body of readers who look to the word for meaning, the reputation is almost sure to be false to the work, composed as it is of the accidents of personality, at best the embodiment of the quality of artist as man. . . .

Hemingway was not just a reputa-tion; he was also an artist, but an artist who faltered and assumed the various masks of his public personality. Acting is a secondary art, depending upon the work of others: in this instance the illusion of a whole work which actual-ly was only partially delivered. Or so it may seem. But this is a half truth. After first reading *A Moveable Feast* I thought his publishers had done him a disservice. I now feel the book is ex-tremely revealing: the public personali-ty was there from the start; even in his apprenticeship it was there, the strug-gle between the ego and its transfor-mation in the artefact. Most craftsmen suffer this conflict, and either end up as artists or personalities. Apparently Hemingway never made the choice, ev-en if he was aware that a choice exist-ed. It is always hazardous to read the inward decisions in the outward ac-tion, but there is a curious evasion in the introduction to this book. The reader is given the choice by Heming-way of reading *A Moveable Feast* eith-er as a memoir or as fiction. Obviously this is a false choice. Was he trying to get himself off the hook, or had he come to think that he might over-ride all forms in the self-regard of that car-nal omniscience of his?

There are too many hooks to get free of; so it must be the devouring omniscience which defines the pathos of the action here. These early days in Paris were wonderful days. So we are told, and we are prepared to believe them so, until we begin to wonder at the wonders. There is not an associate of his, who conceivably might be his rival, or to whom he owed anything, that receives anything but denigration of character or profession. Not once does he show any human sympathy or charity towards his fellow man. The method is very workable. The professional competence of each is betrayed through the deficiencies and follies of a personal and private nature.

* * *

Now why is it that Hemingway wants to be the only one, the only artist and the only man? Why does he want Paris without people? Nor is he content to be the patron of the living and his elders in the crafts, but the past too he wants to envelop in so far as he recognizes what he considers his kind of virility there. But how can anybody, without the severest delusion, speak of Marshall Ney, as Mike Ney, as if he and Ney were old buddies and messmates? It has puzzled me a long time, Hemingway's hatred, at least contempt for tourists. It has seemed so inordinate and actually so irrelevant to the actions of his fictions, for example, *The Old Man and the Sea*. After reading *A Moveable Feast* I think I know. The tourist can go home. Hemingway couldn't. He lived in exile and the kind hardest to bear, self-exile. His residence at Key West was barely in the country; then Cuba, just outside. Later the far isolated West, where the home-tourists matched the International set he wrote about. Why this is so is nobody's business. He had doomed himself to the life of the perpetual tourist, forever in foreign parts, wandering to and through the wonders advertized. No scene, no mountain, not any city, even Paris, could be home. It is pathetic, his

self-identity with Paris, with the restaurants, the streets and parks, as if they were laid out for his pleasure and sole appreciation. He in this book named the streets, the two ways to a given destination, to show his knowledge and control, against all those tourists intruding upon his exile. He only showed by this his isolation.

* * *

Checklist of Additional Reviews

Julius Blum. "Paris—In the Twenties." *Nashville Tennessean*, May 3, 1964, p. 29-D.

Christian Century, 81 (May 6, 1964), 608.

Ruth Smith, "Moveable Feast or Portable Bar?" *Orlando Sentinel*, June 14, 1964, pp. 10, 12, 13F.

Patricia Bunker. *Saturday Review*, 47 (December 5, 1964), 54.

Earl Rovit. *Books Abroad*, 39 (Winter 1965), 91-92.

George Wickes. "Ernest Hemingway Pays His Debts." *Shenandoah*, 16 (Winter 1965), 46-54.

William P. Sears. *Education*, 85 (February 1965), 332.

James Korges. "Hemingway: Down the Street and Across the River." *Critique*, 7 (Spring-Summer 1965), 77-80.

Publishers Weekly, 199 (February 1, 1971), 73.

Best Sellers, 31 (August 1, 1971), 216.

BY-LINE:
ERNEST
HEMINGWAY

Selected Articles and Dispatches of Four Decades

EDITED BY WILLIAM WHITE

CHARLES SCRIBNER'S SONS · NEW YORK

By-line:
Ernest Hemingway

Richard J. Thompson.
Library Journal, 92
(May 1, 1967),
1934.

"Hero as Celebrity."
Time, 89
(May 19, 1967),
133, 134, 136.

This potpourri of Hemingway's journalism from the 1920's to the 1950's will be interesting to Papa-cultists ever searching for new sources of anecdote and biographical fillip; more important, it will be required reading for scholars who want to locate original accounts of the Pamplona afternoons and Parisian dusks that were to be caught in the amber of his novels. But chiefly this worthy book is for the so-called general reader who will be charmed and moved and astonished by Hemingway's talent for *teaching* about wine, food, shooting, fishing, travel, writing, and European customs and pastimes. Hemingway knew an impressive amount about the myriad small things that go to make up the totality of a man's life, and he loved to pass on his lore to the uninitiated—sometimes the habit becomes showy in his fiction and his three book-length essays. Here the matter is perfectly suited to the medium. Recommended for all general collections.

By-Line: Ernest Hemingway, a 77-piece assembly of Papa's journalism edited by William White, is the second course of literary leftovers served up by the author's widow, three years after *A Moveable Feast*. It will be interesting as source material for Hemingway biographers and thesis hunters, but it has intrinsic value for general readers as well. Hemingway could tell a good story and could make the sea and forest seem God's heaven. He even had an occasional wise word for aspiring writers: One of the two absolute necessities for writing is real seriousness; the other, however, is talent. But the author is the main interest. The collection graphs the rise, peaking out and decline of Ernest Hemingway as prose stylist.

The early reports from Europe in the Twenties for the *Toronto Star* were basic Hemingway: clear as glass and ominously perceptive about the aims of such European politicians as Mussolini. After his successes with *The Sun Also Rises* and *A Farewell to Arms* he had the image of the tough and masculine writer-sportsman to live up to. After his period of self-imposed isolation in Key West and Africa he went to Spain to cover the Civil War for the North American Newspaper Alliance and did his best reporting. He wrote journalism so well that two of his pieces later reappeared as short stories.

After that it was all downhill. His China stories for *PM* took on an all-knowing air and his World War II pieces for *Collier's* made him, not events, their subject. He told how Hemingway landed on the beaches on D-day, how Hemingway beat the Allied armies across France, how Hemingway liberated Paris. After the war he was Papa unzipping his ego in public. Out of control, he became a parody of himself, scrambled his syntax, ran off at the mouth in military jargon and let posturing take over his writing like a curse. Crawling out of the jungle after his 1954 plane crash, he shouted his survival in two *Look* articles but Hemingway was clearly on the ropes.

Thirty years after his feast in Paris, Hemingway remembered Gertrude Stein's warning him to get out of journalism. It would use up the juice he needed for writing, she said. But he didn't take the advice. Instead, he became a gossip columnist with himself as major celebrity. (Summary)

Charles Poore. "Portrait of a Man and Some Pieces of Paper." *New York Times,* May 25, 1967, p. 45.

Except for the timeliness of the Canadian material in connection with Expo 67, the journalism in "By-Line: Ernest Hemingway" runs a familiar course. Included are pieces from the Toronto Star, written in the twenties, Esquire letters from the early thirties, NANA dispatches from Spain during the Civil War, PM and Collier's material from World War II. Not included is the stuff that won Hemingway a Nobel Prize—the novels and stories that brought new cadences to English.

The probable and unhappy effect of publishing such material, one fears, is a new attempt to judge Hemingway from these fugitive bits. To do so, however, is like an archaeologist's projecting a town from a plinth or a paleontologist's reconstructing a prehistoric ancestor from a thigh bone.

The better use of Hemingway's journalism is to share his enjoyment in living. What's remarkable is his ability to feel at one with the life of the place he wrote about, whether it was the Chicago underworld, Paris in liberation, China in wartime or Madrid under siege. By early 1922, for example, he was so much the Old Paris Hand that he could look with superior amusement at the pretensions of American bohemians gathered at the Rotonde.

At about midpoint in Hemingway's career, critics began to say he was repeating himself. Every time a new Hemingway book came out they said it again with new satisfaction—fascinating notion! No one seemed to notice the critics repeating themselves. What we can see now with this new collection is that Hemingway has a massive and unfair advantage over his antagonists. To put it bluntly, he had a lot more to repeat. (Summary)

Granville Hicks. "The Novelist as Newspaperman." *Saturday Review*, 50 (May 27, 1967) 23-24.

For some time now, it seems to me, I have been unable to comment on either books by or books about Ernest Hemingway without expressing rather serious misgivings concerning the man and his career. It is, therefore, a pleasure to report that *By-Line: Ernest Hemingway*, a selection of his journalistic writings edited by William White, contains 478 pages that I have read, for the most part, with marked satisfaction.

White, a professor of journalism at Wayne State University, candidly repeats what Hemingway said around 1930 to a bibliographer: that the "newspaper stuff I have written . . . has nothing to do with the other writing which is entirely apart. . . ."

The first right that a man writing has is the choice of what he will publish. If you have made your living as a newspaperman, learning your trade, writing against deadlines, writing to make stuff timely rather than permanent, no one has any right to dig this stuff up and use it against the stuff you have written to write the best you can." But, White points out, Hemingway sometimes made use of this journalistic "stuff" in his serious books. What is more important, his journalism taken as journalism is almost always first-rate, and sometimes it is as truly literature as anything he ever wrote.

* * *

From 1920 to 1924 he supported himself by writing articles for the *Star Weekly* and the *Daily Star* of Toronto, and White has selected twenty-nine of the 154 pieces he wrote for these publications. They demonstrate that he was an honest reporter and an increasingly skillful one. Most of the time he wrote what used to be called "human interest stories," rather than analyses of international developments, though there is a prescient portrait of Mussolini in 1923. . . .

It is important to remember that while he was writing these dispatches Hemingway was working on the short stories that appeared in 1925 as *In Our Time*. Many of these stories, as Philip Young and others have demonstrated, reveal Hemingway's preoccupation with the most somber fears and doubts. Of course he was too sensible to parade his woes in the *Star*. He wrote about the things that interested and excited him, and he wrote about them with great gusto. In later years his gusto sometimes seemed forced, but here it is quite genuine. This gaiety was as much a part of Hemingway as the unhappiness that shows through the stories and the novels.

* * *

There are many newspaper articles, expecially from the early years, that White has not included. I can't speak about them, of course, but most of the seventy-seven pieces that he has republished are good reading. This is a volume that could be enjoyed if the by-line were Joe Doakes, but it inevitably has a special interest for students of Hemingway and for all his admirers. Writing was probably the only thing in life that Hemingway was consistently serious about, and many witnesses have told us how hard he worked when he was trying to do his best. What this collection makes us realize is that he worked just as hard as conditions permitted w ien he was writing for newspapers and magazines. He need not have worried that this "stuff" might be used against him, for the volume can only enhance his reputation.

Carlos Baker.
"His Beat Was The World."
New York Times Book Review,
May 28, 1967,
pp. 1, 16.

"I get around," Hemingway used to say, and it was a fact as well as a boast.

Over forty years he traveled on five continents. The American Red Cross paid passage on his first crossing in 1918. After that, editors of newspapers and magazines were glad to underwrite his globe-trotting in order to print articles with the Hemingway by-line.

Like a number of other previous American novelists, Hemingway was proud of his association with journalism. Altogether he wrote more than a million words for newspapers and magazines. Writing journalism helped him get around, all right; it also helped meet his need for personal publicity and it helped him find a way to say things that haunted his mind.

So this volume is a welcome addition to the list of posthumous books by Hemingway. Rescued from forgotten newspaper and magazine files, the pieces shine like gold coins still bearing the maker's stamp. After all the years, most are still mint-fresh with the author's personality and zest for living.

Here are the young reporter shivering with fever and crawling with lice on a rainy night in Adrianople; the hiker lunching on fried veal and apple pie in the Black Forest; the fisherman dropping a troutfly in the snow-fed Rhone Canal; the back-packer knee-deep in snow at the St. Bernard Pass; one of the boys at the Anglo-American Press Club in Paris. All these experiences and more became the stuff of articles that the folks back home in Canada or America were eager to read and to share the experiences vicariously. It was like that until he was sixty and had taken readers with him through hunts in Africa, wars in Spain,

France and Germany, fishing on the Gulf Stream and bullfighting at Malaga.

The difference between journalism and imaginative writing was not so great as Hemingway at times liked to believe. As editor William White notes, Hemingway's journalism was creative writing too. That helps explain why years afterward the pieces still make fresh and lively reading. To borrow Ezra Pound's phrase, it was news that stayed news. (Summary)

Philip Young. "Hemingway by Moonlight." *Bookweek*, 4 (May 28, 1967), 6-7.

It was a dirty trick on a fellow, this digging up his journalism. Or so in effect Hemingway wrote his first biographer, Louis H. Cohn, even though all the poor man wanted was to enter the titles on a list. Nobody had any business resurrecting that stuff, Hemingway went on, to put it in competition with what he had written for keeps.

Thirty-six years have passed since that little outburst, and behold. Most of what Hemingway wanted buried as he left it has conspicuously been exhumed by the very publishers whose prize author he was.

* * *

But the publishers, having brought out a book that is not going to do a thing to devalue anything else Hemingway ever wrote, are making perfectly good sense. . . . All that's needed is that those who read it should read it for what it is: writing that was at first the meal ticket, before long the moonlighting, of a man who really had a different job.

Hemingway was frequently uncomfortable in journalistic disguise. At times he appears to have taken the role as a way of getting in on the action. In the heat of fighting the Germans an American soldier asked a question for everyone: "What are you doing here if you don't have to be here?" The response, "Lots of Money," is not the answer nor was meant to be. But even in war, where for this writer the action so often was, he admitted that "sometimes it doesn't seem the right man in the right place. . . ."

Nevertheless, he was now and again a marvelous correspondent. After the sorcerer's apprenticeship during which, short of his 21st birthday, he began to turn out feature stories that are even now not particularly embarrassing, he became overnight quite as good as professional. Almost in spite of himself, then, and without the enormous pains he took with his fiction, he turned out good copy. If it was no less minor than he thought, it was certainly less ephemeral. That is what this book clearly establishes.

The evidence is in five parts, beginning with the Toronto newspaper stories, 1920-1924, which skip lightly from this continent to Paris, thence all about Europe clear to Constantinople.

Some political reporting is extraordinary for the precocious shrewdness of a writer who is supposed to have no politics. But our man abroad was just as concerned with cultivating hotels, fishing, bullfights, etc. And some of these preparatory pieces, shortly to mature in *The Sun Also Rises,* are already perfectly ripe in their own way. By Part Two, 1933-1939, practically everything has changed. An obscure cub has taken off into the trees. All of a sudden a famous man of letters is writing to *Esquire*—making, as it were, his first appearance in person. And at the apogee of his career. At least that's what we used to be told. Some serious folk were offended by all that big-game hunting and deep-sea fishing, during a depression, with a war on the way.

The truth of the matter is that Hemingway wrote some satisfactory things for *Esquire*. And they are here; often carrying pleasant shocks of recognition. For instance, there is the nugget out of which *The Old Man and the Sea* was much later fashioned. More important, *By-Line* offers a good opportunity to reconsider that bothersome business of the hairy chest. Not every reader is going to care so passionately as Hemingway if sailfish "tap a bait" or not. (Definitely not!) And surely he misfired in his "Notes on Dangerous Game," which is one of a few items that should probably have been excluded from the book. But a good deal of the fishing and hunting is so fresh and warm that even if one does not practice these sports it is not hard to find vicarious gratification in them. . . .

Dispatches for NANA, 1937-1938, on the war in Spain make up most of the third section. None of them measures up to "Old Man at the Bridge," which so far is the latest of Hemingway's stories to be elevated to the canon of his *Collected Short Stories*. But like the story several of these reports were cabled out of the battle for the Ebro Delta, and it is a tribute to them that they remind one of the story without suffering from the comparison. Part Four is war once more: analyses of the big picture in China (1941) for the late PM, close-ups in the European Theater for *Collier's* (1944). The Chinese dispatches display a hitherto unexploited talent for the clarification of large problems. Those from Europe begin with the long, tense, fouled-up day "we took Fox Green beach," continue through the liberation of Paris and beyond, and reveal that quick sharp eye for immediate problems for which Hemingway had long been famous.

Abruptly the last section begins (and ends) with life and Miss Mary in Cuba, but consists substantially of "The Christmas Gift," which some will recall reading years ago in *Look*. This long, rambling, really awful, but awfully funny, account of his two plane crashes in Africa has many curious features, among them a striking piece of self-analysis occasioned by the reading of his own obituaries. . . .

But the sense that a personality is writing—is nearly always present in his fiction, and even more so in his non-fiction, where little stands between reader and that distinctive self who has been so intensely interesting for better than four decades. In that sense *By-Line* makes interpreters of us all, and few will come away with preconceptions intact. Better late than never, one reader (this one, who seldom fishes and has never hunted) was startled to see, at rare moments, description of these activities become evocation and then suddenly revelation. Somehow one fails to respond properly to the bulls, but it is all at once clear on reading *By-Line* that taking the lives of fish and animals was for Hemingway an essentially aesthetic experience that brought emotions entirely comparable to those aroused by the experience of great painting or music. The "whirr of wings that moves you ... more than any love of country," the beauty of a great marlin, whose every jump was a sight to stop the heart, and at whose boating one is "purified," and welcome in the brotherhood of the "very elder gods," these things are not faked. The long, broad gap between Hemingway the sportsman and Hemingway the writer has closed for at least one of his students. This book doesn't often get outside the perimeters of its genre, and every bit of it is prose. But in many passages artist and man-outdoors are indivisible.

William Kennedy. "The Clear Heart of Reporter Hemingway." *National Observer*, 6 (May 29, 1967), 19.

"Newspaper work," Ernest Hemingway once told an interviewer, "will not harm a young writer and could help him if he gets out of it in time. ... Journalism, after a point has been reached, can be a daily self-destruction for a serious creative writer."

The attack on journalism by novelists is an old one, often valid. Each morning the reporter empties his head of yesterday's work; each story has its own set of ethics, often different from the reporter's and he must reflect them honestly. Also, and probably most important, the relentless, horizontal newness of everything becomes a force field against the ruminative, vertical thought essential to fiction.

Yet Hemingway wrote journalism for 40 years. Was he pulling our leg about its self-destructive qualities? Not at all, for he was never the conventional journalist, and in all but his early years he practiced the trade irregularly, mainly as a means to an interesting life or extra income.

* * *

But it was not the range of his subject matter that made Hemingway unconventional. Many journalists make much out of equally good material. Rather it was that even as a journalist Hemingway had what someone once called "a clear heart," which made for an almost instant point of view, and he put his personality, his tastes, even his prejudices into his articles. In the early years the story was refracted through Hemingway; in later years the story became a means of listening to the Hemingway mind.

And so most of his dispatches are still lively and readable, 20, 30, even 40 years later. They often take fictional form in terms of description, dialog, and narrative thread. They are vignettes, not news stories, though they tell the news.

* * *

The action, the scene, the detail of Hemingway's best fiction is present in his best journalism. When he tries to check in at a German inn in Bavaria in 1922 he pictures the German hostility to foreigners with a memorable, five-page vignette that reads like fiction. He is conveying the thing that made the German arrogance important to him; he is illustrating it, not talking about it. . . .

* * *

True, this journalism is not topdrawer Hemingway. But it is fascinating, for here in raw form are the bulls running in Pamplona's streets, the pseudo artists in Paris, the cowardly lion hunters, the old fisherman who loses his great catch to sharks, and much more that Hemingway transformed so magically into stories and novels.

"Prose is architecture, not interior decoration." he once said. As a jour-

nalist, he was just decorating the room. Later on he built his castles.

Melvin Maddocks. "Perishable Papa." *Christian Science Monitor,* June 1, 1967, p. 15.

It is too bad that the last impression of a writer nowadays is so often a posthumous scrapbook of fugitive pieces—souvenirs from the bottom drawer best left there. It is particularly unfortunate when the publication of a writer's worst work coincides with the critical devaluation of even his best.

The present selection of Hemingway's journalism (1920-1956) lays him wide open to all the familiar complaints of current anti-Hemingwayism. Here are 478 pages of exactly the Hemingway whom admirers would like to forget.

* * *

All life becomes a kind of backdrop against which "your correspondent" intrusively poses, like a guide standing in front of the painting he is commenting upon. The only people tolerated on the scene are those who know their place: the straight-men, the walk-ons, the Hemingway repertory stock players—hard cases with "a lot of style" who know better than to upstage the star. (One of the saddest things about the book is the recitation of the friends whose names occurred to Hemingway after one of his African smashups: Leonard Lyons, Toots Shor, Walter Winchell.)

As crammed with names as a gossip column, these pages exude a peculiar loneliness. As pasted with far-off destinations as travel luggage, they give off a panicked feeling of dead-end. A hollowness of heart, a sinking sense of purposelessness seem to lie just beneath the loudly confident swagger.

The good things—"Christmas in Paris," the tribute to Conrad, a few dispatches from Civil War Spain—stand out almost embarrassingly. It might have been kinder if they were not here. But they do serve to make the point: It is not his critics but Hemingway himself in top form who shows up Hemingway at his worst.

* * *

At his best, Hemingway silences both hostile critics and apologies. And surely he has now earned the privilege of all dead writers—to be reread only at his best.

New Yorker, 43
(June 3, 1967),
145-46.

Hemingway didn't think his journalism was worth reprinting: "No one has any right to dig this stuff up," he once said. But with recent publication of By-line: Ernest Hemingway, present readers have to ask again whether the "stuff" is worth reprinting. The verdict must be a modified yes: it is worth seeing again. The quality of his journalistic writing ran generally parallel to that of his fiction. With only a

few exceptions pieces written during the twenties and thirties for the Toronto Star and Esquire are quick, sharp and rich, with much of the same acuteness of vision and detail one finds in the early stories. But the World War II correspondence and the later more general pieces seem dated, loud and flat. (Summary)

Walter Havighurst.
"A Generous Sampling of
Journalism."
Chicago Sunday Tribune
Books Today, 4
(June 4, 1967),
1.

In "The Best Times" Dos Passos recalled Hemingway in Paris in the middle 1920s. "He was a moody kind of fellow even then. Sorry for himself. One of the things he got sorriest for himself about was not having been to college. I used to tell him he was damn lucky. Think of all the things he hadn't had to unlearn."

In those years Hemingway was educating himself. Europe was his university and newspaper writing was his discipline. While sending news dispatches he was learning languages and literatures, he was looking at the world and at himself and he was finding his way to his own kind of writing. Even as a reporter he shaped his material with his own feelings and imagination. . . .

* * *

His dispatches show a young reporter with a shrewd eye and a skeptical, independent mind. In 1923 the Lausanne conference met in a chateau "so ugly that it makes the Odd Fellows' Hall of Petoskey, Michigan, look like the Parthenon." There he took a hard look at the scowling Duce from Rome. "Mussolini," he wrote, "is the biggest bluff in Europe."

At 25 Hemingway could unmask political pretensions, and he could see the hollowness of generalities. "No history is written honestly. You have to keep in touch with it at the time, and you can depend on it just as much as you have actually seen and followed."

In the Milan winter he saw foxes, deer, pheasants, rabbits hanging frozen before the butcher shops, he saw cold troops wandering down the streets from the Christmas leave trains, and he heard a babel of voices in the cafes. Here are the perceptions and the feeling that would soon shape his stark short story, "In Another Country." His first bull fight was reported in 1923. "It is a good deal like grand opera for the really great matadors, except they run the chance of being killed every time they cannot hit high 'C.' " On that trip to Spain he saw the running of the bulls in Pamplona—and a reader has a fore-glimpse of "The Sun Also Rises."

* * *

This book is indispensable for any Hemingway fan.

Saul Maloff. "Farewell to Arms." *Newsweek,* 69 (June 5, 1967), 102.

These 77 pieces of Hemingway's journalistic writing show the muffled echo of a famous style struggling to find its destiny, and often failing.

Even as early as 1920 Hemingway could strike a pure, clarion tone in a description of a wilderness pool but could not sustain it for long. Two years later, in an account of refugees in Thrace, he found his great subject— men at war—and instinctively seized the bare, necessary images of earth and weather to convey a stark sense of chaos. By 1924 he was not only confident but beginning to be arrogant. He knew how he was, where he stood, what he could use to praise Joseph Conrad at the expense of T. S. Eliot.

This collection reflects the interests of a 40-year career and presents writing so wildly uneven that Hemingway's reputation would have been better served by a more rigorous selection. For his best writing was inevitably done when he was most involved with his subject: bullfighting, hunting and fishing, and chasing wars in Spain, China and Europe. Chasing wars was his consuming passion; he was drawn to them as some men are drawn to the scenes of their disasters. They were what he needed as much as what he dreaded.

But he was always the artist compelled by the knowledge of what he needed for his art, and though he was on assignment, he always took note of the crucial detail that could later become the germ of fiction. Part of the joy of the book then is glimpsing the sure promise of literary riches to come.

Later, though, some of the zest went out of the journalism as it went out of the art. Hemingway became too much the world figure, the jovial and gregarious "Papa" one-upping the generals on the road to Paris. The role didn't help his lonely art. If the war dispatches are any indication, prospects are not good for the big war novel he is supposed to have written. By 1945 he was almost depleted and had made his real farewell to arms a generation before. (Summary)

Stanley Kaufmann. "Before and After Papa." New Republic, 156 (June 10, 1967), 18, 35.

By-Line: Ernest Hemingway, a selection from the novelist's journalism, is likely to serve as evidence for whatever the reader wants to prove about Hemingway. For those who like him, it will show his education in seeing, hearing and recording his world and will provide glimpses into the sources of much of his fiction. Those who dislike him will find substantiation for the view that he was the perennial youth trying to believe that bullfighting and big game hunting were the emotional equivalents of war.

Both views may be true. Quite early in his career Hemingway became a public fool, a "character" in his own imagination, a scavenger on his former self. But he was also a genius, and it would be hard to justify averaging out his career like a sociological chart when what matters is his best work. When he was good, his work was epoch-making and exemplified a ruthless modernism toward which literature for the last century has been moving.

One tends to see in the early work portents of later qualities. This is true of the *Star* dispatches, for example, when in his 1923 article on bullfighting he could write, "It was very exciting, sitting out in front of a cafe your first day in Spain with a ticket in your pocket that meant that rain or shine you were going to see a bullfight in an hour and a half." It took calm nerve to write, "It was very exciting," coldly and baldly like that, and then go on with the rest of the sentence to build the effect of restrained joy. It seems common enough now, but that was before Hemingway had altered the stylistic taste of his time.

Much of his reporting was incisive too. His view of Mussolini playing dictator was unusually prescient. His articles on the Sino-Japanese war showed a knowledge of warfare, of Chinese problems and of the key importance of character. He read character acutely also in his account of the Genoa conference in 1922; the descriptions of statesmen's personalities are clearly and quickly cut.

At the same time, some of his travel writing now seems oddly dated. This may be the result of a shift in the world's experience more than of Hemingway's observations. Instead of accounts by the intrepid explorer of Mediterranean byways the modern reader looks for hints on what he can do next summer when he is there too.

The material basically divides into two kinds: that written before Hemingway was Papa and that afterwards. The first, written when Hemingway had made or was about to make the break with full-time journalism, had a family to support and an unrecognized style to forge, certifies the courage of such a decision. After 1933 his journalism is sad with the half-recognized knowledge that he was building the unattractive Papa character to keep his eyes off the vacancies inside him. Although he seemed to need wars to stimulate him to do his best work, his World War II reports, like his war novel *Across the River and Into the Trees,* marked the nadir of his work as correspondent and artist.

This view of Hemingway before and after he was Papa confirms the value of *A Moveable Feast.* The journalism he wrote in the twenties, at the time of his Parisian feast, underscores the daring of his decision to write powerfully and insouciantly without security. The later journalism emphasized the gap between the daring man and the arrived author. The pathos of *A Moveable Feast* is in the consciousness of that gap. The memoir shows he knew what had occurred; this collection shows it happening. (Summary)

Best Sellers, 27 (July 1, 1967), 148.

* * *

There is an interesting modification in the Hemingway style as he grows older. The first reports from Paris, for instance, have more vitality, less self-consciousness, more (shall we say) independent opinion than the later pieces. The war despatches, too, are vivid, sometimes even electric. The subjects range from fishing (trout, tuna, marlin), hunting, reporting the Geneva Conference, meeting and interviewing some of the great of the day (Ishmet Pasha, Mussolini, King George of Greece), Christmas in Paris and in a chalet in Switzerland. The book will probably sell on Hemingway's reputation and, perhaps, as a volume of nostalgia for the above fifty reader. For journalism classes it should be required reading.

Edward Weeks. " 'Captain' Hemingway." *Atlantic,* 220 (July 1967), 109-10.

Ernest Hemingway was a good journalist and knew how to use his correspondent's credentials to get where he wanted to be. But once on the spot, he knew how to put himself in command of a situation and could see how to embellish reality to make a good story even better. His war reports from the Spanish Civil War, for example, have not only their admirably terse factuality but also a sense of pity and a foreboding of defeat.

His was an uneven record though. He was at his most appealing in accounts of fishing for marlin in Cuba or for trout in Europe, in reports on the Spanish War, and in descriptions of how the army broke through the Siegfried Line. At times like those he wrote with a toughness that came from his identification with and love for the fighting man. That he sometimes went beyond the conventions governing correspondents explains how to his readers as well as to the French partisans he was "Captain" Hemingway. He was not always equally persuasive, however. His accounts of killing the larger animals in East Africa are somehow distasteful, and when as self-appointed commander of the situation he tells the veteran landing craft lieutenant where to put in on Fox Green Beach, it is hard to believe it happened that way. (Summary)

David Cort.
Commonweal, 86
(August 11, 1967),
499-500.

Since Hemingway's suicide has prompted a sad re-assessment of his character and purposes, one wonders whether his beneficiaries might have better hesitated over publication of his weaker output. The effect of such a collection of journalism as we have here is likely to devalue the other assets of the estate, except for *The Sun Also Rises* and some stories. The journalism risks revealing too much about the man.

There may be advantages to young writers, though, in seeing Hemingway's progress as a writer opened to scrutiny. His blunders and successes with the language may be far more instructive than all his aphorisms on the art. His bleakly hack early pieces may furnish some small comfort to the tyro, whatever twinges they might bring to Hemingway in being brought back to view. But Hemingway soon gained confidence, his eyes began to clear, and in his savage sketches of the Swiss, Germans, Paris Bohemians and Genoese Communists he became the writer learning what he had to do, or die. He discovered the magic of honesty and with new vision saw doctrinaire men as men while their doctrines faded.

In his search for the action, Hemingway habitually turned outside himself rather than to his own ego and gathered as friends celebrities like Toots Shor, who debased him. That is one of the sad things the book shows so clearly. Still, in his early days he was a connoisseur on where the action was—Ataturk's Constantinople, Mussolini's Italy, the bulls in Spain. By the thirties he was no longer the ominous nobody looking level at the world but the Big Man writing for *Esquire* sort of as a favor and then for NANA and *PM*, calling the shots on war in Europe and the Pacific. Between the time of his forecasts in the late thirties and early forties and the time of his reports on the American invasion of Nazi France, the world had turned itself around. His pieces on the new Americans in Europe showed the best of his talents as journalist coming together at once. After the war his African pieces showed a return to ponderous irony, coy boasting and a tendency to write private jokes in a kind of code language.

Yet for all the reservations noted, the book, particularly in light of the current state of publishing, has rewards for the reader. (Summary)

Bruce Cook.
"Why Not Send What's-his-name?"
Critic, 26 (August-September 1967), 75-76.

By now one of the truisms of critics most consistently misunderstood is the relationship between a writer's journalism and his "real" work. As critics would have it, journalism prevents the writer from doing his serious work or at best serves only as a source of peculiar situations and colorful characters for his fiction. Time, they say, is what a writer needs to produce a work of art, and journalism takes time. But we need only look at the proliferation of academic novels by writers who chose the flight to ivy halls instead of journalism to see the awful truth about the relationship of time to quality. Remember, too, that Stendhal wrote *The Charterhouse of Parma* in six weeks.

Browsing through this collection of newspaper and magazine articles written by Ernest Hemingway over four decades will remind us again of the part played by journalism in the writer's biography. Hemingway quit the Toronto *Star* just in time, we have learned from Charles Fenton's *The Apprenticeship of Ernest Hemingway*. But in less than ten years he had done most of his best work, from *In Our Time* to *Winner Take Nothing*. With his return to journalism in 1933 for *Esquire*, so the critical scheme goes, he began his decline as a writer in favor of Papa the celebrity. But his North American Newspaper Alliance dispatches on the Spanish civil war were much better. He worked close to his subject, kept the wisecracks and expert opinion at a minimum while he described the Loyalist collapse. The rhythm, syntax and diction of these dispatches were equal to those of the short stories written a few years before. Then again there was the swing to his worst in the Guntheresque pieces of big-picture journalism for *PM* on China.

What the collection shows is that in his tough, laconic articles for the Toronto *Star* Hemingway was perfecting *the* new prose style for his newspaper readers at the same time he was perfecting it in short stories for readers of the old *Transatlantic Review*. For him journalism was not more virulent than any other kinds of writing. It is the *man* who does the writing and he cannot hide his difficulty in writing by turning away from novels to do a bunch of magazine pieces. The faults of the man show up in the writing, whatever it may be—short stories, news articles, magazine pieces or novels. Finally, it is all simply writing. (Summary)

Bernard S. Oldsey. "Always Personal." *Journal of General Education*, 19 (October 1967), 239-43.

* * *

Critics and scholars are going to read this collection by playing the game of which pieces gave rise to which short stories and which sections of the novels. Journalists are going to read it and find just how sharp, sometimes stinging, sometimes comic a roving reporter could be. Sportsmen will have a field day with the expected accounts of fishing, hunting, skiing, hiking, lugeing, and bull fighting.

There is, as blurb writers love to say, something here for everybody. Political types, who may remember that Hemingway once gave up on politics by claiming they were "too hard to do," will be surprised at his understanding of pacts, alliances, and geopolitics, as well as Greek kings, Russian diplomats, Chinese war lords, and assorted dictators. . . .

Maybe, though, the literary historians and educators have the subtlest lesson to learn from this book, because Hemingway was a graduate of what used to be known as the poor boy's college, that of printer's ink and public press.

The honor roll of American journalism includes such distinguished alumni as Ben Franklin, Walt Whitman, Mark Twain, Bret Harte, William Dean Howells, Ambrose Bierce, Harold Fredric, Stephen Crane, Theodore Dreiser, Ring Lardner, John O'Hara, William Faulkner (from the Sunday supplement and sketch division), and Ernest Hemingway. So many of our writers of fiction started this way that we could divide most of them into two large groups, the "reporters" and the "collegians." Reporting was not a bad way to get an education in a day before novelists became standard university products and appendages. It placed fact before fiction and life before symbol.

This is not to say that everything was just fine back in the good old days of journalistic upbringing. A check back to the reporters (as opposed, say, to the likes of Saul Bellow, John Updike, John Hawkes, and John Barth) reinforces the impression of intellectual flatness, reveals the insecurities of the partially educated, and points up their need to write experientially toward some kind of transcending lift.

* * *

How Ernest Hemingway achieved his own lift from journalism to literature is part of what we can learn from this collection, neatly and unobtrusively edited by William White, professor of journalism at Wayne State. White has selected 77 articles, representing about a third of Hemingway's identifiable journalism.

* * *

Moreover, if you read closely from beginning to end, you get some idea of how Hemingway's style started fresh, gained in almost lyric compression, staggered in self-parody, and then came back to the exact and piercing thing made of it in *A Moveable Feast* —which is probably a collaboration of the young man who made the observations in the twenties and the old man who brought them firmly together when he himself was going to pieces in the fifties and sixties. . . .

Perhaps what is most noticeable in the reporting is that it is always personal—freshly and humorously in the earliest pieces, more knowingly and self-seekingly in the later ones. The Toronto *Star* paid half a cent a word for the fresh, punchy stuff. It is quite a bit different from what we got later under the demandingly compressed style of the fiction.

* * *

The NANA stuff is very good, very precise and often evocative. One dispatch takes the reader to an irrigation ditch in the Ebro delta, where boys who will become men in a day quietly await the assault on Tortosa, amid "this year's crop of frogs" and the as yet undisturbed spring onions. This piece and "A Program for U.S. Realism," a war college kind of analysis done for *Ken*, gave us the big and little picture of war.

Of the World War II account, the one done for *Collier's* called "Voyage to Victory" is excellent. Hemingway gave fictional treatment to actuality long before Truman Capote thought of it, earlier in *Green Hills,* and here again in this attempt to show what it was like to come ashore on D-Day, June, 1944, in one LCV(P). Journalist and fiction writer collaborated in this arti-

cle to produce as good a piece of combat writing as we have had.

* * *

To understand how Hemingway transcended journalism and yet made it part of his artistic intent, we need simply read this advice of his to an aspiring writer ("Monologue to the Maestro," *Esquire*, Oct., 1935): "The more [the writer] learns from experience the more truly he can imagine. If he gets so he can imagine truly enough people will think that the things he relates all really happened and that he is just reporting."

Calder M. Pickett. *Journalism Quarterly*, Autumn 1967, pp. 579-80.

Back in the early forties as some of us aspired to literary greatness we always looked to the shining name of Ernest Hemingway. The name doesn't shine today the way it used to, especially among American literature people, and this book of uneven writing may be one reason why that's so.

I stress the "uneven." It's a book that is extremely absorbing, sometimes exciting, sometimes embarrassing. Anybody in journalism should read it, but don't expect to find out what separates journalistic man from literary man. Some of the journalism reads like literature, and Hemingway, as he got older (like Sinclair Lewis or Dos Passos), slipped a lot.

* * *

Except for some of that early writing Hemingway did on the Kansas City *Star* (which up until recent years seldom honored its city staff with by-lines), this is a representation of the great man's journalistic writings, from Toronto days up to the rickety stuff he wrote from Africa in the fifties.

Literary people are tagging him a "primitive" (which isn't as complimentary among literary people as it is among the *artistes*). Right from the start he was a primitive. Fishing and wild animal stuff, even when a young man for the Toronto *Star*.

Some of us will have our students digging into this book for one reason or another, and we'll find some revealing things. . . .

There is some fine reading in the forepart of this book, and you ought to have the book on your shelf in any case.

* * *

E. R. Hagemann. "By-Line E. H." *American Book Collector*, 18 (Summer 1968), 6.

All of us know Joseph Conrad's famous statement in his "Preface" to *The Nigger of the Narcissus*: "My task which I am trying to achieve is, by the power of the written word to make you hear, to make you feel—it is, before all, to make you *see*. That—and no more, and it is everything."

It is "everything" in fiction and Ernest Hemingway achieved this "task" beyond all cavil in his novels and stories. Now *By-Line*, a generous sampling of his journalism from 1920 to 1956, intelligently edited by Professor William White, Wayne State University (Detroit), reminds us forcibly that Hemingway for a good part of his life also achieved this task as a first-rate working reporter and correspondent. One recalls that Stephen Crane did the same thing with equal skill and aplomb in his war dispatches in the Spanish-American War and Graeco-Turkish War, as well as the New York City sketches.

* * *

These 77 dispatches in *By-Line*, many of them still fresh and valid even in 1968, written in that now so-famous style which one wit once described as a "Scotchman's telegram," differ astonishingly, say, from the lamentable prolix, long-winded, loud-mouthed, "I-am-always-right" *New Yorker-Esquire-New York Review* crowd.

* * *

I just want to mention for citations of some kind his Spanish Civil War dispatches, wherein politics is at an absolute minimum, and his marvelous account of D-Day, 6 June 1944, when he hit Fox Green Beach with the U.S. Army, which catches the confusion and the bravery, all told in a flat, emotionless voice. I want to mention, too, "The Christmas Gift" (For *Look* in 1954) which relates his near-death in two plane crashes in Africa and which is very funny and very serious. I want to point to "Monologue to the Maestro" (*Esquire*, 1935) in which Hemingway discusses writing. This piece has been too long overlooked.

I mention these pieces (not forgetting the others and once again acknowledging Professor White's editing skill) because they all tell us, only too truly, what we lost so tragically on 2 July 1961, in, of all places, Idaho.

Checklist of Additional Reviews

Kirkus, 35 (March 15, 1967), 374.

Booklist, 63 (July 1, 1967), 1126.

G. E. LaRocque. *English Journal*, 56 (November 1967), 1216-17.

Social Education, 31 (November 1967), 655.

American Literature, 39 (January 1968), 591.

H. H. Waggoner. "Hemingway and Faulkner: 'The End of Something.' " *Southern Review,* 4 (Spring 1968), 458-66.

Publishers' Weekly, 193 (June 24, 1968), 69.

Clarence Petersen. *Book World*, 2 (July 21, 1968), 13.

Notes

The
Fifth Column

and Four Stories
of the Spanish Civil War

ERNEST HEMINGWAY

CHARLES SCRIBNER'S SONS · NEW YORK

The Fifth Column
and Four Stories
of the Spanish Civil War

Kenneth Paul.
"Vintage Hemingway."
Newsweek, 74
(September 8, 1969),
88.

The Loyalist cause in Spain was a magnet for liberals and radicals from Europe and America during the late thirties. Hemingway was drawn there as fervently as was Robert Jordan in "For Whom the Bell Tolls," and like his hero found the war a mix of hope, cynicism, distrust and apprehension. Now thirty years later, with the Hemingway ethic under question and Carlos Baker's biography on the best-seller lists, Scribner's has collected the play and four stories Hemingway wrote while present at the debacle. They are still a sometimes forceful statement of the emotional tensions and moral dilemmas spawned by that war.

An unresolved period piece, "The Fifth Column" now seems talky and shallow, its quirky dialogue less dramatic than that of the stories. The lovers Philip Rawlings and Dorothy Bridges are at best rollicking Hemingway clichés. But among the stories "Night Before Battle" stands out as vintage Hemingway; its staccato, wine-blurred talk approaches poetry as it marvels at the war down at the end of the street. Beneath the bravado in the stories, light-headed fear bubbles, especially in "The Butterfly and the Tank," which uses the two images as metaphors of the soldiers' distracted gaiety and taut seriousness in the unorthodox war. What Hemingway saw in the rear guard as at the front convinced him that all the kinds of escape —work, sex, alcohol, nostalgia—do little to brighten a world less diminished than completed by death. (Summary)

Carlos Baker.
"The Fifth Column and
Four Stories of the
Spanish Civil War."
Saturday Review, 52
(September 20, 1969),
36-37.

* * *

Except for fulfilling Hemingway's prediction about wars, the years have not been kind to *The Fifth Column*. Its level of credibility now approximates that of *The Mark of Zorro*—to which, oddly enough, it bears some other resemblances.

With the stories, however, we enter another realm. Hemingway garnered the materials for them while he was working on *The Spanish Earth* with Joris Ivens and John Ferno in and around Madrid in the spring of 1937. Between bouts of assisting the filmakers he continued to report the progress of the war for NANA. At the same time, as was his invariable custom, he concentrated on keeping his eyes, his ears, and his literary sensibilities alert for people and situations that were in his judgment too good to waste on newspaper dispatches, that might indeed provide the material for genuine works of art.

The four stories from this period that he considered worthy of survival are "Night Before Battle," "Under the Ridge," "The Denunciation," and "The Butterfly and the Tank." Read as a series they provide an interesting test case for one of Hemingway's favorite public statements about the art of fiction: that if a writer merely reported on an incident he had personally experienced, his work would be flat; only "invented" stories could achieve the requisite roundness and depth. But "invention" for Hemingway never meant abnegation of the actual; he would have agreed with Wallace Steven's dictum that "the real is only the base, but it is the base." With Hemingway invention was largely an architectonic process—the reconstituting of the original elements to form a new superstructure reared on the foundations of the actual.

The least "inventive" story in this group, "Night Before Battle," is also the longest. . . . The story turns upon Edwin Henry's attempts to cheer up Al Wagner, an American Communist tank officer who must renew the attack against Rebel positions next day. It is a good story, incorporating an astonishing amount of information about the life of foreigners in wartime Madrid while achieving unity by keeping Wagner and his problems in central focus.

What especially distinguishes "Under the Ridge" and "The Denunciation" is Hemingway's skill at synecdoche, the art of suggesting the universal by means of the particular. "Under the Ridge," based on one of his photographic expeditions with Ivens and Ferno into the hilly Jarama sector, concerns the fierce resentment of a Loyalist soldier from Badajoz against the cold-eyed "discipline" of a pair of Russian battle police, who execute a deserter with no more compunction than they would have about shooting a rabbit. The ridge of the title becomes in effect a line of demarcation between the native Spaniards and the "foreigners," and the story subtly dramatizes the essential conflict between these two groups in the Loyalist ranks.

In "The Denunciation" a waiter at Chicote's denounces to Seguridad headquarters a devil-may-care customer whom he recognizes as a Fascist spy. A frequent visitor in Spain, Hemingway had many friends on both sides and was constantly struck by the ironies of civil war, particularly that one which turned people he had admired into enemies. . . .

Hemingway's powers of invention were memorably engaged by an incident he knew only from heresay. A light-hearted civilian named Pedro who was squirting waiters at Chicote's with eau de cologne from a flit gun was first beaten and then murdered by three humorless, trigger-happy soldiers. The story struck Hemingway so forcibly that he told it twice—rather lamely in the first act of *The Fifth Column*, and at length in "The Butterfly and the Tank," which John Steinbeck told Hemingway was one of the best short stories of all time: merely to have *seen* it as a story was an act of triumph; to have written it so superbly was "almost too much." Hemingway's skill in developing metaphors from the circumstances of his narrative was one of the hallmarks of his genius. Here, as Steinbeck undoubtedly recognized, the basic metaphor is evolved unerringly from a matrix of invented or observed particulars, raising the story well above the level of mere reportage, even if not to the height at which Steinbeck rated it.

The appearance in book form of these four stories ought to add appreciably to our sense of Hemingway's future as a writer of short fiction. It is our misfortune that he never made good on his original plan to write *The Fifth Column* as a short novel rather than as a play. As fiction, it might have succeeded; as drama, it unhappily does not.

Philip Young.
"The Fifth Column."
New York Times Book Review,
September 21, 1969,
p. 6.

There was a time when Hemingway had doubts about this play and these four stories. He complained that the stories "wouldn't come" and said he was tempted to name the play "The Four-Ninety-Five Column Marked Down From Five." He wished he had used the material of the play for a novel, though his original intention to make it a shorter piece of fiction was a better idea. Despite his doubts, it is good to have these stories of the Last Great Cause in book form, even some three decades after their original publication.

Hemingway's presence dominates the stories and gives the book its sharp distinction. The author never appears undisguised but the leading characters of all the pieces owe much to the writer's sense of identity with them. The narrator Edwin Henry is, of course, E. H. Philip Rawlings' adventures in counterespionage are wishful invention. In the other stories the fictional experience is close to the actual. The difference between this autobiographical fiction and the autobiographical journalism of the Spanish Civil War reports lies more in quality than in kind. Although in theory Hemingway distinguished between his journalism and his fiction written for the record, the distinction in practice was mainly that the fiction was done with more care.

"The Denunciation" shifts from an ostensible feature story on Chicote's bar to a genuine fictional incident when it picks up the espionage interest. "The Butterfly and the Tank," like "Night Before Battle" and "Under the Ridge," raises the question whether it is completely written. With all the talk in the story about the need to write a story based on the observed experience of the narrator, it seems more like a plan for a story than a story itself. It may be, though, that Hemingway found a different way to tell a tale. John Steinbeck thought "The Butterfly and the Tank" one of the "very few finest stories" ever written. Grim, lively, even at times funny, the stories are deft and absorbing enough to stay with the reader.

"The Fifth Column" is something of an autobiographical drama and suffers from not being recollected in tranquillity. Written in the Hotel Florida in Madrid while the city was being shelled daily, the play makes it seem as if the author were living on stage, and that's an impossible place to write. Still, he gets good comic mileage out of the speech of the hotel manager and others for whom English is not the native idiom. Even the horseplay is amusing. But the impact of the play depends on the reader's belief in the hero's romantic political convictions: Philip Rawlings renounces Dorothy for the cause. Hemingway's identity with his heroes and his marrying Dorothy's real life counterpart make us believe otherwise.

What he is trying to tell us through Philip, though, is about the things that would break our hearts because of the hell of war. If his stories don't quite break our hearts, they reach deep enough to touch them. (Summary)

Stephen Spender. "Writers and Revolutionaries: The Spanish War." *New York Review of Books,* 13 (September 25, 1969), 3-7.

The events of the thirties have the curious quality of being sufficiently remote enough to seem "historic" and of being sufficiently near to be discussed by some who participated in them. To others the parallels between the moral-political issues of that decade and this seem instructive on the need to commit themselves to causes. Writers who went to Spain submitted to the test by terror there, even at the risk of being destroyed in the test.

Although Ernest Hemingway went to Spain with the declared intention of writing about the war, he did not have to submit to the test of terror as ultimate reality. His qualifications as expert on the horrors of war were already public knowledge. The test in Spain for him was Whether He Was Still Up To It. The question was probably of greater interest to himself than to others, but in any case, he passed easily.

Part of Hemingway's view of war was the conviction that people who go to war should not complain about what they find there. He quarreled with Dos Passos in Spain for being outraged because one of his friends was shot as a spy. In "The Denunciation" Hemingway as a thinly disguised narrator who is also a well-known writer seems to take responsibility for getting someone shot. His moral seems to be that in a war one yields up his friends to the secret police to be shot without demanding the niceties of a trial. The writer's "evidence" is all surmise and circumstance and guilt by association. After the denunciation the writer calls the secret police and asks that the friend be told it was the writer, not a waiter at Chicote's, who denounced him. He wants the friend not to be bitter or disillusioned about the waiters before he dies. The conceited smugness of the ending makes it one of the most morally repugnant stories ever written.

But when in "Under the Ridge" Hemingway uses his experience and imagination instead of preaching toughness, he gets at truth without moralizing. His story of the Frenchman who had simply seen enough and walked away from battle avoids the hideous inverted sentimentality of "The Denunciation" and moves to deep imaginative insight. (Summary)

Eugene McNamara. *America*, 121 (October 18, 1969), 333.

Since Hotchner's depiction of "Papa" Hemingway, too much has been made of the real, true presence of Hemingway in his work. Looking again at *The Fifth Column*, one finds it tempting to read Hemingway for Philip Rawlings in the swaggering hero's role. But whatever his life was, Hemingway's work was fiction and it has to be judged on that ground.

Readers can first of all be thankful that Hemingway did not pursue a career as dramatist. The play comes off as a self-parodying romantic melodrama, complete with all the stock stage props of sandbagged windows, maps with pins on them, off-stage explosions and reckless drinking. Only things missing are a Colonel Blimp and Vera Lynn singing "We'll Meet Again." More seriously, Hemingway seems uncertain whether he is writing comedy or social comment. The play probably would not have made it in the thirties and is less likely to do so today. Even Hemingway finally recognized that, and the play is interesting now only as a curio of the decade.

The best thing about the play is how it sets off the stories. "The Butterfly and the Tank" subtly interweaves the war story with the writer's problem of turning ordinary reality into enduring fictional art. It does so with immediacy and irony and deftly handled characters and setting. "Under the Ridge," probably the best of the four stories collected here, tells without self-consciousness of the tangled political motives in war and of the bitterness of the Spanish people, victimized, used for larger, cynical purposes, but rising above their normal limitations. Such stories, with all their tightness and control, gain appreciably from being put in unwilling proximity to *The Fifth Column*. (Summary)

John W. Hughes. "Age of the Emotive Man." *New Leader*, 52 (November 24, 1969), 19-20.

Like some back-trailing conquistador, Ernest Hemingway marched through the literature of the Old World, selecting from its valuables and fusing them with his own exotic experience. Especially he took pains to learn about the gold in irony he took from Flaubert and Turgenev. Yet the end of his wanderings was a return to the American heartland and his tragic sensibility was never able to extend beyond the personal. Though he might adorn his authorial vision with the forms and techniques of the European ironists, it remained basically non-European, primitive, and even solipsistic. The emotional logic of Western literary traditions remained alien to him.

The Spanish Civil War served as a spiritual barometer for Hemingway's art and character. In *The Sun Also Rises* he had been able to avoid sexual-emotional commitment to the deca-

dent Europe embodied in Lady Brett through Jake's castration. In his play of the Spanish war, *The Fifth Column,* Philip Rawlings renounces the pleasantly bitchy heroine Dorothy, not because he is a castrate like Jake but because he had devoted himself, however offhandedly, to the Communist cause. Though Communism serves as a way to get rid of another mistress, Dorothy's bourgeois tendencies, like Eliot's politics, do not matter. In Spain the cause was a matter of emotions, not reason, and Hemingway's heroes, like a whole generation of English poets following Auden's Spanish war poems, left rational thought to the commissars. Hemingway's romantic attachment to the cause becomes clear in his portrayal of Dorothy; he subscribed to what George Orwell would call emotional Stalinism.

The emotive men, the romantics and the emotional Stalinists neglected the larger realities of the war and left them to be handled by the bureaucrats. As a result, *The Fifth Column*, though good reading, demonstrates the moral and political vascillation of withdrawal from rational thought. At the same time, the play provides a useful introduction to the short stories gathered here. Hemingway's impressionistic journalism enabled him to capture the mysterious selfhood of a person or thing. At times he lost the overall effect of a scene through concentrating too much on what Hopkins called the "inscape." In only a few scenes was he able to fuse the inner and outer realities of character and larger perspective. "Under the Ridge," one of his all-too-infrequent best, shows him surmounting his irony and cynicism to sympathize with the victims of human tragedy. But his callous detachment, the real badge of the emotive man, intrudes in "The Butterfly and the Tank." By the end of the story the thoughtless murder of a civilian by soldiers is lost in the complications of Hemingway's ironic techniques. The two other stories suffer the same fate. In trying to express tragic emotions through ironic perspective, Hemingway leaves himself open to being misunderstood. (Summary)

John Hollander. "Books in Brief: Fiction." *Harper's*, 239 (December 1969), 146.

Of all the Hemingway material to be posthumously unveiled, short stories dating from before World War II would surely be the most welcome. This awkward volume brings together four previously uncollected stories mostly set in Madrid during the siege, with *The Fifth Column*, Hemingway's play set in the same scene. This last is already familiar to us through inclusion in the canonical old Modern Library Giant edition of forty-nine short stories (until Scribners removed it, for undisclosed reasons when they took over the collected stories reprint again in the Fifties). These four stories are all a bit long-winded; they are neither of the genre of the World War I sketches nor of, say, "Hills Like White Elephants," with its almost visionary anti-

cipation of contemporary Italian cinematic exposition. They propound a world of desperation, military blunders, a senseless slaying of a civilian in a café, the necessary dirtiness of turning in a spy, and the crippling aspect of the International presence on the Loyalist side. Within that world, familiar Hemingwayan acts of grace occur, in a kind of low-keyed way, and the genuine people are mostly being hurt. The Spaniards all speak the patented Hemingway dialect, no contractions and *muy formal*. But the stories are authentic enough, and are quite better than the worst of those in the collected volume. It only seems a pity that these were not included in it, instead of appearing in this somewhat artificial format. "The Denunciation," "The Butterfly and the Tank," "Night Before Battle," and "Under the Ridge" together take up 62 pages. In any event, once the publishers were committed to such a presentation, they might at least have included a note on the publishing history of its contents.

Checklist of Additional Reviews

Publishers Weekly, 196 (July 14, 1969), 164.

Kirkus, 37 (August 1, 1969), 797, 866.

Bert C. Bach. *Library Journal*, 94 (September 15, 1969), 3083.

M. Thomas Inge. "Not Quite Vintage Hemingway." Nashville *Tennessean*, September 21, 1969, p. 9-R; Richmond *Times-Dispatch*, September 28, 1969, p. F-5.

Booklist. 66 (November 15, 1969),
· 377.

Richard Sale. *Hudson Review,* 22
(Winter 1969-1970), 709.

Choice, 7 (July 1970), 685.

Best Sellers, 30 (October 15, 1970),
295.

Saturday Review, 55 (April 29, 1972),
74.

Notes

ISLANDS IN THE STREAM

Ernest Hemingway

New York

CHARLES SCRIBNER'S SONS

Islands in the Stream

Charles W. Mann, Jr.
"Once Again the Familiar
Hemingway Is With Us."
Library Journal, 95
(September 1, 1970),
2827.

In this long-awaited posthumous novel divided into three sections, the Bimini portion is a fishing idyll of prewar life, alive with all the fervor and deceptive simplicity we associate with Hemingway. Once again strong, careful men, thoroughly at home with the difficult task of game fishing, pass their days in hesitant and careful talk about life and art, and at night indulge in a faint dissipation which they wash clean each dawn in the fresh coolness of the Gulf Stream. Readers will find this first section fine and familiar ground. The dialogue and the intensely felt images of sea and sky display a practiced mastery. The crux is in the performance of a delicate rite in which a painter named Thomas Hudson comes to terms with his three young sons by two marriages. A sense of loss is aching and real between each word, and it is no surprise that all the sons are dead before the middle section is underway. The protagonist from that point is a hollow man, and the book almost takes on the same characteristic. But the central section of drink and daydream in Cuba, an essay in sodden, lonely misery, is succeeded by a taut, structured pursuit of survivors of a sunken German submarine. Again familiar territory in which a mixed crew of flawed men with a strong leader painstakingly and superbly perform a dirty job.

Those who wish to can find flaws, can complain that the three divisions are not perfectly wed, that some of the scenes verge on self-parody, that a blonde ex-wife is all Dietrich, "complete with handles," as Hemingway sometimes would say, and that Thomas Hudson is more often Ernest Hemingway than a painter. But they would be wrong. This is a big, impressive, and haunting book; it may not be the masterpiece we wanted, but the peculiar world of Hemingway is much with us in these pages. The novel is certain to be in demand in all libraries, and it deserves many readers.

Christopher Lehmann-Haupt.
"The Case of the Missing Annotations."
New York Times,
September 30, 1970,
p. 45.

Despite all inclinations to believe in miracles (Hemingway Back From the Dead with Lyre intact and Manuscript in Hand!), it is hard to approach "Islands in the Stream" with serious expectations. It was written during the time (around 1950) when Hemingway's fires as a fiction writer were dying (only "The Old Man and the Sea" would be pulled from the embers). The author himself did not think "Islands" nearly ready for publication, as can be inferred from Carlos Baker's recent biography. So its appearance now has the smell of exploitation about it, and one approaches it with all the doubts one brings to newly discovered plays by Eugene O'Neill or new formulas for turning lead to gold. One's fears are confirmed by reading it. Oh, there are pleasant things to be said for the book. There is a superbly controlled description of a deep-sea fishing expedition. There are some good reminiscent passages on the old days in Paris. There are amusing moments of he-manly horseplay and a genuinely delightful exchange between the novel's painter-hero and his favorite bartender in which subjects for epic paintings are dreamed up. And it's good in a nostalgic sort of way to

re-encounter the old Hemingway humbug—the yearning for the truly good and fine and beautiful and true, the strong, if fatuous, sense of honor, and the sanctification, through loving detail, of food and drink (even Coca-Cola gets it here).

But otherwise, "Islands in the Stream" proceeds from fair to bad to worse to horrible, and I wouldn't wish it onto anyone's fall reading list. The first and by far the best section, "Bimini," in which Thomas Hudson is visited at his island retreat by his three sons, has something of the old Hemingway polish and control. But even "Bimini" is tainted by excesses of sentiment, mannered dialogue.... ("There's a lot of wickeds at large. Really bads.... You know evil is a hell of a thing. Tommy. And it's smart as a pig."), and a pervasive tone of pity for its Hemingway-surrogate hero....

And after "Bimini," all semblance of finished work vanishes ... "At Sea," in which Hudson and his cronies chase and kill a U-boat crew, is simply dull and embarrassing and should have been led out behind the stable and destroyed.

So what we have in "Islands in the Stream" is the first or second draft of a novel in which Hemingway had not yet decided who, besides Thomas Hudson, was to star, which of Hudson's sons was to die (in "Bimini" it is the two younger ones; in "Cuba" and "At Sea" it is the oldest one), or what the themes and issues were to be. As an example of Hemingway's fictional art, it should simply not have been published.

Yet to read it against the background of Hemingway's life is not without interest. To learn how he selected, rearranged and transmuted actual incidents and people from his experience; to consider how an actual unfounded rumor of the death of one of his sons in action preoccupied him and how he had not yet discovered how to dramatize its effects artistically; to observe how he splits himself into two characters, the painter Thomas Hudson and his writer friend, and then to watch him comparing the two media; to know finally that "The Old Man and the Sea" was written during the same period (and was, it is suspected by scholars, first intended to be part of "Islands") and then to compare the two works—all this is most useful to understanding both Hemingway's life and his art.

"Islands in the Stream" is a failure (if one may pronounce judgment on so crude a draft) because its author had not yet found any universal meaning in the still-private experience it records. Yet it remains interesting to see how he recorded that experience, how self-dramatization was the first crude step in Hemingway's creative process, how almost adolescent day-dreaming was his first gesture toward art.

No surprise, all this, and hardly peculiar to Hemingway. But it provides the semblance of an excuse for the publication of "Islands." And it also makes one wish that the book had been published as an annotated edition. For if it had been, one would not have needed to draw on memory and skip around in Carlos Baker's volume to justify the time it took to read this very unmiraculous posthumous publication.

Robie Macauley. "100-Proof Old Ernest, Most of It Anyway." *New York Times Book Review,* October 4, 1970, pp. 1, 51.

Back in 1924 Ernest Hemingway wrote on the occasion of Joseph Conrad's death how he had saved up his Conrad to read when he was sick of writing. And then when Conrad died, the young writer felt, after reading all of "The Rover" in one night, that he had used up his Conrad like a drunkard, like a young man who had wasted his patrimony. That was the feeling too of most Hemingway admirers when news of the suicide came: now there would be no more stories. But it has turned out that Hemingway left quite a few unopened bottles of potent stuff.

Confirmed Hemingway drinkers probably would have settled for any small beer remaining, but "Islands in the Stream," with its blend of strong narrative and reflective melancholy, is 100-proof Old Ernest, most of it. Even though the book probably had been stowed away for further aging, it is a complete, well-rounded novel and among his very best.

One possible reason why Hemingway delayed publishing the novel is the slow pacing of the first two sections. "Bimini," the first, has a leisurely plenitude of incident and conversation founded on almost total recall by the author's alter ego, Thomas Hudson. This is different from Hemingway's classic strategy of telling the reader less than he wants to know and making him work for the rest of it. Now we sometimes know more than we want to. But Hudson is fully realized both as painter and man. That rare thing in literature, a believable artist, Hudson generally falls short of the heroic effort we want of him as a man. The tension of this verging on failure, however, provides much of the enduring interest of this first section. That struggle with failure is climactically dramatized in the long fight of David Hudson, the painter's younger son, with the giant swordfish. After a day's battle he loses the catch but has passed through the manhood-by-trial scene and we are emotionally, if not circumstantially, ready for his death in an auto accident. The boy who has become a man is dead.

In the second section, "Cuba," Thomas Hudson draws on the strategy of Nick Adams in "Big Two-Hearted River." Told that his son Tom has been killed in the war, Hudson forces himself into painful concentration on minor actions to guard against the enveloping pain. As in the first section, though, the long, wandering conversations at the Floridita bar and the interior monologues show a lack of pacing.

The third and finest section, "At Sea" moves from desperate inaction to a long, tense stalk of the German submarine crew along the Cuban coast. The pursuit has little to do with the larger war. The Germans are rather a kind of dangerous big game to test Hudson's lonely desperation and to draw him to his own half-consciously desired death.

There is little new here. You know Thomas Hudson if you know Nick Adams, Robert Jordan, Frederic Henry and Anselmo. Hemingway's tormented hero provides the consciousness that holds everything together. Our delight in reading Hemingway is to see the familiar thing done all over again with as much freshness and force as if it had never been done before. (Summary)

Timothy Foote. "Papa Watching." *Time*, 96 (October 5, 1970), 90-91.

Islands in the Stream is the remainder of that big novel Hemingway was rumored working on during the late 1940's and early 1950's. It was at one time described by the author as three loosely linked narratives called *The Sea When Young, The Sea When Absent* and *The Sea in Being*. He later published *The Sea in Being* separately as *The Old Man and the Sea* but never released the first two narratives. The estate's decision to release them now may be challenged, for *Islands in the Stream* is a stunningly bad book.

Hemingway the writer sometimes instinctively knew that Papa Hemingway the public figure was his worst literary creation. His hero Thomas Hudson, with all his sins, sons and sub-chasing, greatly resembles Hemingway, and one suspects the artist in Hemingway would have eventually slashed the novel by a third or a half.

Yet for Papa watchers the book is not all loss; its publication seems a commendable act of nostalgic piety as well as commerce. Even though Hudson is soon taken over by Papa Hemingway and navigates in full anecdotage without benefit of plot, the book fills in scenes of a true summer idyl, drenched in martini golds and Gulf Stream blues, and shows in the last section the powers that made Hemingway the era's best descriptive writer about military action.

Not in any sense a well-made novel, *Islands in the Stream* is more a muted literary reflection on the preoccupations of a working lifetime—death and love, work and action. Though it is filled with self-indulgent garrulity, it also recalls the Hemingway who could push a moment of humor to the edge of comedy and who could convey his love for things of the world without having to explain. In some ways also a rambling family anecdote, the novel shows Hemingway the father, not Papa, concerned for his sons and trying to weave some sort of protective magic about them. By imagining in advance such disasters as may come to them, he seeks to avert tragedy and to protect his children by holding them steadily in mind and heart. When he does so, he escapes his own self-preoccupation and moves into a wider world of love. (Summary)

Roderick Nordell. "Hemingway's View of Himself." *Christian Science Monitor*, October 8, 1970, p. 13.

After all the caveats have been entered, "Islands in the Stream" remains as likable and heartbreaking a book as Ernest Hemingway ever wrote. An inescapable part of this impression lies in the resonance between the novel's hero and a reader's memories of the author's own finally tragic life—even as the autumnal present events of the story resonate with the hero's memories of greener times. But there are also, along with much that is unworthy of Papa, many passages that stand firmly on their own.

The latter occur mainly in the first and last of the book's three loosely linked narratives. But even the lamentable middle one, "Cuba," awash with barfly self-pity and shore-leave lusts, has moments of wildly comic dialogue and Hollywoodishly effective theater —in contrast with some spouting of the now printable words that Hemingway used to complain he couldn't use, and an unbelievable bout of sentimentality with a pet tomcat.

* * *

Until the abrupt pathos of the ending, "Bimini" is Hemingway of unusual mellowness, humor, and even happiness. The relentless descriptions of drinks, the seminars in toughness fade in a glow of father-and-son feeling, children asking to be reminded of what they don't quite remember (in this case, Paris conversations with Mr. Joyce and Mr. Pound and Mr. Ford), days at the beach with a touch of danger, brotherly teasing, friend-of-the-family fun.

The friend, Roger Davis, is a writer and fighter, adding more echoes of Hemingway, as if Hemingway were split into Hudson and Davis—and maybe among other characters such as a crew member with wounds recalling the author's. Perhaps this was to be a kind of testamentary work, Hemingway's view of himself from all angles—the middle-aged man and the sea, a presence that tests and solaces like life itself. What was written might have been changed by him—removing bits of self-parody from the stylized prose, refining the dialogue, which seems to have been brought to a point of narrative functioning but not always with the Hemingway resources of characterization.

* * *

The word from Hemingway is the same at the end as at the beginning. "I don't have to be proud of it," thinks Thomas Hudson, contemplating his wartime task. "I only have to do it well."

It's not enough, really. On the other hand, it is a great deal for a man not to say more than be believes. And somehow, for all its faults, this book leaves one feeling closer to the man than before.

Christopher Ricks. "At Sea with Ernest Hemingway." *New York Review of Books*, 15 (October 8, 1970), 17-19.

Carlos Baker says that when Hemingway wrote the narratives later to be published as *Islands in the Stream*, he wrote each section as an independent unit and hoped later to weld them into a unified whole. But nothing could weld them together. They don't fit. And that may be a clue why Hemingway had to write the book and why he couldn't publish it. The cracks between the parts can't be welded, not even leaped.

Thomas Hudson says there aren't any answers at all. When he says it, though, Hemingway means there are no questions he can afford to ask. There are lots of questions—too many —but they conceal more than they divulge. Devious and secretive, *Islands in the Stream* evasively refuses to say what is the matter with Thomas Hudson (and at the same time, with Ernest Hemingway), It proliferates in good reasons for him to be all at sea—broken marriages, continuing love for his first wife, sons killed, work threatened by drink and lack of discipline, joyless participation in a war that doesn't matter personally. But except possibly for the work reason, they sound like *ex post facto* rationalizations rather than living pains. Hudson's creator, with that kind of protectiveness which is actually self-protection, refuses any painful exploration of the real cause. Instead, he spreads out the reasons until they are so thin they fail to hide the cracks in his story and in his own personal vision. As in T. S. Eliot's view of Hamlet's flaw, Hemingway-Hudson fails to find an objective correlative to serve as the formula of his particular emotion. Hudson's sons die for the cruelest of reasons—authorial escape. They are tossed off the sled so that Hudson-Hemingway can get away. But even their loss doesn't explain Hudson's hopelessness. He doesn't really want to live whether they live or not.

With all his losses, Hudson keeps telling himself not to think about them. He says it so much finally that one suspects he really means he'd better not think. Hudson fingers his concealed wound so unremittingly he never reaches for his bow. With Hemingway, though, one suspects he has become all wound and no bow. (Summary)

Jonathan Yardley. "How Papa Grew." *New Republic*, 163 (October 10, 1970) 25-27.

If American literature has anything approaching an authentic tragic hero, Ernest Hemingway is that man. The claim is not new: "Hemingway's tragedy as an artist," and similar allegations, are familiar stuff. The assumption is that by his thirtieth birthday Hemingway had done virtually all the important work he was to do, that the remaining three decades were to be spent in ever more fruitless and frustrating pursuit of glories and triumphs past.

* * *

The image that Hemingway lived on for thirty years was a gigantic thing. Nothing in American literature rivals its dimension: not London's, not Wolfe's, not (but *oh* how he is trying) Mailer's. In part undoubtedly it was created by his retinue of sycophants and his journalistic imitators, but there can be little doubt that its principal architect was the master himself. It lives so vividly in American myth, right up there with Babe Ruth, Gary Cooper and Teddy Roosevelt, that it may well be Hemingway's masterpiece.

As much as anything else, *Islands in the Stream* seems to have been motivated by an urge to shore up, magnify and embroider the legend. Written around 1950, it is a clearly unfinished three-part novel set in the Caribbean in World War II. Artistically it is ordinary postwar Hemingway, with dialogue which parrots Hemingwayisms . . . and prose which lacks the care and resilience of the best short stories. There are some very good passages in the first section, "Bimini"; the second, "Cuba," is a bore; and the third, "At Sea," is a diverting adventure tale. Overall, it seems unlikely that Hemingway would have wanted to publish the book in this form, not merely because it needs much cutting and refining but because it so obviously anticipates both *A Moveable Feast* and *The Old Man and the Sea* that it seems almost a working draft.

The real interest *Islands in the Stream* holds is as the definitive delineation of the *papier maché* Hemingway, drawn for us not by Baker or Hotchner or *Life*, but by the image himself. The central character, Thomas Hudson, a painter, is clearly to be read as Hemingway; so, to a lesser extent, is his best friend Roger Davis, a writer. Their conversations (Hemingway talking to Hemingway!) and actions are designed to reveal Hemingway in all his aspects to create the Official Portrait.

* * *

It is impossible to separate the Hemingway image from his work, but he was right in claiming that his personality interferes with clear critical judgment of his literary influence and durability. It does not seem coincidental, however, that the brilliant early work—the two great novels and the incomparable stories—is also the work in which he was least self-absorbed; much of it is autobiographical, admittedly, but it is largely devoid of the self-promotion that not long after became his main preoccupation. It also has an objectivity that is essential to its clarity, an objectivity one does not find in *Islands in the Stream*. But then, though it is amiable enough, *Islands in the Stream* does not offer much of anything except the legend. It provides no new keys to Hemingway's literary importance. Its narrative is competent (at narrative Hemingway was *never* incompetent), and it contains just e-

nough flickering reminders of his wasted genius to make reading it a frustrating and saddening experience.

* * *

John W. Aldridge. "Hemingway Between Triumph and Disaster." *Saturday Review*, 53 (October 10, 1970), 23-26, 39.

* * *

Knowing that this may well be the last new Hemingway novel we will ever see, one approaches it with a mixture of wariness, awe, and considerable anxiety, hoping that through some charity of the gods it will turn out to be very good, but knowing also the chances against the novel's being other than very bad. It would be nice homage to be able to pronounce it a masterpiece. There is diminishment for each of us in the possibility that the book might prove a disaster. But the worst diminishment of all: if honesty forces it upon us to be equivocal, finicky, and faint, to say, as unfortunately one must, that the book is neither very good nor very bad, but that it is both, in some places downright wonderful, in others as sad and embarrassingly self-indulgent as the work of any sophomore.

In this respect it resembles *For Whom the Bell Tolls* perhaps more closely than it does any of the earlier novels. There are other obvious similarities between the two books, but they are most strikingly similar in the way each brings together in a single narrative—at times within the space of a single page—some of the best and worst features of Hemingway's writing. The interesting thing, furthermore, is that these features relate in both books to the same kinds of material. Those sections that are devoted mainly to the description of physical action are almost invariably excellent. Those in which the physical action is interrupted to give Robert Jordan and Thomas Hudson an opportunity to *think*, to analyze their feelings or to find intellectual justification for doing what they are about to do, are as vapid and pretentious as such passages nearly always are in Hemingway. Luckily the two kinds of material are not present in equal amounts in either book: the passages describing physical action far outnumber the passages of intellectual analysis in both. But the element that finally saves *For Whom the Bell Tolls* is missing from *Islands in the Stream.*

In the latter there is no coherently formed or sufficiently compressed narrative structure in which the action can take on the intensity or the meaning it would seem potentially capable of developing. There is also no thematic design strong enough to support the weight of Hudson's sagging cerebral muscles or to give his thoughts the kind of relevance to the action that Jordan's can finally be seen to have. Where *For Whom the Bell Tolls* is held together by the rigid economy of the form and the tightly interlocking relationship of events occurring over a period of a few days, the new novel is composed of episodes much more widely spaced in time and only vaguely connected by an evolving plot. The result is that such dramatic tension as may be generated in any one of the episodes tends to be dissipated in the lapse of time separating it from the next. The problem is not simply that the book is divided into three parts but that, as a novel, it *disintegrates* into three parts or long short stories, and these are related only by the fact that Hudson is the central if somewhat opaque character in all of them.

Yet taken separately, as, given the looseness of structure, they must be taken, many of the episodes contain the most exciting and effective writing Hemingway has ever done. There is a marvelous ocean-fishing sequence in Part I, the account of a protracted and agonizing struggle by one of Hudson's young sons to bring in a giant fish. The pathos of the boy's almost superhuman effort—which of course ends in last-minute failure—is brilliantly evoked, and one realizes that here is a dimension of Hemingway one has seen before but perhaps not often enough, that side of his nature which was capable of responding not merely to bluster and bravado but with admiration for bravery in the weak and with tenderness toward weakness in the brave. There are also some nicely comic scenes in a Havana bar that are reminiscent of the better moments of *To Have and Have Not*, and the best sustained piece of writing in the book, the long story of the search for the German submariners ending in the gun battle. This is one of the most impressive descriptions of physical action to be found in Hemingway, comparable to the finest of them all, the account of El Sordo's last stand on the hilltop in *For Whom the Bell Tolls.*

Yet in spite of the high quality of individual episodes, one still senses a deficiency in the whole, which another comparison with *For Whom the Bell Tolls* may help to clarify. When he wrote that book, Hemingway was still close enough to the values and emotional responses of his early career to be able to use them to give a plausible edge of tragedy to Robert Jordan's story. Jordan was the climactic Hemingway hero and the last of the heroes able to embody convincingly the old attitudes about life, love, courage, and death. Even so, one saw that the old attitudes were being stretched extremely thin in Jordan. Already the Hemingway style, which had once been not merely a certain choice and arrangement of words but the verbalization of a distinct metaphysical view of experience, showed signs of hardening into a stance. The conviction was beginning to drain out of it, and it was obvious that Jordan, in those rather maudlin moments of introspection, was struggling hard to keep his old attitudes intact.

But one also saw that this very feature of the novel, this element of ideological strain, helped to provide it with its considerable dramatic tension. There was the conflict, never finally resolved, between Jordan's World War I negativism, the rather effete *Weltschmerz* of Jake Barnes and Frederic Henry, and the requirement imposed by his situation that he be positive and idealistic in his beliefs. Jordan had continually to persuade himself that

he believed in the Loyalist cause, just as he had to persuade himself that he believed in the war and, with less success, in "Life, Liberty, and the Pursuit of Happiness."

Then there were the other sources of dramatic tension: the conflict between the desires of love and the demands of duty; the difficulties Jordan encountered in trying to persuade the guerrillas that they should help him perform a mission in which he himself could not entirely believe; the poignancy of all emotions in the face of danger and the threat of death. There was all that Jordan stood to lose by the action of blowing the bridge. There were Maria and his possible future with her. There were all the experiences of life he had always enjoyed and wished to be able to enjoy again. These elements helped to convert what was in some ways a too heavily melodramatic novel into a work that had some real artistic complexity and truth.

But the situation of Thomas Hudson is very different, and the difference helps to account for what is most wrong with the new novel. Hudson is primarily the product of his past losses, sorrows, and mistakes. He has already lived a long life, and he has been much damaged in the process. No longer positively committed to the early Hemingway values, he yet retains the early skepticism which in him is fast souring into hopelessness. The simple fact is that, unlike his predecessors, he no longer believes in life and no longer enjoys life. By the time he is faced with his own certain death, he is carrying nothing but grief over the death of his three sons, the failure of his marriages, and all the emotions he is no longer able to feel. Nothing motivates him to take action except a vague stubborn sense of duty. He does not believe in this war or in any wars, and the idea of Life, Liberty, and the Pursuit of Happiness has become for him a sad joke indeed. Consequently, Hudson confronts his death like an automaton. He has gone through the motions and put on a good show, but he has had nothing to lose from the start. Hence, his actions have had no meaning. When he dies, he will be ready to die, not for the cause, not in order to save the girl he loves, but because he is tired to death of life. There is sadness in this but no real tragedy, because there is no sense of missed possibility, no conceivable alternative to dying.

* * *

William MacPherson.
"He Played It Again, Sam."
Miami Herald,
October 11, 1970,
p. 7-G.

* * *

Islands in the Stream is not a novel in any familiar sense—certainly not the major novel its publishers claim; it is, rather, the draft of a novel that the author never completed and certainly never attempted to publish, which indicates that his critical lights, however much they may have wavered from time to time, were not completely extinguished.

* * *

Uneven as it is, "Bimini" is the best section. The second (and worst), "Cuba," takes place mostly over a lot of frozen daiquiris "with no sugar" (Hemingway had a philosophical prejudice against sweetness) in the Floridita Bar, where Hudson is mourning the death of his last and eldest son, killed flying a Spitfire over England early in the war.

In the third section, "At Sea," sometimes reminscent of the worst in *To Have and Have Not,* Thomas Hudson is chasing the survivors of a German U-Boat in the Caribbean.

* * *

True, there are occasional flashes of the old brilliance in the writing, but a lot more of the old flim-flam. The tried and true Hemingway themes—grace under pressure, the importance and meaning of being a man (even the fish are male here), the battles against insuperable odds—have been pulled out for another go but they refuse to make it around the course. In his best work Hemingway transmuted this sort of material into art; in his worst he made it ridiculous. Unfortunately, this is his worst, and it should have been published as a volume of uncollected odds and ends, not as a major novel.

* * *

**Joseph Epstein.
"The Sun Also Sets."**
Book World, 4
(October 11, 1970),
1, 3.

Ernest Hemingway was the first of the American writers we came to know too well. In twentieth-century America he practically invented the role of the novelist as celebrity, and in this regard he was most truly Papa, the daddy of a great many novelists to come. During the last twenty or so years of his life Hemingway's celebrity most closely approximated that of a movie star, with consequences that were mixed at best. One lingering result is that today, more than nine years after his death, the experience of reading him is akin to watching a favorite actor—Humphrey Bogart, say, or Gary Cooper—on the late show. As with Bogart and Cooper, two highly stylized actors, so with Hemingway, a highly stylized writer, one doesn't really expect any surprises but instead looks for the old solid performance, anticipates the same marvelous moves that first captivated us so many years ago.

In *Islands in the Stream* one finds very few surprises but most of the old Hemingway moves intact. Although this ample, somewhat rambling, posthumously published novel offers no radical departures from the body of Hemingway's work, its appearance, nonetheless, is salutary for his reputation. Since his death by suicide, the critical line on Ernest Hemingway has been drawn extremely taut; so taut, indeed, as to constitute a noose, leaving his literary repute dangling from the gallows of contemporary criticism. Briefly, the current critical line on Hemingway has reduced him to being the author of one good novel (*The Sun Also Rises*) a handful of excellent stories, and the originator of a once elegantly simple prose style that over the years dried up and flaked off in self-parody. Such are the sweeping swings of critical opinion that in less than a decade Hemingway's reputation appears to have gone from that of major (if not *the* major) American novelist to that of a writer of little consequence; from—to use a boxing analogy of the sort he was so fond of—the heavyweight champ to just another bum.

* * *

More than any other modern American writer, Hemingway illustrates the hazards of personality in literature—the hazards, that is, of the writer interposing himself between his books and their audience. While he lived, he was his own best press agent; since his death, this same press agentry has been the principal obstacle in the way of his books getting a fair reading. Theoretically, nothing about a writer's personal life ought to affect the way one reads his work; in point of fact, almost everything one knows about a writer affects one's reading of him. It was Hemingway himself who sedulously encouraged the close identification between his own life and that of his fictional characters. A writer can probably do his work no greater disservice. While fashions in writers' personalities change—Hemingway's emphasis on his own excessive virility today seems merely embarrassing—good writing remains good writing. Thus Hemingway's personality, which once added an extra luster to his writing, has in recent years threatened to obliterate it.

But once Hemingway's personality is set aside, what becomes clear is that he was neither so great a writer as he pretended nor so inconsequential a writer as the current critical reevaluation of his work would have him. This fact emerges from *Islands in the Stream*, the first of Hemingway's fiction to be published since his death. What is so useful about the novel's appearance is that it allows us to gauge afresh his achievement and his faults— and in a way that rereading his earlier books, which have all been filmed, discussed, and "explicated" half to death, no longer allows. In all fairness, it should be pointed out that *Islands in the Stream* is not an altogether "completed" novel; it was originally worked at during the late 1940s and early 1950s, and had Hemingway lived long enough he may well have taken it out of his bank vault, where he used to place all his manuscripts to age and mellow before returning to polish or otherwise rework them for publication. Yet as it stands the novel contains all of Hemingway's strengths and weaknesses—his worst, which can be terrible, and his very best, which can be no less than wonderful.

Islands in the Stream is a novel of three parts—the first magnificently executed, the second merely interesting, and the third quite trashy.

* * *

Detached from the remainder of the novel, "Bimini" would be one of the best longish short stories Hemingway wrote, standing alongside "The Short Happy Life of Francis Macomber" and "The Snows of Kilimanjaro." It has, to be sure, some of the traditional Hemingway faults: the rather too easy division of the world into good guys and bastards, the rampant use of the word "fine" in lieu of description for any thing or person the author approves of, occasionally stilted dialogue, etc. But so clean and clear and powerful is the rest that these minor points come to matter very little. The quality of insight, which is used sparingly to begin with, is high and the description of land and seascape can be dazzling—the natural world is most truly Hemingway's real element, and his is perhaps the only significant modern body of modern fiction that does not depend upon an urban setting. On a sheerly technical level, he has never been better than he is in long stretches of "Bimini." There is a scene in which Hudson's second son puts up a six-and-a-half-hour battle with a giant fish that, in perhaps one-twentieth of the space, shows up *The Old Man and the Sea* for the pseudo-Biblical second-rate goods that that novel is.

* * *

Somewhere early in the "Bimini" section one of Hudson's sons remarks, as he is retelling the story of his early life in Paris, "Make something happen, then, pappa," and one wants to say the same to Hemingway throughout the last two parts of the novel, which are so very inferior to the first part. . . .

The third part of the novel, "At Sea," is a simple disaster—a prolonged mistake. In it Hemingway has Hudson, in writing reminiscent of the shoddiest prose from *To Have and Have Not*, chasing the crew of a wrecked German submarine around the Caribbean. It is characteristic of Hemingway at his most limited that he could conceive of no other way to end this beautifully begun novel than to put the by-now totally bereft Hudson through the paces of a somewhat empty exercise in physical courage.

As long as a writer is alive, it makes sense to judge him by his worst work, holding it up to him as an example of his cheating on the promise of his talent. When a writer is dead, however, it is his best work that ought to be remembered. And parts of *Islands in the Stream* offer a solid reminder of how good Hemingway could be when he was working well. That he did not always work well he himself seemed to know better than anyone, despite the bravura pose he must have felt it necessary to put on. In his biography, Carlos Baker tells how once, during a blocked period near the end of his life, the tears streamed down Hemingway's face because he could not write and believed he would never be able to again. He was a pro—and if not a great writer of the caliber of Stendhal, Turgenev, or Flaubert, an important and a damn good writer nevertheless.

Geoffrey Wolff. "Out of the Desk." *Newsweek*, 76 (October 12, 1970), 118-19.

Since "Islands in the Stream" is a posthumously published novel (the rest of the novel Hemingway wrote after World War II and from which he drew "The Old Man and the Sea" to publish separately), it calls for special ground rules. In its unrevised state it was not in Hemingway's view good enough to be published. No one can say for sure what he would have produced in revision, but it is certain he would have tightened his sentences. Since he did not have that opportunity, the book has to be read with the indulgent eye of a man who goes through a friend's desk to read his mail.

But that is not to say the work should never have been published. Rather it should be taken for what it is, an unfinished draft in untidy and ambiguous circumstances.

The Hemingway rituals are all present in this story of artist Thomas Hudson—the stylized codes for drinking, fighting, talking, loving—though more humane and less exacting than in the early stories. But because he is less certain of the moral stance behind the rituals, the style reflects that uncertainty. Indeed, the prose is so loose-gaited that at times it seems even the author's attention wanders.

The first section with its superb description of the struggle against the swordfish and the few passages of in-spired comic dialogue is the best, but Hudson, Hemingway's persona, is a shadowy presence, a non-stop talker, a machine for rote memory. The talk with Honest Lil, the Whore-With-a-Heart-of-Gold, seems even more end-less in the second section. In the third the talk, if not so long, is equally maudlin. By then we know: it is a very bad novel with a few bright moments. (Summary)

John Updike. "Papa's Sad Testament." *New Statesman*, 80 (October 16, 1970) 489.

This book consists of material that the author during his lifetime did not see fit to publish; therefore it should not be held against him. That parts of it are good is entirely to his credit; that other parts are puerile and, in a pained way, aimless testifies to the odds a-gainst which Hemingway, in the last two decades of his life, brought any-thing to completion. It is, I think, to the discredit of his publishers that no introduction (the American edition does carry a very terse, uninformative note by Mary Hemingway) offers to describe from what stage of Heming-way's tormented later career *Islands in the Stream* was salvaged, or to esti-mate what its completed design might have been, or to confess what editorial choices were exercised in the prepara-tion of this manuscript. Rather, a gal-lant wreck of a novel is paraded as the real thing, as if the public are such fools as to imagine a great writer's ghost is handing down books intact from Heaven.

So we are left to perform the elemen-tary scholarly decencies ourselves. . . .

What we have, then, is a trio of large fragments crudely unified by a Caribbean setting and the nominal pre-sence of Thomas Hudson. "Bimini" is a collection of episodes that show only a groping acquaintance with one an-other; "Cuba" is a lively but meander-ing excursion in local colour that, when the painter's first wife material-ises, weirdly veers into a dark and pri-vate region; and "At Sea" is an adven-ture story of almost slick intensity. Hudson, if taken sequentially, does not grow but dwindles, from an affec-tionate and baffled father and artist into a rather too expertly raffish wa-terfront character into a bleak man-hunter, a comic-book super-human holding unlooked-for-bubbles of stoic meditation and personal sorrow. Some conscious attempt is made to interlock the characterisations—the manhunter remembers that he is a painter, and gives us some hard-edged seascapes to prove it; the bar clown intermittently recalls that he is drowning his grief at the death of a son—but the real con-gruence of these masks is involuntary: all fit the face of Ernest Hemingway.

Whereas an achieved novel, how-ever autobiographical, dissolves the author and directs our attention be-yond him, *Islands in the Stream*, even where most effective, inspires us with a worried concern for the celebrity who wrote it.

* * *

Hemingway of course did not invent the world, nor pain, mutilation, and death. In his earlier work his harsh obsessions seem honorable and necessary; an entire generation of American men learned to speak in the accents of Hemingway's stoicism. But here, the tension of art has been snapped and the line between sensitive vision and psychopathy has been crossed. The "sea-chase story" is in many ways brilliant, but it has the falsity of the episode in Hemingway's real life upon which it was based. . . . Everything in "At Sea" is true, except the encounter with Germans and the imperatives of the mission, which was not demanded from above but invented and propelled from within. Such bravery is not grace under pressure but pressure forced in the hope of inducing Grace.

And even love becomes a species of cruelty, which divides women into whores and bitches on the one hand and on the other a single icy-perfect adored.

* * *

Love and death: fused complements in Hemingway's universe. Yet he never formulated the laws that bind them, never achieved the step of irony away from himself. He tried; this book opens in a mood of tonic breadth and humour, and closes with a sharp beatific vision of himself, Hudson, dying and beloved:

"I think I understand, Willie," he said.

"Oh shit," Willie said, "You never understand anybody that loves you."

The new generations, my impression is, want to abolish both war and love, not love as a physical act but love as a religion, a creed to help us suffer better. The sacred necessity of suffering no longer seems sacred or necessary, and Hemingway speaks across the Sixties as strangely as a medieval saint; I suspect few readers younger than myself could believe, from this sad broken testament, how we *did* love Hemingway and, after pity feels merely impudent, love him still.

Archie Satterfield. "Hemingway Legend Lives in New Book." *Seattle Sunday Times*, October 18, 1970, p. 4-H.

During Hemingway's last years he frequently mentioned his "big" book. This, apparently, is it. And for those who enjoy storytelling at its best, "Islands" will be well worth its inflated price.

The novel is in three parts, each with an American painter named Thomas Hudson as the central character.

* * *

Each section could stand alone, but Scribner's and Hemingway's widow wisely decided to publish them together. In this way, the reader can feel the full impact of Hemingway's genius as a storyteller.

Comparison with other Hemingway novels is inevitable, but the astute reader will avoid it. This is a novel that stands alone. It is a positive work. Its characters have great dignity. If things don't go well for them, they do not complain.

One of the more interesting of Hemingway's talents is to show through dialog not only what men think but how they think. Thus, there is an emphasis on anticipation—for a meal, a visit, an event. The anticipation becomes more interesting and revealing than the event.

The book is filled with memorable scenes. There is a fishing scene that runs 30 pages and is equal to anything in "The Old Man and the Sea." The search for the Germans and the resulting battle are superb. And no one has been able to write love scenes more convincingly than Hemingway; there is a mutual concern shown between man and woman for which few critics give him proper credit.

In this reader's opinion Hemingway wrote three truly great novels: "A Farewell to Arms," "For Whom the Bell Tolls" and this present book.

Pearl K. Bell. "Hemingway's Abortive Resurrection." *New Leader*, 53 (October 19, 1970), 16-17.

When a writer's widow is also his literary executor, he doesn't need an enemy. It was a monstrous lapse of judgment on her part to publish this disastrously bad novel and pretend it is worthy of being added to the canon.

Coming as it does nine years after the author's death and three decades after Hemingway began confusing his heroes with himself, *Islands in the Stream* is sure to further muddy his troubled reputation.

The writing is, with only a few exceptions, feeble, lame, morally fatigued. Hemingway can find only exhausted platitudes to characterize his hero, Thomas Hudson, tiresomely referred to by his two full names throughout the book. The only moments to take on even the faintest breath of life in the first section come in the deep-sea fishing account, a sort of *Young Man and the Sea*, when the painter's middle son makes a heroic but futile effort to boat his swordfish. In the second section, heavy with pompous simplicities, Hudson mourns the loss of his eldest son, downs several hundred double daiquiris, talks for hours with his favorite Cuban whore and ends with an idyllic interlude of lovemaking with his exwife, the dead son's mother. Not until the last section, with the focus on the action of pursuit and on the treacherously beautiful Cuban coastline, does the novel rise above mean water level and resemble even dimly the work of the master who wrote *A Farewell to Arms* and the wonderfully crafted stories of *In Our Time*. When Hemingway gets beyond the stupefyingly sententious narcissism of the Hemingway-Hudson catechism, his prose is at least readable and at best sinewy and vigorous.

Hemingway's performance here raises again the tantalizing question why so many immensely talented American writers of this century have gone into a crippling decline of repetitious, degrading banality and egoism. Partly the reason is that fiction concentrated on the muscular pleasures of heroic action is especially subject to the law of diminishing returns. When writers rule out contemplative possibilities and aggressively discard a sense of society, they find themselves, as Leslie Fiedler wrote in the mid-50s, imprisoned in the cult of experience and the only way to go is down. Written out of these limitations, *Islands in the Stream*, his dull, pathetic worst, will only obscure Hemingway's former greatness. (Summary)

Bernard Oldsey. "The Novel in the Drawer." *The Nation*, 211 (October 19, 1970), 376, 378.

Ernest Hemingway once declared that a writer's best gift was "a built-in, shock-proof shit detector." He himself had a good one and he was not above using those of others, like Ezra Pound, Getrude Stein and F. Scott Fitzgerald. So just a certain amount of bad Hemingway was published during his lifetime—mainly during his *Esquire* period, and then later in *The Fifth Column* and *Across the River and Into the Trees*. Now more of it than has ever before been brought together in one book has been published as something of a novel, *Islands in the Stream*.

* * *

Hemingway must have understood that this material was not worth publishing, or not ready for publishing. He worked at it from 1947 to 1951, and probably longer. He published *Across the River and Into the Trees* (1950) and *The Old Man and the Sea* (1952); he was severely criticized for the first and received the Nobel Prize after the second (1954). So it is not improbable that he withheld the present material because it was not finished and because, even with more work, it might have damaged his shaken and re-established reputation. But there could very well be another reason: these manuscripts were even more rawly autobiographical than his usual fiction.

Thomas Hudson is a hardly disguised Hemingway—a world-famous painter, living in Cuba and Bimini, who has three sons and has had three wives. The first section of *Islands in the Stream*, "Bimini," details a period when Hudson has all three of his sons with him for an extended visit, just before the outbreak of World War II. From the very beginning the prose is familiarly good, and consistent with the kind of description Hemingway said he learned to do from painters.

* * *

But what is not familiar—in fact is markedly absent from almost all of his fiction—is the paternal love of "Papa" Hemingway, which here produces some happy and humorous family vignettes, as well as a long episode, a tribute to a son, that might have been subtitled "The Young Man and the Sea," and deserves to be read as a companion piece to old Santiago's story.

The second section of the book is named "Cuba," where Hudson lives in a house very much like the *finca* in which Hemingway lived. . . . Even more certainly autobiographical is Hudson's involvement in espionage and sub-chasing activities of the very kind Hemingway engaged in during the early days of World War II, when he had his yacht *Pilar* equipped with makeshift depth charges, and under the guise of oceanographer went in search of German U-boats off the coast of Cuba. Carlos Baker in his biography of Hemingway makes these activities seem buffoonish and inept; and yet it is these, transmuted into fiction of fairly high order, that make for the best section of *Islands in the Stream.*

"At Sea," this third section, consists of the kind of material Hemingway could always handle well—physical action, and men without women in a quest for life surrounded by death. . . .

Ernest Hemingway's semi-professional knowledge of the sea and his novelist's knowledge of men at war make this last section of the book worthy of canonization among his battle pieces. But what else of this book deserves to be placed within the Hemingway canon, rather than the corpus? With the exceptions noted, not much. In fact, publication of *Islands in the Stream* raises serious questions about the posthumous presentation of works an author did not see fit to publish.

* * *

Even in its present form, *Islands in the Stream* is the work of an estimable writer. Its gaga humor belongs with that of *The Torrents of Spring*, its moribund and democratic message echoes *For Whom the Bell Tolls*. Issuing from the vaults of some Manhattan bank, Hemingway's voice is still effective, hauntingly so. It takes us back to that time in our international history when men could still play at war, although they had begun to suspect it was truly a sickness unto death.

Robert Emmet Long. *Commonweal*, 92 (October 23, 1970), 99, 100.

* * *

Islands in the Stream has without doubt, and perhaps even as its chief pleasure, the grand Hemingway manner—the sharp, chiseled style that has been one of the most admired and imitated in the world and is what one means when one speaks of American prose fiction as "modern."

* * *

The impeccable, painterly style of the opening introduces us to a fictional world where the waters off Cuba (a region treated in *To Have and Have Not* and *The Old Man and the Sea*) become distinctively Hemingway terrain, as Paris, Italy, Spain, and Africa had in his earlier fiction. At the center of the work is a successful painter, Thomas Hudson, who is visited by three sons, children of two earlier marriages which ended in divorce. For Hudson one could substitute Hemingway, since the hero is autobiographical in many ways, and is even referred to as "papa." . . . For the most part, however, "Bimini" is concerned with Hudson's relations with his sons. One of the sons loses a four-hour duel with a thousand-pound fish, and the physical details of this struggle are meticulously recorded. But the scene seems too drawn out, and the boys themselves never become quite real. One of the boys is compared to an otter, and that is about as close as Hemingway comes to giving a living sense of them. They all talk in a stylized speech, and in Hemingway's syntax. They ask their father about his early days in Paris, and this occasions a great deal of reminiscence, some of it quite charming and humorous, as when the oldest boy, Tom, Jr., recalls his meetings with James Joyce. But it is essentially memoire writing, and appears to have been written for its own sake, as if Hemingway had forgotten he was writing a novel.

* * *

In some ways, *Islands in the Stream* seems designed as a more cosmopolitan version of *The Old Man and the Sea*. Each of the protagonists is dedicated to his craft, suffers and endures defeat. Yet because *Islands in the Stream* is overwhelmed by retrospection and obsessed by death, it gives the impression of a subconscious death wish.

Islands in the Stream is a formless and sprawling work which dispenses with the usual structure and architecture of the novel; its three major sections are really vignettes extended to hundreds of pages. It is as if Hemingway, at the end of his career, had come full cycle from the dramatic conciseness of the short stories in the early 1920s which brought him worldwide attention at an early age. Yet the economy and understatement of the short scene is Hemingway's real strength, and despite brilliant passages in *Islands in the Stream* (passages almost detachable from the novel), the work as a whole suffers from a looseness that suggests a slackness in conception. Some of the characters are weakly created: the Hudson sons seem unreal as people, and when they are rather too neatly killed off, the great sorrow imputed to Hudson seems unreal too. Other characters drift in and out of the novel without explanation. The men on board Hudson's ship at the end have names like Antonio and Gil and Ara, but they are all faceless and interchangeable with one another. Most of all, Hemingway drifts off at times into lengthy memoire-like recollections which not only do not move the novel along, but give the impression of an imperfect fusion of literary forms. The only thing that really is "happening" in *Islands in the Stream* is style, style as an end and pleasure in itself and related weakly, if at all, to a compelling human drama. It is as if, in *Islands in the Stream*, Hemingway's art had survived intact and failed only of a subject.

Irving Howe.
"Great Man Going Down."
Harper's, 24
(October 1970),
121-25.

In Federico Fellini's attractive film *8½* the central figure is a director suffering a crisis of work. He must soon come up with a scenario for a new film, but he has none. He opens his mind to fragments of memory, but he cannot find a way of ordering them into a coherent whole. Then, as if to anticipate and mock his critics, Fellini puts a grubby intellectual into the film who keeps sneering at the director's wish to make something out of his commonplace recollections of childhood. The director, says the intellectual, lacks an idea, by which he means some abstraction that can be linked with Marxism or Catholicism or existentialism.

The director, unstrung, cannot answer. Yet he feels that, while he does indeed lack an idea by means of which to structure his memories, the *kind* of idea for which he is looking isn't at all what the intellectual keeps jabbering about. At the end of *8 ½* the director thinks he has finally found what he needs: an idea isn't really necessary, we must simply accept the wastefulness and gratuitousness of our experience and learn thereby to "embrace" the vibrant chaos of our past.

* * *

Anyone who has read the three unfinished romances Hawthorne wrote at the end of his life would probably recognize them as the work of a distinguished writer—but a distinguished writer who has gone to pieces, gripped by some intellectual panic that prevents him from achieving coherence. Hawthorne could not get his stories *to move,* just as Fellini's director cannot get the fragments of his memory to relate.

It is a similar difficulty that afflicts Ernest Hemingway's posthumous novel, *Islands in the Stream*, a very strange book full of both pleasing and disastrous things. Its very title suggests an awareness on Hemingway's part that he could manage, by now, only ill-connected portions of a narrative—at most, separate panels of representation—and that he must therefore fall back on the plea that the chaos of existence provides a rationale for his inability to achieve a unified work of art.

Islands in the Stream was apparently composed during the 1950s, toward the end of Hemingway's life and soon after the critical failure of his extremely poor novel, *Across the River and Into the Trees.* . . .

Hemingway, according to his biographer Carlos Baker, worked during these years in fits and starts, beginning and then putting aside several manuscripts, apparently dissatisfied with all of them. We can now see why. One of these manuscripts has been carved into a book by his last wife, Mary, and though it contains some beautiful things—we are, after all, talking about a master—*Islands in the Stream* isn't going to add much to Hemingway's reputation.

* * *

The book moves—it doesn't move very much—on two planes: the external action, often interesting for pages at a time, and the inner life of Hudson, mostly tiresome. Hemingway's evident desire to probe his own loss of nerve and thereby get away from his encrusted *persona* arouses sympathy and respect; but most of the time his vanity is too overpowering for his desire to be realized and we are brought back to the kid-stuff bravado, the tight-lipped posturing, the endless narcissism of his later books. A small yet telling example: in his years of fame Hudson develops a sort of feudal mentality as all too innocently he keeps telling us about the endless loyalty of his retainers. How they all love him, how they all care for him, this great warrior-artist of many loves! . . .

In "Bimini," the first part of *Islands in the Stream*, we see Hudson in his house, a troubled man who "had exorcised guilt with work insofar as he could" and who now recognizes he has been "undisciplined, selfish, and ruthless." . . . What strikes one, in reading these flaccid and rather ugly pages, is how painful it is that the great master of narrative pacing, the Hemingway who could make tightness of phrase into a moral virtue, should now write so slackly, as if he must hang on to an incident for pages of chatter simply because he doesn't quite know what to do next. There follows, nevertheless, a quite charming section in which Hudson's three sons come to visit, and here

the talk is bright, the feeling pure, and the action vibrant. . . .

Part II, a complete disaster, is set in Cuba during the early years of World War II, with a cloak-and-dagger mystification that could thrill five-year-olds. . . .

Part III, "At Sea," constitutes a notable recovery. It is a tense and exciting story in which Hudson, firm beyond grief, commands his boat of American irregulars searching for some stranded U-boat sailors. . . . These pages I found myself reading with a happy surrender to primitive suspense, as well as with pleasure at seeing Hemingway once again in command of his material. Yet, gripping as this part is in its steady accumulation of narrative tension, it isn't the kind of writing a great writer can ever content himself with. Certainly it isn't what a Kipling or a Conrad would have contented himself with, though a Stevenson might have. And to his everlasting credit Hemingway knows this. . . . Because he knows that he must deepen his adventure through an infusion of consciousness, because he sees that no story of battle can ever achieve in its own right the kind of significance a truly ambitious writer aims for, Hemingway keeps returning to the inner life of Hudson. Alas; it is like moving from shiny pebbles to thick mud.

The book does not move, there is no commanding idea—and not the kind of billboard-idea that Fellini's intellectual wants but the kind of emotionally resonant and personal idea that Fellini's director looks for. Nor is the problem of a kind certain academic or formalistic critics might stress:

that from Part to Part new sets of characters are introduced and the old ones left to flounder, or that no effort is made dramatically to link the materials of each Part. The problem goes deeper and has to do with perceptions less easy to pin down—with the kind of firm and disciplined vision of life which, for example, pervades every chapter of *The Sun Also Rises* or *The Great Gatsby*. This is what Hemingway lost, this is what he struggled to recover, and this is what he did not find.

* * *

In *Islands in the Stream* you can see Hemingway struggling desperately with both his need for some concluding wisdom—what, at the end of our journey, do we take the human enterprise to be?—and his habitual tough-guy swagger in all its sodden mindlessness. I say Hemingway struggled desperately, yet on the face of it this book shows few signs of struggle: the writing is usually smooth and there is little of the *gaucherie* of *Across the River*. Here, for example, is the opening paragraph of "At Sea":

> There was a long white beach with coconut palms behind it. The reef lay across the entrance to the harbor and the heavy east wind made the sea break on it so that the entrance was easy to see once you had opened it up. There was no one on the beach and the sand was so white that it hurt his eyes to took at it.

This is accomplished prose, and its syntax and rhythm are calculated to remind us of Hemingway at his best.

That, I fear, is just the point. One has the impression in reading such passages of a writer caressing the phrases in his hand, the way a gambler who has had a run of bad luck will caress the dice: yes, if I go through the old motions, carefully and slowly, I will recover those insinuating rhythms, those phrases of captivation I used to command. Once the virtuoso of rapidity, Hemingway now writes in a kind of slow motion, especially in the first two Parts, hoping to recapture, through the recollection of old ways, the old assurance of tone.

It is not enough, and he knows it. Some element is wanting, call it idea or vision or coherence, some word that could make the world of his imagining come whole again. Hemingway keeps struggling, Hudson hiding his bewilderment. Hemingway summons the old motions, Hudson slides into age. The conclusion seems to me a terrible one: an artist's, a man's search for moral growth can disable his performance, crippling him with the knowledge of what he doesn't know.

J. Lovering.
Best Sellers, 30
(November 1, 1970),
321-22.

It looks very much as if the big one got away!

For many years the followers of Hemingway were led to believe that the old battler had been working off and on since the late forties on a very big book, likely the biggest of his career. It would be of epic proportions and would have its setting in World War II on land, on the sea, and in the air. Hemingway himself sometimes added to these reports. It appears he interrupted this work when he wrote "Across the River and Into the Trees" (1950) and another interruption occurred when he wrote "The Old Man and the Sea" (1952). Upon the death of Hemingway in 1961 there were conflicting reports about the finished nature of the big book. Whatever the precise facts about the writing circumstances of "Islands in the Stream," it is not a book that comes anywhere near being an important part of the Hemingway canon. And this is what most of the Hemingway critics had expected.

* * *

The events in "Bimini" bring overtones and suggestions of several other Hemingway works. There is the fighting and brawling of "To Have and Have Not." There is the reminiscence of Parisian days as Tom, the youngest son, and his father talk over some memorable moments with great men they had lived with, especially the writer James Joyce. In this part there is a flavoring of "A Moveable Feast." When a great broadbill strikes David's fishing line there is a long narrative sequence of the young man's desperate fight to land the fish and of his final failure, which suggests some of the movement and a little of the magic of "The Old Man and the Sea." But all of these resemblances to other Hemingway performances never come close to uniting "Bimini" into a truly success-

ful piece by itself. It is essentially an uneven work. . . .

"At Sea" picks up in narrative interest and pace and it brings to conclusion the death theme. But again there is a slackness about this section that reminds us that Hemingway has done it all so much better on so many other occasions.

Stephen Donadio. "Hemingway." *Commentary*, 30 (November 1970), 93-99.

The second of Ernest Hemingway's books to be published posthumously, *Islands in the Stream* antedates the first from the point of view of composition by approximately ten years. *A Moveable Feast* (published in 1964) contains memoirs begun in Cuba in the fall of 1957 and ostensibly completed with final revisions in Ketchum, Idaho, in the fall of 1960, not long before the author's death. The present work, a long three-part novel which (according to the account given by Professor Carlos Baker) grew out of Hemingway's conception of a big book about the sea—a conception which came to include *The Old Man and the Sea* as its concluding fourth section—was apparently begun shortly after the period of irritability and depression which followed the bad reviews attending publication of *Across the River and Into the Trees*: though it may contain elements composed several years earlier, the entire book seems to have been written and revised during a "huge working streak" between December 1950 and late summer 1951.

* * *

The reasons for the delay in publication are not certain: it is possible that Hemingway felt that the book required further revision; it is also possible that he regarded it as "life insurance" (as he used to say), that he decided it was something he had written "for the bank" in order to save money on his income tax and spread his income out more evenly over leaner years; and it is possible that he felt that he needed to keep this novel in reserve in case his talent ever failed him. As will be seen, there might have been other reasons, too, reasons suggested by his own peculiar feeling about the book.

* * *

The book's three sections proceed chronologically; taken together they record (through flashback, recollection, and present-tense action) the life of Thomas Hudson, a successful American painter several times divorced, from his youthful, idyllic sojourn in the Paris of the 20's to the brink of death in Cuba during World War II. Anyone familiar with the details of Hemingway's own life will find many of them here. . . .

"Bimini," the opening section of *Islands in the Stream*, is largely concerned with a visit to Thomas Hudson by his three sons. . . . After the boys have left, Hudson finds himself alone again, just how alone he learns as Part I closes, when he receives word that

David and Andrew have been killed in an automobile crash with their mother near Biarritz. . . . That the numbing effect of this news is to carry through the rest of the book is made apparent by Hudson's reaction when someone attempting to console him reminds him that he still has his eldest son: " 'for the time being,' Thomas Hudson said, and for the first time he looked straight down the long and perfect perspective of the blankness ahead." . . .

In Part II ("Cuba"), Thomas Hudson has just learned that his eldest son, Tom, has been killed in the war. The logic of the book's progression has now become clear: first all his sons, then he himself, must die. . . .

"At Sea," Part III of *Islands in the Stream*, is completely taken up with the pursuit of the crew of a sunken German submarine off the coast of Cuba by Hudson and a group of underground commandos posing as scientists. This section of the book is unquestionably the weakest and most tedious, but in retrospect this seems to be because the real function of the plot here is simply to deliver Thomas Hudson into death: the ultimately meaningless pursuit, with all its elaborate strategies and calculations, serves only to delay that inescapable conclusion. . . .

It was this last section which Hemingway had the most difficulty writing, but there is a quality of insomnia about the novel as a whole, an edge of desperation reminiscent of a man driving himself beyond exhaustion. The resulting combination of determination and distractedness probably accounts for the book's uneven momentum: the narrative often seems slightly out of control, as if it had begun growing with a life of its own, bulging out in strange and unexpected blossoms which are then cut back, only to reappear after a time like the heads of the Hydra.

* * *

The real interest of *Islands in the Stream* lies in the emotional life trapped but stirring restlessly beneath its surface, a life which it manages to convey through these passages of prose cut loose and floating free of the particular events of the plot: the events themselves are often (especially in Part III) presented without conviction, and in any case they serve as an inadequate vehicle for the burden of feeling they must bear. But it is precisely the distance between realistically-conceived events in the present tense and feelings suspended in a past whose presence can be reached only in dreams or dreamlike recollections that makes the obsessive drama of the novel so compelling, even when, from a narrow literary point of view, it is least successful. . . .

This ambiguous relation to the action corresponds closely to the rhythm and mood of the last section of the novel, and it may have something to do with the great difficulty which Hemingway seems to have had in completing that section. That he did have difficulty is suggested by the daily word count which he often marked at the end of the typescript pages. . . . But another, more intriguing, bit of information recorded by Professor Baker suggests that the difficulty

which Hemingway experienced at this time was not simply a result of fatigue or lack of inspiration. According to Professor Baker, after the completion of the final section of the book, in an unpublished letter to an old friend Hemingway "later said, somewhat overdramatically, that he had 'dreaded' to write it and even hoped at one time that he would never have to set it down."

* * *

Feelings so powerful, no matter how apparently inappropriate, cannot be dismissed lightly, and it is difficult to keep from speculating that they might have had something to do with Hemingway's decision not to publish what was ostensibly a finished work. Hemingway was, after all, a rather superstitious man, and if this novel really struck him, in some strange way, as a rehearsal—or re-living—of his own death, then it seems understandable that he might have wanted to put the book away for awhile, if only by deciding not to publish it immediately.

* * *

The publication of *Islands in the Stream* will not diminish Hemingway's stature, nor will it add to it appreciably; but it should have the effect of reawakening serious critical interest in Hemingway by altering the dominant, rather schematic conception of the shape of his career and raising important new questions about his life and work and the relations between them. For a number of years many literary people have assumed, not always tacitly, that whatever his early achievements Hemingway eventually became a vaguely punch-drunk braggart lost in his own public image.... Ten years ago the news of his suicide left several generations shaken and forced some tentative, if inconclusive, reconsiderations; but the old refrains are still plainly audible in John Aldridge's 1965 judgment that "it now seems clear that Hemingway was in a state of progressive creative decline for at least the last two decades of his life." ...

Hemingway's immense popularity has also been a problem, especially in the academy, where such things as best-sellerdom and movie rights are often (or used to be, before the inversions of "Camp" and the institutionalized worship of popular culture) superciliously regarded—at least overtly—as the unmistakable visible emblems of uncleanness and aesthetic inferiority; but that is merely one of the elements to be discerned in Leslie Fiedler's astonishing pronouncement made in 1964, that "With a single shot [Hemingway] redeemed his best work from his worst, his art from himself, his vision of truth from the lies of his adulators." Such statements as these and the simple-minded or downright repellent assumptions on which they are based have gone more or less unchallenged in recent years, but it is to be hoped that the publication of new Hemingway works, together with more detailed information about his manuscripts, will make a decisive challenge not only likely but inevitable in the near future.

In this regard, the appearance of *Islands in the Stream* is certain to raise questions about what unpublished Hemingway works still exist in manuscript, especially since there have been so many wild speculations and rumors regarding this matter (some of which will undoubtedly persist despite the published inventory).

* * *

In time, the publication of such previously unknown works, by raising more questions than they seem at first to answer, will undoubtedly effect a serious revaluation of the significance of Hemingway's career. But such a revaluation will require a rereading of his works which has as its object something more than proving that he was an adolescent, woman-hating bully, or that his prose went downhill all the way, or that these books are "successful" and those "fail." It will also inevitably demand a careful study of the manuscripts, when these become more generally available, as well as the letters (which, although Hemingway left his widow specific instructions not to publish any of them, have not been destroyed). And while this ideal process is getting under way, one may permit oneself to hope that Philip Young, who after all his personal difficulties with Hemingway is still engaged in the labor of understanding, will decide to begin writing the unauthorized, definitive biography.

Edward P. J. Corbett.
America, 123
(November 7, 1970),
382-84.

Islands in the Stream, the longest of the more than 300 pieces Hemingway is reported to have left in the vault, was written shortly after *Across the River and Into the Trees* began receiving its drubbing from the critics. Apparently the first draft of a novel rather than a completed work, it was partially published in *Esquire* in October 1970. The editor of that magazine indicated then that the manuscript was heavily annotated with Hemingway's memos for revisions. And in her note at the front of the novel, Mary Hemingway tells that she and Charles Scribner, Jr., made minor corrections in spelling and punctuation, cut some repetitive passages, but added nothing to what Hemingway wrote. Unsporting as it might seem to pass judgment on a work in such condition, one nevertheless has it as Hemingway's writing and must admit it will do little to enhance the novelist's reputation but could diminish it a great deal.

In effect three novellas united by the presence of the painter Thomas Hudson, the book has its bright moments despite the overall disappointment one feels. For dramatic intensity and good crisp prose, the 30-page account of the struggle with the swordfish in Part I rivals *The Old Man and the Sea*. After the utter boredom of Part II, the third section gets back to the muscular action Hemingway was always able to manage best. Episodes from this pursuit of German sailors are reminiscent of *To Have and Have Not.*

That Thomas Hudson is a thinly-disguised *alter ego* for Hemingway is probably the best explanation for both the weaknesses and virtues of the novel. Hemingway always put an element of himself in his heroes, but when he modeled them on his latter-day public image, they became tiresome and pathetic. A better image is that remembered one of the youthful Hemingway and his unposturing heroes in *The Sun Also Rises* and the great short stories. (Summary)

Guy Davenport.
"Hemingway as Walter Pater."
National Review, 22
(November 17, 1970),
1214-15.

Hemingway would have been the Walter Pater *de nos jours* if he had not commited himself for 35 years to a grey, low-voiced, plain prose of severely limited flexibility and puritanical restraint. The original usefulness of this style was its laconic leanness, its clean spareness, its masculine brunt. It also served well to disguise Hemingway's inordinate love of spilt blood and his Paterian chill up the spine in the face of tenderly cherished moment. . . .

Hemingway was Pater in a boxer's body. What Pater dreamed of, he did, breaking practically every bone in his body, and using up more mercuro-chrome than all the soccer teams in Christendom. Pater could get a string quartet going in his gizzard with a blue bowl of daisies. Hemingway needed a maddened bull for the same spiritual uplift, but he was Pater right on, the aesthete stalking his splendid moment.

* * *

But Hemingway never got beyond tuning his nerve set. He sought out sensations, savored them (breaking a bone), and pronounced them good or bad, and uncorked the mercuro-chrome. The ensuing frustration he lumped with hangovers, which must have been his most persistent sensa-tion, and waited for the next encoun-ter.

These collisions with sensations were Beauty. Not even Pater, or that Italian Hemingway, D'Annunzio, pur-sued so assiduously the phantom Beau-ty. It is no wonder that in this posthu-mous novel Hemingway casts himself as a painter who was also a great lover, fisherman, shooter of anything that moved, friend of Joyce and Jules Pascin, soldier, and a drunkard who would have won the astounded admir-ation of W. C. Fields.

Using the same, the only prose he ever wrote, apparently not noticing that it is utterly inappropriate for the tale he's telling, Hemingway has scooped together a rigamarole of his favorite themes, and strung them out like so much washing on the line. And yet this late, wordy, shapeless novel is readable; it is still the old Hemingway of the battlefields, the cafés, the bitchy women, the mercurochrome. It is not Hemingway, but the world that has changed.

* * *

Catharine Hughes. "Hemingway's Coda." *Progressive*, 34 (December 1970), 47-48.

Ernest Hemingway's *Islands in the Stream* is unfortunately no exception to the rule that "literary events" turn out to be less eventful than expected or at best become pseudo-events. Even so, it has more than nostalgic interest and sometimes verges on becoming a very good book.

The rest of Hemingway's big "land, sea, and air novel" after removal and earlier publication of the coda as *The Old Man and the Sea* in 1952, *Islands in the Stream* is formed into three parts—"Bimini," "Cuba," and "At Sea." Though at times agonizingly un-even, they include some of Heming-way's finest and most evocative writ-ing. The first section moves to a pow-erful climax in the struggle of young David Hudson, son of Hemingway's protagonist Thomas Hudson, to boat a huge swordfish. "Cuba," easily the weakest section of the book, settles into a mood of alcoholic sorrow as Hudson mourns the death of two sons in an automobile accident and the last son's death in the European war. In the last section he leads his Q-boat crew in fatal pursuit of survivors of a disabled German submarine, but though Hudson communes with his spirit over the rightness of his sense of duty, his heart is not really in his communings or his pursuit.

For all its occasionally brilliant passages—David's superbly described battle with the fish, the erratic tension of the chase, some of the barroom dialogue—the novel in sum is less than equal to the parts. It has some embarrassingly self-indulgent moments, and its scenes of introspection run from the pretentious to the banal. Its triumphs come in the scenes of physical action, but the action and reflection seldom find mutual resonance. Fragmentation of the narrative diffuses the theme so that the book becomes something more like three long stories than a unified and evolving novel. It is not especially good as a novel nor especially bad as writing. (Summary)

Malcolm Cowley. "A Double Life, Half Told." *Atlantic*, 226 (December 1970), 105-106, 108.

When Ernest Hemingway came back from the wars in 1945, he had, by his own choice and that of his world public, his most difficult assignment. He had to write a novel about the war that would beat *For Whom the Bell Tolls*.

Although he seemed to have all the materials, most gathered at first hand, he also had a number of disadvantages about which his public had little knowledge—poor health resulting from the physical traumas of getting around during the war, frequent interruptions of his work by admirers and interviewers, and the temptations of further time-consuming expeditions to Europe and Africa. That he was able to maintain his discipline at the writing table is a mark of his seriousness of purpose. And one is astonished at how much work he accomplished in spite of these distractions. The longest and best of the works accomplished was said to be "the sea novel," which now appears as *Islands in the Stream*.

Hemingway conceived the idea for the novel while accompaning the American armies across France. It was to be a trilogy about the war on land, on sea, and in the air. Starting it in 1947, he wrote intermittently until 1952. The conception gradually changed to that of a collection of three long stories, perhaps four. *The Old Man and the Sea*, written in early 1951, was intended as a coda to the big novel but was published separately. After revision of the three stories, he declared them finished and ready for the vault. Not really finished, however, they needed further adjustments to serve as parts of a unified novel.

Having read most of the original manuscript, I believe the decisions of Mary Hemingway and Charles Scribner to publish the book and to make only minor corrections in the text were wise. The book in its present form is a delight to have.

Islands in the Stream is Hemingway's induction to the war novel he planned. Not one of his major works except in length, it nevertheless has sustained interest and some admirable scenes. One thinks especially of Thomas Hudson's long talk with the Bimini bartender on how to paint the Last Judgment, of David Hudson's fight with the great broadbill, the bar scene with Honest Lil, and best of all, the sea chase in the last section. Though it merits comparison with the destruction of the bridge in *For Whom the Bell Tolls,* the sequence suffers in comparison finally because Hudson's glum sense of duty and his half-conscious death wish fail to match Robert Jordan's tangle of fierce emotions.

One senses that the real difficulty of the book comes from Hemingway's inability to draw on his subconscious mind. In his early work he could descend to a primitive level of feeling at which natural objects take on symbolic meanings without losing their solid reality. At that level events and figures become archetypes of human experience. His hero was the hero of ancient myths: admired, envied, cast out by his people, condemned to wander impotent, directed by guides and precursors, rejoined to his people finally, and killed while leading them in a great exploit. But after the death of the hero, what then? In *The Old Man and the Sea* he was able to draw once again on that deep realm of feeling to find a new archetype, the hero as a hapless but undefeated old man.

For Thomas Hudson, Hemingway drew not on myth but on legend, the legend of the man whose persona he adopted in his relations with the world. Thomas Hudson fails to provide the resonance of those earlier hero figures. Except for a sense of despair, he

gives little indication of those deeper qualities we look for. Though we understand the despair resulting from the loss of his sons, Hudson's seems of longer standing, and the deaths of the sons seem a kind of blood sacrifice to the demands of fiction.

Despite such a flaw, *Island in the Stream* is yet a bold, sometimes funny, always swashbuckling book that prompts respect for Hemingway's efforts in the later years. With all his handicaps, he kept trying to summon back those early powers. Too deeply wounded to write even one of those magical sentences after a day of standing at the writing table, he continued in that private, puzzled, despairing but disciplined exploration. More appealing than his brilliant persona, he had a sort of greatness that matched his last real hero, Santiago. (Summary)

Edmund Wilson. "An Effort at Self-Revelation." *New Yorker,* 45 (January 1971), 59-62.

It is almost impossible to describe the new posthumous Hemingway book, "Islands in the Stream," from the point of view of what happens in it without making it seem preposterous. It gives us Hemingway as a concoctor of self-inflating fantasies at his most exhibitionistic. You have him in his Cuban residence, very thinly disguised as a painter, one Thomas Hudson, showing his sons how things ought to be done and how to behave like men (his younger brother Leicester has explained how Ernest liked to instruct him); you have him in his favorite bars, where he can bully his hangers-on, subjecting them to his sarcasm and otherwise putting them down, and as captain of his own boat, maintaining a good-natured but effective discipline among a gallant crew that adores him. All this time, he is being brought drinks by his servants, by the waiters, or by the members of his crew. One of the last, who drinks too much, is wisely and firmly checked, and in a moment of equally firm self-discipline Hudson makes the dramatic gesture of throwing "high over the side" and letting "the wind take it astern" a glass of "gin and coconut water with Angostura and lime." In his relations with other people he is always on top, always the acknowledged "champion" that Hemingway aspired to be in his writing when he boasted that he was "trying to knock Mr. Shakespeare on his ___." (I am sorry, in the interests of decorum, to be obliged to leave blanks in my quotations from Hemingway.) The most outrageous departure from plausibility, which is also the weakest of the episodes, occurs when Hudson's first wife, long divorced and now a singer entertaining the troops, makes a point of looking Hudson up and eagerly goes to bed with him. This woman is not in any way recognizable as Hemingway's first wife but all too recognizable as a well-known friend of Hemingway's. But why, one asks, if these two characters in the novel can enjoy such passionate love, did they

ever separate? They are agreed not to talk about the past; they acknowledge that they were both to blame. But why can they not be reunited? Nothing is ever explained.

It has always surprised me that the more or less imaginary Hemingway, the myth about himself that he managed to create by the self-dramatization of his extensive publicity and, in his fiction, by the exploits of some of his heroes, should have imposed on the public to the extent it did. The grumbling or bristling reaction on the part of certain reviewers to Mr. Carlos Baker's biography, which took account of the petty and cruel and ricidulous aspects of his subject, makes it plain that the ideal Hemingway was a living reality to many of his admirers. It is true that he was capable of courage, that he was capable of doing certain things very well. But actually, from the beginning, it was not merely the exploits of his heroes, athletic or sporting or military, that made his best stories compelling; it was the strain they conveyed of men on the edge of going to pieces, who are just hanging on by their teeth and just managing to maintain their sanity, or of men who know they are doomed to inexorable defeat or death. The real heroism of these characters is their fortitude against such ordeals or the honor they manage to salvage from ignominy, humiliation. It is this kind of theme in Hemingway that makes his stories exciting and stimulating. Will the hero last? How long will he last?

Now, with all its preposterous elements, this imperfect work, "Islands in the Stream," makes one feel the intensity of a crucial game played against invincible odds as one has not quite been able to do in connection with any of his last three finished novels— "For Whom the Bell Tolls," "Across the River and Into the Trees," "The Old Man and the Sea." It has never been pulled tight or polished, as Hemingway would undoubtedly have done, for his sense of form was exacting. Everything goes on too long, even the most effective episodes: the boy's struggle with the monstrous swordfish —which he loses; the hunt for the Germans among the reefs at the time of the Second War—which results in Hudson's being shot by them. The barroom conversations are allowed to run on to a length that has no real point and in the course of which our interest slackens. These would all—if Hemingway had taken time to treat them with his characteristic technique—have surely been condensed to far fewer pages. That he knew well how much work there was still to be done is made clear by Mr. Baker's quotations from his letters to Charles Scribner. "The Old Man and the Sea" and "For Whom the Bell Tolls" are more satisfactory from the point of view of form, yet they seem to me a good deal less interesting than "Islands in the Stream."

They are less interesting because only here is Hemingway making an effort to deal candidly with the discords of his own personality—his fears, which he has tried to suppress, his mistakes, which he has tried to justify, the pangs of bad conscience, which he has brazened out. This effort is not entirely successful; hence, I imagine, his putting the manuscript away. You

are never allowed to know exactly what happened in Thomas Hudson's past. He is always admonishing himself that he must not allow himself to think about it, so in order to avoid this he orders a drink. The reader clearly sees the drink but not the memory that is being stifled. One is made to feel acutely, however, an ever-present moral malaise. The painful gnawing, amid jolly scenes of drinking, in affluence and beautiful weather, is perhaps more insistently here made to ache than in any of Hemingway's other books since "The Sun Also Rises." There is something more than needlings of conscience; there is that certainty of the imminent death that has threatened in so much of his writing. And the book is given special force and dignity by one's knowledge of the writer's suicide. He invents for his own family, as they figure in the story, deaths that did not actually occur. Two of Hudson's sons are killed in a motor accident, and a third is killed in the war, whereas in reality, though Hemingway's boys were involved in a motor accident, they were not fatally injured, and one who had served in the war and disappeared for a time turned out to have been only taken prisoner. Hemingway himself was not shot by a German, like his hero in "Islands in the Stream." He did not even ever come to grips with the enemy—though he had formerly suffered injuries so frequent that they seem almost to have been self-inflicted—in his one-man campaign against submarines. He died in retirement, by his own hand. It was the dread, the pressure, and need for death, the looming shadow, no doubt, of the memory of his father's suicide, that drove him so determinedly to meet it.

This book contains some of the best of Hemingway's descriptions of nature: the waves breaking white and green on the reef off the coast of Cuba; the beauty of the morning on the deep water; the hermit crabs and land crabs and ghost crabs; a big barracuda stalking mullet; a heron flying with his white wings over the green water; the ibis and flamingoes and spoonbills, the last of these beautiful with the sharp rose of their color; the mosquitoes in clouds from the marshes; the water that curled and blew under the lash of the wind; the sculpture that the wind and sand had made of a piece of driftwood, gray and sanded and embedded in white, floury sand. But to bunch in this way together these phrases of the section called "At Sea" is to deprive them of the atmosphere of large space and free air and light, of the sun and rain on the water, in which the writer makes us see them, and to see them always in relation to the techniques of fishing and navigation. Though the whole thing centers on Hudson and though Hudson is kept always in the foreground, there is a certain amount of characterization of his family and friends and retinue—especially in the case of the boys, with whom Hemingway can come closest to identifying himself. The ability to characterize with any real insight has never been Hemingway's gift. Of the surface of personalities he has always been very observant, and of voices and ways of talking he is a most successful mimic. In his book of reminiscences of Paris,

he reproduces for one who has known them the hoarse British gasps of Ford Madox Ford, the exasperating nonsense of Scott Fitzgerald so faithfully that one can hear them speaking, and one can also hear the tones and turns of speech of persons one has never known. But one is made aware, particularly in "A Moveable Feast," whose characters are real people, how little their friend—or companion—could actually have known about them: what was going on in their minds, what they were aiming at, what they were up to. And his judgments were almost always disparaging. He wanted to make everyone else look ridiculous or morally reprehensible. It was only Ezra Pound who escaped—rather surprisingly, since Pound had once been useful to Hemingway, and it was usually to the people who had helped him or to whom he owed something in a literary way that he was afterward to make a point of being insulting. But in "Islands in the Stream" he allows himself little scope for malignity. He is able to be fond of most of his characters, since they all respect and obey Thomas Hudson, are glad to be molded or guided by him. " 'Tommy,' " says his second in command, when Hudson is dying, " 'I love you, you son of a bitch, and don't die.' Thomas Hudson looked at him without moving his head. 'Try and understand if it isn't too hard' . . . 'I think I understand, Willie,' he said. 'Oh---,' Willie said. 'You never understand anybody that loves you.' " This is sentimental and "self-serving," but it does show, perhaps, on Hemingway's part an attempt to take account of his non-comprehension of other people.

The mimicry of himself by Hemingway has also been mainly on the surface; the malaise itself has been kept there—sometimes, as in "A Clean, Well-Lighted Place," without any indication of what it is that is troubling the character. We are not even, as in "Big Two-Hearted River," told explicitly that there is any cause for disquiet, yet this idyll, which is simply an account of a solitary fishing expedition, is related to something in the background that is never even referred to, which makes the fisherman concentrate with special attention on every baiting of the hook, every catch, every cooking of the fish in the open air. That something, as Hemingway was later to explain, was the young man's experience of the war. Now, in "Islands in the Stream," the experiences that have been pushed down out of sight are continually rising into consciousness; but not even here, as I have already said, are we told exactly what they are. In order to keep them out of his consciousness, Thomas Hudson takes another drink or plunges on into his program of action. Yet in spite of this the mythical figure of Hemingway is constantly breaking down, becoming demoralized by the memory of past betrayals of women who have trusted and loved him, betrayals of his heroic idea of himself. The situation is made truly tragic by the fact that the mythical Hemingway did have a certain basis in reality. After all, he did not always fail or make a fool of himself, though he needed, I think, an audience, if of only one, to appreciate and applaud him. His triumphs were partly actual

and were of a kind that, for his larger audience, seemed to satisfy two typical American ambitions: that of becoming an accomplished outdoorsman and that of making a great deal of money. What had been lost was a part of an ideal self that had partly been realized.

I do not agree with those who have thought it a disservice to Hemingway's memory to publish this uncompleted book. Nor do I agree with those who, possessed by the academic mania of exactly reproducing texts, declared that Mrs. Hemingway and the publisher should have printed the manuscript as Hemingway left it, without making the cuts she explains. The author is not to be charged with the defects of manuscripts which he did not choose to publish and for which he can now take no responsibility, nor his editors with making those works more coherent if the editing has been done with good judgment. I imagine that this book, in the long run, will appear to be more important than seems to be the case at present, and I believe that Mrs. Hemingway is to be encouraged to go on to publish further manuscripts.

Virginia Quarterly Review, 47 (Winter 1971), viii.

Out of the author's literary remains his widow has disinterred three substantial portions of what appears to have been an uncompleted novel, all written in high Hemingway style on themes long since identified with him. . . . Hemingway's mesomorphic hero, as inescapably autobiographical as in all the previous books, has the simple appeal and force of a folk-figure battling fellow creatures or the forces of nature with grim fortitude. Admirers of the author's work will take infinite pleasure in his demonstrable skills as shown herein, where basic Hemingway in its staggering splendor is encapsulated for all to behold in fewer than five hundred pages.

D. J. Gordon.
Yale Review, 60 (March 1971), 429-30.

Hemingway's posthumously published *Islands in the Stream* was written for the most part between *For Whom the Bell Tolls* and *Across the River and Into the Trees*, and, though in most ways lamentable, is a better book than either. To be sure, its three long Caribbean episodes—a visit by the hero's three sons, ending in the deaths of two of them; scenes of barroom and bedroom conversation, featuring news of the death of the third; and an adventurous chase of a Nazi submarine, climaxing in the hero's own dying—are saturated in vanity and self-pity. Thomas Hudson (the narrator always uses this full proper name but an abbreviated name for every other character) is invariably the idealized chieftain of his little society; others, though they may be temporarily front and center, are

his myrmidons. He is apparently incapable of fellow feeling except for his cat and for sufficiently victimized human beings. Nevertheless there is something moving in his desperate effort to survive, to cope with the rending loss of his first wife, of youth in Paris. If we can empathize with a life felt as a choice between blank despair and marginal survival, we may be able to see as not quite silly the plight of a man who has lost his last seconal tablet, who wonders whether he should order whiskey to get him through shaving, who believes that his sons' visit will undermine the vital prop of his work routine. One feels that the characteristic Hemingway attitudes, which lost all their dignity in *Across the River*, are here at the end of a thin rope. . . . It is a telling comment on the novel that the deaths of the sons, which supposedly crush Thomas Hudson's spirit, do not seem nearly so difficult for him to sustain as daily life. It is as if the real opposition of fate is welcomed because it takes him out of himself whereas the "remorse" of obscure origins which he is otherwise left with is too intimate to be dealth with. The style reflects an end-of-the-tether sincerity. Hemingway frequently uses, for example, a sentence with two non-parallel subordinate clauses introduced by the same conjunction: "The water of the Stream was usually a dark blue when you looked out at it when there was no wind." This is sloppy writing by usual standards, but it is as if the writer sensed that a perfect parallelism would seem too neat and self-possessed, would not register the rhythms of a broken spirit.

Finally, however, there is something inauthentic about Thomas Hudson's suffering. I cannot think of any writer who sets up and then refuses so many opportunities for insight as does Hemingway. His pages beg for psychological probing but crumble under it. He refuses to see what is near enough to be seen. The hero too clearly gets pleasure from his suffering for us to regard him merely as a victim. He is also a fool.

Checklist of Additional Reviews

Kirkus, 38 (August 1, 1970), 120.

Publishers Weekly, 198 (August 10, 1970), 47.

Joan Bennett Doerner. "Hemingway's Scrap Heap Hardly Does Him Justice—Another Novel Scrounged." *Houston Chronicle,* October 4, 1970, p. 18.

Jeffrey Hall. "Papa: Portrait of Author Emerges in 'Islands in the Stream.'" Richmond *Times-Dispatch,* October 4, 1970, p. F-4.

William Hogan. "Hemingway's Unfinished Novel." *San Francisco Examiner and Chronicle,* October 4, 1970, "This World" section, pp. 34, 40.

M. Thomas Inge. "Novel Parodies Creator?" Nashville *Tennessean,* October 4, 1970, p. 10-F; Lansing (Mich.) *State Journal,* October 10, 1970, p. D-5.

Walton D. Porterfield. "In a Big Novel, Ernest Hemingway Returns 'In All His Magnificence,'" *Milwaukee Journal,* October 4, 1970, p. V-4.

Louis D. Rubin, Jr. "New Hemingway Novel Poses Questions." *Washington Sunday Star,* October 4, 1970, p. E-1.

National Observer, 9 (October 5, 1970), 19.

Maurice Duke. "Papa's Last Novel Will Sell Well, But It Is Not Good Hemingway." Richmond *Times-Dispatch,* October 11, 1970, p. F-5.

John Raymond. "Hemingway: Papa's Sea Epic Is Merely a Draft." *Atlanta Journal and Constitution,* October 11, 1970, p. D-8.

Arnold Gingrich. "Publisher's Page: Notes on *Bimini.*" *Esquire,* 74 (October 1970), 6, 12.

Edmund Fuller. "Hemingway: The Good and the Bad." *Wall Street Journal,* November 3, 1970, p. 10.

Saturday Review, 53 (November 28, 1970), 32.

Max Westbrook. *Western American Literature,* 5 (Fall 1970), 234-35.

Book World, 4 (December 6, 1970), 8.

New York Times Book Review, December 6, 1970, p. 101.

Matthew J. Bruccoli. *Fitzgerald/ Hemingway Annual 1970* (Washington: NCR/Microcard Editions, 1970), p. 245.

Nick Browne. *Village Voice,* 16 (January 21, 1971), 6, 46.

Robert Elliott Forbes. "Last But Not Best." *Catholic World,* 122 (January 1971), 220-21.

Choice, 8 (April 1971), 224.

Patrick Cruttwell. "Fiction Chronicle." *Hudson Review,* 24 (Spring 1971), 180.

Mary Silva Cosgrave. *Horn Book,* 47 (April 1971), 189.

Publishers Weekly, 200 (December 6, 1971), 54.

Clarence Petersen. *Book World,* 6
    (February 27, 1972), 9.
Best Sellers, 31 (March 1, 1972), 547.
Saturday Review, 55 (April 29, 1972),
    74.
Jay L. Halio. "First and Last Things."
    Southern Review, 9 (Spring 1973),
    455-58.

Notes

THE
Nick Adams
STORIES

BY

ERNEST HEMINGWAY

PREFACE BY PHILIP YOUNG

NEW YORK

CHARLES SCRIBNER'S SONS

The Nick Adams Stories

Matthew J. Bruccoli.
"Return of Nick Adams."
Chicago Daily News,
April 1, 1972.

The Nick Adams short stories will be read as long as anything Ernest Hemingway wrote is being read. They are superb on their own, and at least two, "The Killers" and "Big Two-Hearted River," are masterpieces. But they have an additional importance because the Nick stories introduce the themes and subjects of much of Hemingway's later work.

That we now have all the Nick stories—plus eight previously unpublished Nick pieces—collected in one volume is cause for rejoicing. But Scribner's has botched the volume by not making it fully useful. I'm not talking about scholarly apparatus; I'm referring to help for the non-scholar.

This collection needs a detailed introduction pointing out the parallels and non-parallels between Nick and Ernest himself—instead of the worthless preface by Philip Young. The stories have been put in the order of Nick's life, which is right; but the reader is not told when they were written or published. They require for full understanding a knowledge of the Walloon-Charlevoix-Horton Bay-Petoskey area in northern Michigan, but there is no map. Place photos would have helped, too.

Nonetheless, "The Nick Adams Stories" is one of the key Hemingway volumes, for it adds these eight significant pieces to the Hemingway canon:

"Three Shots," a three-page companion piece to "Indian Camp," and probably incomplete. "The Indians Moved Away," a 2½-page sketch, complete and splendid. "The Last Good Country," a 63-page fragment and possibly the start of a novel. Nick and sister flee game wardens. Important in terms of the author's final persecution anxieties.

"Crossing the Mississippi," a two-page vignette, complete. Nick on the way to Kansas City. "Night Before Landing," a six-page fragment. Nick on a troop ship. "Summer People," a 12-page story, complete. Sexual encounter between Nick and Kate at Horton Bay. An important addition to the Nick stories—and possibly important for biographical background.

"Wedding Day," a two-page sketch, complete. Nick's marriage to Helen in Michigan. "On Writing"—8½ pages, probably cut from "Big Two-Hearted River." Nick rates the competition. For those inclined to read the Nick stories as almost straight autobiography, there is a warning here: "Everything good he'd ever written he'd made up. None of it had ever happened. Other things had happened. Better things, maybe. That was what the family couldn't understand. They thought it was all experience."

This collection also includes "The Light of the World," a greatly misunderstood and underrated story. But it is not a Nick story in that the narrator is un-named. Rather it is a Nick-type story and should have an explanation.

Please, Mr. Scribner—when you make a student edition out of "The Nick Adams Stories," won't you provide a little help?

Digby Diehl.
"New Helping of Unissued Hemingway."
Los Angeles Times,
April 16, 1972,
p. 45, Calendar section.

There is no doubt that with each posthumous release of material from his unpublished manuscripts, the scope and literary brilliance of Ernest Hemingway dazzles us more. First, the extraordinary mature vision of "Islands in the Stream"; then, the fragments of his African journal, "Miss Mary's Lion" in Sports Illustrated; and now, THE NICK ADAMS STORIES, containing eight previously unpublished stories.

In this collection of 24 stories, written at apparently different times throughout Hemingway's career, the character of Nick Adams is developed from boyhood in the Michigan woods through war experiences and into maturity with a general consistency and completeness that is evident for the first time. . . .

Of the 40% in this book that is new, at least one story leaps up as a powerful and finished (if not "polished") story which stands with his best: "Summer People." It is a bittersweet reminiscence of the emotions between friends swimming on a summer afternoon and of the self-consciously casual sex Nick Adams experiences at approximately age 30. It is the most candid sex I can recall in all of Hemingway, and yet the girl, Kate, evokes in Nick a (postwar?) sense of inability to love and an awareness of his relationship with her. . . .

"The Last Good Country," evidently the beginning of a long unfinished story, gives us a youthful Nick in his more familiar surroundings of the trout stream and the woods. In an idyllic escape from two game wardens who are threatening to send him to reform school, Nick hides in the back country with his kid sister Littless—which is where the story is left hanging. Once again, Hemingway the naturalist takes over, sketching the woods, the fishing and the hideout camp with his sparse, sure strokes. Critics will be running for their Holden and Phoebe/ Franny and Zooey comparative texts when they read the uniquely offbeat sentimental dialog between Littless and Nick. Leslie Fiedler should find material for a new book when she tells Nick she wants to be his brother and live by the stream with him forever. ("Come Back to the Woods Again, Nick, Honey"?)

Not all of the new Nick Adams material advances Hemingway's reputation. There are rough fragments and one eerie section called "On Writing" in which the persona of Nick seems to slip away from Hemingway entirely and he careens out-of-control through memories and irrelevancies until he picks up a thread with Maileresque abandon and brings us back to Nick.

* * *

G. E. Murray.
"Papa's Tales of Nick Adams, His Heroic Alter Ego."
Chicago Sun-Times Bookweek,
April 16, 1972.

At a time when literary "discoveries" have become as commonplace as freshly unearthed arrowheads, Philip Young emerges from his latest diggings with a previously unavailable and complete version of Ernest Hemingway's "The Nick Adams Stories."

We should be accustomed to these kind of unveilings by now. During the past few years, a flood of forgotten or lost manuscripts have been resurrected, mulled over for their authenticity and finally published as expensive coffee-table editions.

But any new work by Hemingway is bound to be hot stuff, and will be for as long as "Papa's" last wife feels obliged to dole it out.

And, of course, Hemingway's reputation still is insurmountable in this country and elsewhere. His posthumous novel, "Islands in the Stream," was a success. In Paris, many of Hemingway's stories have been revived, translated and adapted for radio, causing a sizeable stir among the French.

* * *

The premiere selection of the group is "Summer People," a story that compares favorably with the best of Hemingway's early writing. Here Nick is a blend of local hero, adolescent show-off and philosopher-in-residence, whose self-detachment and boyish misgivings about sex pervade this story of summertime fascinations.

In "Summer People," we also see Hemingway growing in awareness of what his task as a writer is, playing with the possibilities of his pin-neat language, and invoking a familiar obsession with masculine adventure.

The same obsession is present in "Night Before Landing," a minor gem. The story deals with the standard anxieties of a young soldier hours before he embarks to meet the enemy. But even here Nick proves to be a challenging portrayal, facing fear with an unconventional, almost chilling ease. Such is the genius of Hemingway.

"The Last Good Country," the longest story in the book, is probably a false start on a novel Hemingway advisedly shelved. It is sketchy, rambling and unresolved. This time Nick is a youthful poacher on the run from two bungling game wardens, roaming Michigan's Upper Peninsula. There are some moments of brilliance, particularly in several of Nick's interior monologs where fact and fancy collide, but the fiction is far from complete and largely overdrawn.

The new fiction in this volume is, for the most part, second-rate. But even the worst of Hemingway deserves attention, and some interesting biographical notes can be garnered from this collection. . . .

If Hemingway had moments when he felt that unpolished or incomplete work would strip the mystery from his art, if he ever considered the fate of those manuscripts he lost interest in, it is possible that he nevertheless planned to be hunted.

"The Nick Adams Stories" is another valuable clue to that hunt. And it serves to remind us again that Hemingway could write as well as Cezanne painted.

Peter S. Prescott. "Big Two-Hearted Writer." *Newsweek,* 79 (April 17, 1972), 100, 104.

As early as D. H. Lawrence's review of *In Our Time* readers and critics alike have thought of the Nick Adams stories as fragments of a novel with potential coherence if they were put into proper sequence. The present collection not only arranges them in order of the protagonist's development but adds eight new stories or fragments as well. The result is that the parts keep their individual integrity and by reflecting on each other add to our per-

ception of Nick's coming of age. The symbolic detail of "Big Two-Hearted River," for example, becomes easier to grasp when we know about Nick's breakdown in the war, described in stories published later.

The new materials, which are of mixed quality, contain pieces that were properly cut from other stories but that should not be lost. "On Writing" helps explain Nick's aims as a budding writer: he wanted to write the way Cezanne painted, to break down the country into its elements and rebuild it into the real thing. In "The Last Good Country" there are idyllic scenes of Nick and his youngest sister on the run from game wardens, but like any good writer Hemingway abandoned the story when he realized it wasn't going anywhere. "Summer People," though, is a finished story, the one entirely successful new piece, and shows Hemingway in good form. Best guess on why he didn't publish it is the explicit sex, which Gertrude Stein had warned him about in "Up in Michigan." It was *inaccrochable*, she said, but by today's standards both show good taste. (Summary)

Louis D. Rubin, Jr. "A Portrait of Nick Adams and How He Happened." *Washington Star,* April 23, 1972, p. C-6.

Publication of the Nick Adams stories of Ernest Hemingway as a group, with previously unpublished and uncompleted material originally involved in the fragmented saga of Hemingway's first and most autobiographical of fictional protagonists, constitutes a fascinating and valuable bit of creative editing.

* * *

The value of this compilation is at least threefold. In the first place, it gives us insight into Hemingway's creative process and his ideas of what fiction should be. His theory about fiction—that the more that can be "left out" of a story, the stronger what is left will be as art—is dramatically visible for inspection here, and most notably in the case of "Big Two-Hearted River," in which what is left out is why the protagonist is off fishing by himself, and what are the forces that lie behind his obvious state of extreme tension. It turns out that originally "Big Two-Hearted River" concluded with a long semi-stream of consciousness monologue in which Nick Adams, who is clearly Hemingway here, thinks about his literary career, his war experience, and about friendship, marriage, and what he wants to do and be as a writer. The passage is anachronistic—it contains material and experience that chronologically belong long after the time of the fishing trip.

Another valuable result of publishing the material in this form is that it offers us all manner of insight into the sensibility of Ernest Hemingway. A long narrative entitled "The Last Good Country," which was left unfinished, involves the young Nick Adams with his family, in particular his sister, in a way that none of the published Nick Adams stories do. The episode is apparently a greatly augmented development of an actual incident involving the youthful Hemingway's violation of the game laws when he shot and killed a blue heron, and his sister helped him get to his uncle's house before a game warden could apprehend him. Hemingway transforms this into a full-fledged flight into the deepest woods by Nick and his sister, with the crime that occasioned it made more serious and less distasteful. The story gets very close to barely sublimated incest; whether Hemingway recognized this, or whether he abandoned completing it for other reasons, is unknown.

The memorable story entitled "Indian Camp," in which Nick Adams witnesses his father performing a Caesarean operation on an Indian woman, only to have her husband commit suicide because he cannot stand the pain his wife is experiencing, turns out to have had an opening section in which the young Nick is left alone in the camp by his father, who has gone off hunting. Nick's fear of the woods, and of death, and his knowledge that his father had some contempt for his fearfulness, give a new emphasis both to the end of the published story, to Hemingway's insistence in later life on branding his father as a coward, and to the early origins of the famous Hemingway preoccupation with death and heroism.

Several stories and parts of stories set in the period after the first world war, when a still-youthful Nick is living a carefree life with companions male and female, fishing, swimming, and, in one instance, having an affair with one of the girls, give us a glimpse of Hemingway's own experience during a time little written about, but full of significance for the later fiction. I was surprised to find that editor Young places the stories entitled "The End of Something" and "The Three-Day Blow" chronologically in this period, rather than before the war. His reasons for doing so, upon reflection, are obvious, and yet the naivete and innocence of Nick Adams in these stories seem more appropriate to the Hemingway of the pre-Europe days. This in itself is interesting; for the persistence of these qualities in the "mature" Hemingway of the post-war years gives us a different picture from the customary stereotype of the youthful Hemingway being changed overnight into the tough, cynical, winner take nothing adult by the horrors of war on the Italian front.

The third and perhaps the best result of the publication of the unfinished Nick Adams material along with the published stories, however, is that it makes available to us some excellent writing. In particular, I think of the story or novella "The Last Good Country." This contains some of the best writing Hemingway ever did. It is a shame that, for whatever reason, he did not see his way to finishing it. Another good specimen is the story, apparently close to finished form, entitled "Summer People." To be sure, it is not the absolutely best Hemingway —but then, neither is a great deal of his short fiction of the 1920s the best Hemingway. Why Hemingway did not publish it is hard to say; perhaps (most

oddly, considering his usual practice) it was too close to real life, and might therefore have given pain to real persons. In any event, it's excellent Nick Adams, and good to have available.

This is a fascinating collection. The fragmentary nature of the new pieces does not really interfere seriously with one's enjoyment. What we have is a more complete view of Hemingway as Nick Adams—and by this I mean the aesthetic experience of taking part in the writer's creation of himself in this guise. So much of reading Hemingway comes down to just that. No 20th century writer ever projected himself more into his work, not merely with autobiographical material but in the sense of dramatizing, through style and attitude, the persona of the creator.

The famous Hemingway style does not exist in a vacuum; it involves the reader's being able to apprehend the achievement of simplicity out of complexity, grace under pressure. When it is working right, no writer is more compelling. In the Nick Adams stories, written in the 1920s, the style is usually working right, and this not only in the completed, published stories but in much of the new material in this collection. "The Nick Adams Stories" represents an addition to the Hemingway canon of more worth than the unpublished novel "Islands in the Stream," and of at least equal importance as "A Moveable Feast." Which is no more than to say that it offers a great deal of vintage Hemingway, and that is all one can ask.

Margaret Manning.
"Nick Adams—
a Reminder."
Boston Globe,
April 24, 1972,
p. 19.

I suppose publication of Ernest Hemingway's Nick Adams stories is something of a literary gimmick, but it is wonderful to have them all together under one cover, so complaints will be mild indeed.

This is the first time that Nick's experiences have been arranged in chronological sequence, and that is one attribute of the book the publisher is pushing as a reason for its existence. The other is the claim that 40 percent of the book is new material.

The new things are really unfinished, though, and probably were simply abandoned because Hemingway decided he didn't care for them.

There are sketches, snippets, a long, inconclusive and slightly soppy narrative about Nick as a boy running away from home, and a full scale story about Nick and a girl called "Summer People."

Even these, however, are interesting bits with gorgeous nature writing and characteristic comments like: "He had already learned there was only one day at a time and that it was always the day you were in."

* * *

Unlike Frederic Henry or Jake Barnes, Nick Adams doesn't really have an integrated personality. Hemingway never intended these stories to be in a sequence.

To Hemingway, Nick was a way of working through things, thinking them out for the novels, getting to the roots, preparing for greatness.

But for the very reason that Nick's persona is scattered and even incoherent, I believe he more closely resembles Hemingway than any of the novelistic heroes.

To the adult Nick Adams, as to Hemingway himself, art became the ultimate value. Writing was living. It was "the greatest pleasure." He wanted to capture nature in words in the same way that Cezanne painted it.

* * *

No other writer in English has the same sensitivity to climate, to landscape, to natural physical things.

The heart stopping beauty of his descriptions of nature in "Big Two-Hearted River," the primeval violence of the battle scenes and of "The Killers"—these are still powerful and fresh and there is great richness and complexity below the oblique dialogue and the skeletal narrative.

Hemingway, Fitzgerald, Dos Passos, Faulkner, the giants of another generation, seem to have shared an intellectual climate that, looking back, was more buoyant than ours.

Though they often described a society in decay, their work, unlike so much written today, was flowering with life.

It is fine to have this reminder of what we are capable of.

Richard R. Lingeman.
"More Posthumous Hemingway."
New York Times,
April 25, 1972.

Like a murder in Macbeth that will not down, the ghosts of Hemingway's unpublished writings from the past continue to stalk us. Two years ago "Islands in the Stream" became a best seller out of a nostalgia for Hemingway, even though he had set it aside not fully revised. Now we have "The Nick Adams Stories," 24 stories and sketches, a third of which were never before published. Many of the new pieces represent a kind of cannibalization of spare parts, reutilized on their own after being cut out of other stories. Only the estate can look at them without mixed emotions.

"Three Shots," cut from "Indian Camp," was clearly excess baggage in that story and shows its greatest value by prompting our admiration for Hemingway's ruthlessly true artistry in excising it. "On Writing," once intended as a conclusion to "Big Two-Hearted River," would have dragged that superb story into the quicksands of irrelevancy. Like a Siamese twin, it died in the separation but left the better story, unlike a real Siamese twin, whole and healthy. "Night Before Landing" can stand only as a fragment. Part of a novel Hemingway began about his war experience and then abandoned, it is not quite a story, sinking into inconclusiveness as it picks up characters

pregnant with potential future actions. It opens but does not close out our glimpse into the center of the characters' beings. "Summer People," one of the few complete new stories, is pitiless in its insight into the injustices of love. One wonders if this is the story called "Up in Michigan" that was dropped from "In Our Time" at the insistence of the publisher, Horace Liveright, on grounds of obscenity. Its frank sex stands in honorable contrast to some of Hemingway's later sexual scenes in which the earth moves.

In "On Writing" Hemingway rejects autobiographical fiction, prefers to let experience perk in the darker recesses of this subconscious mind and emerge as imagined art. Out of this declaration we can see why he never meant the Nick Adams stories to be autobiographical and why the best stories stand alone, not as links in a chain. The Nick Adams stories thus are good to have but do not create new coherence in our knowledge of Nick. They are likely neither to add to nor detract from our memory of Hemingway's best. (Summary)

John Skow.
"A Moveable Fast."
Time, 99
(May 1, 1972),
81-82.

One of the lessons Ernest Hemingway taught a generation of writers was to make stories strong by leaving out things—not just the weak parts but solid parts too. The remainder held an extrordinary tension and the unsaid resonated in those haunted empty spaces.

Since Hemingway's death, his literary executors have kept busy putting back in. The latest addition consists of eight newly published fragments and tales mixed in a new arrangement of the now standard Nick Adams stories, ordered according to the age of the protagonist. Whatever their motives, the executors have worked mischief. Beyond pretense, the fragments are rejects, mediocre at best when judged beside the stories Hemingway believed in enough to publish, and usually worse than that. Written at the beginning of his career, they were properly written off. He had thirty years to change his mind but didn't. Hemingway held to his principle of leaving out and the technique worked.

If Nick was Hemingway's other self, readers knew little about him or what Hemingway felt about him. But those important missing stretches in Nick's life are what make "Big Two-Hearted River" one of his best. Whether Nick has been to war (the usual guess) or has been living a death in the city, the point of the story is that he does not think where he has been. Chinking the empty spaces provides no improvement. Rather we get three resonance-deadening pages about young Nick's nighttime fears cut from "Indian Camp" or a mawkish shard of an abandoned novel about Nick's skulking in the forest with his sister and indulging in romantic despair about being pursued by improbably Snopesian game wardens.

"Summer People," the only passable new work, is a twelve-page story containing a moderately explicit sex scene. If Hemingway withheld it from publication for fear of censorship, he could have published it almost any time after 1950. But he chose not to and presumably thought it not worth the trouble.

Best justification of the book is the excuse to re-read the good Nick Adams stories: the brief but superb vignette of Nick lying wounded in the street of an Italian town; "Indian Camp" except for the phony suicide at the end; "A Way You'll Never Be"; "Big Two-Hearted River" and the two skiing stories. All very fine.

Beyond that, dead writers and their discard piles should be left in peace. (Summary)

David Madden.
"Some Early Hemingway."
Boston Herald Traveler,
June 4, 1972,
p. V-8.

* * *

In the early volumes of stories, the Nick pieces appeared in no order. "As a result the coherence of his adventures," says Philip Young, pioneer Hemingway critic, in his preface, "has been obscured, and their impact fragmented." Young's arrangement tries to achieve a meaningful narrative in which a memorable character grows from child to adolescent to soldier, veteran, writer, and parent. In some stories Hemingway is faithful to actual experience: in others, his imagination transforms the actual.

Nick's comments in the "new" fragment "On Writing" provide some illuminating insights: "The only writing that was any good was what you made up, what you imagined. That made everything come true." The medium for transformation was a style that evoked emotions and attitudes and implied the broad outlines of events.

* * *

The best of the new pieces, "The Last Good Country" introduces some interesting new characters. It contains many of the motifs developed throughout the rest of the book; whole passages turn up in other stories, especially "Big Two Hearted River," to which it is most closely related.

* * *

In "The Last Good Country," Nick and his sister, "Littless," attempt to elude vicious game wardens who are out to arrest him for shooting deer out of season (he shot it accidentally). Nick and his sister indulge in a little too much of the sentimental talk Hemingway sometimes lapsed into in his other work.

They come, in fact, to the verge of incest. She is jealous of Nick's Indian girlfriend, Trudy. When she cuts her hair so she can be more like a boy and thus more acceptable to Nick, she prefigures Maria in "For Whom the Bell Tolls." She jokes with Nick, saying she used to be a whore's assistant, and vows she'll become his commonlaw wife.

Hemingway's characters need to feel exclusive, as in this brother-sister relationship: "She and Nick loved each other and they did not love the others. They always thought of everyone else in the family as the others." "This is the last good country there is left. Nobody gets in here ever."

The how-to-do-it-the-right-way mystique, prevalent in Hemingway's work, is fully expressed in this story, and the importance of knowing is repeatedly asserted. What you can do and what you know places you in a special group and excludes all others. But this exclusiveness, this subjective aristocracy, is based on improvised rules that only members know exist.

* * *

As for what Hemingway himself would have thought of the idea of publishing fragments (Young argues that perhaps only "Summer People" is a complete story), we might remember that the author himself separated the stories in "In Our Time," first collection, with 16 one-page mock chapters —epiphanies really—one of which is reprinted in the present volume.

Even though the Nick stories were written from 1925 to 1933, we might best regard this collection as a kind of patchwork first novel. Even as a group of interrelated stories, it has more character, narrative, and thematic cohesiveness than Sherwood Anderson's "Winesburg, Ohio."

* * *

Jim Harrison.
"The Importance of Being Young—and Ernest."
Washington Post Book World,
June 4, 1972.

It was certain that he was playing to a much larger crowd than his immediate critical audience or the academic community. It was hard to forgive him this and it would muddle the issue (his true stature) for years afterward, even in 1972. "My god," one would have thought had one been old enough to think in those days, "Hemingway carries on as if he were Lord Byron, Natty Bumppo and Humphrey Bogart all in one."

* * *

It seems we will have to forgive Hemingway his fabled idiosyncrasies in favor of his good works which in the gospel sense are obviously living after him, just as he would have forgiven, or at least not noticed, us for doing nothing much at all.

It is pleasant to see all the Nick Adams stories under one cover and that is justification enough for Scribners' reprinting them. Before, of course, one had to sort through several volumes to find all of them and the chronology was a trifle confusing. Now we have the additional delight of eight fragments and stories hitherto unpublished. Of the latter, I liked "The Last Good Country" best; it runs about fifty pages and serves as a begin-

ning, evidently, of an unfinished novel. In "The Last Good Country" Nick is escaping from two game wardens after killing a deer out of season and selling trout to a hotel. Nick takes his sister with him and, though much is left undeveloped, the main thread is sort of an "if Huck Finn had a sister." It shows an enormously tender, almost maudlin side of Hemingway's character. I'm sure when Leslie Fiedler gets hold of it, and perhaps justly, some mildly incestuous aspects of the story will be drawn to the surface with fury.

But it is most of all a summer idyll, the writing very relaxed and beautiful, and obviously a first draft—Hemingway with his guard down.

There is a not very delicate question in these eight additions of whether unrefined or unfinished work should be allowed to emerge. After reading *Islands in the Stream* and the *African Journal* serialized in Sports Illustrated, I would have to opt for a yes. None of the fragments are without interest, and "Wedding Day" and "On Writing" are fascinating sketches. It's too bad that Philip Young's preface to the volume was not longer and more detailed. Young's prose has all the subtlety of a valve grinder but he perceives some of the joy in Hemingway that was so disastrously missing in the Carlos Baker biography.

After a decade away from these stories, one is struck first by the incorruptible purity of the style, the splendor and clarity of the language as language. We must remember that Hemingway, after all, was a pointy-headed intellectual and artist and his avowed intent was to write like Cezanne painted. The stories have all the Apollonian precision that his gaudy life apparently lacked—but again it is easy to fall into the perverse monism of the book reviewer or professor. Mistakes have been made trying to teach Philosophy 101 out of Hemingway's stories, or errantly gathering, as so many young men have done, a life style from them. Wisdom in a novelist or poet is so often an elaborate type that is only self-applicable. As an instance, one turns to Faulkner again and again, to be enriched, to get pleasure pure and simple—not to find principles of conduct. The Nick Adams stories ˋare a young man's stories written by a young man and enjoyed mostly by other young men.

The faultlessness of their pursuits is an embarrassment to older, wiser souls who miss the full panoply of contemporary attitudes and beliefs that helped them accommodate themselves to the miseries of the 20th century. But at least half the stories wear their durability as art very openly and easily, and "Big Two-Hearted River" would be near the summit of any literature.

* * *

Edmund Fuller. "Hemingway's Nick Adams Tales." *Wall Street Journal*, June 8, 1972.

The questions of judgment involved in the posthumous publication of works by an important writer are complex

indeed. Widely differing problems may be involved. At one extreme we have the case of Franz Kafka, now regarded as a major voice of our century. Little of his work had been published in his lifetime and scant attention had been paid to that. On his deathbed, he gave all his manuscripts, including the three celebrated novels, all unpublished, to his friend and fellow writer, Max Brod. In despair, he instructed Brod to destroy them. Brod ignored that request, procured publication of those works by patient advocacy, and the genius of Kafka has been recognized.

In the case of Thomas Wolfe, who died at 37, at least half of the body of his work was left unpublished. The editing of Wolfe always was a complicated process. . . .

Which leads us up to the case at hand: Ernest Hemingway, whose fifth partly posthumous volume is "The Nick Adams Stories" including eight pieces of material never published before.

* * *

"A Moveable Feast" and "Islands in the Stream" each was a new, large work. The Paris memoir was absorbing and contained excellent writing. "Islands in the Stream," notwithstanding unevenness, also offered passages of his best vein.

This new edition of "The Nick Adams Stories" requires more specialized justifications. Critics often have discussed this related group of tales, but they have always been scattered among several volumes of short stories. This is the first time they have ever been brought together and arranged in the order of their internal chronology, including the material never published before.

Critic Philip Young, in a brief preface, remarks: "Arranged in chronological sequence, the events of Nick's life make up a meaningful narrative in which a memorable character grows from child to adolescent to soldier, veteran, writer, and parent—a sequence closely paralleling the events of Hemingway's own life. In this arrangement Nick Adams, who for a long time was not widely recognized as a consistent character at all, emerges clearly as the first in a long line of Hemingway's fictional selves."

All that is true, though autobiographical aspects in Nick are not a new discovery. Also, we are given a slightly false impression of the degree of continuity, for the gaps are large and great alterations appear in Nick which we simply must accept without seeing their development. Oddly enough, however, the series terminates well. We have a sense of conclusion, of rounding off, when at the close of "Fathers and Sons," Nick's small son, raised in France, now visiting the Michigan country with his father, wants to go and pray at the tomb of his grandfather.

* * *

Obviously the new materials, of which that closing story is not a part, have particular interest to literary scholars and Hemingway specialists. But for general readers, the prime value of this book is the editorial arrangement. No truly important contribution is made to the reader's pleasure or

understanding by any of the newly published items which, in general, are inferior in workmanship, hence left by Hemingway as discards, or unfinished pieces.

* * *

Rest, rest, perturbed spirit. It is good to have the old Nick Adams stories brought together in this arrangement. You can forget about the additions; they impair the better work by seeming to mock it.

William Abrahams. "Hemingway: The Posthumous Achievement." *Atlantic*, 229 (June 1972), 98-100.

The postumous fame of a writer is, as everybody agrees, based on the survival and endurance of his work. But for all its prime importance, the work published during an author's career is only one of several claims to literary afterlife. Another is survival of the writer's legend as a personality, and in Hemingway's case the legend has been kept alive by a flow of gossip and memoirs of those who knew him when. At times the legend of "Papa" has seemed likely to overshadow the work of the artist and probably reached its nadir in the work of A. E. Hotchner. The other claim is posthumous publication of the writer's own work, either previously unpublished or uncollected. Dubious as that enterprise is, it has produced the new collection of Nick Adams stories and it must be counted a literary event, though less impressive than *A Moveable Feast* or *Islands in the Stream*.

Arranged chronologically, these stories are made to serve as chapters in a shadow fictional biography or an auto-biographical novel. The misconception here is in supposing a short story and a chapter in a novel are essentially the same. But the methods of a novelist and a short story writer are different. To the degree that a story is a success-ful work of art it is self-contained in providing all we need to know aesthet-ically. That of course may not be the case if one is determined to read it as a part of the writer's or hero's biogra-phy. Placing "Big Two-Hearted River" after the stories of World War I may help explain Nick's nameless anxiety but it violates the story as a self-con-tained work and somehow reduces the extraordinary depth and poetry of our experience. With its absolute rightness the story has its wholeness to which we can want nothing added. Literal-ism, though crucial to the journalist, may suffocate the artist, and Heming-way was preeminently the artist. He knew the value of suggestion and omis-sion.

Even if the assumptions behind the collection are wrong-headed, there is no denying the pleasure one has in reading one marvelous passage after another in the authentic Nick Adams stories. Beside them the new stories, set in italics to distinguish them from those already published, are recogniz-ably lesser work. It is obvious why Hemingway put them aside. Yet at this

time in his literary fame it was not ill-advised to bring them to light.

Hemingway's reputation would be better served, however, by publication of the Complete Collected Stories, carefully edited and arranged accord-ing to the order of their composition. In a separate grouping, perhaps as an appendix, could be placed the stories he chose not to publish during his life-time. Such a volume would reaffirm his true mastery during the inevitable debate over his "place" in the years to come. (Summary)

Phoebe-Lou Adams. *Boston Review of the Arts*, June 1972, p. 44.

In a world overrun with books that should never have been published, one more is not surprising, but that the excrescence should carry the name of Ernest Hemingway is flabbergasting. Stories by one of the greatest Ameri-can writers of this century? A collec-tion that includes a masterpiece like *Big Two-Hearted River*? How could such a thing happen? The answer, of course, is that Hemingway had nothing to do with it. He is being charged with crimes that he decided not to commit. Mrs. Hemingway, whose devotion to her husband's work and reputation is beyond question, has evidently been misadvised.

* * *

Several of the new pieces are short to the point of nonexistence. Of the longer ones, "Summer People," the complete story, is clearly very early work, still contaminated by that cute mawkishness fashionable in Hemingway's Edwardian youth—the quality that he worked hard to unlearn. "The Last Good Country," a long unfinished story, has the merit of a pair of surly game wardens, incisively drawn, and the meticulous, realistic, and yet magical description of wild country that was one of Hemingway's distinctive achievements. It has the demerit of Nick and his little sister, represented as the most unbelievably affectionate, considerate, perpetually amiable juveniles who ever played babes in the wood. They are, heaven help us, right out of James Barrie, even to the nervous sexual undercurrents. Presumably this story was abandoned because Hemingway saw that it could logically lead only to a swamp of sentimentality or to incest among the trout rods.

The only one of these bits and pieces worth preserving is called "On Writing," and it undercuts the whole premise of the Nick Adams stories as autobiographical revelation. Here is Nick-Hemingway on his art. "The only writing that was any good was what you made up, what you imagined. . . . Everything good he'd ever written he'd made up. None of it had ever happened. Other things had happened. Better things, maybe. That was what the family couldn't understand. They thought it was all experience."

Mr. Young presumably thinks so too. Possibly he thinks that what Hemingway didn't use because it wasn't good must therefore be not made up. A very questionable proposition. Certainly, he thinks, ". . . these pieces throw new light on the work and personality of one of our foremost writers and genuinely increase our understanding of him." But he doesn't think it hard enough to supply the information that would enable a reader to consider the Nick Adams material, old and new, in terms of its actual creation. No dates are given for the original appearance of the published stories, no description of the kind of stories that accompanied them, no dates for the principal events of Hemingway's life, no list of what those events were. A supposedly informative project has seldom been offered with such an airy lack of scholarly apparatus.

The new material does, however, throw light of a sort. It shows that Hemingway knew what was superfluous and cut it; knew what was going to be a poor story, and gave up on it; was, in short, an artist in conscious, sensitive control of his material. Is this news to anybody?

Jeffrey Hart. "Vintage Hemingway." *National Review*, 24 (July 21, 1972), 801-802.

Philip Young's collection of the Nick Adams stories by Ernest Hemingway is both an important and an ambiguous book. As a result of his sifting through the unpublished Hemingway manuscripts, Young has brought to light eight new stories dealing with, in my opinion, Hemingway's most important protagonist and has integrated them chronologically with other known Nick Admas stories. But what he wants to construct is a novel Hemingway never wrote—the account of Nick's development from emotionally-dependent child to emotionally-haunted parent.

Among the pluses of this enterprise is the major find of the uncompleted seventy-page story "The Last Good Country." Despite what earlier reviewers have said of this story, it is early and vintage Hemingway. No matter that the story is unfinished, the great themes are present, unrefined and uncriticized but showing the sources of energy. In the story of young Nick's flight from game wardens and in company with his sister, Hemingway is able to suggest the deeper emotions and cryptic meanings beneath his simplest statements. When Nick tells his sister he doesn't want to hear her warning, he is refusing to bring into words the things he already knows—the physical and psychological threats of a violent world already closing in, the traumas that the later stories will demonstrate in all their killers, bullets in the spine, desires, and suicides.

The Nick Adams stories, scattered by Hemingway throughout the volumes of short stories, contain the premise of the entire Hemingway enterprise: suicide and the need for discipline and professional skill in "Indian Camp," still the need of skill and discipline to avoid thinking of emotional wounds in the climactic "Big Two-Hearted River." In the latter story Nick is trying to put himself together

by drawing on what he learned that night at the Indian camp.

Though the Nick Adams stories are welcome drawn together in this volume, they suffer by removal from their original contexts. *In Our Time* was, after all, a carefully arranged artistic whole. The stories gained immense significance by their placement in the volume. "The Battler," for example, begins with the statement that Nick stood up—after being tossed from the freight train. The previous vignette, though, tells of six executed cabinet ministers who will not stand up. The immediately following vignette describes Nick lying wounded in an Italian street. Seeing the story of Nick standing up in this context adds poignantly to our knowledge that Nick will not always stand up again in a world of war and political executions. The point is lost by Young's displacement of the stories from their original settings.

One surprise in Young's chronological arrangement, and one for which he offers no explanation, is his placing the two clearly adolescent stories "The End of Something" and "The Three-Day Blow" in Nick's postwar period. It is hard to reconcile the young Nick who rejects domesticity for "experience" with the battle-wise Nick who by war's end has had too much experience.

Still it is pleasant to have the new stories and the Nick Adams stories all together. Those of us committed to Hemingway may be grateful to Philip Young. (Summary)

Ronald Weber. "Savoring the Hemingway of the Nick Adams Stories." *Detroit Free Press* (n.d.).

For the serious Hemingway reader the place to begin has always been the stories, and that's the best place to return as well. Of all his work the stories—together with "A Sun Also Rises" and the early parts of "A Farewell to Arms"—have held up best, and some of the most memorable stories belong to a group long classified as the Nick Adams stories. . . .

* * *

Of the new stories, however, only one, "Summer People," can be considered a completed work and in any sense an important one, especially for its further development of the Michigan material that gave Hemingway the background for his first serious fiction. . . .

* * *

The chronology serves a purpose, but a minor one at best—and hardly worth the book's preposterous $7.95 price. It's true that some of the stories have puzzled readers because of their original positioning in Hemingway's work. "Big Two-Hearted River," for example, takes on more clarity when we see it preceded not by "Cross-Country Snow," as it first was in "In Our Time," but by "A Way You'll Never Be" and "In Another Country," stories published much later.

But even arranged in sequence the stories never quite form a complete narrative. They retain a fragmented quality because of the nature of the short story itself—its precise focus on a single incident or a single set of emotional responses rather than ongoing development—and because of Hemingway's special brand of story that was always meant to make the readers sense much more than was actually said.

What is consistent and meaningful, and what one realizes again reading the stories through, is Nick's particular sensibility: a general edginess, heightened by a knowledge of war; a deep attraction to the father and rejection of the mother; sexual bravado yet fear of the entanglements of love; delight in male camaraderie; fear of death's obliteration yet an obsessive attraction to it; and finally and most strongly, a love of the outdoors and a feeling for the landscape, especially the Michigan lakes and woods of his youthful summers. Coupled with Nick's inner struggle to grow up and confront the world honestly, is always his simple delight in those summers he had "loved more than anything."

* * *

Checklist of Additional Reviews

Publishers Weekly, 201 (February 7, 1972), 93.
Kirkus, 40 (February 15, 1972), 224.
Best Sellers, 31 (March 1, 1972), 547.

George V. Higgins. "Rooting in Papa's Closet to Discover . . . 14 Pages?" *National Observer,* 11 (April 29, 1972), 21.

Best Sellers, 32 (May 1, 1972), 53.

Quentin Anderson. "Devouring the Hemingway Corpus." *New Leader,* 55 (May 15, 1972), 13-15.

Erling Larsen. "The End of Something Like Responsibility." *Carleton Miscellany,* 12 (Spring-Summer 1972), 76-81.

Booklist, 68 (June 1, 1972), 847.

Library Journal, 97 (June 1, 1972), 2116.

K. McSweeney. *Dalhousie Review* (Summer 1972), 309.

Choice, 9 (September 1972), 814.

American Literature, 44 (November 1972), 530.

Virginia Quarterly Review, 48 (Autumn 1972), cxxi.

George Monteiro. *Georgia Review,* 26 (Winter 1972), 518-20.

New Yorker, 48 (December 2, 1972), 210.

Book Week, 7 (March 25, 1973), 14.

Floyd C. Watkins. "The Nick Adams Stories: A Single Work by Ernest Hemingway." *Southern Review,* 9 (Spring 1973), 481-91.

Douglas Wilson. *Western Humanities Review,* 27 (Summer 1973), 295-99.

Index